FAMILY LIFE EDUCATION

FAMILY LIFE EDUCATION
Principles and Practices for Effective Outreach

Stephen F. Duncan
Brigham Young University

H. Wallace Goddard
University of Arkansas

SAGE Publications
Thousand Oaks ▪ London ▪ New Delhi

For information:

Sage Publications, Inc.
2455 Teller Road
Thousand Oaks, California 91320
E-mail: order@sagepub.com

Sage Publications Ltd.
1 Oliver's Yard
55 City Road
London EC1Y 1SP
United Kingdom

Sage Publications India Pvt. Ltd.
B-42, Panchsheel Enclave
Post Box 4109
New Delhi 110 017 India

Printed in the United States of America.

Printed on acid-free paper.

Library of Congress Cataloging-in-Publication Data

Duncan, Stephen F.
Family life education : principles and practices for effective
outreach / Stephen F. Duncan, H. Wallace Goddard.
     p. cm.
Includes bibliographical references and index.
ISBN 0-7619-2769-7 (pbk.)
   1. Family life education. I. Goddard, H. Wallace. II. Title.
HQ10.D853 2005
306.8-dc22

                                          2004023046

      06   07   08   09   10   9   8   7   6   5   4   3   2

Acquiring Editor:	Jim Brace-Thompson
Editorial Assistant:	Karen Ehrmann
Project Editor:	Claudia A. Hoffman
Copy Editor:	Barbara Coster
Typesetter:	C&M Digitals (P) Ltd.
Indexer:	Will Ragsdale

CONTENTS

PREFACE

Family life educators (FLEs) are found in many settings. Much important family life education (FLE) is done in school and university classrooms. This book is designed as a practical yet scholarly how-to volume for a different set of FLEs: those who work outside a traditional classroom setting. The broad goal of this book is to help upper-division and graduate students who are preparing to be FLEs as well as FLE professionals who serve on the front lines. This book is intended to develop and enhance the knowledge and skills needed to take FLE principles to citizens where they live and work. To this end, we have tried to incorporate some of the leading scholarship with years of our own professional experiences, to provide a scholarly yet practical guide for the FLE professional and professional-to-be.

This book is based on the assumption that there are specialized skills and knowledge a family life educator needs to succeed with the general public, those persons who are not likely to return to college to learn for family life. The needs and motivations of this audience usually differ from the traditional family science college or high school students. For example, it is known that adult education audiences are more likely to be motivated by a personal or family need (e.g., see Knowles, 1998). In addition, venues for FLE outside the traditional classroom vary greatly, from radio broadcasts and newsletters to home visits and workplace training. Thus, for FLEs to succeed in the business of educating the public requires a somewhat different skill set than teaching students in traditional classroom settings. This book is intended to arm students and professionals with practical, educational experiences in their college curriculum and continuing education to become more effective ambassadors of family science scholarship to citizens of the world.

Various works have been published on FLE prior to the current volume. The comprehensive *Handbook of Family Life Education*, Vols. 1 and 2, published in 1993 and edited by Margaret Arcus, Jay Schvaneveldt, and Joel Moss, provided solid coverage of the scholarship and practice of FLE to that date. These volumes clarified many issues and raised questions that have spawned research and theory in FLE. They also provide a strong academic treatment of FLE with leanings toward college-level FLE. They are more oriented toward basic scholarship than practical application.

A more recent work, titled *Family Life Education: An Introduction*, published in 2001 and written by Lane Powell and Dawn Cassidy, updates several of the content areas of the *Handbook* volumes and provides many useful ideas as a solid primer for the practice of FLE.

Family Life Education: Principles and Practices for Effective Outreach is the first book on FLE to combine both the scholarly foundation and the practical how-tos for successfully carrying out FLE outside a traditional classroom setting.

A comprehensive, scholarly, yet practical how-to text has been needed in the field for a long time, both to train upper-division and graduate-level students how to do FLE but also as a sourcebook to strengthen professionals already in the field. Thus far, many have been consigned to learn the principles and practices of effective FLE through limited university training or the crucible of experience alone.

Family Life Education: Principles and Practices for Effective Outreach had its genesis when we generated a topical outline collected from our professional experiences as Cooperative Extension specialists in four states. We also drew on the experience of colleagues across the country.

The book is organized into 14 chapters and two appendixes. The first chapters lay the foundation for effective outreach work by discussing the historical and philosophical underpinnings of current outreach FLE, guiding readers to develop their own FLE philosophy and role as a family life educator, presenting an integrated framework for developing prevention programs, describing elements of effective FLE resources and programs, and principles and practices for evaluating such programs. The next several chapters help readers learn principles and methods for reaching out to the lay audience, including designing effective instruction, engaging the lay audience, methods for effective FLE, working with the media, writing for the lay audience, and using technology in FLE. The final chapters assist the reader in learning principles and practices for reaching diverse audiences, form effective collaborations, and market family life principles, practices, and programs. The book concludes with an epilogue chapter, designed to highlight the needs of future research and practice in FLE. Each chapter includes an explorations section at the end, designed as a real-life application of the chapter material.

We appreciate and acknowledge contributing authors Tonya Fishio, author of Chapter 8 on media, Steven Dennis and Aaron Ebata, authors of Chapter 10 on technology, and Charles Smith, coauthor of the Statement of Principles found in Appendix A. We are indebted to these colleagues for generously sharing their expertise.

We acknowledge also the individuals who provided reviews both of the original proposal for the book submitted to Sage and the full book manuscript. These include Brent A. McBride, University of Illinois; Linda Skogrand, Utah State University; Karen DeBord, North Carolina State University; Chuck Smith, Kansas State University; Judith A. Myers-Walls, Purdue; Susan Witt, University of Akron; Glen F. Palm, St. Cloud State University; and a few others who wished to remain anonymous. Our reviewers provided many helpful insights that led to important additions that made it a better product for our intended audiences. We express gratitude to Jim Brace-Thompson of Sage for his support throughout the development of the proposal and book. His encouragement has helped us keep on track.

We thank you, the reader, who is committed to helping families in your sphere of influence to live more satisfying and loving family lives. We wish you every success in your FLE pursuits.

Finally, we express appreciation to loving and supportive family members, particularly our wives, Barbara and Nancy, whose constant encouragement is always a major factor in any of our worthy accomplishments.

—Steve Duncan and Wally Goddard
July 2004

CHAPTER 1

FOUNDATIONS AND PHILOSOPHIES OF OUTREACH FAMILY LIFE EDUCATION

Family life education (FLE) that takes place in communities is a unique type of education. The business of outreach FLE involves taking family science principles and practices to the general public—individuals, couples, parents, whole families—in varied educational settings outside the traditional classroom. Some outreach family life educators (FLEs) are employed as field agents or as university campus-based specialists within the Cooperative Extension System. Others may work in social work or other human service agency contexts or as media representatives. Those with an entrepreneurial spirit may develop their own FLE business and market their programs nationally. Still others may hold traditional university positions that include some outreach expectations.

To succeed in educating the public about family life requires a somewhat different skill set than teaching students in traditional classroom settings. With these skills, FLEs become more effective ambassadors of family science scholarship to citizens of the world.

This text endeavors to provide a comprehensive response to the following need: There are knowledge and skills that FLEs need to be most helpful and effective in work with their clientele. To arrive at the response, we generated a content outline that represented our collective experiences totaling nearly three decades as family life Extension Service specialists at several universities. We sent the content outline to other specialists and colleagues and incorporated their ideas. Then we went to work. The result is what we hope is a practical how-to reference volume on effective outreach FLE that you will use for years to come.

This first chapter provides a foundational and philosophical discussion of FLE in outreach settings. We begin with a brief discussion of the definition and history of outreach FLE, followed by the role universities have played in the movement. We next turn to a discussion of various roles FLEs can play in communities. Finally, we discuss elements pertinent to the development of a working philosophy of outreach FLE. At the end of the chapter, you'll have the opportunity to create a personal philosophy of FLE in outreach settings, integrating the various perspectives presented in the chapter.

● DEFINING FAMILY LIFE EDUCATION

Much effort has been expended to define FLE, with definitions dating back over 40 years (Arcus, Schvaneveldt, & Moss, 1993b). Overall there has been little consensus reached on a specific definition, and greater consensus reached on aims or principles underlying FLE (Arcus et al., 1993b). Moreover, no attempt has been made to distinguish FLE taking place in high school and college settings from FLE taking place outside these environments.

We define *outreach* FLE as any educational activity occurring outside a traditional school classroom setting, usually involving adults, that is designed to strengthen relationships in the home and foster positive individual, couple, and family development. Such education comprises many topics, from marriage education to parenting skills, from stress and anger management to strategies for adapting following divorce. In fact, it is any form of education that has as its goal to "strengthen and enrich individual and family well-being" (Arcus et al., 1993b, p. 21) and falls within any of the 10 content areas of FLE set forth by the National Council on Family Relations (Bredehoft & Cassidy, 1995), save that it assumes a lay audience that may not turn to a traditional classroom for FLE. Such education follows the operational principles set forth by Arcus et al. (1993b, pp. 15-20), which we have adopted and adapted for community settings. Specifically, these principles state that FLE (a) is to be relevant to individuals, couples, and families across the life span, (b) is based on the felt needs of individuals, couples, families, and communities, (c) draws on material from many fields and is multiprofessional in its practice, (d) is offered in many venues, including community workshops, video and print media, publications, the Internet, and many other settings, (e) is educational rather than therapeutic, (f) is respectful of diverse values, and (g) requires qualified FLEs to realize its goals.

By now it should be clear that this is a book about how to do FLE in outreach versus traditional classroom settings. The guiding principles for each are identical, but the practices vary widely. However, we don't want to continue repeating "outreach FLE" or "FLE in outreach settings" every time we speak of FLE. Therefore, anytime we use the term *family life education* (or *FLE*) from here on out, we are speaking specifically about *outreach* FLE as we have defined it above.

A BRIEF HISTORY OF OUTREACH ● FAMILY LIFE EDUCATION

Many disciplines have contributed to the history of FLE—traditional home economics, family sociology, social work, marriage and family therapy, social psychology, education, and parenting education (Lewis-Rowley, Brasher, Moss, Duncan, & Stiles, 1993)—which in turn draws upon child development and medicine. Truly FLE is multidisciplinary in focus and multiprofessional in practice.

Early Roots

The earliest FLE efforts in the United States can be traced to a collaboration between church and state to ensure that children were raised according to biblical standards. Self-help books emerged around 1800, how-to books became visible in the 1850s, and child and mother study groups developed, a precursor of what has come to be known as the Parent Teacher Association (PTA) in the public school system (Lewis-Rowley et al., 1993).

Informal discussions among support groups were perhaps among the first community venues of FLE. For example, as early as 1815, groups of parents met in Portland, Maine, to discuss child-rearing practices (Bridgeman, 1930, cited in Lewis-Rowley et al., 1993). Also, mother study groups, termed "maternal associations," were organized in the 1820s to discuss child-rearing approaches (Sunley, 1955, cited in Lewis-Rowley et al., 1993), followed by mothers' periodicals titled *Mothers Assistant* and *Mother's* magazine, believed to be the first known parenting periodicals.

The American Land Grant University System

A more formal FLE movement was also taking place in universities and colleges throughout the United States and some of its territories. The land grant university system was created by the Morrill Act, signed into federal law by President Abraham Lincoln on July 2, 1862. This act provided 1.7 million acres of land to the states so that each might have at least one college that promoted "the liberal and practical education of the industrial classes in the several pursuits and professions of life." Some of the "practical education" was to be taken out among the people where they lived and worked. The signing of the Morrill Act became the catalyst for the establishment of academic programs in home economics throughout the United States. Within this context, home economics/human ecology emerged as a dominant theoretical paradigm at the turn of the 20th century (Lerner, 1995). From a human ecological perspective, put forth first by Ellen Swallow Richards, the family was seen as affecting the well-being of the larger society. Thus, as the home environment could be enhanced, so too could the community at large. Leaders in the home and family movement during this time saw scientific knowledge about the family, which was disseminated to masses, as an important way of correcting or preventing social ills so pronounced in the family (Lewis-Rowley et al., 1993). The "home oekology" (Buboltz & Sontag, 1993) perspective brought many disciplines to bear on the problems pronounced in families.

Cooperative Extension

The Morrill Act also set the stage for an educational delivery system that would transmit knowledge about families to the masses, which came to be known as the Cooperative Extension System. This system, created by Congress through the passage of the Smith-Lever Act in 1914, provided a major federal thrust in the furtherance of FLE in community settings. So enthused was President Woodrow Wilson about the new system that he called it "one of the most significant and far-reaching measures for the education of adults ever adopted by the government." Its purpose was "to aid in diffusing among the people of the U.S. useful and practical information on subjects related to agriculture and home economics, and to encourage the application of the same." Extension work was to consist of "giving practical demonstrations in . . . home economics to persons not attending or resident in said colleges in the several communities, and imparting to such persons information on said subjects through field demonstrations, publications and otherwise."

The underlying philosophy was to "help people help themselves" by "taking the university to the people" (Rasmussen, 1989, p. vii).

Thus, land grant institutions became known as universities *for* the people of the state: the teaching, research, and outreach done there was primarily to benefit the masses in the state (Lerner, 1995). The land grant idea was committed to applying the best science possible to the practical problems of families. Extension home economics agents, later known as family and consumer science agents, were hired to be the conduit through which information about family life could be communicated to the local communities, through the carrying out of community-based FLE programs. Some states hired family living agents, in addition to family and consumer science agents, whose specific charge was to carry out FLE programs. Today there is a county agent in most of the over 3,000 counties of the United States who have at least a partial charge to promote strong family living through extension programs. These agents often carry out their responsibilities in this area in collaboration with other like-minded professionals. FLE programming is carried out through specific curriculum designed for target audiences, fact sheets, bulletins, pamphlets, videos, newspaper series, online learning modules, and other various means. During the late 1980s, Cooperative Extension in the family area was zero funded by the Reagan administration, later to be restored due to a public outcry of support.

Areas of family life emphasis within Cooperative Extension have evolved over the years to meet the needs of the constituency. Beginning in the 1980s, programs became more focused on interdisciplinary national initiatives than disciplinary programs (Rasmussen, 1989). For example, families underwent radical changes over two decades that culminated in the 1980s, which brought about increased stresses and risks for family disruption and dislocation. Complex issues such as these demanded a comprehensive, interdisciplinary response. During this time, family and economic well-being received increased emphasis among local FLEs affiliated with Extension.

Concerns for limited-resource families, defined as families at risk for not meeting basic needs, received increased programmatic emphasis in the early 1990s and continue today. This increased emphasis has led to adopting teaching strategies and practices that are best suited to meet the complex needs of limited-resource families such as peer support, professional and paraprofessional teaching efforts, one-on-one home visits, and working in small groups (Cooperative Extension Service, 1991).

Other recent emphases in the Extension System have included a focus on children, youth, and families who possess greater risks for not meeting basic life needs. The Children, Youth, and Families at Risk (CYFAR) initiative has received federal funding since 1991. Since that time, CYFAR has supported programs in more than 600 communities in all states and territories. Other major family life efforts have been made in the area of parenting education. In 1994, the National Extension Parent Education Model (Smith, Cudaback, Goddard, & Myers-Walls, 1994) was developed. This model made an important contribution to guiding the development of community-based parenting education programs. Web-based FLE to both professionals as well as clientele has also rapidly advanced with the advent of the Children, Youth, and Families Education and Research Network (CYFERNet), making research-based FLE resources available at the click of a mouse. While traditionally, marriage education programs in communities have been offered through the church, more programs are being offered through community adult education and extension programs and other nonreligious settings (Stahmann & Salts, 1993).

Other University-Based Outreach Efforts

In addition to organized efforts within the land grant university system, other outreach activities have been established at universities of recent date that have also contributed to what FLE is today. Perhaps most prominent in this movement has been the explosion of service learning and internship opportunities that, while helping the student, richly benefit the communities that receive the associated services. Service-learning pedagogies, of which internships are a type, enhance traditional modes of learning and actively engage students in their own educations through experiential learning in course-relevant contexts. But they also foster lifelong connections between students, their communities, and the world outside the classroom (Crews, 2002). These experiences enable students to contribute to the well-being of families within the context of their service learning assignment. For example, students in the School of Family Life at Brigham Young University can select from over 300 family- and youth-serving agencies in surrounding communities and in other parts of the United States and the world. Some examples of these agencies include writing for FLE Web sites, designing and marketing FLE curricula, and visiting families one on one to offer direct services.

Community Movements

In addition to developments within the land grant university system, outreach FLE was also fostered by the contemporary expansion of parenting education volunteer groups and community organizations. Certainly one of the earliest aspects of FLE is actually the growth of parenting education (Brock, Oertwein, & Coufal, 1993). For example, the National Congress of

Mothers was founded in 1897 and renamed the National Congress of Mothers and Parent-Teacher Associations in 1908, and was dedicated to promoting the notions of mother love and mother thought (Bridgeman, 1930, cited in Lewis-Rowley et al., 1993). In addition, the Society for the Study of Child Nature had also grown to several chapters, and by 1908 was consolidated into the Federation for Child Study. Among other things, this organization performed FLE functions such as distributing information on children, promoting lectures and conferences, and cooperating with other like-minded groups (Bridgeman, 1930, cited in Lewis-Rowley et al., 1993).

Expansion of FLE continued into the 1920s with the growth of parenting education. In 1924, the Child Study Association held a conference that invited the participation of 13 smaller organizations. The outgrowth of this conference was the National Council of Parent Education, which had as one of its goals to suggest guidelines and qualifications for the training of parents. By 1924, 75 major organizations were conducting parenting education programs (Brim, 1959, cited in Lewis-Rowley et al., 1993). Parenting education grew with the support of the Spelman Fund, and the Child Study Association of America was born, with the primary purpose of development and supervision of the use of parenting education materials. By 1930, there were some 6,000 members of this association acting as parenting educators (Bridgeman, 1930, cited in Lewis-Rowley et al., 1993). Parenting education declined somewhat during the 1930s as attention was turned to financial survival. We also saw the end of the Spelman Fund and some organizations that focused on parenting. Growth picked up again in during the 1940s as a preventive intervention but with largely a mental health perspective (Lewis-Rowley et al., 1993).

Parenting education has come to be both preventive and remedial (Brock et al., 1993). Even some specific parenting programs are more preventive or remedial, depending on the needs of the clientele. In recent decades, parents, churches, courts, and community mental health are turning to parenting education as a remedy. Divorcing couples are being assigned to divorce education to minimize stressful and destructive aspects of divorce on children. Abusive parents are being court-ordered to parenting education classes. More programs are becoming available for teenage parents.

The medical community, namely physicians, have also been active contributors to the FLE movement, often offering child development-related advice to scores of patients. Professionals trained as medical doctors with a specialty in pediatrics have written very popular parenting advice books (e.g., Brazelton, 1992). The American Academy of Pediatrics, a highly respected professional group, periodically issues news releases containing recommendations for parents on such things as limiting the amount of television watched by children under two (see http://www.aap.org).

Linked with the movement of FLE, especially that of early childhood intervention through parenting education, is the family support movement, developing essentially since the middle 1970s (Weissbourd, 1994). During the 1970s, a call for more preventive services, rather than customary crisis mode interventions, led to more family service agencies taking a more active part in FLE. Influenced by a human ecological perspective (Bronfenbrenner, 1979), family support focuses on a strengths-based approach to strengthening and empowering families and communities so that they can foster the optimal development of children, youth, and adult family members (Family Support America, 2003). The family support movement was founded on the following guiding principles (Weissbourd, 1994) that cut across disciplines:

- The most effective approach to families emanates from a perspective of health and well-being.
- The capacity of parents to raise their children effectively is influenced by their own development.
- Child-rearing techniques and values are influenced by cultural and community values and mores.
- Social support networks are essential to family well-being.
- Information about child development enhances parents' capacity to respond appropriately to their children.
- Families that receive support become empowered to advocate on their own behalf.

Family support initiatives strongly rely on the use of collaborations to carry out programs. A number of family support program offerings have emerged throughout the United States. Resource centers for parents in schools and family strengthening services offered through nonprofit agencies have become part of the family life educational landscape. FLE programs in communities following a family support model often use home visits and peer educators as major methods of teaching principles and skills.

Reaching Diverse Audiences

For years, observers have acknowledged that FLE receives "underwhelming participation" from the masses (Bowman & Kieren, 1985). But even more alarming is the finding that FLE is not reaching audiences at greatest need (e.g., Sullivan & Bradbury, 1997). There is a movement afoot to help change that. For example, the CYFAR initiative of the Cooperative Extension System mentioned earlier is an example of taking FLE beyond the traditional audience to meet the needs of groups at greatest risk, who are often socioeconomically and racially diverse. Government agencies are also increasing their efforts in this regard. For example, the Administration for Children and Families (ACF), an agency of the U.S. federal government, has contracted with family scholars, FLEs, and professional organizations to develop, implement, and evaluate programs for strengthening marriage among audiences that historically have been underserved, such as disadvantaged families (Dion, Devaney, & Hershey, 2003), who are disproportionately Black and Hispanic. Practical approaches for working with diverse audience are discussed in detail in Chapter 11.

Web-Based Family Life Education

An overview of FLE is not complete without some discussion of Web-based FLE. Individuals are increasingly turning to the Internet for all kinds of information, including matters of personal and family well-being. Because the Internet is a powerful medium that has much to offer FLEs (Elliott, 1999; Hughes, 1999; Morris, Dollahite, & Hawkins, 1999), over the past few years many FLEs have developed Web sites (Elliott, 1999). In fact, currently there are hundreds of FLE Web sites available online (Elliott, 1999). Some argue that this medium of FLE has revolutionized the manner in which FLE is disseminated to the masses (Smith, 1999). Limited evaluation data suggests that Web-based FLE can positively benefit its audiences, but whether it is an adequate substitute for face-to-face FLE is unknown and an important area of needed research (Steimle & Duncan, 2004). Using technology in FLE is discussed in Chapter 10.

EVOLUTION IN THE DISSEMINATION OF ● SCIENTIFIC KNOWLEDGE ABOUT FAMILIES

The field of family sciences emerged during the 1920s largely with the belief that problems plaguing the family could be addressed through systematic research. The ideal envisioned the university as the institution that could, through research, address the real-life problems and concerns pertaining to children, youth, and families. Doherty (2001) explains: "[Family science] embraced a vision of making the world better through the work of University-trained professional experts who would generate new knowledge and pass it on to families in the community" (p. 319). What evolved, according to Doherty, was a "trickle-down model of research and practice" (p. 319). According to this model, scientific knowledge for families is generated by university researchers, who then transmit this knowledge to practitioners (e.g., FLEs), who then, in turn, disseminate the information to the masses. The strength of this model, according to Doherty, lies in its ability to address problems scientifically when experiential knowledge about a topic is relatively lacking or when the issue is so hotly debated as to prevent a more objective view of an issue. The weakness of this model is that it ignores the collective wisdom of families and communities garnered through experience, although it is from families that much of what we call research data are generated. In addition, instead of being seen as partners in knowledge generation, this perspective relegates families to the "role of consumers of academic knowledge" (p. 321).

There are other dangers inherent in the traditional model of research generation and dissemination. Historically, researchers have failed to engage and partner with communities in the research process, neglecting to study the issues of greatest interest to them (Lerner, 1995). Without community/ family collaboration in the research process, research that becomes available to pass on to communities can become increasingly irrelevant to the needs of real families, causing to go unrealized the vision of scientific information benefiting families. In fact, Richard Lerner (1995) argues that much of the research generated by universities is of little value to communities. Furthermore, this top-down model of knowledge dissemination has been criticized as being inadequate at best, evidenced by the fact that the problems targeted still continue to plague children, youth, families, and communities (Lerner, 1995), even many of the same problems that experts were trying to fix when they first had a vision of a better world, made better with their discoveries.

A new model of taking family scholarship to the people is emerging, critical to effective FLE in community settings. Scholars are now arguing that effective FLE will integrate the best scientific information with the knowledge, lived experience, culture, and expertise of community clientele (Doherty, 2000; Lerner, 1995; Myers-Walls, 2000). To accomplish this requires a community-collaborative approach where there is extensive interface of the worlds of families in communities and institutions where scientific knowledge about these families is generated (Lerner, 1995). Families and professionals become partners in identifying strengths and needs and in mobilizing to address identified problem. FLE professionals bring their expertise not to dominate or give pat or complete answers but as "a potential part of a confederation of community members, a partnership that brings to the 'collaborative table' knowledge-based assets" (Lerner, 1995, p. 114). Hence, such an FLE professional would seek to be "on tap" but not "on top" (Doherty, 2001,

p. 322), viewing themselves as one of the many sources of knowledge in a community, but being careful not to "stifle families' own wisdom and initiative" (p. 322). The next section expands the discussion of the many roles FLEs in community settings can take in their professional role, including those most consistent with the perspectives above.

VARIED APPROACHES OR "ROLES" ● IN FAMILY LIFE EDUCATION

There are many educational approaches one can take, or roles one can play, as a family life educator. These approaches, reflecting various teaching philosophies and paradigms, are based on one's sense of responsibility for program content and methods and the assumptions one has about education, the educator, the learner, and the content. It is important for FLEs to be knowledgeable about each of these various approaches, their strengths and limitations, and when a certain approach might be recommended over another. While by no means exhaustive, these approaches comprise several prominent options: an expert approach, a facilitator approach, a critical inquirer approach, a collaborator approach, an interventionist approach, and an eclectic approach.

The Expert Approach

An expert approach fits a liberal educational philosophy, which is the oldest and most enduring educational philosophy, with roots tracing back to classical Greek philosophy (Price, 2000). A liberal education philosophy emphasizes the development of intellectual powers through the mastery of a disciplinary area of study. According to Elias and Merriam (1995), "[L]iberal education produced a person who is literate in the broadest sense—intellectually, morally, spiritually, and aesthetically" (p. 26).

FLEs operating from an expert approach view themselves as "subject matter authorit[ies] whose function it is to transmit a fixed body of knowledge to the learner" (Price, 2000, p. 3). FLEs are seen as possessors of important knowledge and skills that others do not have and who rely on them to transmit them. Those who follow an expert approach believe that answers lie with informed experts and that the lives of participants will be improved if they will learn the materials and skills, according to their instructions (Myers-Walls, 2000). Thus, materials tend to be highly structured with predetermined curricula and agenda, leading to the acquisition of predetermined knowledge and skills. Most packaged educational programs ostensibly follow this assumption, especially those that are particularly concerned that programs be delivered as written. An FLE teaching parenting using the expert approach to teaching would follow carefully a designated curriculum and insist upon content mastery before moving on to other concepts.

An expert approach makes certain assumptions about learners as well. One tacit assumption is that the audience is relatively uninformed as to the content, or that the experiential knowledge they have regarding a topic is of less importance than the specialized knowledge the expert is bringing to them. Lecture is often a common mode of delivery; the learner's task is to soak up, reflect upon, and analyze the information. This traditional form of education is often referred to as the "banking" model of education, where students are viewed as empty cash receptacles needing to be filled with the instructor's exclusively possessed knowledge. The transfer of knowledge often occurs in a static exchange with little discussion. This FLE perspective also fits with Doherty's (2000) notion of trickle-down research and practice discussed earlier.

The Facilitator Approach

Facilitator-oriented FLEs often have no specific agenda. Instead of facilitators deciding how programs are to proceed, participants decide what is important to them and then set the learning agenda. Facilitators acknowledge that participants are already fairly well informed about a topic. The facilitator, while often possessing specialized knowledge, doesn't seek to share that information except as a coequal and as it fits the flow of the group. Instead, the facilitator seeks to help participants gain access to the knowledge they already have within them. Thus, a facilitator approach may best be used when the audience possesses a substantial amount of knowledge and are highly motivated learners. This approach fits the personalistic paradigm (Czaplewski & Jorgensen, 1993) and humanist educational philosophy (Price, 2000), with its emphasis on maximizing the growth of the total person. Humanist adult educational philosophy is based upon the assumption that human nature is essentially positive and that each person possesses unlimited potential; therefore, humanist educational goals are bent toward the holistic development of persons toward their fullest potentials. Learning is essentially a personal, self-directed endeavor, and while disciplinary knowledge is important, it is bent toward the ultimate goal of self-actualizing individuals (Elias & Merriam, 1995). Learners know best what their learning needs are. Collaborative learning, experimentation, and discovery are all a part of the learning methods used. The learner's background and individual experiences are taken into account. Educators with a humanist philosophy act more as facilitators of individualized learning than as disseminators of fixed knowledge. In fact, the educator is "a colearner in the educational process, and assumes an egalitarian relationship with learners" (Price, 2000, p. 4). A standardized curriculum might not even exist, making evaluation of outcomes more difficult. After welcoming participants to a parenting workshop, FLEs working from this approach would have parents generate the list of topics to explore what would be most beneficial to them.

A related philosophical orientation that fits with a facilitator approach is the progressive philosophy, perhaps the most influential educational philosophy in adult education (Price, 2000). This educational philosophy stresses holistic, lifelong, and life-wide education and an experiential, problem-solving approach to learning as opposed to didactic, passive learning. The experiences of the learner become paramount in determining areas to be learned and problems to be solved. The educator is primarily a facilitator of the learning processes through guiding, organizing, and evaluating learning experiences within which she or he may also be actively involved. Thus, learning is collaborative between the learners and instructors (Price, 2000). FLEs following this philosophy in a class for married couples might present problem scenarios, then have participants identify possible solutions to the problems or have them try out solutions they generate for a time and report back to the group.

The Critical Inquirer Approach

Educators using a critical inquirer approach use questions to help participants think critically about the issues that are presented. This perspective acknowledges that participants have a responsibility to contribute meaningfully to their society and thus need to critically assess issues about them (Czaplewski & Jorgensen, 1993). This approach is tied to a critical/humanist philosophical orientation, which, like traditional humanistic approaches, promotes self-actualization of the learner. Yet for a critical/humanist, personal fulfillment is achieved through "becoming an autonomous, critical, and socially responsible thinker through an emphasis on rationality" (Tisdell & Taylor, 2000). FLEs might use a critical inquirer approach to help participants evaluate proposed or existing public policies designed to strengthen families.

The Collaborator Approach

Falling somewhere in between expert and facilitator approaches, in terms of responsibility for content and methods (Myers-Walls, 2000), is the collaborator approach. This approach recognizes that both FLEs and participants bring specialized knowledge to the learning experience. The educator brings research-based principles to the learning environment, and the participants bring their own lived experience regarding these principles. The collaborative educator brings a prepared agenda and curriculum, but these materials are fitted around the needs of participants. Participants are encouraged to contribute ideas for the agenda, but the educator maintains some control over the schedule and content of the discussion. After presenting the agenda for a Principles of Parenting program, collaborative FLEs might ask, "Are there any additions you'd like to make to the program, any topics you'd like to see covered that aren't listed?"

The Interventionist Approach

Interventionist-oriented FLEs are change agents: they seek cognitive, attitudinal, and behavior change, even transformation of participants through education. They believe that education for family life goes beyond simply learning for knowing, but extends to learning for living (Mace, 1981). Such professionals are not mere knowledge transmitters or discussion facilitators (Guerney & Guerney, 1981). Interventionist approaches can be traced to both behaviorist and radical educational philosophies. For example, a behaviorist philosophy centers on changing behavior though the shaping of the environment to promote the desired behavior. As noted by Elias and Merriam (1995), a behaviorist-oriented educator is a "behavioral engineer who plans in detail the conditions necessary to bring about desired behavior" (p. 88). Such educators extensively use behavioral or learning objectives, model desired behavior, provide behavioral reinforcement for achieving the desired behavior, and use systematic instructional design. Learners are engaged in step-by-step learning of desired behaviors, receiving instructor support and evaluation through the processes. FLEs working from this perspective with couples might teach and demonstrate Five Steps to Handling Conflict, then have couples practice the skills with the aid of a personal coach, who provides both reinforcement and corrective feedback.

Radical educational philosophies form the basis of educational strategies aimed at bringing about social change and combating social, political, and economic oppression of society. Developers of this approach (Freire, 1971; Mezirow, 1995) saw the traditional liberal form of education as limiting and paternalistic, because it treats knowledge as a gift of the learned to those who are not. One such approach deduced from the radical philosophical traditions is transformative learning, which promotes increased self-awareness and freedom from constraints, necessary to help create social equity for the oppressed and for real learning to occur (Christopher, Dunnagan, Duncan, & Paul, 2001). In this context, educators are liberators, not facilitators, who help learners become social activists. This kind of learning occurs in three steps (Taylor, 1997): (1) learners engage in critical self-reflection about assumptions and present approaches, (2) learners transform or revise their perspective, and (3) learners actually adopt new ways of behaving, consistent with their renewed perspective. FLEs working from this philosophy with a group of parents might ask their participants to reflect on the approaches they use to parent their children and reflect on what is effective and ineffective. The FLEs might then discuss a variety of helpful approaches with the group and have parents create parenting plans to try in the coming week.

The Eclectic Approach

Educators coming from an eclectic approach would use elements of all the approaches, depending on the situation. For example, FLEs might wisely use an expert approach to teach others about a topic where little or no experiential knowledge exists or about a topic that is more controversial and needs an expert voice to set the record straight with empirical data (Doherty, 2000). An interventionist approach may be the best approach when working with oppressed and marginalized families who need to realize they have a voice, great opportunities, and unlimited potential.

Which of these approaches do you most readily identify with? Some research shows that most FLEs organize and deliver their curricula based on a collaborative approach (Myers-Walls, 2000). While thematically FLEs may use one approach over another, the approach FLEs use may depend somewhat upon the context. For example, the expert approach may be the approach of choice when it becomes necessary to share information about which the audience has limited knowledge or experience or when expert opinion is important to help solve a controversy. However, it would not be a recommended approach for use in a group of experienced, highly motivated parents—a facilitator or collaborator approach would be more successful. A critical enquirer approach is best when you want the audience to think deeply about an issue, even if it is about the quality of their own parenting; a facilitator approach likely would lack the structure and impetus to help accomplish this. When the learning of skills is part of the plan, interventionist approaches are likely the best. All in all, having all these approaches at one's disposal may be the most ideal situation of all, pointing to an eclectic approach. Thus, FLEs need to be sensitive to the best times to use a particular approach.

● DEVELOPING A WORKING PHILOSOPHY FOR OUTREACH FAMILY LIFE EDUCATION

Having a sense of our role as FLEs and its philosophical underpinnings provides a basis for creating a working philosophy of outreach FLE. It is important for FLEs to take time and ponder their philosophical basis for teaching (Dail, 1984). They need to actively reflect and contemplate over *why* they do what they do (White & Brockett, 1987). Given the practical focus of FLE, some educators may question the relevance of philosophical rumination (White & Brockett, 1987), perhaps even seeing it as primarily an academic exercise they simply don't have time for. However, when we fail to tie FLE practice to philosophical underpinnings, our efforts may take on a mindless, ungrounded quality.

Everyone has some kind of working philosophy that is tied to one's personal values, experiences, and lifestyles and reveals itself in one's professional actions (White & Brockett, 1987). It's wise from time to time to clarify and write down our ideas so that they are subject to our understanding and critical reflection, at the same time realizing that a personal FLE philosophy is ever changing, always subject to modification through experiences and reflection.

Dail (1984) suggested several additional reasons for developing a personal philosophy: It provides a sense of direction and purpose; it helps the educator get in touch with his or her own beliefs and their influence; it helps the educator assess educational problems (e.g., provide a foundation for deciding what to teach about effective parenting); it helps the educator relate FLE to the needs of the larger society; and it provides impetus for the scholarly study of families. "In its essence," says Dail, "a philosophy of family life education provides a deeper meaning to the educator's life" (p. 147).

Dail (1984) provides a framework for the development of a personal philosophy of FLE, which we have adopted and adapted below.

Beliefs About the Family and the Nature and Quality of Family Life

FLEs need to answer for themselves tough questions that even the savviest of politicians would prefer to avoid. For example, what is family? A single father and two children? Grandmother, mother, and daughter? Mom, Dad, and three children? Coparents with each bringing a child to the relationship? The definition of what a family is and/or should be will have profound effects on how an educator relates to clientele, especially those who may be excluded by their definition. Another consideration is the nature of family life. What assumptions do you make about the nature of family life? Are families a mere social arrangement, or do they have greater significance? How important is "family"? Whether family is seen as *the* fundamental unit of society or as one of the major entities among a cast of many players will effect educational practices with families. A third consideration is the quality of family life. For example, what characteristics comprise an ideal family, contrasted with a low-functioning family? Because of our beliefs about how parents ought to treat their children, we could never support coercive parenting as a functional ideal in a family. Your beliefs about the way families should be may lead you to draw the line on some family behaviors.

We think a working philosophy of FLE must also consider the answer to questions at the heart of the human experience. For instance, what does it mean to be human? Since humans have common existence and relationship in families, is membership in a family a key part of what it means to be human? What assumptions underlie our beliefs about human nature?

Beliefs About the Purpose of Family Life Education

FLEs must be clear about what they want to accomplish and why (Powell & Cassidy, 2001), so that appropriate goals and objectives can be created. Preceding goals and objectives are a sense of vision and mission. For example, what value does education about family life have in society? David Mace (1981) envisioned FLE as something that originates from a cloudburst of information that becomes part of the knowledge base of a learner, which then produces personalized insight that leads the learner to experiment with new behaviors in family relationships. When family members coparticipate and mutually reinforce such action, the result is shared growth of members. Thus, does FLE in communities exist to be a catalyst for such a process? Guerney and Guerney (1981) reflected on whether FLEs could be considered "interventionists." That is, do FLEs take some "clearly defined" action "designed to induce some change" (p. 591)? The Guerneys argue that if FLEs believe that their purpose goes beyond mere knowledge transmission "but of changing attitudes/values and behavior," they should "class themselves . . . as interventionists and be willing to stand up and be counted as such" (p. 592). This kind of "intervention" is distinguished from the focused, brief intervention strategies and family therapy that constitute the domain of the clinical professional and is outside the scope of FLE (Doherty, 1995). Thus, an important question at the heart of the purpose of FLE for outreach professionals to raise is how "interventionist" FLE should be.

Beliefs About the Content of Family Life Education

There is no shortage of family-strengthening ideas to teach others. For example, there are literally hundreds of parenting books designed to impart advice to eager readers who want to do the best by their children. Some works are based on sound scholarship, others upon clinical impressions, still others on the simple convictions of the authors. What should be taught in FLE settings? How do you decide what to teach? Of what value is university-based theory and research? Even the best research has limitations in its application to individual/family needs. Much research has been completed with a disproportionate amount of White, middle-class participants. Thus, the data may have systematic bias. Participants in FLE programs also bring with them a rich array of personal experiences. How can the rich learning that is the lived experiences of individuals, families, and communities become part of the content of FLE?

Our personal values may also lead us to choose certain materials to teach certain ideas while ignoring or giving limited exposure to others. For example, if your personal values dictate that teens should avoid having sex outside of marriage and you are called upon to give a 45-minute talk at a high school assembly, your selected material may likely be quite different than it would be if you valued the full, unlimited, but responsible sexual activity of teens.

Beliefs About the Process of Learning for Families and Individuals Within Families

There are many ways to share information about family life in community settings. We can teach in small or large groups, through media channels such as radio, newspapers, magazines, television programs, and videos; through newsletters, publications, the Internet, and leaflets; through one-on-one meetings in homes or an office. How do individuals and families learn most effectively? From a family systems approach, it can be argued that the best learning for family strengthening will occur as a full family group. New knowledge can be colearned and reinforced at home. However, when any member of the family is missing, newly learned attitudes and behaviors are at risk for being sabotaged by the missing member. Still, one person behaving positively can influence the others. In addition, individuals and families differ in terms of their primary learning styles and sensory modalities (Powell & Cassidy, 2001), which effective education must account for. What learning processes invoke positive change in knowledge, attitudes, skills, and behaviors? How important are learning goals and evaluation in these processes? What assumptions do you hold about learners? Are they lights to be lit or cups to be filled?

CONCLUSION ●

Outreach FLE has a long history. It is evolving from an expert top-down approach to addressing family problems to a collaborative, strength-based, community strengthening model that integrates scientific knowledge from family sciences with the values and experiences of families in communities. There are many philosophical bases from which we can craft FLE and varied approaches associated with these philosophies. Generally, the best strategies are community-collaborative in nature, but each approach discussed may have a role depending on the circumstances. Crafting a philosophy of FLE has the potential to purposefully guide and direct our efforts. Following are exercises to help guide you in writing your personal philosophy and approach in FLE.

EXPLORATIONS ●

1. Follow the guidelines below and design your own working philosophy of outreach FLE. Address the questions in your discussion.
   - What are my beliefs about the family and the nature and quality of family life and the human experience?
     - What is a "family"? How important are families? What values do I hold regarding families and the human experience? What does it mean to be human?
   - What are my beliefs about the purpose of FLE?
     - What is the nature of FLE? What value does FLE have in communities? Is it to provide insight, skills, and knowledge? Is it to change behavior? How "interventionist" should FLE be?
   - What are my beliefs about the content of outreach FLE?
     - Of what value is university-based theory and research to families? Of what value is the lived experiences of individuals, families, and communities, and how can it become part of the content of FLE? How do my personal values regarding families and the human experience influence the content I select?

- What are my beliefs about the process of learning for families in outreach settings?
  - How do individuals and families learn most effectively? What teaching strategies have the greatest impact? How important are learning goals and evaluation in these processes? What assumptions do I hold about learners?

2. Describe what you are like as an FLE. Different FLE settings may necessitate different approaches. But most of us will find a place where we are most comfortable and effective. Review the various approaches discussed in the chapter. Which approach best describes you and why?

CHAPTER 2

DESIGNING COMPREHENSIVE PREVENTION PROGRAMS IN OUTREACH FAMILY LIFE EDUCATION

Beyond philosophically grounding our work as family life educators (FLEs), it is important that FLEs place their programmatic efforts in a scientifically supported, organizing framework. This chapter presents an integrative framework for designing family life education (FLE) programs, which includes the following broad stages: problem analysis, program design, pilot testing, advance testing, and dissemination. Found within each stage are many subprocesses. For example, during the problem analysis stage, FLE professionals would be engaged in defining the problem or goal, identifying risk and protective factors, assessing accessibility of the target group, and forming a coalition of stakeholders who work together to address the problem.

● THE SCIENCE AND PROFESSION OF PREVENTION

As a guiding principle, FLEs focus on preventive education rather than therapeutic remediation (Arcus & Thomas, 1993). The modern prevention movement as related to family strengthening is about 20 to 25 years old (Small & Memmo, 2004). L'Abate (1983) was among the first to articulate the concept of prevention in the family field. L'Abate describes three levels of prevention: primary, secondary, and tertiary. Primary prevention-oriented FLEs help families develop the knowledge and skills they need to build strong relationships before any problems or issues present themselves, preventing problems before they occur. For example, most FLE Web sites are primary preventive in focus, as they are geared to transmit information and skills to the audience. Secondary prevention involves working with audiences who have some signs of risk, where intervention would prevent more serious problems from occurring (Small & Memmo, 2004). For example, a program developed to help parents overcome unbridled anger tendencies learned in their families of origin would be operating at this level. Tertiary prevention programs are designed for FLE audiences already experiencing a good deal of distress. Such programs normally are carried out by clinical professionals or FLEs who also have such training. FLEs typically operate at the primary and secondary prevention levels and leave tertiary prevention to family therapy (Doherty, 1995).

The concept of prevention has likewise been found in the fields of public health and the psychological and social sciences. In fact, a new discipline has emerged, termed *prevention science,* whose goal is "to prevent or moderate major human dysfunctions," including those associated with marriage, family, and individual development (Coie et al., 1993, p. 1013).

Prevention science integrates the independent risk-focused paradigm (Hawkins, Catalano, & Miller, 1992) and protective or resiliency factors paradigm (e.g., Werner, 1990). Prevention science when applied to FLE focuses on the understanding of both risk factors and protective factors as a precursor to the development and implementation of FLE programs. Risk factors are variables that increase the vulnerability of individuals, couples, and families to a variety of negative outcomes; protective factors are safeguarding variables that increase an individual's, couple's, or family's resistance to normative, developmental, or unplanned stressors (Bogenschneider, 1996; Rutter, 1987). The presence of risk factors or protective factors are not enough to ensure that a negative or positive outcome will occur, but simply make such outcomes more likely when present. Risk factors increase the odds that negative outcomes will occur; protective factors increase the likelihood that negative states will be thwarted. Protective factors are activated only in the presence of risk factors (Small & Memmo, 2004).

Family science has progressed far enough in its knowledge about marriage and family relationships to be able to detail risk factors and protective factors for the prevention of marital distress, poor child development outcomes, and various psychological disorders. A science of prevention today pertains to marriage and familial disorders as much as it does to the prevention of heart disease and cancer. The most effective FLE programs are those that simultaneously and proactively work to reduce risks while increasing protection.

TWO RELATED PREVENTION EDUCATION MODELS ●

Since the emergence of prevention science, at least two related theoretical models for developing prevention programs have surfaced in FLE literature, appearing in print at about the same time. Each model helps us take family life educational program design beyond a "service mission" to a "scientific enterprise" (Dumka, Roosa, Michaels, & Suh, 1995, p. 78). Dumka et al. (1995) constructed a five-stage process for developing prevention programs, consisting of problem analysis, program design, pilot testing, advance testing, and dissemination. Found within each stage are many other subprocesses. For example, during the problem analysis stage (Stage 1), FLE professionals would be engaged in defining the problem or goal, identifying risk and protective factors, and assessing accessibility of the target group. The first two stages address the formulation of an intervention theory, Stages 3 and 4 (implementation) become a test of the theory, and the final stages assess whether the program works and should be widely disseminated (Dumka et al., 1995). In the second model, Bogenschneider (1996) began with the epidemiological models of risk and protection from prevention science and placed them within the context of ecological systems theory (Bronfenbrenner, 1979, 1986) and developmental contextualism (Lerner, 1991, 1995). The result was an ecological risk/protective theoretical model for the design and implementation of youth development programs. At least four premises derive from this perspective: (1) outcomes are multiply determined, (2) proximal environments have the strongest and most direct influence on outcomes, (3) risk and protective factors occur at different levels of the human ecology (e.g., individual-family-community), and (4) these factors move and change through developmental time. From this basis, Bogenschneider proposes 12 principles for building prevention programs:

(1) identify the real issues or problems facing youth, (2) establish well-defined goals that target the risk and protective processes associated with the identified youth issue or problem, (3) be comprehensive in addressing both risk and protective processes in several levels of the human ecology, (4) collaborate with stakeholders in the community or neighborhood, (5) educate coalition members on current theory and research on adolescent development, prevention programming, and community process, (6) tailor the plan to the community, reducing risks that exist locally and building protective processes that do not exist, (7) involve the target audience in program design, planning, and implementation, (8) be sensitive to cultural, ethnic, and other forms of diversity in the neighborhood or community, (9) intervene early and continuously, (10) select developmentally appropriate intervention strategies, (11) anticipate how changes in one part of the system may affect changes in the system or other settings, and (12) evaluate effectiveness by monitoring changes in risk and protective processes.

Below we integrate the Dumka et al. and Bogenschneider models to form a framework for the design of comprehensive FLE programs. We introduce this framework and provide relevant examples of its use.

● A COMPREHENSIVE MODEL FOR THE DESIGN OF FAMILY LIFE PREVENTION PROGRAMS

Stage 1: Problem Analysis

Identify Problem and Establish Overall Program Goal(s)

It is important to clearly articulate the problem or need one seeks to address through an FLE program. One way to do this is to formulate a brief research-informed problem statement. Students in an undergraduate FLE class crafted the following problem statement for their transition to parenthood program. It is titled Making Room for Two When Baby Makes Three:

> Current research shows that nearly half of all divorces occur within the first seven years of marriage. It has also been shown that the arrival of the first baby to a couple tends to increase the likelihood that either the husband, wife, or both partners will experience a decline in marital satisfaction. Therefore, it is essential that couples become aware of this problem and make their marriage a priority during the transition to parenthood.

Identification of problems certainly comes from investigating extant scholarship. But as Bogenschneider (1996) points out, such problems must be relevant and tied to real issues facing a community. Therefore, concomitant with problem analysis from a research and theory perspective is an analysis of the problem within the specific population we seek to serve, thereby avoiding the potential disconnect noted in Chapter 1. From a human ecological perspective, it is possible that problems identified more broadly may be very unique to local community cultures; thus, FLEs will wisely survey individual targeted communities to learn of their specific problems and needs. Findings from local populations that demonstrate a problem or need may be more likely to motivate community buy-in than more remote research conducted in distant places. Local data collection also is often a more reliable way to determine needs and forestall wasteful spending of prevention dollars. For example, while serving as extension specialists in Alabama, we had the opportunity of conducting a Teen Assessment Project (TAP) survey, modeled after the Wisconsin Teen Assessment Project (Small & Hug, 1991), in various middle and high school locations throughout the state. In one location, school administrators were convinced that they faced a serious drug problem, and were preparing to spend lots of district dollars on prevention programs. They invited us to administer the survey. Surprisingly to them, the survey data suggested that there were other risk behaviors going on that were far more serious, even deadly, leading the district to spend dollars on programs to address this higher-priority concern.

With a problem defined, an overall program goal statement can be developed that points to the general direction a program will take to address the problem. This statement should also make reference to the target audience. For example, the goal of the aforementioned program was stated as follows: "The goal of Making Room for Two When Baby Makes Three is to enhance marital satisfaction among *expectant and new parents* as they face the birth of their first child." Another example: "The ABC program is designed to help *single parents* identify and build upon their parenting strengths, enhancing their sense of competence as a parent."

Identify Risk and Protective Factors, and Extract "Teachable" Ideas

Knowing risk and protective factors associated with the identified problem enables FLEs to target and limit specific processes that lead to negative outcomes and target and increase specific processes leading to positive outcomes. For example, risk and prediction research has identified various negative interaction patterns that place couples at heightened risk for marital disruption, such as escalation, avoidance, withdrawal, and negative interpretations (Gottman, 1994; Markman, Stanley, & Blumberg, 2001). Research has also identified processes that enhance the well-being of marriage, such as nurturing friendship and commitment. Both risk and protective factors will range from those more or less modifiable within the context of an FLE program. For instance, parental divorce is a risk factor in marriage that is not modifiable. However, how a parental divorce plays out in a current marriage is possible to change. To be effective, FLE programs will need to focus on modifiable factors and increasing protection from the influence of negative processes that may have been produced by the factors.

Extract the "teachable" ideas and principles from theories and research, those ideas that are practical and useful in addressing the problem. Some examples include the following: "The more authoritative a parent is, the better off their children will be as they grow." "The more married couples accurately read one another's love language, the better the marriage." "Risks for divorce are reduced when couples learn to handle conflict and disagreements effectively." Teachable ideas such as these are usually embedded within or supportive of broader ideas deduced from theories related or applied to the family, such as family systems theory, communications theory, exchange theory, family development theory, human ecology theory, or social learning theory. FLEs are wise to have a working knowledge of these major theoretical frameworks (for an excellent discussion of using theory to design programs, see Powell & Cassidy, 2001, p. 51).

Establish Well-Defined Program Goals That Target the Risk and Protective Factors Associated With the Problem

With knowledge of the various risk and protective processes, specific goals directed at risk-reducing and protection-enhancing outcomes can be crafted. With the general goal of increasing marital well-being, specific program goals might be established to help achieve it, such as "Reduce self-reported levels of escalation during conflict discussions by 50%" and "By the end of the program, all couples will report having a weekly date and report intentions to continue the practice, without baby around."

Form a Coalition of Stakeholders Who Work Together to Address the Problem

As will be discussed in greater detail in Chapter 12, most family concerns are too complex and need solutions too comprehensive for any single entity to address alone. Wise FLEs will seek to join forces with other like-minded persons in addressing family concerns. As was discussed in the previous chapter, communities bring with them their own special expertise, with FLEs comprising one player at the collaborative table. "Involving local citizens in planning helps ensure that prevention programs fit the community, promotes local ownership, and engenders commitment to seeing that the program is implemented and maintained" (Bogenschneider, 1996, p. 132). Once a coalition is formed, FLEs can use their expertise to educate coalition members on current theory and research addressing the problem. After a coalition to address youth concerns was formed in a small Montana town, an FLE professional shared with them the risk factors and protective factors associated with youth development and worked with them to design and implement a survey that assessed these factors in several high schools in the area. Findings from the survey provided an empirical basis for targeted youth development programs within the participating schools.

Stage 2: Program Design

Consult the Target Group

As a prelude to or concomitant with other aspects of program design is the task of assessing target audience needs. Many FLE programs fail because they do not spend time thoroughly investigating the needs of target audiences (more about this will be discussed in Chapter 13). Consulting the target audience is a way of checking out the fit of the research literature with the actual audience for whom an educational product is intended. There are at least three kinds of needs to assess (Arcus et al., 1993b). *Felt* needs are those sought from audiences in response to direct questioning through questionnaires, interviews, and focus groups. It is what they say they need. For example, the question, "What concerns do you have about parenting teenagers nowadays?" asked of parents of teens would be a question designed to elicit felt need responses, as well as "If a program were designed to help you be a better parent for your teenagers, what would it contain?" *Ascribed* needs are those FLEs may observe because of their specialized knowledge. These are the needs FLEs may attribute to the group as a result of a review of the literature. To continue with the example of parents of teens, a large representative study of teens may reveal that they are much less likely to participate in risky sexual behavior when their parents appropriately monitor their activities. From this data, FLEs might decide that parents of teens need to learn how to monitor their teens, such as using the Who-What-Where-When approach (who are you going to be with, what will you be doing, where will you be going, and when will you be home?). *Future* needs involve the skills and abilities required to accomplish future tasks and perform future roles. The idea of anticipatory socialization suggests that transitions to new roles are easier when we learn as much as we can about a role before we perform that role. Future needs can be tapped by asking such questions as "What do couples preparing for marriage need to know prior to marriage?"

There are numerous ways to consult the target audience, from conducting interviews, sending mail questionnaires, and using existing data about the audience. To aid in the design of their parenting program for high-risk families, after reviewing the literature, Dumka et al. (1995) conducted focus group interviews with various subgroups of their targeted population. A total of 53 parents divided into six groups participated and were asked open-ended questions that probed their needs as parents, their children's needs, as well as the resources in the community currently available to meet those needs. Parents requested a program that would provide information regarding drug and alcohol abuse to parents and children and teach parenting skills such as improved communication and disciplining children. There was some variation in reported felt needs among the groups, and these variations were considered accordingly in program design.

The involvement of the target audience is not only critical in program design but also in the planning, implementation, and evaluation of the program. Wise FLEs will include members of the target audience on their coalition and will seek their input at every stage of the program. When deciding on how best to evaluate the effectiveness of our program to help families on public assistance gain self-sufficiency, a group of FLEs (Duncan, Dunnagan, Christopher, & Paul, 2003) first field tested their evaluation protocol with several low-income, limited-literacy participants, and made some adjustments based on their feedback.

Select Change Objectives

Change objectives refer to the knowledge level, attitudes, behaviors, and aspirations targeted for change by the program. Fulfillment of these objectives lead to the positive outcomes predicted by the theories and research and desired by the target audience. These objectives are stated in specific, action-oriented terms (e.g., what will occur as a result of the program?). Dumka et al.'s (1995) analysis of the literature and consultation with the target group led them to identify several change objectives, written from a leader-centered perspective, such as "Increase supportive parenting" and "Increase consistent discipline."

Select Outcome Evaluation Instruments

The purpose of evaluation is to assess whether a program is showing progress in meeting change objectives. The instruments selected must allow us to evaluate changes in the risk and protective factors that can be attributed to the program and must be directly tied to program objectives. Some tools that have demonstrated reliability and validity can be selected, provided they fit change objectives. Otherwise, they must be created and pilot tested to ensure their usefulness.

In the Making Families Stronger program, I (Duncan) had the goal of increasing the levels of self-reported family life satisfaction through the processes of identifying and building one's family strengths. The change objective was to "increase family life satisfaction levels among participating families." I selected David Olson's Family Life Satisfaction scale as my outcome evaluation tool, which is a reliable and valid measure of family life satisfaction directly tied to the change objective that also incorporated a family strengths approach in the development of the items. Thus, it was the "perfect" tool for my purposes. (See Chapter 4 for a full discussion of evaluation.)

Select Change Methods

Change methods will be wisely tied to change objectives. An important question to ask is, What method would be most effective to accomplish this objective? For example, a skills-related objective calls for a skill-teaching methodology. Steps include the following: (a) describe the skill, (b) model the skill, (c) practice the skill in a nonstressful setting and situation, (d) receive reinforcement and corrective feedback, and (e) use the skill in a real-life setting, that is, at home (also see Chapter 7). Other types of objectives would draw from other methods. Methods effective with adult learners include buzz groups, role playing, and various forms of discussion (see Chapter 7). All methods would be sensitive to varied learning styles, sensory modalities, and developmental needs and abilities (see Chapter 11).

In deciding on the best methods, wise FLEs will also examine existing programs for methods that work with their population, often called "best practices." The process of learning about other programs, methods used, and their effectiveness is critical to identifying these practices. It can also save program development time and energy. Ask yourself: What can I learn from these programs without having to reinvent the wheel, at the same time incorporating my own imagination/creative energy?

Decide Program Extensiveness

Dumka et al. (1995) identify three dimensions of program extensiveness. The first of these is the selectiveness of the program. A *universal program* is designed for everyone. A parenting program following a PTA meeting billed "for all parents" would be such a program. Such a program avoids the risk of inviting only certain parents, and thus parents avoid a labeling stigma. However, it may be too general to make a significant difference among persons needing a targeted program. A *selective* program would be targeted to particular subgroups of participants (e.g., single parents, seniors) or subgroups exhibiting risk factors a program seeks to address (e.g., families receiving public assistance). An *indicated* program would be developed for an audience exhibiting negative outcomes, such as parents court-ordered to participate in parenting programs as an adjunct to counseling. Such audiences may include participants whose needs cannot be effectively met with preventative FLE alone (Dumka et al., 1995). A second aspect of program extensiveness is *breadth,* or the number and range of change objectives. Following an ecological systems (Bronfenbrenner, 1979, 1986) orientation in relation to prevention programs, Bogenschneider (1996) recommends that change objectives range across several levels of the human ecology. For example, a program designed to help employed parents harmonize work and family would also help employers craft family-friendly workplace policies and promote work-family harmony through media channels. A program focused on only one level will likely be limited in impact, as other systems in the social ecology may act to sabotage newfound insights and strategies. For example, the excitement of learning to harmonize family and work in a community workshop may be drained when the workplace refuses to grant flextime.

A third dimension of program extensiveness is *length.* While shorter programs may be the desire of a target audience and more appealing from a marketing perspective, longer programs are more effective in producing reliable, longer-lasting changes. For example, in marriage education, where the audiences tend to be of lower risk for marital disruption (Carroll & Doherty, 2003), longer programs involving over 12 contact hours produce somewhat better outcomes than shorter programs (Guerney & Maxson, 1990). Where audiences are of greater risk, the ideal length of contact may be much longer. For programs to have a significant impact on families at risk of child abuse, some argue that programs should be at least 6 to 18 months in length. It has been found that parents who participate for a longer duration (~ 2 years) and who used all services offered (at least 3-5 programs) had better outcomes than those receiving less intense and shorter-term services (Whipple & Wilson, 1996). The National Research Council (1993) reviewed several child abuse prevention programs and found that programs that were short term and low in intensity did not change long-term relationships between parents and children.

Design Recruitment/Retention Strategy

One of the greatest challenges FLEs face is recruitment and retention of audiences. As part of needs assessments surveys, wise FLEs will consult the target audience about the best ways to recruit and retain an audience. Dumka et al. (1995) followed this strategy during their focus groups and were given several suggestions: (a) include both parents and children in the program so they could talk about what they were learning, (b) help parents develop a support group so they could help each other during and after the program, (c) provide child care and refreshments, and (d) offer the program close to home with no more than one meeting a week.

Tailor Program Content and Delivery

Programs designed after a "one size fits all" model are doomed to failure. Program content and delivery must be tailored to the needs of the audience and the community. For example, the content and approach should be sensitive to cultural, ethnic, and other forms of diversity (see Chapter 11). To maximize participation, implementation strategies should be based on target audience felt needs and preferences. For example, a standard curriculum was not acceptable in one community until after the inclusion of recruitment meetings (drummed up by current participants where recruits were invited by current participants), teachers from the same culture, and home visits for those participants facing transportation barriers. In one program for limited resource families (Duncan et al., 2003), educators kept the material simple and to the point because of the vast differences in participant educational levels. Materials were adjusted to relate to very basic levels of life skills. Written materials were written at a low reading level or were simple enough that they could be easily adapted or interpreted.

Stage 3: Pilot Testing

Once programs have been developed, they are ready for testing in the field. The goal of pilot testing is to "implement the prototype program with participants and in contexts as similar to the targeted participants and contexts as possible" (Dumka et al., 1995, p. 84). Dumka et al. recommend doing three kinds of evaluation at this stage: recruitment and retention, process, and formative evaluation.

Recruitment and Retention Evaluation

This is the process of assessing whether your recruitment strategy designed during Stage 2 is working. Since FLE in community settings often suffers from underwhelming participation, and participation is vital for the existence of the program, this piece of evaluation is of vital importance. If the recruitment strategy you used for a parenting program included circulating a flyer to all parents of fourth graders and only 3 of an eligible 100 parents showed up for the program, it would be clear that recruitment strategies need changing. The Dumka et al. strategy noted above resulted in over 53% of parents participating in five or more sessions—quite successful for a program such as this.

Process Evaluation

This kind of evaluation provides information about the overall management of the program to assess if the program is functioning as designed. It would include an adjudicated assessment of instruction (e.g., is quality information being taught?), logistics (evaluation of the meeting place, food, and transportation), how evaluation processes are perceived by participants (e.g., do participants find evaluation questions too personal or complex?), level of community support (e.g., media pieces supporting the program), support from stakeholders (e.g., county commissioners giving the program attention), and a host of other elements. Feedback on processes from staff and clientele are both important. We call this kind of evaluation "project quality control."

Formative Evaluation

This kind of evaluation assesses participants' direct experience with program material and learn what modifications may be necessary to improve their learning experience. At a pilot testing stage, it is appropriate for FLEs to administer a brief questionnaire at the end of each session and ask whether the participants learned something new, what were the strengths in the program, and suggestions for improvement. Both process and formative evaluation are part of the "program clarification" tier of evaluation (Jacobs, 1988), which will be fully discussed in Chapter 4.

Program Revision

Process and formative evaluation will likely point to needed changes. FLEs need to identify and decide what they are going to do differently, based on the pilot feedback they receive. Data may suggest needed content, implementation, or evaluation changes. For example, formative evaluation of a Web site led to changes in the format of the articles and the adding of some user-friendly features (such as the ability to e-mail an article to a friend or family member). In another program, process evaluation revealed that many participants complained about being expected to complete pretests and posttests that were long and tedious. The evaluators decided to provide a nominal financial incentive of $10 per completed questionnaire.

Stage 4: Advanced Testing

After integrating changes suggested during pilot testing, a program is ready for more advanced assessment. The goal of advanced testing is to evaluate the ability of a program to make significant changes in targeted risk factors and protective factors. In other words, it asks the question, Does the program truly accomplish the stated change objectives? For a parenting program, this may mean the enhancement of not only reported parenting skills but also translation to better outcomes long term among participating parents' children. To answer these kinds of questions requires an assessment sophistication greater than pilot testing.

Advance testing includes the processes of choosing an experimental design, implementing the revised program, analyzing the data, and continuing to refine the program. While some programs collect data that masquerade as impact data (Small, 1990), advance testing of program impact requires an experimental research design. This is because experimental designs most effectively control competing explanations for what may be positive outcomes. Perhaps the most common experimental research design is the pretest, posttest, control group design. If a program is important enough to collect experimental design data, the data deserve more sophisticated treatment as well, to help answer more definitively important questions. For instance, a common FLE question, beyond one of general program impact, is, For whom is the program most effective? Analyses such as multivariate analysis of variance (MANOVA) can help answer that question.

Stage 5: Dissemination

Imagine this: You have developed a program for families with widespread community support. You have field tested it with the families for whom it was intended and have made some adjustments in the program and how you carry it out, as a result of the candid input from program participants and staff. You have taken the revised program, continued to make refinements, and have subjected it to an ultimate test: an evaluation using an experimental design. Findings from your evaluation suggest that the program successfully meets change objectives and is significantly reducing some risk factors among parents (e.g., harsh discipline strategies, lack of social support) and significantly increasing protective factors (e.g., use of affirming, loving messages with youngsters, more shared parenting). Your program is a success and you feel justifiably proud of the effort you and your coalition have made with families in your community. You are now ready to take your program forward to the masses, to export it and what you have learned to other communities, so that your efforts might strengthen families in those communities as well.

The goal of the dissemination stage is the widespread adoption of the program. Programs beginning in one area expand to other communities and often become institutionalized and part of community culture. Dissemination involves identifying potential users of the program, promoting the program (through publications and other targeted venues; more about promotion and marketing is discussed in Chapter 13), publishing results of evaluation studies in scholarly journals, and providing technical assistance to those interested in adopting the program.

Table 2.1 summarizes the steps we have discussed.

TABLE 2.1   A Comprehensive Framework for Designing Family Life Prevention Programs

Stage 1: Problem Analysis

Identify Problem/Establish Overall Program Goal

Program goal should clarify the audience (e.g., The ABC program is designed to help single parents identify and build upon their parenting strengths, enhancing their sense of competence as a parent)

Consult the Scholarly Literature

Identify current theories/research addressing the problem/goal

Risk factors/protective factors, predictors of positive outcomes, etc.

Extract the "teachable" ideas/principles from theories/research, those that are practical/useful in addressing the problem. Examples:

"The more authoritative a parent is, the better off their children will be as they grow."

"The more married couples accurately read one another's love language, the better the marriage."

"Risks for divorce are reduced when couples learn to handle conflict and disagreements effectively."

Establish Well-Defined Program Goals and Objectives

Goal: Significantly reduce levels of escalation in the relationship. Objective: All couples who participate in the Fair Fighting enrichment program will reduce measured levels of escalation by 50%

Form a Coalition of Stakeholders Who Work Together to Address the Problem

Educate coalition members on current theory and research addressing the problem

Stage 2: Program Design

Consult Target Group—Assess Their Needs

Assess needs using focus groups, interviews, questionnaires, existing data, etc.

Felt, ascribed (those you discern because of your specialized knowledge), and future needs (e.g., what do couples preparing for marriage need to know?)

Involve the target audience in program design, planning, and implementation

Seek their input at every stage

Select Change Objectives

    Knowledge, attitudes, behaviors/skills, and aspirations targeted for change

    Tied to promote the positive outcomes predicted by the theories and research and desired by target audience

    Stated in specific, action-oriented terms (e.g., what will participants be able to do as a result of the program?)

Select Evaluation Tools

    Formative and summative

    Instruments directly tied to program objectives

Selecting Change Methods

    Tied to objectives—a skills objective need skill development method

    Review existing programs to find "best practices"

    Use adult learner methods—buzz groups, role playing, discussion group, skill practice, etc.

    Give attention to learning styles, sensory modalities, and developmental needs/abilities

Decide Program Extensiveness

    Selectiveness: Universal (y'all come), selective (audience exhibiting risk factors), or indicated (audience exhibiting negative outcomes)

    Breadth: Range of change objectives: e.g., comprehensive, in terms of level of human ecology, or more focused on one or two levels

    Length: Shorter or longer?

Design Recruitment/Retention Strategy

    Ask the target audience what is best way to recruit and retain an audience

Tailor Program Content and Delivery

    Tailored to needs of audience/community

    Sensitive to cultural, ethnic, and other forms of diversity

    Implementation strategies, based on target audience needs and focus group findings, to maximize participation

        Recruitment meetings

        Teachers of same culture

    Home visits

Stage 3: Pilot Testing

Implement Program

Recruitment and Retention Evaluation

    Is it working? Are people coming and staying or returning?

Process Evaluation

    Project quality control

Formative Evaluation

Program Revision

(Continued)

TABLE 2.1 (Continued)

Stage 4: Advanced Testing

Select Experimental Design
Implement Program
Analyze Data
Refine Program

Stage 5: Dissemination

Widespread Adoption of Program

Source: Adapted from Dumka, Roosa, Michaels, & Suh (1995) and Bogenschneider (1996).

● CONCLUSION

It is important for prevention-oriented FLEs to ground their work in a scientific framework of program design. This chapter has presented a practical framework for the design of comprehensive family life educational programs in outreach settings. The following activity can help you translate these ideas into your own program development efforts.

● EXPLORATIONS

1. Identify a problem topic and create a rough outline of your program strategy in Stage 1 and Stage 2 of the framework. Try it out with topics of widespread importance in communities, such as strengthening single parents, preventing adolescent drug use, marriage preparation for second-timers, and managing stress and crisis in families.

2. Do an inventory of existing family life programs. Identify the levels of prevention at which they operate (primary, secondary, and tertiary) and how extensive they are (universal, selective, indicated).

3. The authors recommend analyzing the problem through exploring related research and theory *prior to* consulting the target group to assess their needs. What are some advantages and disadvantages of doing this? How can the disadvantages be addressed?

CHAPTER 3

ELEMENTS OF QUALITY FAMILY LIFE EDUCATION RESOURCES AND PROGRAMS

Countless family life education (FLE) resources of one kind or another exist today. These resources include workshop curricula, newsletters, videos/video-based curricula, books, lay publications, support groups, and Web sites. The materials cut across many content areas, from parenting and marriage education to individual development. Family life educators (FLEs) are faced with the decision of whether to adopt and adapt existing resources or to create materials of their own. Many of these resources have been developed in educational outreach settings, such as land grant universities, while others have been developed and distributed commercially. However, these materials are of varying quality, not always following high development standards (Hughes, 1994). How do FLEs determine the quality of existing resources as they consider the many options available to them? Or alternatively, if they decide to develop their own resources, what elements would appropriately be included?

Beyond materials is the broader FLE program, which we define as comprehensive, multilevel, collaborative, community-based educational efforts for children, youth, families, and communities. While many of these kinds of comprehensive programs have been created, few meet the test of time (Lee, Mancini, Miles, & Marek, 1996). What are the elements of successful, sustained programs, and how can we infuse those essentials into our efforts in communities?

Chapter 2 provides a framework for the design of comprehensive FLE prevention programs. In this chapter, first we take the discussion a step further to spotlight and evaluate the specific features of quality FLE resources. Second, we review the elements that research shows hold comprehensive programs together once they are in place, and provide examples of programs around the United States that contain these elements.

● THE NEED FOR STANDARDS OF QUALITY FOR FAMILY LIFE EDUCATION RESOURCES

Most fields have standards of quality, often embodied in professional bylaws and licensure criterion. For example, the professions of social work and marriage and family therapy have long had established criteria for practice. In FLE, progress has been made over the past two decades in the professionalization of FLE. For example, in 1984, the National Council on Family Relations (NCFR) became the first professional organization to establish criteria and standards for FLEs, later giving birth to its Certified Family Life Educator (CFLE) program. Certification requires at least a bachelor's degree, completion of college courses spanning 10 different family life substance areas, and an internship, plus the equivalent of 2 years of full-time related work experiences. In 1993, Family Service Canada followed suit by announcing its own Canadian Certified Family Educator (CCFE) program. In addition to these professionalization efforts, recent efforts have also specified the ethical and professional standards of FLEs and family science professionals in general (Adams, Dollahite, Gilbert, & Keim, 2001; Brock, 1993). Advances have also been made in clarifying the content of FLE, teaching, and evaluation strategies (Hughes, 1994).

Despite these developments, recommendations for accepted standards of FLE practice have lagged behind (Hughes, 1994), specifically the nuts and bolts of how to put together quality family life educational resources. Such standards are important to guide development efforts if implementers are to maximize their effectiveness. Such a model would suggest minimum standards whereby the quality of a resource might be judged. Thus, a model would serve both as a helpful resource development device as well as a tool by which one could make decisions about adopting a particular set of materials for use in one's community FLE setting.

ELEMENTS OF QUALITY FAMILY ●
LIFE EDUCATION RESOURCES

Work by Hughes (1994, 1997) provides a useful basis for the assessment of a wide variety of educational products, be it a workshop series, video, Web site, or other educational media. These elements include content, implementation process, instructional process, and evaluation. Some of the elements are consistent with the program design framework discussed in Chapter 2 and are repeated here as part of the assessment process. While some of the elements have a more direct application to program curricula, we agree with Hughes (1994) that most of the items can be applied to most any FLE resource.

Content

When evaluating the quality of an FLE resource, there are three elements of the content that are important to consider: the theoretical/research base, the context-sensitivity of the information, and the practice base.

Theoretical/Research Base

Is the resource based on current scholarship on the topic? Quality FLE resources will have a clear link to leading-edge scholarly thinking and, where appropriate, will clearly indicate a specific theory and research base that undergirds the resource. The scholarly base is then woven into the goals, objectives, and activities of the materials. Undergirding such resources are specified, widely demonstrated ideas about how positive predictable change occurs under certain conditions. The job of the materials is to provide those conditions that facilitate desired change. For example, a research- and theory-based marriage education program curricula to enhance the quality of participants' marriages and protection against divorce would seek to address, through knowledge and skills, the documented risk factors for marital trouble (such as mishandling of marital differences) and enhance protective factors (such as nurturing love and friendship). Thus, materials based on leading-edge theoretical principles and research, rather than someone's intriguing ideas or good intentions, are more likely to produce the outcomes we want as FLEs. These principles become the "teachable" ideas for the lay audience—ideas the audience really needs to know.

Context

Materials based on sound theory and research can miss their mark if their principles are not applicable to the diversity of individuals or groups in the target audience. Thus, the research and theories must be evaluated for their applicability to either a wide diversity array of individuals or to the specific target audience (Myers-Walls, 2000). This effort is especially critical, since much of social science research that undergirds FLE materials is biased toward White, middle-class families. For example, FLEs developing curricula to help lower-income families make transitions from welfare dependency to self-support would make sure that the theory, research, and interventions are based on an understanding of the complex needs of limited resource families (limited in terms of education and perception of personal resources as well as income) at different levels of their social ecology (at the individual, family, and community levels) (Christopher et al., 2001). A parenting newsletter series for single parents would include an understanding of the challenges and strengths single parents bring to parenting, as well as general principles emerging from parenting research across groups.

Practice

Quality FLE resources employ not only leading-edge theory and research but also the best practices/interventions available (Hughes, 1994). Whereas the theory and research articulate *what* needs to be taught, the practice part of an educational resource details *how* the ideas are to be taught or what methods have been used most effectively to teach the principles. For example, in developing a multisession workshop series for strengthening single parents, FLEs would review the practice literature that details how such workshops for single parents have been taught in the past, the specific methods that were used, and how effective they were. Then such methods would be incorporated into the program.

Instructional Process

Teaching Plans

Hughes (1994) warns that even materials based on strong scholarship and best practices can fall flat if the design for delivery (e.g., teaching plan for a workshop series) is ill conceived or the material is presented poorly. As a beginning, well-designed teaching plans would include goals and specific, measurable learner-centered objectives, focused on producing changes in participant knowledge, attitudes, behavior/skills, and aspirations (Bennett & Rockwell, 1995). Directions on how to facilitate the learning process would be included, including the amount of time to be spent on each teaching activity. A variety of teaching activities and formats would be used, allowing for varied learning styles, sensory modalities, and developmental needs/abilities. These activities would be closely tied to goals and objectives. A variety of teaching aids might also be used, including visuals and video clips (see Chapters 4 and 7 for additional discussion on goals, objectives, and methods).

Presentation

According to Hughes (1994), two important presentation features are the readability of participant materials and the appropriate use of examples. When the written word is used to convey FLE information, it must be accessible to all within a target audience, neither talking over their heads nor talking down to them. It's also important to cull resources to find and share the examples and stories that fit the life experiences of the participants. From comic strips to photos and video media, care should be taken to illustrate a wide variety of situations without any demeaning reference to any racial, ethnic, or economic group or type of family. Instead, a wide portrayal of a variety of groups is appropriate, or portrayals especially suited to the target audience. Attractiveness of the resource is also important. For example, the visual appeal of an FLE Web site may be the most important element initially to encourage further exploration. Although the material must be tied to sound scholarship, it doesn't have to look or sound that way. For example, the best research for marriage education audiences can be placed in reader-friendly, engaging language instead of stilted, scholarly writing and say much the same thing.

Implementation Process

Well-designed and presented materials may still fail if they are not implementation savvy. Hughes (1994) argues that "failures in implementation" are likely "the most important point of failure" of FLE programming (p. 77). Many programs are doomed before they start because of their failure to consult the target audience and assess their needs (Duncan, Box, & Silliman, 1996). In fact, wise FLEs will consult with the target audience at every stage, from program design and implementation to evaluation. Quality resources will show evidence that FLEs have formulated their implementation approach based on the assessed needs of the target audience. Characteristics of the target audience would also be described in materials such as age, developmental level, ethnicity, gender, social class, and family life stages. Also important are data regarding groups for whom the material would not be appropriate, or guidelines for implementation for other groups (e.g., how a marriage enrichment program could be adapted for remarried or cohabiting couples). All of this information should trace back to information from consulting the intended audience, including data gathered directly from potential participants in a community as well as other data sources already available, such as community demographics collected by a city.

Having a marketing plan is also an important key for implementation. Program resources might field test and include recruitment and marketing ideas in their materials. Programs will give attention to the various aspects of marketing (Weinreich, 1999) and provide guidelines to implementers as to how to carry out such a plan. Some of these aspects include information such as product characteristics (the total program package, including the topics taught and how), price (cost in terms of time and money), place (where a program should be located), promotion (what is the best way to get the word out about the program?), publics (whose support in a community do we need to implement the program?), partnership (with whom should we partner or collaborate in order to reach the most people?), policies (what policies support the delivery of the program or would need to be addressed for the program to be successful?), and purse strings (where would funding be found for a program like this?). Details of marketing plan development are discussed in Chapter 13.

Evaluation

Quality FLE resources include some provision for determining if the materials benefit others. For example, a new FLE curricula for a workshop series will include, at a minimum, data collected on target audiences and how these data led to the existing design of the program, and tools for conducting both formative and summative evaluations. Evaluation tools would be clearly tied to program goals and objectives. The tools would collect data about program utilization (e.g., how many attend a program and their characteristics?), client satisfaction (e.g., how useful was this Web site for you?), short-term impact (e.g., what changes have you noticed in your marriage that you believe resulted from the Strengthening Your Marriage program?), and long-term impact (e.g., maintenance of program outcomes a year later) (Jacobs, 1988). More mature curricula would include additional quantitative and qualitative data that demonstrate program effectiveness.

The adapted tool used to evaluate family life education resources is provided in Table 3.1.

(Text Continues on Page 47)

TABLE 3.1   Family Life Education Program Resource Review Form

Use this form to assess the level of quality of outreach FLE resource materials, including curricula, videos, Web sites, and other resources. Not all items will apply equally to all resources.

Reference Information

Title: _____

Author: _____

Source: _____

Intended Audience. Please note the audience for which the resource is intended. (Check all that apply.)

_____   Parents (Type _____)
        (Single, Step, Adoptive, Teenage, All, etc.)

_____   Children (Age Range and/or Family Type) _____

_____   Married Couples

_____   General Public

_____   Other (Specify: _____)

Delivery Method. Indicate the type of resource. (Check all that apply.)

_____   News release

_____   Short brochure

_____   Long brochure

_____   Slide/Video

_____   Program curriculum

_____   Web site

_____   Other _____

Ratings of the Resource. Please rate the educational resource on the following dimensions. Keep in mind the intended resource and the type of delivery method when making these ratings.

(Continued)

TABLE 3.1 (Continued)

Content: Theory and Research	Low/Poor			High/Excellent		
1. Prevention/intervention theory is clearly stated.	1	2	3	4	5	N/A
2. Resource is based on current research findings.	1	2	3	4	5	N/A
3. Resource includes the major and/or most important research resources.	1	2	3	4	5	N/A
4. Resource accurately uses the findings from research (or other sources).	1	2	3	4	5	N/A
5. Resource clearly presents the findings from research and other sources.	1	2	3	4	5	N/A
6. Resource draws appropriate implications from the research and other sources.	1	2	3	4	5	N/A
7. Resource notes limitations of research findings and conclusions.	1	2	3	4	5	N/A
Content: Context						
8. Contextual information regarding the families' involvement in relevant settings (school, work, child care, church) is appropriately considered.	1	2	3	4	5	N/A
9. Culture and social class influences are appropriately considered.	1	2	3	4	5	N/A
10. Political, economic, and other macrosocial influences are appropriately considered.	1	2	3	4	5	N/A
Content: Practice						
11. Resource adds something new to the practice/ intervention approaches on this topic/issue.	1	2	3	4	5	N/A
12. Resource builds on appropriate existing program resources (e.g., other programs, professionals, clinical research).	1	2	3	4	5	N/A
13. Resource accurately uses findings from clinical research/practice.	1	2	3	4	5	N/A
14. Teaching/intervention strategies and techniques are based on clinical research/practice.	1	2	3	4	5	N/A
15. Resource notes current limitation of clinical/ practice knowledge in regard to this program/topic.	1	2	3	4	5	N/A

Comments:

Instructional Process: Teaching Plans	*Low/Poor*			*High/Excellent*		
1. The topic is important for the intended audience.	1	2	3	4	5	N/A
2. There are clear goals and objectives for instruction or the interactive/teaching elements of the Web site.	1	2	3	4	5	N/A
3. Activities/interactive features fit the goals and objectives.	1	2	3	4	5	N/A
4. Activities/interactive features are appropriate for the intended audience(s) (age group, family type, gender, ethnic group).	1	2	3	4	5	N/A
5. Directions for conducting (or doing online) teaching or learning activities are sufficient.	1	2	3	4	5	N/A
6. A variety of activities and teaching formats are used.	1	2	3	4	5	N/A
7. Balance between giving information, discussion, and learning activities is achieved.	1	2	3	4	5	N/A
8. Structured and/or unstructured approaches are used appropriately.	1	2	3	4	5	N/A
9. Sufficient time is allowed to cover topics/ activities (not too much or too little).	1	2	3	4	5	N/A
10. The structure of the content is logically organized and easy to follow.	1	2	3	4	5	N/A
11. Teaching aids (visuals, materials, handouts, etc.) are appropriate.	1	2	3	4	5	N/A
12. Potential teaching/practice problems are discussed and solutions suggested.	1	2	3	4	5	N/A
13. Appropriateness of the length of the resource for the topic and the intended audience.	1	2	3	4	5	N/A

Instructional Process: Presentation

14. Appropriate readability for the intended audience.	1	2	3	4	5	N/A
15. Appropriateness of the examples for the intended audience.	1	2	3	4	5	N/A
16. Attractiveness of the resource for the intended audience.	1	2	3	4	5	N/A
17. Appropriate portrayal of a range of racial/ethnic groups.	1	2	3	4	5	N/A
18. Appropriate portrayal of a range of family types.	1	2	3	4	5	N/A
19. Effectiveness of pictures/graphs, etc.	1	2	3	4	5	N/A
20. Quality of the overall design and layout.	1	2	3	4	5	N/A

Comments:

(Continued)

TABLE 3.1 (Continued)

Implementation Process	Low/Poor			High/Excellent		
1. General information in regard to using the program is provided.	1	2	3	4	5	N/A
2. Appropriate audience for program is outlined.	1	2	3	4	5	N/A
3. Limits are provided about audiences that would not be expected to benefit from the program.	1	2	3	4	5	N/A
4. Marketing/recruitment materials and suggestions are provided.	1	2	3	4	5	N/A
5. Logistical issues in implementation are clarified.	1	2	3	4	5	N/A
6. Budget issues are explained clearly.	1	2	3	4	5	N/A
7. Community or agency issues in implementation are explained.	1	2	3	4	5	N/A
8. Potential implementation problems are discussed and solutions suggested.	1	2	3	4	5	N/A
9. If appropriate, staff or volunteer training guidelines are sufficient.	1	2	3	4	5	N/A
10. Background material and/or resources are provided to implementers/trainers.	1	2	3	4	5	N/A

Comments:

Evaluation	Low/Poor			High/Excellent		
1. Evidence of needs assessment process with appropriate audience(s) is provided.	1	2	3	4	5	N/A
2. Utilization data are provided.	1	2	3	4	5	N/A
3. Accountability procedures are provided to track utilization of the program.	1	2	3	4	5	N/A
4. Results of client satisfaction are provided.	1	2	3	4	5	N/A
5. Procedures for assessing client satisfaction are provided.	1	2	3	4	5	N/A
6. Feedback from staff trainers, other stakeholders is discussed.	1	2	3	4	5	N/A
7. Procedures for obtaining feedback from staff trainers and other stakeholders are provided.	1	2	3	4	5	N/A
8. Evaluation of critical program features is provided.	1	2	3	4	5	N/A
9. Effectiveness of the program for specific audiences is clear.	1	2	3	4	5	N/A
10. Limits of the effectiveness of the program are clear.	1	2	3	4	5	N/A

Evaluation		Low/Poor				High/Excellent	
11. Guidelines for impact evaluation are provided.	1	2	3	4	5	N/A
12. Evaluation tools (formative and summative) are provided.	1	2	3	4	5	N/A
13. Summative evaluation tools are tied to goals and objectives.	1	2	3	4	5	N/A

Comments:

Overall Evaluation of the Resource

____ This resource should not be used at all.
(Describe the major problems.)

____ This resource would be useful with the following modifications.
(Describe the needed modifications.)

____ This resource would be useful in the following circumstances and
with the following audiences. (Describe circumstances and audiences.)

Source: Adapted from Hughes, 1994, 1997.

APPLICATION OF ASSESSMENT TO ● EXISTING FAMILY LIFE EDUCATION RESOURCES

As mentioned at the outset, there are many FLE resources, yet none of them are known to have been subjected to a thorough, independent assessment using the Hughes (1994, 1997) approach. A comprehensive review of the many actively used materials is beyond the scope of this chapter. However, we wanted to determine the extent to which these elements of quality were present in at least a few well-known and often used FLE resources. Our selection of these resources should not be seen as an endorsement of them. Our purpose here is not so much critical as it is educational—to illustrate how the assessment tool can be used to make decisions about the selection of materials, taking into account both program strengths and limitations. Undoubtedly, resources that meet these criteria to perfection do not exist; many resources not fully meeting the criteria are undoubtedly useful, effective materials.

FLE is a multifaceted, multidisciplinary field with many different content areas (Arcus, Schvaneveldt, & Moss, 1993a), but much of the programming is done in marriage and couple relationships and parenting and family strengths. We chose two widely used program curricula for review: the Prevention and Relationship Enhancement Program (PREP) and the Strengthening Families Program (SFP).

The Prevention and Relationship Enhancement Program

PREP is one of the best known marriage education resources available, and also has an extensive research program demonstrating its effectiveness (for a review, see Stanley, 2001). The program was designed to teach couples communication, conflict resolution, and problem-solving skills shown to be linked to marital strength. PREP attempts to reduce risk factors and raise protective factors through addressing topics such as commitment, handling conflict using the speaker/listener technique, gender differences, forgiveness, fun, friendship, and sensuality. The basic PREP program is organized into one full-day session followed by two 2-hour weekday evening sessions, totaling 12 hours of contact.

PREP Content

In terms of content, the PREP program material presents a clear scholarly background for the program, embedded in cognitive-behavioral and communication theory, with years of research and clinical practice underlying the general principles and the interventions used in the program, primarily consisting of skills training in the active listening skill they call the speaker/listener technique (Markman, Stanley, & Blumberg, 1999). Extensive references to up-to-date sources are included. Limitations of the scholarly findings and conclusions supporting the program are also discussed, such as cautioning readers regarding positive PREP outcomes based on short-term results. The PREP evaluation studies have measured many outcomes but have found modest benefits on only a few. In addition, the communication approaches promoted by PREP have been strongly challenged in the scholarly literature. The authors also provide their response to the debate surrounding the use of active listening skills in marriage education and therapy (see Gottman, Coan, Carrere, & Swanson, 1998), but place this discussion in a box within the instructional material yet provide no indication as to the implications of this concern for applying the material. There is little evidence of change in approach in concert with the emerging findings.

In terms of practice, the PREP program develops communication skills, using the behavioral techniques of modeling and coaching. Practice strategies are closely aligned with behavioral marital therapy, and the use of skill training is a commonly used strategy within a cognitive-behavioral framework. The research on PREP itself has also provided encouragement to those who engage in community-based marriage education, since participants receiving the program from PREP-trained clergy and lay leaders had equal or better outcomes than those trained by PREP developers (Stanley et al., 2001).

PREP offers little guidance addressing the contexts in which this program can be used effectively. The developers claim and their research also shows that the program can be effectively implemented among premarital, marital (at various life stages), and remarital groups and in Westernized culture (i.e., the United States and Europe). The accompanying videotape uses couples from different races in early-to-later stages of marriage. However, the program material does not address how it can be used with groups of various cultures, races, socioeconomic background, or literacy levels. While program materials state that PREP is best used with couples with lower risks, there is no indication of how the program might be used among truly disadvantaged populations or risk groups as an adjunct to counseling. However, a recent study not cited in this version of the program does point to its usefulness among couples with at least some risks (Halford, Sanders, & Behrens, 2001).

PREP Instructional Process

The program material is formatted around a one full-day and two 2-hour weeknight sessions. The instructional design of PREP largely consists of minilectures embellished by the use of video clips, overheads, and humorous cartoons that illustrate concepts (also available on PowerPoint for PREP trainees) and dyadic skill training (couples together, assisted by behavioral "coaches"). Program materials provide helpful overviews of the three sessions, materials needed, and a checklist for setting up a room. There is a program outline/schedule for lectures and coached couple interactions using a variety of alternative formats, including weekend only, one-day, and so on. The program outline has clear indications where video and overhead segments are to be used.

The delivery process instructions lack clearly articulated, learner-centered goals and objectives. Leader-oriented goals are mentioned in the implementation materials (and called "objectives"), but no specific, measurable objectives are associated with the specific sessions and lectures. Thus, it is difficult to determine the fit of the program activities with goals and objectives of the program. In addition, there are no specific times for activities mentioned, so facilitators would need to determine the times for themselves, including the approximate length of video clips.

The lecture outline is somewhat sketchy and seems to assume the leader has a substantial background in the content area. This lack of detail is perhaps related to the fact that professional training in PREP is required before interested parties are contractually allowed to present the full program. Nevertheless, the material lacks specific detail that would be helpful in instructional processes, such as a suggested script. The outline by itself suggests a largely didactic approach to teaching, involving little input from or direct engagement with the audience (e.g., asking for participants' questions or opinions).

There are various supportive materials for the program. A *Couple's Notes* booklet provides a useful way for couples to follow lectures and jot down ideas they want to remember that are associated with key concepts of the program. In addition, couples receive "The Floor" (a small card), which couples pass back and forth as they practice the speaker/listener technique. Written on The Floor are the rules for speaking and listening that couples are to follow as they practice the skill, a helpful structuring and memory device.

PREP Implementation Process

A useful feature of the PREP program is a fairly detailed leader's guide. This material includes information on staff requirements, participant eligibility, recruitment ideas, the role of leaders, ideas for delivering lectures (which the PREP people call "talks"), program resources, and program logistics. Based on the format selected (weekend, weekday evening, etc.), there is a listing of what leaders need, what the couples need, and various presentation materials, sample schedules, and times for each element. In addition, there is an outline for a booster session, also shown to be a best practice (Carroll & Doherty, 2003; Giblin, Sprenkle, & Sheehan, 1985).

PREP Evaluation

PREP program materials include a review of research that supports the program's effectiveness. In addition, included are a variety of tools, many of them with established reliability and validity, that FLEs could use to evaluate PREP effectiveness, depending on the objectives identified for the specific program. Some of the tools include a marital satisfaction instrument, a confidence scale, a problem inventory, and a relationship dynamics scale. However, it is difficult to know how these tools apply to the goals and objectives of PREP, since there is weak discussion of both.

Missing from the PREP material was any discussion of an effort to investigate the needs of the target audience prior to or concurrent with program development. Thus, while appearing to address many of the common risk and protective factors in marriage relationships, it is unknown if or how the needs of the target audience were considered, nor do program leaders receive any guidance in assessing needs.

Parenting and Family Education: The Strengthening Families Program for Parents and Youth

The Strengthening Families Program for Parents and Youth 10 to 14 (SFP) is a parent, youth, and family skills-building, video-based curriculum designed to prevent teen substance abuse and other behavior problems, strengthen parenting skills, and build family strengths. Like the PREP program, SFP has been carefully evaluated in many studies as one of the programs used in the acclaimed Project Family project (Molgaard & Spoth, 2001).

SFP is comprised of seven sessions, each 2 hours in length, plus four booster sessions. During the first hour, parents and youth meet separately and then come together during the second hour to practice skills and have fun. Thus, a special feature of this program is that parents and their youth get to learn together.

SFP content

In terms of content, SFP states it is based on 20 years of research on risk factors and protective factors for youth behavior problems (Molgaard, Kumpfer, & Fleming, 2001). A review of this research is provided in the materials, but it is very brief and fails to note the specific risk and protective factors the program addresses. The program ostensibly draws upon other theoretical/research bases such as social learning and behavioral management (use of reinforcements and penalties), humanistic psychology (mutual empathy activities), communication theory (I-messages), and Adlerian perspectives (family meetings). However, these bases are not delineated in the review. An extensive reference list to published studies and sources undergirding the program is provided. Limitations of the scholarly findings supporting the research is not included. However, the developers do report on their efforts to modify the program consistent with the needs of other audiences (i.e., African Americans and Hispanics).

In terms of practice, the SFP curricula are video based and use skill training, homework assignments, and a variety of other teaching methods to accomplish its goals. This approach appears to be consistent with current best practices in parenting and family education, but the sources influencing their decisions about program practices is not mentioned, nor is reference made to other similar successful programs in this area. An important omission is the lack of discussion about the theoretical and empirical rationale behind the specific structure of SFP, namely holding separate groups for youths and parents for part of the time, coupled with a family gathering. Similar to PREP, professional training is required before one may be a certified SFP leader. Trained leaders who have conducted SFP may in turn train others who work with them.

In terms of context, SFP appears to be sensitive to the various ethnic and sociodemographic groups. The Leader Guide details research on SFP with samples that included a high percentage of economically disadvantaged families and also details several program revisions undertaken following the research to make the curriculum appeal to a wider audience (specifically, Hispanics and African Americans, as well as Whites). These revisions included using actors for the videos from different races and more informal and game-like activities.

SFP Instructional Process

The seven sessions have three separate teaching plans for parents, youth, and family. The first page of each session contains a Contents and a Materials Needed section, plus learner-centered session goals. The parent sessions employ video clips throughout, the youth sessions use videos during two of them, and the curriculum otherwise uses a variety of teaching and activity formats, handouts, and home practice activities. The Leader Guide, list of materials, and the manner in which the sessions are scripted provide ample direction for carrying out the instruction, including the length of time needed to complete each segment. A video script is included within the session so it is easy to refer to ideas mentioned there. Clear instructions are provided throughout the program, with icons signaling a particular segment in the material (such as a TV screen to signal when the video is to start).

SFP curricula are written in a simple, direct manner, so the materials are easy to understand for the audience and educator alike. The videos are of high quality and provide both positive and negative examples of the concept being taught. The situations are lifelike and relate to parents' experiences. The materials have a very professional appearance. All the handouts needed to facilitate the instructional process are professional looking and separated by session.

SFP Implementation Process

A useful feature of the SFP is the Leader Guide, which contains much helpful information regarding many of the more practical and logistical considerations for implementing the program, such as securing funding, finding a place to meet, roles of facilitators, scheduling, booster sessions, recruitment, registration and fees, meals/snacks, child care, transportation, incentives for attendance, and many other useful ideas that might easily slip one's mind if they were not brought up. The program contains ordering information for materials, evaluation tools, and a summary of the evaluation research and list of curriculum references.

SFP Evaluation

While the SFP was developed to address the various risk factors facing young people at this age, little information is mentioned regarding how the program was developed. For example, there is no evidence that the program was developed to address felt needs of a target audience. No details regarding how target audience perspectives and needs were sought are included in this material. However, the SFP reports positive results in controlled studies of program effectiveness.

No formative evaluation tools allowing facilitators to assess participant perceptions of individual sessions with an eye to improving them is included in the evaluation materials. The evaluation tools include a 14-item questionnaire for both parents and youth, asking them to compare the knowledge and skills they had before and after the SFP. In addition, a 3-month follow-up phone evaluation is also included. Program leaders randomly select a few participants and ask them questions similar to the other questionnaire. These evaluation tools are directly tied to program goals.

In summary, both PREP and the SFP have many elements of FLE resource quality but also some limitations. For example, both programs have strongly evident scholarly bases, but both fail to report how the needs of the target audience were considered during program design. Both programs ostensibly have goals and objectives, but only the SFP clearly delineates them. PREP instructional outlines are general, while SFP's suggested guide is quite detailed. FLEs can use this kind of evaluative approach to weigh the strengths and limitations of curricula or other resources they may be considering for their audiences. Table 3.2 summarizes the strengths and limitations of these curricula. We now turn to a discussion of the characteristics of strong, sustainable, comprehensive FLE programs.

TABLE 3.2   Assessment of FLE Curricula Using Hughes (1994, 1997) Assessment Approach

Resource	Content	Instructional Process	Implementation Process	Evaluation
Prevention and Relationship Enhancement Program (PREP)	Strengths: Clear scholarly base Weaknesses: Discussion on active listening caveat limited; no discussion on using with various group	Strengths: Program materials, overheads, video, varied format suggestions; booklet for couples Weaknesses: Lacks goals and objectives; lecture outline lacks detail; largely didactic, weak instructional design	Strengths: Detailed leader's guide Weaknesses: None noted	Strengths: Tools, evaluation research data Weaknesses: Unclear how tools tied to goals and objectives; no information on assessing needs of audience prior to implementation
Strengthening Families Program (SFP)	Strengths: Ostensibly strong scholarly base; video and skill training appropriate and context sensitive Weaknesses: Research and theory not clearly delineated; limitations of research not discussed, nor applications to varied audiences; no rationale for family-youth approach given	Strengths: Curricula organization very clear; clear content; learner-centered goals and objectives; clear instructions for facilitator Weaknesses: None noted	Strengths: Excellent leader's guide, containing practical and helpful information Weaknesses: None noted	Strengths: Reports of results from controlled studies; evaluation tools directly tied to program goals included Weaknesses: Little information on how program was developed or how target audience needs were assessed

CHARACTERISTICS OF STRONG, SUSTAINABLE ●
FAMILY LIFE EDUCATION PROGRAMS

As important as it is to have strong program curricula comprised of a strong theory and research base, clear goals and objectives, methods consistent with objectives, attention to diverse audiences, a guide for implementation, and evaluation tools tied to the objectives, program curricula is only part of successful, sustainable FLE programs. There are many elements of quality comprehensive programs that transcend specific curricula. Drawing on the published literature and experiences of leading community-based programs, Lee et al. (1996) identified eight characteristics of quality community-based programs. These characteristics are important to keep in mind as you seek to build a comprehensive FLE program in a community that will stand the test of time. Some of these characteristics are also reiterations and extensions of important elements found in quality community-based FLE curricula.

1. Successful community programs are community based and carried out in collaboration with many community partners.

Successful programs emerge from the needs of the community rather than from the desires of outsiders. Instead of "one size fits all," these programs are flexibly implemented and adapt to community needs. They embed themselves in the local community, becoming part of a network of supportive services carried out by collaborative professionals and volunteers (Lee et al., 1996). This collaborative approach minimizes turf issues, brings more resources to bear on a community issue, maximizes effectiveness in program planning and implementation, and increases the likelihood that a program will stand the test of time (Duncan et al., 2003).

Montana Extension's Educating Families to Achieve Independence in Montana (EDUFAIM) is an example of a community-born collaboration that fits this approach (Duncan et al., 2003; Woods, 1998). EDUFAIM communities identified the needs of those moving from public assistance dependence, and then held visioning and strategic planning meetings involving community professionals, the target audience, and volunteers. Up to 40 different agencies in some areas collaborated in the planning and carrying out of the program. Community professionals were also supported by a collaborative group of university faculty from 11 disciplines and state agency personnel. Thus, a close university-state agency-community partnership emerged. Chapter 12 provides more discussion about the process of creating collaborations.

TABLE 3.3   Elements of Strong, Sustainable, Comprehensive Programs

---

Successful community programs are community based and carried out in collaboration with many community partners.

Successful community programs are comprehensive in scope, based on an ecological or systems view of individuals, families, and communities.

Successful community programs are inclusive of program participants in program planning, delivery, and evaluation.

Successful community programs are preventive in nature through successfully interfacing service and education, and recognizing and building on participants' strengths to enhance skills.

Successful community programs are developmentally appropriate and based on current research.

Successful community programs are accessible to participants with a mix of program deliveries based on participant needs.

Successful community programs are accountable to stakeholders and are able to demonstrate positive outcomes in participants and community environments.

Successful community programs have leaders with vision.

Source: Lee et al., 1996.

---

2. Successful community programs are comprehensive in scope, based on an ecological or systems view of individuals, families, and communities.

The best programs operate at many levels (e.g., individual, family, and community) and incorporate not only specific family-based programs but efforts to strengthen the community context as well (Lee et al., 1996). Clientele are viewed as individuals within families within communities, and programs are designed accordingly. Successful, long-lasting prevention results are most often the result of consistent, multilevel, multifaceted efforts. For instance, in addition to parenting skills, a comprehensive Parenting Teens program might also provide peer mentoring to encourage prosocial teen activity, newsletters for parents and other caring adults who work with teens, and media messages promoting positive parent-teen relationships. Successful efforts at adolescent drug abuse prevention would seek to minimize or eliminate risk factors occurring at the individual level (e.g., low self-efficacy), the family level (e.g., uninvolved parenting), and the peer group level (e.g., peers who use drugs) as well as enhance protective factors at the same levels (individual: religious commitment; family: involved parenting; peer: peers who are nondrug users). Likewise, during program design stages, program developers would include persons in their task forces representing different levels of the social ecology, including parents, youth, school personnel, and other adults who have an interest in the development of youth. Many researchers report that such an approach is critical to the success of prevention programs (Lee et al., 1996).

One program described by Lee et al. (1996) that exemplifies this approach is the Hampton Family Resource Project in Hampton, Virginia. The program consists of three components reflecting a multilevel approach to meet a wide range of family needs: Healthy Start, Healthy Family, and Healthy Community. During the Healthy Start or early intervention segment, the project provides services to pregnant women and their families and tracks children up through their fifth year. Family support workers are assigned to teach the family skills (home management and parenting) during the pregnancy and provide emotional and practical support, and to serve as role models. During the Healthy Family or "individualized prevention education" section, parenting education classes are provided to families with children 5 years of age and younger, through classes, in-home visits, family resource centers in libraries, and child development newsletters. "The promotion of community values that support positive child development" is the focus of the Healthy Community component. This value is in part fostered through a Healthy Stages newsletter, available to all Hampton residents who have children 5 years of age and younger.

3. Successful community programs are inclusive of program participants in program planning, delivery, and evaluation.

Successful programs involve participants at every level of program development, from predesign stages to implementation and evaluation. Even if programs are employed in different areas, clientele from those specific communities are involved so that the program is responsive to local needs. In addition, there is what Lee et al. (1996) refer to as an "integrative approach" to program planning. Local leaders are identified and trained, and local participants are fully involved in the planning and decision making regarding a program or its policies, philosophy, or procedures.

Youth Opportunities Unlimited of Manchester, New Hampshire, is mentioned by Lee et al. (1996) as an example of this approach. Providing after-school activities to at-risk children and youth, this program actively involves parents and young people in program direction, deciding the nature of program and family activities, and planning monthly meetings. In the process of creating a research and faith-based Web site, developers conducted numerous 2-hour focus groups to determine what the site would look like and contain. Once the site was launched, visitors had the opportunity to provide ongoing feedback on every aspect of the site. Then developers used this feedback to make revisions (Steimle & Duncan, 2004).

4. Successful community programs are preventive in nature through successfully interfacing service and education, and recognizing and building on participants' strengths to enhance skills.

Successful programs designed to foster resiliency and limit risks among children, youth, and families accomplish their goals through preventive, empowering means rather than through remediation. Thus, these programs aim to stop problem behaviors before they get started, often as early intervention (Lee et al., 1996). In addition, some of these programs focus on helping clientele identify and build upon strengths they already have.

The focus on empowerment and strength building transcends a program. As Lee et al. (1996) explain:

> Agency workers attempt to create momentum for positive change based upon individual, family, and community strengths. Participant autonomy is encouraged through community participation in decision-making affecting program development and administration. Empowering agencies educate people about their rights and responsibilities, education about their individual and social resources, about the barriers to obtaining and using those resources, and enable people to develop the skills to use the power they do have or to create new power, individually and collectively. (p. 10)

Lee et al. (1996) discuss the Southside Boys and Girls Club as an example of a program that has a clear prevention thrust. Their efforts aim to get children off the streets and into meaningful programs that build their educational competence and their abilities to get along with family and community members, and enhance their sense of self-worth.

5. Successful community programs are developmentally appropriate and based on current research.

Successful programs are based on best practice models of effective programming noted in the scholarly literature and on the specific needs of their community. The research is comprised of community needs assessments, the existing scholarly literature, and on the best strategies for reaching a target audience. Needs assessments may include existing data already available (e.g., state child abuse data) as well as new data collected from the target audience to refine an understanding of the issue for a specific community population, as well as how to best reach them.

Such programs often follow a community-university partnership model, where the community presents the issue in a unified context and university-based researchers provide the expertise of the scientific literature to address the community need.

Project Uplift of Greensboro, North Carolina, follows such an approach. As a facilitative organization of many different services and educational programs, ranging from GED classes to computer literacy to parenting, the program is undergirded by current family support research, theory, and evaluation. Program leaders are part of a network of professionals seeking to identify best practices in their service, including trainers, academics, policymakers, and funders (Lee et al., 1996).

6. Successful community programs are accessible to participants with a mix of program deliveries based on participant needs.

To be effective, FLE programs must be accessible to their intended audience (Lee et al., 1996). Clientele may face significant barriers that prevent them from attending programs located at community centers or other venues. Increasing accessibility may mean that the program is held in small groups or one-on-one in the homes of clientele. For many clientele, location may be a critical factor as well as its perceived safety, ease of access via public transportation, and free parking nearby.

Other aspects of accessibility are also important. Successful programs consider language needs, literacy rate, and educational level of the participants and then gear the material accordingly (Lee et al., 1996). For example, instructional classes might be offered in small groups or one-on-one, as needed, allowing for more individualized attention and for materials to be more effectively adapted to individual participant needs. Other strategies include keeping material simple and to the point and using a variety of hands-on activities and support groups in and out of a learning setting. Successful programs also use existing services as a means to achieve its ends, such as community forums, newsletters, conferences, and workshops.

Many of the programs noted by Lee et al. (1996) use home visiting as a means to maximize accessibility. Some programs are held in the public schools in the neighborhoods being served, and fit around the day and evening schedule of participants. When participants' native language, culture, or socioeconomic background is something other than middle class

Anglo-American, effective programs use speakers of those languages or persons from those cultures or life experience to enhance understanding and more effectively meet individual needs. For example, in one program, an instructional team consisted of a master's-prepared professional with considerable experience in working with low-income persons, paired with a person who had life experience as a recipient of public assistance (Duncan et al., 2003).

7. Successful community programs are accountable to stakeholders and are able to demonstrate positive outcomes in participants and community environments.

To be sustained, comprehensive community-based programs need to demonstrate some defensible measure of effectiveness. They need to be able to show stakeholders that the results achieved have been worth the investment in time and money. Such programs incorporate an ongoing evaluation of what works, what does not work, and what changes need to be made to improve services to clientele and the community. These data are often both quantitative (e.g., statistics showing improvement in parenting competence attributed to a parenting course) and qualitative in nature (success stories of family budgeting principles in practice), and report data not only from program participants but also from staff, partners or collaborators, and stakeholders.

The Southside Boys and Girls Club (Lee et al., 1996) shows its success by holding up members who have succeeded in business or higher education. Another program called Cities in Schools began its evaluation by getting baseline data as participants enter the program, and it holds yearly parent, child, teacher, and tutor surveys. The survey instrument used was designed by university partners, and they have continuously documented their successes (Lee et al., 1996).

Evaluation data can also be used to market a program. A successful program can produce a video to document its success and distribute the video to key agencies and organizations where the program might play a role. The video can give an overview of the program and feature participants telling their own stories of how the program shaped their lives. In addition, collaborating partners can be interviewed who highlight the value of the program to their community. Evaluation data on the program are woven throughout the video. Accompanying the video is a popularized report that presents both quantitative data in simplified tables and success stories. Such a video is appropriate if vital stakeholders include many laypersons or if broad awareness is an objective.

8. Successful community programs have leaders with vision.

This final characteristic of strong, sustainable programs has more to do with leadership than with program substance. Leaders of these programs are, according to Lee et al. (1996),

able to think through an organization's mission and establish it clearly and visibly. They serve as models, symbolizing a group's unity and identity. They view themselves as ultimately responsible and therefore surround themselves with strong associates and subordinates who function ably and independently and whose development they encourage. They function in a team relationship. Importantly they demonstrate long range vision, showing an ability to think beyond the day's crises, beyond the quarter. They are able to reach and influence constituents beyond their jurisdictions. They think in terms of renewal, seeking the revisions of process and structure by an ever-changing reality.

These leaders offer strong and committed leadership, keeping the program's vision in front of decision makers over years, being consistent with service at various sites, facilitating partnerships and ongoing community collaboration, bringing key partners together to renew and articulate program visions and strategies, and developing consensus.

The Family Resource Development Association of Cedar Rapids, Iowa, enjoys strong and committed leadership (Lee et al., 1996). The leader sees his role as a facilitator of partnership planning, ongoing community collaboration, and maintaining an environment of consensus around a shared vision.

CONCLUSION ●

While there are numberless resources available for FLE, not all materials are of equal quality. Resources constructed with careful and appropriate attention to elements, such as a strong theory and research base, clear goals and objectives, methods consistent with objectives, attention to diverse audiences, a guide for implementation, and evaluation tools tied to the objectives, are likely to serve FLE audiences better than those that do not, and certainly improve FLE practice. FLEs can use these guidelines to help them assess the quality of existing resources or to develop their own. In addition, when FLEs seek to establish comprehensive community-based programs that transcend curricula, they are wise to model programs that utilize the eight characteristics discussed in this chapter.

● EXPLORATIONS

1. Identify an FLE resource (curricula, Web site, etc.) and, using the review form provided in Table 2.1, do a "quality elements" assessment. Based on this evaluation, discuss whether or not you would use the resource and how you would improve it. Use the review form as a checklist for ensuring the quality of your own resources.

2. Locate and investigate comprehensive FLE programs in your community. Evaluate these programs against the eight characteristics of strong, sustainable programs discussed in this chapter. Find out how long the programs have existed. Do the longer-lasting ones have more of the characteristics?

CHAPTER 4

PRINCIPLES OF PROGRAM EVALUATION

EVALUATION AS FRIEND AND FOE: ● STEREOTYPES AND OPPORTUNITIES

FLEs who enjoy program evaluation are rare birds. Evaluation is generally viewed as a necessary evil. It requires time, provides sobering and often disappointing feedback, is difficult to design, and may seem impossible to analyze. Evaluation arouses deep dread in most FLEs. But it is required by most funders.

There is another way of thinking about evaluation. It can be seen as a process for gathering information to make your program stronger. It can provide vital data about what parts of the program are working well and which need tweaking. It can provide data that justify further funding. It can provide priceless information about how to match program options to program clients. According to this view, evaluation is our friend.

Evaluation is a systematic gathering of information that can be used to inform good decisions. It is much more than pretests and posttests, numbers and charts. In this chapter you are introduced to many different ways of getting and using information to strengthen your programs.

● ESTABLISHING THE TARGET: VISION AND GOALS

A respected parenting program funded by the Alabama Children's Trust Fund took part in the field test of a new evaluation instrument. The instrument was designed to measure a broad array of outcomes that are common in parenting programs. It was used with program participants both before the program began and again at the conclusion of the program. The instruments were sent for analyses, and a report was returned to the program site.

When the program director received the report, she called the instrument developers in a panic. "Your report shows that program participants only had significant improvement on 49% of the variables. That is failure by any standard! Are we really that bad?"

There is no simple answer to that question. The fact is that it depends. If the 49% of the variables on which there were significant changes are the variables that are important to the program leaders, then they are a remarkable success. If, in contrast, most of the variables of interest for the program are a part of the 51% in which there was no significant change, then the program leaders have cause for serious reflection. There simply is no way to interpret any outcome without having goals and objectives as a standard.

Even goals and objectives should be embedded in a larger picture of the desired outcome. That larger picture might be called a vision. One of the characteristics of effective program leaders is that they can articulate the big picture of their program efforts (Lee et al., 1996).

● DEVELOPING A VISION

Vision statements are shared expressions of a program staff. The vision describes what they want the program to accomplish by focusing on the end result. A shared vision is essentially the answer to the question What do we want to create?

Vision statements generally have the qualities of being lofty, big picture, and ambitious. They are also dynamic, needing revisiting and renewal periodically. When people share a vision, they are connected by a common aspiration. It can focus the energy and guide the decisions of the organization.

The meaningful vision statements are created by persons who have a stake in the program, such as program staff, partners, and recipients of services. Vision statements focus and express the shared hopes and dreams for the program.

Imagine gathering all the people together who are involved in delivering a program, inviting them to spend a morning around a conference table sharing how they would like the community to be different as a result of their program over time. Do you think the group would quickly converge on a common vision?

Experience suggests otherwise. When people united in a common cause begin to share their vision with each other, there are often a lot of surprises. Each person has a very different vision. While this person may think that the group is doing what they are doing "in order to help people in our community break the cycle of poverty," a colleague involved in the same program may see the central purpose as "arming citizens with a clear sense of purpose." Another person may see the core cause as "strengthening family bonds in our community."

Those visions are not necessarily incompatible. Each person in a work group may be driven by a personal vision that is different from that of anyone else in the group. Such diversity can enrich both collegiality and the quality of work.

The differences in vision can also lead to meaningful discussions about the core purposes that unite the work group. In the course of the discussions, each person is likely to enlarge and enrich his or her vision. As the group converges on core purposes, members will be better able to work in unified support of those purposes. Those core purposes can inform program activity and guide evaluation efforts.

Just a note of caution: Any attempt to come up with a single statement of vision for which all members of the group will express complete support will often be difficult. The discussion may be more important than a totally unified statement. The reasonable goal for this vision discussion is to better understand each other and to identify some common purposes.

One Montana family program for promoting self-sufficiency gathered together the program, staff, state and local collaborators, and Extension administrators for a "visioning and strategic planning" meeting. Each invitee was encouraged to develop his or her own vision statement prior to attending the meeting. At the meeting, each person shared his or her statement in small groups and recorded the shared elements. In the large group, elements of the visions were shared. The group worked together to form a statement that represented the shared vision. It read, "Supportive Montana communities that empower families to develop skills, knowledge, and competencies necessary for managing family resources and progressing toward a self-supporting lifestyle."

Another vision statement might say, "Our vision of our community is a place where parents show love and care for their children." Elements of the Administration for Children and Families (ACF) vision statement (which ACF calls a mission statement) include the following: "[F]amilies and individuals empowered to increase their own economic independence and productivity; strong, healthy, supportive communities that have a positive impact on the quality of life and the development of children" (Administration for Children and Families, n.d.).

● GETTING SPECIFIC: PROGRAM GOALS AND OBJECTIVES

With some common vision in hand, the process can move to the next stage of specificity: program goals and objectives. Goals are one step more specific than vision. They express general purposes for specific programs. For example, a community program may have as its vision a community where parents are closer to their children. A goal in that program might be to teach the concept and use of languages of love to program participants. An objective is the most specific level of intent. For a program such as the one described, the objective might be that every parent who takes part in the program will be able to name three languages of love and identify the one or combination that best helps him or her connect with each child in the family.

Objectives are the place where our thinking must get most clear and specific. It is an unusual person who finds the writing of objectives to be fun. The creation of objectives requires very careful thinking yet allows us to design and assess more effective programs.

Maybe the process is made more unpleasant when we require that objectives fit some preestablished pattern. The objectives only exist to make program delivery and evaluation more in alignment with the program goals and ultimate program vision.

A good objective is clearly tied to the goal, should be specific enough to be measured, and usually describes some action or knowledge that a participant would gain by participation in the program. Some objectives specify an exact level of performance: "Participants will report involvement in daily renewal rituals (yoga, exercise, or meditation) for at least 15 minutes per day at least 4 days per week." Such exactness is important for programs that have both well-developed programs and well-developed measures.

Another dimension to objectives is the time span of effects. The more immediate effects of programs are called outcomes. The long-term effects are called impacts. For example, an outcome objective might be that couples involved in a program commit to set aside time every week for enjoyable activities together. The impact might be that participants report feeling closer to their partners 1 year after the completion of the program.

AN EXAMPLE OF AN EVALUATION ●
FRAMEWORK IN PARENTING

One example of the development of program goals and objectives is in the area of parenting. The Cooperative Extension System has been interested in supporting parenting education for many years. In 1994, four Extension specialists (Smith, Cudaback, Goddard, & Myers-Walls, 1994) worked together to create the National Extension Parent Education Model (NEPEM), which defined six categories of vital parenting behavior. The document also included sample objectives. But there was still a substantial distance between coming up with objectives and having an effective evaluation system.

It was not until 2002 that a group of Extension leaders attempted to develop more detail as part of the Evaluation and Accountability Systems for Extension (EASE). A group of specialists took the six categories from NEPEM and developed both objectives and measures. While a comprehensive evaluation system would provide many objectives related to each critical parenting practice and each objective could have many different evaluation questions, the evaluation questions in this example are suggestive of an evaluation framework in three areas of the national parenting model.

Table 4.1 shows some representative impacts, objectives, and evaluation items. There are dozens of meaningful objectives that might be written in each vital area of parenting. For each objective, many different items could be written to evaluate the accomplishment of the objectives.

Matching the Parts

Some of these objectives and some of the evaluations items will not be suitable for some audiences. That is a vital point. The objectives must match the program mission. The evaluation items must match the objectives. And the objectives must be suitable for the specific audience in reading level and appropriateness of the target behavior.

Of course, there is another vital match: The program with all its instructional activities should match the objectives and the evaluation (Goddard, Smith, Mize, White, & White, 1994). If a program sets its objectives to build stress techniques but instead teaches car repair and, for evaluation, measures height and weight of participants, the resulting data will be hard to interpret. They will tell us almost nothing about the effectiveness of the program—unless we decide that weight loss is our real program objective. (The theoretical connection between car repair and weight loss will still require attention.)

TABLE 4.1 Examples of Parenting Impacts, Goals, Objectives, and Evaluation Items

Impact: Parents will provide appropriate nurturance and guidance to their children and youth, resulting in positive development and achievement.

Impact A (NEPEM *Care for Self* dimension): Parents will become more effective in caring for self.

Goal A: Parents report they are managing personal and family stress (more) effectively.

Objective A1. Parents will increase their awareness of exercise as a means of dealing with stress.

Sample measurement item:	*Never*				*Always*
I exercise to lower stress.	1	2	3	4	5

Objective A2. Parents will develop awareness of their need to take time out and to get control of their own feelings.

Sample measurement item:	*Never*				*Always*
When I get upset with my child, I take a minute to calm down before I deal with him or her.	1	2	3	4	5

Objective A3. Parents will know some stress-reduction techniques (i.e., getting organized, changing attitudes or expectations, changing environments or people whom you associate with, limiting the number of things on your to-do list, setting priorities, physical exercise, humor).

Sample measurement item:	*Never*				*Always*
When I feel myself getting angry, I have some things I do to help me calm down, like going for a walk, listening to music, or calling a friend.	1	2	3	4	5

Objective A4. Parents will know techniques to support themselves and to cope effectively in times of personal difficulty (e.g., calling a friend and letting off steam, positive self-talk, hot bath, take or plan a vacation, call crisis center).

Sample measurement item:	*Never*				*Always*
I know what to do or whom to call when I feel like I can't take it anymore.	1	2	3	4	5

Impact B (NEPEM *Guide* dimension): Parents use appropriate positive discipline techniques.

Goal B1: Parents apply their knowledge of child development to support their children's developmental progress—framing choices, setting limits, and monitoring their children's activities appropriately.

Objective B1. Parents will increase the use of positive strategies for learning self-control such as allowing their children to make decisions and avoiding force.

Sample measurement item:	Never				Always
I let my child make his or her own choices whenever possible.	1	2	3	4	5

Objective B2. Parents will learn characteristics of effective discipline, including being positive, teaching, and giving choices.

Sample measurement item:	Never				Always
Even though I must sometimes correct my child's behavior, I show lots of love to him or her.	1	2	3	4	5

Objective B3. Parents will increase their use of praise, encouragement, and other supportive language.

Sample measurement item:	Strongly Disagree				Strongly Agree
I try to notice and encourage the good things my child does.	1	2	3	4	5

Objective B4. Parents will decrease scolding, punishment, and harsh, punitive, and controlling parenting behaviors.

Sample measurement item:	Strongly Disagree				Strongly Agree
I say far more positive than negative things to my child now than before this class.	1	2	3	4	5

Objective B5. Parents will increase their knowledge of different ways to help their children develop responsibility and use these techniques, such as allowing their children to make decisions, not being overly intrusive, allowing their children to experience the world as a lawful place and allowing their children to suffer the consequences for their actions in order to help children understand the relationship between actions and consequences.

Sample measurement item:	Strongly Disagree				Strongly Agree
I believe that letting my child make many little decisions on his or her own is a good way to teach responsibility and self-control.	1	2	3	4	5

(Continued)

TABLE 4.1 (Continued)

Impact C (NEPEM *Nurture* dimension): Parents show affection and nurturance to their children.

Goal C1: Parents listen and attend to their children's feelings and ideas.

Objective C1.1. Parents will know that talking with their children is very important to help children feel significant as well as to help children develop language, intellectual, and social skills.

	Strongly Disagree			Strongly Agree
Sample measurement item:				
My child learns a lot from something as simple as talking to me. 1	2	3	4	5

Objective C1.2. Parents will know that talking with their children is very important to help children feel significant as well as to help children develop language, intellectual, and social skills.

	Never			Always
Sample measurement item:				
I take time to just talk pleasantly with my child. 1	2	3	4	5

Objective C1.3. Parents will increase their knowledge and use of the varying techniques for providing encouragement/nurturance through both verbal and nonverbal means.

	Strongly Disagree			Strongly Agree
Sample measurement item:				
I have learned new ways to encourage and praise my child in the last few weeks. 1	2	3	4	5

Goal C2: Parents show love and caring for their children.

Objective C2.1. Parents will know that praise should be sincere.

	Never			Always
Sample measurement item:				
I tell my child about the good things I see in him or her. 1	2	3	4	5

Objective C2.2. Parents will learn to be sensitive to the ways their children get the message of parental love, including taking time to do things that their children love and taking time to understand their children's feelings.

	Never			Always
Sample measurement item:				
I try to show love to my child in the way that works best for him or her. 1	2	3	4	5

Reprinted from National Family Consumer Sciences POW Impact Committee, 2003.

The matches might be illustrated as follows:

Vision—Goals—Objectives—Instructional activities—Evaluation measures

When all of these program elements are in alignment, greater gains and more meaningful data are more likely.

DEFINING THE KIND OF INFORMATION ● NEEDED: THE EVALUATION QUESTIONS

There are many reasons to gather evaluation data, including assessment of participant progress, guiding program decisions, refining program processes, specifying effective program elements, establishing the merit of specific viewpoints, or maximizing program effects. (See Herman, Morris, and Fitz-Gibbon, 1987, for more details on each of these purposes.) When we merely do evaluation because it is expected or because it is considered good form, it is not likely to have the benefits that may accrue when we carefully preconsider what data we need and how we expect it to be used.

Common questions that can guide evaluation include the following:

1. What are the ways in which participants are prepared to function better in their family life as a result of our program? (attitudes, knowledge, skills)

2. In what ways do the participants actually function better as a result of our program? (behavior)

3. What elements or combination of elements have the greatest impact?

4. What needs related to program objectives remain unaddressed in spite of program efforts?

5. What evidence do we have that our program satisfies the objectives of our funders?

Meaningful answers to questions such as these are not found readily. In fact, Francine Jacobs (1988) has argued that many discouraging outcomes in evaluation are not necessarily evidence of inadequate programs; the outcomes may be evidence that we have asked the wrong questions at the wrong time. When we apply comprehensive outcome measures to still-developing programs, we should not be surprised that we have disappointing results. Jacobs suggests that evaluation should grow with the program. In fact, she describes five tiers of evaluation.

In the first level of evaluation, called the preimplementation tier, data can be gathered to establish community needs. While often not thought of as a part of evaluation, it puts all program efforts in the larger context.

There are many sources of data for such a needs assessment. Socio-demographic data may indicate community problems and risks in the program area. Local press coverage can provide an indication of community awareness and concern. Interviews with community leaders (social service agencies, faith communities, business managers, etc.) can provide vital information on both the problems and previous efforts to address them. In some cases, it may be helpful to conduct a community survey. For example, some communities have surveyed both youth and parents about youth challenges (Olson, Goddard, Solheim, & Sandt, in press) in order to better target youth-serving interventions.

The second level of evaluation, the accountability tier, involves "the systematic collection of client-specific and service-utilization data" (Jacobs, 1988, p. 54), answering the question, Who is getting what services? Data includes not only the number of people served, but their characteristics. As a result, it may be possible to determine the extent to which the program's target audience is being served with the intended intervention. This level may not seem like serious evaluation in the traditional sense. Yet such data are essential for understanding the progress of the organization toward its goals. For a beginning program, this may be some of the most helpful feedback than can be obtained.

A vital part of all evaluation is the gathering of "use" information from program personnel. Effective evaluation includes asking instructors and participants about the pattern of service delivery and client participation. It is possible, for example, that program objectives are not being met simply because the program is offered at the wrong time of day or in the wrong location. This is not information that will readily emerge from a paper-and-pencil test given to those who do attend the program.

Some (Thomas, Schvaneveldt, & Young, 1993) have argued that Jacobs may emphasize the ways that programs impact participants and neglect the ways in which program participants impact the program. Programs are certainly impacted by the participants, including ways that may have an enduring impact on programs and delivery. It can be useful to gather data about the ways that the program has adjusted to accommodate participants.

On the third level, the program clarification tier, program staff and participants provide feedback on how to improve program content and delivery. This level includes close scrutiny of program goals and objectives. The essential question is, How can we do a better job serving our clients? (Jacobs, 1988, p. 57). Both staff and participant feedback are essential to answering this question.

Client satisfaction data are valuable on this level. It is often helpful to gather data not only from active program participants but also from those who registered but dropped out of active participation. Such interviews may yield important clues for greater effectiveness. For example, sensitive inquiry may determine that the current, middle-class, college-educated teacher is not the right person to deliver this program for limited-resource, young, Hispanic mothers. There may be language and cultural barriers that need to be addressed.

At Level 4, the progress-toward-objectives tier, more mature programs give careful attention to outcomes, including the questions "Which participants achieved which of these proximate objectives? Are there differential program effects based on participants' ages, races, or opinions?" (Jacobs, 1988, p. 59). This intensity of evaluation is suitable for programs that "are longer lived, more experiences, and relatively secure financially" (Jacobs, 1988, p. 59). While these are the activities that most think of as standard evaluation activities, such intensive evaluation requires greater program maturity than most programs have.

Level 4 evaluations will often require the help of professional evaluators or others with specialized knowledge of evaluation. Measures may include items such as those listed above in the discussion of EASE. Careful measurement and statistical analysis can provide evidence that program clients are making progress toward stated program objectives.

Jacobs makes the point that, while standard measures may be an important part of the evaluation, customized measures that tap the unique character of the program are essential.

The final level, the program-impact tier, is the most rigorous. It often entails random assignment of participants to treatment and delayed treatment groups, longitudinal data collection, and complex analyses. In evaluation-intensive funded projects, as much as 30% to 40% of the total budget may be allocated to evaluation activities. Such investment of resources can support careful, exacting analyses with persuasive conclusions.

It is clear that this is not the right level of evaluation for a young, still developing program. It is no more reasonable to ask a toddler to wear adult shoes than it is to ask a developing program to do effective, comprehensive outcome evaluation. McCall and Green (2004) argue that, in our rush for such rigorous testing, we may have undervalued other methods of evaluating programs.

One of the commonest problems in the evaluation of FLE may be placing evaluation burdens on programs that are not prepared to support them. Evaluation should be matched to the program. It is also wise to educate funders and other stakeholders to expect the kind of evaluation that is appropriate for the maturity of the program.

Most programs fail to get enough information from program staff. Careful scrutiny of the delivery process may include not only staff discussions but observations of teaching or service delivery by fellow staff members.

● THE LOGIC MODEL APPROACH TO EVALUATION

Jacobs's five-tiered model of evaluation sensitizes program developers to the need to match evaluation efforts to the maturity of the program. It encourages program evaluators to gather and use different kinds of data. It also provides a philosophical context for the enterprise of evaluation. It does not provide a step-by-step process for evaluation.

One popular method for conceptualizing program and evaluation efforts is the development of a logic model. Logic models were first developed by Edward Suchman (1968) and have become increasingly popular.

Logic models commonly begin with a description of the situation and priorities. The situation statement can result from an effective needs assessment. Priorities are related to the vision of the program. This section of the logic model may also include a list of stakeholders and a summary of research or best practices related to the identified problem.

The next step in the model is to specify inputs. What are the human, financial, material, and knowledge resources that can be applied to the problem?

Next are outputs that are divided into activities and participants. What are the processes that will be used to effect change? Will the program use newsletters, group meetings, conferences, home visitation, or some other process? Related to participants, who will take part, what agencies will be involved, who are the customers of services?

Next are the outcomes or impacts divided into short term, medium term, and long term. Clearly, the short-term results are easiest to measure. What are the changes in knowledge, attitudes, skills, and aspirations (Rockwell & Bennett, 2004)? Medium-term results such as changes in behavior or social policy are generally more difficult to measure. Long-term impacts include changes in communities such as lowered divorce rates or teen pregnancy. They are clearly the most difficult to impact and to measure. Since there are many factors outside those affected by the program, it is especially difficult to establish that a specific program had a societal impact. Such forces are labeled external factors in some logic models.

Undergirding the other elements of the logic model are assumptions. Many programs struggle under a load of unchecked assumptions. For example, the assumption that raising self-esteem will remedy a wide range of social problems has wide appeal and popular support. Unfortunately, it has not been supported by research (Kohn, 1994; Mecca, Smelser, & Vasconcellos, 1989).

Logic models are one way of organizing the various elements of a program. They provide a framework for organizing thinking and planning evaluation. For an effective and more detailed introduction to logic models, consult the University of Wisconsin Web site at http://www.uwex.edu/ces/ lmcourse/#.

INNOVATIONS IN EVALUATION ●

Transformative Learning

Sometimes we think of professional evaluation as paper-and-pencil tests used to get quantitative measures of progress. But there are many other ways to get very useful information. One way is to invite program participants to meet with an interviewer (someone besides the educator or program delivery person) sometime after the completion of the program. Details of how this evaluation might be done are given in an article by Joy First and Wendy Way (1995). The interviewer can sit with those individuals who are willing to visit and ask questions such as the following:

- About how many times last week did you talk about the class, or anything you had discussed at the class, with friends or relatives?
- Do you talk to friends or relatives about any changes in your parenting as a result of the class? Can you tell me a story about those changes like you might tell a friend or relative?
- What are the most important things you feel you learned by going to the class? Can you remember any feelings you had when you were at the class?
- Has attending the class made parenting any easier? Has it made it more difficult? How?
- Can you tell me about any experiences that show how the class has affected your life—either parenting or in other ways?
- What is your best experience from the class? What is your worst experience?

(For First and Way's full list of interview questions, see page 109 of their article.)

Such information gathered by a sensitive interviewer can provide very valuable information about the strengths of the program and ways to improve it. Themes can be tallied and presented in reports to stakeholders. Such information should also be reviewed by program staff in order to get fuller feedback than quantitative data provide.

Results Mapping

Success stories have the ability to add flesh to evaluation bones. But success stories have been suspect for many reasons. They are not systematic and may capture more about the author's enthusiasm than the program's effects.

Barry Kibel (1999, n.d.) has developed a process of results mapping as a creative blend of quantitative and qualitative methods of evaluation. Results mapping is not held hostage to the limiting assumption of quantitative methods that a standard treatment has a significant effect on all recipients. This process allows portraits of different kinds of benefits from similar or customized services of an agency.

In results mapping, the storyteller explains "how the program first got involved with the client, what actions it subsequently initiated to promote client health and growth, and how the client responded to these actions" (Kibel, n.d., p. 12). The coding system even provides a results ladder with seven levels, from providing general information to attaining mastery level.

The following is an example of a story used in results mapping:

Frances is a 78-year-old [who, after surgery,] received warm lunches through the meals-on-wheels program operated by our senior center. This was her first contact in Cincinnati with adults her own age. The volunteer who delivered the meals encouraged her to visit the center after she got well. She arrived one day, stayed a few hours, then left. A week later she was back, and remained most of the day. She has been a regular ever since. For the past two months, she has been volunteering in the kitchen helping to prepare the meals we deliver. (Kibel, n.d., p. 9)

Posttest First Methods

The gold standard of evaluation has traditionally included a pretest and posttest. There are times when a posttest without a pretest may be the preferred way to evaluate. For example, parents under the supervision of a social service agency or mandated by a judge to participate in classes may not be willing to complete a pretest with candor. They may be suspicious of program personnel and the objectives of data collection.

There may also be problems with participants' interpretation of pretest items. Consider the case of a parenting class where improved empathic listening is a major objective. If we ask parents how well they are doing at empathic listening before they start the program, they may think they are doing very well. But as the program progresses and the parents learn more about what empathic listening involves, they may realize that they have much more to learn. They may give themselves a lower score on the posttest than the pretest even though they may actually be doing better. The lower score represents not diminished skill but heightened expectation. Participants' definition of empathic listening was changed by the program.

This phenomenon, called response shift bias, has been the subject of concern for many scholars (Cronbach & Furby, 1970; Doueck & Bondanza, 1990; Golembiewski, Billingsley, & Yeager, 1976; Howard & Daily, 1979; Howard, Ralph, Gulanick, Maxwell, Nance, & Gerber, 1979; Howard, Schmeck, & Bray, 1979; Robinson, 1994; Sprangers, 1989; Terborg, Howard, & Maxwell, 1980). While the most advanced evaluation requires sophisticated designs, the present point is that there are good reasons that a person may choose some design besides the traditional pretest and posttest.

Response shift bias should be less of a problem when parents are merely asked to describe their behavior. For example, if we ask how much time a parent spent with a child in a play activity requested by the child, the answer should be less vulnerable to definition bias than questions that ask the participants to evaluate their subjective performance. When the program participants' definition of a behavior is changed by the program, it may be wise to ask participants after the program how well they are doing at that behavior (a posttest). After each such question, the participants could be asked how well they were doing on the same behavior at the beginning of the program (a retrospective pretest). This can allow a comparison of the two ratings to see if there has been any change. Alternatively, change can be assessed directly. Participants could be asked to tell whether they are now doing worse, about the same, or better on that behavior. These approaches avoid the problems associated with a changing definition of the behavior since pre and post assessments are asked at the same time with the same definition of the target behavior in mind.

The following is a simple example of a posttest and a retrospective pretest:

How well do you accept influence from your partner?

_____ Very poorly
_____ Poorly
_____ Well
_____ Very well

Before you began this program, how well did you accept influence from your partner?

_____ Very poorly
_____ Poorly
_____ Well
_____ Very well

The following is a simple example of posttest and change:

How good are you at listening to your child's feelings?

_____ Very poor
_____ Poor
_____ Good
_____ Very good

Compared to when you started this program, how good are you at listening to your child's feelings?

_____ Much worse
_____ Worse
_____ About the same
_____ Better
_____ Much better

● USING EVALUATION DATA

Not only should evaluation be designed with its end use in mind, but also careful attention should be exercised to the amount, depth, and style of presentation based on its purpose. A presentation to a lunch meeting of the general membership of a civic club that has helped fund a program will probably be quite different from the written report submitted to a governmental agency. In the former case, the appropriate presentation may include a slide show describing the objectives and activities of the program, providing a success story or two, and a very few statistics, together with an invitation for continued support. In the latter case, a complete tabulation of data may be appropriate. Even though gains may not have been shown in some areas, the narrative may justify the finding with the statement that those were secondary or even incidental objectives. The case could be made for continued or expanded funding to better address those objectives.

If you or someone in your office has a reasonable sophistication in statistics, your report might be prepared by your staff. If the organization does not have such expertise in house, you might supplement the expertise you do have with consultants who have successful experience with evaluation reports (see Morris, Fitz-Gibbon, & Freeman, 1987).

CONCLUSION ●

There are many ways to evaluate. Complex and ambitious evaluations may not be the best method for gathering the information you need. As you apply your good sense and your knowledge of your program and the participants, you can design the evaluation program that meets your information needs and will be effective at communicating with important stakeholders.

EXPLORATIONS ●

1. Visit a community program that delivers FLE. Ask about program objectives. Examine evaluation instruments that are used. Examine any reports on the program. Decide which tier of evaluation (Jacobs, 1988) is appropriate for the program's development and the level on which the program is trying to operate. Consider what information should be collected to facilitate the program objectives.

2. Create a flow chart of evaluation processes or a logic model you would recommend to guide a community FLE program you would like to initiate.

CHAPTER 5

DESIGNING EFFECTIVE INSTRUCTION

I f you were invited to provide training or to prepare a publication on the subject of nurturing the developing child, how would you organize or structure your presentation? Are there rules or guides for making it effective?

Many of us would begin with a definition of *nurture*. We might then summarize what is known on the subject of nurturing children, including effective nurturing practices. If we are effective teachers, we will probably include stories to make our instruction more interesting and pertinent. And we will invite listeners or readers to apply the principles to their own situations. But is there something more than intuition and raw experience to guide this process?

The answer is yes. There is a substantial and growing science of instructional design. In fact, there is far more science behind instructional design than average FLEs need to know. So while FLEs do not need to become entirely focused on instructional design, they can be far more effective if they are familiar with many of the core principles.

This chapter is dedicated to discussing and applying two bodies of work by M. David Merrill, professor of instructional technology at Utah State University. His theory or framework is the centerpiece of this chapter because it is widely used in the instructional design industry, has been substantiated by research, and provides practical recommendations to those who are preparing instruction.

COMPONENT DISPLAY THEORY ●

David Merrill has developed a system of instructional design that is called component display theory (CDT) (1983, 1994). There are parts of CDT that are beyond the purview of this chapter and most FLEs. However, Merrill's discussion of primary presentation forms can provide a very useful guide in the development of short presentations, extended training, and publications—any form of FLE.

If you are a person who understands tables readily, Table 5.1 will summarize the key elements of CDT in a simple form. If you do not readily comprehend the table, the text below should make the ideas clear without the table.

Let's use Merrill's CDT theory to guide the development of a lesson or publication on the topic named above: nurturing the developing child. A common way to begin would be to share a principle with the learners. Merrill calls this an expository generality (EG), which simply means that the teacher tells (called "expository" mode) some general idea, principle, concept, truth, or process (a generality). So the generality might be that "Children are most likely to grow into compassionate, productive adults when they are cared for by people who are sensitive to their needs, are committed to them, and build close relationships with them."

This simple statement undergirds the most important process in parenting (Peterson & Hann, 1999). Nothing matters as much as nurturing. A clear, direct, simple expression of this principle (EG) is a good way to start the teaching—though not the only way.

For those who are familiar with scholarship on the subject, the clear statement of principle is rich with meaning. For the typical learners, the meaning of the statement and its applications to their lives may not be clear. The typical learner will need far more instruction than a mere statement of principle.

Using Stories That Teach the Principle

In order to help learners understand just what the principle means, the teacher may next choose to provide examples (Eeg or expository instances) that illustrate the major points. If, for instance, we wanted to illustrate the importance of sensitive caregiving in the development of children, we might tell a story about a caregiver who responds to infant distress with support, soothing, and patience and the beneficial effects of such care. For the sake of clarity, we might also tell a contrasting story of care that is brittle, angry, and impatient and the negative consequences of such care.

TABLE 5.1   The Component Display Theory

		Kind of Content	
The Primary Presentation Forms of Component Display Theory		Generality (G), rule, definition, principle, or procedure	Instance (eg), a specific example of an event, process, or principle
Mode of Delivery of Presentation	Expository (E): present, tell, or show	1. EG: Tell a rule or principle	2. Eeg: Give an example or story that supports the principle
	Inquisitory (I): question, ask, or learner practice	3. IG: Invite learners to express the rule in their own way	4. Ieg: Ask learners to think of their own experiences that illustrate the principle

Source: Adapted from Merrill, 1994, p. 121.

In order to provide parents with an application of the principle, we might tell about a little boy named Riley who had colic. His parents didn't have much experience with babies or with colic. At first they wondered if they had a bad child. They wondered if they should just ignore the boy's crying in order to break the habit. But they had been told that infants sometimes get colic and need soothing. So Mom and Dad took turns rocking, singing, and patting Riley when he had colic. They helped and supported each other. When they were both worn out, they might lay Riley down in his crib for a few minutes. But even in this stressful situation, both parents made real efforts to be sensitive to Riley. Within a few weeks, the colic began to fade. While it had been a difficult time for the family, Riley had developed a sense that his parents would respond sensitively to his distress. What a great foundation for trust!

Teaching is made more interesting and effective by the use of appropriate stories. They can help learners see how an abstract principle applies to real life. They can also help learners remember the general principle. We learn through stories.

The colic story is especially appropriate for parents of infants who are likely to have children with similar problems. Multiple stories with diverse situations might be helpful. For example Ellyn Satter has written a book (1999) and developed a video (1995/1997) that illustrate sensitive feeding of children.

In the video she shows a parent whose sole objective appears to be to get the bottle of baby food inside the baby as quickly as possible. The parent does not talk with the child or wait for the child's signs of interest in food. The parent just shovels the food into the child. In fact, it seemed clear that the child ran out of interest in the food long before the food ran out. The parent continued to shovel the food into an increasingly unhappy child. That is a good example of nonsensitivity.

In contrast, Satter also shows parents who are sensitive to the child. They engage the child in playful conversation. They offer the food so the child can see it. They allow the child time to process the food. They notice when the child loses interest in the food. Her principle related to sensitive feeding is that nutrition has a way of falling into place when people are the priority rather than the rules that govern them. In a workshop teaching situation, Satter's video might be used or stories from her book might be shared. If you are preparing a publication on this subject, you might tell your own stories (or the stories of parents you know) or seek permission to reprint Satter's stories.

If your audience includes parents of school-age children, the stories would naturally revolve around the challenges and opportunities they will face with their children. For example, they might involve sensitivity to the children's challenges at school, their disappointments, rivalries, or difficulties in getting chores done. Even in such situations, the same general principle presides: When parents are sensitive to their children and their needs, the children are more likely to grow into socially competent people.

Each of the subparts of a principle can be taught in the same way. The principle as stated above has at least three major subparts dealing with the importance of sensitivity, commitment, and close relationship. Stories can be shared to illustrate each part of the general principle. As you can imagine, there might also be additional subprinciples taught along the way. For example, in teaching about the importance of close relationships, the teacher may teach about the characteristics of effective listening or about taking time with children. Each lesson may have one central principle and a network of supporting principles.

As you select stories to illustrate principles, it makes sense that you would use stories that your clientele can relate to. You are not likely to share stories of parents dealing with teens' careless driving if you are teaching parents of young children. In some cases, you may have a very diverse audience, including parents of a broad age range of children and very diverse life situations. It makes sense to offer a range of stories, but it also leads to another mode of learning, the mode that Merrill calls the inquisitory mode, suggesting that the teacher is inviting participation by the learners.

Helping Learners Take the Principles Home

Let's start with inquisitory generalities (IG). This step could involve asking participants to recall or repeat the rule or principle about nurturing young children. It should go beyond parroting back the original statement and invite learners to express the principle in their own words and way. Answers may be very diverse. One participant may express the principle as "Ya gotta love 'em." Is that expression of the principle acceptable? The answer is, it depends. We might ask the participant, "Will those words help you remember to act in the ways we have talked about?" If the answer is affirmative, then that expression of the principle is satisfactory. If not, the participant might suggest how to modify his or her statement to capture the full meaning of the original principle.

The objective is not to push participants toward our words but toward actions congruent with the principle. That is why we ask, "Will those words help you remember to act in the ways we have talked about?"

Each person may have a different way of expressing the principle: "I gotta notice my kid." "I must stop being in a hurry." "I need to take time for my children." While those words may each express something very different from the original principle, each may capture that part of the principle that the participant is ready to live. The object of all instructional activity is to move participants toward actions congruent with principles.

Once the participants have their own handle on expressing the principle, effective application can be advanced by encouraging them to think of situations from their own experience where they can see the principle at work. Since we are asking the learners for their stories, Merrill calls this inquisitory instances (Ieg). Participants may tell their own stories related to the principle. An able teacher will help learners see the principle (EG) at work in their stories.

Some of the participants' stories may not seem to illustrate the principle very well. We can invite them to make the connection clear: "Do you see the principle of nurturing young children in that story?" Or if the story simply does not illustrate the principle at hand very well, a sensitive teacher might respond, "That story beautifully illustrates another principle of parenting that we will discuss later in this series. Do you have any stories that illustrate the power of love to help children grow and develop?"

Finding Instructional Balance

One way of thinking about Merrill's CDT is as a reminder to balance. Related to mode of delivery, the theory reminds us to balance the leader talk with participant talk. Certainly each participant has something valuable to contribute. The leader should bring expert knowledge as well as facilitation skills. The learners bring their own discoveries, creativity, expertise, and wealth of experience. When they work well together, great discoveries can be made.

Balance between leader and participant does not necessarily mean equal time. Instead, it suggests that each be involved in ways that advance learning. In the early stages of a class, the leader may need to take more initiative. As participants become more comfortable, they may contribute more and more to the class.

Related to the kind of content, Merrill's theory reminds us to balance generalities with instances. We have all been bored by lectures that described laws and principles but never touched down in human experience. Perhaps we have also heard presentations that were filled with stories but failed to clearly identify any general principles. When there is a healthy balance of the two, learning is facilitated.

Instruction Outside a Classroom

Much of the foregoing discussion presumes that the instruction will be delivered in face-to-face instruction. It is also useful to use CDT in organizing print materials. While a print teaching process does not allow for full-fledged interaction, many effective FLF publications provide questions that invite participant thought and reaction. Many such publications provide a place for participants to write their reactions. They may also invite participants to discuss the ideas with other family members, respected peers, or potential mentors.

When learning is done in an electronic mode, responses can be programmed into the computer software. Or in the case of online learning, there may be interaction between the students and between students and teaching assistants.

In Chapter 6 we explore additional ways to support and encourage learner participation. The focus of this chapter is designing instruction that is likely to help learners understand and apply principles for better family life.

Mixing the Elements of Instruction

The foregoing discussion may seem to suggest a lockstep march through a process. The reality of effective teaching is much more random and exciting. A teacher may choose to mix the instructional elements to fit the learners and the subject. For example, a teacher may choose to begin with one or more stories (Eeg's) before making a statement of the principle (EG). Beginning with interesting stories may be an effective way of engaging learners' interest.

A lesson may also begin with an inquisitory generality. For example, you might invite learners to respond to the question "What do you think is the most important thing parents can do to help their children turn out well?" If the teacher or leader dismisses answers that are not the one he or she has in mind, participants are likely to be turned off. However, a skillful teacher can respond to every answer positively: "What an important principle!" "You have probably seen that make a real difference!" Each can be written on the board or flip chart.

In the course of the discussion, someone is likely to nominate the principle that is the subject of the session, to which the teacher can respond, "That is very important. And it happens to be the one that I would like us to talk about today." An inquisitory generality may be a good way to begin if you want to get participants thinking about the general lessons they have learned.

A lesson might also begin with an inquisitory instance. We might ask, "Would you tell me stories from your parenting experience that taught you important lessons of parenting?" After listening to several stories, the leader might comment, "Thank you for sharing your stories. One of the themes I see in many of them is the importance of nurturing children." Beginning with their stories may allow the learners to see from the beginning that the general principle (EG) is tied to their lives.

Each approach has advantages and disadvantages. It requires a skillful teacher to begin in the inquisitory mode. It may also require more time to get to the central point. Yet this approach may be useful for some audiences and some subjects.

● FIRST PRINCIPLES OF INSTRUCTION

Based on decades of experience in instructional design, David Merrill (2000, 2001) has created his own nominations for the first principles of instruction. He has compared his recommendations with those that come from prominent instructional models, and found the common themes across most of the models. In the balance of this chapter, we consider how these principles might be applied to the challenges faced by FLEs.

Instruction Addresses Real Problems

Merrill's first principle (2001) states that "learning is facilitated when the learner is engaged in solving a real-world problem" (p. 461). In this arena, school learning is disadvantaged. Most problems that are presented in school classrooms are artificial. (Think of those story problems in algebra or analyses of poems done in literature classes.) FLEs have a big advantage in this arena. Family life is filled with real-world problems. Family problems tend to be real and personal. In fact, it is characteristic of family life that our relationships are close and continuing—just the right combination to present real-world problems.

Consider ways of applying this first principle to FLE. Imagine that you are teaching a class about the importance of commitment in couple relationships. You might set the stage by sharing a story from your own life or from a print source that illustrates the challenges of commitment.

For example, you might share a story from John Glenn's autobiography (1999). He tells that his wife was bashful in part because of a problem with stuttering. He was often in the public eye. There were times when he had to choose to be involved in his profession the way people expected him to be or to be sensitive to his wife's preferences. He chose to honor his commitment to his wife.

You can invite participants to consider times when they were discouraged with their partner relationship, when they felt like giving up. Rather than have them share stories that could be painful for their partners, you could invite them to list some of the difficulties couples face that could challenge their commitment to each other. Such a discussion is likely to make the issue very real for all participants; it would be the rare participant who would not think of his or her own challenges with commitment.

Each person could be invited to identify a specific situation in which he or she found it difficult to show commitment—and make either a mental or written note. Then class members could be invited to share ideas for sustaining commitment. As the group suggests ideas, each person is invited to make note of those ideas that could be useful in his or her relationship.

Of course, group discussion is not the only path to learning. The work of Lev Vgotsky (see Rogoff, 1990) underscores the importance of learning from experts. In many arenas of activity, skill is learned through apprenticeships. FLEs can invite people to interview those who have succeeded at the processes under study. A young couple might interview a seasoned couple, asking them about ways they have shown commitment to each other. Younger couples can also be invited to be quiet observers of couples who have learned to work well together.

FLEs may also be involved with problem solving in after-class discussions or in home visits. For example, on a periodic home visit, a parent may ask the visitor what to do about a lazy daughter. The wise educator will not spout some canned wisdom but will model problem solving with her carefully chosen questions. "Tell me more about what your daughter is like." "In what situations is she lazy?" "Are there situations where she is not lazy?" "What have you tried to help her do better?" "Have any of those efforts paid off?" "Can you see any special reasons why she might not do well in the areas where she has seemed lazy?"

All of these questions are intended to help the parent move beyond frustrated judgment of a child to productive problem solving. They set the stage for the most important question: "Can you think of anything you can do to help your daughter function better [i.e., be less lazy]?" The parent might not have ready answers. A helpful educator might suggest some possibilities: "Do you think she fails to do certain chores because she hates those particular tasks? Or because she doesn't like to be rushed? Or because she doesn't know how?" Effective FLEs facilitate their participants' real-world problem solving.

Of course, it is generally unwise to start education with the most emotion-invoking and long-lasting problems. Merrill (2000) recommends that learners deal with "a progression of carefully sequenced problems" (p. 5). That is one reason that it is advantageous to start FLE preventively. When a parenting or partner relationship has been toxic for years, it is difficult to turn the tide.

Activating Existing Knowledge

Merrill's second principle is that learning is facilitated when existing knowledge is activated as a foundation for new knowledge. For example, if we were interested in teaching a group of parents to tune in to their children's languages of love, we might begin by inviting them to think about times in their childhoods when their family members tried to show them love. We would encourage them to think about efforts that were more or less effective. While all of the efforts to communicate love might be sincere, some were probably effective and others may have been counterproductive. We might discuss what made the difference.

Participants would probably recognize that some efforts were well tuned to our preferences and some were not. If a family member who knows I am on a diet still buys me a candy bar as a gift, I might not be appreciative. By recognizing the importance of attunement to the other person—awareness of that person's needs or preferences—we can become more effective at showing love.

To take this idea one step closer to the parents' task of showing love to their children, we might ask the parents to think about efforts they have made to show love to their children that have been more or less effective. By analyzing their efforts to show love to their children, they might determine their children's preferences or languages of love.

While the discussion of previous experience does not create new knowledge, it does bring existing knowledge to a more conscious level and organizes it into a form that can guide intentional action.

In some cases, it may be useful to create a new experience for learners as a foundation for the new learning. For example, family members in a weekly class might be asked to wear some special mental glasses that allowed them to only notice the good things that their partner or children do. Imagine that the glasses entirely block out annoyances and disappointments. Notice the good, record it, and return to the next session to discuss what they noticed and experienced.

It is possible that such an assignment would set the stage for teaching class members about the processes by which humans judge the motives of others and about the power of the mind to interpret and filter experience. It could provide personal experience relevant to the lesson to be taught.

The Power of Demonstration

Merrill's (2000) third principle states that learning is facilitated when new knowledge is demonstrated to the learner. It is not uncommon for people in classes to be taught a new principle, presented with a dilemma, and asked to tell how to respond. The task may seem easy to those who are familiar with the principle and have tried to apply it for years. But the jump from current experience to new performance can be daunting for many learners.

For example, it is common in both parenting and couple relationship trainings to teach people about empathic responding. We teach people to attend to the emotional experience of their child or partner and try to express in words what that person may be feeling. It may seem easy enough—but decades of experience can work against ready application of the principle.

Imagine that we have taught parents about empathic listening in parenting. In order to give them a chance to practice, we ask them to imagine that one of their children has come home from school with slumped shoulders and confessed to getting in trouble at school. In fact, the teacher yelled at your child and called him names. At this point, you invite parents in your class to tell what they would say if they were responding empathically to the upset child. We suspect that the natural parental tendency to play like a cross-examining investigator will swamp the valuable lessons parents may have learned in a parenting class. Habit regularly trumps new learning.

Especially as participants learn new and difficult skills, it might be useful to invite them to tell what they would normally say under such circumstances. "Under normal circumstances, what might a parent say in response to a child who has come home and reported trouble at school?" Parents can report their automatic response. For example, one parent might respond, "I would find out what my son did to get into trouble!" Your response as an educator can open the way for the new learning: "That is a very normal reaction. Let's think about how it would work. How do you think your son would feel if you quizzed him about what he did to get himself in trouble? Would it effectively convey your compassion and understanding? Would it prepare him to try better behavior?" The answer should be obvious to any parent who is not defensive.

As the ineffectiveness of our automatic reactions becomes clear, the way is open for the educator to invite new thinking: "What might a parent do that would show more compassion?" In response to any answer, you can direct the person to the effect on the child. This process demonstrates just how difficult new skills can be while pointing the parents to the ultimate test of their actions: How do the actions affect the child?

As a family life educator, you can also suggest parent responses while inviting the parents to test them by the same standard. "How would your child feel if you said, 'Oh, son! You must have felt humiliated to be chewed out in front of your classmates!'" Truly empathic listening is so contrary to humans' automatic and egocentric responses that it takes lots of practice. But "learning is facilitated when new knowledge is demonstrated to the learner" (Merrill, 2000, p. 2). Many demonstrations over many sessions may be necessary for effective learning.

Applying New Knowledge

Merrill's (2001) fourth principle states that "learning is facilitated when the learner is required to use his or her new knowledge to solve problems" (p. 463). There are no written tests that qualify a person as a good family member. The application of knowledge is the end goal of FLE.

Between sessions of FLE it is common to make assignments to participants. For example, after teaching about the importance of thinking positively about one's partner, each participant might be encouraged to think of a quality or behavior that is most appreciated in the partner. Once the quality is identified, each participant can be encouraged to think of a way to prompt remembering that quality in the hours and days ahead. Some might choose to tie a string around a finger or carry a keepsake in a shirt pocket. Participants are encouraged to use the prompt to remember the quality regularly, especially in times of stress. Each is asked to make a mental or written note of successes and struggles that might be shared with the class in the next meeting of the group (whether face to face or online).

Merrill (2001) observes that "appropriate practice is the single most neglected aspect of effective instruction" (p. 464). The new behavior needs to be practiced. Gottman (1994) refers to extensive practice as overlearning. He recommends that partners overlearn their new skills so that they have a fighting chance when they face a challenge and are tempted by habit to fall into unproductive if overritualized patterns.

Practice can happen in both instructional and real-world settings. FLEs can facilitate such field learning by providing learners a standard by which to judge their performance. For example, an educator might teach participants in a parenting class to judge any responses to parenting problems by a two-part test: (1) Is the solution likely to improve the behavior? (2) Does the solution show respect for the child? When the parents have a standard for judging their new solutions, they are more likely to turn to new behavior rather than fall back on old habits.

Turning again to Merrill (2000): "Most learners learn from the errors they make, especially when they are shown how to recognize the error, how to recover from the error, and how to avoid the error in the future" (p. 8). Many of us have spent decades trying to get better at practicing what we preach. We can patiently provide relevant practice to help our participants apply knowledge to their lives across time.

New Knowledge Integrated Into the Learner's World

Merrill's (2000) fifth and final point is that "learning is facilitated when new knowledge is integrated into the learner's world" (p. 2). Learners may benefit from making specific and practical plans for integrating their new knowledge into their family lives. They can engage in periodic discussions with colearners or support groups. They can keep a journal of their performance.

They may also benefit from teaching their newfound knowledge to others. There is nothing quite like teaching to force us to understand a principle and how it works. Your participants might be invited to give a minilesson to the class, to teach a group at work or in their faith community.

Merrill (2000) observes that there is no satisfaction quite like moving from student to teacher or mentor. "The real motivation for learners is learning. When learners are able to demonstrate improvement in skill, they are motivated to perform even better" (p. 8). The combination of integrating the skills into everyday life and sharing them with others cements the lessons.

● CONCLUSION

When instruction—whether oral or written—is designed according to established principles of instructional design, the message is more likely to be effective. In addition, the instruction is more likely to be enjoyable for both the educator and the participant.

● EXPLORATIONS

1. Now that you are familiar with all four elements of Merrill's CDT, take a speech, lesson plan, or outline—any deliberate instruction—and identify the four elements: EG, Eeg, IG, and Ieg. Evaluate whether adding more of one or another of the elements would have made the presentation more effective for the purpose it was delivered.

2. Develop a lesson plan or pamphlet to teach a principle with which you are familiar. In fact, it would be useful to select a subject that you have taught before or are likely to teach in the future. Create the instruction using (and labeling) all four elements of Merrill's CDT. Describe your audience and justify your combination of elements based on the needs of your target audience and your instructional objectives. Share your work with a classmate for feedback. If you have created a lesson plan, seek an opportunity to use the plan to teach a group and invite a classmate or colleague to give you feedback.

3. Review the lesson that you created using the component display theory above for its consonance with Merrill's first principles of instruction. Enlarge or refine your lesson as necessary. Identify the way you will facilitate learning in each of the ways described in Merrill's five principles by placing a numeral 1 through 5 next to the part of your lesson plan that facilitates learning in that way.

CHAPTER 6

ENGAGING AN AUDIENCE

There is much that could be written about processes for engaging an audience; it is as much art as science. There are four broad themes in this chapter. The first deals with the art of teaching—and special considerations with the adult learner. Next is a short section about personality theories; if we hope to change people with our teaching, we can benefit from insights into human nature. The third section of this chapter reviews some of what is known about "joining" or relationship building as a precondition to effective helping. In addition, Ginott's method of applying these principles is reviewed. Finally, the chapter concludes with some practical application of the principles to teaching and print efforts.

THE ART OF TEACHING ●

Reflect on your best learning experiences—classes, workshops, or lectures. Do you learn best when a teacher relentlessly pounds facts into you? Have you gained the most when you felt cowed and intimidated by a dismissive teacher? Do you prefer to be a silent, unengaged observer?

One of my (Goddard's) favorite teachers in high school was Ray Gilbert. He taught trigonometry—not a subject that is automatically riveting. He was a tall, gangly man who typically began each class period by sitting on his desk and chatting with us. He might talk about a ball game or a snowstorm or some world happening that impacted us all. He seemed to genuinely enjoy us, which was a rare experience for high school students.

Mr. Gilbert was excited about trigonometry. He described the ways we could use trig to track the path of, for example, a potato shot from a potato gun. He talked and laughed easily. The experience I remember most clearly from his class was a day when several of us had written problems from our homework assignment on the board. Each of us in turn discussed the steps in our solution. When it was my turn, I began to trace through the steps but was only midway through the problem when I realized that I had misunderstood the problem and done it all wrong. A blush began at the top of my head and was rapidly working its way through my soul as I stammered my way to the end of the problem. I felt humiliated.

Mr. Gilbert stood up at the back of the classroom, took a deep breath and said, "Wow. In all my years of teaching, I have never seen that problem done that way." I felt relieved. I might not get credit for accurate trig, but I had gotten credit for creativity.

A Formula for Engaging an Audience

A person can scan the leading guides for family life educators (FLEs) and parenting educators (e.g., Arcus et al., 1993b; Bornstein, 2002; Fine, 1980, 1989; Fine & Lee, 2000) and fail to find any practical formula for teaching. There are skills approaches (Campbell & Palm, 2004), but no guiding principles.

If I were to provide a simple formula for effective teaching, it would include three elements: relevance, respect, and participation. Mr. Gilbert certainly honored that formula. He got us involved in solving problems, he respected us—even when we made mistakes—and he tried to make trig relevant.

Family life education (FLE) may likewise benefit from considerations of relevance, respect, and participation. FLE enjoys the inherent advantage of being relevant for everyone; everyone is tied to a family in some way.

Respect is also a vital element. It would be painfully ironic to try to teach respect in families using methods employing scorn and contempt. We must model the respect that we invite participants to take to their family relationships.

Participation is fundamental to FLE. Family life is more than book learning; it is a personally engaging enterprise that is best learned in participatory ways.

This formulation for engaging lay audiences can take many forms. Some years ago, I (Goddard) was invited to talk to a group of parents about teens and sexuality. I showed up at the appointed time and place with facts, figures, and discussion questions. As I entered the classroom, I found that there were about 20 teens and no adults. I asked the program organizers about the sudden change of audience. "We had these teens from a residential facility show up and thought that they would benefit from a presentation by you about the role of sexuality."

I felt a great urge to panic. Nothing I had prepared for the parents fitted this new audience. My mind raced while I unloaded my books and papers. When I could delay no longer, I introduced myself and went to the board and drew one horizontal line from one end of the board to the opposite end—about 12 feet long. I told the teens that I wanted their opinions about the meaning of sexual behavior. At one end of the continuum I put the word *Never*. "Some people believe that sex is never good. It is best to avoid it your whole lifetime."

I walked to the opposite end of the board and wrote the word *Always*. "Some people believe that sex is always good with another consenting person. Anytime you can get it, take it."

Putting a mark near the middle of the line, I said, "Some people believe that sex is good in some kinds of committed relationships. In other words, sex is good if you are in love or married."

I invited the teens to tell what they thought was the ideal role for sex. Was it always bad? Was it always good? Was it good only under certain circumstances? Of course, I did not encourage them to describe their own sexual behavior, only their beliefs about the appropriate role of sex.

A lively discussion ensued. Students challenged and questioned each other. Many were clearly reflecting on their own position for the first time. In the course of the discussion, one boy who had endorsed an almost predatory view moved to a more conservative and considerate position. Others developed greater clarity about their beliefs.

Of course I do not believe that we settled all issues in that 1-hour discussion. And such a discussion should not be held without appropriate safeguards such as careful guidance by an experienced teacher. However, the effectiveness of the session at clarifying student views was the result of the teens' lively participation. A lecture probably could not have elicited the reflection and insight that came from the hour-long discussion.

Engaging the Adult Learner With Family Life Education

FLE can happen in settings as diverse as an eighth-grade health class, a church-sponsored marriage retreat, a community fathering class, or a prison mothering class. Traditionally, much of FLE has been done with adults.

Hopefully, many more young people will be involved in FLE in the future. Since the people who are married or parenting are most likely to be adults, and since those who have traditionally enrolled for FLE have often been adults, it is important to be aware of unique considerations for adult learners.

Knowles (1998) summarizes some of the classic observations about adult learners. "In conventional education the student is required to adjust himself [or herself] to an established curriculum; in adult education the curriculum is built around the student's needs and interests. The resource of highest value in adult education is the learner's experience. Experience is the adult learner's living textbook" (p. 39). Knowles also observes that "adults have a deep need to be self-directing" (p. 40). "Adult learners are precisely those whose intellectual aspirations are least likely to be aroused by the rigid, uncompromising requirements of authoritative, conventionalized institutions of learning" (p. 38).

Some might be tempted to suggest that participants in FLE merely gather and share ideas—an open sharefest. There are times when that may be effective. Yet active participation does not preclude leadership. While a group leader or educator may have more knowledge of research than any of the class members, participants "as a group have more solutions than we do" (Curran, 1989, p. 20). The ideal learning environment will bring the knowledge and facilitation skills of the educator together with the experience and problem-solving capacity of the participants. A specific method that provides such a learning environment is described later in this chapter.

● WHAT CHANGES PEOPLE? CHALLENGING IDEAS FROM PERSONALITY THEORIES

There are no simple answers to the question of what changes people. The complexity is due to both the complexity of people themselves and the diversity of views on the subject. Different psychological schools of thought would offer very different recommendations for changing human behavior on the basis of their assumptions about human nature and motivation.

For the purposes of this discussion, the work of Salvatore Maddi is helpful. He has divided the many theories of personality into three broad categories. The first group of theories are called conflict theories. One of the most prominent conflict theorists was Sigmund Freud, for whom the core tendency in humans is "to maximize instinctual gratification while minimizing punishment and guilt" (Maddi, 1989, p. 627). This puts humans in conflict with society, which must manage individuals' drives if the common good is to be maintained.

While there are many other versions of conflict theories in addition to Freud's, an educator who subscribed to a conflict model of human behavior would frame the task in terms of the inherent conflict between family members' interests or between an individual family member and the family as a whole. Complicating the educator's job, many conflict theorists believe that psychological defenses would make it impossible for participants and family members to access their true feelings and motivations.

The task of FLEs who subscribe to conflict models of human behavior would be to teach family members to gratify their own needs while respecting the needs of others. "The best that [families] can do is aim for cooperation and order so as to maximize gratifications for all" (Maddi, 1989, p. 51). The way to engage learners in a class would be to offer ways of reducing tension while minimizing their guilt and punishment.

In contrast to conflict models, consistency models posit that all humans want to reduce the tension or difference between expectation and reality. The best-known conflict model is probably the cognitive dissonance model, which asserts that humans want to minimize the large discrepancies between expectation and occurrence while maximizing small discrepancies between them. Said differently, people like small surprises but they do not like to be shocked. The activation version of consistency theories suggests that humans seek to maintain a level of activation to which they are accustomed. When people are underactivated, they seek more stimulation. When they are overactivated, they seek to reduce stimulation.

Consistency models might be applied to FLE in a couple of ways. Interest can be stimulated by presenting situations that challenge participants' traditional ways of thinking. For example, parents in a parenting class might be provided with information that challenges their familiar thinking, such as "If it is true that children generally do what seems right to them, how do we explain the way children sometimes hurt their siblings?" By presenting two "truths" that are at odds with each other, we can often stimulate our participants to think in more complex ways.

Consistency models can also consider the level of stimulation that is optimal for each learner in a class. While the optimal level will vary from learner to learner, important clues can be gained by observing the class. Are they understimulated or overstimulated? During the course of a session, having a variety of activities is probably optimal. Consistency models sensitize us to the fact that learners will learn best when they are neither bored nor overstimulated. The old adage may be true that it is the educator's job to comfort the afflicted and afflict the comforted.

Maddi's third way of understanding human behavior is the fulfillment model. Rather than seeing the world as two great forces at odds with each other, fulfillment models focus on one great force, the realization of one's abilities or the striving toward ideals. Carl Rogers and Abraham Maslow are prominent names associated with this view.

Fulfillment models have implications for engaging and teaching family life audiences. Maslow suggested that we do not move to higher levels of functioning when lower needs are gnawing at us. Assuring class members of safety, belongingness, and our esteem for them might make it easier for them to participate. In those cases where they carry burdens and worries from home to class, it may be useful to help them process them. "It looks like you're worried about things at home."

The other practical application of the fulfillment model to engaging the audience is to paint a picture of personal possibilities for participants. What Maddi (1989) has said about therapy might also be applied to FLE:

> In [FLE], it is very helpful—for [participant] and [educator] alike—to believe in a view of the [person] as unlimited in what it can become. It is helpful because you are already dealing with a [participant] who [may be discouraged] and has lost conviction about becoming anyone worthwhile. In such a situation, it is necessary to hold out a view of life that is extreme enough in its opposition to the client's view to be able to serve as the needed corrective. (p. 102)

Comparing the Personality Theories

We are tempted to ask which of the personality theories best describes human reality. Maddi (1989) finds "considerable empirical support for both versions of the fulfillment model and the activation version of the consistency model" (p. 532). Yet savvy FLEs know that there are valuable lessons to be learned from each of the views.

For example, the conflict models remind us that there is often a conflict within families and within classes. We can help participants meet their needs while respecting the needs of the group. The consistency models encourage us to be mindful of the activation levels of class members. The fulfillment models offer an optimistic portrait of personal development that can give us and our participants renewed hope.

Each family life educator will form a unique combination of models to form a personal philosophy. Many FLEs subscribe to fulfillment models because of their positive portrayal of humans as having inherent strengths and unlimited potential for growth. Such educators are likely to see themselves as collaborators or facilitators, as described in Chapter 1.

Participants in FLE settings likewise may resonate with this philosophy that credits them with much that is good. So, as Myers-Walls and Myers-Bowman (1999) have suggested, there is merit in assessing learners' models of human functioning and matching them to the curriculum and teaching style that best fits them.

RELATIONSHIPS AS THE BASIS FOR HELPING •

Prelude to Effective Education

In FLE, it is common to focus on the content to the neglect of process. The relationship between the educator and the learner may be more important than the content of the lesson. As DeBord et al. (2002) observed, "[I]nstructors will be more likely to provide appropriate content and learning experiences if they have developed a relationship with participants, can identify their strengths and challenges, and can modify the program to fit the specific needs of the audience" (p. 32).

This should not be surprising. In family relationships, nothing matters as much as the quality of the relationship. As Smith, Perou, and Lesesne (2002) observe about parent-child relationships: "[W]hat is essential for a child's well-being [is] stable loving relationships with parents who provide nurturing, reciprocal interactions" (p. 406).

It is also the quality of the relationship that seems to be the biggest factor in helping relationships, whether educational or therapeutic. FLE is clearly distinct from therapy but employs some of the methods that are successful in therapy. In a study of solution-focused therapies, Miller, Duncan, and Hubble (1997) found that relationship matters more than technique:

> While therapists tended to attribute therapeutic success to the use of solution-focused techniques (e.g., specialized interviewing techniques, miracle questions), the clients consistently reported a strong therapeutic relationship as the critical factor in treatment outcome (e.g., therapist acceptance, non-possessive warmth, positive regard, affirmation, and self-disclosure). (p. 85)

So research confirms that the quality of the relationship matters more than the specific techniques used. Brammer and MacDonald (1999) report that "all authorities in the helping process agree that the quality of the relationship is important to effective helping" (p. 49). In the absence of a positive, affirming relationship, growth is less likely. In therapy, this relationship is established through the process of joining. Minuchin and Fishman (1981) observed:

> Joining a family is more an attitude than a technique, and it is the umbrella under which all therapeutic transactions occur. Joining is letting the family know that the therapist understands them and is working with and for them. Only under this protection can the family have the security to explore alternatives, try the unusual, and change. Joining is the glue that holds the therapeutic system together. (pp. 31-32)

Hanna and Brown (2004) suggest that "the personal rapport or empathy that therapists develop with those they are trying to help remains the single most proven variable determining the effectiveness of psychotherapy" (p. 89). Jacobson and Christensen (1996) similarly make the case for viewing clients compassionately in integrated couple therapy:

> The skilled ICT therapist has to develop the ability to find compassion and sympathy in each person's story, no matter how unsympathetic and contemptible one partner may appear. Our position is that the vast majority of people act badly in relationships because they are suffering. (p. 99)

To the extent that participants in FLE settings examine personal feelings and assumptions as part of a change and growth process, the same principles can be expected to apply. In fact, a vital process for connecting may be identifying and appreciating family strengths.

Below are Hanna and Brown's (2004, p. 95) six processes for joining, together with commentary on their application to FLE:

1. "Emphasize positive statements reported by family members."

   We are all encouraged and energized when people notice and appreciate the good in us and our families: "I am impressed with your resilience."

2. "Encourage family members to share their story about themselves."

   It may be especially useful to notice ways that the family has adapted or coped with problems: "It seems that your family has great determination when difficulties arise."

3. "Note family interactions that reflect strength and competency."

   Each story tells something about the difficulties families face but also about the resources they use to meet them: "I like the way you involve your family in solving problems."

4. "Emphasize those times that family members enjoy together."

   Explore the positive experiences that family members describe; help them put a frame about the best in their family life: "It sounds as if your family enjoys laughter together."

5. "Reframe problems or negative statements in a more positive way."

   Help family members find a positive interpretation for their experiences: "Your worry was a sign that you really care about your children."

6. "Emphasize what families do well."

   Invite them to talk about their successes: "Please tell us more about how you overcame that challenge."

The Boundary Between Therapy and Family Life Education

While FLE may draw on some of the techniques and findings of therapy, it is not the same as therapy. In fact, there are ethical issues that require educators to carefully establish a boundary between their educational efforts and the methods of therapy. Bill Doherty (1995) has described the dilemma in this way:

> In order to accomplish its purpose, parent and family education must have more personal depth than other forms of education, but too much depth or intensity risks harming participants, or at least scaring them away. Participants must be able to tell their stories, express their feelings and values, and be encouraged to try out new behaviors. However, if they recount in detail their most traumatic memories, ventilate their most painful and unresolved feelings, or take major behavioral risks, the experience can be damaging. (p. 353)

Doherty describes five levels of his family involvement model, from least involvement to greatest:

> Level 1: Minimal emphasis on family might include a parent-teacher conference in which the school conveyed policies or information.

> Level 2: Information and advice is the level at which the educator undertakes training of the recipients.

> Level 3: Feelings and support add to the information of Level 2, the processing of feelings. This is not the intense processing of personal and painful experience. This is the level on which much FLE takes place.

Level 4: Brief focused intervention "represents the upper boundary of parent and family education practiced by a minority of professionals who choose to work with special populations of parents and seek special training in family assessment and basic family interventions" (p. 355).

Level 5: Family therapy is beyond the scope of FLE.

While warning FLEs against moving into Level 5 interventions, he observes that "a strictly content oriented training program [for FLEs] cannot adequately prepare professionals for affective work with families" (p. 356). FLEs need to know how to facilitate the processing of personal family experience with their participants.

A Specific Method for Capitalizing on Emotion in Family Life Education

Haim Ginott, famous for his classic book *Between Parent and Child,* spent years working with children in play therapy and with their parents in therapy. Over the years, he came to the conclusion that most parents need education rather than therapy; they are not mentally ill, they are merely uninformed (Goddard & Ginott, 2002).

Ginott conducted parenting groups in New York City for many years and developed a process for working with parents that combines the principles of trust building with emotional education. While Ginott's work focused on parenting education, the same principles apply in delivering couples' education or other kinds of FLE. Ginott's approach helps FLEs model the behaviors they are encouraging participants to practice in their family lives.

Ginott's method, described by his student and colleague Arthur Orgel (1980), suggested that there are four steps in the process of supporting parents. Ginott's method has particular merit because it is based on his top-rated (Norcross et al., 2003) parenting books (Ginott, 1965, 1969; Ginott, Ginott, & Goddard, 2003) and because of his experience as a family life educator (Goddard, 1999). The same processes can be effective in couples' education and other forms of FLE.

1. *Recitation is the first stage of FLE.* In this stage, parents (partners or other participants) are encouraged to talk about their challenging experiences as parents. This allows parents to discover that all parents have problems. It also allows the parenting educator to model attention, understanding, and acceptance. Many parents have never had someone sensitively listen to them before. It is important for parents to feel heard and understood.

Such sensitive listening may not be easy for the parenting educator. The educator must listen carefully, resist the temptation to correct or preach, and be skillful in remaining supportive and encouraging: "Wow. That must have been very difficult." "You probably wondered what to do." "Yes. Parenting can be very challenging!"

The objective at this stage of a discussion is not to teach new skills to the parents but to allow them to talk about their challenges while feeling understood, accepted, and valued. This skill is especially important when parents have many challenges or are mandated to participate in a parenting education program. When a parenting educator is supportive and encouraging, parents can embrace their unique strengths and feel safe enough to explore strategies to address their challenges.

Sometimes class members lack confidence in their parenting skills and worry that they make many mistakes. The effective parenting educator recognizes, values, and encourages parents' desires, even as their skills are still emerging. Effective FLEs help family members discover their strengths and build on them.

In fact, insightful psychologist Martin Seligman (2002) suggested that our growth may be more tied to effectively using our strengths than to remedying our weaknesses. In fact, our strengths may define our weaknesses. We may not be able to surgically remove our weaknesses without damaging our strengths.

The central task of the first step in FLE is to give participants the experience of being authentic and still being valued. This is the foundation upon which better parenting and better partnering can be built.

2. *Sensitization is the second phase of Ginott's method.* This second stage of parent (partner or family) education can begin after participants begin to feel accepted, valued, and safe—which may take 30 minutes, a whole session, or many weeks or months. In this second stage, the educator turns the attention of the parents to understanding their children's feelings. "How do you think your daughter felt in that situation?" "Why might that have been especially difficult for your son?"

The parenting educator may help the parents understand their children's feelings by asking them how they might have felt in similar situations. "How might you feel if you worked all day to get the house clean and your husband (or a friend) only noticed a dirty window?" Parents may come to better understand their children's feelings when they relate them to their own experiences in an environment where they feel understood.

Everyone has struggles and disappointments. One of the challenges of family life is to apply our own human struggles to understanding how our children and partners feel. While we will never completely understand how an experience feels for others, we can appreciate how real the pain (or joy or confusion) is.

Family life is often made more difficult when family members react to each others' behavior without taking time to understand. Under such circumstances, the person is likely to become angry and resistant. In contrast, when the person feels understood, family members can work together more effectively.

In the first stage, a family member feels understood and valued. In this second stage, that family member learns to understand and value others in the family.

3. *Learning of concepts comes next.* Parents can learn principles that will help them be more effective. For example, "Nurturing strengthens relationships" is a principle that can help family members relate to each other more effectively. FLEs may have a series of principles to suggest. (A list of principles related to human development and family life is provided in Appendix A.) They can involve the group by asking them to apply the principles to situations in their homes. The educator may even invite participants to customize the principles and apply them to their family realities.

4. *The teaching and practice of better skills is the final stage of Ginott's process.* Participants learn how to use their new skills and get practice in applying the principles. They may get practice by responding to situations presented by the educator and other parents. They may also get practice by developing ways to deal with situations with their own children.

A wise educator will not try to be the source of all answers but will ask participants for their ideas. For every situation there are many ways of responding. It is good for class members to hear many different ideas for dealing with a specific problem. If skills are thought of as tools in a tool box, then it is important for participants to have many different tools and to know how to use them well. Each of us has different tools and different skills in using them. We can learn from each other.

It is also important for participants to learn how to evaluate their various options. For any idea that is suggested, you might invite participants to consider two critical questions: "Would that work for me and my family? Does it show respect for all of us?"

The main objective of Ginott's four-step process in parenting education was to provide parents with the personal experience of a warm, caring environment in which they can learn effective, respectful strategies. Then they will be prepared to go home and create a warm, caring environment in which their children can learn more strong and humane ways of acting. In a way, the parenting educator is a parent to the parents. In that role, the parenting educator can be a model of a good parent.

Sometimes there will be parents in a class who are very angry or hostile (just as there will be children in a family who sometimes are very angry or hostile). An angry parent provides a parenting educator a great opportunity to model effective ways to deal with anger. "I can see that you feel very strongly about this." "This must be very upsetting for you."

There are extreme cases when parents feel so angry or stressed that they are not able to participate effectively with others in the classroom. These participants may benefit from individual therapy. Rather than acting as an individual therapist in this setting, educators are encouraged to provide appropriate referrals to trained professionals.

PRACTICAL APPLICATIONS ●

Our objective is to foster growth and learning. Transformative learning theory suggests that this is most likely to happen with "(a) teachers who are empathetic, caring, authentic, and sincere and who demonstrate a high degree of integrity; (b) learning conditions that promote a sense of safety, openness, and trust; and (c) instructional methods that support a learner-centered approach that promotes student autonomy, participation, reflection, and collaboration" (Christopher et al., 2001, p. 135). There are practical ways to make this happen.

Drawing the Best Out of Your Participants: Some Practical Tips

It is common to see educators as the source of solutions and participants as the source of problems. In this view, participants bring their ignorance and their problems to educators, who bring their knowledge, answers, and suggestions to the participants. You can see problems with this approach:

- Participants know far more about their own lives, challenges, and resources than the educator does.
- Any solutions imposed by the educator without the conviction and commitment of the participants will not be effective.

Some of the most important answers in any training will come from participants. The most important answers are those that represent the participants' best thinking and commitments to growth.

Sometimes participants do not volunteer answers to questions because they are not sure how they will be treated. Will they be embarrassed by the educator? Will they be corrected or condemned? If they can't express themselves clearly, will they be humiliated by an insensitive educator?

Educators earn trust with all participants by the way they treat each participant. It is natural for participants to be reluctant to comment until they feel safe with an educator. A skilled educator will set participants up for success by asking questions that allow for many different answers. They ask questions like the following:

- "What do you think will work?"
- "What have you seen people do in this situation?"
- "Do you have an idea of how to apply this principle?"

After asking a good question, an educator looks at the participants. Sometimes it is clear that one or more of them have ideas but are reluctant to volunteer. We can gently encourage them: "Reba, it looks like you have an idea."

During this first silence, if the educator jumps in with answers, participants learn that the educator doesn't really want to hear from them. They are less likely to answer in the future. If an educator genuinely welcomes input from participants, most quickly warm up. When participants make a comment, the educator encourages effort by honoring every comment.

The best way of thinking about teaching is as an opportunity for people to gather to solve problems. An educator should bring important research-based knowledge. But, equally important, an educator should bring an ability to draw the best answers and enthusiasm for growth out of the participants. When teaching is understood in this way, there are several things educators should do to bring out the best from the participants:

1. Educators should feel and show a great respect for the efforts, skills, experiences, and challenges that participants bring. This respect can be shown by listening carefully and humbly to participants' comments. It can be shown also with statements such as
   - "You face so many difficulties!"
   - "I admire your courage to keep trying."
   - "You have tried many things to make your life better."
   - "I don't know if I could survive what you face."
   - "You have a lot of good ideas."

2. Educators honor participants (and bring out their best) by inviting them to be creative problem solvers. While educators teach true principles, they always invite the participants to find good ways of applying those principles to their lives.

   - "What do you think would work with your family?"
   - "How would you apply that principle to make your family better?"
   - "What have you learned from your experience?"
   - "Can you think of other things you would like to try?"

The best educators help the participants find ideas within themselves.

3. There are times when a participant will make a statement that the educator disagrees with. This is the place where master educators shine. It is also the place where all educators work to be better. A great educator will honor that part of the statement that is true or will honor the participant's efforts while inviting the participant to other possibilities. For example, if a parent in class suggests that "What kids these days need is a good whopping!" there are many things a master educator might say:

   - "I agree that children need to know limits. What do you think is the best way to get children to respect those limits?"
   - "Letting children know that you are serious about limits is important. In my experience, children are more likely to follow the rules when they understand them and believe that they are important. How can we help children with this?"
   - "Respecting rules is important. Can you think of the experiences you have had that helped you want to follow the rules?"
   - "You really want your children to respect the boundaries. What do you do that works best for that?"

Application to Print

While much of this chapter presupposes a face-to-face teaching context for FLE, the same principles apply to print materials that can radiate accusation and austerity or warmth and encouragement. For example, in the Introduction to his classic parenting book (1965), Haim Ginott offers warm compassion to his reader:

No parent wakes up in the morning planning to make a child's life miserable. No mother or father says, "Today I'll yell, nag, and humiliate my child whenever possible." On the contrary, in the morning many parents resolve, "This is going to be a peaceful day. No yelling, no arguing, and no fighting." Yet, in spite of good intentions, the unwanted war breaks out again. Once more we find ourselves saying things we do not mean, in a tone we do not like. (p. xiii)

● CONCLUSION

When educators combine compassion for the participants with a passion for the subject, participants are likely to leave the experience wanting to be better, wanting to grow, and wanting to return for more help to improve their family lives. When educators have both an understanding of human development and skill at conveying, they are likely to be effective at encouraging growth in their participants.

● EXPLORATIONS

1. Think about your greatest learning experiences—whether classes, informal sharing, or solo discoveries. When you have several experiences in mind, consider what they have in common. Visit with others in your group about their experiences. See if you can extract some common elements of great learning experiences.

2. Based on your experiences, what would you add to this chapter's formulations for effective FLE?

3. Explore your personal strengths by completing the VIA Signature Strengths Survey in either Seligman's book *Authentic Happiness* (2002) or his Web site (www.authentichappiness.org).

4. Consider your strengths as a family life educator. For example, do you have an energetic personality? Deep sincerity? Broad knowledge? Wide experience? Creativity? Skill at writing? Compassion? Emotional intelligence? Describe the way you could use your strengths to be an effective family life educator. Get feedback from those who know you and have observed your efforts to share family life principles.

5. As you read this chapter, which ideas or principles would you like to apply to your practice of FLE? How could you try out those ideas in your personal and professional activity? Whom could you take as a mentor?

6. Recall a time when someone shared with you a challenge in family life. Consider how you could employ the six recommendations from Hanna and Brown (2004) mentioned earlier to help the person identify and appreciate family strengths. Write out specific statements and discuss with classmates or colleagues.

CHAPTER 7

TEACHING IN OUTREACH FAMILY LIFE EDUCATION

Mechanics and Methods

I n previous chapters, we discussed the importance of creating a context of caring in a family life education (FLE) setting and of attending to instructional design principles to bring quality education to the lay audience. In this chapter, we turn our attention to the mechanics and methods of outreach FLE. We first discuss how family life educators (FLEs) decide what to teach the lay audience. For example, what is the appropriate blend of scholarship, moral thinking, and lived experience? How will the life experiences of participants be integrated with theory and research-based instruction provided by the family life educator? Next, we discuss how to create learner-centered goals and objectives for instruction that are specific and measurable. Finally, we discuss a selection of numerous methods that are especially suitable for outreach FLE and provide examples of their use.

CRITERIA FOR SELECTING ● USEFUL AND VALID INFORMATION

In any outreach setting, from traditional workshops to Web sites, FLEs must address the question, What do people need to know about this topic? Adult

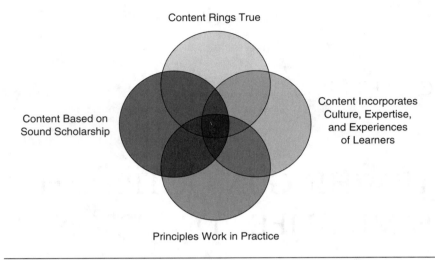

Content Rings True

Content Incorporates Culture, Expertise, and Experiences of Learners

Content Based on Sound Scholarship

Principles Work in Practice

Figure 7.1   Selecting Content for Outreach Family Life Education

audiences usually have already formed their opinions about many topics we address and in many cases have real-life experiences to support them. For instance, parents have experiences being parents, and FLEs who do not take that into account, regardless of how powerful their ideas are, will risk alienating their audiences. We believe FLEs should seek out and find the principles that their clientele need to know the most. While many factors influence our content selection decisions, we believe that the most useful and valid FLE information is found at the intersection of the following four elements: (1) ideas are grounded in sound scholarship, (2) ideas ring true, or fit with our values and instincts, (3) ideas fit with and incorporate the knowledge, culture, expertise, and lived experience of the learners, and (4) ideas work in practice (see Figure 7.1).

Are the Ideas Grounded in Sound Scholarship?

In the area of family life, there is an explosion of information, some credible, and some incredible, even unbelievable! Many persons are willing to be called a family "expert" through bringing forth armchair theories and ideas of their own design. In contrast, FLE programs must be grounded in the latest scholarship. We emphasize the importance of sound scholarship as an element of quality FLE resources in Chapter 3. In fact, the insistence upon a scholarly base may likely be the single most important element that distinguishes professional FLEs from other persons committed to family strengthening. The latest scholarship is not simply the niftiest, trendy idea that landed unexpectedly in a moment of inspiration. Nor is it a single study. The most reliable and valid ideas for an outreach audience are those that can be summarized from a wide array of well-conducted studies. The ideas are both theoretically and empirically sound. We call these ideas "principles." Principles take on almost a timeless quality, although their application continues to be timely. Principles are well tested and verified through a considerable amount of scientific research, involving more than a single study or author. For instance, while Grandma knew that loving and caring parents are critical for a child's development, every study we know of has found some connection between parental love and positive outcomes for children. Therefore, we would feel confident putting forth the principle "Every child needs a relationship with a loving, supportive parent."

FLEs may become overwhelmed if they attempt to review every piece of scholarship about a topic. Instead, a scholarly review should seek to identify the *teachable* ideas or principles, those ideas that lend themselves to dissemination and that we judge as important for the targeted audience to know and live by. For example, a review of scholarship on the topic of parent-adolescent relationships might emphasize the leading predictors of quality relationships between parents and their adolescent children, such as the recognition of a teen's need for autonomy and privacy.

The trouble with the scholarly base is that it is often fraught with limitations that, in turn, limit the amount of confidence that can be placed in the identified principles. For example, prior to the 1990s, when scholars became more sensitive to the differences between family needs based on their race or culture, much of what we had known about the characteristics of strong families was derived from studies of White, middle-class, two-parent families. Even today, some of the best conducted research available may be biased toward a certain kind of family type. Large, national studies are often touted for their quality and the ability they provide to researchers to do complex, comprehensive analyses. But it is risky to overgeneralize and apply such studies to a specific community, family, couple, or individual. As important as a scholarly foundation is to quality FLE, because the scholarly canon is not complete, FLEs should exercise caution when they use such material as the basis of an outreach education offering. The conclusions from research are by nature tentative and subject to modification through additional studies or reformulation of theories. Thus, instead of teaching research-based principles as *the way things are,* wise FLEs will use more tentative references to the principles with words such as, "Current research supports . . ."

Do the Ideas Ring True?

As FLEs, we often strive to empower parents to trust their own values and instincts as they parent their children, and we are challenged to design learning experiences where they can find parenting solutions within the context of their values (DeBord et al., 2002). The same recommendation seems to apply to us as we endeavor to select the best and most useful information to share with our outreach audiences. FLEs can critically inquire: "Does the information or research recommendations fit with my own values and instincts? Do the ideas ring true?"

For example, there may be ideas that appear in the scholarly literature that FLEs may feel are simply "wrong" for families. There is a moral and ethical dimension to FLE (Doherty, 1993) about which many can agree, a sense of what is valuable or "right" and damaging or "wrong" for families. Nevertheless, all FLEs will make their own judgments about the rightness or wrongness of ideas. An example of a "wrong" idea that has appeared in the scholarship, in our opinion, is the notion put forth by author Judith Harris (1998) that the way parents bring up their children has almost no bearing on how the children develop. We might ask ourselves, "Does this proposition seem correct, or 'right,' regardless of the scientific basis? Does it fit my own instincts?" To us, such a proposition, at a minimum, is counterintuitive and is also at substantial odds with our own experiences, but it also ignores a substantial body of literature suggesting that parents have a strong influence on the social development of children (see Hart, 2000).

Another example is the finding that spanking when combined with reasoning is an effective parental discipline strategy with 2- to 6-year-olds (Larzelere, 2000). Some view any form of spanking as an assault on children. Thus, if your moral position as a family life educator is that under no circumstances is hitting a child ever justified, then you will feel uncomfortable putting such an idea forward in a workshop.

On the other hand, occasionally there will be cases when research-based practice that rings true to us will not ring true to some in our audiences. For example, with the spanking illustration, some may openly disagree with the general position from research that discourages spanking as a parenting strategy, arguing that "it works for me." In such situations, to invite open discussion of the variety of ways parents strive to handle children's misbehavior, ending the discussion by stating, "There are many ways of responding to children's misbehavior. Parents use many ways to handle their children's misbehavior and are in the best position decide what is right for them. However, the research shows that children fare best when their parents rarely or never use spanking."

It makes sense for FLEs, as much as is possible, to choose to teach those scientifically supported principles that they truly believe are correct. Thus the ideas, when taught, will carry some passion and conviction. For example, for years author Duncan has taught audiences characteristics of strong families that have emerged from research, partly because of their fit with his own values and convictions about effective family processes.

Incorporating the Knowledge, Culture, Expertise, and Experiences of the Learners

In Chapter 1, we emphasize that most effective FLEs incorporate the best scientific information with the knowledge, lived experience, culture, and expertise of families in communities (Doherty, 2000; Lerner, 1995; Myers-Walls, 2000). In selecting from scholarly materials, FLEs will seek to choose materials as free from bias as possible and general enough in principle that they can be applied in a variety of settings and cultures. Part of this involves care in reviews of literature to ensure that the basis of our material is as representative as possible of the audiences we seek to serve. However, beyond this, when FLEs are in teaching settings, they will need to find ways to incorporate what participants bring with them into the educational setting. Part of this includes involving the clientele in the development of community-based programs (DeBord et al., 2002). The other part involves FLEs taking steps as group leaders in the educational setting to draw out from participants their experiences, knowledge, expertise, and unique perspective. David Mace (1981), a pioneer in the field of FLE, reminds us that the word *education* derives from Latin verbs and prefixes that together mean to draw out from learners what is already in them, in terms of capability or potential.

For example, there is widespread agreement in the scientific literature that children need love, limits, and latitude for optimum development (Hart, Newell, & Sine, 2000). After presenting this idea to parents, we can then check this idea out with group: "Does this principle make sense to you? Does it fit with your experiences?" We can then invite parents to share their experience with the idea by asking, "What experiences do you have with setting limits for children?" As parents share their experiences, they become a fruitful resource to each other and to FLEs of ideas for strengthening parenting in the community, beyond what the research and instructor may bring. Participants in FLE benefit from the collective wisdom of others. "The group itself benefits from listening to individuals' . . . perceptions, whether they are based on unique cultural history or keen personal sensitivity" (DeBord et al., 2002, p. 31).

Alternatively, at times the real-life experiences and wisdom of participants in an FLE program may run counter to scientifically based recommendations. FLEs will need to respect the experiences and culture of participants but not be afraid to challenge them with an idea that may broaden their experience. For example, most parents have used spanking as a mode of child discipline, and some parents may scoff at the idea of using less aversive means (e.g., reasoning, time-out) to control the undesirable behavior of children. Some may say something like, "Reasoning never worked for me. I spank 'em and they toe the line!" We can ask participants what the potential good and bad outcomes of this approach might be. Then FLEs can facilitate a discussion of different ways of doing things that have been used by other parents (e.g., using time-out, reasoning, or distraction) to help learners see that misbehavior can be handled in a variety of ways. Participants can then be invited to test if the new ideas work for them. On the other hand, in some cultures parents may spank more because they feel they must make their children obey or they will not respect the culture's values. It is important for the FLE to understand cultural values underlying different parenting practices and determine how these practices intersect or conflict with the current scholarly literature.

Do the Ideas Work in Practice?

Experiences with principles may have taken us only so far, and there are ideas our FLE audiences may hear from us or from one another that they haven't tried out. We can encourage them to experiment with the ideas they hear. Part of assessing the validity of an idea is to test it out in our own lives. It may be based on many studies and it may ring true, and it may be reinforced by the experiences of many, but we have to ask ourselves if it will work for me. Of course, no one strategy works for everyone under all circumstances. But if a tool proves useful in some instances, it can be kept handy to use when needed. We test the idea out in the laboratory of our own experience so we know whether or not it works for us.

● DECIDING HOW TO TEACH

Formulating Learning Goals and Objectives

Regardless of whether we are leading a workshop, writing a news column or Web article, or appearing on television, FLEs are teaching. *Every aspect of outreach FLE has a teaching component.* Successful teaching requires that we have clear goals and objectives.

Program goals and objectives are discussed in the context of program evaluation in Chapter 4. We revisit that discussion briefly in the context of designing significant learning experiences (Fink, 2003) for our FLE audiences.

FLEs may be tempted to make a simple list of topics as a means of guiding their instruction. A learner-centered approach changes this focus and invites the educator to specifically identify what learners should get out of the learning experience (Fink, 2003). Goals articulate general purposes of instruction. For example, a goal or purpose of a family strengths program (or Web or news article series) might be "[t]o help families gain greater happiness in their family life through identifying and building upon their strengths."

Learning objectives are more specific and measurable, and include active verbs (e.g., learn, understand, apply, practice, identify, compare and contrast, critique, do). There are several dimensions of learning that are of importance to FLEs. Perhaps you want your audience to gain knowledge, change their attitudes and values, change behavior, develop skills, or some combination. Thus, as you formulate learning objectives, there are certain questions that are important to ask (adapted from Fink, 2003):

Knowledge

What do you want your learning audience to know (or think about, reflect upon)? For example, what key information (facts, terms, concepts) is important for the learners to understand and remember? What key ideas or perspectives are important for learners to comprehend?

One educator wanted his workshop audience to understand the difference between a problem-focused perspective and a family strengths perspective to building a strong family, and he formulated the following specific learning objective: "Participants will be able to distinguish between a problem-focused approach and a family strengths perspective to strengthening their family."

Caring

What changes would you like to see in what your learners care about, as expressed in their attitudes, values, and feelings? What attitudes and values do you want them to develop or reconsider? What affective experiences do you want them to have with the material?

One educator wanted to change her audience's attitudes toward housework from one of "mere drudgery" to "an opportunity for family connection." Thus, a primary learning objective became "Participants will view housework as a potential setting for family members to strengthen their relationship with each other."

Application

What behaviors would you like them to change? What important skills do you want them to learn?

Interventionist-oriented FLEs will often be interested in structuring instruction in ways that evoke change in behaviors and development of skills. FLEs leading parenting workshops may want their parents to learn authoritative approaches to parenting. A learning objective appropriate for this area might be the following: Participants will learn and practice three skills pertinent to authoritative parenting: establishing connection, regulating children's behavior, and promoting autonomy. Perhaps in the same program, FLEs are interested in promoting the use of positive approaches to discipline, including reducing the use of corporal punishment as a strategy. A possible learning objective would be the following: Parents will learn and practice numerous options for dealing with difficult child behavior.

● SELECT METHODS FOR OUTREACH FAMILY LIFE EDUCATION

With content selected and goals and learning objectives established, we are ready to select delivery methods. While numerous methods of teaching family relationships have been generated over the years (e.g., Klemer & Smith, 1975), a recent and thorough anthology of methods in FLE does not exist. This section of the chapter reviews several methods we and others have found especially useful and applicable in FLE settings. We have attempted to select a wide variety of methods that would suit a wide variety of learning styles and cultures. Many of the following methods are limited to use in more traditional outreach settings, such as community workshops. (We are indebted to Brynn Steimle for her collection of many of the following methods.)

Leading Group Discussions

Discussion invites active involvement in the learning process (McKeachie, 1999). It allows learners to clarify their thinking through making comments and through listening to the comments of others (Klemer & Smith, 1975). One way to initiate a planned discussion is by presenting a thought-provoking problem statement or question (Harris, 2002; Hobbs, 1972, p. 112; McKeachie, 1999, p. 50). Such questions may begin with words such as *give evidence, explain, interpret, compare, analyze, evaluate, how, why, what* (Hobbs, 1972, p. 112).

During the course of a discussion, appropriate and respectful responses by the educator to student comments will encourage future response (Powell & Cassidy, 2001). Important group discussion skills (Alabama Cooperative Extension, 1996) include the following:

Structuring

Make clear the purpose and goals of the discussion, to keep discussion within boundaries. You need to be continually aware of what is happening and judge whether or not it is appropriate to a group's purpose. You need to limit and redirect discussion when participants wander too far astray.

Linking

Linking identifies the common elements in the group's questions and comments. Listen for themes that are similar and help members see that they share feelings and beliefs. Linking also promotes interaction between participants.

Summarizing

Summarizing, like repetition, promotes learning. Emphasize the most important ideas dealt with during the session. A summary may reveal points to group members they missed earlier. Also, ask participants to summarize what they have learned; this allows the leader to assess their understanding and clarify misconception.

Answering Questions

You can be an effective group discussion leader without answering every question directed to you. In fact, when you are occupying a collaborator or facilitator role, it's good to try and get the group to answer the questions. Turn the question back to the group by saying, for instance, "Does anyone have any ideas on that?"

Fish Bowl

A fish bowl is a special adaptation of group discussion and provides the opportunity to learn empathy and understanding of another's point of view. First, the group is split into two groups, often with opposing views about a topic. Two circles of chairs are formed, one inside the other. One group takes a seat in the inner circle, and the other sits on the outside. Participants in the center circle (the fish) are observed by those in the outer circle. If the nature of the room makes this arrangement of chairs inconvenient, the fish may simply go to the front of the room while the observers stay in their seats. Once in place, the educator facilitates a discussion with the fish while the rest of the group observes, taking note of what is being discussed and how it is being done (McKeachie, 1999, p. 211). Members of the inner group talk to one another about some topic suggested by the facilitator while the outer circle group is asked to listen to the discussion without interrupting. After about 10 to 15 minutes, the discussion should be halted and the members of the inner circle asked to be silent while the others discuss what they have heard and understood about the point of view of the inner group, or what new ideas/information they have learned that was previously unknown. Then the groups switch places and repeat the process. After each group has had the opportunity to share their views and to be heard by those in the outer circle, the entire group is brought back together to discuss what was learned from the experience.

One educator used this technique during a parenting workshop with parents and their preteen children. He first asked the parents and youth to imagine they were asked to write books respectively titled *What Kids Expect of Parents* and *What Parents Expect of Their Kids*. What would be the major points of the books? The kids were in the inner circle first, and responded to the question "If you were to write a book titled *What Kids Expect of Parents*, what would the Table of Contents read?" Parents often bit their tongues as they listened to their children's frank comments, and some started to interrupt on occasion. The educator then asked the parents what they heard their youth say, which led to increased understanding of their children. Then it was the parents' turn to speak and the preteens to listen and paraphrase their understanding. Parents and teens experienced an increased level of mutual understanding, resulting from truly listening to one another.

Buzz Groups

Buzz groups are another variation on traditional discussion. Buzz groups, or several small groups within a larger group, allow participants to discuss an issue among themselves (Hobbs, 1972; McKeachie, 1999). Buzz groups usually last for 5 minutes or less (McKeachie, 1999). An educator may request that each individual contribute one idea to the group, and then a group spokesperson can summarize the group's discussion for the rest of the participants (McKeachie, 1999).

Also, dilemmas can be used to allow students to solve a problem using skills they have learned in the session (DeBord, 1989). For instance, in a parenting workshop you could present a scenario and have a group work to a solution such as the one below:

> Your 13-year-old daughter seems to have been distancing herself from the family lately. One day you get a call from the mother of your daughter's male friend saying she has just discovered they are sexually involved. You have taught your daughter the importance of abstinence. What are possible ways you might handle this situation?

This sort of scenario could also be used in a role play (see below).

After group reports, the educator summarizes the discussion as a whole (Hobbs, 1972). To help groups stay on focus, the educator may want to place the problem scenario on an overhead or computer projector. Also, it's helpful for the educator to walk around the room, observing each of the groups during the buzz session (Hobbs, 1972; McKeachie, 1999).

In a balancing work and family program, an educator divided participants into groups of five and assigned them different scenarios. For example, one scenario read,

> Your job takes you away from home several times a month, and your spouse and child have begun to complain about your regular absences. You are feeling stressed each time they raise the issue.

The groups worked together to identify the work-family stressor (e.g., not enough time for family) and then ran it through an ABC model of stress by asking questions such as "How can I ALTER the source of stress? Do I need to ACCEPT the stressor as inevitable? Do I need to BUILD resources? CHANGE perceptions?" The groups selected a spokesperson to share their scenario, the stressor identified, and how they collectively decided to meet the challenges. If the same scenario was used across groups, the educator had the first group report, and successive groups report only those ideas that were unique to them.

Personal Narrative: Stories of Life

Personal narrative, or stories from one's own life and from the lives of others, grounds abstract principles in reality. Stories have an emotional quality that reaches the heart of participants more quickly than didactic teaching can. Some evidence suggests that stories are effective family life educational tools and motivate good parenting (Grant, Hawkins, & Dollahite, 2001).

Personal narratives might reveal FLEs' own struggles with an issue or problem (e.g., "I struggle to be the kind of parent I want to be") and how they have gone about dealing with challenges or solving problems (e.g., "When I was too harsh with a child, I've gone to him or her and sought forgiveness"). Sometimes the stories have a "moral" to them—an essential punch line (Thomas & Arcus, 1992). Stories with moral content also build the moral intelligence of adults and children alike (Coles, 1997). The oral tradition of storytelling is found in numerous cultures and is useful for teaching many family life ideas. Some cultures use elders to tell these stories. Thus, FLEs might act as a catalyst for family members to begin telling and sharing their own personal and family narrative.

Here's one of our favorite stories (from the life of author Goddard), illustrating the importance of loving children in ways they want to be loved:

Wally, a high school math teacher, was approached by a young fellow after class. The young man asked Wally to come with him on Saturday at 6 A.M. to the reservoir, crawl through the mud and cattails to the water's edge, and watch the ducks take off. Now Wally thought of other things he'd rather be doing ("sawing logs," for instance), but since he liked to take pictures, he agreed to go. It was a good experience. Wally took lots of great photos. About 2 weeks later, this same young man told Wally that his dad was taking him to hunt big game. Wally responded, "Wow, you must be pretty excited!" The young man thought a moment and said, "Not really. I'd really like my dad to come with me to the reservoir some mornings and watch the ducks take off."

In a workshop, parents could then be asked to share their impressions about the story and what major messages or principles could be derived from the story. Then a discussion about how to learn and respond accurately to a child's love language could ensue.

Here is a personal narrative of the benefits of marriage preparation, from the life of author Duncan. In this case, the marriage preparation was unintentional:

During my master's program, I took an Introduction to Marriage and Family Therapy course. One assignment was to attend five "enrichment" sessions with a partner. The partner could be anyone, but immediately I thought of several women I knew. I decided to ask Barbara.

Barbara and I had been friends for over a year and just recently felt attracted to one another. I assured Barbara that the enrichment experience was just for a class, for "science," I joked. She agreed to participate.

During the first session, we explored our families. We mapped out our families on the chalkboard and described the relationships we had with each member. Our first assignment was to go out and get to know each other. We talked for hours about our families and backgrounds.

We spent the next day together too, having dinner with her grandparents and father, who just happened to be in town. The sessions helped us get to know each other from the inside out. We also benefited from the hour-long ride to and from the university, when we talked about many important matters.

Through this assignment I gained something far more important and valuable than an A on the paper. Barbara and I became engaged and married a few months afterward. This unintentional premarital counseling experience set the stage for understanding, kindness, consideration, friendship, and sharing that continues to be an important part of our very satisfying 22-year marriage.

FLEs could use a story like the foregoing as a real-life illustration of the benefits of marriage preparation, after citing research that predicts a 30% increase in outcome success among those who participate in focused preparation for marriage (Carroll & Doherty, 2003). Such stories make the statistical data meaningful.

Stories are everywhere to be found. Look for them in magazines and books. Seek them in the lives of others, but also in your own life as a family member and from grandparents and other family "historians." Then share them. As FLEs are open with their own imperfections as parents, spouses, and family members, they encourage an accepting "we're all in this together" climate that increases participants' sense of safety.

Skill Training

FLEs often have the opportunity to help participants gain skills they need for successful marriage and family life. Here is a common approach based on social learning methods (Dumka et al., 1995):

- Describe the skill

  Example: Listening to children with the head and heart is an important skill for a parent to have. Elements of the skill include giving full attention, acknowledging feelings, inviting more discussion, and showing understanding by paraphrasing.

- Model the skill

  Example: As a parent, I'm going to demonstrate this skill in a role play with one of you as my child, who has had a particularly awful day at school and wants to talk with a parent about it.

- Practice the skill in a nonstressful setting and situation

  Example: Let's break up into parent-child pairs and practice this skill, using a scenario you come up with.

- Receive reinforcement and corrective feedback

  Example: I'll come around and visit you, to see how you're coming along.

- Use the skill in a real setting

  Example: For homework this week, practice head and heart listening with your children. Come prepared next time to report how it went.

Family Councils/Meetings

Long recommended by family experts, family councils provide a choice opportunity for clarifying family responsibilities and expectations. Family councils can be used to set goals, distribute household work, resolve family problems, and celebrate one another's successes. When councils are conducted properly, they allow each person to voice his or her opinions and feelings and be involved in solving problems and making decisions.

You can use an FLE program to model and practice a family council for use at home, and/or you can use it as a teaching method. For example, one Building Family Strengths seminar held on one Sunday evening drew an overflow crowd of whole families at the local elementary school in a rural area. The family life educator began the evening by asking family members, "What makes families strong?" Answers varied among children and adults. Then the educator shared nine characteristics of strong families, many of which coincided with strengths identified by the participants, and illustrated the characteristics using personal stories and examples shared by participants. Refreshment time arrived, to be held in the school lunchroom. Here is where the second part of the program began. The families sat together as the educator asked, "If you wanted to build strengths in your family, what would you do first? Identify your strengths!" The families worked together family council style to identify where they were strong and where they needed improvement. Then they decided together on one or two areas of strength that needed work, and set goals for doing activities that build the strength.

As a take-home assignment, you might ask participants to begin holding regular family councils. Here are some guidelines for holding them:

- Schedule a regular time for family councils, say every other Sunday or once a month.
- Councils shouldn't always be used to air concerns and solve problems. Try to talk about fun things too—like planning family activities.
- Set and follow an agenda. Rotate conducting responsibilities between parents and older children.
- Prior to the council, encourage family members to write down things they want on the agenda for discussion. You might post a large piece of paper on the refrigerator or a bulletin board for this.
- Set ground rules for the council such as (a) everyone is free to express his or her opinions and feelings without fear of being blamed or insulted for what they say, (b) everyone is expected to listen to what is being said. Interruptions are not allowed.
- Limit the council to an hour, and end on a cheerful note—with a joke or refreshments.

Role Playing

Role playing is a technique to use when FLEs want participants to see how people would act in a given situation. They learn generalizations about behavior, and they begin to understand feelings. It includes both prepared or scripted role plays and spontaneous role plays. Role playing also allows participants to practice using a principle that has been learned (Vance, 1989), so that when they encounter a real situation requiring its use, they will be better equipped to respond (Klemer & Smith, 1975). While many feel uncomfortable with using or participating in role plays, they are effective in rehearsing effective strategies, and one can visualize and anticipate the effects of behavior on others.

The classic manner of role playing is to select a vignette or problem and explain the situation to the group, explain to the actors their role, explain the audience's role, have the role players start the role play, end the role play, and then facilitate a discussion of the role play. For example, if the role play involved a parent-child scene, it would be good to discuss how the child felt and how the parent felt. Role plays are useful to contrast a negative example (e.g., ineffective parenting) against a positive example (e.g., effective parenting).

Seven guidelines for all role playing, whether it be classic or some variation of the classic type, follow (Institute for Mental Health Initiatives, 1991; Klemer & Smith, 1975; Vance, 1989):

1. There must be a reason for using role playing other than entertaining the group, such as teaching a principle of behavior and/or helping participants gain insight into their own beliefs.

2. The situation must be emotional; that is, participants must feel an emotional investment in the outcome.

3. Be careful when selecting actors. Use role players (through selecting or volunteering) who will not feel threatened by playing the role.

4. Give the role players a little time to get into the role. They will need to think about the age, the personality, the pressures of the moment on that role, and the reaction that the person might make.

5. Part of good management of role playing is the selection of the stopping place. The point of role playing is to dramatize some behaviors and not to fill up time. When the players have shown several reactions in an attempt to solve the problems stated, stop the role playing before it drags.

6. Facilitate discussion of the role play. For example:
   a. What was the conflict/problem?
   b. What was going on with each person? Ask the group how they think persons would feel in this situation. Ask the role players to describe their feelings as they enacted their roles.
   c. Was the situation handled effectively or ineffectively? Why or why not? What could be improved? Discuss the practices that would improve the situation.
   d. Role-play the situation again and incorporate the principles and practices discussed.

7. If the roles played were very emotional and out of character for the players, they must be "de-roled." That is, either call each one by name or ask each of them to say to themselves, "I am [my name]." This process may sound unusual, but a peculiar feeling remains with some people if they are not brought back into their own roles.

Movie Clips

Many years ago, pioneer FLEs Richard Klemer and Rebecca Smith (1975) argued that using movies "is a way of studying family relationships . . . including interaction of specific people in specific situations. . . . Students can identify or empathize more easily with the people in [movies] than they can with abstract concepts" (p. 25). FLEs can use short clips from popular movies to illustrate important points regarding marriage and family relationships. For instance, during a marriage preparation program, a clip from *My Big Fat Greek Wedding* could be used to initiate a discussion on the importance of similar backgrounds between a man and woman considering marriage. In this movie, the man and woman considering marriage and later marrying come from arguably incompatible backgrounds. The movie does a great job at illustrating the differing backgrounds but fails to point out that this will create a lot of complications and difficulties throughout their married life. FLEs could engage the group in a discussion of some of these potential complications that result from lack of similarity.

It's important to introduce the clip well, so that participants understand what the clip is about and how it fits in the process. FLEs might also encourage participants to look for certain things in the clips. After a clip has been shown and discussed, it's useful to reiterate the point the clip illustrated before moving on to another instruction.

At the end of this book is Appendix B, listing some of our favorite movie clips, topics they address, and how the clips could be used. You can think of many others!

Educational Videos

Many FLE curricula have companion videos or a strong video component. Not all videos are of equal quality and content (such as discussed in Chapter 3), but many excellent educational videos are available for stand-alone instruction or enhancements of a program. Videos should be carefully chosen as aids to accomplish specific objectives, not merely to fill instructional time.

There are various educational videos available to FLEs. One source for accessing such videos is *Audiovisual Resources for Family Programming* (Jordan & Stackpole, 1995). Another refereed source of educational videos is the journal *Family Relations.* Each January issue, this journal publishes a listing of award-winning educational videos that have been reviewed and rated by a committee of FLEs.

Music and Pictures

The psychological and therapeutic benefits of music are well known. Music can have a calming, mood-altering influence. From a family life educational perspective, music can also be used to help individuals come to understand themselves and others (Klemer & Smith, 1975). Playing songs can help learners explore issues or ideas. For instance, through listening to a medley of various songs, an educator could help a class see the various kinds of love that are discussed (motherly love, deep-rooted love), as well as other things often called love (i.e., sexual attraction).

Music clips can also be used to explore various philosophies of life (Klemer & Smith, 1975) and to generate discussion of the impact that holding these philosophies has on marriage and family life. For example, author Duncan uses a song series as part of his marriage education programs to illustrate approaches to marital commitment. Since he's a reasonably good musician, he sings and interacts with the audience while accompanying himself on the piano. After posing the question "How can and does modern Western culture influence our approach to keeping marital commitments" and allowing some discussion, he sings excerpts from songs that illustrate lax commitment in relationships:

"Love on the Rocks" (Neil Diamond)

Excerpt:
> You need what you need
> You can say what you want
> Not much you can do when the feeling is gone

Analysis: Shows a lax commitment to marriage by suggesting that there's little that can be done to restore absent love feelings.

"Why Don't We Live Together" (Barry Manilow)

Excerpt:
> Why don't we live together
> Only the two of us, we'll learn to trust
> Don't have to say forever
> 'Cause we know the rain could start and break our hearts
> But we'll never find the future if we hesitate
> We'll spend our lives waiting

Analysis: Shows a lax commitment in relationships by suggesting the relationship doesn't have to be permanent.

"Then You Can Tell Me Good-Bye" (Neal McCoy)

Excerpt:
> But if you must go I won't tell you no
> Just so that we can say we tried

Tell me you love me for a million years
Then if it don't work out
If it don't work out
Then you can tell me good-bye

Analysis: Shows a lax commitment in relationships by suggesting that promises are kept so long as things work out.

He also provides a song critical of this lax approach:

"What's Forever For?" (Michael Martin Murphy)

Excerpt:
But I see love-hungry people
Trying their best to survive
While in their hands is a dying romance
And they're not even trying to keep it alive
So what's the glory in living
Doesn't anybody ever stay together anymore
And if love never lasts forever
Tell me what's forever for

Analysis: A commentary on the state of affairs in relationships: Commitment in relationships is so lax that people aren't really trying to keep love alive.

After this final number, Duncan then leads participants in a discussion of nurturing commitment and protecting marriage from the widespread consumer culture that threatens it.

Many popular songs have family themes that could be incorporated into FLE. Some include "Butterfly Kisses" by Bob Carlisle (fatherhood, parenthood), "Cats in the Cradle" by Harry Chapin (father influence), "Do You Love Me?" from *Fiddler on the Roof* (marriage), and "Through the Years" by Kenny Rogers (marriage).

Pictures can also be used to enhance FLE. For example, they can be used as a storytelling aid. One family life educator told a story of a family that lost all their worldly goods due to a natural disaster, yet still had each other, while showing photographs of the destruction such disasters leave in their wake. The story was used as a springboard into a discussion of the importance of commitment to family (Krysan, Zill, & Moore, 1990), especially during the toughest times. Another use of pictures is to teach generalizations about family relationships (Klemer & Smith, 1975). For example, another educator showed photographs of family members from around the world, where fathers and sons, mothers and daughters, siblings, and entire family groups were posing or engaged in activities, and then asked participants to identify the commonalities among the pictures. In this photo illustration, some commonalities emerged: family members were touching, there was a theme of togetherness, and all appeared happy together. The overall principle taught was that family bonding is a universal desire and can be nurtured through meaningful time together.

Books, Plays, and Short Stories

A variety of books, plays, and short stories depict themes that would be fruitful for outreach FLE. Some examples are *A Doll's House*, by Henrik Ibsen (good illustration of onset of marital decline, Helmer and Nora's relationship), *I Never Sang for My Father,* by Robert Anderson (teaching how adult children and their aging parents relate), and *A Piece of Strong*, by Guy de Maupassant (illustration of the costs of being unforgiving). Check book reviews to identify other sources.

Comic Strips and Cartoons

Comic strips and cartoons often grab the attention of learners and are useful discussion starters. We can invite participants to comment about the cartoon, such as to what degree they agree or disagree with the sentiment. Also, because of their humorous nature, cartoons can help reduce tension among participants (Warnock, 1988). There are many cartoons that serve as commentaries on family life. For instance, by exaggerating reality, *Calvin and Hobbes* helps illustrate many issues pertaining to parenting. *For Better or Worse* has very realistic portrayals of grief after losing a lifelong spouse, older adult courtship, and marriage adjustments related to the birth of the first child. *Family Circus, Peanuts,* and *Dennis the Menace* are other useful cartoons.

Editorial cartoons also provide useful illustrations of themes and occasionally present interesting ironies. For example, one cartoon (find it in Larson, 2000, p. 179) shows a picture of a small car alongside a gigantic flying machine labeled "marriage." The caption reads, "Which one doesn't require a special course of instruction to operate at age 16?" Discussion can ensue on the benefits of preparing for marriage at least as thoroughly as most states prepare young people to drive.

Games

Games can be used as ice breakers (DeBord, 1989), to interest students in a topic (Grieshop, 1987; O'Neill, 2003), or to facilitate active learning

(McKeachie, 1999). Games can be presented following a format similar to television game shows (DeBord, 1989). When this is done, the familiarity of the game may encourage greater participation (DeBord, 1989).

Miner and Barnhill (2001) describe one game, Dollars for Answers, developed by county agents at Utah State University. In this game, the educator asks for a volunteer to come to the front of the classroom, then proceeds to ask the volunteer multiple choice questions relating to the workshop topic. When a question is answered correctly, the volunteer receives a $1 prize. Giving this small prize makes the game more interesting and reduces the formality. After the question is answered correctly, the educator can take whatever time he or she wants to elaborate on the answer. If the volunteer answers incorrectly, the educator explains the correct answer, and again, has the opportunity to teach the class. The volunteer can be given the chance to answer more than one question before another volunteer is chosen. An alternative is to ask the entire class to vote on what they think is the correct answer, rather than putting one individual on the spot.

Another extension specialist (O'Neill, 2003) provides extensive instructions for creating an interactive Jeopardy-like PowerPoint quiz game at (see http://www.joe.org/joe/2003april/tt2.shtml).

Object Lessons

Object lessons engage participants in the learning process. For example, one family life educator, when teaching about work and family balance, introduces the session through the use of an object lesson. He asks for a volunteer to participate. He then proceeds to place books on the volunteer, wherever he can hold them—a few in each hand, one on his or her head, one on an uplifted knee, and so on. Through a dialogue with the volunteer, he then establishes how easy it is to become overwhelmed when multiple tasks are placed upon us from all directions. He ties this into demands from home, work, one's faith community, civic obligations, and so on.

Object lessons can also cause participants to reflect on and question assumptions in ways that have the potential to promote action. Author Duncan uses a driver's license to illustrate the need to prepare for marriage. He contrasts the requirements for a driver's license with the requirements for a marriage license. It takes far more time, effort, and (usually) money to obtain a license to drive than to obtain legal permission to marry. As participants wrestle with the issue, they may come out more motivated than ever before to consciously prepare for marriage.

Homework Assignments and Learning Contracts

Wise FLEs give participants something to work on between sessions or, if one session is all you have, an assignment or challenge to complete at home. Use the beginning of the next session to review how the homework assignment went. For example, following an Emotion Coaching (Gottman, 1997) session for parents on becoming aware of children's emotions, one educator assigned participants to keep a journal of the emotions either they perceived or their children reported experiencing each day of the following week, noting also the events or other circumstances that may have triggered the emotion. Prior to moving on to another skill, each parent was given the opportunity to report on his or her experiences and receive feedback from the educator.

Some participants are reluctant to complete homework assignments. FLEs who use a homework approach are wise at the beginning of the sessions to explain to participants that homework assignments provide a vital opportunity for them to practice the skills they learn in the program at home, and that they will get the most benefit from a program if they complete homework assignments during the week after each session. Alternatively, commitment to homework completion can flow naturally from the use of learning contracts (Knowles, 1998). Learning contracts comprise the following eight steps:

1. Diagnose learning needs ("Where am I today as a parent and where would I like to be, in terms of knowledge and abilities?").

2. Specify learning objectives ("What do I want to be able to *do* as a result of this program?").

3. Specify learning resources and strategies ("What activities in and out of class would help me accomplish my objectives?").

4. Specify evidence of accomplishment ("What can I use to show I have gained the knowledge and skills I sought?").

5. Specify how the evidence will be validated ("Who will verify that I have the knowledge and skill?").

6. Review the contract with a consultant (show the educator the five steps).

7. Carry out the contract.

8. Evaluate your learning.

As participants create their own learning objectives and then consider what they need to do to accomplish them, they may be more self-motivated to engage in the learning strategy of practice at home (Step 3) and demonstrate their learning in the following session, receiving facilitator feedback (Steps 4 and 5).

Idea Reinforcers

Take-home session reminders are helpful in reinforcing key ideas from a session or presentation. One approach is to type the main ideas and memorable subpoints on a bordered half sheet of paper or on the same size cardstock and include a visual on it that would add to their recollection. For example, a presentation on Timeless Principles of Parenting might read like the one in Box 7.1.

Box 7.1

Timeless Principles of Parenting

1

Learn and Speak Your Child's Love Language

Watch them, ask them, don't mind-read!

2

Correct With Love

How you say it matters

3

Use Consequences

Natural, logical, individualized

Myth Versus Reality

FLE programs offer the opportunity to correct mistaken perceptions about family issues. For example, FLEs can help deconstruct many myths that have arisen regarding marriage that a young adult marriage preparation audience may embrace. Some of these myths might include "there is a one-and-only" or some other myth (Larson, 1988). Belief in myths can lead to expectations built upon false ideas and can become a risk factor in marriage (Larson, 1998). Some older persons carry myths about aging (e.g., all older people become senile if they live long enough) that, if embraced, may limit their ability to have a maximum quality of life.

Author Duncan developed a program called Myths of Aging that was built around this method. The program first began with a quiz, which participants were to answer on paper "True" or "False." In checking the answers, he provided not only the answers but an explanation of the answer using research.

● CONCLUSION

This chapter has detailed some of the mechanics and methods of putting together educational materials for FLE settings. FLEs need to be selective in deciding what to teach and how to teach it, being clear in what they want to accomplish in terms of learner-gained knowledge, attitude and behavior change, and learning skills. Finally, we detailed several methods that can be used in community workshop settings for delivering FLE.

● EXPLORATIONS

1. Create a sample instructional outline appropriate for a workshop setting. Write the overall goal, followed by two or three learning objectives following the pattern in the chapter. Make sure the objectives are measurable and contain active verbs—what you actually want participants to *do.* Then, for each learning objective you list, select a different instructional method and practice teaching with your class and colleagues.

2. Go on a methods treasure hunt for a few weeks and create a chest of Family Life Education Methods. Many excellent books developed for adult learners contain ideas that can be adapted to FLE settings. One favorite is Mel Silberman's *Active Learning: 101 Strategies to Teach Any Subject* (1996).

3. Develop a habit, like radar, of checking for story illustrations when reading magazines, books, newspapers, and other literature; checking comics (in newspaper and at online sources), watching movies and videos. Friends and family may think you obsessive, but FLEs often can't help looking for teaching elements in all these materials.

CHAPTER **8**

WORKING WITH THE MEDIA IN FAMILY LIFE EDUCATION

By Tonya Fishio

T he Air Force would never send a pilot to fly an F-16 without hours of instruction, study, and training. However, millions of people take a seat in the cockpit of family life having previously only ridden as a passenger. Not only do they lack formal training, but there is no instruction manual in the glove compartment to refer to. While some figure it out as they go, others are headed straight for destruction, hoping to find the eject button before impact.

Unfortunately, a family life education (FLE) professional cannot be at the other end of each headset offering suggestions, guidance, and encouragement. They can, however, utilize a very powerful communications tool to reach millions of these volunteer pilots—the mass media.

"The best and most powerful way of attaining success and conveying your message to the largest audience is by using the mass media" (Berman, 1977, p. 16). The most common mass media outlets include newspapers, magazines, television, radio stations, wire services, trade publications, and the Internet.

Because the Internet is such a growing and pervasive venue for FLE, it is addressed separately in Chapter 10. In this chapter, we discuss principles and practices for disseminating family life educational information through newspapers, television, and radio.

You have a wealth of information that can change lives, alter futures, strengthen families, and improve society, but it lives dormant as gray matter in your brain or as black ink characters stored on your office shelves. Your accumulated intellect, research, and experience has great potential to impact thousands or even millions if only you had a way to share it with those who need to implement it in their personal lives. Your knight in shining armor has arrived—the media; but note, he may be carrying a few toads in his pocket with warts that you will have to work around.

Although approaching the vast world of the mass media may seem intimidating, once you understand a little about how the media works, opportunities will demand your attention. When you learn to facilitate the needs of the media, it will be more willing to facilitate your needs.

● MASS MEDIA AND OUTREACH FAMILY LIFE EDUCATION

Family life educators (FLEs) face both promise and peril (Myers-Walls, 2003) in taking their message to the general public. Certainly the promise is signaled in part by the proliferation in the amount of family life materials available for public consumption. For example, according to a recent analysis (Simpson, 1997), it is estimated that there are over 1,500 parenting books in print, comprising 20% of the psychology market, and over 200 magazines that devote themselves to parenting and family matters. These numbers do not include the magazines that occasionally feature such material. Studies show that parents and families want information about families in this format. Additional advantages of mass media for outreaching the FLE message include the capability for reaching many people at once and the findings that media as part of a mosaic of actors can and does influence behavior (Simpson, 1997).

But there is a potential quagmire. As far-reaching as mass media is, it also tends to provide a more superficial coverage of topics, limited by the length of sound bites and print inches. Parenting advice offered through media channels is often confusing and conflicting (Simpson, 1997). Some experts favor a more permissive parenting approach and trumpet their philosophy, while another just as loudly proclaims that parents need to reassert authority.

Because of the potential for success as well as failure when utilizing mass media channels, FLEs need specific guidelines to follow for navigating the dangers and realizing the promise of FLE.

UNDERSTANDING THE MEDIA: ●
WALK A MILE IN ITS SHOES

Deadlines! Deadlines! Deadlines!

You've been up since 4 a.m. and you're on the air in 30 minutes with a breaking story, but your source hasn't returned your calls all morning, so you quickly move to Plan B and call someone else. "Four, three, two, one and you are on the air." Sorry, missed opportunity for your original source. Next time you won't even waste your time calling him in the first place.

———◆•●•◆———

Your newspaper story is due to the editor by 4 p.m. To present a well-rounded story, you need a source to represent another viewpoint. Who do you call? Not the guy who interrupted you while you were rushing to meet yesterday's deadline and insisted on rambling on about some fluff release he had just sent. Instead, you remember a source you previously used who returned your phone calls promptly, provided an insightful perspective, and even recommended another source. You know he is respectful of the deadline pressures you are dealing with.

Media representatives are always under a deadline—one that is typically measured in minutes and hours rather than days or weeks. There is no time for writer's block, pushy publicity seekers, or unresponsive sources. If media representatives leave you a message, call them back as soon as possible. One simple call communicates that you are responsive and media friendly. If, however, you are calling for your own purposes (to encourage coverage of your organization, research, or program; to follow up on a release; or to establish a relationship), always ask if they are on a deadline. If they are, ask when you should call back. The last thing you want to do is annoy media representatives dealing with deadline pressures. Such actions will most likely get your name remembered—along with a loud alarm shouting, "Royal pain . . . Avoid this person!"

A phone message returned "tomorrow" is usually not worth returning. (Fox & Levin, 1993, p. 54)

It is easier to be respectful of deadlines when you know when the deadlines are—so ask. If you don't have the opportunity to ask, there are some general guidelines you can refer to. Reporters working for a newspaper distributed in the evening typically must have their stories to their editor by noon. Reporters working for a morning paper (the more common of the two) have a late afternoon or evening deadline. A typical day for morning paper reporters begins with them in the office by 10 a.m., out pursuing a story by noon, in front of the computer madly writing by 3 p.m., and finally submitting a story to their editor by 5 p.m. for an overnight print. In such an instance, calling between the hours of 3 and 5 p.m. would be the worst time. As for media representatives working in broadcast and radio, they typically arrive at the office in the early morning and spend the day developing a story to be submitted by 3 p.m. for editing and production before it airs on the early evening news.

With such a hectic schedule, is there ever really a good time to contact the media? While there may not be a perfect time, it is better to contact representatives anytime outside the 2 to 3 hours they are on deadline. The more you work with the media, the sooner you will learn to facilitate the media's needs so representatives will be more willing to make time for you. "Although many media representatives may not want to admit it, they need you as much as you need them. Media can't create their stories without experts, interesting individuals and reliable information" (Berman, 1977, p. 17).

Information Flood

You walk into the office at 10 a.m. and there are already eight releases waiting for you on the fax machine. Grabbing them as you walk by, you head for your desk with the flashing phone message light that greets you each morning. While your computer boots up, you quickly glance through the releases, keeping the recycle paper bin close by. After spending approximately 5 to 30 seconds per release, you narrow the eight releases down to three to read later. Now your e-mail account has 21 new messages; thank goodness for the Subject line allowing you to delete at a glance. Finally, you have to acknowledge the persistent red light on the phone. Whew, and the mail hasn't even arrived yet.

Every day media representatives are bombarded with information coming from all directions: phone, e-mail, fax, courier, and traditional mail services. While technological advances have made it possible for the media to gather and share information in a matter of seconds instead of days, these advances have also created a mountain of information for each representative to sift through. Because it would take more than a full-time job to carefully review all the information, media representatives have developed strategies to weed out nonessential information. To keep your release from the recycle bin, you need to be aware of the strategies they use and then appeal to their sense for news. The media's first line of defense is assessing how newsworthy the information is, based on general industry guidelines.

Newsworthy Guidelines

Information has to fit into only one of the following categories to be considered newsworthy:

1. *Proximity*. These are "local" stories, where information is relevant to an audience in a specific area or region targeted by the publication or broadcast station. Sometimes media representatives are willing to cover a story that seems out of proximity if a local angle is present. For example, when Covenant Marriage legislation passed in Arkansas, it naturally fit the proximity criteria in that state. However, a newspaper in Oklahoma may have also carried a story if its own legislators were intent on presenting a similar bill.

2. *Timeliness*. An event happening today or tomorrow is fresh; one that happened yesterday is already old news. Occasionally, major events have a 2-day life span; however, this is the exception rather than the rule. Also, research published in the current issue of the *American Medical Association* or other peer-reviewed academic journals is timely; a study published in the previous issue is usually past its time.

3. *Value/Importance*. What kind of an impact will the information have on the media outlet's audience? How many people will be affected? Who is involved (prominent figures add to newsworthiness)? All these questions help determine the value or importance of the information and whether or not the media outlet will cover the story.

4. *Conflict/Controversy*. Conflict and controversy are natural magnets for media outlets. Such information, if it is true, is almost always guaranteed a time in the spotlight. While most companies or organizations want to avoid controversy, sometimes it can play to your advantage if you are trying to get the media to cover your perspective on a specific issue. For example, author Judith Ruth Harris raised the age-old debate on nature versus nurture when she published *The Nurture Assumption* (1998). The book supported the notion that parents do not have a large impact on the outcome of their children. While the

debate was not new, the book offended good-intending parents and enraged family life professionals across the country. The controversy opened the door for family life experts to contact their local media and present their viewpoint. Newspaper and broadcast reporters as well as radio talk show hosts were eager to gather a local perspective on what had become a much larger controversy.

5. *Unusual*. The unexpected, remarkable, rare, strange, and even outstanding people or situations can merit media coverage. This newsworthy criterion is why Clonaid's claim to have successfully created the first human clone received so much media coverage, despite the company's evident lack of credibility.

6. *Human interest*. If a story has emotional appeal, it doesn't have to be earth-shattering to receive media attention. Audiences appreciate stories that make them feel something. Often these stories introduce elements the audience can relate to, inspiring them and subtly encouraging action. Human interest stories can also make the audience feel connected with the world. A mother who chooses to leave her professional career to stay at home with her children may not seem like breaking news. However, when presented with the rising trend of the modern 1950s woman, her transition back into the full-time homemaking role is the perfect human interest story.

News is tomorrow's history done up in today's neat package. News is the best record we have of the incredible meanness and the magnificent courage of man. . . . [N]ews is the timely, concise, and accurate report of an event; it is not the event itself. Mitchel Charney Reporting (Calvert, 2000, p. 13)

Although general guidelines are established to determine newsworthiness, you can never escape a certain level of subjectivity. No matter how objective reporters try to handle information, news decisions are influenced by reporters' background, previous experiences, and personal judgments. Unfortunately, this leaves you with no guarantee for media coverage. The most you can do is make sure your information fits clearly within at least one of the given criteria.

Story Ideas

It's a national holiday, and while it seems everyone else in the country is off, here you are with your colleagues thumping your fingers trying to come up with a story idea for today's deadline. With most people at home, the usual faxes, e-mails, and phone calls are at a standstill.

You have three stories in the works, but due to the holiday, you won't get any quotes from your sources today. It is definitely a slow news day.

With the usual steady flow of information, it's hard to believe that a media representative would struggle for a story idea. However, the pressure to continually generate news is not an uncommon one. Unfortunately, many of the releases received by the media are thrown out because the reporter does not deem the release as newsworthy, the release is poorly written, or it is an obvious attempt for free publicity. The mountain of information and story ideas can quickly shrink, often leaving a reporter to dig deep for fresh ideas.

In addition, national holidays and other slow news days can torture the media, but they are a great opportunity for you. Sending information during these times increases the likelihood of coverage. Even if your efforts do not result in a story, media representatives are more likely to remember your name and organization or company without all the other voices competing for their attention. Holidays are also a great time to recycle information to the media. For example, you may have sent the media a release several months ago regarding a relationship assessment you developed. If the story did not receive coverage at that time, be creative and write a human interest story that ties the assessment with Valentine's Day or spring weddings and send it again. You can also contact targeted publications and ask what special issues they have scheduled for the year. Special issues focus on a specific topic and are geared to generate additional advertising revenues for the publication.

Author and professor Jeffry Larson's publisher issued a press release announcing his new book, *The Great Marriage Tune-Up*. A second release was distributed in February to targeted media that had not yet run a story on the book. The second release connected the book's content with Valentine's Day and resulted in additional local coverage. Following is a section of the release:

"Romance is over-rated," jokes BYU professor and marriage therapist Jeffry Larson, author of "The Great Marriage Tune-up Book." He says research shows that romantic love is just one component of a successful marriage.

"Our society sells romance and Valentine's Day and we don't see the reality. After they are married, most couples are really disillusioned when the romance begins to simmer down and they start to deal with everyday issues," he says.

(Press release, Brigham Young University)

● WORKING WITH THE MEDIA: PLAYING ON THE SAME TEAM

Mutually Beneficial Relationships

"Many reporters grow to rely upon credible communicators at universities and nonprofit agencies almost like field correspondents. They count on their sources to keep them abreast of the latest trends and steer them to front-page stories" (Calvert, 2000, p. 15).

Just as you need the media to get your message out, the media needs you, but don't expect it to admit it as readily. So, how do you get media representatives to recognize the value you can contribute to their job as a trusted source they seek after?

The first step is to build a relationship. If they don't know who you are, they will never come knocking at your door. Identify the local media representatives with whom you want to work and invite them to lunch. Some representatives do not accept lunches or are not allowed to by their employer. In such cases, don't be offended; simply shift gears and arrange to meet them without the food or to have a tour of their bureau. One-on-one meetings are the perfect opportunity to put faces with names for both parties. Once media representatives have an identity to associate with the information that crosses their desk, they are more likely to take note and possibly cover your stories.

Use this opportunity to introduce yourself and your organization. Provide the media representative with contact information for yourself as well as others within your organization who might serve as a valuable source. Make sure to include areas of specialty or expertise for each contact.

Most important, ask questions. Find out what kind of stories media representatives look for. Are they more interested in human interest stories or only the latest research? Do they like stories that offer advice to the readers or only represent the facts? Is a feature or a straight news story more likely to receive coverage? Media representatives may cover a wide range of topics, so find out how frequently they cover topics related to your area. Once you have a greater understanding of what media representatives are looking for, have a conversation about how your organization can help facilitate representatives' needs.

Other questions to ask during a meeting with media representatives include how they like to receive information (i.e., fax, e-mail, traditional mail, wire service, etc.), do they mind follow-up phone calls, when is the best time to call, when are deadlines, and what are the demographics of their media outlet?

After establishing a relationship with a media representative, don't forget to maintain that relationship through good media etiquette. While contact is important, it is more important not to become an annoyance. Send information whenever you have it, but limit pitching a story over the phone to those times when you have your most important information. When it is appropriate to pitch a story, offer an angle the media representative can pursue rather than just the topic or facts. If you follow up on a release over the phone, never ask "Did you receive the release I sent you?" Instead, tell the reporter why you thought the information would be of interest specifically to his or her outlet's audience.

Other tips on media etiquette include the following:

- Respect deadlines and call at appropriate times.
- Respond quickly to media inquiries.
- Send thank-you cards for coverage received and at other appropriate times.
- Recommend another expert or source when you don't have the information or simply think it would be helpful.
- Tell the truth at all times, without exception (nothing burns bridges with the media more quickly than an untruthful or evasive response).
- Never exaggerate your qualifications, accreditation, or title.

Information Tools

The media is dependent on the information it receives. There are a variety of tools employed to distribute information to the media. Each tool has its own purpose, advantages, and disadvantages. You must become familiar with the various tools in order to effectively select the one that fits your message. We cover the following tools in this section: press kit, press release, column article, radio program, letter to the editor or opinion editorial, and public service announcement.

Press Kit

A press kit is a package for media representatives of written materials created to introduce and provide background on your company, organization, program, or service. Press kits may be distributed to media representatives prior to a major event, with a release announcing the launch of a new program, when you meet with media representatives during the relationship-building phase, or upon request. A press kit may contain (but is not limited to) the following materials:

- Fact sheet or backgrounder
- Current releases
- Biography sheet
- Recent media clips
- Brochures/pamphlets

Fact Sheet or Backgrounder. A fact sheet is a one-page brief overview of a company, organization, program, or issue. It must contain the 5Ws and 1H: who, what, when, where, why, and how. Fact sheets are written in third person in a very direct, concise manner, implementing an outline format, with each section of information easily identified. Readers must be able to find the specific information they are looking for without having to read the entire document. You may customize information sections according to your needs. For example, a fact sheet for the BYU Family Studies Center emphasizes the broad range of research topics the center supports, whereas a fact sheet for RELATE, a relationship assessment tool, highlights the instrument's features (see Figure 8.1).

A backgrounder is longer than a fact sheet, provides more details, and is written in a traditional paragraph format rather than the outline format of a fact sheet. However, backgrounders are still written in a concise, direct, factual manner. The backgrounder may provide additional history of an organization or issue. For example, a nonprofit organization sponsoring premarital education courses may expand upon the history of the organization, why the organization was created, the value and impact its educational courses have had on couples over the years, including research findings, and the need for such programs.

Current Releases. A press kit may contain one general release about the company, organization, program, or issue, or it may contain several releases recently distributed to local media. (More details regarding the format, writing, and distribution of releases are included in the Writing Guidelines section below.)

Biography Sheet. A biography sheet provides background on an individual who may be a spokesperson, expert, presenter, researcher, or other individual whom a media representative may use as a resource. Information may include current position, educational background, published research or areas of expertise, awards, and professional credentials. "Its purpose is to describe the individual's expertise in a credible way; to make the spokesperson or employee believable in the eyes of the reader" (Derelan, Rouner, & Tucker, 1994, p. 66).

CONTACT: Tom Holman
(801) 422-6704
RELATE@byu.edu

RELATE
FACT SHEET

PURPOSE   To help strengthen marital and premarital relationships by identifying and evaluating specific strengths and challenges in the relationship.

HISTORY   Developed at the BYU Family Studies Center, RELATE was released in 1997 and is the third version of a comprehensive relationship instrument developed by the Marriage Study Consortium. The first version, called Marital Inventory, was developed in 1980. Tens of thousands of couples and individuals have completed one of the three versions of the questionnaire in the last 20 years.

The framework of RELATE is based on the comprehensive review of research regarding the premarital predictors of marital quality from the 1930's to today.

FEATURES   Covers more than 60 aspects of the relationship and 100 percent of the premarital predictors, **making it the most comprehensive relationship assessment tool of its kind.**

Evaluates relationship in four major categories including personality and values, support from family and friends, communication and conflict resolution; and family background.

Provides a four-section report with interpretive graphs, charts, and an assessment of problem areas.

Easy to take and administer.

COST $5 per person/$10 per couple

AVAILABLE   *Mail:* The Marriage Study Consortium
Box 25391
Provo, UT 84602-5391
Telephone: (801) 422-4359
Email: RELATE@byu.edu
Internet: http://relate.byu.edu

Figure 8.1   Sample Fact Sheet

Recent Media Clips. Media clips are copies of articles that feature information you provide to the media or that mentions your organization. These are only applicable if you have recent clips from prominent media outlets. If you are distributing the press kit to local media, then local clips are sufficient. However, if you are distributing the kit to national outlets, including only local clips may diminish the impact. Media clips serve to illustrate the newsworthiness of your content. If a targeted media outlet notices that other notable outlets are covering your information, then the targeted outlet may be more inclined to take note and also run a story. If you intend to distribute a media clip in mass quantities, you need to contact the original outlet and receive permission. Some may require that you submit your reprint request in writing.

Brochures/Pamphlets. Include any brochures or pamphlets you have printed about your organization or program. Although these printed materials are general and may target a different audience, they still provide valuable information that the media may find of interest.

Press Release

Writing and distributing a press release to media outlets is the most common method for providing information and breaking into the news network. It remains the most common method because it works. It is the most effective tool available. However, don't expect your release to be used right away or to be printed word for word, if it is used at all. As we have already explained, many of the releases sent out are simply thrown away. To help keep yours out of the recycle bin, make sure it fits at least one of the newsworthy categories provided earlier in the chapter. It is also important to follow the standard format for releases, which we discuss in this section, making sure it is well written and without spelling errors.

Once your release makes it through the first media screening, it may be held for future use. Media representatives often maintain a round file (a file to hold those releases that are interesting but that don't fit an immediate need). Releases in the round file are often used to generate future story ideas or as a reference for related topics.

A release that generates immediate coverage is rarely printed verbatim. More commonly, an editor of a daily paper assigns the story to a reporter, who investigates the information. The reporter researches the topic and contacts additional sources for a well-rounded story. The story may remain focused around the information you sent, or the reporter may decide to use only a portion of the information in a larger story.

When a release was distributed to national media regarding research on how women inhibit greater father involvement in family work, a writer for the *New York Times* was assigned the story. After investigation, she broadened her story to focus on how working mothers deal with the stress of after-work responsibilities. When the article ran, only three paragraphs and one quote included information from the original release.

Standard Release Format. See Figure 8.2 for a sample press release using the following format guidelines:

- Use company or organization letterhead. If you do not have letterhead, include the organization's name, address, e-mail, Web site, and telephone number at the top of the first page.
- Place contact information for the individual handling media inquiries in the top right corner. Include name, phone number, and e-mail address.
- Center a headline that catches the attention and provides insight into the content of the release.
- Use a larger font for the headline than you use for the text. Headlines are also often set in bold type.
- Include the date the information is released and the city of origination in parentheses before the first sentence of the text.
- Indent all paragraphs five spaces.
- Use double spacing.
- Limit the "lead," your door opener, to the first one or two paragraphs.
- The body of the release fills in all remaining details. It typically applies the principle of the inverted pyramid, providing information in descending order of importance.
- Limit the release to two pages when possible, printed only on one side.
- At the bottom of Page 1, center "-more-," indicating there is an additional page. If you choose to ignore the two-page limit, continue to center "-more-" at the bottom of each page except the final page.
- Include the page number (i.e., -2-, 2–2–2, or Page 2) at the top of each page following the first page.
- Center "###" at the bottom of the final page, indicating there is no more information.

Headline. The headline is a short, catchy summary of the information presented in the release. Headlines are set in bold type and set in a larger font than the text. They do not have to be written as a complete sentence, and they do not include a period at the end. Headlines are the bait to entice

CONTACT INFORMATION

Elizabeth Thompson
MRDAD.COM
Visit Our Site
866-836-6255
Email us Here

**New Book Gives Men the Tools and Support
They Need to Be the Best Dads Ever**

Announcing the release of the essential resource for new dads. This new book gives dads the tools, support, and encouragement they need to be the best dads possible.

(San Francisco, CA—June 14, 2004) Fatherhood expert Armin Brott's groundbreaking book, THE NEW FATHER: A DAD'S GUIDE TO THE FIRST YEAR, has been completely revised, updated, and expanded. The new edition features the latest research on hundreds of topics, from what's going on at the hospital right after childbirth to how a dad can support his partner when she's having trouble breastfeeding. THE NEW FATHER: A DAD'S GUIDE TO THE FIRST YEAR includes updated advice for dads in the military and others who are separated from their babies, information on preemies and multiples, and specific guidance for adoptive, divorced, and older dads. It also provides invaluable information and practical tips on such issues as:

- The baby's physical, intellectual, verbal, and social development
- Understanding fathers' emotional and psychological development
- Analyzing the baby's temperament
- Planning finances and choosing the right life insurance policy
- Understanding how the new mom is feeling and how the baby will change your relationship
- Being involved even if you're only able to see your baby for a short time every day
- Juggling work and family
- Introducing the baby to reading, music, and even art

"Becoming a father is one of the most dramatic changes a man will ever experience," says Brott. "And the first year of fatherhood is critical, because that's when the initial bonds between father and child form and the foundation of a lifelong relationship is built."

Written with the same thoroughness, accessibility, and humor that have made Brott's NEW FATHER series the most popular fatherhood books in the country, THE NEW FATHER: A DAD'S GUIDE TO THE FIRST YEAR (paperback, $12.95, hardcover, $18.95) incorporates the latest scientific research, the author's personal experiences, and those of the hundreds of new dads he's interviewed. The series, which also includes the best-seller THE EXPECTANT FATHER, is the gold standard in its field. And with over one million copies sold, Brott's books are the essential resource for new dads—and moms—everywhere.

For additional information, review copies, or to schedule an interview with Armin Brott, contact Elizabeth Thompson at MrDad.com

# # #

Figure 8.2　Sample Press Release

media representatives or gatekeepers into reading the release. Media representatives may scan several releases, reading only the headlines. This brief introduction to the information is used to determine whether it is worth their time to read more.

Most consumers of print media handle articles written in newspapers and magazines the same way. Think of the last time you picked up a newspaper. Did you read it cover to cover? Or did you scan the headlines to determine if you were interested in reading the article? If you're like the majority of information consumers, you scanned. When you create a headline for a release, think of how you handle information and what catches your attention. If a headline doesn't interest you, it's guaranteed not to entice the media. To help you gain a greater understanding of what the media looks for, pick up a daily paper and read today's headlines.

Another tip to help you write a captivating headline is to write it last. Just because the headline is the first information a media representative notices doesn't mean you have to write it first. If you're sitting in front of a blank screen and can't seem to capture the essence of your information in one short statement, give your brain a break and move on to the text. Ideas for the headline will come as you develop the personality of your release. Media outlets work in this same manner. All the articles you read are written before a headline is even considered. And if you're lucky enough to have your story printed by a media outlet, don't be surprised when they don't use your original headline.

A standard headline is sufficient for many releases; however, others require a subheading. Subheads are also centered and printed directly below a main headline. Most subheads are typed in a font size slightly smaller than the headline but still larger than the text. Subheads are included when there is a prominent, secondary point of interest in the release or when you determine it's necessary to further detail the content of the release. However, the subhead should never simply restate the headline.

Following are a few samples of headlines with and without subheadlines.

"PHEROMONES IN MALE PERSPIRATION REDUCE WOMEN'S TENSION, ALTER HORMONE RESPONSE" (University of Pennsylvania release, March 14, 2003)

"HAPPILY EVER AFTER . . . WHAT EVERY COUPLE SHOULD KNOW Research Identifies 25 Factors to Predict Marital Satisfaction" (Courtesy BYU Family Studies Center)

Lead. The headline is the bait to lure the media representative into reading the release, but the lead provides the news hook. From the lead, media representatives determine if the information is newsworthy and significant

Why the stress on the lead of the press release?

(Simon, 1983, p. 7)

enough to investigate. The lead must raise public need, concern, or interest and leave media representatives eager for more information. If you don't have a good lead, you might as well not waste your time writing the remainder of the release, because no one will look at it.

"Why the stress on the lead of the press release? The answer is that you are a guest in the mediums' house, and the lead is your calling card. You are also an uninvited guest, and the average daily newspaper and radio-television station receives scores of uninvited guests in every day. Your release competes with many other releases for an editor's attention. The average editor has neither the time nor the inclination to read through scores of press releases. A quick glace through the lead tells the experienced editor if the release will be of any use to him" (Simon, 1983, p. 7).

There are two kinds of releases and thus two kinds of leads—the straight news story and the feature story. A release for a straight news story is direct and to the point. The lead for such a story should contain the 5Ws and 1H: who, what, where, when, why, and how. The most important of these six elements should be included in the first paragraph; the remaining elements may follow in the second paragraph.

Straight news stories, and thus their leads, implement a concept we referred to earlier as the inverted pyramid, where information is presented in descending order of importance.

In other words, they place the most important points first; the second most important point next; and so on, down to the least important.

(Calvert, 2000, p. 18)

When writing in an inverted pyramid, the lead should contain the climax or conclusion of the story, allowing subsequent paragraphs to fill in the details. Supporting material that expands upon the lead may include examples, quotes, statistics, and other facts that build your story. It is important to use the inverted pyramid when you send a release to media representatives because it is the same concept they apply when writing an article. The inverted pyramid provides readers with the essence of the story so they have the most important information regardless of when they quit reading—and quit reading they will.

Once again, place yourself in the shoes of the audience and think of how you consume information. How frequently do you move on to another article before completing the first article you started to read in a newspaper or magazine? Don't expect your audience to be any different. Write your release knowing you most likely will not get in the last word. In addition to the attention factor, the second reason to implement the inverted pyramid is that printed information is cut from the bottom up when there is limited column space. If the climax of your story is at the end, it may get lost in the editing room.

Straight news stories and leads are good for conferences, conventions, professional meetings, awards, new developments, some research, and other breaking news. Following is an example of a straight news lead:

WASHINGTON (AP)—Unmarried couples—whether same-sex or opposite-sex—are far more likely than married couples to mix race or ethnicity, Census Bureau data shows.

About 7% of the nation's 54.5 million married couples are mixed racially or ethnically, compared to about 15% of the 4.9 million unmarried heterosexual couples. The percentage is only slightly lower for the nation's nearly 600,000 same-sex couples. (Associated Press, March 13, 2003)

Historical Note: The media first implemented the concept of the inverted pyramid during the Civil War as field correspondents sent their stories via telegraph. After numerous stories were interrupted due to the enemy cutting communication lines or the system simply malfunctioning, correspondents began sending the most vital information over the wire first. This allowed important information to be relayed to the waiting public regardless of whether or not some of the supporting details were received.

(Anderson & Itule, 2003, p. 44)

A feature story or soft news must also answer who, what, where, when, why and how; however, this information does not necessarily need to be included in the feature's lead. Features are commonly about people, which lends them perfectly to marriage, family, and human development stories. When writing a lead for a feature story, search for a human interest angle that the audience can relate to. You want to make them feel and generate emotion as much as possible. An effective feature lead uses narrative, descriptive language and mental imagery, composing words to develop a picture in the audience's mind. However, be careful not to use too many descriptive or flowery words. Strong verbs are often more effective than an abundance of adjectives. Once the lead captures attention, the supporting information paragraphs must follow with the details.

Following is an example of a feature lead that captures its audience's attention and draws them into the story:

With a wave of the wand and a dance in the night, Cinderella found herself in the arms of Prince Charming and they lived happily ever after . . .

maybe. We missed the follow-up story, but according to 20 years of research, the fantasy most likely got locked in the attic with the glass slippers.

While many enjoy their Cinderella moment as they are swept off their feet, they often find that marriage doesn't chase their problems away with the stepmother. Unresolved issues linger long, much longer, than the echoing of the wedding bells.

You may also use anecdotes or create a scenario to capture the reader's attention. If you can involve the readers in the story, they are more likely to read on to the next paragraph. As a feature lead typically cannot stand alone, make sure to follow a story, anecdote, or scene with an explanation of its significance to the information you are presenting in the remainder of the release. You may find it challenging to make feature leads effective. They often take the longest time to write, but they can also be the most rewarding because of the creativity they require.

Although feature leads typically are not written in an inverted pyramid, the remaining body of the release often presents the information in descending order of importance.

Quotations. Quotations are an essential element to every release. An actual statement from an expert or third party lends credibility to the presented information. Media representatives often look for interesting sound bites to add interest and personality to a story. By providing them with such sound bites, you are more likely to get your message across your way. A direct quotation is the only information from your release that has to be printed verbatim if the media representative chooses to use it. To increase the likelihood of a quotation's inclusion in a media story, write specific, vivid, descriptive statements that reflect the source's personality. Make sure the quotation contains accurate information and that it is easy to understand. If a statement sounds too academic, uses jargon not familiar to the average reader, or belabors a point, it will not be used. Incorporate a quotation into the first page of a release and continue to moderately use them throughout. Use transition paragraphs to lead into a quotation as well as to separate two quotations.

Distribution. Now that you understand the basic principles behind writing a release, how do you distribute it to targeted media outlets? First, you must determine who your targeted outlets are and identify the type of media outlets you want to cover your story: daily newspapers, weekly community papers, magazine, specialty publications, television/radio, and so on. Each type of media outlet has its advantages and disadvantages.

Daily newspapers have a greater circulation and reach a broad range of people; however, the number of subscribers who actually read the paper daily is significantly lower than the circulation numbers imply. Also, of those who do read the paper, studies indicate that they read approximately one fourth of the paper, skipping a majority of information. Dailies are also inundated with information, causing many stories to go uncovered.

On the other hand, weekly community papers have a smaller circulation, but they have a more loyal audience. Weeklies are also more likely to print a release verbatim, as they have a smaller staff and do not receive the mounds of publicity seekers knocking at their door.

Magazines have a longer shelf life than newspapers—typically 3 to 5 weeks. Feature stories frequent magazine pages, and the articles are typically longer, allowing for greater detail or more sources.

Specialty publications directly target your audience. Also, those reading the publication are often actively seeking information.

Television will summarize your information into a sound bite lasting between 30 and 90 seconds. Due to the limited time, television stories focus on the highlights and have to eliminate much of the detailed information. Television is also interested in strong visuals.

Radio seeks for a local connection to the issues it covers and often allows sources to share their message points by participating in a live, on-air, talk show program. However, if your information is simply covered in the news segment, it is subject to the same time limitations as in broadcast television news (approximately 30 seconds or five sentences).

Once you determine the type of media outlets you want to target, it's time to get specific and create the media lists. Start by creating a local media list. From there, create additional media lists to include national outlets that target your intended audience. For example, you may have a media list that focuses on a specific state or region of the country. You may have a magazine media list targeting a specific demographic such as wedding and bridal magazines, health magazines, or family publications. You may also have to adapt your media distribution list each time you send out a release, depending on the topic.

Before distributing a release regarding the latest research findings on siblings of children with disabilities, we researched special-interest publications that went to families of children with disabilities. Our media distribution list was significantly smaller for this particular release (only 11 publications); however, it was also much more targeted. When one of these publications ran a story on the research, the information directly reached those families that were interested and could find personal application, thus making a greater impact on individual lives.

What information do you include in a media list? You want the name and contact information for each media outlet. You also want the name of the specific editor or producer covering your area. The features editor typically filters all family-related information; however, some publications have a reporter dedicated specifically to family matters. You can find all this information in Bacon's media guides. Your local library should have current copies, or you may contact Bacon to purchase your own copy at Bacon's Information Inc., 332 South Michigan Ave., Chicago, IL 60604 (telephone 312-922-2400).

As you create a targeted media list, it is helpful to contact each outlet by phone and verify that the contact information is correct, including the specific media representative to whom you intend to send your information. You will be surprised at how many changes you will have to make even though Bacon's updates the information in its guides annually.

There are also newswire services, such as PR Newswire, willing to distribute your release for a cost. If you can afford it, this is the easiest way to distribute a release, as you don't have to do any of the footwork outside of sending the wire service your release and identifying the type of media outlets you would like to receive the release. You may contact your local PR Newswire representative through the company's Web site, e-mail, or toll-free number: www.prenewswire.com, information@prnewswire.com (telephone 1-888-776–0942).

Newspaper Column Article

As an expert, you can work with your local newspaper to print a regular column on a given general topic (e.g., family, marriage, parenthood). If the paper agrees to run the column after they have seen a sample of your writing, be prepared to generate fresh ideas constantly. You can't just decide one week that you are too busy or that you don't have an idea to write about, because a good column will eventually generate a loyal audience. You are committed. Once you have agreed to write a regular column, start keeping an idea folder for those times when your mind is in a drought for ideas.

Column articles often offer advice, insights, answer questions, and sometimes simply entertain with anecdotes and personal experiences related to the topic. A column is a great opportunity to share your personal yet professionally informed opinion with a large number of people whom you otherwise would never reach. Column writing is casual, like a letter from one friend to another. The writing should also give its readers insight into the columnist's personality. Existing FLE programs you are already doing can form a basis for articles you write.

You may be surprised at the impact a simple column article may have. One family life educator had a regular biweekly article called "Family Matters" that was sent out via university communication services and ran in an average of 13 Montana newspapers per release, as well as in a few regional papers. His photo accompanied the articles, so he was occasionally recognized as he traveled the state. At a conference in Billings, a marriage and family therapist from a remote rural area approached the educator and told him that articles the educator wrote were leading people to realize that changes in family life were needed and they were coming to the therapist for counseling.

Radio Programs

Radio programs are short, prerecorded informational segments or they are question-and-answer programs focusing on a specific topic. For example, Zion's Bank of Utah records a radio program featuring a different local business each day. The program does not promote the bank other than mentioning that it is the sponsor of the program. Another example is Intermountain Health Care recording a daily health tip.

Radio scripts follow a basic structure, including an introduction, a teaser or headline, the main information or advice, a billboard, and a closing, including identification. Here is an example of a prerecorded radio script:

From the Montana State University Extension Service, here's Steve Duncan with a tip on balancing work and family.

Ever feel bombarded when you come home at the end of a hard day? Try taking 15 minutes to unwind before attacking the new demands of home. It may be one of the best things you can do for your family. The shift from work to family is largely mental, but there are some physical things you can do to help it along.

Before you leave work, make a list of everything you need to do the next day. This will help you leave those tasks behind and clear your mind for home activities.

Have a predinner snack such as fruit, vegetables and dip, cheese and crackers, or a cup of soup. This will stave off that starving feeling and you won't have to jump immediately into preparing dinner.

Play your favorite music, get a cool drink, and relax while you read the mail.

Walking, bike riding, swimming, or playing tennis may offer time with our spouse or children, as long as it relaxes you.

I'm Steve Duncan, Family and Human Development Specialist, with the MSU Extension Service.

Letter to the Editor or Opinion Editorial

If you have a strong opinion about a specific topic, especially one covered in a publication's editorial pages or by a radio talk show host, you're always welcome to submit a letter to the editor. As with all press materials, there is no guarantee that your letter will be printed or read on the air. If the editor does decide to include your letter, it will be printed or read verbatim. Keep all letters to the editor short. Get directly to your point of view and don't ramble. Sign the letter and include your city of residence.

Opinion editorials are similar to letters to the editor because you have control of the content. One advantage to an opinion editorial is that you can expand on your point of view a little more with 500 to 750 words. One disadvantage is that op-ed articles are harder to place. Not all papers include space for them. You can request a listing of the papers that do by writing to the National Survey of Newspaper Op Ed Pages, Post Office Box 213, Saguache, CO 81149. Include your title, affiliation, and contact information at the end of your op-ed.

Public Service Announcement

The Federal Trade Communications Commission (FCC) on its Form 303, Statement of TV Program Service, section IV, page iii, defines a public service announcement (PSA) as "[a]ny announcement for which no charge is made and which promotes programs, activities or services for federal, state or local governments or the programs, activities or services of nonprofit organizations and other announcements regarded as serving community interest, excluding time signals, routine weather announcements and promotional announcements."

It is important to note that a PSA is not free advertising for a company or organization. A PSA may mention the name of the company or organization, but all other content must focus on serving the community interest. An intended audience will never hear or see a PSA that appears too commercial.

With limited airtime, most radio PSAs are limited to short scripts read by the announcer. Television PSAs may also be submitted as scripts to be read by a television personality or announcer, or they may be prerecorded spots comparable to any paid advertising commercial. In television, submitting a script is the least expensive route, but a prerecorded spot has greater impact and is more likely to be used. Antismoking and antidrug spots are common PSAs seen in today's programming.

WRITING GUIDELINES ●

Regardless of the communications tool(s) you select to distribute to the media and reach your end target audience, you need to follow some basic writing guidelines. First, all media materials are written according to the *Associated Press (AP) Stylebook.* Some common AP rules include not using a comma before the last item in a series of three, spelling out all numbers under 10, not capitalizing official titles such as president or vice president of individuals in a company if it follows their given name, and using only an individual's last name after the first reference. These are only a few of the hundreds of guidelines listed in the stylebook. Copies of the *AP Stylebook* are available at most bookstores. You can also write and request a copy from Associated Press, AP News Features Department, 50 Rockefeller Plaza, New York, NY 10020.

Second, write tight, short, and clearly. Sentences should average 15 to 20 words. Once you get 30 or more words in one sentence, you start to sacrifice readability. Break up long sentences with more periods. If this is not possible, use a dash or colon to create a bite-sized thought. A sentence shorter than 20 words may be used on occasion if it adds impact, but be careful not to lose your message. Keep your paragraphs short as well. Media outlets print most information in columns. A long paragraph can seem uninviting in such a narrow space. Pick up a newspaper and look at the length of the paragraphs. Although they vary from one sentence to several sentences, they remain relatively short. Remember, space is a premium, so there is no place for redundancy, an abundance of adjectives, or nonessential information.

Third, use common, simple words. Two simple words are often more readable than one complex or technical word. This is sometimes difficult for individuals who are used to writing for peer-reviewed journals. Remember, when writing for the media, your audience is not comprised of colleagues who are familiar with the topic and issues. Rather, you are trying to reach individuals, parents, and families who may have no background related to the topic but who are interested in and need the information. If there is a word that you would not typically use when talking outside of work, then don't use it when writing for the media.

Following is an example of two sentences that are too technical and use unnecessary jargon:

- We live in a world of objects and events that are multimodal and dynamic.
- Organisms make sense of this flux of stimulation by perceiving events that are unitary despite changing stimulation to multiple sensory systems.

Such writing limits your audience and the value of your message significantly. Only those involved in the research or the study of similar areas would understand the intent of these two sentences.

Review the following two sentences and determine which one clearly communicates the intended message:

- Depending on whether the tempo was seen, heard, or seen and heard, infants would stare or lose interest during various times.
- Infants maintained or lost interest in the event depending on whether both their visual and auditory senses were used or just one of the two senses was stimulated.

Fourth, use the active voice, where the subject acts upon the object. The active voice can help keep your sentences short as well as maintain interest. It is always better to demonstrate an action rather than just tell about it. Also, active verbs invite the reader into the story more than *to be* verbs.

Finally, edit and rewrite all press materials. There is always a better way to write a sentence or explain a concept. Don't become so attached to your first draft that you can't scrap it for a better one. As you read through your press materials, look for ways to shorten, simplify, and add action. Imagine that you'll receive a dollar for every word you eliminate without changing the meaning of the content. It may surprise you how many wasted words were included in the first draft. Double-check all facts and spelling of names. Make sure there are absolutely no spelling or typographical errors.

Broadcast writing for both television and radio employs many of the same basic writing guidelines as print; however, there are a few differences.

Robert Gunnings: Ten Principles of Clear Writing

1. Keep sentences short on the average.

2. Prefer the simple to the complex.

3. Prefer the familiar word.

4. Avoid unnecessary words.

5. Put action into your verbs.

6. Write the way you talk.

7. Use terms your reader can picture.

8. Tie in with your reader's experience.

9. Make full use of variety.

10. Write to express, not to impress.

(Anderson & Itule, 2003, p. 32)

The primary factor dictating these differences is that broadcast writing is heard rather than read; it is written for the ear, not the eye. Broadcast writing has a very limited amount of time to capture and maintain the audience's attention while simultaneously giving information. Visual images are created with words to help the audience experience the story, not just hear it. Simple, direct visual language paints word pictures.

Writing for Television and Radio

First Sentence:
The Grabber: Summarize the story in one sentence in a way that entices the viewer or listener to want to hear and see more.

Second Sentence:
Visualization: Describe the video the viewer sees on the screen for television or use words to create the video in the listeners' mind for radio. Enhance the visual image or create the visual image.

Third Sentence:
The Facts: List the important facts about what happened in a short sentence.

Fourth Sentence:
The Setup: Set up the sound bite or actuality. In radio you need to use the person's name and title so we understand from whom we'll hear and why we should care. In television you can use a blind lead.
Sound Bite or Actuality: Select the portion of the interview to tell the story. This should not run longer than 10 to 20 seconds. It should not contain facts, because the reporter can tell the facts. It should contain emotional or editorial statements the reporter cannot make.

Fifth Sentence:
The Big Finish: Summarize what will happen or what will likely happen in the future because of the foregoing information.

Source: Courtesy of Robert Walz, KUTV Channel 2 reporter and BYU Professor of
        Communications.

When writing for broadcast, the inverted pyramid is not necessary. Facts are not presented in descending order but rather are incorporated into a complete package that holds the audience's attention throughout. It is essential that the information is presented in a fluid, easy manner for the viewer or listener to follow. Scripts must also be written for easy reading by the broadcaster.

Other writing guidelines that pertain to television and radio writing include the following:

- Use a conversational tone and write as if you were talking to a friend. You need to write with simple, common words that the viewer or listener will understand the first time. Broadcast audiences do not have the option to go back and reread information they missed or did not understand as print audiences do.
- Keep all sentences short. In print you want to vary the length of your sentences for interest. However, using short sentences in broadcast ensures that the meaning is not lost.
- Simplify and round off complicated numbers. "Three and a quarter million dollars" is easier for viewers or listeners to hear than is "3,243,975 dollars."
- Use the phonetic spelling of uncommon or complicated words and names. Viewers and listeners will never see the phonetic spelling, but it helps the broadcaster pronounce it properly.
- Summarize statements instead of using quotation marks.
- Place the title of an individual before his or her name.
- Avoid abbreviations to eliminate confusion. Only use acronyms that are more common than the actual name (i.e., FBI, NCAA, CNN). When it is necessary to use a common acronym, place a hyphen between each letter (i.e., F-B-I).

● MEDIA INTERVIEWS

Now that you have learned how to build relationships with media representatives, catch their attention with newsworthy information, select the right press materials, and write clearly and succinctly, you can sit back and relax. Right? Sure you can, that is, until a media representative calls you wanting a "live" interview. Those beads of sweat appearing on your forehead are for a good reason. You have seen too many people stammer around not knowing what to say or, worse yet, get trapped by an unexpected, leading question. What if you make a mistake or sound dumb? Fear is a natural reaction to a request for an interview, but it is a manageable fear with a little research and preparation.

Research

Start by researching the interview medium and environment. Television and radio interviews may be live, with no editing, or taped, allowing the producer to edit at will. Live interviews are more intimidating because there is no room for mistakes. Everything you say and do is seen and/or heard by the audience. However, this may also serve as an advantage, as a producer cannot edit out any comments you want the audience to hear. A taped interview may not make you as nervous, but many of your comments will be cut. You may be disappointed when a half-hour interview results in a 30-second sound bite.

Television

Television interviews are shorter than other media due to the fast-paced nature of television news. Each story typically lasts from 30 to 90 seconds. In a television interview, you must pay attention to your appearance and mannerisms.

Radio

On a radio talk show, there are many interruptions. You have to pause for every commercial as well as for scheduled news or traffic and weather breaks. You will also have to listen to the talk show host's comments and opinions in between his or her questions. Many shows allow listeners to phone in with comments and questions. While many callers make a valuable contribution, be prepared for the occasional caller who may take you off guard.

Print

Interviews for print media are typically a little longer than broadcast, as the media representative is allotted more space to elaborate on a topic. Some journalists prefer to interview in person, but more are conducting interviews over the phone and asking sources to fax or e-mail additional information. With more time for interviews and more space allotted for the story, you are also more likely to have many of your message points included in the story. Unfortunately, in print media there is also a greater likelihood of a journalist misquoting you than when you are taped for television or radio. For this reason, it is wise to inform reporters that you are taping the conversation and they are welcome to reference the recording when they write the story.

Next, research interviewers. Review material previously produced by interviewers to get a feel for the type of stories they present. Do they primarily cover controversial issues? Are their stories fair and well rounded, or leading and somewhat biased? Do they have a reputation for getting the dirt and asking all the tough questions? It is also appropriate to directly ask interviewers what type of a story they are preparing and who else they are interviewing. Once you understand the direction media representatives want to take the story, you can begin shaping your messages.

Preparation

Target Audience

Determine your primary, target audience. Be specific—a "general" audience does not exist. Think about who you want to hear your message so you can direct all comments to them rather than the media. If the story is about children coping with divorce, are newlywed couples your target audience? Probably not.

Self-Interest

Once you determine your target audience, identify the audience's self-interest in relation to the topic. What motivates them? Using our first example of children coping with divorce, you decide your target audience is divorced parents or parents in the process of getting a divorce. Their self-interest is dissolving a marriage with the least amount of emotional damage to their children. Now you can develop specific message points tied to the target audience's self-interest.

Primary Message Points

Although you may have many facts you would like to share with your target audience, it is important to try to limit your main message points to three. These three points are what you want your audience to remember if they don't retain anything else. Main message points are not the details but rather general statements that may serve as headings or even memory joggers for your supporting information. To help the audience remember your three primary message points, tie them in to the audience's self-interest and repeat them often in an interview. Politicians and talking heads are usually well trained on message repetition and can serve as good examples. The next time you watch a news program, listen to how frequently the individual being interviewed repeats the same sentence. Media representatives often try to elicit a different response by altering the question slightly. However, a well-trained spokesperson will not fall for this trick but will rather stick to the message point and repeat it until the interviewer moves on. The more you repeat a message point, the more likely the audience is to remember and the less likely you are to get off track or to make a comment you later regret. Although you want to stick to your message points, you may support them with additional information, including examples, anecdotes, statistics, and quotes. Remember to repeat, repeat, repeat.

Who is in control of the interview is up to you. Although the interviewer asks the questions, your answers direct the flow of information. If an interviewer tries to take a story in another direction than you prefer, simply come back to your message points. Answer the interviewer's question, followed by a main message. Following are a few examples:

- "Yes [the answer], and in addition [message point]."
- "No [the answer]; let me explain [message point]."
- "I don't know about that, but what I do know is [message point]."

Even with repetition, a lot of information is given in an interview. It is important to help your audience remember the main message points by emphasizing and summarizing them. For example:

- "That is interesting, but I think it is most important to remember . . ."
- "It boils down to this . . ."
- "Let me emphasize . . ."
- "It is critical to remember . . ."

Interview Control

To reiterate a main point from the previous section, when you are in an interview situation, get your message points across. An answer plus a key message equals your response. To ensure that the integrity of your message is maintained, it is acceptable to tape all interviews. Taping an interview is like taking out misquote insurance. Although it doesn't guarantee that your words will never be taken out of context, it does extend a safety cord for recourse. If this does happen to you, request a retraction or correction statement.

Also, keep your cool at all times. Never act defensive when an interview turns hostile or you are put on the hot seat. If you stay in control and stick to your message points, you maintain credibility with the audience. In addition, know when to stop talking. Experienced media representatives have mastered the power of the "silent pause." They have found that when they allow silence to linger, human nature taunts the individual they are interviewing to fill the pause. It is during these ramblings that the media obtains its juiciest quotes and the interviewee pulls away from message points and may speculate or make a statement that he or she later regrets. Once you have answered the question and stated a key message, then stop and wait for the next question, regardless of how long the silence hangs (it's probably not as long as you think it is anyway).

You need to maintain a high level of energy throughout an interview. A low-key response may be fine in a normal conversation, but it appears negative and boring in a radio or television interview. You should also maintain eye contact with the interviewer and sit erect or even lean forward slightly. Don't fidget; it's annoying. You can, however, use natural hand movements, just not so many that it distracts from your message. Also, don't forget to listen. If you're too busy thinking of what you're going to say next instead of listening, you may miss the boat and say something unrelated, or worse yet, miss an opportunity for a better comment than the one you're rehearsing in your head.

Finally, people wonder what to wear for an interview. Dress in your typical business attire for a print or radio interview. Dress conservatively for a television interview. You don't want what you wear to distract from your message. If you choose to wear a print, keep it simple and unobtrusive. Although it might be uncomfortable for a man, allow the station to apply makeup if they offer. You'll be glad you did when see yourself on the television.

Interview DON'Ts

1. Never say, "No comment." "No comment" means "guilty" to most people who hear it.

2. Never say anything off the record. Assume all microphones are live. The most important rule is never say anything you don't want to see on TV or read on the front page of a newspaper.

3. Never lie to a reporter.

4. Never lose your temper. Be polite, but firm.

5. Never use profanity or slang. Don't tell jokes. Don't say anything that could even remotely be constructed to be off color, sexist, or racist. Don't comment on anyone's age, religion, or politics. Tell jokes ONLY if they are self-deprecating.

6. Never say "uh." Drop all the "uhs" from your speech.

7. Never wave your hands. Don't bob and weave your head around. Sit still.

8. Never answer hypothetical questions. Don't speculate. Be specific. Stick to what you know.

9. Never comment on what others have said—particularly if you haven't seen or heard it. Don't verify something that might not be true.

10. Never use doublespeak, government-speak, or jargon. Use numbers in an interesting way. Make your information easy to understand. Personalize your information. Relate it to the reporter or the target audience. Humanize it.

11. Never talk to a reporter without doing your homework. Prepare. Turn the interview into a "sales call."

12. Never stop talking after you've answered a yes or no question. Keep going. Say something like, "Yes, but you should also know . . ." or "No, but let me elaborate . . ."

Interview DO's

1. Do your homework before you talk to a reporter. Be prepared for the reporter's worst questions with three positive points you want to get across. Practice what you want to say. Remember, you're selling your activity. Talking to a reporter is an "opportunity."

2. Speak in short sentences using plain English. For TV and radio, think in terms of 20- or 30-second answers. This ensures that the reporter will use what you say.

3. Smile. Act like you enjoy what you're doing. Call reporters by their first name; reach out and physically touch the reporter. Look interested in what you're doing.

4. Tell a POSITIVE story. You do a lot of good things; tell the reporter about your three positive points.

5. If you don't know the answer, say, "I don't know." If you do know the answer and can't tell it now, tell the reporter when you can give him or her the answer. Refer the reporter to someone who does know the answer or offer to find out who does.

6. If a TV station offers you makeup, accept it. The TV camera will add 10 years and 10 pounds. Remember, the TV pros all wear makeup.

7. Dress conservatively and simply. Be remembered for what you said, not what you wore. Ignore this rule if you're a rock star.

8. Stop talking when you've made your point. Let the reporter worry about empty air space. Stick to your subject. Don't speculate.

9. If a reporter asks several questions in a row, pick the one you want to answer. Or ask the reporter to repeat the question.

10. Have show-and-tell material. A simple pie chart works well. Have a videotape? Take it too.

11. Take advantage of the opportunity at the end of the interview when the reporter asks if there is anything you'd like to add. Repeat your three positive points and summarize.

(Calvert, 2000, p. 107)

● CONCLUSION

Communicating FLE messages through media channels represents tremendous opportunities to reach large audiences. Knowledge of the media and skill at crafting messages for public use via print, radio, and television is necessary if FLEs are to have the greatest impact for good.

● EXPLORATIONS

1. Read the following headlines. Determine which stories are newsworthy and identify the standard criteria you applied to make your decision.
   a. Former Vice President Al Gore to Speak on New Book, "Joined at the Heart: The Transformation of the American Family," at Local University
   b. Parenting Workshop to Be Held at Panguich Civic Center
   c. Las Vegas Chapel of Love Reports an Increase in Wedding Ceremonies
   d. Massachusetts Legalizes Same-Sex Marriage
   e. Marriage, the New Social Status According to Trend Reports

2. Determine a holiday, event, or time of year that is appropriate to repackage and pitch research on playground aggression to the media for additional coverage.

3. Change the following sentences to the active voice:
   a. The shy child was shunned by the kids at the playground.
   b. The premarital assessment will be completed by the couple before they marry.
   c. They were focused on each other's problems before receiving counseling.

4. Simplify and clarify the following sentence:

A ubiquitous example is the use of clinical and psychometric diagnoses to account for students' lack of learning.

5. Write a 30-second radio script on a topic related to your field of study. You may elect to write a script for a radio PSA or a radio program.

6. Given the following information,
   a. Identify the target audience,
   b. Identify the three primary message points,
   c. Write an interesting lead that grabs the reader's attention.

You, along with a team of researchers and professionals, have developed a program, Marriage Focus, to help couples strengthen their marriage while weathering the transition to parenthood. The program includes an educational video and a workbook. The program is divided into four sessions. Each session focuses on a quality (identified through research) that may enhance a couple's marriage as they become new parents: friendship, generosity, fairness, and loyalty. The value of strengthening a relationship in preparation for parenthood is stressed throughout the program. The program is administered in conjunction with your local hospital's childbirth classes.

CHAPTER 9

WRITING FOR
THE LAY AUDIENCE

T he written word forms a conversation between a writer and a reader. At times the words may feel like a stern lecture. Other times the conversation may seem pointless, dense, or wrong-headed. Yet, at best, the written conversation expresses the writer's soul, engages and enriches the reader, and builds a bridge between both.

The first part of this chapter provides suggestions for effective writing. The latter part of the chapter provides samples of excellent writing in very different styles.

● PURPOSES OF WRITTEN MATERIAL

I (Goddard) was asked to evaluate a short Web course on parenting that was intended for a general audience. Several considerations seemed important in evaluating any stretch of writing.

What is the target audience like? For example, is the audience primarily first-time parents of newborns? Or are there likely to be many readers who are parents of school-age children or teenagers? Are the readers seeking general information, or are the parents seeking answers to specific problems because the Web site caters to parents of problem teens?

What do the parents already know? What is their previous experience with this Web site or other parenting materials?

What are the objectives of the course or article? The obvious answer may be "to give parents information that will help them be more effective." But the article may have additional objectives. Maybe a primary objective is to motivate the reader to be a regular visitor to the Web site. Maybe the article is intended to promote a certain book, program, or product. Maybe the article is intended to challenge a common idea that is presumed to undermine the parents' parenting efforts.

Unfortunately, our writing experiences for university classes often have a very different objective: to prove to professors that we know more than we do. In service of that cause, we may write in great depth and length, using technical jargon and barely related references. Those practices are rarely effective in writing for professors and will surely be unhelpful in writing for a real-world audience.

Evaluating the Course

The title of the course that I reviewed was Identifying Your Parenting Style. The Web site was designed to help primarily parents of teens who were in trouble. I assumed that the course would provide some process for identifying the readers' parenting style and challenges and would make recommendations for more effective parenting. I was surprised to find that the course was focused on summarizing Diana Baumrind's work. It defined and frequently used terms such as *authoritative, authoritarian,* and *laissez-faire*. The objective seemed to be to enable parents to name and describe Baumrind's categories of parenting.

Such depth and jargon may be more appropriate for a college course than for a lay audience, especially since the terms can be confusing. In writing for a lay audience, we usually want to provide readers with clear understanding and move them fairly quickly to action steps. Extensive background information may not be necessary.

There are many ways to approach the subject. I have a colleague who uses objects to illustrate parenting styles: the marshmallow parent may be sweet but melts under heat and squishes under pressure; the jawbreaker parent may be tough but is brittle and inflexible; the tennis ball parent is flexible but has reasonable boundaries. The useful question is not whether those categories map perfectly onto research designations, but whether the idea will be clear, memorable, and useful in moving parents toward actions that are supported by research.

Another approach is to discuss important parenting dimensions. The central dimensions in child guidance are (a) warmth, nurturance, and support, together with (b) monitoring and firmness (see Peterson & Hann, 1999). An effort to educate parents might describe ways to be both warm and firm.

While research provides the skeleton of our recommendations, our real-life experience provides the flesh. From our experiences we draw stories, metaphors, and an intuitive sense of ways to apply the research. For example, in writing for a lay audience, we might observe that most parents find either warmth or firmness to come more naturally. We can use our strength while developing and managing our weaker side.

● TIPS ON WRITING

It is tempting to hope that there is some tidy formula for writing effectively for lay audiences. Just as in all processes with humans, there are sensible steps but no magic formulas.

Rico and Volk (1999) have described a "natural" process to turn thoughts into written words. This approach may be especially helpful for those who are daunted by a blank page.

For those who have the words but want guidelines, LaRocque (2003) may be useful. She provides a dozen guidelines to good writing such as keep sentences short, avoid pretensions (don't write as if you were writing for a professor!), use active verbs, and get right to the point. In addition to the dozen guidelines, LaRocque also provides useful helps on storytelling. Her book is filled with practical examples from her experience as a writing coach.

In addition to the guides described above, there are other recommendations that make your writing more likely to be effective.

Read Widely to Develop Your Own Style

To become an effective writer, it is useful to be an active reader. Read articles from newspapers and magazine. Note what works for you and what doesn't. Save those that you consider to be both most effective and most similar to the voice you want to develop.

You may favor a lively and irreverent style such as Dave Barry's (1991): "So most married couples, even though they love each other very much in theory, tend to view each other in practice as large teeming flaw colonies" (p. 208).

Carol Tavris's (1989) writing is clear and richly visual: "The individualism of American life, to our glory and despair, creates anger and encourages its release; for when everything is possible, limitations are irksome. When the desires of the self come first, the needs of others are annoying. When we think we deserve it all, reaping only a portion can enrage" (p. 69).

Many readers enjoy the writing of Sam Quick (Quick & Lasueur, 2003): "Peace is still possible in the hustle and bustle of modern life, but it thrives on the quiet times. Preferably in the morning before the activities of the day claim you, cultivate a state of inner quietness. You might read briefly from an inspirational source, enjoy a period of meditation and prayer, or keep a journal about something wonderful and close to your heart" (p. 1).

You may choose to write with the power and directness of Martin Seligman (1991): "Freud's speculations were built on very little observation and a very free use of imagination. He claimed that depression was anger turned against the self. . . . For all its hold over the American (particularly the Manhattan) imagination, I have to say that this view is preposterous" (pp. 10-11).

Some of the passages above were written for an educated and informed audience. They may be too complex for some of the people we serve with family life education (FLE). In many cases, FLE is written to an eighth-grade reading level. LaRocque (2003) has written about writing with simplicity and clarity. She argues that "short words are small, strong, and suited to story telling. . . . We should trust them more" (p. 31).

Each of the authors above has developed a voice that is distinctive and effective for his or her purpose and personality. Martin Seligman would probably not succeed at efforts to write Dave Barry's humor columns. Dave Barry does not have the technical knowledge or disposition to write a thorough treatise such as Tavris has written. Reading widely can help us find and develop our own voices, whether it is closer to one of those above or one very different.

Some writers use a more formal style, some use a more conversational one. Some write objectively. Some feel comfortable with a personal and disclosing style. Just as in all relationships, we use our unique style to deliver a message that speaks to our audience.

It is tempting to recommend one process of writing. Many people recommend a thorough outline. There are others who prefer to let the material lead them to unexpected places. It takes hundreds of hours of experience to develop a writing voice.

In the latter part of this chapter are samples of very different styles of writing about family. You may get ideas for your unique style by examining these samples.

Know Your Audience

It makes a great deal of difference whether your audience is readers of a metropolitan newspaper, a technical company newsletter, or an elderly homemakers' book of hints. It is important to know the audience. But even a thorough demographic profile is not enough. What are the current issues? What is their history (e.g., what are the articles they have previously read? What historical cohort are they a part of?)? What is the culture of their group?

Clearly there are no simple or easily accessible answers to these questions. That is why it is wise to ask questions of members of the group and those who have worked with them or written for them.

I (Goddard) have written articles that I thought were clear and direct. A helpful editor has responded with a multitude of questions: "Who is this person? Why should we trust him?" "What does this word mean in this context?" "What is the background to this idea?" We may get so accustomed to communicating with our professional peers that we lose touch with the language of our audience. A good editor can alert us to communication failures. It can also be useful to have our material read by members of the target audience who are brave enough to be honest.

In some cases, you may be writing for a low-literacy audience. While all the suggestions for writing for lay audiences in general apply to writing for this audience, there are special considerations in writing effectively for those with limited literacy. For additional information on writing for low-literacy audiences, see specialized instructions, such as Gaston and Daniels (n.d.).

In one case I was asked to prepare a message for Title I parents in a poor, rural Alabama school district. In preparation, I drove to the community, walked around the neighborhoods, asked questions at a convenience store, and interviewed a mother of two children in the school. The experience was humbling. I may know something about research on parenting, but if I do not understand my audience, I am not very likely to help them. Their day-to-day challenges and experiences are very different from mine. I know my message was humbler, and I think it was more helpful because of my efforts to understand the audience.

Clearly Define Your Purpose

Very often we have something we want to say but we are not quite sure what it is. It is more a flurry of impressions than a distinct message. Try to express in one sentence exactly what you would like your audience to know, feel, and do. For example, with a workplace newsletter, your objective might be to "challenge old ideas in the area of couple relationships so that the readers will be anxious for more information as delivered through future columns."

In addition to the single-objective statement, it is often very useful to identify two or three supporting ideas per article or chapter. "1. Readers will understand the limitations of frank communication for improving relationships. 2. Readers will understand the importance of kindness in relationships. 3. Readers will be encouraged to identify three ways to effectively show kindness."

Write Simply and Clearly

For our colleagues it may be effective to write, "Research shows that marital quality and stability is primarily related to the occurrence and maintenance of positive feelings, interactions, and behaviors that promote attraction, closeness, and personal support of another person." How would you communicate the same idea to a lay audience?

The idea could be communicated with a simple statement: "Strong marriages come from finding positive ways of being together." It might also be useful to use an anecdote to illustrate.

Another example: "The famous religious thinker Martin Luther once declared, 'Marriage is the school of love.'" The same idea might be communicated more clearly with the words "Marriage can help us learn valuable lessons about love."

Still another example: "William James, known by some as the father of modern psychology, once stated, 'The deepest craving of human nature is the craving to be appreciated.' In marriage, we long to feel that our partner respects and appreciates us. How can marital partners meet this craving for appreciation in ways that build and strengthen the relationship?" Instead, we could simply ask, "Do people like to be appreciated? How can you show appreciation that supports your partner?"

EXAMPLES OF EFFECTIVE WRITING ●

As you read the following examples of writing for a lay audience, notice the distinct characteristics of each piece. Consider those factors that would make it effective for some audiences and less effective for others. You will note that some of the passages are written in a more professional voice and others in a more conversational voice. As you study them, you will probably find that one or more of them feel very comfortable to you. Look for writing that uses a voice you might like to use.

Martha Beck, from *The Joy Diet* (2003, pp. 92-93, 192-193)

These days, I'm less like a nurturing, nondirective therapist than a skydiving instructor who stands at the open door of an airplane and methodically shoves terrified students into thin air. Experience has taught me that the way to a joyful life is always fraught with fear, that to find it you must follow your heart's desires right through the inevitable terrors that arise to hold you back. If you don't do this, your life will be shaped by fear, rather than love, and I guarantee, the shape will be narrow and tiny compared with your best destiny.

I once had a client named Pierre who wanted very much to find the right woman but was terrified of rejection. We were both thrilled when Pierre met Emily, the aerobics instructor of his dreams, and their first three dates went beautifully. Then catastrophe struck, at least from Pierre's perspective: Emily called to say she'd have to take a rain check on their next evening out, because her uncle had died and she had to go out of town for the funeral.

"Pretty obvious what's going on, isn't it?" Pierre said after telling me this.

"Um, well, I guess so," I said. "Her uncle died. She has to go to the funeral."

Pierre snorted derisively. "Oh please. It's my hair. She figured out I'm losing my hair." He was so convinced of this that he was planning to end the relationship.

I reacted so strongly to Pierre's biased interpretation of his interaction with Emily (I think I laughed out loud for a full minute) that he decided to do a little research before he passed judgment. He found a website for the newspaper in the town where Emily's uncle had supposedly lived and died. Sure enough, they had run a recent obituary for someone with Emily's surname, and the funeral was on the very day she had claimed to be attending it. Pierre's relationship was back on.

H. Wallace Goddard, an excerpt from "The Cat Door" in *The Great Self Mystery* (1995), a five-part program intended to help adolescents discover and use their gifts

Kesha studied the room wide-eyed. Never had she seen so many gadgets. Sam laughed at her. "Haven't you ever seen a lab before?" Kesha shook her head in amazement. "What do all these things do?"

"My mom's an inventor," Sam explained. "She thinks of new ways of doing things. Like this." Sam led Kesha to a table covered with motors, metal rods, wires, and miniature doors. "Mom is developing an automatic door for cats to enter the house."

Kesha half scowled and half smiled. "That seems so silly."

"Maybe. But even the electric can opener seemed pretty silly years ago," Sam replied.

"But what if some other animals come along? The door will open and you'll have families of armadillos and skunks and possums in the house!"

Sam shrugged. "That's what inventing is all about, I guess. Trying to find some ways to solve old problems without making new ones."

As they continued through the lab, Kesha marveled at all the projects. "And your mom does this for a living?"

"That's right. She has a lab right here in our home and she invents."

"I love the creative part of this, but . . ." Kesha hesitated, "how does her inventing pay all the bills?"

"That's a good question for you to ask her sometime." Sam led the way from the lab through the living room to the kitchen. "Here, have a cookie."

Kesha eyed the cookie suspiciously. It looked like a normal chocolate chip cookie. "So, Sam, are you going to be an inventor like your mom?"

Sam looked surprised. "Oh, no! I'm not an inventor! I'm very different from my mom! Mom has all kinds of new ideas and she's great with machines."

"So . . . what are you good at?"

"Hmmmm . . ." Sam thought for a long time. "That's a good question. I'm not sure. But I know I am no good at inventing."

Martin E. P. Seligman, excerpt from Chapter 11, "Love," from *Authentic Happiness* (2002, pp. 185-186)

Work can be a source of a level of gratification that far outstrips wages, and by becoming a calling, it displays the peculiar and wondrous capacity of our species for deep commitment. Love goes one better.

The tedious law of *homo economicus* maintains that human beings are fundamentally selfish. Social life is seen as governed by the same bottom-line principles as the marketplace. So, just as in making a purchase or deciding on a stock, we supposedly ask ourselves of another human being, "What is their likely utility for us?" The more we expect to gain, the more we invest in the other person. Love, however, is evolution's most spectacular way of defying this law.

There is a time in life (later, we pray, rather than sooner) that we all go into a tailspin. We age, sicken, or lose our looks, money, or power. We become, in short, a bad investment for future payouts. Why are we not immediately set out on the proverbial ice floe to perish? How is it that we are allowed to limp onward, enjoying life often for many years beyond these times? It is because other people, through the selfishness-denying power of love and friendship, support us. Love . . . is the emotion that makes another person irreplaceable to us. Love displays the capacity of human beings to make commitments that transcend "What have you done for me lately?" and mocks the theory of universal human selfishness. Emblematic of this are some of the most uplifting words it is ever vouchsafed for a person to say: "From this day forward, for better, for worse, for richer, for poorer, in sickness or in health, to love and to cherish until death do us part."

William J. Doherty, from *Take Back Your Marriage* (2001, p. 105)

I think of long-term marriage like I think about living in my home state of Minnesota, in Lake Wobegon, perhaps. You move into marriage in the springtime of hope, but eventually arrive at the Minnesota winter with its cold and darkness. Many of us are tempted to give up and move south at this point. We go to a therapist for help. Some therapists don't know how to help us cope with winter, and we get frostbite in their care. Other therapists tell us that we are being personally victimized by winter, that we deserve better, that winter will never end, and that if we are true to ourselves we will leave our marriage and head south. The problem of course is that our next marriage will enter its own winter at some point. Do we just keep moving on, or do we make our stand now—with this person, in this season? That's the moral, existential question we face when our marriage is in trouble.

A good therapist, a brave therapist, will help us to cling together as a couple, warming each other against the cold of winter, and to seek out whatever sunlight is still available while we wrestle with our pain and disillusionment. A good therapist, a brave therapist, will be the last one in the room to give up on our marriage, not the first one, knowing that the next springtime in Minnesota can be all the more glorious for the winter that we endured together.

John M. Gottman, from Chapter 8, "Strengthening the Foundations," in *Why Marriages Succeed or Fail* (1994, pp. 224-225)

Finding the Glory in Your Marital Story

One sure sign of a strong marriage is a couple's tendency to "glorify" the struggles they've been through together. In interviews, we found that a stable couple will describe their marriage in terms of a worthwhile journey, a saga in which they face adversity and become closer because of it. They tell detailed stories about certain traumas or intense experiences that bonded them to one another. They say they've come through troubled times feeling more committed and hopeful about their relationship.

It's not that couples who glorify their marriages actually faced more troubles than less stable pairs. But they seem to garner more meaning and inspiration from their hardships than others might.

The point is that stable marriages become even stronger in the telling of the tale. Stable couples' stories serve to bolster their faith in one another and their union.

Charles A. Smith, author's description of *Raising Courageous Kids* (2004)

Too often in this perilous world we hear the faint drumbeats of approaching danger, a call beckoning those whose hearts are filled with hate. Yet at the moment when these merchants of misery release inexplicable pain in the world, men and women with courageous hearts appear. Their heroism rekindles hope and reminds us that good will and decency remain alive.

Alana Franklin rescues a six-year-old boy from a gunman who invaded his home. *Fallon Richards* pulls a bed-ridden elderly man from his bed to safety during a fire in his mobile home. *Terreatha Barnes* leaps into a runaway vehicle containing two preschool children and brings it to a halt by pushing on the brake with her hands (breaking her jaw as she does so). What do these three individuals have in common? Other than being courageous females, Alana, Fallon, and Terreatha were all eleven or twelve years old. Their example shows us that the same heart that prompted passengers on Flight 93 to rise up against their captors, firefighters to march up the steps of the World Trade Center, and two men to bring a woman in a wheelchair down 70 floors at the WTC to safety, beats inside young people as well.

We are not born with courage. Threads of power, devotion, integrity, honor, and valor were combined and woven into the tapestry of our lives from the moment we were born.

H. Wallace Goddard, excerpt from "Something Better Than Punishment" (1994, pp. 1-2)

When we think of discipline, we may think of threats and punishment. They may be the most common ways that parents deal with their children's misbehavior.

What is wrong with threats and punishment? One thing that is wrong with them is that they teach children bad things. Can you think of some bad things that are taught to children by the use of threats and punishment?

Consider threats. It is common for parents to get frustrated with their children and yell at them. "If you do that one more time I'm going to whip you, young man!" "I've told you a thousand times. If I have to tell you once more . . ." Threats are bad because they insult children. They are likely to make the child feel dumb and put-down. The child may feel angry with the parent for treating him that way. Threats are also bad because they may tell the children that we yell a lot but we never do anything. Consider the following story.

(Continued)

(Continued)

A mother was loading her children in the car to go to the store. Just as she got them all in the car, the neighbor came over to talk to her. As the two ladies talked, the children became restless. One of the boys began to climb out the car window. The mother yelled for him to get back in the car. Then she returned to talking with the neighbor. The boy sat in the window and played. The mother yelled at him to get in the car and threatened to spank him. He sat still while his mother yelled at him, but as soon as she returned to talking, he climbed out the window onto the hood of the car. The mother continued to talk to the neighbor.

This boy did not think his mother was very serious. She yelled a lot. But she never did anything—unless she became really angry. It's common for parents to be yelling, "Don't touch that!" "Leave her alone." "Go away." Using threats may teach children that parents are unkind and that they don't mean what they say.

There are also problems with punishment. Sometimes parents punish because they are angry. They may spank their children in anger. What does spanking teach a child? For many children it teaches that the world is a cruel place. It may also teach them that parents are mean. It may teach them that it is all right for big people to hurt little people. Those are not the things we want to teach our children. The most effective parents rarely or never use spanking.

When a parent spanks a child for bad behavior, the parent may think that making the child suffer teaches him or her not to do bad things. What it usually teaches the child is to feel angry or unsafe. Or it may teach the child not to do bad things when the parent is around. But it does not teach the child to be helpful or to have self-control or to feel safe.

There is something better than making children suffer. It is teaching. We want to teach our children that rules are important, that people can work together and solve problems without using physical means.

Teaching is more than talking. It includes how we act. In this publication are some ideas to help you more effectively teach children respect for rules. You can use these suggestions to find better ways to discipline your children—ways to be sure you are helping, never harming your children. You can help your children develop into strong, caring people you will be proud of. [Five principles of guidance follow.]

Haim Ginott, excerpts from Chapter 1, "The Code of Communication: Parent-Child Conversations," in *Between Parent and Child* (Ginott, Ginott, & Goddard, 2003, pp. 5-8)

Children's Questions: The Hidden Meanings

Conversing with children is a unique art with rules and meanings of its own. Children are rarely naive in their communications. Their messages are often in a code that requires deciphering.

Andy, age ten, asked his father, "What is the number of abandoned children in Harlem?" Andy's father, a lawyer, was glad to see his son take an interest in social problems. He gave a long lecture on the subject and then looked up the figure. But Andy was not satisfied and kept on asking questions on the same subject: "What is the number of abandoned children in New York City? In the United States? In Europe? In the world?"

Finally it occurred to Andy's father that his son was concerned not about a social problem, but about a personal one. Andy's questions stemmed not so much from sympathy for abandoned children as from fear of being abandoned. He was looking not for a figure representing the number of deserted children, but for reassurance that he would not be deserted.

Thus his father, reflecting Andy's concern, answered, "You're worried that your parents may someday abandon you the way some parents do. Let me reassure you that we will not desert you. And should it ever bother you again, please tell me so that I can help you stop worrying."

On her first visit to kindergarten, while her mother was still with her, Nancy, age five, looked over the paintings on the wall and asked loudly, "Who made these ugly pictures?" Nancy's mother was embarrassed. She looked at her daughter disapprovingly, and hastened to tell her, "It's not nice to call the pictures ugly when they are so pretty."

The teacher, who understood the meaning of the question, smiled and said, "In here you don't have to paint pretty pictures. You can paint mean pictures if you feel like it." A big smile appeared on Nancy's face, for now she had the answer to her hidden question, "What happens to a girl who doesn't paint so well?"

Next Nancy picked up a broken fire engine and asked self-righteously, "Who broke this fire engine?" Her mother answered, "What difference does it make to you who broke it? You don't know anyone here."

Nancy was not really interested in names. She wanted to find out what happened to children who break toys. Understanding the question, the teacher gave an appropriate answer: "Toys are for playing. Sometimes they get broken. It happens."

Nancy seemed satisfied. Her interviewing skill had netted her the necessary information: This grown-up is pretty nice, she does not get angry quickly, even when a picture comes out ugly or a toy is broken, I don't have to be afraid, it is safe to stay here. Nancy waved goodbye to her mother and went over to the teacher to start her first day in kindergarten.

Carol, age twelve, was tense and tearful. Her favorite cousin was going home after staying with her during the summer. Unfortunately, her mother's response to Carol's sadness was neither empathic nor understanding.

(Continued)

(Continued)

CAROL (with tears in her eyes):	Susie is going away. I'll be all alone again.
MOTHER:	You'll find another friend.
CAROL:	I'll be so lonely.
MOTHER:	You'll get over it.
CAROL:	Oh, Mother! (Sobs.)
MOTHER:	You're twelve years old and still such a crybaby.

Carol gave her mother a deadly look and escaped to her room, closing the door behind her. This episode should have had a happier ending. A child's feelings must be taken seriously, even though the situation itself is not very serious. In her mother's eyes a summer separation may be too minor a crisis for tears, but her response need not have lacked sympathy. Carol's mother might have said to herself, "Carol is distressed. I can help her best by showing that I understand what pains her. How can I do that? By reflecting her feelings to her." Thus she would have said one of the following:

"It will be lonely without Susie."

"You miss her already."

"It is hard to be apart when you are so used to being together."

"The house must seem kind of empty to you without Susie around."

Such responses create intimacy between parent and child. When children feel understood, their loneliness and hurt diminish. When children are understood, their love for the parent is deepened. A parent's sympathy serves as emotional first aid for bruised feelings.

When we genuinely acknowledge a child's plight and voice her disappointment, she often gathers the strength to face reality.

Shirley Jackson, from *Life Among the Savages* (1997, p. 1)

Our house is old, and noisy, and full. When we moved into it we had two children and about five thousand books; I expect that when we finally overflow and move out again we will have perhaps twenty children and easily half a million books; we also own assorted beds and tables and chairs and rocking horses and lamps and doll dresses and ship models and paint brushes and literally thousands of socks. This is the way of life my husband and I have fallen into, inadvertently, as though we had fallen into a well and decided that since there was no way out we might as well stay there and set up a chair and a desk and a light of some kind.

CONCLUSION ●

The best written materials read naturally and effortlessly. What is hidden behind the text is the time spent gaining the knowledge, finding a voice, writing the ideas, and refining them. There is no royal road to effective writing. It takes thoughtful effort.

EXPLORATIONS ●

1. If you were designing a Web course for families such as those described at the beginning of this chapter, what knowledge of parenting do you think is most important for them to have? How would you make it memorable? What strategy would you use to help the parents apply the knowledge to their parenting challenges?

2. Identify samples of writing that speak to you. Describe characteristics of the voice in those samples.

3. Select a family topic on which adult family members are likely to have an interest. Have each member of the class write an 800- to 1,000-word article on that subject as if it were being prepared for a local newspaper (or some other agreed-upon outlet). After each person has had a few days or a week to prepare the article, make enough copies for your class members or colleagues. Share them. Discuss the strengths and limitations of the various pieces. As a follow-up activity, refine your article and submit it to a print source.

4. Discuss with a classmate or colleague your reactions to the several writing samples. What do you like about each? Do you have some other sample of writing that especially appeals to you? How would you describe the style you have developed or hope to develop?

CHAPTER 10

FAMILY LIFE EDUCATION ON THE TECHNOLOGICAL FRONTIER

By Steven Dennis and Aaron Ebata

W hat is history's greatest technological advance? Is it the plow, which gave birth to leisure time and creative thought? Is it the printing press, which fueled education for the masses? Or is it the microcomputer and global communication resulting from the massive electronic network known as the Internet? Each arguably has changed the course of history. Each has altered the way families interact and learn about their duties and relationships. In this chapter, we explore the role and effective use of technology in family life education (FLE).

Often when we hear the word *technology* we imagine electronic devices, computers, software, hardware, or some amazing piece of equipment that has become a tool for humankind. Although such devices qualify as technology, in the truest sense, technology has a broader definition. It is the application of science. It is scientific advances applied to commerce, industry, education, and daily life. Technology considers both physical tools and research-based principles. It is both hardware and processes. However, since the science of sound instructional principles is addressed elsewhere in this book, this chapter focuses primarily on the technological trends and Web development tools and processes that are central to FLE via the Internet and other distance education technologies. Web addresses are given for many examples throughout the chapter. Although all were active at the time of publication, the Internet is ever changing. Any discontinued sites or broken links attest to the challenge of providing FLE via the dynamic world of the Internet.

THE TECHNOLOGICAL LANDSCAPE ●

History

In 1953, only about 100 computers existed in the entire world. They were huge machines that filled rooms but had less power than many handheld computers today. Since IBM's introduction of the personal computer, or PC, in 1981, the cost, power, versatility, and usage of computers has exploded. Much of the growth can likely be attributed to the rapid expansion of the Internet. The Internet began as a military project in 1970 but was soon opened up to military contractors and university research partners. By the late 1980s, most universities and many businesses came online. But it wasn't until the advent of the World Wide Web in 1992 and the commercialization of the Internet by Internet service providers in 1993 that growth rocketed and the Internet truly became the information superhighway.

Computer Usage and Internet Access

In 2000, a Census Bureau (U.S. Census Bureau, 2001) report estimated that 54 million households, or 51% of all households in the United States, had one or more computers. Approximately 44 million, or 42% of households, had Internet access. By comparison, in 1997, 36% of households had computers and only 18% of households had Internet access. Amazingly, Internet access had more than doubled in 3 years. It is unlikely that growth has slowed considerably in recent years. In fact, a recent Nielsen NetRating (2003) report estimates that nearly 109 million users have Internet access at home. The greatest growth has occurred among those connecting via high-speed or broadband connections, such as DSL, cable modems, or satellite systems. Internet access by modem has declined, particularly in urban settings. Mobile phones and PDAs with wireless Internet capabilities are further expanding the possibilities of access.

Some have cautioned that unequal access to technology has resulted in a digital divide in our society (Roach, 2003; Strover, 2003; Van Dijk & Hacker,

2003). Women, minorities, and poor youth and families may be disadvantaged in a high-tech world. A report from the U.S. Department of Education, National Center for Education Statistics (2003), found computer and Internet use continues to be divided along demographic and socioeconomic lines, with gender being a notable exception. During most of the 1990s, males were reported to use the computer and the Internet more frequently. Ono and Zavodny (2003) found that although the gender gap for access to computers or the Internet disappeared by 2000, gender differences still exist. They found that women access the Internet less frequently and for shorter periods of time. Women appear to be less intense about their online experience. The 2000 Census Bureau survey found Internet access to be more common among married-couple households with school-age children. Access is also more common in suburbs than in either central cities or rural areas. Households in the West are most likely to have access, and households in the South least likely. White non-Hispanic and Asians are more likely to have access than Blacks or Hispanics. And finally, while usage and access increases with age during childhood, the trend reverses among adults, with those over 65 least likely to either own a computer or have access to the Internet. E-mail (87%) and searching for information on the World Wide Web (64%) are the primary uses of the Internet for adults. (U.S. Census Bureau, 2001). Undoubtedly, as computers and communication technologies expand, the variety of uses and value of access will increase.

It is important to recognize that the Internet and its use is amazingly dynamic. Already these use and access statistics are dated. More individuals and families are connected than ever. But while the digital divide may be closing on one front, it will always exist on another. When a new technology emerges, it is first embraced by those with the greatest resources. Only as use and demand increase does it become more affordable and accessible to all.

So although the Internet is expanding, some are being left behind. Family life resources distributed solely through the Internet will likely miss many of those with the greatest need. Some lack the money to get connected, and others lack the desire. They may see no personal benefit to Internet access or may lack confidence in operating computers or maneuvering the Internet. For others, the primarily text-based material available on the Internet may not be their preferred format for information, because they read marginally or cannot type.

A recent evaluation of an FLE Web site points to the danger of making assumptions about who would most likely use or benefit from Web-based programs. In examining participant ratings of their site, Steimle and Duncan (2004) found greater changes in self-reported attitudes and behaviors among non-Whites and those with less than college educations.

Future Trends

Although family life educators (FLEs) must be sensitive to the resource divide that may result with any new technology, several trends will likely reduce the disparity of at least computer ownership and Internet access:

1. The Internet is increasingly becoming a multimedia-rich environment. High-speed broadband connections that accommodate multimedia are quickly becoming the standard. Text information is increasingly being supported by audio, video, and graphical supplements. Riley and Bogenschneider (1992) suggest in their review of effective delivery methods that print materials are more appealing to educated individuals, whereas broadcast media or video formats are preferred by those with less education. A multimedia-rich environment will make the Internet more appealing to a broader audience.

2. The applications for computers and the Internet have expanded. Computers are no longer just for data processing. Software applications and potential uses have expanded to thousands of possibilities, from digital imaging and photography to educational games and simulations. Nearly everyone can find a use for a computer.

3. The number of computer networks has expanded. Metcalfe's Law states that the value of a network grows in proportion to the square number of users (Metcalfe, 1996). Just as the value of a telephone depends on the number of other users with a telephone, so the value of a computer network increases with the number of users. Wireless networking via mobile phones or PDAs will continue to expand the reach and value of the Internet.

4. Computers and other hardware technologies are getting faster and smaller. The number of transistors on a chip has doubled approximately every 12 to 18 months for the past 30 years (National Science Foundation, 2002). Performance increases with the number of transistors per chip. Furthermore, this process of miniaturization has led to smaller but more powerful handheld devices. FLEs will soon be able to give media-rich presentations using devices that may fit in their pockets.

5. Alternative input methods such as touch screens or voice and handwriting recognition continue to improve. Individuals who cannot type or prefer alternative input methods may soon find that the inability to type is no longer a significant barrier to computer use.

6. Technologies are merging. A single unit may soon serve as a radio, television, DVD player, stereo system, camera, and telephone. Ninety-eight percent of households in the United States have a television. Its popularity

can partly be explained by its low cost and by the diverse programming that accommodates low-literacy audiences. As computer and Internet access costs decline and efforts to reach diverse audiences are expanded, the computer may become as popular as the television. In fact, we may increasingly find that our television is a media-rich computer connected to a vast communication network. As such, television or computer programming in the future will likely become more individualized. Consumers will watch what they want asynchronously. Instead of broadcasting generally over cable or satellite systems, on-demand programming will be delivered by broadband Internet access. Hence, in the future, owning a television may be synonymous with owning a computer and being connected to a global digital network.

Learning and Information Delivery in a High-Tech World

Technological changes have and will continue to facilitate cultural changes. Although the way we learn may be tied more to our biology and cognition than technological advances, the context of learning and methods for disseminating information will continue to change. Smith (1999, pp. 31-34) suggests that technology has changed the cultural conditions in the six following ways:

1. The locus of information control has shifted form the expert to the consumer.

2. Learning is becoming anarchistic and chaotic.

3. Information has become a global business.

4. Learning is now embedded in a culture of speed.

5. Infoglut and corresponding information anxiety is a challenge.

6. New technologies create new communication communities.

Each of these cultural changes will shape the responsibilities and methods of FLEs. Let's consider each in greater detail:

1. *The locus of information control has shifted from the expert to the consumer.* Increasingly, the consumer will determine when, where, and how to access information. Experts can no longer organize, package, and deliver information in controlled manners that are based more on their own preferences than the needs and preferences of consumers. With potentially thousands of options, consumers are in control and will access information according to their needs and way of thinking.

2. *Learning is becoming anarchistic and chaotic.* In the past, educational resources have been largely linear. They have clear objectives, a logical plan, and a predictable conclusion. Such resources are neat and tidy and have an obvious start and ending. Increasingly, learning is nonlinear. Hypermedia allows learners to follow multiple paths—each with a different ending. The learning objectives and paths are determined by the interests of consumers. Although customizing the path of learning to meet the preferences, desires, and needs of individual learners sounds appealing, there are concerns. Chen and Dwyer (2003) warn that there is little empirical evidence to show that a hypermedia learning environment improves learning outcomes. In fact, Astleitner and Leuner (1995) suggest that hypermedia may deter learning in several ways. For example, hypermedia makes goal attainment less defined. Learners may miss key points because they are distracted by huge amounts of less pertinent or unnecessary information. A learning objective is most easily met when the target is clearly identified. In a hypermedia environment, there may be no specific targeted objective.

In addition, learners may become spatially disoriented by the complex node-link structure of hypermedia. After selecting a few embedded links, learners may lose sight of where they came from, where they are, and where they should go. In short, they become lost in hyperspace. Finally, hypermedia may contribute to cognitive overload resulting from the high memory demand. Although hypermedia may be an ideal structure for information retrieval, it may not be equally effective as a means of knowledge acquisition or learning.

3. *Information has become a global business.* Geographic and organizational boundaries are fast becoming meaningless. Organizations and educators who seek to protect their turf will find there is no turf in the digital world. Consumers can electronically access material from libraries, universities, or organizations around the world with greater speed than they can drive to their county Extension office. FLEs will find their target audiences spanning the world. To attract consumers, organizations will need to pool resources and expertise in collaborative ways. Already collaborative efforts such as CYFERnet exist (see http://www.cyfernet.org). The CYFERnet Web site brings together peer-reviewed research-based child, youth, and family resources from all the public land grant universities in the country. Likewise, institutions of higher education are collaborating to offer degree programs. For example, the Great Plains Interactive Distance Education Alliance (GPI-DEA) (http://www.gpidea.org) offers multiinstitution programs in family financial counseling, gerontology, and youth development. The Cooperative Extension Curriculum Project (CECP) (http://cecp-online.org) is another collaborative effort by the Southern Region Program Leadership Network, the Association of Extension Administrators, and the Association of Southern Region Extension Directors to extend the reach of family life and other

Cooperative Extension programs. In addition, many states have developed virtual universities or campuses (see http://www.adec.edu/virtual.html). These universities attract students from around the world and connect them to leading experts without ever requiring the student to leave home.

4. *Learning is now embedded in a culture of speed.* For whatever reason, our culture places great value on quick results, immediate access, and instant gratification. Whether we are trying to lose weight, purchase consumer goods, or expand our learning, it seems that sooner is better. Although distributed learning opportunities increase the likelihood that information will be presented when and how it is needed, the window of opportunity is small in a culture of speed. FLEs must be ready with accessible resources when the need arises. For example, following the September 11 terrorist attacks on the World Trade Center, professionals were scrambling to provide parents with resources to help themselves and their children appropriately discuss and cope with the devastating event. The window of opportunity was small. Many excellent resources have been developed since, but fewer were available at the time they were most needed. To be successful, FLEs must be ready when the window of opportunity opens—whether it opens for one or a thousand.

5. *Infoglut and corresponding information anxiety is a challenge.* Information on nearly every subject can be easily found in minutes. In fact, peddlers of information no longer wait for you to come to them. Aggressive approaches that use spyware and unsolicited spam messages have added to infoglut of the Internet. Sifting through the enormity of information to determine if it is accurate, credible, and useful is an ominous task. Many have likely asked which of the 350,000 hits to an online search have what they need. Effective search and filtering strategies have become increasingly important. Many professional organizations and academic centers are struggling to find ways to screen, endorse, or implement criteria standards for acceptability. For example, the Child & Family WebGuide (http://www.cfw.tufts.edu) was created by librarians and child development faculty at Tufts University in an effort to help parents and professionals find credible and useful information about family life, parenting, and child development. Graduate students and faculty have evaluated thousands of Web sites using four criteria: authority, content, ease of use, and stability of the site.

Although the technology exists for search engines to search only among preapproved or credentialed sites (see http://www.surfmonkey.com), it has generally only been used to screen inappropriate content from children, not the quality and credibility of family life content. Numerous Web site awards have been created to lend credibility and recognition to Web sites. But unlike the Oscars, Grammys, or Emmys, Web surfers are generally unaware of which awards truly represent a significant or credible honor. In fact, the Web Credibility Project at Stanford University (http://www.webcredibility.org) sponsored a study that found that the average consumer paid far more attention to the superficial aspects of sites, such as visual cues, than to its content. For example, nearly half of all consumers (or 46.1%) in the study assessed the credibility of sites largely on visual design, including layout, typography, font size, and color schemes (Fogg et al., 2002). It appears that many consumers believe that if it looks dazzling, the content must be good. More rigorous criteria is less common among professionals and consumers. One study found that preservice and inservice teachers considered the credibility and usefulness of Internet resources to be equal to information found in textbooks (Iding, Crosby, & Speitel, 2002). This may or may not be the case.

Fetsch and Hughes (2002) suggest that consumers evaluate the quality of family life content by comparing it to recognized standards or corroborating sources. Consumers should look for biases, emotional appeals, and conflicts of interest that are common to commercial or ad-sponsored sites. Fetsch and Hughes also recommend that consumers be wary of dramatic claims that oversimplify the nature of family life or suggest that there is only one way to handle a problem.

6. Smith (1999) notes that *new technologies create new communication communities*. Newsgroups, chat rooms, listservs, Web logs (or blogs), and other electronic forums have provided new ways for people to meet, discuss ideas, and share their feelings. As with any educational approach, what attracts some may alienate others. Some prefer to discuss ideas and share feelings through the anonymity of the Internet. Others prefer the personalization that comes with face-to-face interaction. The new and expanded communication options provided by the Internet and other technologies are undoubtedly most effective when passed on to the learner in the form of choices. Variety, flexibility, and alternative approaches will help each learner individualize a plan that works best for him or her.

Designing Effective Resources

At a time when almost endless information is at our fingertips and technologies and communication networks are expanding, it is easy to become enthralled with the latest advances in hardware and software. But the effective use of any technology requires that it be applied with sound principles. Effective FLE that incorporates the Internet, computer-based applications, or other media-rich approaches must maintain a solid foundation in the principles of instruction. Five are suggested here:

1. *Develop and market the value of credibility.* Today's consumers have numerous access points for information. When competing against the information provided by thousands of others, the sources considered most credible will capture the attention of consumers. Credibility may even be more important in settings of anonymity or minimal personal contact. When developing a Web site, or other resources, Fogg (2002) recommends 10 guidelines for enhancing the credibility:

- *Make it easy to verify the accuracy of the information on your site.* Use citations, references, and clearly identify source materials.
- *Show that there's a real organization behind your site.* List a physical address, or post a photo of your office.
- *Highlight the expertise in your organization and in the content and services you provide.* Share the credentials and affiliations of the experts who are on the team. Avoid links to less credible sources. Your site may become less credible by association.
- *Show that honest and trustworthy people stand behind your site.* Identify the real people behind the work. Share bios that convey their involvement and trustworthiness.
- *Make it easy to contact you.* Having a physical address, phone number, and email address will show that you welcome personal contact and have nothing to hide.
- *Design your site so it looks professional.* Pay attention to the layout, typography, images, and consistency in design. Make sure your overall design matches the purpose of the site.
- *Make your site easy to use and useful.* Find ways to help the user locate information quickly and intuitively. Keep it simple.
- *Update your site's content often.* People assign more credibility to sites that show they have been recently updated or reviewed.
- *Use restraint with any promotional content.* If possible, avoid having ads on your site. If you must, clearly distinguish the sponsored content from your own. Avoid pop-up ads.
- *Avoid errors of all types.* Typographical errors and broken links hurt a site's credibility more than most people imagine. It's also important to keep sites up and running.

2. *Engage your learners.* Active learning strategies require something of the learner. Learners can be engaged with lively discussions or hands-on games or activities, but they can also be engaged mentally with thought-provoking questions, captivating stories, or analogies or metaphors. Learners can also participate through role playing, simulations, or case study analysis. Web-based courses, teleconferencing, Web casting, and other technology-based

approaches can all be designed with engagement in mind. Whatever the approach or delivery method, effective FLEs will find ways for learners to reflect on or apply the information. Active strategies will increase participant learning. The goCyperCamp (http://gocybercamp.org/) Web-based learning environment developed by the 4-H Youth Development Program is an excellent example of an engaging Web site.

3. *Incorporate variety and extend choices.* Each learner has a favorite way of learning. By designing educational materials with a variety of learning activities and methods, a richer learning environment is created, especially when learners are given an opportunity to choose among the various options. Levin, Levin, and Waddoups (1999) found that "multiplicity" may decrease efficiency in the short run but may encourage the development of powerful new learning and teaching environments in the longer term. They define multiplicity as multiple contexts for learning, multiple instructional media, multiple instructional formats, multiple learning activities, and multiple assessment techniques. Levin et al. believe that multiplicity results in both a broader and deeper representation of content to be mastered. Parent 2 Parent (http://p2p.uiuc.edu/), developed by the University of Illinois, is an excellent example of a parent education and support Web site that incorporates a variety of learning methods.

4. *Provide learners with instructional maps.* In a hypermedia environment, one can easily get lost, but sound instruction in any environment requires a clearly charted course. Using menus, sidebars, summary tables, graphical representations, transitional cues, outlines, video examples, or other content organizers can help learners to clearly identify key points and the direction of the content. Appropriate menus with an easy way back can keep learners from being lost in a sea of embedded menus and hyperlinks. Providing learners with a clear instructional map will help them reach their learning destination effectively.

5. *Provide broad support.* Smith (1999) noted that "the Internet is a great informer but a poor coach" (p. 33). The methods in which FLE is provided may change, but humans will always need the specific guidance, feedback, and support of mentors and teachers. Similarly, Dhanarajan (2001) warns that commitment to leading-edge hardware and software is not enough. Mastering the tools of distance education technologies requires significant training and support for both the designer and end users to become proficient and master such tools. Although many independent learners have the determination and skill to learn with only minimal support, effective FLE will require more. Speaking of distance education in higher education, Dhanarajan notes:

A passionate teacher, a personal computer, a server, and connections can spawn an instant course. . . . While these may be excellent for those learners seeking enrichment and personal pleasure who have greater skills to "learn" through cyberspace, they are far from satisfactory for those who are intent on gaining credits and qualification. Such people need an assurance of institutional commitment to provide all the other services of a healthy and supportive learning environment such as access to mentors, libraries, laboratories, assessment, and opportunities to gain recognized credit. A chat room is not a substitute for the range of services provided by committed institutions. (pp. 64-65)

Indeed, the successful FLEs of the future will not only provide a board level of support to learners but will develop and deliver content in proven ways. Adequate planning and preparation is a must. In the next section, we share more specifically the design and planning considerations for developing a successful online course.

● DEVELOPING ONLINE PROGRAMS FOR FAMILY LIFE EDUCATION

As the American population becomes increasingly wired and turns to the Web to seek information and learn new skills, having Web-based programs may be an essential part of an overall outreach effort. But without careful planning, a Web-based effort can lead to unforeseen problems as well. We emphasize that the Web is a delivery medium that makes it easy to do certain things, but the impact and educational value of a program still depends on the quality of the content and the extent to which the program can effectively fulfill some educational need.

In this section, we apply some of the findings and suggestions summarized in the previous section and outline practical issues that need to be considered when developing an online outreach effort. First, we examine the advantages and disadvantages of Web-based efforts and compare online programs with more traditional programs. We then use a program development model to offer steps that educators should take in designing a Web-based program. Next, we address the need for promoting and marketing the effort, and then how developers can evaluate their efforts. Finally, we conclude by commenting on some developing issues in Web-based delivery of FLE.

Why Should Family Life Educators Consider Online Programming?

There are a number of advantages that a Web-based program can have as compared to more traditional ways of delivering education and information:

- It can be convenient for consumers. A Web-based program is potentially available 24 hours a day, 7 days a week. Users can seek information when they need it, at a time and a place that is convenient for them and not the providers.
- An online program can provide support to and enhance other kinds of more traditional efforts like parenting classes or presentations.
- By using the hyperlinking and multimedia features of the Web, online resources can potentially offer richer, more flexible learning experiences or more useful ways of structuring or presenting information.
- A Web-based information warehouse can potentially be easier to maintain, update, and distribute compared to print resources.
- A Web-based effort can be cost effective and build on existing resources.
- A Web effort can reach new audiences that traditionally may not have been served.

One of the biggest disadvantages is that an online resource will not reach certain populations. However, there are some other important disadvantages or potential barriers that need to be considered:

- Online resources are only available when all of the links in the technological chain are working. Thus, all of the following must be in place and operating for a user to be able to use a Web-based program: (a) the computer server that houses the site and the network (or Internet service provider) that distributes the information, (b) the Internet network or backbone and nodes through which information passes, (c) the user's Internet service provider, (d) a working telephone or cable lines or unobstructed satellite or radio transmission paths through which digital signals must pass, and (e) the user's computer system. All of these parts rely on electrical power, of course!
- The promise of online support or enhanced programming may promote expectations or demands that are difficult or costly to meet. There is greater pressure to be (or at least appear to be) current and dynamic—with new content appearing regularly.

- Having an online delivery system does not guarantee that the content is useful, credible, or meets any criteria or standard for quality (technically referred to as "junk").
- New audiences may have different needs and expectations compared to audiences we have traditionally served and may create additional demands on an educator. Educators may put faith in the importance of certain factors that make a resource credible or useful (e.g., that it is research based), but studies described earlier show that consumers may be using other criteria to make judgments of credibility. Having a Web presence means having a *global* presence, which can make it difficult to *limit* your audience or to handle requests or communications with a broader pool of clients.

In sum, although a good Web-based program can be effective and efficient, it may also be costly, difficult to maintain, and may require new resources and expertise to successfully sustain the effort. At its best, Web-based resources can effectively touch the heart to motivate, inspire, and provide support as well as develop new knowledge and skills. At its worst, these resources can be dull, inaccurate, or reinforce myths and misconceptions about family life.

Models and Methods for Web-Based Delivery

An important first step is to consider how a Web-based effort fits into the overall educational strategy that an individual or organization might have. In general, a Web-based effort can serve to (a) provide support to existing educational offerings (e.g., workshops, printed materials), which might involve supplemental information or opportunities for communication and/or (b) provide information or educational programs that can stand alone. We focus on three kinds of information or learning experiences:

1. Information that can be used as reference (links, fact sheets, background papers, brochures, documents) where users decide when and how to interact with the materials in an unstructured fashion

2. Structured learning experiences (online classes, curriculum modules, lessons) that provide some kind of planned framework or guided interaction with the materials to achieve some learning goal

3. Opportunities for interactions with an expert, authority, or instructor, or with other users

Educators can use different methods and tools to provide these kinds of experiences. The most common method of delivering content on the Web is still text (occasionally illustrated with graphic images). Although there may be links within the text that can easily take users to other sources of information, most of the family life content on the Web is essentially electronic versions of what you might see on a printed page. The Web can also be used to distribute formatted or illustrated text (brochures, newsletters, etc.) that can be downloaded and saved for viewing or printing (i.e., using Adobe's PDF or Macromedia's Flashpaper). Family-info.org (http://www.family-info .info) is a good example of this model.

Links to other sources of information is a common and powerful feature of Web-based programs. Most Web sites feature links to other resources on the Web, but some sites are primarily designed to refer users to other sources of information. These portals, or directories, are guides to other sources of content. The value of a good directory or portal is that it makes it easier for users to find the kinds of resources that they would find most helpful. Most good portals provide (a) a structure or way of cataloging and labeling sources into categories that can be browsed by a user and (b) a good search feature that lets users enter a set of keywords. Examples of portals for FLE include CYFERNet (www.cyfernet.org), Teen-Link (web.aces.uiuc.edu/ p2p/teenlink), and the Tufts University Child & Family WebGuide (www.cfw .tufts.edu).

Multimedia (audio, video, animation) elements have the potential for being a powerful tool that might engage users, but the advantages and disadvantages of the use of any type of media remain the same regardless of how it is actually delivered. For example, a video of talking heads will probably have the same impact if viewed on the computer as if viewed on TV. The advantage of having video available over the Web is that of convenience and potential timeliness. More recently, a variety of software tools (like Macromedia's Breeze) make it easy to develop and deliver narrated Power-Point presentations over the Web. Unfortunately, this tool cannot ensure that these presentations will be effective or, at the least, entertaining.

Message boards, discussion forums, chat rooms, or Web logs can facilitate communities of like-minded others or fellow seekers trying to find answers to specific questions or problems. The Web has the potential of facilitating communities of shared expertise and support and bridging social and geographic barriers. These tools can be used for communication between an educator and a client or user and for communication between users. For issues where there may be many right answers in addition to expert advice (e.g., coping with an infant who won't sleep through the night, trying to manage the stress of caring for a disabled parent, etc.), shared experience can provide a sense of support and can normalize what might be perceived by an individual as an abnormal or an isolated experience.

The Web also provides the potential to engage learners by providing more interactive experience. Here we define *interactive* as the ability to customize, shape, select, or change information or experience provided by the Web site based on individual input. Examples include the following:

- Being able to customize features of a Web site, personalize an online experience, or get customized information based on user input. For example, the Parenting News Web site (parenting.uiuc.edu) allows users to customize the content of the site by having users select topics of interest during a registration process. By entering the birth date of a child, users can also choose to get e-mail notification and/or electronic delivery of an issue of the *Parenting the First Year* newsletter (developed by University of Wisconsin Extension) that is specific to the age of their child.

- Quizzes, surveys, questionnaires, or smart guides or wizards that provide a different set of information, advice, or referrals based on a diagnosis of responses from a user. This type of tool might help users narrow down a complex set of paths or choices (like trying to choose a TV or figuring out what a medical symptom might mean or how to deal with a child who bites or how to conduct a program evaluation). The Parent Self-Assessment (PSA) (see http://psa.uaex.edu/) is one example of an assessment tool that channels parents to educational resources based on the assessment profile. Similarly, a variety of assessments at Martin Seligman's Authentic Happiness Web site (see http://www.authentichappiness.org) help users learn their signature strengths.

- Gamelike experiences that lead to different outcomes based on choices made during different parts of a story. These structured-choice scenarios might be as simple as a branching story or as complex as a computer game (like the Sims). Games that have nonviolent or prosocial story lines or agendas are rare. However, recent examples include September 12th (http://www.newsgaming.com/news games.htm), which examines some of the consequences of a war on terror, and Real Lives 2004 (http://www.educationalsimulations.com), an "interactive life sim" that enables a player to "live" in any one of 190 different countries. Rather than focusing on entertainment, these simulations provide experiences for exploring "understanding and compassion in an increasingly global society."

- Community recommendations and ratings. These might include user recommendations or ratings of different sources of information, advice, or ideas similar to user reviews of books and merchandise found on commercial sites such as Amazon.com or on Epinions.com.

Freedom Versus Structure

Part of the appeal of the Web is the ability to freely make unrestricted choices amid what often seems to be an infinite universe of chaos and anarchy. Being able to find critical information quickly and easily, without having to go through barriers erected by others, is at the heart of this idea. At the same time, educators often believe that learning certain types of skills or content can be facilitated by structured experiences. Examples of structured courses, or educational modules, include an online marriage class from Utah Marriage (http://www.utahmarriage.org/) and courses on discipline and anger management for parents from the Kansas State's WonderWise Parent (http://www.ksu.edu/wwparent/courses/index.htm).

The Web is also well suited for formal online distance learning coursework that uses many of the tools and methods outlined above. A variety of courseware or authorware are available to schools, colleges, and corporations and provide instructors with tools for constructing or supporting Web-based learning (e.g., WebCT, Blackboard, Macromedia). Educators have the option of constructing modules or courses that are entirely on demand (essentially a self-study model where the user determines the time and pace of study), in real time (where students may be geographically dispersed but expected to be connected to the instructor and other classmates via technology at a certain time), or some combination of both. The use of synchronous (i.e., real-time) and asynchronous (anytime) methods of facilitating participation still assumes that some guided interaction by the instructor, and interaction between students, is beneficial for learning. A good source for additional information is the University of Wisconsin Extension's Distance Education Clearinghouse comprehensive source for resources on distance learning (http://www.uwex.edu/disted).

Program Planning and Development for the Web

In this section, we focus on the issues that educators must address in developing their own Web-based resource. We recommend following a typical program development or curriculum development process, with additional consideration given to issues that are unique to the Web.

There are three basic ways that an educator could develop and build a Web-based effort. The first method is to do it yourself. In some cases, individuals or groups of individuals have designed, built, and maintained their own sites as well as provided the content for the site (with some technical support from others or an institution). A good example is the WonderWise Parent (www.ksu.edu/wwparent/index.htm) developed by Dr. Chuck Smith at Kansas State University. Despite the proliferation of software tools to help those who are not technically inclined, a sustained effort typically requires developing some technical expertise and a passion for creative expression. Most others will (or should) either (a) hire technical staff and manage the development themselves (or with a team) or (b) outsource the project to experienced designers and programmers.

Whatever method you choose, there are some important issues that you will need to consider and communicate with those who will be developing the effort. Rather than focusing on the specific elements of good design (e.g., aesthetics, ease of navigation) that we mentioned earlier, here we focus on broader issues of program development for the Web. We organize our discussion around a process that should help an educator develop a plan that can function as (a) a strategic road map for keeping track of progress, (b) a document that will serve as the basis for working with a Web designer and programmer to develop a more specific set of requirements, and (c) a tool that can be used to describe the effort to stakeholders and potential funders.

Assessing and Defining Needs

Being able to articulate the rationale for a program and providing support for an effort that addresses some need is the basis for most grant proposals and should be addressed to justify the time and effort on a project—particularly when time and effort could be spent on other types of programs or delivery methods. Conducting some type of needs assessment will allow a developer to evaluate whether even embarking on a project is worth the time and effort. This process might include a review of existing information, a survey of the literature, or obtaining new information for (or from) a specific population.

This process can be useful for (a) clearly identifying a target audience or the characteristics of a population that would place them in greater need, (b) identifying and prioritizing particular issues or specific aspects of broader issues that need to be addressed, and (c) identifying potential methods, mechanisms, or processes that might be particularly useful or not useful.

Defining Goals, Objectives, and Potential Methods

In planning a Web-based program, it may be useful to start by developing a logic model or to use a program or curriculum development process outlined elsewhere in this volume. The following questions should be addressed:

- Who is the primary audience or target for this program? Is there a secondary audience?
- What are the primary goals and specific objectives (or learning outcomes) for this program? What do you hope to accomplish? Are there any secondary goals that you have for the project?
- What methods do you anticipate using to address or achieve these goals or outcomes?
- Are there any existing methods, resources, or other sites that could be used to address these goals? How would the proposed effort be different from, complement, or improve upon existing methods?
- What are the financial resources, personnel, or sources of support that you will be able to draw on for developing and maintaining this effort?
- How will you evaluate the effort? What will you need built into the site to help evaluate the effort?
- How do you intend to manage the site once the development phase has been completed?

Once these questions have been answered, the actual design and development of the program can begin.

The Web Development Process

Like the development of any program or curriculum, the development of a Web-based effort will go through stages that feed back to other stages. These stages would include the following:

- A strategic planning stage, where overall goals and objectives are identified and clarified and where strategic options are considered.
- A definition phase, where a preliminary design and prototype might be developed and evaluated by the educator and representatives of the potential audience. During this stage, functional requirements may be specified and technical needs determined. An estimated budget and tentative time line or schedule may be outlined in this stage.

- A development phase, where an initial version or prototype is built and content is developed and implemented into the site. Small-scale testing and feedback from users can be used to make modifications in the design, and a "final" model is determined and built.
- During the implementation phase, the Web site is reviewed and tested and finally launched.
- This cycle is then repeated for the next phase or the next version of the site.

Before meeting with a Web designer or developer, it can be useful to prepare a written document that tries to capture your vision of the program in a concise way (in addition to documenting goals, objectives, and methods). Come up with possible names or titles for the program that will clearly convey the site's purpose or contents. You might also consider a short tagline, or subtitle, that clarifies or adds to a user's understanding of the purpose of the site. Next, develop a single-sentence (or short-paragraph) description of the purpose of the site and what a user can expect to find there. This information will be useful to a Web designer, and can serve as an early draft of materials that can eventually be used in news releases and promotional materials. Next, develop a list of keywords that someone might use to describe and access your site. Finally, make a list of existing sites that you would want a designer to look at, either because (a) they have elements that appeal to you, (b) they would be sites that have similar content and would compete with your program, or (c) they have elements that exemplify what you do NOT want to see in your program.

Practical Considerations for Managing Content

The belief that a Web-based program will somehow be easier to maintain or manage than some other type of program is a mistaken one. Although Web delivery makes certain kinds of tasks easier (or less relevant), many educators who have turned to the Web have discovered that these types of programs sometimes take more attention than print materials that can sit on a shelf or a curriculum that is already in use by others. Web users assume that information on the Web is dynamic and changing, so it is important for educators to plan for managing change. More specifically, educators need to plan for how the site will be managed once it is up and running. Specifically,

- Who will be responsible for making decisions about the contents of the site and authorizing changes in the design of the site or its contents (i.e., managing the site)?

- What process or procedure will be used for evaluating existing content and determining the need for revising or developing new content? How often should existing content be evaluated? When do the materials expire? What process will be used to determine when things should be deleted or revised? How often should the site be updated with new content? Who will be responsible for developing, reviewing, and editing new content?
- Who will be responsible for actually putting content online or actually making changes in the design or functionality of the site? Will there be a formal process or procedures for keeping track of which changes need to be made and when and how these changes were accomplished?
- Who will be the primary contact for the program?

The answers to these issues may suggest using a certain type of model for managing the site and may have implications for the actual design of the site itself. For example, sites that will have frequently updated content can be designed to be database driven so that the content in a site can be updated by contributors who do have special technical skills. In these sites, a shell is designed with specific sections or components that draw content from a database. An educator can then enter new content into the databases using a form, and the content is automatically formatted and served to a Web page. This type of site is more complex and more expensive to design and build, but it has the advantage of not having to rely on someone with technical skills to change the content of the page.

Sites can also be designed so that content can be updated or changed using site management tools such as Macromedia Contribute or Microsoft Front Page or other similar product. In these types of sites, templates can be designed to make it easy for the less technically inclined to add or change content in certain sections of pages and to prevent accidental damage to the site itself.

Disseminating and Marketing

What if you offered a great class or workshop and no one came? Like any other program, educators need to consider how a program will be disseminated. We have already discussed things that educators should consider while designing and building the resource itself. Once the resource is ready to be deployed, educators need to identify their target audience (or market), decide how to best promote the resource, and determine how they can evaluate their marketing efforts.

A Web-based program must be promoted like any other type of educational program. Although we would like to believe that the quality of the site will speak for itself, the quantity of information available on the Web makes it easy for good information to be hidden unless conscious, strategic efforts are made to promote the program. Efforts could include the following:

- Direct marketing to the primary (target) audience using electronic methods (e-mail announcements, information on other Web sites that serve the same audience) as well as traditional methods (print announcements using mailing lists, flyers and brochures, media spots, etc.)
- Marketing to secondary audiences that might recommend or provide information about the site to the target audience (other sites, services, providers, consumer guides, reviewers, etc.). For FLEs, this would mean promoting the resource to other professionals, institutions, agencies, and businesses that serve families
- Personal appearances, demonstrations, and participation in public and professional events that might garner media attention

It is useful to think of a marketing effort as a promotional campaign that has several coordinated parts. News releases and media attention can be useful, as many newspaper and television stations have Web sites that provide additional information and links to viewers who may have seen part of a news article or broadcast.

It is especially important to be able to generate electronic word of mouth so that other Web sites provide a link to your resource. As we discuss next in the section on evaluating Web-based family life programs, although different search engines have different methods of finding and ranking the relevance of particular Web sites in search results, two of the most important determinants remain (a) how many other Web sites refer to you and (b) whether the Web sites that refer to you are themselves highly ranked.

A Framework for Evaluating Web-Based Family Life Programs

We have been discussing the potential of Web-based programs and have outlined issues and procedures that should be kept in mind when developing Web-based family life programs. Although Web-based efforts have proliferated, there is relatively little published data on the effectiveness of these types of programs (Hughes, Ebata, & Dollahite, 1999). In their report of an evaluation effort, Steimle and Duncan (2004) note that of the handful of articles focusing on the evaluation of family life Web sites (i.e., Hughes, 2001; Morris, Dollahite, & Hawkins, 1999), only one other published study collected information from users to evaluate effectiveness (Grant, Hawkins, & Dollahite, 2001). These studies suggest that the use of the Web as a medium for education and outreach is promising, but systematic efforts to evaluate Web-based programs are rare and provide unique challenges and barriers.

For evaluating Web-based programs, Steimle and Duncan (2004) have adapted Jacobs's (1988) five-tiered model for evaluating family programs, and offer helpful guidelines and recommendations based on their development and evaluation work. Here we summarize some of these recommendations and make additional comments for specific stages.

Tier 1, the *Web site preimplementation stage,* includes needs assessment, preliminary research, and pilot testing focused on developing and improving a program. This stage might include the use of focus groups, individual interviews, surveys, and walk-through usability studies of prototypes.

Tier 2, the *Web site utilization stage,* focuses on whether and how a site is being used. The most common method of assessing utilization would be to examine Web log statistics that are commonly collected (and often misinterpreted). Originally designed as a means to assess load, traffic, or demand put on a Web server (the computer that hosts a Web site), these statistics have been used to estimate the number of visits a site receives, which parts of a site get the most visits, the time spent on each visit, and where the visitor was previously before coming to the particular site. Hughes (2001) provides a "layman's guide" to the kinds of statistics that are available from Web logs and shows how these kinds of data can be used in formative evaluations. He also points out the limitations of Web log statistics.

Tier 3, the *Visitor satisfaction stage,* involves collecting user information (which could be qualitative or quantitative) that would help improve a program and provide additional information that might complement information on Web site utilization. The use of Web-based surveys or quick feedback ("How helpful was this article?") would be helpful at this stage.

Tier 4, the *Progress-toward-objectives state,* focuses on "determining whether the program is successful in meeting its goals." This might include user reports of knowledge, attitude, or behavioral change or anecdotes and success stories that attribute change to the program. Although not addressed by Steimle and Duncan (2004), another object of attention at this stage would be an assessment of how successfully disseminated or visible the site might be. This can be thought of as an assessment of relative impact of a site in comparison to other sites that might have similar objectives.

A quick and dirty assessment might include an examination of page rank in a Google search (using keywords that you think should bring up a particular site). It could be argued that this method assesses relevance or visibility by taking into account the extent other sites link to (i.e., recommend) a target site. More graphic methods for assessing the relationship between a particular site and referring sites (and perhaps the centrality of your site) is to use applications that provide graphical, maplike representations of links between sites, such as VisIT (http://visit1.vp.uiuc.edu) and KartOO (http://www.kartoo.com) or blinkx (http://www.blinkx.com).

For these types of assessments (and for usage statistics described for Tier 2), developers will be faced with trying to make sense of their results. Often inferences about whether some number or statistic is "good enough" or "needs improvement" can only be made when compared to the ranking, visibility, relevance, or centrality of other sites. Even here, however, the developer will need to define the appropriate universe for comparison. One developer might feel that it is unfair to compare the relative impact or visibility of a site developed by an educational institution (with a meager budget) with a commercial site funded by a major corporation or federal agency. Another developer might reason that consumers may not initially care about these considerations when doing a search on the Web and that a site must compete for visibility with ALL other sites. These developers would have quite different universes for comparison, and while the actual performance of their sites might be similar, their relative performances based on comparisons might be quite different.

Tier 5, the *Website impact stage,* focuses on long-term outcomes that might use experimental or quasi-experimental methods. Although a systematic treatment-outcome model that uses a pre-post comparison group design with random assignment might be the ultimate test of the effectiveness of a Web-based program, Jacobs (1988) points out that only certain types of "mature" programs might warrant this kind of effort. At this stage, a developer might consider what the most appropriate model for evaluation might be by thinking about how one might evaluate comparable or analogous offline programs or resources. For example, if the site provides unstructured, on-demand content that consists primarily of text in short articles, comparable offline analogs might include fact sheets or brochures, newsletters, magazine articles, or popular trade or self-help books. How would these types of resources be evaluated? Would one have the same expectations for impact that one might have for a site that is comparable to a structured, intensive, long-term intervention that uses multiple methods and supportive relationships with professionals and peers and is based on evidence-based principles?

Peer Review and "Critical Acclaim"

A final method for evaluating a Web-based program is to have the program reviewed by knowledgeable authorities or experts. In the early days of the Web, sites proudly displayed awards and reviews from self-appointed organizations or individuals that purported to recognize the "best of" what was available on the Web. The identity of these individuals and organizations, their credentials for making judgments, and the criteria used for ratings or inclusion into categories were often vague or nonexistent. Although a developer might seek a review for evaluation (and marketing), there are some important questions to consider:

- What are the relevant disciplines, industries, professional societies, or consumer organizations that are relevant to the site?
- Are there standards or criteria that have gained the endorsement of people or organizations that matter?
- Which individuals or organizations are qualified to provide a credible review? Are they experts in a content area or subject-matter experts? Do they have Web development or design expertise or experience?
- If a program is to be compared with others, what is the appropriate universe for comparisons? Should your program be compared to commercial sites?
- What does a developer do with a review? Is it used purely for improving the program? Can or should the review be used to foster credibility or to promote the program?

These questions and recommendations come during a period of rapid growth and evolution in Web-based programs, and it is clear that innovative methods that bridge traditional convention and an ever-changing technological landscape will need to be developed.

CONCLUSION •

For FLEs, the use of technology could make this the best of times, but it also brings the potential to easily make it the worst of times. While technology provides a wealth of opportunities to both consumers and providers of information, it provides greater power to consumers who can afford to view information as a commodity. An important issue to FLEs and other information providers is whether they can add value to information that could easily be obtained from a variety of sources. In the past, educators may have had the advantage and luxury of relying on certain badges of credibility (educational credential, affiliation with a university or organization, claims of being research based, etc.) or having relationships of trust to market a limited resource to familiar audiences. The increased availability of information makes it essential that educators explore and perhaps embrace some of the methods used by commercial providers and marketers in order to engage new audiences who will make the final judgment about whether an educational program is credible and useful and whether a provider can be trusted to provide useful information in the future.

● EXPLORATIONS

1. Perform an Internet search on "family life education" or visit some of your favorite family life sites. Using the Web credibility criteria outlined in the chapter, assess the credibility of the sites. Which sites do you trust? What could be done to enhance the credibility of the sites?

2. Visit your organization's Web site. Assess the freshness of the content. Schedule an appointment with the Webmaster for your site or one of interest. Ask about policies and procedures for keeping content up-to-date.

3. Develop an evaluation plan for an FLE Web site or Web course that is of interest to you. Using the five-tier approach discussed in the chapter, determine what information needs to be collected at each tier. Consider who and how the information can be collected. Determine an approximate time line.

CHAPTER 11

WORKING WITH DIVERSE AUDIENCES

Diversity is an essential part of being human. In one way or many ways, we are all different from each other. When we speak of diversity, we often think of ethnic diversity. Mindel, Haberstein, and Wright (1998) define an ethnic group as "those who share a unique social and cultural heritage that is passed on from generation to generation. . . . In America, the core categories of ethnic identity from which individuals are able to form a sense of peoplehood are race, religion, national origin, or some combination of these categories" (p. 6).

Yet ethnic diversity is not the only kind of diversity. It may not even be the most important kind of diversity for the work of family life educators (FLEs). Diversity of family experience plays a central role in people's experience of family and life (Hart & Risley, 1995; Peterson & Hann, 1999). Factors that could substantially affect one's experience of family as well as one's approach to family creation include experience of abuse, parental incompetence or mental illness, family mobility, parental conflict, poverty, stress, family size, spacing of children, proximity of extended family, social support, belief systems—the possibilities are innumerable. Of course, there is no tidy formula that connects difficult early family experience to dysfunctional adult family functioning Werner and Smith (1977, 1982, 1992, 2001) found that many of the stressed children they studied later flourished. Their resilience apparently resulted from various combinations of dispositional and environmental resources. Wide diversity of experience combines with great diversity of disposition and resources to make for very different outcomes.

In addition to accounting for ethnic diversity and family experience, Silver, Strong, and Perini (2000) recommend that effective educators should factor in multiple intelligences and learning styles. In their framework, they use Howard Gardner's eight multiple intelligences and four Jungian learning styles akin to Myers-Briggs's personality classifications. The challenge of dealing with diversity can be overwhelming if it is seen as somehow calculating and accommodating differences in ethnicity, family experience, gender, learning styles, and multiple intelligences. There simply is no formula for processing this myriad of factors to create educational recommendations. This is one of the reasons that we must invite learners to take substantial responsibility for their learning.

● SENSITIZING TO DIFFERENCES

It is useful to be familiar with cultural proclivities. For example, Native American families (especially traditional ones) are more likely than many American families to include extended family, a communal family economy, low educational attainment, reverence of nature and ancestors, strong interdependence, and strong loyalty to family (John, 1998).

African American families are more likely than many American families to operate without marriage, have woman-headed households, be based on consanguineal relationships, suffer poverty and poor-paying employment, and have limited education (McAdoo, 1998). Hispanic families in America are more likely than many American families to have strong religious beliefs, value cooperation, interdependence and loyalty to family, and strong extended family relationships (see Mindel, Habenstein, & Wright, 1998). However, the astute reader will recognize the limits of these generalizations. Consider the differences between, for example, Mexican Americans (many of whom live along the southern border of the United States), Puerto Ricans (who are more likely to live in New York City), and Cuban Americans (who are likely to live in Florida). Even with the Cuban American group, there are substantial differences between the backgrounds of those who came in the first wave as Castro took power in Cuba (more likely to be wealthy and educated) and those who came later (Suarez, 1998).

A similar point can be made about Native Americans. "Native Americans represent a large number of tribes with different linguistic and cultural heritages. There is no one kind of Indian, no one tribe, no one Indian nation" (Hildreth & Sugawara, 1993, p. 165).

DIVERSITY OF LEARNING STYLES •

In the effort to help FLEs work more effectively with various ethnic groups, there have been attempts to describe distinct ethnic learning styles (see Guion et al., 2003). For example, African Americans are said to learn through movement, humor, emotion, imagery, holistic, and oral approaches. In contrast, Asian American learning styles are described as high motivation to achieve, use of intuition, self-discipline, concentration, showing respect or conformity, and use of problem solving. Hispanic/Latino learning preferences include cooperative learning, interdependence, affection, intuitive, and based in tradition. Native American learning preferences include cooperation, holistic orientation, harmony seeking, visual and symbolic, as well as storytelling.

The great danger of generalizations is that they may mask the great individual variation within a group. Social scientists are fond of observing that the variance within groups exceeds that between groups. For example, while there may be some difference in spatial aptitude between men and women (the issue is still debated), the differences among men and among women are so great that knowing the sex of the person tells you almost nothing about the likely spatial aptitude of a given person.

There is an old saying that "All Indians walk single file. At least the one I saw did." Humans tend to be naive psychologists who use their limited experience to form general laws (Heider, 1958). While it may be useful and necessary to see patterns in experience, human history is littered with the wreckage of us-them thinking. Any attempt to reduce a group of people to a few descriptors is certain to leave us unprepared to appreciate the rich diversity within the group. When attempts to describe a group of people cause us to be categorical and prejudiced, they are counterproductive. When attempts to describe a group of people cause us to be humble and appreciative, they prepare us for mutual learning.

ETHNICITY AND VALUES •

It is useful to be aware that each person we meet brings a unique set of experiences and sensitivities to any interchange. Family life education (FLE) deals with inherently personal and value-laden subjects. We should be prepared to understand the worldview and logic of those we serve.

McDermott (2001) has described several values pertinent to family life that show considerable variation:

- Individual as the primary unit in society
- Competition
- Communication standards
- Action orientation
- Time orientation
- Work ethic
- Family structure

The Individual

The dominant North American culture places a high value on the individual as the primary unit of society. Many other cultures are more socio-centric, valuing a couple, a family, or a community as the basic unit of society. A related value is competition. While much of American culture values winning, many people within our culture and in other cultures value cooperation and teamwork more highly. Effective FLEs will be aware that many participants within a class may be very sensitive to the well-being of all participants. Not only will they not want to see others humiliated, but they may not want to compete with each other. Common American teaching techniques that emphasize competition such as quiz bowl may raise anxiety and discomfort with such audiences.

Communication Standards

Related to communication standards, some participants may be reluctant to participate because their English is limited. Some may be uncomfortable with self-disclosure. Some may see strong statements and direct questioning as harsh. Sensitive FLEs will observe carefully the patterns that participants use and will strive to communicate in a way that honors participants' preferences.

Action Orientation

The dominant culture values an action orientation. We tightly program ourselves to avoid wasting precious time. Some cultures are more reflective. They may value being over doing.

Culturally observant FLEs will consider the action orientation of potential audiences in the selection of program content and methods. Once I

(Duncan) was invited to do a seminar on time management on the Crow Indian Reservation in Montana by a county Extension agent who was also a member of the Crow tribe. She wanted me to help her audience use their time better. As I prepared, I felt that in-vogue practices of effective time management developed by upper-middle-class Whites with a business orientation would have limited applicability among poor single parents on the reservation. While teaching them, I found that instead of being time oriented, participants were event oriented. They organized their lives around events of the day (e.g., mealtimes, beginnings and endings) instead of by hours and minutes. So instead of framing the discussion around the management of time, we talked about getting things done. Such an approach helped them learn new things about accomplishing more with their lives within the context of their cultural values.

Time Orientation

Time orientation is also an important value. Some cultures are very focused on honoring the past. History and ancestors are highly honored. The dominant American ethos tends to look to the future. Optimism and foresight are valued. Since we are likely to have persons in groups comprising all of these perspectives, wise FLEs can honor each through the wise selection of stories and examples illustrating the virtue of each viewpoint.

Work Ethic

The dominant culture has a strong work ethic. Those who work hard are respected. The great danger is the assumption that hard work translates into success. There are many who work hard (or want to work hard) but are seriously disadvantaged. Poverty is not a sure sign of laziness. Success is not sure evidence of industry.

Family Structure

Family structure is another value that can lead to misunderstanding. Americans tend to value autonomous households. Many cultures value the rich interdependence of extended family households. We should resist the temptation to impose our meaning on living configurations that may be different from our own.

An awareness of these values can sensitize us to preferences and values of those we serve. There is no paper-and-pencil assessment that allows us to pigeonhole them. Given the diversity that can be expected within a seemingly homogeneous group, there is no single method that will be effective with a specific group. There are, however, processes that help us discover and honor the diversity we will find among those we serve.

● SKILLED DIALOGUE

Barrera and Corso (2003) have developed a process that they call skilled dialogue. While their process was developed for use in early childhood education and special education, the principles clearly apply to FLE.

Skilled dialogue challenges the notion that cultural competence is primarily the result of extensive knowledge about cultures. "The belief that one must have information about others before one can be culturally competent is itself a cultural artifact" (p. 42). Beyond cultural education, Barrera and Corso recommend dialogue that includes respect, reciprocity, and responsiveness. "Respect is expressed as a willingness to acknowledge a variety of perspectives as equally valid to achieving a particular goal" (p. 67). Reciprocity "requires entering into interactions ready to learn as well as to teach, ready to receive as well as to give" (p. 69). Responsiveness focuses on communicating both respect and understanding of the others' perspectives.

Sometimes our subject matter expertise works against us. The more we are socialized to the scholarly ways of thinking, the more we may be ready to prescribe solutions before we fully understand those we serve. We may develop hardening of the categories.

Barrera and Corso give examples that are pertinent for FLEs. One example that is especially pertinent for home visitors involves Betsy, who visited Karen, a single mother from Puerto Rico, weekly. Betsy laments: "When I ask her to tell me what she'd like for her child Maya or when I ask her to work with Maya, she says that I am the expert and that I should tell her what needs to be done. Sometimes she'll even leave me alone with Maya. I know that Karen cares about Maya and is just expressing her respect for me, but how can I get Karen more involved in Maya's activities while I am visiting" (p. 43)?

The instinctive response to Karen might be to explain the importance of her participation and request (or insist) that she remain and participate while Betsy works with Maya. Since the objective of Betsy's visits is not only to help Maya directly but also to train Karen to work more effectively with her, the request seems entirely reasonable. But there is a wonderful opportunity for skilled dialogue here.

The first quality of skilled dialogue is respect. Respect entails believing that people do what they do for reasons that make sense to them. We may not understand the reasons—we may not even know the reasons—that Karen keeps her distance. But if we respect Karen, we believe that her reluctance to take part in Maya's treatment is not a sign of indifference. Karen might not take part because she feels very inadequate in the presence of an expert. (Have you ever felt inadequate in the presence of an expert?) Or she might use Betsy's visits as a chance to get a welcome break. There are many reasons Karen does not take part. We do not have to agree with those reasons. We can identify tension points without making any judgments about the character of the other person.

Reciprocity, the second quality of skilled dialogue, acknowledges that every person has experience and perceptions of value. We don't have to prove that we are right and they are wrong. If we are skilled at listening and understanding, there is much we can learn from Karen. We can observe the ways in which she does interact effectively with Maya. We can ask questions to help us understand. "How would you feel about hanging around while I work with Maya? I would like you to tell me what things I am doing that you think might be helpful to her." Such a request acknowledges that Karen knows more about Maya than we do. It invites her to be a partner in the process of helping Maya.

Responsiveness requires humility, or what Barrera and Corso describe as being open to mystery. We listen. We observe. We ask questions. We know that we need knowledge that the mother has as much as she needs the knowledge that we bring. We know that we don't have all the answers. We seek to understand and to communicate that understanding by asking such questions that may begin with "What do you think . . .? Do you think it would help if . . .?"

Such skilled dialogue can lead to "anchored understanding of diversity"—not the generalizations about cultures but a specific knowledge and appreciation of someone who is different from us. "Simply knowing about something tends to leave one detached, standing outside with a relatively general and perhaps even stereotypical picture" (Barrera & Corso, 2003, p. 54). Such anchored understanding does not come from a textbook; it can only come through personal relationships.

With an anchored understanding of diversity, we are prepared to enter what Barrera and Corso call "3rd Space." Rather than dragging the parent to our view or abdicating to the parent's view, we look for the new place that incorporates the best of both of our experiences. Third Space invites us "to make a fundamental shift from dualistic, exclusive perceptions of reality and to adopt a mindset that integrates the complementary aspects of diverse values, behaviors, and beliefs into a new whole" (pp. 75-76). Betsy may need to set aside any agenda for Karen until she understands her world. She may offer to help her prepare dinner or wash dishes while they chat.

● GROUP FAMILY LIFE EDUCATION EXAMPLES

I (Goddard) was invited to teach a series of parenting classes to a group of parents whose teens were in trouble with the law. The parents did not come to the class gladly. They were mad at their teens and mad at the judge who required their attendance at parenting classes.

With respect to the issue of diversity, the organizer of the classes had serious reservations about whether a college professor with a happy family would be able to speak the language of angry, working parents who were experiencing hell at home. It was reasonable for him to worry. If I had given university lectures on socialization processes, I would have alienated the parents.

We began the first session with introductions and a question: "Is parenting hard or easy?" The question energized the parents. All agreed that parenting is tough duty. Some of them volunteered their stories. Over the course of several sessions, most of them shared their struggles.

One of the fathers—a tough, crusty, and outspoken man—told that every night he propped a chair against his bedroom door and kept a weapon under his pillow because he was afraid that his daughter might break into his room in the night and stab him.

There are many ways to react to such a statement. One natural reaction might be "If you weren't such a brute, you wouldn't have to worry about your well-being!" On some level, we might be "right." But such an approach is only helpful in silly movies. If we apply Barrera and Caruso's quality of respect (above) together with Ginott's process of sensitization (as described in Chapter 6), our reaction would be very different. I tried to imagine what that man might be feeling. Based on my effort at empathy, I could reply from the heart, "Ouch! It must be very painful to have such an awful relationship with your daughter when you want so badly to be a good dad."

Actually, there was nothing in his statement that spoke to his aspirations as a father. But I speculated that the reason he told that story—and the reason it was so painful for him—is that he would like to have a caring relationship with his daughter. I know how painful it would have been for me if I had been in his shoes. Over the course of the series of classes, that father moved from resentment toward hope.

I am convinced that our effectiveness in FLE has less to do with the match of our education and experience to that of our participants than it has to do with our willingness and ability to be genuinely compassionate. While each of the participants in that class had a different story to tell, each of their stories was about hopes, struggles, and disappointments. Those are stories that should draw compassion out of all of us.

I (Duncan) was invited to one of Montana's Indian reservations to teach a half-day workshop on personal development. I find Abraham Maslow's conceptualization of the self to be very powerful and helpful, and was in the process of presenting some of his ideas in a way I thought understandable to my group. At one point, I chose the metaphor of an apple to lead participants into an exercise where they would identify characteristics of their true or "core" selves. I said, "I am like an apple, and at my core you will find . . ." I then invited participants to complete the phrase by listing their core personal characteristics, which Maslow maintains are always positive and "uncreated." Instead of beginning to write, several smiled awkwardly and some even chuckled softly. So I asked them what they found funny. They were comfortable enough around me to tell me directly what was on their mind. Apples are red on the outside (at least many varieties) and white on the inside. So my asking them to imagine they were an apple was the like asking them to pretend they were American Indian only on the outside but actually White on the inside. We dialogued about what metaphors for the self would be more meaningful to them, and found that metaphors representing human connection to the earth and other living things held significance. Although some things we will learn only by experience, this one taught me the importance of checking out assumptions with others from the target audience.

PROGRAMMING FOR DIVERSITY ●

The primary challenges for programming for diversity are twofold: (1) create FLE materials and use approaches that are inclusive of heterogeneous groups audiences or (2) be on target with materials developed or adapted for homogeneous groups. In addition to the perspective and strategies we have already discussed, here are several specific guidelines for diversity programming in FLE (Myers-Walls, 2000).

Know Your Audience

There are literally dozens of dimensions on which FLE audiences may vary. Some typical ones include age, income, and marital or parental status. From an ecological systems perspective (Bronfenbrenner, 1979), a true understanding of FLE audiences moves well beyond knowing their simple social address. Effective FLE programming involves understanding audiences in the context of their surroundings (Schorr, 1988, 1997). It also includes being sensitive to the unique construction of meaning for each participant. Understanding diversity moves to an awareness of the multiple and intersecting ways in which audiences and individuals within audiences may vary.

All of us have membership in a variety of different groups based on our gender, race, religious beliefs, income, and educational levels. To these group variations can be added the additional diversity noted earlier in the chapter, such as learning styles and communication standards. Myers-Walls (2000) has summarized some of these cultural contextual variations and possible values that spring from them (see Table 11.1).

Perhaps the best time to begin learning about audience diversity is during the needs assessment process, where attitudes, values, meanings, and expectations can be explored. Data collection during needs assessment should be representative of the diversity of persons for whom that program is being designed. Wise FLEs will also include members of the intended audience on the assessment team to ensure sensitivity to the kinds of questions that should be asked members of particular subgroups. However, needs assessments alone are insufficient to meet diversity needs. To be effective, FLEs must remain flexible during teaching situations and continually assess the fit of the principles they share with the life experience and meanings of participants.

Know Yourself

Myers-Walls (2000) suggests learning who we are, what we know, and how we feel pertaining to diversity matters. Learning who we are involves identifying our personal characteristics and the various sociocultural groups to which we belong. We can identify the various ways we intersect and overlap with audiences as well as how we differ from them, and the implications for FLE. A self-evaluation of what we know and do not know about the various audiences we seek to reach is another important step. When the knowledge gap is too great, then we work to reduce that knowledge gap through greater study of the audience. Some of this beginning knowledge gap may be closed though learning about various cultural perspectives such as those shared at the beginning of the chapter. Assessing how we feel is about asking ourselves questions regarding our attitudes and values such as we explored in Chapter 1. According to Myers-Walls (2000), "A central question with which to begin a self-assessment is whether one views diversity as a problem to be solved or an opportunity to be realized" (p. 371).

TABLE 11.1   The Cultural Context of Families

Dimension	Possible Values
Population-Environmental Context	
Population mix	Homogeneous versus heterogeneous
Geography and climate	Uniting or separating families and individuals
Socioeconomic status	Mix of haves and have-nots
Religious orientation	Homogeneous versus heterogeneous, along with specific religious values and practices
Age/maturity of the community	Long history versus recent establishment or change
Community resources	Many versus few resources and services available
Levels of racism and discrimination	High versus low
Views of Children	
Child-rearing responsibility	Individual parents, extended family members, the community, tribe, or other
Investment in child rearing	Demanding of time and energy versus easy and requiring little effort
Children's contributions	Children as producers of goods and services versus as consumers who receive more than they return
Children's role	Blessing versus burden
Interpersonal Relationships	
Means of dealing with conflict	Physical versus social techniques
Whose needs predominate?	Children, adults, or the group?
Sharing problems with others	Seen as a request for help, a sign of weakness, or entertainment
Means of working together	Cooperation versus competition; communalism versus individualism
Views on gender	Men dominant, women dominant, or shared roles; sons or daughters more highly valued or both valued equally

Source: From "Family Diversity and Family Life Education" by Judith A. Myers-Walls, from *Handbook of Family Diversity*, edited by David H. Demo, et al., copyright © 2000 by Oxford University Press, Inc. Used by permission of Oxford University Press, Inc.

Explore Your Limits

FLEs may be flexible and comfortable with a certain level of diversity but uncomfortable when diversity exceeds certain personal, ethical, and empirical boundaries. Knowing who we are as FLEs involves knowing where these specific boundaries lie for ourselves. For example, we might never recommend that parents spank their children for any reason because we personally consider spanking disrespectful of children. Professionally, we may consider it unethical to recommend a strategy that potentially could do harm, despite lack of evidence that spanking is always damaging to children. We may believe there are certain values, attitudes, and behaviors in families that are better and healthier than others, and we are not willing to recommend less effective strategies. For that reason, we might tell participants, "Spanking is probably never the best solution." It is probably not productive to argue against a group's cultural values, but it may be useful to invite group members to consider even better techniques that are consistent with their group and individual values.

Evaluate Program Material for Diversity

There are at least three important questions to ask when evaluating FLE program material for diversity (Myers-Walls, 2000):

1. *Are the goals and objectives of the program appropriate for the individuals and groups in the audience?* FLEs need to assess whether the material shared will benefit all groups equally or whether it will tend to favor specific groups. Goals and objectives should be written to incorporate the various groups' (or targeted groups') values and aspirations.

2. *Are the content of the program and sources of information or knowledge base applicable to the audience? How inclusive and applicable are they to a heterogeneous group? How might the program be adapted to meet the needs of a different homogeneous or targeted audience?* The ideas on which FLE programs are based are only as good as their scholarly foundation. Many ideas commonly accepted as truth in family science are based mostly upon research of the White middle class. FLEs should examine source materials for their breadth and inclusiveness (e.g., did the summary of studies underlying a parenting idea include data from a diversity of respondents?). For targeted audiences (e.g., single parents with young children), FLEs should examine whether the foundational material applies to the targeted population.

I (Duncan) was working as an Extension specialist in Montana and had been asked to deliver a series of Making Families Stronger workshops at several elementary schools and a middle school in my hometown. The workshop series was based on well-known family strengths literature, prominently based on findings from mostly two-parent, first marriage White families. The workshop series was well publicized in anticipation of the events. One afternoon I received a phone call from an interested person who asked whether the workshop would be relevant only to traditional families with a mother and a father and if the examples would feature only that family form. She mentioned that she was interested in attending with her female partner. I told her that while the research underlying the program originated primarily from two-parent, heterosexual parent-headed families, it also included some stepfamilies and single-parent families. Beyond those families, it was unknown precisely how the family strengths ideas would apply to other family forms. However, I hastened to add my professional position that the strengths were about family processes, not family structures, and that the ideas were relevant for any close human relationship. I was pleased to see her and her partner attend my middle school workshop and seem to enjoy the discussion.

3. *Are the teaching methods and styles respectful of and effective with the audience?* If an audience had limited educational background, methods might be chosen because of their effectiveness with visual and auditory learners, rather than relying on written materials. For example, wise FLEs might include a variety of visual media such as videotaping and movie clips, telling stories that relate to participant experiences, hands-on activities, group activities, group games, and role playing to present ideas. Educators would keep the material simple and to the point because of the vast differences in participant educational levels. Written material would be written at a low reading level or be simple enough that it could be easily adapted/interpreted.

Be Flexible

Effective FLEs will need to respond flexibly to a variety of educational needs. Avoid the one-size-fits-all approach to programming. An individualized approach based on family need rather than a uniform approach across family should be used, especially when working with limited resource families (Schorr, 1988, 1997). Some ideas may go untaught in workshop settings, but human needs will be met. To accomplish this, sessions might be offered in small groups or have built-in one-on-one time, as needed, allowing for more individualized attention and for materials to be more effectively adapted to individual participant needs.

● CONCLUSION

All of us share something in common: We are alike and different in many ways. To effectively meet the needs of an increasingly diverse FLE audience, family life professionals need to become sensitive to diversity on many fronts, including cultural differences, learning styles, cultural contexts, and values. Important skills FLEs need to program for diversity include using skilled dialogue, knowing the audience, knowing themselves, knowing their limits, and how to evaluate program materials for diversity. Characteristics important for working with diverse audiences include empathy, compassion, and flexibility. The following explorations will help you strengthen your abilities to work with diverse FLE audiences.

● EXPLORATIONS

1. Think of a group with which you have worked or with which you expect to work. What are some of the unhelpful judgments you have been tempted to make of those you served? How can those judgments be framed differently as you try to apply the qualities of anchored understanding?

2. In leading a training, one mother told of difficulties when her strong-willed child had a tantrum at the grocery store. The educator asked what she had tried and what effect they had had. She told him. He suggested additional possibilities. She insisted that nothing would work. He recommended some alternatives—and did it with greater certainty. She became more resistant. What might the educator have done to be more effective, based on the ideas you have gained from this chapter?

3. As you anticipate the difficult situations you will face in your professional activities, what challenges are you likely to face in connecting with the people you serve? How can you prepare yourself to respond helpfully and sensitively? Discuss with your colleagues and classmates what challenges they have faced and how they have dealt with them. Develop your own plan for growing and maintaining an anchored understanding of diversity.

4. Imagine you have been asked by your family coalition to provide parenting education in your community. In your search for an optimal program, you come across a program called Principles for Parenting

Success. As you review it, you notice some good general principles, but they need adapting to fit your community, which is racially, culturally, educationally, and economically diverse. Describe how you would modify this program for diversity based on the social ecology of your community. First, discuss how you would modify the program to make it more inclusive, then discuss how you would alter it for a specific target audience within the community. Describe how you would modify goals and objectives, content, teaching methods, and evaluation approaches.

5. What are some of the signs when you are teaching a workshop that the content or presentation is not reaching the audience? What can a workshop leader do to adjust to the audience?

CHAPTER 12

CREATING EFFECTIVE COLLABORATIVE PARTNERSHIPS

With all the challenges facing families today, wise family life education (FLE) professionals realize that they cannot fully address these concerns single-handedly. We need the help of like-minded others. How do we go about bringing our contributions to the collaborative table and synergize with them to effectively serve families in our communities?

Stated succinctly, "Community-based organizations, [FLEs], and agencies that share common goals can expand their outreach and effectiveness through collaboration, partnerships, linkages, and networking. Educational . . . needs of . . . families are interrelated and complex. Since no one system alone can effectively address the multiplicity of needs and problems of families, the collaborative process is a recognized and practical approach. The collaborative process involves agencies, corporations, and volunteer groups working together to provide comprehensive approaches to the complex problems of families. From this process, new alliances, partnerships, and networks evolve, and ultimately benefit . . . audiences" (Cooperative Extension System [CES], 1991, p. 4).

There are many ways to work together to address family issues. Because effective collaboration is a key characteristic of strong, sustainable community-based programs, as noted in Chapter 3, we devote special attention to working together collaboratively in this chapter. We begin by defining the collaborative process in addressing complex family issues and discuss its advantages and challenges. We next present a taxonomy for working with others (ranging from networking to full collaboration) and strategies for building effective collaborative partnerships. Finally, we provide a discussion of principles for successful collaboration and examples of effective collaborative partnerships in action.

At the conclusion of the chapter, readers have the opportunity to select a family life topic reflecting a community need (e.g., better parenting of young children) and create a community linkage plan that pulls together important stakeholders (e.g., parents, preschool teachers, head start representatives), decision makers (e.g., legislators), and agency representatives (e.g., child protective service agencies) to address the topic.

DEFINING THE COLLABORATIVE PROCESS •

Problems facing families today rarely involve simple, silver bullet solutions. No one group or discipline can effectively or successfully address the multiplicity of needs and problems of families (CES, 1991). Family concerns that attract the preventive attention of FLEs have multiple causes, with both risk factors and protective factors occurring at different levels of the social ecology (see Chapter 2; Bronfenbrenner, 1986). Because family issues are multilevel and multidisciplinary in scope, the best solutions to address them are likewise multifaceted and holistic. For example, a family-serving organization with the goal of helping parents balance work and family will have less success on its own than it would have if workplaces joined it by adopting family friendly policies and radio stations provided helpful balancing hints to commuting parents. Not surprisingly, therefore, many individuals and groups recommend working together to form strong problem-solving relationships to enhance the benefits to children, youth, families, and communities (Borden & Perkins, 1999; CES, 1991; Extension Committee on Organization and Policy [ECOP], 2002). In fact, more and more initiatives at the local, state, and federal levels expect multiple sector agencies to collaborate (Borden & Perkins, 1999). While it may not be possible in terms of time or resources to address all problems from a systemic perspective and work at multiple levels simultaneously, the most effective and comprehensive FLE offerings would address both risk and protective processes at several closely interrelated levels of the human ecology (Bogenschnieder, 1996).

Collaboration has been defined as "a process through which parties who see different aspects of a problem can constructively explore their differences and search for solutions that go beyond their own limited vision of what is possible" (Gray, 1989, p. 5). All parties bring to the collaborative table their own knowledge, training, understanding, and experiences; collaboration is a process whereby those strengths and gifts are placed on the table and fused with others. Effective collaborations are full partnerships, where all parties throw down institutional, disciplinary, and agency barriers and individual agendas to develop a shared vision, common goals, and strategic plans. The players "invest a relatively equal amount of tangible and intangible resources" to the partnership (Ritter & Gottfried, 2002, p. 7). Leadership is shared and the successes of respective partners are interdependent (Evans et al., 2001). If the ultimate goal in FLE is the restructuring of existing programs and services toward comprehensive, integrated service delivery for families, then full collaboration represents the ideal situation (Melaville & Blank, 1991).

● ADVANTAGES OF COLLABORATION

There are many advantages that accrue when FLEs work together collaboratively with like-minded others to address the needs of families.

Opportunity to Bring Together a Wide Range of Expertise on Behalf of Clientele

Family issues are complex, and all members of a collaboration, with their unique training and experiences, will bring a different view of the problem and solution. The varied perspectives release the group from parochialism of perspective that can result within a single agency or disciplinary focus. Ideally, the collaboration also includes members of the targeted audience, who bring with them their own experiences and expertise that need integration into the professionals' views.

Decisions at Every Level of the Program Are Better

At every level of program design, decisions are made about content, process, and so on. Because the problem or concern is likely to be fully defined and details not missed and multiple perspectives drawn upon, programmatic solutions are likely to garner better results.

Can Harness and Combine Financial and Human Resources

When integrated FLE services to families is the goal, a collaboration allows for various agencies to allocate a portion of their funds and a portion of the time of employees to addressing the issue.

Enhance Likelihood of Community Buy-In

When many sectors join together collaboratively, a community sees that efforts go beyond the work or ideas of one person or group. With many community sectors represented and included, participation levels increase.

Increase Likelihood of Institutional Change

Members of collaborative partnerships can establish goals within their own organization to institutionalize the participation of personnel in collaboration through line-item budgets, work plans that include ongoing participation, human and financial, in collaborations serving families.

Increase Likelihood of Program Dissemination

Members of collaborations bring with them their own clientele, which become instant clientele of the collaboration. Thus, participation is multiplied as the collaboration grows.

Improves the Quality of Programs and Is Worth the Effort

As part of its effort to evaluate efforts across its funded programs, the Children, Youth, and Families at Risk (CYFAR) Evaluation Collaboration conducted surveys of Extension Service professionals in 45 states and territories in late 1997 and early 1998. Respondents were asked if working together rather than alone improved work and if it was worth the effort. When asked how strongly they agreed with the statement "Working with other Extension staff has improved our programs for children, youth and families at risk," 78% agreed or strongly agreed. When asked whether collaboration with other community, county, state, and federal organizations is worth the effort, 82% agreed or strongly agreed that it was.

CHALLENGES TO COLLABORATION ●

A decision to collaborate is not without its challenges. These challenges must be recognized and addressed if a collaborative partnership is to work effectively and be sustained over time. Here are several challenges that need attention (Meek, 1992a):

Turf Issues

Sometimes members of collaborations become concerned with getting credit or owning for themselves a particular domain. As a popular saying goes, "It is amazing how much can be accomplished when no one cares who gets the credit." For fullest accomplishment, turf protection and mistrust must be overcome. If collaborative partners mistrust each other, they will not be willing to share resources or be receptive to one another's ideas. Most of the advantage of working together will be lost; in fact, there may be a negative outcome.

One such negative outcome occurred when a successful program designed to help families transition from public assistance to self-sufficiency was blocked from expansion and permanence when a previously collaborating group decided on competing for grant dollars against the collaboration. The outcome was the closing down of the successful program in that area and the subsequent limiting of services the program provided to needy families.

When individuals and groups join a collaboration, they typically are committed at the outset to the ethic of working together harmoniously, sharing power, program ownership, and other resources. The processes that follow of creating a shared vision, mission, and strategic plan are often all that is needed to reduce turfism. Turf battles do occur, however, and when they concern substantive issues in the collaboration, such as goals, resources, or methods, they can usually be resolved with ordinary problem-solving strategies (e.g., identify and clarify the concern, suggest solutions, choose one a collaboration thinks will work, carry out the solution) (Meek, 1992b). Of course, full collaboration requires the goodwill and cooperation of all collaborating organizations. If one organization refuses to cooperate, it cannot be coerced. It can only be invited.

Reaching Consensus

It takes time to reach agreement on a general course and direction, followed by specific goals, objectives, roles, and other related decisions. Sometimes partners lack the authority to make decisions on behalf of their sponsoring organization, and must return to get clearance for their involvement. Depending on how well the collaboration communicates or how often it meets, decision by consensus could make acting on a problem slow and ineffective.

Similar to overcoming turfism, a key to consensus building is the strategic planning process that first begins with the creation of a shared vision that truly incorporates the diversity of perspectives represented. A shared vision provides a strong foundation for a collaboration, and once it is in place, achieving consensus on mission, goals, and objectives receives impetus.

In facilitating the planning for a local healthy marriage initiative for Hispanics, a strategic planner first defined and gave examples of vision statements. He then asked members of the budding collaboration to answer four questions to probe their perspective (adapted from Callor et al., 2000):

Vision Statement: A written statement that describes the community as it could be at some future point.

Examples:

A community committed to putting family first.

Married couples love, support, and respect one another.

All children and youth live in families that promote their positive development.

Answer the following:

Where do you hope the Healthy Marriage Initiative will be in 5 years?

What is the purpose of the initiative? What problem does it address?

What do you hope the initiative will offer over and above what other programs offer?

Write your vision statement.

The resulting two-part vision statement read: "Married couples living together in love and respect who support each other and their children; Communities that empower couples with knowledge, attitudes, skills, and resources necessary for successful marriage."

Limited Resources

It is possible that otherwise valuable partners will decide not to collaborate because they lack the finances to do so. Such potential partners are faced with the decision of devoting resources to a collaboration or keeping the funds within their own organization to address their own high-priority projects. If a collaboration is funded through extramural funds, where partners' involvement is paid for by those dollars, these concerns can be partially overcome. Otherwise, a looser connection among the partnership that does not involve the sharing of financial resources may be advised.

Divergent Views

As efforts toward reaching consensus ensue, some may adopt a policy position that is inconsistent with one of the partners and may cause the partner to be uncooperative, ineffective, or to simply drop out. Preventively, these challenges can be addressed through establishing core values of the collaboration during the visioning process, among which might be stated, "We honor and value the unique gifts, talents, and perspectives each individual, group, and organization brings to the collaboration." The core values guide the development of the ground rules a collaboration might adopt, which might include an occasional reminder to members to respect and hear one another's views.

Member Difficulties

Members in crisis may cause cooperation to decrease. Human service organizations are often at the top of agencies targeted for budget cuts. Thus, collaboration member agencies may suffer challenges of their own, such as the elimination of their own jobs. As organization administrations change, so too may the attitude of the participating organization toward the collaboration, which may pose problems if the new administrator does not favor or does not understand the nature of the collaboration.

For a collaboration to be successful, it must have sustained committed membership. Extracting written commitments from individuals, groups, and organizations indicating their commitment of time, people, and revenue may be necessary. In addition, collaborations will want to develop membership guidelines governing terms of office and replacement of members (Bergstrom et al., 1995).

● A COMMUNITY LINKAGES FRAMEWORK

While there is much to be desired in full collaborative partnerships to comprehensively address family concerns, it would be inaccurate to suggest that full collaboration is necessary or best for every program. There are a variety of ways of working together for families in communities, and certainly some problems, goals, or issues may benefit from more limited partnerships. The level of partnership selected depends mostly on the purposes of the program (Betts et al., 1999). FLEs should ask themselves what level of collaboration is necessary for program success.

A useful model describing the levels of collaboration is the Levels of Community Linkages model, developed by the National Network for Collaboration (Bergstrom et al., 1995), showing a continuum of possible levels of partnership in projects, as well as the purpose, structure, and process of such linkages. Other authors (e.g., Melaville & Blank, 1991) have also discussed a variety of approaches in working together. We present an adapted model in Table 12.1 and discuss it below.

TABLE 12.1   Levels of Community Linkages

Levels of Partnership	Purpose	Structure	Process
Networking	Dialogue and understanding Share information between agencies	* Loose/flexible link * Roles loosely defined * Community action is primary link among members	* Low-key leadership * Minimal decision making * Little conflict * Informal communication
Cooperation	Match needs/limit overlap of services	* Central body of people as communication hub * Semiformal links * Roles somewhat defined * Links are advisory * Group leverages/raises money	* Facilitative leaders * Complex decision making * Some conflict * Formal communications within the central group
Coordination	Share resources to address common issues or create something new	* Central body of people consists of decision makers * Roles defined * Links formalized * Group develops new resources and joint budget	* Autonomous leadership but focus in on issue * Group decision making in central and subgroups * Communication is frequent and clear
Coalition	Share ideas and resources over a multiyear period	* All members involved in decision making * Roles and time defined * Links formal with written agreement * Group develops new resources and joint budget	* Shared leadership * Decision making formal with all members * Communication is common and prioritized
Collaboration	Build a program together to accomplish a shared vision and impacts	* Consensus used in shared decision making * Roles, time, and evaluation formalized * Links are formal and written in work assignments *A full partnership	Leadership high, trust level high, productivity high * Ideas and decisions equally shared * Highly developed communication

Source: Adapted from Bergstrom et al., 1995; Betts et al., 1999; Melaville & Blank, 1991.

Networking

At the network level of partnership, the purpose of the relationship is dialogue toward mutual understanding, passing along information that is helpful to each other's work. While it is possible that networkers are part of groups that have similar goals, goal similarity is not a prerequisite to networking. This level of working together is entirely appropriate if all one wants to do is to let one know what the other is doing. For example, one community organized a services network for Hispanic families, meeting each week to provide each other with information about services each organization offered, to calendar upcoming events, and to discuss needs. FLEs might only need or want to network, when at this point all FLEs want to do is inform others of the services they provide and share ideas during networking meetings.

Cooperation

Relationships move from networking to cooperation when organizations begin to match needs and efforts to avoid overlap. They work to help each other realize their goals but do not change the basic services they provide or the rules that govern their organizations (Melaville & Blank, 1991, p. 14). For example, while two FLEs operating in the network's organizations may very capably provide parenting education, cooperating FLEs might decide that one should specialize in programs for parents with children birth through age 11 while the other might focus on parents of adolescents. They would refer clientele to one another.

Coordination

From cooperation to coordination involves increasing the depth of interdependence of partners. In addition to doing what cooperators do, coordinators also share resources (human and/or financial) to address issues of shared concern or to create something new by virtue of the association. Typically, the associations are temporary and time limited. Thus, if FLEs' effort and involvement is intended to be short lived, coordination may be the appropriate level of partnership. For example, members of an ongoing youth services network who had concerns about higher risk youth in the inner cities met together to identify issues facing the youth. The group decided to elicit the help of family and human development Extension specialists to conduct a survey of youth attitudes and behaviors corresponding with these issues. The specialists summarized the findings in a reader-friendly report, complete with tables and recommendations based on the findings. From recommendations, the specialists suggested various FLE program offerings that could be used to address the identified needs.

Coalition

Coalitions essentially involve long-term coordination. Members share ideas, leadership, and resources over several years. In the aforementioned example, the youth agency network becomes a coalition simply as it continues to remain in existence over many years and continues to address youth needs as they arise. The FLEs brought in to help address the needs would continue in their advisory role.

Collaboration

Perhaps the feature that most distinguishes a collaboration from other levels of linking together is the focus on building a program together to accomplish a shared vision and outcomes. Parties gather together from conceptualization stages, creation of a shared vision and mission, strategic plans, continuing on through the implementation and evaluation of programs. They recognize and honor unique contributions and share credit for accomplishment (ECOP, 2002). Collaboration is ideal when the needs of an FLE audience require a seamless, comprehensive response. For example, one family-based program designed to prevent child abuse involved an initial home visit to assess needs, which could vary from parenting skills to knowledge of nutrition to housekeeping skills. Drawing on resources collected and developed by the collaboration, the home visitors proceeded to provide the in-home education to empower the families.

ASSESSING THE EFFECTIVENESS ● OF YOUR COLLABORATION

Effective collaborations have key characteristic processes (Borden & Perkins, 1999). Once a collaboration is in place in a community, FLEs can take steps to evaluate the strength of an FLE collaboration. Each of the following 13 factors (Borden & Perkins, 1999) can be rated on a scale of 1 to 5 (1 = strongly disagree to 5 = strongly agree) to assess how well a collaboration is functioning:

1. *Goals.* The collaboration has clearly defined goals. It has developed a shared vision and mission, strategic plan, and intended outcomes. The strategic plan is followed carefully and referred to and updated annually.

2. *Communication.* The collaboration has open and clear communication. There is an established process for communication between meetings.

3. *Sustainability.* The collaboration has a plan for sustaining membership and resources. This involves membership guidelines relating to terms of office and replacement of members.

4. *Research and evaluation.* The collaboration has conducted a needs assessment and has obtained information to establish its goal, and the collaboration continues to collect data to measure goal achievement. They share this evaluation data with members of the collaboration, stakeholders, and funding agencies.

5. *Political climate.* The history and environment surrounding power and decision making is positive. The political climate may be within the community as a whole.

6. *Resources.* The collaboration has access to needed resources. Resources refer to four types of capital: environmental, in-kind, financial, and human.

7. *Catalysts.* The collaboration was started because of existing problem(s), or the reason(s) for collaboration to exist required a comprehensive approach.

8. *Policies/Laws/Regulations.* The collaboration has changed policies, laws, and/or regulations that allow the collaboration to function effectively.

9. *History.* The community has a history of working cooperatively and solving problems.

10. *Connectedness.* Members of this collaboration are connected and have established informal and formal communication networks at all levels.

11. *Leadership.* The leadership facilitates and supports team building and capitalizes upon diversity and individual, group, and organizational strengths.

12. *Community development.* This community was mobilized to address important issues. There is a communication system and formal information channels that permit the exploration of issues, goals, and objectives.

13. *Understanding community.* The collaboration understands the community, including its people, cultures, values, and habits.

Reprinted from Borden, L. & Perkins, D., "Assessing your collaboration: A self evaluation tool," from the *Journal of Extension*. Reprinted with permission.

GETTING STARTED: STEPS FOR CREATING ●
EFFECTIVE COLLABORATIVE PARTNERSHIPS

Visit With Parties Who Share Goals and Interest

Inventory the organizations in the community (and state, depending on the scope of the program) and identify those that share similar goals and interests to those of your organization. Arrange an opportunity to meet with them to discuss jointly working together. If your interest is in parenting education, what other groups or individuals share the goal of helping parents effectively nurture their young?

Agree on Desired Outcomes

In the process of discussion and synergizing your ideas with your collaborative partner, agree on outcomes that members of the group are jointly committed to. One outcome a parenting collaborative group might target is "Equip parents with effective, positive child guidance tools and, in the process, substantially reduce use of corporal punishment as a discipline strategy."

Have a Shared Vision, Mission, and
Strategic Plan for Achieving Outcomes

Although, as noted in Chapter 4, arriving at a shared vision takes time, such a process is important to invite the commitment of all collaborative parties. Once that is achieved, the next vital step is the development of a mission statement (where we define what the organization is and does) and strategic plan (specific steps the program will take to achieve the desired outcomes, in line with the project vision and mission).

Pool Resources (Human and Financial) and
Jointly Plan, Implement, and Evaluate Programs

The best collaborative partnerships approach the ideal of seamlessly fusing parties together. Participating agencies devote a substantial amount of the parties' time and job effort to the collaboration. After the preliminary work of creating the vision, mission, and strategic plan is accomplished, the parties continue to work together to put the flesh on the skeleton of the program, including development of the materials, implementation and dissemination of materials, and determining whether the program accomplished targeted outcomes.

Involve Participants in the Collaboration

A serious weakness in many family life educational efforts is the failure to include the target audience in predevelopment stages of a program. As a result, such programs are destined to fail from the beginning (see Chapter 13 for a fuller discussion). However, in addition to assessing participant needs, it is also critical to involve them in the collaboration, where the participant voice can be heard not only with respect to how an FLE program is developed but also how it is implemented and evaluated.

Focus on Participant Needs and Outcomes

The felt and ascribed needs identified during needs assessments conducted at the program predesign stages become the focus of attention and effort. Without meeting participant needs and achieving intended outcomes, the program will fail.

Build Ownership at All Levels
(Local, County, State, etc.)

The antidote to turfism is shared ownership. Shared ownership is fostered through full participation of all parties at the visioning and strategic planning stages, and each participant is delegated individual responsibility for the outcomes of the joint effort (Melaville & Blank, 1991).

Recognize and Respect Strengths of Members

Each member of the collaboration will bring unique strengths, perspectives, and skills to share as part of the project. Taking time to appropriately acknowledge the contributions of each member of the group for good ideas and so on is an important part of building positive morale among group members. For collaborations to thrive, a perceptive and cooperative facilitator is a key resource.

EXAMPLES OF EFFECTIVE FAMILY ●
LIFE EDUCATION COLLABORATIONS

As you will recall from Chapter 3, effective collaboration is an important component of effective, sustained, community-based FLE programs. Many community partners are involved. Below we present two examples of effective FLE collaborations that utilize many of the principles and steps outlined above.

Alabama's Begin Education Early and Healthy (BEE) Program

The BEE program (Abell, Adler-Baeder, Tajeu, Smith, & Adrian, 2003) targets geographically isolated, limited resource (low-income and/or limited education) families with preschool-age children (2-5). The key thrust of the BEE program is to assist parents in becoming more effective in meeting their goals for the development and well-being of their children. Specific goals of the project are to increase parental capacity to (a) provide appropriate guidance, emotional support, and involvement in school readying behaviors, (b) initiate contact and interact productively with community services related to children's health, and (c) develop effective coparenting relationships across a variety of family forms and structures.

The project envisioned communities in Alabama where children and youth can lead positive, secure, and productive lives. The mission statement reads: *"Sharing parenting information about early childhood education and development with rural, underserved families to increase parents' abilities to guide and nurture their young children's learning readiness."*

The BEE program uses one-on-one parenting education modules and a unique van-based delivery system as its core programming content. These modules focus on providing parents education in support of their effectiveness as caregivers and first teachers of their young children, as well as parents' health literacy and coparenting relationships. Health modules address the development of knowledge and skills that parents need to interact effectively with the health care system, to follow the instructions and advice provided, and to use complementary components of the health care system. Learning module objectives focus on building strengths among participant families through the development of practical knowledge and decision-making skills that form and sustain healthy adult relationships, family relationships, and nurturing environments for children.

Delivery of the core BEE program is done by a trained paraprofessional BEE educator, who recruits and works one-on-one with caregivers and at least one child aged 2 to 5. Up to 15 families are recruited and are enrolled for 10 weekly 1-hour sessions. Each family attends their sessions aboard a van, renovated to be a classroom on wheels, which travels to their homes. On the BEE van, the child takes part in hands-on developmentally appropriate activities while the educator and the parent discuss parenting and child development. BEE health and relationship modules are delivered in a group setting in faith-based or community-based locations identified through the work of the BEE collaboration coordinator. Potential group leaders or educators are recruited and identified by community agencies and organizations and trained to conduct learning modules by project codirectors with the assistance of the BEE collaboration coordinator.

Three counties (Wilcox, Macon, and Perry) were selected as sites for the BEE project. These counties are located in Alabama's Black Belt, an area defined by its fertile black soil that was once the backbone of the state's agricultural economy but is now plagued by pervasive poverty and economic stagnation. Extension and community leaders in these counties have shown an interest in grassroots efforts designed to address communitywide concerns and recognition of the need to develop more cohesive community collaborations to address families' security, health, and educational needs.

A key group in the BEE program are the BEE advisory boards, critical for expanding community involvement and collaboration. These boards involve community members in advising program staff and serve as a mechanism for involving the broader community in creative support and expansion activities.

Educating Families to Achieve Independence in Montana (EDUFAIM) Program

The EDUFAIM program (Duncan, Dunnagan, Christopher, & Paul, 2003) is a second example of an effective collaborative. Formed to help families make transitions from public assistance to self-reliance, EDUFAIM is designed to help limited-resource families gain the knowledge, attitudes, and skills needed for effective family resource management and progress toward a self-supporting lifestyle.

This collaboration first began with simple discussions among parties interested in improving the plight of limited resource families in Montana. In early 1995, specialists at the Montana State University Extension Service met with the Department of Public Health and Human Services (DPHHS) public assistance directors to discuss working together for limited-resource families. Initial meetings focused on nutrition education and food resource management, since most of the state dollars available at that time for the education of limited-resource families were earmarked for nutrition programs. However, it was clear that Montana families coming off public assistance needed more than nutrition education to make a successful transition to self-sufficiency. Extension and DPHHS parties both concluded that many public assistance families now needed educational aid in a number of areas as they made the transition from welfare dependence to self-sufficiency. They decided to seek grants to fund such a transition program in Montana. They were successful in obtaining a State Strengthening grant from the Children, Youth, and Families at Risk Initiative (CYFAR) of the Cooperative State Research, Education, and Extension Service (CSREES). The state-level collaborative partnership had been forged.

While state-level partnership is important, without local collaboration and buy-in, a program will falter. The next step was to select local community sites. State partners contacted county Extension agents and their county welfare directors to assess the level of interest and community buy-in to EDUFAIM. To be selected, sites needed to demonstrate interest and buy-in and have a community infrastructure that would allow for the collaboration of many agencies to carry out the work. In addition, in an attempt to reach the most resource-poor areas of the state, the percentage of children living in poverty at the selected sites needed to meet or exceed 20%. Two sites were selected initially, serving five rural Montana counties.

Specific educational program content for EDUFAIM is determined by the needs identified and prioritized by individual families and communities. Program areas may include, but are not limited to, nutrition and health (e.g., preventive health education, maternal and infant nutrition, food preparation, healthy and low-cost food shopping, and food safety), individual and family development (e.g., parent education, building family strengths, balancing work and family, building self-efficacy and positive expectations, managing stress), resource management (e.g., time management, money management, consumer skills), community development (e.g., small business development), and housing (e.g., housing affordability and availability, protection of housing investment, health-related environmental issues within the home).

Upon entry into the program, families develop a family investment agreement (FIA). The FIAs list the kinds of EDUFAIM courses families believe they need to help them move toward greater self-sufficiency. Classes are taught in small group settings or one-on-one, as needed, by local EDUFAIM staff consisting of an EDUFAIM family educator assisted by an EDUFAIM program aide. The family educator is a professional holding a master's degree with considerable experience working with limited-resource families. Program aides are paraprofessionals indigenous to the limited-resource population who have real-life experience with public assistance. This combination of professional and real-life experience is likely to form the basis of strong, caring associations between educators and participants (Giblin, 1989). The family educator and program aide work collaboratively with the local community advisory council for FAIM, consisting of agency representatives, volunteers, and members of the target audience.

Local staff are supported with educational materials and training, evaluation, and computer technology by the state EDUFAIM team. This team is comprised of resident and Extension faculty representing 10 disciplines—family science, nutrition, adult development, adult education, child development, family economics, community development, housing, youth development, and computer technology. Each site has two computers, one for office use and one for public use. These computers provide Internet connectivity, allowing access to many Web-based resources for their clientele and the ability to stay connected with other professionals locally and nationally. Specialists assist sites by pointing community EDUFAIM staff to resources that help support them in their work with limited resource audiences.

The state EDUFAIM team is in turn supported by college deans, department heads, Extension administration, and state directors of the DPHHS, who together have developed a shared vision and strategic plan for addressing the educational needs of at-risk families in Montana, using EDUFAIM as a vehicle. The vision of the EDUFAIM program is *"Supportive Montana communities that empower families to develop skills, knowledge and competencies necessary for managing family resources and progressing toward a self-supporting lifestyle."* In connection with this vision, the EDUFAIM mission statement reads: *"EDUFAIM is a collaborative effort of the Montana State University Extension Service, Department of Public Health and Human Services, and Community Advisory Councils that provides educational programs to empower FAIM and other at-risk families in attaining knowledge and developing skills necessary for managing family resources and progressing toward a self-supporting lifestyle."* This vision and mission statement form the basis of a comprehensive strategic plan for its accomplishment. The vision, mission statement, and strategic plan are reviewed and updated annually, and course corrections are made when needed.

In turn, local EDUFAIM staff and community advisory councils have developed their own vision, mission mission statement, and strategic plan that are in line with the state vision. They likewise hold regular meetings to review and update their plans.

The federal liaison external to the project termed the EDUFAIM project a "model of collaboration" (Woods, 1998). Several specific collaboration strategies have been used with success in EDUFAIM; five are listed below:

Shared Vision

From the outset, in participating communities, EDUFAIM has been viewed as the catalyst to coordinate the variety of necessary programs to help remove barriers to employment and to help families become self-supporting. Everyone at the table shared the vision that this collaboration would produce superior results.

Focus on Participants' Needs

The collaboration has been working in part because everyone has striven to keep in mind that collaboration exists to meet participant needs in the most effective way possible. Participants were interviewed during the design phase of EDUFAIM to learn from them what they needed to become self-reliant. Their responses, plus their representation as members of community advisory councils, helped form EDUFAIM's entire structure, service delivery approach, and strategic plan.

Use of Most Knowledgeable and Experienced Resources

The partnership utilized the most knowledgeable and experienced resources in the community. Each of the participating organizations and agencies at the local level selected a top member of their team to guarantee a horizontal collaboration among "equals." This was done because it has been their experience that hierarchical collaborations do not work. Because of this egalitarian arrangement, the EDUFAIM partnership was able to recognize and respect their limitations and defer to the core competencies of other collaborators. As a result, EDUFAIM staff participated in an extremely strong referral network.

Compensation Arrangements Discussed in Advance

Issues of ownership were discussed openly. At one site, ownership issues started to become a concern when Welfare-to-Work monies became available and there was the potential for interagency competition. However, because of the shared vision and focus on the needs of individuals, community agencies were able to come together to write the grant, and all compensation arrangements were completely and satisfactorily resolved.

Responsiveness to Clientele

Program leaders discovered throughout the growth of their program that they needed to respond quickly to the needs of clientele and be as flexible in providing services as possible. They found it essential to their success that their working environment was responsive and the communication paths streamlined. Modern technology (i.e., e-mail, faxing, cell phone) helped them to perform optimally with their collaborators and participants.

● CONCLUSION

Given the social problems landscape, there are many opportunities for FLEs to make a difference in communities. Wise FLE professionals realize that their strength and effectiveness with their educational audience is multiplied as they work together with like-minded individuals. This chapter presented several ways to work with others, focusing on the establishment of collaborative partnerships, and provided a few examples of such partnerships in action. One of us alone is never as powerful as all of us together.

● EXPLORATIONS

1. Detail a collaboration plan for your program. The essence of collaboration is to gain community ownership and support of the program, coordinating or collaborating with other agencies and existing efforts in the community to avoid duplication.
   - Identify those persons, agencies, and organizations that would likely share the vision of your program and be interested in similar outcomes. This will be your steering or advisory group. Describe how you will ensure the diversity of the group.
   - Describe how you would initiate a collaboration among the members of the committee. How would you go about creating a shared vision, mission, and strategic plan to direct your program? How will you resolve concerns about program ownership (turf issues)?
   - Describe how you will coordinate, collaborate, partner, network, and so on with other agencies and existing efforts in the community to avoid duplication and extend your reach.

2. Make a list of the kinds of programs FLEs might foster in a community. Identify which efforts might be best approached through networking, cooperation, or other means, including working alone. Assess the advantages and disadvantages of each approach.

3. Scan your community for examples of FLE programs. Identify the projects according to their level of partnership. Make plans to visit several programs and their leaders and observe how effective the level of partnership works, given the program's purpose.

CHAPTER 13

MARKETING FAMILY LIFE PRINCIPLES, PRACTICES, AND PROGRAMS

I n the movie *Field of Dreams* (Robinson, 1989), a voice whispers to the lead character, "If you build it, they will come." Eventually, he discovers that the "it" he is to build is a baseball diamond in the middle of a cornfield on his farm. This diamond becomes a place where the late, great ones gather to play ball. Not only do the players show up, so do the crowds!

In contrast, traditional family life education (FLE), especially that which takes place outside school classroom settings, suffers from "underwhelming participation" (Bowman & Kieren, 1985). Although no reliable figures exist for outreach FLE as a whole, studies of participation in marriage preparation programs have found that only 36% of couples who married in the last 5 years received church-affiliated premarital counseling (Stanley & Markman, 1997). One reason for underinvolvement of participants may hinge on the way FLE programs, principles, and practices are marketed. It is still the FLE professionals themselves, rather than potential clientele, who sense the need and appreciate the benefits of FLE the most. How can we foster a greater application of principles and practices and participation in programs?

Outreach family life educators (FLEs) can learn much from the field of social marketing to help answer these questions. Marketing emphasizes understanding target audiences through research, as a prelude to or concomitant with program development, in order to tailor the programs to the needs of the audience and thus facilitate their acceptance (Kotler & Bloom, 1984, cited in Levant, 1987). Marketing aims at understanding the motivations and underlying values of target audiences in order to encourage widespread adoption of targeted behaviors.

Most businesses and organizations exist only because of their markets (Calvert, 2000). Businesses that ignore consumer needs soon die. It is suspected that FLE programs not designed to meet specific needs of the target population will meet a similar fate (Duncan & Marotz-Baden, 1999). Effective businesses and organizations often spend a significant amount of money to persuade persons in these markets to buy their product. The field of outreach FLE has a different "product" to sell than most businesses: knowledge, principles, and practices important for enriching individual, marriage, and family life. How can FLEs create a market for FLE principles and programs? How do we motivate audience participation in FLE programs? How do we motivate adoption of desired behaviors? How should programs be produced, priced, placed, and promoted, with what partners, and with what funding to reach the target audience most effectively?

Drawing upon the original four Ps of marketing (product, price, place, promotion) and integrated with additional Ps of social marketing (publics, partnership, policy, purse strings) (Weinreich, 1999), we present a discussion of principles and some practical strategies for helping to answer this question, using relevant family life examples. At the end of the chapter, readers use the integrated Ps of marketing to devise a marketing plan of their own.

● THE SOCIAL MARKETING MIX

Social marketing as applied to FLE involves the use of consumer marketing principles to encourage the adoption of a behavior, principle, or practice that will benefit individuals, families, and society as a whole. We distinguish this kind of marketing from traditional forms of marketing in that the target goal is the strengthening of individuals, marriages, and families in their relationships.

Katz (1988) suggests that marketing decisions may be analyzed along four dimensions: product, price, place, and promotion. Marketing research links the four Ps as the framework for data collection on which marketing decisions are subsequently based (Katz, 1988). Marketing research quantifies and qualifies the nature of client needs and monitors the effectiveness of the process of satisfying those needs. If clients' needs are not satisfied, revisions begin with the four Ps (Katz, 1988).

Product

Product is the total package of professional services that is delivered to the client. The quality of these services may be an important factor in the client's decision to participate in a program. The services should have consistently high quality (Kotler & Roberto, 1989) in order to maintain a loyal clientele. In addition to the services themselves, a social marketing perspective also identifies the "product" as the behavior or cluster of behaviors we want participants in FLE to adopt. For example, parenting educators may want participating parents to adopt specific parenting practices, such as better listening and communicating with their youngsters. Leaders of a marriage workshop may want couples to intentionally attend to the "little things" in marriage, such as calling their spouse from work on occasion and making special time for intimacy.

Assessing the Target Audience

An important part of designing a product, in fact in addressing all eight of the Ps of marketing, is to first identify and become knowledgeable about the target audience. Assessing target audience needs ensures that the resulting educational programs are relevant to individuals and families throughout the lifespan and are based on the identified needs of such families (Powell & Cassidy, 2001). Identifying the specific target audience is aided by first segmenting the population (Kotler & Roberto, 1989). Some of the factors by which an audience might be segmented include, but are not limited to, the following (Kotler & Roberto, 1989; Weinreich, 1999):

- *Geographic region:* County, city or SMSA (Standard Metropolitan Statistical Areas—a standard Census Bureau designation of the region around a city); size; density (urban, rural, suburban); climate
- *Demographic:* Age, gender, family size, family life cycle, income, occupation, education, religion, race/ethnicity, social class, language, literacy
- *Psychographic:* Lifestyle, personality characteristics, values, conceptions of social norms
- *Attitudinal:* Attitudes, opinions, beliefs, and judgments about product; benefits sought and barriers avoided, readiness stage (unaware, aware, informed, interested, desirous, intending to buy)
- *Behavioral:* Product user-status, usage rate, occasion for use, other health-related activities.

The segment should be of practical importance to the target audience, the knowledge of which would enhance the potential of developing a product tailored for that need. For example, a balancing work and family program developed with large urban business parents in mind may likely be largely irrelevant to rural, farm family audiences also interested in harmonizing their work and family life. Once a target audience has been clearly identified, the next step is to find out from them what issues trouble them, to assess needs and the ways such needs might be addressed. For example, if we wanted to help working parents better balance work and family, we may want to first find out what concerns they have about balancing work and family, how important they feel it would be to do something about it, and what kind of balancing product would appeal to them the most. "To have a viable product," writes Weinreich, "people must first feel that they have a genuine problem, and that the product offered is a good solution to that problem" (1999, p. 10).

A variety of methods can be used to assess the needs of a target audience. Much can be learned about an audience through collecting secondary research, which does not require any face-to-face contact. Secondary research data is comprised of data that is already available, usually found in scholarly works such as journals and books, but also general social surveys conducted within the community of residence of the target audience. In addition, there are data sets available at the local, state, national, and international level that help to identify needs associated with membership in a target audience. To further tailor a program to the needs of a specifically targeted audience usually requires the collection of additional data from the intended audiences themselves, or primary data collection. Methods of data collection of this sort include telephone or face-to-face interviews and larger-scale surveys of the target population. For example, the Oklahoma Marriage Initiative (Johnson et al., 2002) conducted a large-scale social survey from which valuable information was learned regarding Oklahoman attitudes about a number of factors, but also marriage education, which information was then used to determine how to proceed with outreach efforts. To increase their participation in marriage preparation, young adults have been surveyed in college classroom settings to understand their perceptions of marriage preparation programs from a marketing perspective (Duncan, Box, & Silliman, 1996; Duncan & Wood, 2003). Vital information was learned in these studies addressing how a marriage preparation program might be produced to attract a larger, more diverse audience of young adults.

A primary prevention framework (Dumka et al., 1995) suggests the importance of consulting the target group through focus groups in order to enable program developers to adapt educational program content and processes to the needs, conditions, values, beliefs, and expectations of the audience (Dumka et al., 1995; Morgan, 1996; Morgan, Krueger, & King, 1998). Focus groups are small discussion groups normally consisting of 6 to 12 participants of similar or varied characteristics, depending on the interests of the researcher (Fern, 1982, and Morgan & Spanish, 1984, cited in Lengua et al., 1992). The expressed needs of the focus groups are incorporated into the various elements of program design, including topics, selection of change objectives, length and breadth of program, cost, and recruitment and retention strategies (Dumka et al., 1995).

One approach to conducting focus groups as a method of assessing the family life educational needs of the target audience is illustrated by Duncan and Marotz-Baden (1999). Data collected from county Extension agents and other sources led to the identification of "balancing work and family" as a major family program initiative in Montana. Surveying the research literature revealed that while balancing work and family was indeed a dilemma, the data were badly biased toward urban dwellers. Seriously lacking was data regarding the rural family's experience with the issue, indeed whether it was an "issue" at all. To assist in answering this question for Montanans, county Extension agents led focus groups in six different regions of the state (northwest, southwest, north central, south central, northeast, and southeast). Focus group participants were recruited using a methodology adapted from Community Action Planning (Schaaf & Hogue, 1990) called a "People Matrix." The People Matrix is a tool to assist focus group leaders in identifying and recruiting a broad mix of categories of persons in a community. For the purposes of this study, the authors were interested in recruiting parents from various personal and vocational categories who were likely to be consumers of balancing work and family information. Persons who fit these categories were invited by the county agent facilitators to participate in the focus groups. Participants within each region were recruited from different geographical sites (north, south, east, west), from different cultures (Hispanic, Native American, White, other), and from different age categories (young adult, middle adult, older adult).

Following the four Ps of marketing, an interview schedule was adapted from Lengua et al. (1992). Participants were asked 11 open-ended questions to probe concerns they had about balancing work and family, how programs might be produced, priced, and promoted, and where they might be held, consistent with a marketing perspective. Results revealed that indeed balancing work and family was an important issue, and suggested that a preferred balancing work and family program would involve a modest time investment, be low cost, and involve the workplace, the community, and family members, among other elements. The program would teach personal, resource management, meal planning, and relationship skills that would help participants address their work-family concerns.

The target audience research process will also reveal the methods whereby FLEs can best help participants reach product goals. For example, in regard to information on balancing work and family, researchers (Duncan & Marotz-Baden, 1999) asked focus groups, "How would you like to get this information? What methods would you like to see used?" Respondents were interested in a variety of methods outside of the traditional FLE workshop. The only major theme that emerged was that the methods used not take much time away from family. Options most frequently noted were mini-classes; workshops (short, concise) in a relaxed atmosphere offered during the day at the workplace or during kids' school hours; reading materials for study at home (newsletters, news articles) containing short, quick tips at appropriate reading level; audiotapes; videos; radio spots; and support groups. The involvement of community organizations such as the chamber of commerce, churches, and employers was seen as important.

"Positioning" the Product

In addition to understanding the needs of a target audience, FLEs also need to position their product to maximize its appeal to clientele (Weinreich, 1999). Part of this involves having the target audience help identify the benefits of following the FLE principles and practices and why pursuing these benefits is better than the alternatives—for example, do nothing. These benefits are integrated into how we reveal the product to the public. They need to be able to answer the question "What's in it for me?" For instance, continuing on with the balancing work and family example, if the end product of a program is "greater harmony between work and family settings," what benefits would accrue from greater work-family harmony? Some that might be listed include a stronger marriage, stronger relationships with children, less guilt, more time for family recreation, and greater personal peace.

Price

Price, the fee for services rendered, is determined after examining several interacting factors, such as the cost of offering the product, the price of the competitor's product, the target population's sensitivity to prices, objectives of the organization (profitability vs. market penetration), and capacity to supply services (Kotler & Roberto, 1989; Weinreich, 1999). But it also includes various tangible and intangible costs a client must face in order to receive the intended benefit from the product (Weinreich, 1999). In a balancing family and work workshop series, such costs include the time and energy invested in a workshop, transportation to and from the workshop, competing activities (such as a favorite TV program scheduled at the same time as the workshop), child care costs (if necessary), and the monetary cost of the class. Participants may also need to face the barriers that might stand in the way of actively harmonizing work and family, such as a lack of knowledge about time management, lack of motivation to spend more time and energy at home instead of at work, and a concern about losing status at work if one becomes more family focused. One aspect of human motivation related to price is that the target audience must view the benefits of FLE as outweighing the costs of participation. These benefits include knowledge gains and emotional and psychological benefits (Kotler & Roberto, 1989).

For example, when developing a parenting workshop series for lower-income parents with young children, a sliding scale (as a fee for services) or scholarships could be provided by local businesses to allay the financial costs of programs. Child care services might also be provided at no cost through volunteer partners to likewise reduce the actual and perceived costs of participation. While longer programs tend to be the most effective programs, an assessment could be made of target audience perceptions as to how long in time participants would be willing to commit to a program. Regardless of how effective it might be, if a program demands more than an audience will give, the size of the audience is likely to be diminished.

Once real and perceived costs are understood, an important question is this: How can we best position the FLE product so that it minimizes the perceived costs and the barriers associated with its adoption? Some parents feel overwhelmed with the dilemma of balancing family and work, wondering how it possibly can be done. Tips for parents might include the following: Spending 30 minutes of one-on-one a day can be done; it's not as difficult as you think—just take them to the store with you.

Direct questioning can also provide important data. As part of target audience surveys, FLEs can ask questions such as "How much time and money would you be willing to spend on a program like this?"

Place

Place describes the physical location where services are offered to users. Convenience for clientele may be a key issue in participation in programs. Place includes a variety of "locations": Extension offices, shopping malls, at-home education (e.g., videos, Internet), or even mass media approaches.

Some research indicates that the most favored locations for outreach FLE programs would be in familiar locations—common gathering places for community members (Duncan et al., 1996; Levant, 1987), such as libraries, churches, and universities. One study (Duncan & Marotz-Baden, 1999) asked participants in a balancing work and family focus group, "Where would be the most convenient place to have a program like this?" Familiar community sites (Extension office, library, community centers, schools, courthouses, churches) where a group already meets were preferred. Presentations to organizations also attracted interest. There was a clear preference for programs to be available where parents already are, specifically the workplace or at home (take-home packets and videos), and programs that used new technologies (interactive TV and computer).

Kotler and Roberto (1989) recommend three considerations in terms of place: access, security, and appearance.

Access

FLE services should be easily and conveniently accessible, be they services available at workshop locations or over the Internet. There should be convenient hours of operation, such as an appropriate time for maximum accessibility for whoever the target audience is. The location should be conveniently accessible, as close to the target audience as is possible. Some research (Duncan et al., 1996; Levant, 1987) suggests that maximum distance from home should be within 15 miles. Yet audiences with transportation barriers may need additional help to get to a workshop even if only a moderate distance away from home. Other aspects of accessibility include staff who are not too busy to be responsive to the needs of clientele, and not having to wait long to receive the needed assistance.

Security

Part of what FLEs should do is create a climate of safety for all participants. Clientele want a place that is safe. FLEs can take steps to ensure that the place selected for a workshop ensures the physical safety of participants. Beyond physical safety is the importance of emotional safety of participants. Most FLE in face-to-face settings goes beyond information giving to the sharing of feelings. Participants need to feel that an FLE group is, emotionally, a safe haven. Facilitators can do much to create such a climate, as noted in Chapter 6. Participants should feel assured that their dealings will be kept private. Such safety can be emphasized as facilitators emphasize privacy as part of the ground rules for an FLE group.

Appearance

Aspects of appearance are also important. Recent research on an FLE Web site revealed that appearance was an important consideration for potential users (Steimle & Duncan, 2004). The appearance of physical facilities and educational material, be they print publications, videos, CDs, or Web sites, sends a message regarding the professional nature and quality of the service.

To probe "place" issues during a target audience survey or focus group, FLEs could ask participants, "Where would be the most convenient place to have a program like this?" However, beyond a physical location of services, place also refers to the locations where the target audience is most likely to make decisions about the product (Weinreich, 1999) or the specific practices FLEs wish the intended audience to adopt. For example, for a program promoting harmony between work and family settings, where are some of the places that could be used to get the message across? Some of those might include workplace newsletters to employees, television public service announcements during evening programming, and radio spots during the noon hour and commute times.

Promotion

Promotion is the method of bringing awareness of the service to the service user. Promotional activities, including advertising and word of mouth, must sustain an image of propriety and respectability in order to expand services to a larger target audience (Katz, 1988). It includes the integrated use of advertising, public relations, promotions, media advocacy, personal selling, and entertainment approaches (Weinreich, 1999).

Of the variety of promotional approaches that could be used, research shows that marketing through personal communication, or word of mouth, is the most effective way of getting a target population to adopt a specific action (Kotler & Roberto, 1989; Weinreich, 1999), such as attending a parenting workshop series. Personal promotional approaches, including word-of-mouth and personal invitations by mail or telephone, are the preferred way of hearing about program offerings, according to some studies (see Duncan et al., 1996; Duncan & Marotz-Baden, 1999; Levant, 1987). Word-of-mouth communication can be done by the clientele themselves but also by identifying influential individuals and organizations who can act as opinion leaders, including neighbors, community leaders, radio and television personalities, spouses of governmental officials, and newspaper columnists, as well as by featuring well-known and influential personalities giving testimonials in promotional materials. Word-of-mouth communication is especially effective when it follows a mass communication about the subject (Kotler & Roberto, 1989).

In addition, if timed right, a promotional message is likely to have strong conversational value. For example, a program designed for parents of adolescents would wisely use a promotional strategy that hit on the salient points for parents with teenagers (e.g., how do we help our teens make good choices even when we're not around?). Material on the workshop might be distributed on an evening at the school when many parents are likely to be around and have the potential for conversing about the topic such as after an athletic event.

Targeting of the promotional message to a developmental stage is also important. FLEs will want to promote the program to those parents who are likely to be most interested in the program. For example, parents of newborns will likely not be very interested in learning how to handle the terrific twos, so giving them this information at the hospital would likely not be effective.

The research you conduct with the target audience will be the most effective and reliable source of deciding what mix of promotional sources to use. FLEs can ask the target audience questions such as, "What is the best way to let you know that a program like this is available?"

In addition to the personal approaches noted earlier, one assessment study of balancing work and family needs (Duncan & Marotz-Baden, 1999) noted, in response to this question, additional preferred promotional approaches, including the media (newspaper, radio, newsletter, posters), employers, and community agencies. Other methods of promotion noted in the marketing literature (Weinreich, 1999) for FLEs to consider include advertising (e.g., television or radio commercials, billboards, posters, brochures, grocery bags, fast-food restaurant placemats), public relations (e.g., press releases, letters to the editor, appearances on talk shows), promotions (e.g., coupons for attending parenting seminars), media advocacy (e.g., press events designed to encourage policy change, such as reducing fees for marriage licenses if couples complete marriage education), personal selling (e.g., direct mail campaigns), special events (e.g., health fair or conference displays), and entertainment (e.g., dramatic presentations, songs, television shows).

Beyond the traditional marketing mix, social marketing adds four additional Ps: publics, partnership, policy, and purse strings (Weinreich, 1999).

Publics

For an outreach FLE program to be maximally successful, it needs to be sensitive to the variety of publics that potentially will influence or be influenced by the program. Thus, *publics* refers to groups both internal and external to the program (Weinreich, 1999). The primary group external to the program that FLEs want to influence is, of course, the target audience, those who we want to adopt the principles and practices we teach. However, there are at least three additional secondary groups that are important in marketing considerations. The first group is comprised of persons in the near environs of target audience clientele who have an influence on the target audience's opinions. These persons might include the target audience's partner, parents, relatives, friends, or coworkers. For example, in addition to promoting a marriage preparation program to committed couples in a community, word of the opportunity might also be shared with parents and recently married couples who can encourage involvement. A second group might be public policymakers such as legislators— city and state government officials whose position makes them influential in creating the environment conducive to acceptance of the behavior change one seeks to bring about. For example, laws have recently been passed in the state of Florida requiring high school students to receive some form of relationship education prior to graduation, with the end behavioral goal of moderating marital distress. Such efforts undertaken in other states might begin by seeking buy-in and authorship of a bill by a state legislator. Still another group includes those defined as gatekeepers who have some control over access to public messages that encourage the primary group to adopt a behavior, such as media professionals (public service directors at radio and television stations, local reporters in various media), health professionals, and business owners. In Arkansas, public television station buy-in to the idea of effective parenting was necessary to free up considerable time for broadcast of the popular *Guiding Children Successfully* program series. Thus, winning the buy-in of these secondary target audiences prior to the launch of major FLE initiatives is critical in hastening the acceptance of a program.

The development team of an FLE program may be quite energized about a program. Beyond them, it is necessary to also win over others internal to the program. This group is comprised of staff at all levels of an organization, but especially staff members providing the direct services and the administrators. This kind of buy-in can be achieved by bringing internal staff together to jointly establish a shared vision, mission statement, and strategic plan. For example, one program designed to help lower income families (the primary target audience) move from public assistance to self-sufficiency (Duncan et al., 2003) first sought the buy-in of its Extension Service, its Department of Public Health and Human Services, and university department heads and deans before launching its initiative into the state. These groups met together to jointly create a vision, mission, and strategic plan. Strong buy-in to the program was a prerequisite to communities being selected to participate in the program. The selected local communities likewise met together to establish their own vision, mission, and strategic plan that was closely aligned with the state-level plan.

Partnership

As discussed in Chapter 12 on collaboration, most issues facing families are much larger in complexity than any one organization can handle on its own. Partnership is strategically wise from a marketing perspective in that persons will likely have more confidence in a program that partners with others who have expertise than just with one group. Teaming up with others not only extends human and financial resources but also usually increases access to the target audience (Weinreich, 1999). The task for FLEs is to think of other groups who share the same goals.

For example, if you were desiring to conduct a program to address strengthening marriage at the time of transition to parenthood, you could offer the program on your own. Or you might do as some FLEs did: partner with the state's largest health care organization and offer a low-dosage program called Marriage Moments as part of existing childbirth education classes. Whereas offering the material separately may have been possible, doing it in partnership with an existing agency and infrastructure already used by many new parents has reached far more parents than other more traditional ways of offering the program ever could.

FLEs may want to think about the various organizations they could partner with to expand their reach. Organizations that have similar goals to FLEs' might include school systems, the governor's office, local government offices, businesses (especially after they are shown how strong marriages and families positively influence profitability), state and local agencies, and higher education. Given the many possible roles FLEs may play, they may feel least comfortable in the role of a marketing expert. As FLEs consider who to partner with, it may be wise to include those persons and organizations with marketing savvy, such as businesses and public relations persons.

Policy

For some FLE principles and practices to become maximally integrated into a culture may require more than a public service announcement campaign with Web site material. Sometimes policy change at a higher level is necessary to produce the kind of community support necessary to bring about targeted attitudinal and behavioral change. Culture change as well as individual change is sometimes necessary. FLEs might ask if there are any changes in policies or legislation necessary in order to bring about the change they desire.

Though it is the subject of some controversy in both the scholarly and lay community, some argue that for child abuse to be eliminated requires the legislative prohibition of spanking by parents, notwithstanding that the vast majority of parents have used the approach. An FLE initiative on effective parenting with a specific objective to eliminate spanking among participating parents may find that the accomplishment of that objective quite is elusive without help from greater powers, namely the state. To increase the likelihood that couples consciously prepare for marriage may require a shift in public policy. For instance, some states have proposed a discount on marriage license fees if couples complete marriage preparation through their religious organization. FLEs might present brown-bag seminars on balancing work and family, yet the goals of such programs are likely to be sabotaged if the workplace lacks flexibility in when or where employees must work.

Purse Strings

A variety of sources may be considered to help fund outreach family life educational efforts, including the direct costs to consumers. Most FLE programs are not fully funded by participant fees. Wise FLEs give consideration to the funding of their efforts, especially long-term funding that ensures sustainability of the service. The resources identified as part of the partnership created can form an important source of sustaining funds, especially if the partnership progresses to form a true collaboration, as was discussed in Chapter 12. Beyond that, FLEs need to seek funding from a variety of other sources to maintain the program, such as state and federal agencies, foundations, and donors who are committed to strengthening families. Some FLE efforts sell a product in addition to providing a service as a way to keep the outreach self-sustaining. For example, the RELATE premarital assessment tool (www.relate_institute.org) is the first of its kind totally online assessment device offered at a nominal price that is designed to sustain the Web site.

CRAFTING MARKETING • MESSAGES TO FOSTER CHANGE

In the movie *Field of Dreams* (Robinson, 1989) discussed at the beginning of this chapter, the closing scene features a long line of interested persons heading to a desired location. Something motivated them within to make the decision to come to the soon-to-be-famous cornfield baseball diamond.

Perhaps ideally, FLEs would have many levels of institutional support promoting FLE, making it likely that a target audience will participate. For example, some have even argued for passage of laws necessitating marriage preparation as a requirement to receive a marriage license. Laws of this sort make it easier for targeted behavior (such as attendance at marriage preparation and the subsequent beneficial behaviors) to be performed by the target audience. Laws passed prohibiting smoking in public places certainly have made it more difficult for smokers to light up. With few exceptions, outreach FLE rarely enjoys the same kind of institutional encouragement that accompanies other health behaviors, and hence must rely more on persuasive means to attract its audience (exceptions would be mandated attendance such as court-ordered parenting classes or coparenting classes for divorcing parents). This being the case, it is critical that social marketing messages be crafted based on an understanding of human nature and behavior change theories (Weinreich, 1999).

While theories suggesting approaches for developing social marketing messages in FLE do not exist, several theories have been utilized in the field of health and social behavior that can provide a basis for such messages. Some of the most widely used theories include the health belief model (Strecher & Rosenstock, 1997), theory of planned behavior (Ajzen, 1991), social cognitive learning theory (Bandura, 1986), stages of change theory (Prochaska & DiClemente, 1983), and the diffusion of innovations model (Rogers, 1983). Rather than consider each theory separately, we present a synthesis of characteristics derived from these and other behavior change theories that must be present in a program's messages and intervention, or already be present in the target audience, in order to effect behavior change (Weinreich, 1999).

In describing the characteristics, we will use the marketing of marriage preparation programs as an example. The target audience is engaged heterosexual couples. The product we want them to adopt is a serious, concerted effort toward marriage preparation, leading to enhanced marital outcomes.

Characteristic #1: Believe That They Are at Risk for the Problem and That the Consequences Are Severe

Let's take a couple from the target audience, John and Janet, both in their mid-20s. John just proposed marriage and Janet accepted. They are very much in love and optimistic about their future together. However, both of them come from families where the parents have divorced; likewise, their parents' parents also terminated their marriage. While they are aware of research communicated through media reports suggesting that couples whose parents had divorced are at heightened risk for marital disruption, John and Janet downplay any concerns, insisting their marriage will be much different.

Let us imagine you have announced a marriage education initiative in your community. The initiative includes many facets and educational resources, comprising brochures and bulletins, marriage workshops, a Web site, and referrals to marriage and family therapists as needed. What social marketing messages might be designed to encourage targeted audiences to feel the need for the program, leading them to invest in some aspect of your program offering? Marketing messages would need to convince John and Janet that because of their family backgrounds, they are at increased risk for marital trouble. The increased risks, shown in higher levels of mismanaged conflict, poor communication, and heightened negativity, can lead to the death of a marriage relationship, or divorce. Once a couple's awareness of risk is heightened, a call to action should be included, such as including a telephone number or Web site in promotional materials as a doorway for obtaining more information or registering for a workshop.

Characteristic #2: Believe That the Proposed Behavior Will Lower Its Risk or Prevent the Problem

Once John and Janet are aware of their increased risk, they still must be convinced that investment in a marriage education offering will provide what they need to effectively reduce risks or alleviate potential problems altogether. A marketing message designed to produce this belief might list the various benefits of marriage preparation, such as enhanced ability to manage conflict, higher dedication to one's mate, and greater positivity, as well as a reduced chance for divorce. They might be persuaded to become involved when they learn that participation ups their chances for outcome success by 30% compared to nonparticipants (Carroll & Doherty, 2003).

Characteristic #3: Believe That the Advantages of Performing the Behavior (Benefits) Outweigh the Disadvantages (Costs)

John and Janet have grown up in a culture that has actively perpetuated myths about marriage (Larson, 1998)—such as preparing for marriage should just come naturally, that no special knowledge or skill is necessary—which scholars identify as the myth of naturalism (Vincent, 1973). Besides, Janet and John say, all this serious thinking, assessment, and analysis takes all the romance out of the process. Somehow Janet and John need to be convinced that spending some serious preparation time for their marriage will not remove the good things about the relationship but will only serve to enhance them, including the romance. A marketing message of this sort might acknowledge the myth of naturalism up front (e.g., some think it takes no special knowledge, character, or skill to have a great marriage) and then point to the enhanced benefits among couples who have taken the time to learn how to strengthen their relationships (e.g., "At first, learning to really listen to Barbara seemed like going through the motions. But now I really *know* her, and we feel closer to each other than I ever imagined").

Characteristic #4: Intend to Perform Behavior

According to the theory of planned behavior (Ajzen, 1991), behavioral intention is the strongest predictor of behavior. Intentionality is influenced by three major factors:

1. *Attitude toward the behavior*. This involves the person's weighing the positive and negative consequences of the behavior, similar to Characteristic #3.

2. *Subjective norms about the behavior*. What significant others think about the behavior and how motivated a person may be to fulfill these perceived expectations play a role.

3. *Perceived behavioral control*. This involves a person's perception of the power of external factors to either help foster or distract from the behavior.

To maximize the likelihood of John and Janet participating in some form of active marriage preparation, it is necessary to build their intention to take action. We could try and change their attitude by emphasizing the positive consequences of participation (e.g., better management of conflict, more positivity) and downplaying the negative consequences (e.g., 2 hours a week for 6 weeks is nothing compared to a lifetime of increased happiness in marriage). The positive consequences might be demonstrated by a couple whose actions toward one another make plain the benefits accruing from marriage preparation. John and Janet might be persuaded toward involvement if people important to them (e.g., such as a recently married friend couple who had been involved and benefited from it) recommended their participation. Finally, they might be more likely to be involved if we made their involvement easier, such as offering the program as part of something they were already doing (e.g., as a class in a church they both attend).

Characteristic #5: Believe That They Have the Ability and Skills to Perform the Behavior (Self-Efficacy)

While the benefits of marriage preparation can be trumpeted loudly, John and Janet must believe they have the wherewithal to gain those touted benefits for themselves. In essence, they must possess a sense of self-efficacy, acknowledging to themselves, "Hey, I can do that! I can have that kind of marriage too." We might promote their self-efficacy by first providing peer models of the behavior, such as attendees of marriage preparation programs who, like them, have accentuated marital risks and were skeptical that marriage preparation could enhance their relationship, and what they now realize having gone through the experience and how it benefited their marriage.

Characteristic #6: Believe That the Performance of the Behavior Is Consistent With Its Value System and Self-Image

Although John and Janet are skeptical about the claims touting the benefits of marriage preparation, they are strong believers in the importance of marriage and see themselves as married to each other permanently. Marketing messages that relate to how important marriage is to society, how most people desire marriage for the companionship and intimacy it can bring, and the benefits of facing life together as a couple rather than alone might build this characteristic. Messages with this in mind can then be crafted to show how marriage education provides the knowledge and skills that enable our marriages to start off on the right foot.

Characteristic #7: Perceive Greater Social Pressure to Perform the Behavior Than Not to Perform It (Social Norms)

Janet and John wonder if many people are actually interested in focused marriage preparation, or is it just an interest of a very small minority of people.

Wise marketers of marriage preparation programs can emphasize the research that reveals that a high percentage of young adults report interest in and a need for marriage preparation (e.g., Duncan et al., 1996). Social norms marketing messages found in promotional materials might read like this: "Eighty-eight percent of young adults say marriage preparation is important: How about you?"

Characteristic #8: Experience Fewer Barriers to Perform a Behavior Than Not to Perform It

We need to minimize or eliminate in their minds the barriers to John and Janet's participation in marriage preparation. It is important to give attention to at least three possible barriers (Weinreich, 1999):

1. Physical barriers (e.g., ease of access of materials, transportation, money)

2. Emotional or psychological barriers (e.g., fear of social disapproval for participating in marriage preparation; fear of exposing relationship weaknesses or raising doubts about marriage)

3. Social or cultural barriers (e.g., the only people who attend marriage preparation are problem couples admitting they can't make it on their own; promoting equality in marriage in a culture that specifies constrained gender roles)

● CONCLUSION

Outreach FLE, currently receiving growing but still underwhelming involvement from the public, will remain a fairly empty field of dreams unless FLEs do a better job of applying the principles of social marketing to their work. The eight Ps of social marketing have been discussed with family life educational examples, along with integrating these ideas into the psychological underpinnings of human behavior. We hope our reach can extend even beyond our dreams as we seek with understanding to reach an ever larger audience.

● EXPLORATIONS

1. Use the ideas in the chapter to devise a marketing plan for your outreach FLE program. Consider the following questions, adapted from Weinreich (1999), as you craft your plan:

Target Audience
- Identify your primary target audience, segmenting as appropriate. Also, identify others in the secondary audience (influencers) you might want to involve in marketing your program, such as relatives of the target audience, media professionals, public figures, sports heroes.
- Discuss briefly how you would research the needs of the primary target audience. What information is essential for your research? What primary and secondary data collection approaches would you use to gather that information?

Program Goals
- What specifically do you want to accomplish with your target audience? How many in the target audience will adopt the targeted behavior?

Product
- What is the product or behavior you are asking the target audience to adopt?
- What are the key benefits the target audience would receive from adopting the product?
- What is the competition for your product in the target audience's eyes? Competition in FLE might include other FLE offerings or simply competing activities (such as a favorite program on TV held at the same time as a workshop) or no desire to learn ("I already know how to parent effectively! No one can tell me what I don't already know").
- How is your product different from and better than the competition's?

Price
- What are the costs or other barriers that the target audience associates with the product?
- How can you minimize the costs or remove the barriers?

Place
- What are the places in which the target audience makes decisions about engaging in the desired behavior?
- Where do target audiences spend much of their time?
- How will the target audience receive the product? How can existing delivery systems be used, such as a company newsletter, school Web site, or a toll-free hotline? What approaches to product dissemination will be most efficient for reaching target audience members?

Promotion
- Which communication channels do target audience members pay the most attention to and trust the most?

- What promotional techniques (e.g., marketing tools and strategies, media and community contacts) are the best for conveying your message?
- Who are the most credible spokespeople to address your target audience?

Publics
- Who are the people or groups (in addition to primary and secondary target audiences) outside your organization whose support you need for your program to be successful?
- Who are the people or groups inside your organization whose support you need for your program to be successful?

Partnership
- Which are the most promising organizations to join forces with?

Policy
- What types of policies (organizational or governmental) should you address in your social marketing program?

Purse Strings
- From which organizations will you seek further funding, if necessary?

2. Choose a program topic and desired product or targeted behavior. For each of the characteristics derived from the synthesis of behavior change theories that must be present in a program's messages and intervention, devise marketing messages designed to motivate change in participants toward accomplishment of your program's product.

CHAPTER 14

IMPROVING THE PRACTICE OF FAMILY LIFE EDUCATION

O ver a decade ago, in their concluding chapter of Volume 1 of the *Handbook of Family Life Education* (Arcus & Thomas, 1993), Arcus and Thomas asked, "What issues and problems need to be addressed and what critical challenges must be surmounted if the [family life education] movement is to continue to serve families well?" (p. 229). In this epilogue chapter, we ask a similar question: What are the practical issues that need attention if family life education (FLE) is to be successful in strengthening individuals, couples, and families where they live and work, well into the 21st century?

Many would say that these are both the best of times and the worst of times. Families face unprecedented stress. Yet FLE has powerful new allies with new discoveries in FLE and technological resources. While the field will continue to grow and be refined, we have tools today that can be used to make important differences for those we serve.

To us, there are five issues that require attention: professionalization, program rigor, program effectiveness, marketing, and reaching the neediest audiences. We give special attention in this concluding chapter to the professionalization of FLE. The remaining areas have also been developed as themes in various chapters in this book. We revisit them here for emphasis.

● PROFESSIONALIZATION OF FAMILY LIFE EDUCATION

Major efforts need to continue to be made to increase the value and understanding of FLE as a profession, and these understandings yet need institutionalization within community consciousness. There is too little information about what family life educators (FLEs) are and do and why the public should care. Efforts are being made to address these deficits. One major effort toward professionalization of FLE has been the certification of FLEs. Perhaps the most comprehensive and notable effort in the field has been the certified family life educator (CFLE) program sponsored by the National Council on Family Relations. Established in 1984, the program identifies 10 areas within which FLEs need a knowledge base (Bredehoft & Cassidy, 1995): families in society, internal dynamics of families, human growth and development over the life span, human sexuality, interpersonal relationships, family resource management, parent education and guidance, family law and public policy, ethics, and FLE methodology. College and university programs seeking recognition as "approved academic programs" orient their courses to help students develop competencies in these 10 areas. At graduation, students may apply for provisional certified family life educator status and thereby gain national recognition from a national credentialing body. Today there are approximately 1,300 active certified family life educators (CFLEs) and over 500 provisional CFLEs (Cassidy, 2003). As of spring 2004, there are over 80 approved CFLE programs at colleges and universities across the United States (Gonzalez, 2004). Other professional organizations have been engaged in broad-based certification that have relevance for FLEs. For example, the American Association of Family and Consumer Sciences offers a certification in family and consumer sciences (CFCS).

Even though the theoretical importance of certification for the development of the discipline of FLE has been demonstrated (Cassidy, 2003), and the benefits of certification for applicants and the field are touted (see www.ncfr.org), convincing others of its practical importance has proven to be quite a different matter. For example, in 2001, the National Council on Family Relations commissioned the Human Resource Research Organization (HumRRO, 2001) to conduct a market analysis that, among other things, asked employers to report their preference for hiring certified FLEs over those not certified. Respondents completed a survey by mail or via the Internet. Only 7% of the potential sample responded to the survey, seriously limiting the usefulness of the data. However, findings revealed that only a small minority of potential FLE employers (2.7% of mail survey respondents,

11.5% of Internet respondents) expressed a current preference for hiring CFLEs, with a larger minority (13% of mail survey respondents, 30% of Internet respondents) expressing a preference for hiring CLFEs in the future. Evidently, the need for credentialed professionals in family life has not risen to the felt need of credentials for those in social work or clinical professionals, where such credentialing is part of a state's statutes and community consciousness. More work remains to be done to demonstrate convincingly the benefits of certification to potential employers, FLEs, and the public.

A related alternative to broad-based certification for FLEs is the movement to recognize professional development in an FLE subspecialty, such as parenting and marriage education. In the same market analysis cited above, employers were asked to report the extent to which they would favor employees with either certification as a parenting educator or a marriage educator. There was greater preference for the parenting educator certification, perhaps because the respondents were more familiar with the field of parenting education than marriage education. However, before such efforts with other certifying approaches were made, the marketing study findings indicated that NCFR should continue to support the CFLE credential and do so solidly before taking on other credentials (Cassidy, 2003).

Some groups are not waiting for national professional organizations to act on specifying a course and direction in subspecialty professional development and certification. In 2002, a group of eight family life and human development Cooperative Extension specialists began to ask what knowledge and skills parenting educators need to be effective with parents and children. The result of these discussions is the National Extension Parenting Educators' Framework (NEPEF) (DeBord et al., 2002), comprised of six *content* dimensions drawn from the National Extension Parent Education Model (care for self, understand, guide, nurture, motivate, advocate) and six *process* dimensions (grow, frame, develop, educate, embrace, build). Developers see NEPEF as a framework for helping to tailor existing degree programs in colleges and universities but also as a structure for credentialing programs. For example, in North Carolina, through focus groups, parenting educators helped design a four-level credentialing system. To become credentialed, parenting educators must demonstrate they have education and experience with each of the NEPEF areas in addition to references and a personal statement with their application. The North Carolina Parenting Education Network has taken this on as part of building the field. Their vision is that court judges and others will begin to recommend that parenting education be delivered by credentialed parenting educators. North Carolina now has over 55 credentialed parenting educators (Karen DeBord, personal communication, June 15, 2004).

Networking provides another opportunity to strengthen the profession of FLE. The profession and service to clientele benefit when we can share and learn ideas from other FLEs locally, statewide, nationally, and internationally, with whom we are bound by a common vision and mission. An example of the kind of networking that needs to take place is the National Parenting Education Network (NPEN) (www.npen.org). This organization promotes four tenets: networking, to facilitate linkages among practitioners; knowledge development, to expand the base of research and knowledge and increase its accessibility; professional growth, to address issues such as ethics, standards, certification, and education; and leadership, among parenting educators and with policymakers, media, and the public. NPEN has been a catalyst for states to establish their own networks.

Another movement in the professionalization of FLE is training in specific FLE program curricula, either commercial or university based. For example, Smart Marriages (www.smartmarriages.com) posts both a substantial listing of program resources and sponsors pre- and postannual conference training in many different programs for couples, parents, and families. FLEs can take advantage of this training and incorporate them as part of their programming repertoire. Increased professional capabilities make FLEs more useful to their clientele and put them in a position to promote FLE. Of course, professional training opportunities such as these need to be screened for their credibility and programs for their design (as discussed in Chapter 3). Yet many outstanding programs exist where FLEs can be trained in specialty programs that bring them independent professional recognition. We applaud these movements because we believe they will hasten the speed at which FLEs can be recognized for their expertise. We invite national professional organizations to underwrite such options for their membership.

Colleges and universities can expand their content and practical training in FLE in concert with the times. With the venues of FLE becoming increasingly diverse, it is clear that training programs in FLE need to adapt to adequately prepare students to enter frontline FLE positions in communities as members of nonprofit agencies and other organizations with community FLE missions, as well as preparation for teaching FLE in high school and college settings. While the principles guiding FLE are similar, the practices differentiating outreach FLE and classroom-based FLE are significant. For example, few academic programs help budding FLEs develop skills at working with the media, networking and collaboration, or developing FLE Internet sites.

Beyond certification, improved networking, training in specialty programs, and expanded academic offerings, FLEs can build the profession of FLE by being more proactive about their line of work. Cassidy (2003) suggests several ways this can be done.

Promote and Support Standards of Practice

Becoming certified as a family life educator or some other subspecialty helps to accomplish this. Among other things, certification increases credibility as a professional by showing that the high standards and criteria needed to provide quality FLE have been met. The designation can be included in one's resume, on professional stationery and business cards, and the instructional material one uses.

Educate Employers and the Public

As discussed in Chapter 13 on marketing, FLEs are in need of marketing themselves to a perhaps inattentive public. They need to take the opportunity to explain what FLEs are and do, what their academic training prepares them to do, and why having certification is critical in a world of ideas with questionable foundations about families.

Partner Family Life Education With Other Intervention Services

FLEs might seek to offer their prevention programs as an adjunct to the counseling services offered by the same agency. For example, a married couple might be directed to FLEs for relationship skill building while using the counseling sessions for clinical issues.

Family Life Educators as Providers in Response to Legislation

Occasionally, a public policy may be enacted that opens the door for increased FLE involvement. For example, one legislative proposal provided a discount on marriage license fees if couples completed a marriage education course. FLEs could be identified as providers of such a course.

A final effort with the promise of increasing the awareness of FLEs as unique professionals has just begun. NCFR has been working with the Department of Labor (DOL) to create a new job classification. The new occupation is to be titled certified family life educator. According to Dawn Cassidy (2004), NCFR Certification Director, once a CFLE is part of the DOL's classification system, statistics such as employment settings, educational requirements, and salaries can be more reliably collected, enabling NCFR to more accurately track and promote the profession of FLE.

● PROGRAM RIGOR

Over a decade ago, Arcus and colleagues (1993a) expressed concern about a weak scholarly basis for programs. As we mentioned in Chapter 7, "In the area of family life, there is an explosion of information, some credible, and some incredible, even unbelievable! Many persons are willing to be called a family 'expert' through bringing forth armchair theories and ideas of their own design. In contrast, FLE programs must be grounded in the latest scholarship."

Recent decades have hosted a revolution in our understanding of family process. New insights into development and well-being challenge old notions of self-esteem (e.g., Baumeister, 1992; Seligman, 2002). Old recommendations in couple relationships have been dramatically altered (e.g., Gottman, 1999). Scholars of parent-child relationships are developing an integration of nature and nurture approaches (e.g., Maccoby, 2002). Yet many of these discoveries do not get beyond a small group of scholars. The greatest discoveries need to find their way to the homes, minds, and practices of family members everywhere.

Since the Arcus et al. (1993a) writing, important advances have been made and models recommended to encourage the development of FLE programs that have strong scholarly foundations (Bogenschneider, 1996; Dumka et al., 1995; Hughes, 1994). In addition, a number of FLE resources have been developed that are founded on solid research (see example programs in Chapter 3). Helping FLEs develop and enhance their skill in developing scientifically rigorous programs has also been a major emphasis in this book. Yet there continue to be family life resources developed for the general public that have questionable scientific foundations, some of which earn considerable money for the authors. This undermines the credibility of the profession of FLE while failing to provide value to those who pay the bills. FLEs will advance the trustworthiness and usefulness of the field to the public to the degree they follow rigorous practices in the design, implementation, and evaluation of their programs.

For FLEs to truly make a difference in communities, more programs need to be developed systemically, that is, are comprehensive and multilevel in focus. To make a meaningful difference for families will require more than a single program focused at a single level. To be sure, this kind of systemic programming is complex and expensive. However, more and more of our programs should consider educational intervention at more than one level.

For instance, reduction of marital risks and promotion of strengths requires interventions at different levels of the social ecology: individual (e.g., reducing personal beliefs in marital myths), couple (e.g., dealing calmly with couple differences and challenges), community (e.g., provision of marriage education programs in religious and nonreligious community settings), and national (e.g., the establishment of family-friendly policies). In addition, a comprehensive approach would entail the provision of interventions of differing levels of involvement at the personal/couple level depending on clientele need, ranging from basic information (e.g., marriage fact sheet or video) to couple therapy (Doherty, 1995).

PROGRAM EFFECTIVENESS ●

A key question for FLE among the public is this: Does it work? There is a need to do better evaluations to better answer that question. Many programs are developed without first assessing the needs of the targeted audience and then marketed without evidence that they really work. The importance of assessing needs prior to or concomitant with program development is emphasized in Chapters 2, 4, and 13.

Once FLE resources are developed in concert with up-to-date scholarship and input from the targeted audience, they need rigorous evaluation appropriate to their developmental stage, as emphasized in Chapter 4. Chapter 4 provides many helps for improving the quality of FLE evaluation. Among them is the importance of linking program processes from visioning to goals to objectives to program activities to evaluation items.

There are still too many programs doing evaluations that don't match the maturity level and objectives of FLE programs, limiting the ability to answer important questions about program effectiveness. This circumstance must change if FLE is to become embedded in communities as an indispensable component of strengthening families.

For example, we don't know what kinds of programs work best for what populations, in the short term and the long term, although the pleading for this kind of evaluation has persisted for years (e.g., Carroll & Doherty, 2003; Guerney & Maxson, 1990). We can begin to answer this question even at the formative stages of program evaluation (e.g., Steimle & Duncan, 2004). In addition, we know almost nothing concerning the comparative effectiveness of programs. Little is also known to what degree FLE actually may make matters worse instead of better (e.g., Halford et al., 2001).

Evaluation sophistication must also increase. The better the evaluation, the more that FLEs can declare with confidence to funders and the public that their program accomplishes its vision and mission. Combining multiple methods of program evaluation, quantitative and qualitative approaches, using approaches that follow best evaluative practices, and, as appropriate, publishing them in leading journals are important directions to take. Certainly as programs become mature, FLEs are wise to spend considerable funds demonstrating the impact of the program and communicating findings in understandable ways to decision makers and the public, as well as professional audiences.

● MARKETING OF FAMILY LIFE EDUCATION PRINCIPLES, PRACTICES, AND PROGRAMS

As mentioned in Chapter 13, it is still the FLE professionals themselves, rather than potential clientele, who sense the need and appreciate the benefits of FLE the most. We must do a better job of marketing FLE principles, practices, and programs if the field is to grow in communities.

To apply these principles requires FLEs to first and consistently assess the needs of the target audience, as emphasized in Chapter 13. This audience will tell us most about how important the issue is and how to best reach them with the FLE information we seek to share with them.

As we continue into the future, FLEs will need to give increasing attention to when, where, and how programs will be offered. They will need to move beyond traditional modes of delivery of FLE and expand efforts in other areas. For example, the Internet is a primary "place" where FLE currently and in the future will take place, and this book devotes some emphasis to its use. However, currently nothing is known about the relative effectiveness of Web-based FLE versus traditional FLE (Steimle & Duncan, 2004). As this and other resources are developed, we will need to take care that the quality of the educational experience is not sacrificed. Other places that likely will experience increased emphasis are mass media (multimethod such as radio and TV public service announcements with corresponding evaluation), piggybacking FLE with other content areas (such as intertwining marriage education with childbirth education), and home visits to higher-risk clientele needing a one-on-one tailored approach.

Also, when considering traditional FLE, it is clear from some research that audiences prefer short programs. Yet longer programs tend to produce the strongest, most reliable effects on participants. More thoughtful attention must be given to the economy of a program, making it more efficient without reducing effectiveness. For example, can programs be trimmed to bare necessities elements of programs that are responsible for producing the greatest benefits?

More effective assessment of educational needs together with precision education may allow users to get the information they need in a format that works for them just as they need it. While growing technological resources will enable new options, it seems clear that family life will always be a uniquely human enterprise.

Finally, as FLEs we must work harder to position the strengthening of families at the forefront of public attention. Polls suggest we could be successful with a well-coordinated social marketing effort. According to one recent international poll conducted for the World Congress on Families II, most of the world's citizens agree that the family is the fundamental unit of society (Wirthlin Worldwide, 1999). Recent U.S data reported that 92% of Americans agree we can only go forward in this country if families are strengthened (Wirthlin Report, 2000). Using research to frame the health of families as a public health issue may be an important step in the development of social marketing messages. For example, studies show that poor social relationships are as damaging to physical health as cigarette smoking (House, Landis, & Umberson, 1988, cited in Doherty, 1997). It is likely that few in the general population are aware of this research. Knowing such facts may promote greater interest in strengthening their family through education.

REACHING DIVERSE, UNDERSERVED AUDIENCES ●

Potential FLE audiences are becoming increasingly diverse. For example, between 1980 and 2000 the minority population grew 11 times faster than the White, non-Hispanic population. While the general population witnessed a 24% growth, there was a corresponding 31% growth among African Americans, 142% among Latinos, and 204% among Asian and Pacific Islanders (Hobbs & Stoops, 2002, cited in Wiley & Ebata, 2004). If trends continue, FLEs can expect the White middle class, as a proportion of their anticipated FLE audience, to decrease in size. To be effective, FLEs will need to carefully examine their personal values and biases in response to growing diversity, as well as assess program goals and objectives, content, teaching methods, and marketing strategies for their fit with the specific audience (Myers-Walls, 2000; Wiley & Ebata, 2004).

There is also evidence that the populations most needful of FLE, including ethnic minorities, are being underserved. For example, individuals and couples who participate in premarital education tend to be at lower risk for marital distress and dissolution (Carroll & Doherty, 2003; Sullivan & Bradbury, 1997). Where the needs are greatest, the opportunities for positive outcomes and impacts increase. We must do a better job in reaching those who are most in need of FLE.

We agree with the four categories of strategies proposed by Wiley and Ebata (2004) to improve FLEs' efforts to reach underserved audiences. First, efforts must be made to increase access of underserved audiences to existing FLE resources. It is possible that the underserved audience simply does not know about the resources ("Did you know that the parenting group meets at the elementary school every Thursday evening at 7:00 P.M.?"), which begs the question of how well materials are being marketed to them. Second, assuming access to a resource, we need to carefully select the resource, making sure it is sensitive to the unique characteristics and needs of the underserved audience. A program for parents in general may not be the program of choice for father strengthening. The third strategy involves modifying the resources or services to fit the audience. Modifying a resource may require language and cultural sensitivity adjustments. Finally, it may be necessary to develop a program from the ground up, because existing programs or modifications thereof are simply inadequate to address the needs of the underserved audience.

For FLEs to more effectively carry out their charge to strengthen families among an increasingly diverse citizenry, they will need enhanced professional training. College and university degree programs will need to give increasing attention to diversity training. Citizens of a diverse society need greater sensitivity to different worldviews. Certification criteria may need reexamination; professional associations can play an important role in the inservice training of its membership (Wiley & Ebata, 2004).

● CONCLUSION

In this book we have attempted to provide background for the essential skills needed for effective outreach FLE. We have spoken about the need for a working philosophy to guide our work as FLEs, for programs to be scientifically designed as well as service oriented, and for curricula and programs to follow after established quality guidelines. We have addressed evaluating and creating significant learning experiences that engage audiences using a variety of methods. We have written about the important role of media and use of technology in FLE, as well as building sensitivity to diversity, a need for collaboration, and marketing family life educational principles, practices, and programs. Finally, we have highlighted some important areas of concern as we try and move FLE into the future.

We hope all of this helps us improve our craft and capabilities to strengthen individuals and families with whom we have the chance to work. We wish you every success in the vital work of FLE.

EXPLORATIONS ●

1. Do a personal inventory of your professional strengths and potential in reference to the various skills and ideas presented in this volume. Consider how to best use your strengths. Select an area where you would like to grow in the coming months. You might devote extra study time to the area, observe the work of admired models, practice the skill, or meet with a mentor. Develop in that area until you are comfortable that it has become a strength.

2. If you have not already done so, join a professional association that supports and provides linkages to other FLEs, such as the National Council on Family Relations and the American Association for Family and Consumer Sciences. Study articles in the journals sponsored by these organizations that have particular relevance to work as FLEs.

3. Seek opportunities for state and local networking with FLEs. Check to see if affiliates of NPEN are located in your state and how you can connect with them. Or consider starting your own association with like-minded individuals.

APPENDIX A

A Statement of Principles

By H. Wallace Goddard
and Charles A. Smith

This appendix is quite different from the chapters in this book. While all the chapters amass the scholarly thinking and evidence behind certain practices, this appendix lists, describes, and applies a set of principles. These principles are much like assumptions. They may fit with the informed good sense of many scholars and practitioners, but we do not undertake to prove them. We suggest that they be used as discussion points in clarifying thinking or developing programs. In considering program coverage and recommendations, the principles can act as a helpful guide.

For example, when outlining a program for teen parents, planners might examine this list of principles. They might identify those with special application to the specific audience and objectives of the program. They might consider how to honor all the principles in the process of developing the program. The same kind of reflection might be done in designing activities for the program.

The principles can also guide our own development and professional practice. We must grow if we are to help those we serve to grow. Consider those areas where you would like to make greater application of principles in your practice of family life education (FLE).

THE PRINCIPLE OF ORDER: BEHAVIOR ● HAS PREDICTABLE CONSEQUENCES

Elaboration: The laws of nature and the laws of relationships follow systematic principles. By working with the laws, we get the outcomes we seek. A farmer who fails to provide wise and consistent attention to his crops is likely to harvest more weeds than grain.

Marriage example: A couple that tries to operate over the years on initial infatuation without continued investments of understanding and connection is likely to drift apart. A person who chooses to blame is likely to experience alienation.

Parenting example: Children who do not have a close personal relationship with at least one adult who talks to them, loves them, and respects them as special people are likely to grow up emotionally and socially limited. It is important for children's development that there be adults who interact positively with them.

FLE application: Family members who fail to gain knowledge and act deliberately are likely to have more family problems than if they seek information and act intentionally. To impact outcomes, it is important to understand the laws of development and apply them. Family life educators (FLEs) can appeal to people's intuitive sense of this law in marketing programs by asking, "Do you want your family outcomes to be left to chance?"

THE PRINCIPLE OF EMPATHY: ● A FUNDAMENTAL ACT OF CARING IS TAKING TIME TO LOOK AT THE WORLD THROUGH ANOTHER PERSON'S EYES

Elaboration: Our fundamental separateness as humans cannot be overcome without the effort to understand the feelings and unique experiences of those we care about. It is a fundamental act of hostility or indifference to fail to see or try to see the world from another person's perspective.

Marriage example: It is common in marriage to interpret partner behavior based on its effect on us. Until we take time to discover what that behavior means to the partner, we do not understand our partner and cannot respond helpfully.

Parenting example: When a child comes home from school feeling humiliated by a bad experience, we can increase our intimacy and show support for the child by taking time to understand what that experience means to the child. The parent begins with "You've had a bad day" and follows by restating the child's experience in words that lets the child know that the parent can relate to the child's experience.

FLE application: This principle not only undergirds the content of much FLE, but it is vital in the delivery of FLE. Participants can be expected to respond more positively to facilitators who are compassionate and understanding. The same principle may be applied in dealings with ourselves. When we interpret our own lapses in patient, empathic ways, we are less likely to get discouraged (see Seligman, 1991).

● THE PRINCIPLE OF AGENCY: PEOPLE ARE FREE TO MAKE CHOICES

Elaboration: No one can make a person think, feel, and usually even act in ways contrary to that person's choices. A person's choices can be better understood by knowing the past but are not bounded or dictated by what has gone on before.

Marriage example: Our partners' anger does not require our reaction in kind. We can choose to be reflective, understanding, and helpful rather than angry, resentful, or spiteful.

Parenting example: Parents can help children recognize their options and make choices based on their values rather than thoughtless, automatic reactions.

FLE application: Much of FLE—and self-help in general—invites participants to make choices. One way humans create problems for themselves is by telling themselves victim stories in which they suffer at the hands of others. Another is to create villain stories in which other people are especially bad and take away our power of choice. A third kind of story is helpless stories, where we see ourselves as powerless.

There is some truth in all of these stories. We do suffer from other people's misdeeds. We do work with some people who are very difficult. We do not have complete control of our experience.

But the key to growth in any setting—family, community, or work—is using the power we do have. Rather than feeding the monster stories that make us—or those we serve—feel powerless, hopeless, and resentful, we can identify our space for action and act within it. (see Patterson, Grenny, McMillan, & Switzler, 2002).

THE PRINCIPLE OF MOMENTUM: ●
THE PATTERN OF ONE'S LIFE IS DEFINED
BY THE ACCUMULATION OF CHOICES

Elaboration: Patterns of choices have a cumulative effect. Some choices are made more difficult because of a pattern of previous choices. The person who has often chosen anger as the reaction to differences of opinion may find that reaction becoming automatic.

Marriage example: The emotional bank account is a good example of the principle of momentum. Those partners who consistently invest in the relationship through acts of thoughtfulness, kindness, and consideration will have an account balance superior to those who make only sporadic deposits or periodic withdrawals.

Parenting example: Children can be taught to be aware of momentum. One small act of kindness can lead to another, and then to another, until kindness becomes interwoven in the pattern of a person's life.

FLE application: A participant in a workshop may be very discouraged at the difficulty of a new approach. The new skill can be compared to a new language. It may be learned slowly and used imperfectly but, persisted at, can become natural over time. Some FLEs recommend overlearning, that is, practicing a new skill until it becomes automatic (see Gottman, 1994). This a way to develop momentum in a different, more helpful direction.

THE PRINCIPLE OF LOSS: SOMETIMES ●
THE BEST CHOICE TO SUSTAIN AND
AFFIRM LIFE REQUIRES RISK OR SACRIFICE

Elaboration: It is easy to suppose that good choices are always easy. That is not always true. Good usually entails some cost. For example, the willingness to stand up for principles may entail the loss of certain friendships.

Marriage example: Some people avoid close relationships because of the risk of being hurt. The fact is that we can limit our risk and manage our investment, but in so doing, we limit the potential for growth and intimacy.

Parenting example: Close relationships are based on the willingness to give and share with another person. One loses, or risks losing, something in order to gain something even more important—the respect and affection of another person. When parents allow children time to tie their shoes on their own, parents are slowed down. When a parent allows a teen the opportunity to drive the family car, the parent risks damage to the car and injury to an inexperienced driver.

FLE application: It can actually be reassuring to participants that there is risk in undertaking new skills. "No one does this perfectly. We all goof up more or less often." In a counterintuitive finding by Wilson and Linville (1982), students who were told that it was normal to experience some failure as they adjusted to a new process (in their case, university education) actually performed better than those who were not told. It can be reassuring that failure does not signal unique stupidity or ineptitude. It may only mean that we are learning and growing.

● THE PRINCIPLE OF INTEGRITY: ACTING CONSISTENT WITH INTERNAL PRINCIPLES OF RIGHT AND WRONG AND OUT OF COMPASSION FOR ALL LIFE BUILDS HEALTHY RELATIONSHIPS

Elaboration: A sense of right and wrong is the accumulated wisdom of experience with life. The key is to put these moral concepts into action and monitor their application in terms of how they affect oneself and others.

Marriage example: A man who tells his wife he loves her and works to show his love in his actions toward her is likely to have a strong relationship with her.

Parenting example: Parents may emphasize the importance of consistency between what their children say and do. If children, for example, say they will or will not do something, they are obligated by integrity to follow through consistently. In a similar way, when parents make a promise to a child, parents assume the obligation to do as they said, no matter how challenging it might prove to be.

FLE application: Participants who are evaluating any particular course of action in family life might consider two questions: "Is this action likely to get me what I want? Does this action show respect for the other people involved?" According to Hoffman (2000), humans can develop an internalized concern for others when they are treated with empathy and taught to understand the feelings of others. We can invite participants to draw on their own inner voices of compassion by asking, "What do you feel best about? In your heart, what do you think would show respect for that person?"

THE PRINCIPLE OF MOVEMENT: LIFE IS MOVEMENT ●

Elaboration: Short of cryogenic freezing, humans do not hold still. Life cannot be captured in a shadow box. People move actively toward one set of goals or another. The key is to move briskly and wisely toward carefully chosen goals. To stop growing is to die.

Marriage example: Relationships do not coast to bliss. Failure to invest in a relationship entails moving toward other goals, whether they are as vacuous as television watching or as demanding as career development. In any case, we move either toward or away from each other.

Parenting example: Children are growing and changing every day. Knowing a child means rediscovering him or her afresh in each encounter.

FLE application: It is popular to observe that the only constant is change. In FLE, we can teach people to use change as an ally rather than an enemy. Some of the difficulties in children (colic, diapers, and tantrums) will be outgrown with a little patience and perspective. Some of the difficulties in marriage (severely limited resources, tiredness) pass if we are patient. Rather than let today's discontents become the theme of our family story, we can learn to move forward while watching for sunnier weather (see Gottman, 1994).

THE PRINCIPLE OF GOODNESS: ●
THERE IS AN INCLINATION IN THE HUMAN
SPIRIT TOWARD LIFE-SUSTAINING BEHAVIOR

Elaboration: Healthy human beings fight to protect and preserve life. Healthy human beings flinch at the sight of suffering and waste. While decay is real, so also is the drive toward goodness, connection, and growth.

Marriage example: There are strong survival instincts that partners have for their relationship. When those instincts are swamped by despair and hopelessness, the relationship may end. However, even when discouragement is strong, the flames of hope can be fanned into new warmth, especially when determination is joined with fresh ideas.

Parenting example: Young children smile and reach out during the first months of life. The parent can encourage that inclination by responding warmly and sensitively to the child.

FLE application: Some scholars have argued that inborn empathy is the basis of moral development (see Hoffman, 1983). If that is true, there is a solid basis for believing that humans can learn to live together. Family members who learn perspective-taking may be able to move beyond competitive thinking to cooperative efforts. FLEs who show compassion for participants can help participants show compassion to other family members (see Chapter 6 in this volume and Maddux, 2002).

● THE PRINCIPLE OF CHAOS: THE WORLD IS NOT ALWAYS TIDY

Elaboration: It is wise to make allowances for imperfection and untidiness in life and relationships. Expecting Hollywood endings in all life struggles sets a person up for disappointment.

Marriage example: We never know our partners completely. We never work together perfectly. There are irresolvable differences in every relationship. Insisting on perfection guarantees disappointment. Accepting differences, even unpleasant ones, encourages more peace and better cooperation.

Parenting example: As we work with children, we make allowances for the inconvenience and challenge of living with little people who will not fit tidily into our adult schedules. Parents who adjust their schedules and expectations in order to synchronize with their children will find greater harmony and growth. Also, despite our good intentions and best efforts, some problems will remain.

FLE application: There certainly is untidiness in FLE. Many participants do not understand (or do not accept) our recommendations or may implement them imperfectly. Any growth is incremental. FLEs are wise to calibrate expectations. It may be helpful to think about the whole context in which participants live and to acknowledge the challenges of change (for ideas on change processes, see Prochaska, Norcross, & DiClemente, 1994; for ideas about limits on human change, see Seligman, 1995).

● THE PRINCIPLE OF READINESS FOR CHANGE: PROBLEMS ARE BEST SOLVED WHEN FAMILY MEMBERS ARE MENTALLY AND EMOTIONALLY READY TO GROW AND WHEN FAMILY MEMBERS ARE FEELING SAFE AND VALUED

Elaboration: True and enduring change cannot be achieved through physical or psychological force. Individual perspectives have to be respected and problems addressed at a time when those involved can listen, think, and learn. We cannot impose growth.

Marriage example: Marital conflict is more likely when partners are tired, frustrated, unhappy, hungry, or upset. To attempt to address chronic marital differences when people are in such a state may be like trying to read the paper while sitting in a burning house. There is wisdom in approaching differences when we feel peaceful—when we are under the influence of our nobler nature.

Parenting example: Children do not learn well or gladly when they are tired. Bedtime is not the best time to confront misbehavior and teach limits. Children learn best when they are alert and when we approach them with respect and kindness.

FLE application: It is natural to use a medical model in working with participants in FLE. We diagnose their failings and make specific recommendations. The challenge in working with humans is that the focus on problems can make people feel discouraged or resistant. Seligman (2002) has challenged such medical approaches: "I do not believe that you should devote overly much effort to correcting your weaknesses. Rather, I believe that the highest success in living and the deepest emotional satisfaction comes from building and using your signature strengths" (p. 13). Participants in our FLE efforts may be helped more by appreciation and encouragement of their strengths than by incisive diagnosis of their shortcomings. At the very least, our positive relationship with participants provides us the trust capital that will make us better change agents when participants are prepared to change.

THE PRINCIPLE OF DISCOVERY: ● THERE ARE ALWAYS MORE POSSIBILITIES THAN OUR PERSONAL EXPERIENCES SUGGEST

Elaboration: No one person has sufficient experience to know everything about a problem. No one person can see all points of view. That is why it is vital for us to learn from each other.

Marriage example: Many couple conflicts involve imposing our personal "musts" on the relationship. "We must get up early." "We must celebrate the holidays elaborately." "We must have a large house." When we are truly open to other people's experiences and perspectives, we discover many roads leading to growth, intimacy, and satisfaction.

Parenting example: Rather than dictate behavior to children, we can help them discover options. Children should not be flooded with more choices than they can process. But they can be helped to discover multiple pathways through life. In addition, there are many different ways to successfully raise a child.

FLE application: If the only valued tools in an FLE experience are those held by the facilitator, there are likely to be many problems that don't get fixed. The most capable FLEs draw on the life experience and creative thinking of the participants. Each participant brings a unique set of tools and perceptions.

● THE PRINCIPLE OF SYNERGY: WHEN WE ACT TOGETHER, WE DISCOVER POSSIBILITIES THAT NONE OF US WOULD DISCOVER ALONE

Elaboration: When people turn from proving they are right to working toward joint possibilities, they often discover remarkable options. Our differences have important clues to guide our growth and discovery. When we work alone, we limit our reach.

Marriage example: For vacation, he wants to go fishing with the kids. She wants to visit her mother. They can fight about the virtue of their respective preferences. Or, working together, they can discover a better way. Maybe he will find a fishing hole near her mother's place. Maybe she will visit her mom at a different time. There are surprising possibilities when we join creative forces.

Parenting example: Even when parents feel that they cannot allow a child to participate in a certain activity, they can ask the child to suggest alternatives. They can join the child in exploring possibilities. "What would be an activity that we might both feel good about?" The principle of synergy suggests that making children our partners makes for more successful problem solving.

FLE application: This is the 3rd Space concept that is discussed in Chapter 11. It is also the synergy concept effectively popularized by Stephen R. Covey (1989). Those who are not bounded by their own poverty of options but who effectively draw on the wealth of possibilities in the group are likely to be effective FLEs.

● THE PRINCIPLE OF LEGACY: OUR ULTIMATE WELL-BEING DEPENDS ON MAKING AN INVESTMENT IN OTHERS

Elaboration: Under the sway of the self-esteem movement, many have determined to meet their own needs at all costs. The self becomes the standard of judgment. Yet generativity and integrity in life depend on the investments we make in other people and in relationships. When we live only for ourselves, we never discover the satisfactions that come from service.

Marriage example: Rather than see marriage as a partnership where two relatively autonomous adults share some part of their lives as long as it is profitable, we can see marriage as the place where flawed and imperfect people commit to join and help each other in a journey. Marriage can be more than a convenient and pragmatic partnership; it can be a commitment to being together, growing together, and serving together. In serving we grow.

Parenting example: When children are involved in service, they are less likely to have serious adjustment problems. Children can be involved in helping others in many ways. In the early years, they may join their parents in visiting the sick, elderly, or lonely. As they get older, they may contribute their own energy and talents to improving life for those in their circle of experience who are in need.

FLE application: Erikson (1963) recognized generativity as one of the great accomplishments of adulthood. While many participants will come to FLE with some measure of sorrow and disappointment, we can invite them to "find the glory in their [family] story" (Gottman, 1994, p. 224). Perhaps they have not triumphed, but certainly they have grown. In fact, Gottman recommends several ways that couples can strengthen their futures by celebrating the best of the past.

THE PRINCIPLE OF EVIL: ●
THERE IS POTENTIAL FOR EVIL IN PEOPLE

Elaboration: To ignore evil is to be unprepared for the challenges of life. Each of us can be forgiven for an occasional self-serving pursuit of personal goals. None of us is totally selfless. Some individuals, though, twisted by harmful conditions during their formative years, have made the choice to commit themselves to self-serving goals, destructive behavior, and indifference to human suffering. Although not inherently "evil," children who are not treasured, nurtured, and loved can become inhumane. Even though individuals with this destructive personality are a distinct minority, their presence has to be acknowledged and understood.

Marriage example: Partners in a relationship can cherish each other knowing that there is an element of danger in the world. Their marriage can provide solace and comfort and provide a secure base for managing any threats to family well-being.

Parenting example: In the absence of active, committed adults in their lives, children are not likely to develop their potential for compassion and caring. They may even become brutish and heartless.

FLE application: Some people have suffered in ways that make immediate growth through FLE unlikely. They may need help getting unstuck. Wise FLEs learn when to refer participants to mental health professionals (see Doherty, 1995).

● EXPLORATION

Create a set of principles to which you subscribe. The principles may be modified from this list or be a very different set. Consider how the principles you have chosen or developed would guide your efforts as a family life educator in areas where you plan to work.

APPENDIX B

Favorite Movie Clips for Outreach Family Life Education

1. *Fiddler on the Roof* (Jewison, 1971), "Do You Love Me" clip. Use to illustrate differences between perceptions and practices of marriage then (in Teyve's time) and now. Ask participants to think of examples of "married love" from the clip. Were there examples of commitment, devotion, service, sacrifice? How did love manifest itself in the clip? How would you contrast it to the manner that love is talked about nowadays?

2. Show scenes from Disney films, such as *Cinderella* (Jackson, Luske, & Geronimi, 1950) and *Sleeping Beauty* (Geronimi, Larson, Reitherman, & Clark, 1959), where the heroines meet princes and fall instantly in love (with barely a "hello") and are shown in the end marrying these men they hardly know and yet somehow "live happily ever after." Discuss how the media and society can distort an appropriate understanding of marriage preparation and mate selection. Then show the video *Fanny's Dream* (Baker, 2000), a very different fairy tale about marital happiness.

3. Show scenes from the film *Runaway Bride* (Marshall, 1999). Possible scenes: Richard Gere's "ideal proposal" acknowledging there will be challenges during married life; scenes where Richard Gere's character discovers Julia Robert's character's tendency to lose herself in relationships (shown by her egg "preferences"), and then the scene where she tries to discover her true self, including what kind of eggs she really likes.

● FAMILY STRENGTH BUILDING

1. *Fiddler on the Roof* (Jewison, 1971), "Tradition" clip. To illustrate the role traditions play in family unity, development of personal identity, and a sense of responsibility. This movie can also be used to demonstrate what can happen to families if traditions become so rigid that they lead to intolerance.

2. Show the scene from the TV film *Les Miserables* (Jordan, 1978) (with Anthony Perkins) where Bishop Bienvenu, to prevent Jean Valjean from going back to prison, gives Jean the silver Jean had actually stolen from him. Discuss compassion with the class and its impact on people—those who are compassionate and those who receive their compassion. The most obvious effect on Jean was powerful and immediate—he would not return to prison. However, deeper results are likely as well. (Ask students for their ideas as to what these could be.) For example, his faith in humankind was restored, his hope for the future was brightened, and he was blessed by the love he, no doubt, now felt for the bishop. He was essentially reborn to a new life of goodness and love rather than hate, anger, and violence. Discuss the sacrifice the bishop had to make in order to be compassionate. Discuss the relationship of this story to the need for love and compassion at home.

3. Show segments from *Life Is Beautiful* (Benigni, 1998) to depict family love and compassion. Examples include the husband picking flowers for his wife from cracks in sidewalks; the wife's devotion to her husband shown by her joining him in a concentration camp; although separated at the camp, the husband's efforts to communicate love by opening the window and playing her favorite song; the father's protection of his son by turning the concentration camp experience into a game.

● PARENTING

1. *Mary Poppins* (Stevenson, 1964), "Grind at that Grindstone." Show scenes from *Mary Poppins* to illustrate the importance of parental involvement with children and spending time together as a family. Show the scene where Bert (Dick Van Dyke) has just completed sweeping the Banks's chimney, then gives Mr. Banks some advice

about his "little tykes" when he sings "You've got to grind, grind, grind at that grindstone." Ask for class/participant impressions of the clip. Discuss the pressures fathers (and mothers) feel to succeed in the world of work and the time bind that is a reality. Also discuss what can happen when time with children is not prioritized, because, as Bert says, "Childhood slips like sand through a sieve."

2. Show a "parental nurturing" clip from *Sixteen Candles* (Hughes, 1984), the scene where the father, by listening and talking with Sam, nurtures her when she is going through a hard time and can't sleep.

3. To illustrate the importance of preparing for parenthood, show a video clip from *Penny Serenade* (Stevens, 1941). This humorous scene depicts a couple bathing an infant whom they have just adopted. It is evident that the couple knows little about caring for babies.

4. Show clips that illustrate different types of parenting styles: authoritative (*The Sound of Music* [Wise, 1965], where Captain von Trapp whistles for his children), permissive (*Willy Wonka and the Chocolate Factory* [Stuart, 1971], the "Blueberry" girl), indifferent (*Matilda* [DeVito, 1996], the scene where her parents sign over her custody to Miss Honey), and authoritative (*Friendship's Field* [Baker, 1996], opening scene).

5. *Hook* (Spielberg, 1991), two scenes: Scene 1, the scene that opens at the daughter's play and concludes with Dad showing up late to the baseball game; Scene 2, the troubling phone call from America and Dad yelling at the kids, followed by a pointed discussion between husband and wife about Dad's lack of involvement. Great illustration of how parenting suffers from work and family imbalance.

FAMILY CRISES ●

1. Use several snippets from the ending of *Shadowlands* (Attenborough, 1993) to illustrate the family crucible of grieving for a loved one. First, the "Golden Valley" scene to show the good times in the marriage. Then to the scene after the wife's cancer returns and she is dying at home. Then a brief clip after his wife's death of C. S. Lewis struggling with the meaning of it all and digging into his faith to accept it. Finishing with the ending scene with C. S. Lewis and his

stepson talking about how they miss their wife/mother and grieving for her. These clips allow for an discussion of grief using an neutral example.

Several modern films depict crucible experiences and the way individuals and families deal with them, and may be valuable to discuss in class, such as *Steel Magnolias* (Ross, 1989), *Lorenzo's Oil* (Miller, 1992), *Stepmom* (Columbus, 1998), *My Life* (Rubin, 1993), *Regarding Henry* (Nichols, 1991), *Life Is Beautiful* (Benigni, 1998), *The Deep End of the Ocean* (Grosbard, 1999), and *Beaches* (Marshall, 1988).

● GENDER ISSUE

1. If you want to illustrate many gender issues in the modern world, show some clips from *Mr. Mom* (Dragoti, 1983).

REFERENCES

Abell, E. E., Adler-Baeder, F., Tajeu, K., Smith, T. A., & Adrian, A. M. (2003). *Begin education early and healthy (BEE): Strengthening rural Alabama families.* Narrative report. Retrieved from http://www.cyfernet.org/databases/cyfarreporting/Public/narratives/display.asp.

Adams, R. A., Dollahite, D. C., Gilbert, K. R., & Keim, R. E. (2001). Development and teaching of ethical guidelines for family scientists. *Family Relations, 50,* 41-48.

Administration for Children and Families. (n.d.) *ACF Mission.* Retrieved June 14, 2004 from http://www.acf.hhs.gov/acf_about.html#mission.

Ajzen, I. (1991). The theory of planned behavior. *Organizational Behavior and Human Decision Processes, 50,* 179-211.

Alabama Cooperative Extension Service. (1996). *PEP leader's manual.* Auburn, AL: Author.

Anderson, D. A., & Itule, B. D. (2003). *News writing and reporting for today's media* (6th ed.). New York: McGraw-Hill.

Arcus, M. E., & Thomas, J. (1993). The nature and practice of family life education. In M. E. Arcus, J. D. Schvaneveldt, & J. J. Moss (Eds.), *Handbook of family life education* (Vol. 2, pp. 1-32). Newbury Park, CA: Sage.

Arcus, M. E., Schvaneveldt, J. D., & Moss, J. J. (1993a). Family life education: Current status and new directions. In M. E. Arcus, J. D. Schvaneveldt, & J. J. Moss (Eds.), *Handbook of family life education* (Vol. 2, pp. 199-213). Newbury Park, CA: Sage.

Arcus, M. E., Schvaneveldt, J. D., & Moss, J. J. (1993b). The nature of family life education. In M. E. Arcus, J. D. Schvaneveldt, & J. J. Moss (Eds.), *Handbook of family life education,* (Vol. 1, pp. 1-25). Newbury Park, CA: Sage.

Astleitner, H., & Leuner, D. (1995). Learning strategies for unstructured hypermedia: A framework for theory, research, and practice. *Journal of Educational Computing, 13*(4), 387-400.

Bandura, A. (1986). *Social foundations of thought and action: A social cognitive theory.* Englewood Cliffs, NJ: Prentice Hall.

Barrera, I., & Corso, R. M. (2003). *Skilled dialogue: Strategies for responding to cultural diversity in early childhood.* Baltimore: Brookes Publishing.

Barry, D. (1991). *Dave Barry talks back.* New York: Crown.

Baumeister, R. (1992). *Meanings of life.* New York: Guilford.

Beck, M. (2003). *The joy diet.* New York: Crown.

Bennett, C., & Rockwell, K. (1995). *Targeting outcomes of programs (TOP): An integrated approach to planning and evaluation*. Unpublished manuscript, Lincoln, NE: University of Nebraska.

Bergstrom, A., Clark, R., Hogue, T., Perkins, D., Slinski, M., Iyechad, T., et al. (1995). *Collaboration framework: Addressing community capacity*. Washington, DC: National Network for Collaboration, Cooperative State Research, Education, and Extension Service, U. S. Department of Agriculture.

Berman, S. (1977). *How to create your own publicity*. New York: Frederick Fell Publishers.

Betts, S. C., Marczak, M. S., Marek, L. I., Peterson, D. J., Hoffman, K., & Mancini, J. A. (1999). *Collaboration and evaluation: Application of research and evaluation for community-based programs*. Tucson, AZ: University of Arizona Extension Service.

Bogenschneider, K. (1996). An ecological risk/protective theory for building prevention programs, policies, and community capacity to support youth. *Family Relations, 45,* 127-138.

Borden, L. M., & Perkins, D. F. (1999). Assessing your collaboration: A self-assessment tool. *Journal of Extension, 37*(2). Retrieved from http://www.joe.org/joe/1999april/tt1.html.

Bornstein, M. H. (Ed.). (2002). *Handbook of parenting: Vol. 4. Social conditions and applied parenting*. Mahwah, NJ: Lawrence Erlbaum.

Bowman, T., & Kieren, D. K. (1985). Underwhelming participation: Inhibitors to family enrichment. *Social Casework, 66*(10), 617-622.

Brammer, L. M., & MacDonald, G. (1999). *The helping relationship: Process and skills*. Boston: Allyn & Bacon.

Brazelton, T. B. (1992). *Touchpoints*. Reading, MA: Addison-Wesley.

Bredehoft, D., & Cassidy, D. (Eds.). (1995*). College and university curriculum guidelines in Family Life Education Curriculum Guidelines* (2nd ed., pp. 12-14). Minneapolis, MN: National Council on Family Relations.

Brock, G. W. (1993). Ethical guidelines for the practice of family life education. *Family Relations, 42,* 124-127.

Brock, G. W., Oertwein, M., & Coufal, J. D. (1993). Parent education theory, research, and practice. In M. E. Arcus, J. D. Schvaneveldt, & J. J. Moss (Eds.), *Handbook of family life education* (Vol. 1, pp. 1-25). Newbury Park, CA: Sage.

Bronfenbrenner, U. (1979). *The ecology of human development*. Cambridge, MA: Harvard University Press.

Bronfenbrenner, U. (1986). Ecology of the family as a context for human development: Research perspectives. *Developmental Psychology, 22,* 723-742.

Buboltz, M. M., & Sontag, M. S. (1993). Human ecology theory. In P. G. Boss, W. J. Doherty, R. LaRossa, S. K. Steinmetz, & W. R. Schumm (Eds.), *Sourcebook of family theories and methods: A contextual approach* (pp. 419-448). New York: Plenum.

Callor, S., Betts, S. C., Carter, R., Marczak, M. S., Peterson, D. J., & Richmond, L. S. (2000). *Community-based project evaluation guide*. Tucson, AZ: University of Arizona Extension Service.

Calvert, P. (Ed.). (2000). *The communicator's handbook*. Gainesville, FL: Maupin House.

Campbell, D., & Palm, G. F. (2004). *Group parent education: Promoting parent learning and support*. Thousand Oaks, CA: Sage.

Carroll, J. S., & Doherty, W. J. (2003). Evaluating the effectiveness of premarital prevention programs: A meta-analytic review of outcome research. *Family Relations, 52,* 105-118.

Cassidy, D. (2003). The growing of a profession: Challenges in family life education. In D. J. Bredehoft & M. J. Walcheski (Eds.), *Family life education: Integrating theory and practice.* Minneapolis, MN: National Council on Family Relations.

Cassidy, D. (2004, Spring). Directions. *CFLE Network, 16*(2), 1.

Chen, W.-F., & Dwyer, F. (2003). Hypermedia research: Present and future. *International Journal of Instructional Media, 30*(2), 143-148.

Christopher, S., Dunnagan, T., Duncan, S. F., & Paul, L. (2001). Education for self-support: Evaluating outcomes using transformative learning theory. *Family Relations, 50,* 134-142.

Coie, J. D., Watt, N. F., West, S. G., Hawkins, J. D., Asarnow, J. R., Markman, H. J., et al. (1993). The science of prevention: A conceptual framework and some directions for a national research program. *American Psychologist, 48,* 1013-1022.

Coles, R. (1997). *The moral intelligence of children.* New York: Random House.

Cooperative Extension Service. (1991). *Reaching limited resource audiences.* Washington, DC: Author.

Covey, S. R. (1989). *The seven habits of highly effective people.* New York: Simon & Schuster.

Crews, R. J. (2002). *Higher education service-learning sourcebook.* Westport, CN: Oryx Press.

Cronbach, L. J., & Furby, L. (1970). How we should measure "change"—Or should we? *Psychological Bulletin, 74,* 68-80.

Curran, D. (1989). *Working with parents.* Circle Pines, MN: American Guidance Service.

Czaplewski, M. J., & Jorgensen, S. R. (1993). The professionalization of family life education. In M. E. Arcus, J. D. Schvaneveldt, & J. J. Moss (Eds.), *Handbook of family life education,* (Vol. 1, pp. 51-75). Newbury Park, CA: Sage.

Dail, P. W. (1984). Constructing a philosophy of family life education: Educating the educators. *Family Perspective 18*(4), 145-149.

DeBord, K. (1989). Creative teaching: Simulations, games, and role playing. *Journal of Extension, 27*(2). Retrieved June 13, 2003, from http://www.joe.org/joe/1989 summer/tt1.html.

DeBord, K., Bower, D., Goddard, H. W., Kirby, J., Kobbe, A., Mulroy, M., et al. (2002). *National Extension parenting educators' framework.* Raleigh, NC: North Carolina State University.

Derelan, D., Rouner, D., & Tucker, K. (1994). *Public relations writing: An issue-driven behavioral approach* (2nd ed.). Englewood Cliffs, NJ: Prentice Hall.

Dhanarajan, G. (2001). Distance education: promise, performance and potential. *Open Learning, 16*(1).

Dion, M. R., Devaney, B., & Hershey, A. M. (2003, November). *Toward interventions to strengthen relationships and support healthy marriage among unwed parents.* Paper presented at the Annual Meeting of the National Council on Family Relations, Vancouver, BC.

Doherty, W. J. (2000). Family science and family citizenship: Toward a model of community partnership with families. *Family Relations, 49,* 319-325.

Doherty, W. J. (2001). *Take back your marriage.* New York: Guilford.

Doherty, W. J. (1993, November). *Moral discourse and family life education.* Paper presented at the Extension Pre-Conference at the Annual Meeting of the National Council on Family Relations, Baltimore.

Doherty, W. J. (1995). Boundaries between parent and family education and family therapy: The levels of family involvement model. *Family Relations, 44,* 353-358.

Doherty, W. J. (1997). *The scientific case for marriage and couples education in health care.* Retrieved from http://www.smartmarriages.com/hpmarr.html.

Doueck, H. J., & Bondanza, A. (1990). Training social work staff to evaluate practice: A pre/post/then comparison. *Administration in Social Work, 14*(1), 119-133.

Dumka, L. E., Roosa, M. W., Michaels, M. L., & Suh, K. W. (1995). Using research and theory to develop prevention programs for high-risk families. *Family Relations, 44,* 78-86.

Duncan, S. F., Box, G., & Silliman, B. (1996). Racial and gender effects on perceptions of marriage preparation programs among college-educated young adults. *Family Relations, 45,* 80-90.

Duncan, S. F., Dunnagan, T., Christopher, S., & Paul, L. (2003). Helping families toward the goal of self-support: Montana's EDUFAIM program. *Families in Society, 84,* 213-222.

Duncan, S. F., & Marotz-Baden, R. (1999). Using focus groups to identify rural participant needs in balancing work and family education [Electronic version]. *Journal of Extension, 37*(1). Retrieved from http://joe.org/joe/1999february/rb1.html.

Duncan, S. F., & Wood, M. M. (2003). Perceptions of marriage preparation among college-educated young adults with greater family-related risks for marital disruption. *Family Journal, 11,* 342-352.

Elias, J. L., & Merriam, S. B. (1995). *Philosophical foundations of adult education.* Malabar, FL: Krieger.

Elliott, M. (1999). Classifying family life education on the World Wide Web. *Family Relations, 48,* 7-13.

Erikson, E. (1963). *Childhood and society.* New York: Norton.

Evans, G. D., Rey, J., Hemphill, M. M., Perkins, D. F., Austin, W., & Racine, P. (2001). Academic-community collaboration: An ecology for early childhood violence prevention. *American Journal of Preventive Medicine, 20,* 22-30.

Extension Committee on Organization and Policy (ECOP). (2002). *The extension system: A vision for the 21st century.* New York: National Association of State Universities and Land-Grant Colleges.

Family Support America. (2003). Retrieved from http://www.familysupportamerica.org/content/home.htm.

Fetsch, R. J., & Hughes, R., Jr. (2002). *Evaluating family life web sites.* Consumer Series, No 10.253. Retrieved November 26, 2003, from http://www.ext.colostate.edu/pubs/consumer/10253.html.

Fine, M. J. (1980). *Handbook on parent education.* New York: Academic Press.

Fine, M. J. (1989). *Second handbook on parent education: Contemporary perspectives.* New York: Academic Press.

Fine, M. J., & Lee, S. (2000). *Handbook of diversity in parent education: The changing face of parenting and parent education.* New York: Academic Press.

Fink, L. D. (2003). *Creating significant learning experiences.* San Francisco: Jossey-Bass.

First, J. A., & Way, W. L. (1995). Parent education outcomes: Insights into transformative learning. *Family Relations, 44,* 104-109.

Fogg, B. J. (2002). *Stanford guidelines for web credibility.* Retrieved November 27, 2003, from http://www.webcredibility.org/guidelines/index.html.

Fogg, B. J., Soohoo, C., Danielson, D., Marable, L., Stanford, J., & Tauber, E. R. (2002). *How do people evaluate a web site's credibility.* Retrieved November 27, 2003, from http://www.consumerwebwatch.org/news/report3_credibilityresearch/stanfordPTL.pdf.

Fox, J. A., & Levin, J. (1993). *How to work with the media.* Newbury Park, CA: Sage.

Friere, P. (1971). *Pedagogy of the oppressed.* New York: Herder & Herder.

Gaston, S., & Daniels, P. (n.d.). *Guidelines: Writing for adults with limited reading skills.* Retrieved December 11, 2003, from http://www.cyfernet.org/research/writeadult.html.

Giblin, P. (1989). Effective utilization and evaluation of indigenous health care workers. *Public Health Reports, 104,* 361-367.

Giblin, P., Sprenkle, D. H., & Sheehan, R. (1985). Enrichment outcome research: A meta-analysis of premarital, marital, and family interventions. *Journal of Marital and Family Therapy, 11,* 257-271.

Ginott, H. G. (1965). *Between parent and child.* New York: Macmillan.

Ginott, H. G. (1969). *Between parent and teenager.* New York: Macmillan.

Ginott, H. G., Ginott, A., & Goddard, H. W. (2003). *Between parent and child.* New York: Three Rivers Press.

Glenn, J., with Taylor, N. (1999). *John Glenn: A memoir.* New York: Bantam Books.

Goddard, H. W. (1994). Something better than punishment. In series, *Principles of parenting.* Auburn, AL: Alabama Cooperative Extension System.

Goddard, H. W. (1995). *The great self mystery.* Auburn, AL: Alabama Cooperative Extension System.

Goddard, H. W. (1999). Haim Ginott. In C. A. Smith (Ed.), *Encyclopedia of parenting theory and research* (pp. 202-204). Westport, CT: Greenwood Publishing.

Goddard, H. W., & Ginott, A. (2002). Haim Ginott. In N. J. Salkind (Ed.), *Child development.* New York: Macmillan Reference.

Goddard, H. W., Smith, B. L., Mize, J., White, M. B., & White, C. P. (1994). 1. Getting started; 3. Parenting goals/objectives; 5. Level of evaluation; 7. Parenting measures. In *The Alabama Children's Trust Fund evaluation manual.* Auburn, AL: Auburn University.

Golembiewski, R. T., Billingsley, K., & Yeager, S. (1976). Measuring change and persistence in human affairs: Types of change generated by odd designs. *Journal of Applied Behavioral Science, 12,* 133-157.

Gonzalez, N. (2004, Spring). Academic program review NEWS. *CFLE Network, 16*(2), 13.

Gottman, J. M. (1994). *Why marriages succeed or fail and how you can make yours last.* New York: Simon & Schuster.

Gottman, J. M. (1997). *Raising an emotionally intelligent child.* New York: Simon & Schuster.

Gottman, J. M. (1999). *The marriage clinic.* New York: Norton.

Gottman, J. M., Coan, J., Carrere, S., & Swanson, C. (1998). Predicting marital happiness and stability from newlywed interactions. *Journal of Marriage and the Family, 60,* 5-22.

Grant, T. R., Hawkins, A. J., & Dollahite, D. C. (2001). Web-based education and support for fathers: Remote but promising. In J. Fagan & A. J. Hawkins (Eds.), *Clinical and education interventions with fathers* (pp. 143-170). New York: Haworth.

Gray, B. (1989). *Collaborating.* San Francisco: Jossey-Bass.

Grieshop, J. I. (1987). Games: Powerful tools for learning. *Journal of Extension, 25*(1). Retrieved June 13, 2003, from http://www.joe.org/joe/1987spring/iw2.html.

Guerney, B. G., Jr., & Maxson, P. (1990). Marital and family enrichment research: A decade review and look ahead. *Journal of Marriage and the Family, 52,* 1127-1135.

Guerney, B., & Guerney, L. F. (1981). Family life education as intervention. *Family Relations, 30,* 591-598.

Guion, L., Broadwater, G., Chattaraj, S., Goddard, H. W., Lytle, S. S., Perkins, C., et al. (2003). *Strengthening programs to reach diverse audiences.* Gainesville, FL: University of Florida Cooperative Extension Service.

Gunnings, R. (1968). *The technique of clear writing.* New York: McGraw-Hill.

Halford, K. W., Sanders, M. R., & Behrens, B. C. (2001). Can skills training prevent relationship problems in at-risk couples? Four-year effects of a behavioral relationship education program. *Journal of Family Psychology, 15,* 750-768.

Hanna, S. M., & Brown, J. H. (2004). *The practice of family therapy.* Belmont, CA: Brooks/Cole-Thomson Learning.

Harris, J. R. (1998). *The nurture assumption: Why children turn out the way they do.* New York: Free Press.

Harris, V. W. (2002). *Creative ways to teach marriage and family relations.* Logan, UT: EnVision Entertainment.

Hart, B., & Risley, T. R. (1995). *Meaningful differences in the everyday experience of young American children.* Baltimore: Brookes Publishing.

Hart, C. H. (2000). Parents do matter: Combating the myth that parents don't matter. *Marriage and Families.* Retrieved September 8, 2003, from http://as3.lib.byu.edu/~imaging/marriageandfamilies/issues/2000/aug00/aug00frameset.html.

Hart, C. H., Newell, L. D., & Sine, L. L. (2000). Proclamation-based principles of parenting and supportive scholarship. In D. C. Dollahite (Ed.), *Strengthening our families: An in-depth look at the proclamation on the family* (pp. 100-123). Salt Lake City, UT: Bookcraft.

Hawkins, J. D., Catalano, R. F., & Miller, J. Y. (1992). Risk and protective factors for alcohol and other drug problems in adolescence and early adulthood: Implications for substance abuse prevention. *Psychological Bulletin, 112,* 64-105.

Heider, F. (1958). *The psychology of interpersonal relations.* New York: John Wiley & Sons.

Herman, J. L., Morris, L. L., & Fitz-Gibbon, C. T. (1987). *Evaluator's handbook.* Newbury Park, CA: Sage.

Hildreth, G. J., & Sugawara, A. I. (1993). Ethnicity and diversity in family life education. In M. E. Arcus, J. D. Schvaneveldt, & J. J. Moss (Eds.), *Handbook of family life education, Volume 1: Foundations of family life education* (pp. 162-188). Newbury Park, CA: Sage.

Hobbs, C. R. (1972). *The power of teaching with new techniques.* Salt Lake City, UT: Deseret Book.

Hoffman, M. L. (1983). Affective and cognitive processes in moral internalization. In E. T. Higgins, D. N. Ruble, & W. W. Hartup (Eds.), *Social cognition and social development* (pp. 236-274). Cambridge, UK: Cambridge University Press.

Hoffman, M. L. (2000). *Empathy and moral development: Implications for caring and justice.* Cambridge, UK: Cambridge University Press.

House, J. S., Landis, K. R., & Umberson, D. (1988). Social relationships and health. *Science, 241*, 540-544.

Howard, G. S., & Daily, P. R. (1979). Response-shift bias: A source of contamination of self-report measures. *Journal of Applied Psychology, 64,* 144-150.

Howard, G. S., Ralph, K. M., Gulanick, N. A., Maxwell, S. E., Nance, D., & Gerber, S. L. (1979). Internal invalidity in pretest/posttest self-report evaluations and a reevaluation of retrospective pretests. *Applied Psychological Measurement, 3,* 1-23.

Howard, G. S., Schmeck, R. R., & Bray, J. H. (1979). Internal invalidity in studies employing self-report instruments: A suggested remedy. *Journal of Education Measurement, 16*(2), 129-135.

Hughes, R., Jr. (1994). A framework for developing family life education programs. *Family Relations, 43,* 74-80.

Hughes, R., Jr. (1997). *A guide to evaluating the quality of human development & family life web sites.* Retrieved from http://www.hec.ohio-state.edu/famlife/technol/guide/standard.htm.

Hughes, R., Jr. (1999). Frequently asked questions about the use of information technology in family life education. *Ohio State University Extension: Human Development & Family Life Bulletin, 5,* 4-5.

Hughes, R., Jr. (2001). A process evaluation of a website for family life educators. *Family Relations, 50,* 164-170.

Hughes, R., Jr., Ebata, A. T., & Dollahite, D. C. (1999). Family life in the information age. *Family Relations, 48,* 5-6.

Human Resources Research Organization (HumRRO). (2001). *Market analysis of family life, parenting, and marriage education for the National Council on Family Relations.* Alexandria, VA: Author.

Iding, M., Crosby, M. E., & Speitel, T. (2002). Teachers and technology: Beliefs and practices. *International Journal of Instructional Media, 29*(2), 153-170.

Institute for Mental Health Initiatives. (1991). *Anger management for parents: The RETHINK method.* Champaign, IL: Research Press.

Jackson, S. (1997). *Life among the savages.* New York: Penguin.

Jacobs, F. H. (1988). The five-tiered approach to evaluation: Context and implementation. In H. B. Weiss and F. H. Jacobs (Eds.), *Evaluating family programs* (pp. 37-68). Hawthorne, NY: Aldine De Gruyter.

Jacobson, N. S., & Christensen, A. (1996). *Acceptance and change in couple therapy: A therapist's guide to transforming relationships.* New York: W. W. Norton.

John, R. (1998). Native American families. In C. H. Mindel, R. W. Habenstein, & R. Wright, Jr. (Eds.), *Ethnic families in America: Patterns and variations* (4th ed., pp. 382-421). New York: Prentice Hall.

Johnson, C. A., Stanley, S. A., Glenn, N. D., Amato, P. A., Nock, S. L., Markman, H. J., et al. (2002). *Marriage in Oklahoma: 2001 baseline statewide survey on marriage and divorce* (S02096 OKDHS). Oklahoma City, OK: Oklahoma Department of Human Services.

Jordan, B., & Stackpole, N. (1995). *Audiovisual resources for family programming.* New York: Neal-Schuman.

Katz, B. (1988). *How to market professional services.* New York: Nichols Publishing.

Kibel, B. M. (1999). *Success stories as hard data.* Boulder, CO: Perseus Publishing.

Kibel, B. M. (n.d.) *Success stories as hard data.* Retrieved June 14, 2004, from http://www.pire.org/resultsmapping/abridge.htm.

Klemer, R. H., & Smith, R. M. (1975). *Teaching about family relationships.* Minneapolis, MN: Burgess.

Knowles, M. S. (1998). *The adult learner* (5th ed.). Houston, TX: Gulf Publishing.

Krysan, M., Moore, K. A., & Zill, N. (1990). Identifying successful families: An overview of constructs and selected measures. Washington, DC: Child Trends.

Kohn, A. (1994). The truth about self-esteem. *Phi Delta Kappan, 76*(4), 272-283.

Kotler, P., & Roberto, E. L. (1989). *Social marketing: Strategies for changing public behavior.* New York: Free Press.

L'Abate, L. (1983). Prevention as a profession: Toward a new conceptual frame of reference. In D. R. Mace (Ed.), *Prevention in family services: Approaches to family therapy and counseling* (pp. 46-52). Beverly Hills, CA: Sage.

LaRocque, P. (2003). *The book on writing.* Oak Park, IL: Marion Street Press.

Larson, J. H. (1988). The marriage quiz: College students' beliefs in selected myths about marriage. *Family Relations 37,* 3-11.

Larson, J. H. (2000). *Should we stay together?* San Francisco: Jossey-Bass.

Larzelere, R. E. (2000). Child outcomes of nonabusive and customary physical punishment by parents: An updated literature review. *Clinical Child and Family Psychology Review, 3*(4), 199-221.

Lee, T. R., Mancini, J. A., Miles, C. S., & Marek, L. I. (1996, June). *Making a difference: Community programs that last.* Paper presented at the Linking Families and Communities Conference, Louisville, KY.

Lengua, L. J., Roosa, M. W., Schupak-Neuberg, E., Michaels, M. L., Berg, C. N., & Weschler, L. F. (1992). Using focus groups to guide the development of a parenting program for difficult-to-reach, high-risk families. *Family Relations, 41,* 163-168.

Lerner, R. M. (1991). Changing organism-contest relationships as the basis process of development: A developmental contextual perspective. *Developmental Psychology, 27,* 27-32.

Lerner, R. M. (1995). *America's youth in crisis: Challenges and options for programs and policies.* Thousand Oaks, CA: Sage.

Levant, R. F. (1987). The use of marketing techniques to facilitate acceptance of parent education programs: A case example. *Family Relations, 36,* 246-251.

Levin, J., Levin, S. R., & Waddoups, G. (1999). Multiplicity in learning and teaching: A framework for developing innovative online education. *Journal of Research on Computing in Education, 32*(2), 256.

Lewis-Rowley, M., Brasher, R. E., Moss, J. J., Duncan, S. F., & Stiles, R. J. (1993). The evolution of education for family life. In M. E. Arcus, J. D. Schvaneveldt, & J. J. Moss (Eds.), *Handbook of family life education* (Vol. 1, pp. 26-50). Newbury Park, CA: Sage.

Maccoby, E. E. (2002). Parenting effects: Issues and controversies. In J. G. Borkowski, S. L. Ramey, & M. Bistol-Power (Eds.), *Parenting and the child's world.* Mahwah, NJ: Lawrence Erlbaum.

Mace, D. R. (1981). The long, long trail from information-giving to behavioral change. *Family Relations, 30,* 599-606.

Maddi, S. M. (1989). *Personality theories: A comparative analysis.* Chicago: Dorsey Press.

Maddux, J. E. (2002). Stopping the "madness": Positive psychology and the deconstruction of the illness ideology and the DSM. In C. R. Snyder & S. J. Lopez (Eds.), *Handbook of positive psychology.* New York: Oxford University Press.

Markman, H. J., Stanley, S. M., & Blumberg, S. L. (1999). *Prevention and relationship enhancement program (PREP) leaders manual.* Denver, CO: PREP Educational Products.

Markman, H. J., Stanley, S. M., & Blumberg, S. L (2001). *Fighting for your marriage.* San Francisco: Jossey-Bass.

McAdoo, H. P. (1998). African-American families. In C. H. Mindel, R. W. Habenstein, & R. Wright, Jr. (Eds.), *Ethnic families in America: Patterns and variations* (4th ed., pp. 361-381). New York: Prentice Hall.

McCall, R. B., & Green, B. L. (2004). Beyond the methodological gold standards of behavior research: Considerations for practice and policy. *Social Policy Report, 18,* 1-12.

McDermott, D. (2001). Parenting and ethnicity. In M. J. Fine, & S. W. Lee (Eds.), *Handbook of diversity in parent education* (pp. 73-96). San Diego, CA: Academic Press.

McKeachie, W. J. (1999). *Teaching tips: Strategies, research, and theory for college and university teachers* (10th ed.). Boston: Houghton Mifflin.

Mecca, A. M., Smelser, N. J., & Vasconcellos, J. (1989). *The social importance of self-esteem.* Berkeley, CA: University of California Press.

Meek, J. (1992a). *How to build coalitions: Collaboration.* Ames, IA: Iowa State Extension Service.

Meek, J. (1992b). *How to build coalitions: Turf issues.* Ames, IA: Iowa State Extension Service.

Melaville, A. I., & Blank, M. J. (1991). *What it takes: Structuring interagency partnerships to connect children and families with comprehensive services.* Washington, DC: Education and Human Services Consortium.

Merrill, M. D. (1983). Component display theory. In C. M. Reigeluth (Ed.), *Instructional design theories and models.* Hillsdale, NJ: Lawrence Erlbaum.

Merrill, M. D. (1994). *Instructional design theory.* Englewood Cliffs, NJ: Educational Technology Publications.

Merrill, M. D. (2000). First principles of instruction. In *Second generation instructional design.* Retrieved February 2, 2004, from http://www.id2.usu.edu.

Merrill, M. D. (2001). First principles of instruction. *Journal of Structural Learning and Intelligent Systems 14,* 459-466.

Metcalfe, R. (1996). *The Internet after the fad: Remarks of Dr. Robert Metcalfe at the University of Virginia May 30, 1996.* Retrieved November 23, 2003, from http://www.americanhistory.si.edu/csr/comphist/montic/metcalfe.htm#me7.

Mezirow, J. (1995). Transformation theory of adult learning. In M. Welton (Ed.), *In defense of the lifeworld: Critical perspectives on adult learning* (pp. 39-70). Albany, NY: State University of New York Press.

Miller, S. D., Duncan, B. L., & Hubble, M. A. (1997). *Escape from Babel: Toward a unifying language for psychotherapy practice.* New York: Norton.

Mindel, C. H., Haberstein, R. W., & Wright, R., Jr. (1998). *Ethnic families in America: Patterns and variations.* Upper Saddle River, NJ: Prentice Hall.

Miner, F. D., Jr., & Barnhill, J. V. (2001). Dollars for answers. *Journal of Extension, 39*(6). Retrieved June 13, 2003, from http://www.joe.org/joe/2001december/iw6.html.

Minuchin, S., & Fishman, H. C. (1981). *Family therapy techniques.* Cambridge, MA: Harvard University Press.

Molgaard, V., Kumpfer, K., & Fleming, E. (2001). *Strengthening families program leader guide.* Ames, IA: Iowa State University Extension.

Molgaard, V., & Spoth, R. (2001). Strengthening families program for young adolescents: Overview and outcomes. In S. I. Pfeiffer & L. A. Reddy (Eds.), *Innovative mental health programs for children: Programs that work* (pp. 15-29). Binghamton, NY: Haworth Press.

Morgan, D. L. (1996). Focus groups. *Annual Review of Sociology, 22,* 129-152.

Morgan, D. L., Krueger, R. A., & King, J. A. (Eds.). (1998). *Focus group kit.* Thousand Oaks, CA: Sage.

Morris, L. L., Fitz-Gibbon, C. T., & Freeman, M. E. (1987). *How to communicate evaluation findings* (2nd ed.). Newbury Park, CA: Sage.

Morris, S. N., Dollahite, D. C., & Hawkins, A. J. (1999). Virtual family life education: A qualitative study of father education on the World Wide Web. *Family Relations, 48,* 23-30.

Myers-Walls, J. (2000). Family diversity and family life education. In D. H. Demo, K. R. Allen, & M. A. Fine (Eds.), *Handbook of family diversity* (pp. 359-379). New York: Oxford University Press.

Myers-Walls, J. (2003, November). *The perils and promise of using mass media for family life education outreach.* Paper presented at the Annual Meeting of the National Council on Family Relations, Vancouver, BC.

Myers-Walls, J. A., & Myers-Bowman, K. S. (1999). Sorting through parenting education resources: Values and the example of socially conscious parenting. *Family Science Review, 12,* 69-86.

National Research Council. (1993). *Understanding child abuse and neglect.* Washington, DC: National Academy Press.

National Science Foundation, Division of Science Resources Statistics. (2002). *Significance of information technology* (No. NSB 02-01). Arlington, VA: Author.

NetRatings Inc. (2003, May). *Nearly 40 million Internet users connect via broadband, growing 49 percent, according to Nielsen/NetRatings.* Retrieved November 26, 2003, from http://www.netratings.com/pr/pr_030618_us.pdf.

Norcross, J. C., Santrock, J. W., Campbell, L. F., Smith, T. P., Sommer, R., &.Zuckerman, E. L. (2003). *Authoritative guide to self-help resources in mental health.* New York: Guilford.

Olson, J. R., Goddard, H. W., Solheim, C. A., & Sandt, L. (in press). Making a case for engaging adolescents in program decision-making. *Journal of Extension.*

O'Neill, B. (2003). How to create and use an interactive PowerPoint quiz game. *Journal of Extension, 41*(2). Retrieved June 13, 2003, from http://www.joe.org/joe/2003april/tt2.shtml.

Ono, H., & Zavodny, M. (2003). Gender and the Internet. *Social Science Quarterly, 84*(1), 111.

Orgel, A. R. (1980). Haim Ginott's approach to parent education. In M. J. Fine (Ed.), *The handbook on parent education* (pp. 75-100). New York: Academic Press.

Patterson, K., Grenny, J., McMillan, A., & Switzler, R. (2002). *Crucial conversations.* New York: McGraw-Hill.

Peterson, G. W., & Hann, D. (1999). Socializing children and parents in families. In M. B. Sussman, S. K. Steinmetz, & G. W. Peterson (Eds.), *Handbook of marriage and the family* (2nd ed.). New York: Plenum Press.

Powell L. H., & Cassidy, D. (2001). *Family life education: An introduction.* Mountain View, CA: Mayfield.

Price, D. W. (2000). Philosophy and the adult educator. *Adult Learning, 11,* 3-5.

Prochaska, J., & DiClemente, C. C. (1983). Stages and processes of self-change of smoking: Toward an integrative model of change. *Journal of Consulting and Clinical Psychology, 51,* 390-395.

Prochaska, J. O., Norcross, J. C., & DiClemente, C. C. (1994). *Changing for good.* New York: Avon Books.

Quick, S., & Lasueur, A., Jr. (2003). Take time to be slow and quiet. *A world of possibilities.* Retrieved July 5, 2004 from http://www.ca.uky.edu/agcollege/fcs/areas/hdfr/articles/Media_Article_8.htm.

Rasmussen, W. D. (1989). *Taking the university to the people: Seventy-five years of cooperative extension.* Ames, IA: Iowa State University Press.

Rico, G., & Volk, T. (1999). *Writing the natural way: Turning the task of writing into the joy of writing.* New York: Tarcher.

Riley, D., & Bogenschneider, K. (1992). *Reaching and teaching parents of teens: Which delivery method is best?* (North Wisconsin Youth Futures, Technical Report No. 5). Madison, WI: University of Wisconsin-Madison/Extension.

Ritter, S. H., & Gottfried, S. C. (2002). *Tomorrow's child: Benefiting from today's family-school-community-business partnerships.* Greensboro, NC: Regional Educational Laboratory at SERVE.

Roach, R. (2003). Digital divide rooted in home computer ownership. *Black Issues in Higher Education, 20,* 50.

Robinson, E. A. R. (1994). Implications of the pre/post/then design for evaluating social group work. *Research on Social Work Practice, 4,* 224-239.

Robinson, P. (Director). (1989). *Field of Dreams* [Motion picture]. United States: Universal Studios.

Rockwell, K., & Bennett, C. (2004). *Targeting outcomes of programs.* Retrieved June 16, 2004, from http://citnews.unl.edu/TOP/index.html.

Rogers, E. (1983). *Diffusion of innovations* (3rd ed.). New York: Free Press.

Rogoff, B. (1990). *Apprenticeship in thinking.* New York: Oxford University Press.

Rutter, M. (1987). Psychosocial resilience and protective mechanisms. *American Journal of Orthopsychiatry, 53,* 316-331.

Satter, E. (1995/1997). *Ellyn Satter's feeding with love and good sense* [Video and teacher's guide]. Madison, WI: Ellyn Satter Associates.

Satter, E. (1999). *Secrets of feeding a healthy family.* Madison, WI: Kelcy Press.

Schaaf, K., & Hogue, T. (1990). *Preparing your community: A guide to community action planning in Oregon.* Salem, OR: Positive Youth Development of Oregon.

Schorr, L. (1988). *Within our reach: Breaking the cycle of disadvantage.* New York: Anchor Press.

Schorr, L. (1997). *Common purpose: Strengthening families and neighborhoods to rebuild America.* New York: Anchor Press.

Seligman, M. E. P. (1991) *Learned optimism.* New York: Alfred Knopf.

Seligman, M. E. P. (1995). *What you can change and what you can't: The complete guide to successful self-improvement.* New York: Ballantine Books.

Seligman, M. E. P. (2002). *Authentic happiness.* New York: Free Press.

Silberman, M. (1996). *Active learning: 101 strategies to teach any subject.* Boston: Allyn & Bacon.

Silver, H. F., Strong, R. W., & Perini, M. J. (2000). *So each may learn: Integrating learning styles and multiple intelligences.* Alexandria, VA: Association for Supervision and Curriculum Development.

Simon, R. (1983). *Publicity and public relations worktext.* Columbus, OH: Grid Publishing.

Simpson, A. R. (1997). *The role of mass media in parenting education.* Boston: Center for Health Communication, Harvard School of Public Health.

Small, S. A. (1990). Some issues regarding the evaluation of family life education programs. *Family Relations, 39,* 132-135.

Small, S. A., & Hug, B. (1991). Research-based youth programming. *Journal of Extension, 29,* 27-29.

Small, S. A., & Memmo, M. (2004). Contemporary models of youth development and problem prevention: Toward an integration of terms, concepts, and models. *Family Relations, 53,* 3-11.

Smith, C. A. (1999). Family life pathfinders on the new electronic frontier. *Family Relations, 48,* 31-34.

Smith, C. A. (2004). *Raising courageous kids.* Notre Dame, IN: Sorin Books. Retrieved July 5, 2004 from http://www.ksu.edu/wwparent/programs/courage/Media %20guide.pdf.

Smith, C. A., Cudaback, D., Goddard, H. W., & Myers-Walls, J. A. (1994). *National extension parent education model.* Manhattan, KS: Kansas Cooperative Extension Service.

Smith, C., Perou, R., & Lesesne, C. (2002). Parent education. In M. H. Bornstein (Ed.), *Handbook of parenting* (2nd ed.), *Volume 4: Social conditions and applied parenting* (pp. 389-410). Mahwah, NJ: Lawrence Erlbaum.

Sprangers, M. (1989). Subject bias and the retrospective pretest in retrospect. *Bulletin of the Psychonomic Society, 27*(1), 11-14.

Stahmann, R., & Salts, C. (1993). Educating for marriage and intimate relationships. In M. E. Arcus, J. D. Schvaneveldt, & J. J. Moss (Eds.), *Handbook of family life education* (Vol. 2, pp. 33-61). Newbury Park, CA: Sage.

Stanley, S. M. (2001). Making a case for premarital education. *Family Relations, 50,* 272-280.

Stanley, S. M., & Markman, H. J. (1997). *Marriage in the 90s: A nationwide random phone survey. A marital research poll by PREP, Inc.* Denver: PREP.

Stanley, S. M., Markman, H. J., Prado, L. M., Olmos-Gallo, P. A., Tonelli, L., St. Peters, M., et al. (2001). Community-based premarital prevention: Clergy and lay leaders on the front lines. *Family Relations, 50,* 67-76.

Steimle, B. M., & Duncan, S. F. (2004). Formative evaluation of a family life education website. *Family Relations, 53,* 367-376.

Strecher, V., & Rosenstock, I. (1997). The health belief model. In K. Glanz, F. M. Lewis, & B. Rimer (Eds.), *Health behavior and health education* (2nd ed.). San Francisco: Jossey-Bass

Strover, S. (2003). Remapping the digital divide. *Information Society, 19*(4), 275.

Suarez, Z. (1998). The Cuban-American family. In C. H. Mindel, R. W. Habenstein, & R. Wright, Jr. (Eds.), *Ethnic families in America: Patterns and variations* (4th ed., pp. 172-198). New York: Prentice Hall.

Suchman, E. A. (1968). *Evaluative research: Principles and practice in public service and social action programs.* New York: Sage.

Sullivan, K. T., & Bradbury, T. N. (1997). Are premarital prevention programs reaching couples at risk for marital dysfunction? *Journal of Consulting and Clinical Psychology, 65,* 24-30.

Tavris, C. (1989). *Anger: The misunderstood emotion.* New York: Simon & Schuster.

Taylor, E. (1997). Building upon the theoretical debate: A critical review of the empirical studies of Mezirow's transformative learning theory. *Adult Education Quarterly, 48*(1), 34-59.

Terborg, J. R., Howard, G. S., & Maxwell, S. E. (1980). Evaluating planned organizational change: A method for assessing alpha, beta, and gamma change. *Academy of Management Review, 5*(1), 109-121.

Thomas, J., & Arcus, M. (1992, November 5-10). *Teaching as storytelling: Personal narratives in family life education.* Paper presented at the Annual Meeting of the National Council on Family Relations, Orlando, FL.

Thomas, J., Schvaneveldt, J. D., & Young, M. H. (1993). Programs in family life education: Development, implementation, and evaluation. In M. E. Arcus,

J. D. Schvaneveldt, & J. J. Moss (Eds.), *Handbook of family life education: Foundations of family life education* (Vol. 1, pp. 106-130). Newbury Park, CA: Sage.

Tisdell, E. J., & Taylor, E. W. (2000). Adult education philosophy informs practice. *Adult Learning, 11,* 6-10.

U.S. Census Bureau. (2001). *Home computers and Internet use in the United States: August 2000* (No. P23-207). Washington, DC: Government Printing Office.

U.S. Department of Education, National Center for Educational Statistics. (2003, October). *Computer and Internet use by children and adolescents in 2001* (No. NCES 2004-014). Washington, DC: Government Printing Office.

University of Wisconsin. (2002). Enhancing program performance with logic models. Retrieved June 16, 2004 from http://www.uwex.edu/ces/lmcourse/#.

Vance, B. (1989). *Planning and conducting family cluster: Education for family wellness.* Newbury Park, CA: Sage.

Van Dijk, J., & Hacker, K. (2003). The digital divide as a complex and dynamic phenomenon. *Information Society, 19*(4), 315.

Vincent, C. E. (1973). *Sexual and marital health.* New York: McGraw-Hill.

Warnock, P. (1988). You don't have to be funny to use humor. *Journal of Extension, 26*(2). Retrieved June 13, 2003, from http://www.joe.org/joe/1988summer/f1.html.

Weinreich, N. K. (1999). *Hands-on social marketing: A step-by-step guide.* Thousand Oaks, CA: Sage.

Weissbourd, B. (1994). The evolution of the family resource movement. In S. L. Kagan & B. Weissbourd (Eds.), *Putting families first: America's family support movement and the challenge of change* (pp. 28-47). San Francisco: Jossey-Bass.

Werner, E. E., & Smith, R. S. (1977). *Kauai's children come of age.* Honolulu, HI: University of Hawaii Press.

Werner, E. E., & Smith, R. S. (1982). *Vulnerable but invincible: A longitudinal study of resilient children and youth.* New York: McGraw-Hill.

Werner, E. E., & Smith, R. S. (1992). *Overcoming the odds: High risk children from birth to adulthood.* Ithaca, NY: Cornell University Press.

Werner, E. E., & Smith, R. S. (2001). *Journeys from childhood to midlife: Risk, resilience, and recovery.* Ithaca, NY: Cornell University Press.

Whipple, E. E., & Wilson, S. R. (1996). Evaluation of a parent education and support program for families at risk of physical child abuse. *Families in Society, 77,* 227-239.

White, B. A., & Brockett, R. G. (1987). Putting philosophy into practice. *Journal of Extension, 25 (2).* Retrieved October 15, 2001, from http://www.joe.org/joe/1987summer/a3.html.

Wiley, A. R., & Ebata, A. (2004). Reaching American families: Making diversity real in family life education. *Family Relations, 53,* 273-281.

Wilson, T. D., & Linville, P. W. (1982). Improving academic performance of college freshmen: Attribution therapy revisited. *Journal of Personality and Social Psychology, 42,* 367-376.

Wirthlin Report. (2000, August). *Americans rank strengthening families as highest priority.* Reston, VA: Author.

Wirthlin Worldwide. (1999, September/October). *International survey on marriage and the family.* Reston, VA: Author.

Woods, B. (1998). *Feedback on EDUFAIM: Montana's state strengthening project.* Unpublished manuscript.

NAME INDEX

SUBJECT INDEX

ABOUT THE AUTHORS

Dr. Stephen F. Duncan is a Professor in the School of Family Life at Brigham Young University. He has authored or coauthored numerous outreach publications for lay audiences and professionals, written hundreds of articles for newspaper columns, been interviewed numerous times for television, radio, and magazine outlets, and directed nationally recognized outreach family life education programs. He served as an Extension Family Life Specialist at Auburn University in Alabama for 5 years and held a similar position at Montana State University for over 7 years. At BYU he teaches undergraduate and graduate courses in family life education, conducts research geared to improve the practice of family life education, and directs Web-based and community-based family life education projects. He has certification as a Family Life Educator.

He is a well-published family life education scholar, authoring numerous articles on outreach programs and evaluation, many of which have appeared in leading family life education/outreach outlets. He serves or has served on several editorial boards, including *Marriage and Families,* an outreach-oriented journal, the Children, Youth and Families Education and Research Network (CYFERNet), the national family Web site of the Cooperative Extension System, and *Family Relations,* widely recognized as the world's leading applied family research/practitioner journal.

Dr. H. Wallace (Wally) Goddard is a Family Life Specialist at the University of Arkansas Cooperative Extension Service. He served as an Extension Family and Child Development Specialist at Auburn University for over 6 years, during which time he developed Principles of Parenting, a broad parenting program that has been adopted by several states, and The Great Self Mystery, a youth identity program that has been adopted by national organizations. He was also one of four scholars invited to develop the National Extension Parent Education Model, which is the base document for all Extension parent education. He writes monthly columns for several Web magazines on various family subjects and has authored general audience family books.

In addition to work in Extension, he also provided content expertise to Stephen R. Covey when he worte *The 7 Habits of Highly Effective Families.* Experience in both university and business settings has provided a wealth of background in family life education. He also has graduate training in instructional psychology and certification as a Family Life Educator.

Since accepting a position with the University of Arkansas Cooperative Extension Service, he has developed extensive Web-based parent education and has been involved with the national team that is developing national standards for parenting educators. He is also involved in the development of a model and national curriculum for couples' education. He has served as chair of the Education and Enrichment section of the National Council on Family Relations, the premier family professional organization in the world. He currently serves on the editorial board for the Children, Youth and Families Education and Research Network (CYFERNet) and has served as Book Review Editor for *Family Relations.* He has taught graduate courses on family life education.

Steven Dennis is an Extension Family Life Specialist with the University of Arkansas, Division of Agriculture, Cooperative Extension Service. He received graduate training in both instructional technology (MS, 1992) and family science (PhD, 1995) from Utah State University. Prior to joining the Cooperative Extension service, he worked as a faculty member of the School of Human Environmental Science at the University of Arkansas, Fayetteville, and the Center for Persons with Disabilities at Utah State University. He currently directs the Best Care child care training programs and the Family and Community Connections mentoring program. He is also activity involved in the statewide asset-building network, Raising Arkansas Youth (RAY), and other parenting, family, and youth development efforts of the Cooperative Extension service.

Aaron T. Abata is an associate professor of social development in the Department of Human and Community Development at the University of Illinois at Urbana-Champaign, where he also holds an appointment as an Extension Specialist with University of Illinois Extension. He received his B.S. degrees in biology and psychology from the University of Hawaii and completed his M.S. and Ph.D. degrees in human development and family studies from Penn State. Dr. Ebata came to Illinois in 1990 after completing a research fellowship in the Department of Psychiatry and Behavioral Sciences at Stanford University. A former elementary and preschool teacher, Dr. Ebata has conducted applied research on how children and families cope with stress and now develops outreach programs for parents and conducts training for professionals who work with children. He is married and the father of two young sons.

Tonya Fishio is a public relations professional who has worked in the field for 10 years. After receiving her communications degree from Brigham Young University, she worked in the New York office of Edelman Public Relations and at Nu Skin International in Utah. She has held positions in internal communications, international relations, crisis management, and media relations. Specializing in media relations, she currently manages the media outreach efforts for the Family Studies Center in the School of Family Life at BYU. In this capacity, she uses both the local and national media to share family research findings and university-sponsored family-related programs with target audiences.

Charles A. Smith is a Professor and Parent Educator in the School of Family Studies and Human Services at Kansas State University. He holds a BS in psychology from the University of Dayton and both an MS and PhD in child development from Purdue University. He has worked extensively with young children as director of the Child Development Center at Texas Tech University, as a preschool teacher, and as a play therapist in a children's hospital. *Raising Courageous Kids: Eight Steps to Practical Heroism* (2004) is the most recent of his five books. His Web sites, The WonderWise Parent (http://www.ksu.edu/wwparent/) and Raising Courageous Kids (www.raising coura geouskids.com), provide additional information about his programs.

Research Methods
for Generalist Social Work

ABOUT THE AUTHOR

Christine Marlow was born and raised in England and received her under-graduate education in anthropology from the University of Wales, University College Swansea. She came to the United States in the early seventies and worked as a social worker in Maine for several years. After receiving her M.S.W. and Ph.D from the University of Chicago, she taught in Indiana and then New Mexico. At New Mexico State University she teaches primarily in the research sequence at both the undergraduate and graduate levels. In 1994 she spent a year in Zimbabwe as a Fulbright Scholar. She has now adopted southern New Mexico as her home.

SECOND EDITION

Research Methods for Generalist Social Work

Christine Marlow
New Mexico State University

Brooks/Cole Publishing Company

I(T)P® An International Thomson Publishing Company

Pacific Grove ■ Albany ■ Belmont ■ Bonn ■ Boston ■ Cincinnati ■ Detroit ■ Johannesburg
London ■ Madrid ■ Melbourne ■ Mexico City ■ New York ■ Paris ■ Singapore
Tokyo ■ Toronto ■ Washington

Sponsoring Editor: *Lisa Gebo*
Marketing Team: *Deborah Petit, Jean Thompson*
Editorial Assistants: *Terry Thomas, Shelley Bouhaja*
Production Editor: *Keith Faivre*
Manuscript Editor: *Cathy Cambron*
Permissions Editor: *Cathleen C. Morrison*
Interior Design: *Carolyn Deacy*

Cover Design: *Roy Neuhaus*
Cover and Interior Photos: *Leslie Parr*
Art Editor: *Lisa Torri*
Photo Editor: *Bob Western*
Typesetting: *G&S Typesetters, Inc.*
Printing and Binding: *Malloy Lithographing, Inc.*

For more information, contact:

BROOKS/COLE PUBLISHING COMPANY
511 Forest Lodge Road
Pacific Grove, CA 93950
USA

International Thomson Publishing Europe
Berkshire House 168–173
High Holborn
London WC1V 7AA
England

Thomas Nelson Australia
102 Dodds Street
South Melbourne, 3205
Victoria, Australia

Nelson Canada
1120 Birchmount Road
Scarborough, Ontario
Canada M1K 5G4

International Thomson Editores
Seneca 53
Col. Polanco
11560 México, D. F., México

International Thomson Publishing GmbH
Königswinterer Strasse 418
53227 Bonn
Germany

International Thomson Publishing Asia
221 Henderson Road
#05–10 Henderson Building
Singapore 0315

International Thomson Publishing Japan
Hirakawacho Kyowa Building, 3F
2-2-1 Hirakawacho
Chiyoda-ku, Tokyo 102
Japan

Printed in the United States of America.

10 9 8 7 6 5 4 3 2 1

Library of Congress Cataloging-in-Publication Data

Marlow, Christine.
    Research methods for generalist social work / Christine Marlow. —
2nd ed.
        p.   cm.
    Includes bibliographical references and index.
    ISBN 0-534-34953-6 (alk. paper)
    1. Social service—Research—Methodology.   I. Title.
HV11.M3493   1998
361'.0072—dc21   97-9557
                                                              CIP

Contents

5

Designing Needs Assessments   71

6

Designing Program Evaluations   85

7

Designing the Evaluation of Practice   111

8

Selecting the Participants in the Research   133

9

Collecting the Data   157

11

Analysis of Qualitative Data   209

12

Analysis of Quantitative Data: Descriptive Statistics   225

13

Analysis of Quantitative Data: Inferential Statistics   247

14

Research Writing   265

15

Using Research Findings in Practice and Evaluating Research   289

Appendixes

To Mike and Sam for their patience

My reason for writing this text is not unusual. After several years of seeking a social work research methods text and unsuccessfully trying a new text each year, I gave up and started to write. From teaching the same course repeatedly, I had developed a number of ideas of what a text needed. These ideas became crystallized through many discussions with students and colleagues and through my experiences with the Council on Social Work Education (CSWE) accreditation process. The following themes emerged, which have been joined by additional themes in this updated second edition.

THEMES AND ORGANIZATION

A Focus on generalist practice. Undergraduate and foundation graduate courses in social work programs usually are taught from a generalist perspective. Research methods must also be taught within this framework; consequently, the text includes examples from generalist practice. The relevance of research to the rest of the curriculum is thereby increased.

Emphasis on the practice-research link. When the parallels between generalist practice and research are emphasized, research becomes more accessible because practice is often perceived as more intuitive and understandable. Consequently, the text illustrates these parallels. Throughout the text, examples emphasize the link between research and practice by presenting real-life social work studies.

Discussion of production and consumption. The text presents research methods from the perspective that social workers can be both producers and consumers of research. This also ensures compliance with the CSWE accreditation requirements for the research curriculum.

Agency focus. In line with ensuring the relevance of research methods, the text discusses the application of research methods in agency rather than academic settings, because agencies are where the majority of social work graduates will be employed.

Ethics content. Ethical issues are included for each stage of the research process; that is, they are integrated into each chapter and not viewed as separate, discrete topics.

Human diversity content.   Similarly, issues concerning human diversity as they relate to research methods are included. Although partly addressed through discussions of alternatives within and to the scientific method, this content (as with the ethics content) is considered for each stage of the research process.

Discussion of the different approaches to research.   This second edition covers different research approaches more explicitly, and it is clearer than the first edition in distinguishing between the more traditional approaches (in this text called positivist) and alternative approaches (here designated interpretist). The use of these terms is somewhat arbitrary, and they are used here in a general sense. The term *positivism* is used in a general sense to include its variants, such as *postpositivism* and *quantitative methods; interpretism* is similarly used in this general sense to include *constructivism* and *qualitative methods.* Some may find this distinction rather elementary. A beginning text in research methods cannot engage in epistemological debates; what is important for the student to understand is that research can be conducted using different methods and within different paradigms.

International content.   As universities become increasingly conscious of internationalizing their curricula, social work programs are also adopting global perspectives. Thus this new edition incorporates some content from outside the United States, particularly in the examples.

Content on participatory approaches to research.   Recent years have seen increased use of research methods that empower clients and research participants through their engagement in the research process. These approaches vary in name and form; they include action research and empowerment research. This new edition includes content on these approaches.

A chapter on needs assessments.   This edition includes a new chapter on the design of needs assessments or surveys to accompany the chapters on the design of program evaluations and practice evaluations. This new edition has also added approaches to evaluating practice that go beyond single-system studies and expanded content on writing literature reviews.

The book is written so that each chapter can stand independently if necessary. The statistics chapters (Chapters 11 and 12) may be omitted if students have already completed statistics courses. Important terms appear in the text in **boldface** type and are defined there. These terms also are included in the glossary at the back of the text. Each chapter includes a references section, as well as a summary, further reading, and study/exercise questions. If possible, students should complete the exercises as a group; a group effort often provides a richer educational experience.

ACKNOWLEDGMENTS

Completion of this new edition depended on many people (too many for me to name them all), but I would like to thank the following specific individuals and groups: Pat Sandau-Beckler, associate professor at New Mexico State University, co-authored Chapter 15; Donnelyn Curtis, reference librarian at New Mexico State University, contributed the bulk of the literature review and library resource material.

The reviewers of the manuscript contributed critical comments as the book progressed, and I would like to thank Jane Kronick, Bryn Mawr College; Stephen M. Marson, University of North Carolina, Pembroke; David Miller, Liberty University; Phyllis Solomon, University of Pennsylvania; Katherine Tyson, Loyola University of Chicago; Robert Vernon, University of Indianapolis; and Marilyn Wedenoja, Eastern Michigan University. Special thanks go to Colin van Rooyen at the University of Natal, Durban, South Africa. He helped me shift from being too "U.S.-centric" to adopting more of an international perspective; he also offered many practical suggestions. Thanks also to the social work students at the University of Natal who offered several of the research study examples.

Other contributors include all the students who have enrolled in the research methods courses I have taught over the years in the United States and in Zimbabwe where I was a Fulbright Scholar in 1994. In many ways, the students wrote the book by teaching me how the material could be presented so that it would make sense to them.

Lisa Gebo at Brooks/Cole was wonderfully understanding and supportive. I would like to thank Leslie Parr, Loyola University, New Orleans, for the superb photographs. Leslie and I have been friends for many years; her photography continually reminds us that social work research has to do with people rather than numbers. I would also like to extend special thanks to Vernalynn Andrews for her clerical assistance with the drafts of the manuscript. I cannot thank her enough for her patience and thoroughness.

Finally, to my family: son Sam and partner Mike. Thanks for your great patience during the times I was inseparable from my computer.

Science and Social Work

■

"The social work research methods course was the one
I dreaded the most. I didn't want to take it."

—*social work student*

INTRODUCTION

The attitude reflected in this student's statement is not unusual in social work classrooms. Social workers often express inherent suspicion, or even a phobia about research. Have you ever skimmed over articles in social work journals, because you were intimidated by the language and the displays of results? Have you ever shuddered at the thought of undertaking a research project? If so, you are not alone. Because research is typically associated with mathematics, you may not be enthusiastic about applying what is perceived as a cold impersonal approach to human needs and problem solving. After all, most social workers want to work with people, not numbers. Research, however, is simply a means of gaining knowledge, and in social work practice, we need all the knowledge we can muster if we are to be optimally responsible to ourselves, our clients, and our agencies.

Once you understand the research process, you will have access to a vast amount of information in the literature. Articles that once eluded you with discussions of "validity" and "correlation coefficients" not only will become accessible, but will make available information that you can apply to your practice.

When you are equipped with the knowledge and skills to apply research methods, you will also know how to answer many of the questions that arise in your role as a generalist social worker, such as these:

■ Are my visits to Mrs. Garcia really helping her cope with the death of her husband? What is her experience of the grief counseling?

■ How effective is program X in providing services that support and protect victims of domestic violence? What are the experiences of the clients receiving these services?

■ What are the needs of adolescent fathers in City Y? What is it like to be a teenage father in City Y?

This book emphasizes the strong links between the processes of research and practice, helping you answer these types of questions and understand social work research. The steps of generalist social work practice have their equivalents in social work research.

Thus, the following chapters help you learn the steps of research in a process similar to the way you learn the steps of practice.

Certain themes of this text will help explain research methodology and its relevance to your practice as a generalist social worker:

■ The research process and generalist practice are connected.

■ You may be either a consumer or producer of research.

- Research examples throughout the book are those you will encounter as a generalist researcher.
- Different research approaches may apply depending upon the type of question being asked.
- Special issues are involved when you conduct research in agencies.
- Ethical issues are associated with each stage of the research process.
- Human diversity issues are also involved with each stage of the research process.

These overlapping themes support the mission of the book: to present research methods within a generalist social work framework.

Many new concepts are introduced in this book. These terms are boldfaced in the text where they are first defined; they are also listed in the glossary at the end of the book. Each chapter includes an overview, a summary, recommended further readings, and study/exercise questions. This chapter will discuss the following topics:

- types of understanding
- conceptions of science
- positivist approaches to science
- interpretive approaches to science
- the choice of a scientific approach in social work

COMMON TYPES OF UNDERSTANDING

In our attempt to understand the world, we have developed many different ways of understanding and thinking about human behavior. These types of understanding include using values, intuition, past experience, authority, and the scientific approach. Social work can involve any or all of these types of understanding, and it is important to know about them and the role they play in generalist social work practice.

Values.   **Values** are beliefs about what is right and wrong. They are closely tied to our respective cultures. For example, among many cultures, a strong value is placed on children's having respect for their elders. Among some groups, formal education is highly valued, whereas among others education within the family is emphasized.

Values can be institutionalized by religion. For example, certain values characterize Christianity, such as the Protestant belief that work is a means of gaining societal and individual worth, and the Catholic belief in the forgiveness of sins. Buddhists value reincarnation, and this belief affects how people live their present lives. Other religions involve a form of ancestor worship, whereas others strongly value the natural world around them, revering the plants and animals that make up their worlds.

Although values may be fundamental to a culture's tradition, these traditions can change over time. For example, in a number of cultures, many people now recognize that women should have the same career opportunities as men. This was not the case a hundred years ago, or even ten years ago in some countries.

Social work as a profession is based on certain values. These include fundamental notions about the most desirable relationships between people and their environment. Social work values include respect for the individual's dignity and uniqueness; recognition of the client's right to self-determination; and confidentiality.

Intuition.   **Intuition** can be defined as a form of insight: when we intuitively know something, we understand it without recourse to specialized training or reasoning. Intuition may also be based on past experiences. In some cultures, intuition is a powerful tool for understanding and explaining the world. People with strong intuition may be seen as having magical powers. If they also exhibit experience and skills, they may enjoy special status in a culture. An example is the *curandera,* a woman who is perceived to possess healing powers in the Hispanic culture in the Southwest and Mexico. Similarly, in South Africa among the Zulu people, the *sangoma* is thought to be able to understand the world using special intuitive powers.

Sometimes we call upon intuition in social work practice. Although it's unlikely that we would act on intuition alone, we might use it to give ourselves leads to investigate further. For example, we might have an intuition that a child is being sexually abused. It may be hard for us to explain this feeling rationally, but the insight can provide a base or starting point for gathering information, which may or may not support the intuition.

Experience.   **Experience** can be defined as firsthand, personal participation in events that provide a basis for knowledge. You often use this experience to guide present and future actions, particularly when the experience had a successful outcome (even though you may not understand why it was successful). Clearly, these experiences vary from individual to individual and according to the type of situation. Experience is highly valued in most cultures. Elders are often highly regarded because of their experience; employers often use experience as a criterion for assessing job applicants. In the practice of social work, this experience is often referred to as practice wisdom. Although highly valuable as a source of knowledge, it is risky to use practice wisdom as the sole guide to practice and as the only resource for making practice judgments.

Authority.   Sometimes events and circumstances are understood by referring to outside sources of knowledge or to an **authority** on specific topics. The authority is credited with an understanding we do not directly possess. Thus, in lieu of direct understanding—whether obtained through values, intuition, or experience—we accept an explanation by virtue of our confidence in authorities.

Who or what the authority is depends upon the nature and context of the problem.

In practice, social workers rely on authority in a number of ways. We identify experts in different fields of practice and seek their opinions and knowledge, either by consulting with them personally or by reading their publications. There is vested authority in the social work professional organizations, such as the National Association of Social Workers (NASW) in the United States and the National Institute of Social Work in Great Britain. We use their authority to direct us in different areas, for instance in adhering to a prescribed code of ethics.

Science.   Specific characteristics of science distinguish it from other forms of understanding discussed in this section. **Science** refers to both a system for producing knowledge and the knowledge produced from that system. It is guided by a set of norms that include the following (Neuman, 1994).

Universalism.   Regardless of who conducts scientific research or where it is conducted, it is judged solely on its scientific merit.

Organized skepticism.   All scientific evidence should be challenged and questioned.

Disinterestedness.   Scientists should be able to accept other scientific evidence that runs against their position.

Communalism.   Scientific knowledge must be shared with the public, including the methods used.

Honesty.   Scientists demand honesty in all research.

As well as being characterized by these norms, science consists of theories and research methods. **Theories** describe or explain logical relationships among phenomena in our world. Theories help guide our thinking about many aspects of social work practice and include theories of human behavior, such as developmental theories, and theories underlying practice, such as systems theories. Theories are to be distinguished from values, which are concerned with what should be rather than what is. Instead, theories attempt to understand and explain logical and persistent patterns in phenomena.

Theories cannot stand alone in science, however. They need to be supported by the other component of science: **research methods.** Research methods adhere to the following principles:

1.   Information is collected from *observing* the world. This observation can be carried out in different ways, but it is different from philosophizing, or speculating.

2. The steps of the research process are *systematic,* not random or haphazard.
3. Studies should be *replicated;* repeating studies a number of times determines whether the same results will be found.

People think about the relationship between research methods and theory in different ways. Just as different types of theories explain different phenomena, so different research methods may apply to different topics. These different methods and ways of conceptualizing science will be discussed in the next section of this chapter.

Science is the focus of this text because it is the dominant type of understanding today. Many individuals and organizations throughout the world depend on science. For example, the medical profession relies on knowledge derived from the application of science. Businesses use scientifically based theories and strategies. Social work is no exception; the profession has historically recognized the contributions of the scientific approach.

Before proceeding with a more detailed description of the scientific method, it is important to note that although the scientific approach dominates the thinking in many countries, this has not always been the case. For example, Greek rationalism once dominated Western thought, offering logic as the test of truth and not relying on scientific evidence. Even today, scientific thinking is not dominant in all cultures. For example, in some American Indian cultures, direct experience of an event is the primary means of explanation. Among some other groups, including the Zulu, scientific explanations are not always accepted. For example, existence of HIV (the human immunodeficiency virus) in the body is not always seen as evidence of a person's being HIV positive (van Rooyen & Engelbrecht, 1995).

CONCEPTIONS OF SCIENCE

Although science is unified by its shared norms, the actual doing of science varies. Up until about 25 years ago, this was not the case. One model or approach was used in the social sciences; this model was broadly referred to as positivism. (Variations and other terms include logical positivism and empiricism.) **Positivism** rests on a number of different principles about how science should be done. One central principle is that science depends upon the collection of observations that support theories. These observations need to be made objectively. **Objectivity** refers to the condition in which, to the greatest extent possible, researchers' values and biases do not interfere with their study of the problem. Another principle is that the theories and observations remain separate. A theory ultimately needs to be supported by observations, resulting in laws and rules that help make sense of the world.

Over the years, however, the positivist approach and its principles have been questioned. Throughout the social sciences, including social work, positivism's claim to be the same thing as the scientific method and empirical science has raised skepticism. The questioning derives from two major sources:

first, students of the history of science; and second, people who traditionally have been excluded from the scientific community, members of diverse, often minority groups, including women. Each of these sources will be discussed.

Thomas Kuhn explores the issue of values in *The Structure of Scientific Revolutions* (1970). From studying the history of science, Kuhn concluded that other factors besides specific observations and theoretical necessity lead to the emergence and acceptance of the "best theory." These other factors include values. Kuhn wrote about paradigms, defining a paradigm as "the entire constellation of beliefs, values, techniques and so on shared by members of a given [scientific] community" (Kuhn, 1970). Paradigms function as maps, directing us to the problems that are important to address, the theories that are acceptable, and the procedures needed to solve the problems. Kuhn proposed that paradigms shift over time. Paradigms reflect changing values, countering the idea that a fixed reality exists out there to be objectively observed. Objective reality appears to change as paradigms change.

An example of a paradigm shift occurred in social work during the last 50 years. In the 1920s and 1930s, the prevailing paradigm or framework for social work practice was psychoanalytic and was tied closely to a medical model. In the 1960s, a more ecological systems framework was adopted. This paradigm shift has important implications not only for how social workers conceptualize their practice but also for how research is conducted. Research questions deriving from a medical model differ substantially from those deriving from a systems perspective.

The views of diverse groups, which previously had been virtually denied access to the traditional scientific paradigm, have had an increasing impact on how science is perceived. Many argue that the types of questions asked are influenced by the social context of the researcher (Kuhn's point) and that different groups bring different experiences to the research, influencing the types of questions asked.

Many **feminist researchers**—for example, Davis, 1986, and Belenky, Clinchy, Goldberger, & Tarule, 1986—are also affecting how science is viewed. They argue that men and women experience the world differently, and that the objective model of science is more compatible with men's ways of thinking. Because women see the world more in terms of relationships and interaction, feminists think that a relationship is formed between the researcher and subject, which results in the formation of a constructed reality between them. Thus, according to feminist researchers and many others, no facts exist out there that can be objectively observed.

This questioning of the principles underlying the positivist approach to science resulted in the adoption of alternative research models by people in the social sciences, including social work. Positivism has not been rejected, but alternatives to positivism are now considered also to be part of the scientific norm. Just as positivism embraces a number of different variations, for example postpositivism, so several models have also been developed as alternatives to positivism. **Interpretism** is the term used here to denote these alternatives. In the next two sections, the positivist and interpretist approaches will be examined, and the different principles guiding the two approaches will be discussed.

THE POSITIVIST APPROACH TO SCIENCE

Positivism is traditionally equated with science and is the approach predominantly used in the natural sciences. Some principles of this approach were described in the previous section; here positivism will be presented in more detail.

According to positivism, observations of the world can and must be carried out objectively. Biases and values must be eliminated as much as possible. Positivist research methods are designed for this purpose. Many of these methods rely on a clear distinction between the researcher and the subject, with any contact between the two being strictly formalized. In positivist research, the subject actually becomes the object of study. The science is researcher-driven (Guba, 1990); the subjects have little say about how the research is carried out.

The goal of science is to search for causes of phenomena. Such a search is possible because it is assumed the world has an order that can be discovered, so that it is possible to explain and predict what goes on in the world. The strongest theories are predictive. **Causality** means that changes in some factor or factors (A) produce variations in another factor or factors (B). The following conditions have to exist in order to infer the existence of a causal relationship:

- A statistical association has to exist between the factors. (The intricacies of statistical association will be explained later.)
- Factor or factors A must occur prior to factor or factors B.
- The relationship between the factors A and B must not be spurious. In other words, the relationship must not disappear when the effects of other factors are taken into consideration.

A deductive approach is used to build knowledge. **Deductive reasoning** involves drawing conclusions from the general to the particular. A theory generates questions; these questions are then compared with observations. For example, various researchers have investigated whether Piaget's theory of child cognitive development is valid across different cultures (Mangan, 1978), testing through observation whether Piaget's theory describes what occurs in different cultures. The results are then fed back into the theory.

The observations collected are usually **quantitative.** To gather quantitative observations or data, categories of the phenomena under study are created prior to investigation. Numbers are assigned to these categories, which are then statistically analyzed.

The positivist approach requires studying large numbers of subjects, because a central concern is that one should be able to **generalize** the results of the research to as large a group as possible. Findings from a study can be generalized if they can be applied to other groups rather than being specific to those in the current research. For the findings to be generalized, the subjects being studied need to be representative of the groups to which the researcher wants to generalize the findings. Certain techniques in positivist research ensure this representativeness. Large groups are also needed because the statistical tests used to analyze the quantitative information usually gathered by positivist research are designed for large numbers of subjects.

As discussed earlier, the positivist approach has come under increasing criticism in recent years, particularly in the social sciences. In general, critics have questioned whether a positivist approach is applicable when studying human beings. Recently there has even been some question about whether positivism can be used as the only research approach in the natural sciences. One main group of alternative approaches to science is offered in the next section.

A Positivist Study in Social Work

Feldman (1990) evaluated intensive family preservation programs in New Jersey. He was trying to identify those factors (or causes) that resulted in successful outcomes for families served. He used a number of objective measures to assess service outcomes; the resulting quantitative data were tested using statistical procedures. He used a positivist approach to try to establish causality, so that the results of the study could be generalized to other family preservation programs.

THE INTERPRETIVE APPROACH TO SCIENCE

There are several branches of interpretive science, including hermeneutics, ethnomethodology, constructionism, phenomenology, naturalistic inquiry, and qualitative methods. Here we need not be concerned about the distinctions among these approaches (see Patton, 1990, for a good discussion), but rather with their overall assumptions and methods of interpretation.

For the interpretive researcher, reality is based on people's definitions of it, rather than being something externally present. The **subjective** experience is what needs to be studied, rather than the objective one. For the interpretists, observation takes on a different quality than it has for the positivists. People's behavior cannot be observed objectively; instead, the researcher and subject create a reality through their interaction. Because reality is perceived as interactive and constructed, the subject's role in the research process is more active. Instead of being researcher-driven as in the positivist approach, the research process is instead subject-driven. Subjects become partners with the researchers and empowered in the process. In addition, interpretists explicitly acknowledge the researcher's biases and values. These are stated explicitly rather than ignored.

Interpretists are primarily interested in **description** rather than explanation. Because of the assumption that reality is socially constructed and is in a state of being mutually shaped, causes cannot always be definitively established. Instead the interactive reality is discovered and described.

Interpretists usually build knowledge inductively. **Inductive reasoning** uses observation to examine the particulars of a phenomenon and then develops generalizations to explain or describe relationships among the particulars. Inductive reasoning involves finding patterns common to separate phenomena. For example, certain similarities may be seen in children with behavioral problems in school. After collecting case examples, a theory is developed that states the children have other characteristics in common besides the behavior problems. The majority may be found to be new immigrants whose parents do not speak English, and their behavioral problems may result from teachers' failures to appreciate the children's difficulty in making the transition from home to school. Thus, a theory is built from observations, rather than developed through generating questions that are then answered through observations.

Interpretive researchers usually collect **qualitative** information. Qualitative information involves the nonnumerical examination of phenomena, using words instead of numbers, and focusses on the underlying meanings and patterns of relationships. Often these underlying patterns are disguised if categories are formed before numerical observations are made. Analysis of qualitative information consists of creating categories after the verbal material has been collected. When qualitative information is collected, the number of subjects in the study is often small, because the focus is on collecting in-depth information from each subject so as to understand the subject's subjective experience of the phenomena under study.

Interpretive Research in Social Work

Hyden (1994) in Sweden studied 20 couples in which the husband repeatedly beat the wife. Hyden learned about the two parties' characterizations of the situation, their reflections on what happened, and their interpretations of the meaning of the events for their marriage. Hyden collected data over two years through intensive, detailed interviews. She then analyzed these narratives, with the focus on describing and understanding the couples' experiences.

See Figure 1.1 for an illustration of the relationship between the interpretist and positivist approaches. Remember that the distinction made between the two approaches here is a fairly crude one. As mentioned earlier, different terms are often used in different ways, and what they denote is subject to considerable debate. The complex field of the philosophy of science is beyond the scope of this book.

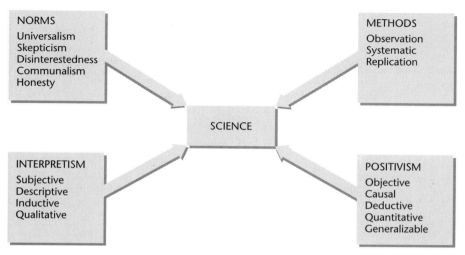

Figure 1.1   **Different approaches to science**

THE CHOICE OF A SCIENTIFIC APPROACH IN SOCIAL WORK

Having described two basic approaches to science, how do you reach a decision about which one to use for social work? Over the last few years there has been quite a debate in social work about this very question. Some argue that social work will lose its credibility as a social science if it abandons the positivist approach, and that positivism is the only method that develops sound knowledge on which to base social work practice (Scheurman, 1982; Hudson, 1982). Others defend and promote alternative perspectives, arguing that only they can capture the essence and meaning of social work (Heineman, 1981), reminding us that human behavior is complex and not always observable and measurable. Their argument is that the basic principles underlying the interpretive, alternative approaches are more compatible with social work in that they empower the subjects and reflect more accurately the diversity of opinions and perspectives within the field.

The position behind this book is that both positivism and interpretism offer the potential to build knowledge in social work. Just as different models exist to guide practice, each offering its strengths and weaknesses, so in research, different methods have advantages and disadvantages. Each is a response to different perceptions of reality. Neither positivism nor interpretism can offer the ultimate "truth."

Since both approaches offer advantages, the question becomes which one to use when. The decision depends on the type of question being asked. Some questions are more suited to a positivist research method, and some to an interpretive one. Take the three sets of questions at the beginning of this chapter. The first part of each question is asking for information that goes beyond the particular to the general. The answers need to be as generalizable as possible. The focus, at least in the first two questions, is on explanation—in other words, whether and how the programs and interventions are working. The intent of these questions is to produce information that is as objective as possible in order that funding decisions can be made and programs developed.

The second part of each question is a very different matter. The second part focuses more on the subjects' experiences, and the goal is to understand rather than explain. These questions are less concerned with objectivity and the ability to generalize the findings.

Sometimes the type of question to ask and subsequently the type of approach to use depends upon the level of knowledge we have about the area under study. For example, suppose the phenomenon under study is battered women. Initially, Walker's (1979) theory, that "learned helplessness" can explain why battered women stay in violent relationships, was developed using an interpretist approach. It was only after the theory was developed through interpretist observation that the theory was tested using a positivist approach. Thus the generation of knowledge can be seen to be cyclical, with both approaches integral to the development of concepts and theories.

In this book, both approaches will be described, and you will be given guidance about times when one might be more appropriate than the other. Both approaches require specific skills, experience, and planning. The appropriate choice depends upon the question under study and the overall purpose of the research. As with practice—where, for example, behavioral interventions require a different knowledge base and are appropriate to different circumstances than psychodynamic interventions—no one approach is always better or right.

SUMMARY

This chapter introduces the themes in this book. Different types of understanding are based on sources of knowledge including values, intuition, experience, authority, and science. The positivist and interpretist approaches to science can both offer advantages in addressing the different types of research questions asked in generalist social work.

STUDY/EXERCISE QUESTIONS

1. List the five different types of understanding presented in this chapter and discuss how you use each of them in your practice.

2. Go to a public place and observe the people for 15 minutes. Report back to your class. Note the similarities and differences in what each student

observed. Discuss the implications of these observations for the concept of objectivity.

FURTHER READING

Davis, L. (1986). A feminist approach to social work research. *Affilia, 32–47.*
One of the first articles that specifically discusses the principles of the feminist approach to research in social work.

Guba, E. G. (1990). (Ed.). *The paradigm dialog.* Newbury Park, CA: Sage.
A good discussion of some different paradigms that have dominated the social services.

Kuhn, J. (1970). *The structure of scientific revolutions.* Chicago: University of Chicago.
As discussed in this chapter, a landmark book that provided a new perspective for conceptualizing science. This short book is exciting and very informative.

Patton, M. Q. (1990). *Qualitative evaluation and research methods.* Newbury Park, CA: Sage.
A very clear guide to the different forms of qualitative research (in this chapter referred to as interpretive methods).

Reinharz, S. (1994). *Feminist methods in social research.* Oxford University Press.
An excellent book that includes different applications and approaches to feminist research.

Tyson, K. (1994). *New foundations for scientific social and behavioral research.* Boston: Allyn & Bacon.
Katherine Tyson has collected materials relating to the debate between the positivists and those holding alternative views of science. She presents the heuristic paradigm as a way of conducting research in social work.

REFERENCES

Belenky, M., Clinchy, B., Goldberger, N., & Tarule, J. (1986). *Women's ways of knowing: The development of self, voice, and mind.* New York: Basic Books.

Davis, L. (1986). A feminist approach to social work research. *Affilia, 32–47.*

Feldman, L. H. (1990). Evaluating the impact of intensive family preservation services in New Jersey. In K. Wells & D. Biegel (Eds.), *Family preservation services.* Newbury Park, CA: Sage.

Guba, E. G. (1990). (Ed.). *The paradigm dialog.* Newbury Park, CA: Sage.

Heineman, M. (1981). The obsolete scientific imperative in social work research. *Social Service Review, 55,* 371–397.

Hyden, M. (1994). Woman battering as a marital act: Interviewing and analysis in context. In C. K. Riessman (Ed.), *Qualitative studies in social work research.* Newbury Park, CA: Sage.

Kuhn, J. (1970). *The structure of scientific revolutions.* Chicago: The University of Chicago Press.

Hudson, W. (1982). Scientific imperatives in social work research and practice. *Social Service Review, 56,* 246–258.

Mangan, J. (1978). Piaget's theory and cultural differences: The case for value based modes of cognition. *Human Development, 21,* 170–189.

Neuman, W. L. (1994). *Social research methods.* Boston: Allyn & Bacon.

Scheurman, J. (1982). Debate with authors. *Social Service Review, 56,* 144–148.

van Rooyen, C., & Engelbrecht, B. (1995). The impact of culture on HIV/AIDS social work service delivery: Emerging themes from a study in progress. *Social Work Practice, 3.95,* 2–8.

Walker, L. (1979). *The battered woman.* New York. Harper Row.

Research and Generalist
Social Work Practice

■

One problem in understanding the research process is that it is often viewed in isolation, rather than as being closely linked to practice. In this chapter the link between research and practice will be explored. In addition, close parallels between the practice process and the research process will be examined. This chapter discusses the following:

- generalist practice
- the purpose of research on generalist practice
- research roles in generalist practice
- research and generalist practice processes
- values in research and practice
- research and human diversity

GENERALIST PRACTICE

Before discussing how research is linked to generalist practice, we need to explain what is meant by **generalist social work practice.** "The roots of the generalist concept go as deep as the social work profession itself" (Landon, 1994, p. 1101). Social work from its inception has been committed to both addressing individual competencies and implementing social change. Today, generalist practice is the form of social work practice taught in undergraduate programs in the United States and in many other parts of the world as a basis for professional social work education.

Over the years, various views have developed about what constitutes generalist practice. Several writers have tried to clarify its components (Schatz & Jenkins, 1987; Baer & Federico, 1978) and proposed different conceptualizations (Johnson, 1995; O'Neil McMahon, 1996; Compton & Galaway, 1994; Miley, O'Melia, & DuBois, 1995), but there still is no single accepted model of generalist social work.

Schatz, Jenkins, and Sheafor (1990) drew from some of these studies and conceptualizations and suggested that generalist social work is marked by the following:

- It is informed by socio-behavioral and ecosystems knowledge.
- It reflects ideologies such as democracy, humanism, and empowerment.
- It is theoretically and methodologically open.
- It involves direct and indirect intervention.
- It is client-centered and problem-focused.
- It is research-based.

Generalist social workers are expected to be competent in doing the following:

- Engaging in interpersonal helping
- Managing change processes
- Using multi-level intervention modes
- Intervening in multi-sized systems
- Performing varied practice roles
- Assessing and examining their own practice
- Functioning within a social agency

THE PURPOSE OF RESEARCH IN GENERALIST SOCIAL WORK PRACTICE

As generalist social workers, why do we need to be concerned with research? Because the dominant way of understanding the world is through science, building a strong research base for practice helps legitimize the profession and gives it credibility to others. Relying on research, however, does not mean dismissing other forms of understanding. Beyond its legitimizing role, research fulfills a number of other functions for generalist social work practice, promoting a strong knowledge base, fiscal and ethical responsibility, and clients' empowerment. Each of these will be discussed in turn.

Building Scientific Knowledge

Scientific knowledge is built through applying research methods to support and develop theories. In the last chapter, two different research approaches were discussed. Each builds knowledge rather differently from the other. The positivist approach generally uses the deductive method of building theory, deducing premises from the theory and testing those premises. The interpretist approach uses the inductive method, in which observations are made and, from those systematic observations, theories are built.

The development of knowledge through research is a central function of research in social work. This knowledge about the extent, nature, and causes of social problems, and the effectiveness of various interventions and programs, significantly enhances social work practice. Without this research-based knowledge, social workers would have to rely on the other sources of understanding described in the last chapter. Although each of these sources has its own contributions to make to practice, generalist social work would suffer without scientifically based knowledge.

For example, if you were employed in Child Protective Services as an investigator, a critical part of how you make decisions about intervention with the family is based on risk assessment tools. These tools, such as the Child Well-Being Scales (Magura & Moses, 1986), are based on previous research and are tested using scientific methods. Without such tools, your decision might have to be based on your authority as an investigator, your intuition, your values, or your past experience with similar situations—all important components in the final decision but weakened by the absence of the scientific component.

Entire programs are developed on the basis of research. For example, early intervention programs for new parents are based on research that indicates that parent training and support can help reduce the incidence of child abuse and neglect. The training itself is based on theories of child development that are supported by research.

On a larger scale, major welfare reform decisions need to be based on information gathered from previous studies. For example, Chilman (1995) critically reviewed studies concerning the working poor. As a result of this review, she proposed further legislation to help move recipients of welfare from economic dependency to self-sufficiency through employment.

Ethical Issues

Social workers need to be knowledgeable about research for ethical reasons. Social workers are ethically responsible for providing the best possible services to their clients. In the United States, the National Association of Social Workers' Code of Ethics (1997) specifically addresses this issue.

- Social workers should educate themselves, their students, and their colleagues about responsible research practices.
- Social workers should monitor and evaluate policies, the implementation of programs, and practice interventions.
- Social workers should promote and facilitate evaluation and research to contribute to the development of knowledge.
- Social workers should critically examine and keep current with emerging knowledge relevant to social work and fully use evaluation and research evidence in their professional practice.*

To abide by the NASW Code of Ethics, the social worker needs to be proficient in social work research methods.

Fiscal Accountability

As long as social work practice is predominantly funded by government and charitable contributions, accountability will be a critical issue in the field. In recent years, fiscal accountability has become even more important. Funds allocated to the human services are decreasing rapidly, and different organizations must compete for smaller and smaller pools of money.

---

*Material from the National Association of Social Workers throughout this textbook and in Appendix E reprinted with permission from the National Association of Social Workers (NASW), 1997.

Two aspects of social accountability must be considered. First, social workers are expected to demonstrate that they are spending money responsibly, including the assurance that a social program's goals are being met and funds are being distributed in the most efficient way to meet those goals. The agency or the individual practitioner may be responsible for this accountability. Second, generalist social workers are often called upon to establish new services and programs, particularly in rural areas. To do so, and to solicit funds for the purpose, you need to substantiate your claim by providing clear evidence of need and a strong basis in research for the proposed program.

Ensuring Fiscal Responsibility Through Research

Hagen and Lurie (1995) examined the Job Opportunity and Basic Skills Training Program (JOBS) introduced as part of the Family Support Act of 1988, which attempted to help move welfare organizations from promoting welfare dependency to self-sufficiency. The study examined the views of frontline workers and found that they strongly support the JOBS program and its goals. They did have reservations about the program's effectiveness, suggesting that education and training services were inadequately funded and that their local communities lacked employment opportunities.

Empowering Clients

Not only can research be indirectly empowering to clients—through building knowledge and ensuring fiscal and ethical accountability—but certain research methods can be directly empowering as well. Subjects (often clients) can be directly involved in the research process from its planning to its implementation. Some research strategies involve clients more than others do. We discussed in the last chapter how the interpretive approach tends to be more subject- rather than researcher-driven. This tendency derives in part from the assumption that meaning emerges from the interaction of subject and researcher, rather than from the researcher's objective observations alone. Through use of the interpretive approach, clients become empowered because they are not being used as subjects but instead as direct participants in the research.

Another opportunity for clients' involvement in research, and subsequent empowerment, is through **participatory action research.** This approach to research has three aims, all intended to empower clients. The first is to produce knowledge and action directly useful to groups of people. A second aim is to encourage people to construct and use their own knowledge for empowerment. The third aim is to promote collaboration throughout the research process. Participatory action research originated and grew in developing countries, where it continues to be a standard approach to research. Increasingly, participatory action research is being adopted in other parts of the world. In the United States, corporations have used this type of research as a way of motivating workers to adopt new productivity strategies. For example, in a case study of Xerox Corporation, White (1991) demonstrated how labor, management, and the researcher worked as a team to help increase productivity, instead of the researcher's simply going in with a plan and recommendations from management's perspective. Participatory action research is particularly compatible with generalist social work in that the approach emphasizes empowering systems of different sizes, from individuals through whole communities. Usually, the people under study participate actively with the researcher throughout the research process, from the initial design to the final presentation and dissemination of results. Note that a number of different research methods can be used within the participatory action research framework, including either the positivist or interpretist approach.

RESEARCH ROLES IN GENERALIST PRACTICE

As we have seen, generalist social work practice is based in research, and practitioners must be able to assess or examine their own practice in terms of research. To accomplish this goal, the generalist social worker needs to adopt two roles with respect to research: the consumer and the producer.

The Consumer

As was discussed earlier, the scientific approach is essential in building a knowledge base for social work. To use this knowledge in an informed manner, social workers need to understand research methods so they can evaluate the extent of a theory's research base. Even if the theory has apparently been validated and supported by research, there is no guarantee this research is of high quality. A social worker who is knowledgeable about research can better evaluate the quality of that research base. In their users' guide to social science research, Causer, Cook, and Crouch (1991) point out, in a section entitled "The literature is probably worse than you think," that many mistakes and errors occur even in published research. Your research instructor can undoubtedly confirm this statement.

Critical analysis of research is also useful in the social worker's assessment of specific practice techniques. For example, home-based services are commonly provided by generalist practitioners, and there exists a whole body of literature and research about these services. The practitioner informed about research can turn to this research for guidelines for practice. Using research in this way, the practitioner may be able to answer a question such as "How do I know whether home visits to 85-year-old Mrs. Garcia will help prevent her being placed in a nursing home?" This ability to evaluate theories is known as the consumer function of research knowledge. The details of how to consult research to enhance practice are provided in Chapter 15.

The Producer

The second reason social workers need to know about research methods is the most obvious one. Armed with this knowledge, social workers can then use the methods directly in their own practice to answer questions that arise. This ability to use research methods is vital whenever answers cannot be found in the existing literature, as is frequent in social work, whether or not the social worker is engaged in generalist practice. Social workers often need to carry out their own research on the effectiveness of many interventions they use. In addition, generalist social workers are often required to demonstrate the need to provide new services or to improve existing services. Clearly, this type of inquiry also demands a knowledge and implementation of research methods.

In sum, generalist social workers, acting as producers of research, can begin to build new knowledge for practice. Though such a task may seem overwhelming to you at this point, this book will describe how to produce research step by step. You will be provided with the tools to become not only a producer of research, but also a critical and intelligent consumer.

Remember that social workers use many of the skills and techniques described in this book routinely, without formal research training or education. Social workers act as consumers of the literature, for example, when they read reports and gather relevant information. As producers, social workers gather data from multiple sources. In addition, they document progress toward clients' goals, write reports, and engage in many other activities that, as we will see, are all included in the larger activity of research.

RESEARCH AND GENERALIST PRACTICE PROCESSES

Social workers are often intimidated by research, in part because they think it involves very different types of knowledge and skills from those of practice. In fact, as we are about to see, the processes of practice and research are very similar, particularly for generalist social work practice.

Although the generalist perspective is conceptualized in different ways, as we discussed in the last section, authors of generalist social work texts are in basic agreement in recognizing a general process for practice. This process is usually conceptualized sequentially, as consisting of progressive stages leading to certain goals. This concept originated with one of the founding mothers of social work practice theory, Helen Harris Perlman (1957), who proposed "operations" as part of the practice process. Later others modified these operations; for example, Pincus and Minahan (1973) described "guideposts for the process," Shulman (1992) and Egan (1994) proposed "stages" or "phases," and O'Neil McMahon (1996) discussed the "general method." The practice process itself is generally referred to as the "problem-solving process"; although some generalist writers have reframed the idea as "empowerment-based practice" (Miley, O'Melia, & DuBois, 1995), the problem-solving process remains central to generalist practice.

The problem-solving process and its associated steps follow very closely those of practice. For the purpose of comparison, we will refer to the steps in the problem-solving process as set out by Johnson (1995).

Preliminary Statement of the Problem

A critical step in the preliminary statement of the problem in practice is to arrive at as much precision as possible. As Johnson stated: "The more precise the statement and the more individualized the situation, the more relevant and salient can be the goals and desired solutions. Usually, as one proceeds to further steps, the need and opportunity for greater precision of the problem statement arises, and this step is returned to for restatement of the problem" (1995, p. 69). The first step in research is also to develop a preliminary statement of the problem or question. As in practice, the statement needs to be made with precision and care.

For example, we might be interested in investigating the problem of children with AIDS. Instead of simply conceptualizing the question as "the problem of children with AIDS," we need greater clarity. For example, the question might be stated thus: "To what extent are the needs of children with AIDS being met?" The issue of continually refining the problem in practice also occurs in research. As we proceed with the research, new insights occur and new information is gathered, which in turn may lead to a reformulation of the problem. For example, the question may change to focus on evaluating the services of a specific agency: "To what extent is program X serving the needs of children with AIDS?" This question may then become even more specific: "How effective is program X in advocating for children with AIDS?" This issue of question development and formulation is further discussed in Chapter 3.

Preliminary Assumptions

The next step in practice is to acknowledge implicit assumptions we have made about the nature and cause of the problem. "As the problem is stated, implicit assumptions are made about its nature and cause" (Johnson, 1995, p. 70). One such assumption might be in the meaning of certain terms that we often use in social work, such as *support* or *depression,* or even a concept as apparently simple as *family.* We all assume certain meanings for these terms; these assumptions need to be clearly stated.

This process of acknowledging assumptions also occurs in research. Clear definitions of terms and explicit statements of assumptions underlying the research question help reduce bias, an important consideration whether adopting the objective stance of positivism or the empathic neutrality of interpretism. Although assumptions can be made at all stages of the research process, clearly stating what is assumed during the initial stages of the research is particularly useful.

One strategy for acknowledging assumptions is to state very carefully the nature of the question and to identify its different components. In our example concerning children with AIDS, we would need to define the term *advocating*. We may have a number of different assumptions about this function of social work, but how does the agency see this role and how can it be defined so all concerned are in agreement? What do we mean by *effective*? That all children with AIDS referred to the agency receive advocacy services? Half the children? How are children with AIDS defined? Are we concerned with children who are infected with the HIV virus or those with AIDS symptoms? What ages will be included in this study? This issue of assumptions will be further discussed in Chapter 4.

Selection and Collection of Information

Although we are often tempted to stop at this stage and jump in with an intervention assessment, Johnson (1995) stated: "There is a need to determine and accumulate relevant evidence about the situation, and this evidence needs to be related to the salient features of the situation and to the presented concern of need" (p. 70). In practice, the social worker collects this evidence or information. Johnson suggested a number of perspectives that the social worker might adopt in collecting information: historical, social-psychological, biological, economic, political, religious, and ethical.

In research the collection of information is also critical. It consists of three tasks: data collection, sampling, and design. Data collection for the project concerning children with AIDS might include interviewing or administering questionnaires to the children's caretakers. The sample from which the data are collected might be relatively small, perhaps ten or so caretakers, and their selection will need to be considered carefully. The design of the research might include a comparison group of caretakers of children with AIDS who do not receive services from program X, which provides services specifically to those with AIDS, but instead receive services from a more generic type of agency. Each of these steps in research will be discussed further in Chapters 5, 6, 7, 8, and 9.

Analysis of Available Information

In practice, analysis includes examining the information or data collected and reaching some conclusions about those findings. This step is often referred to as assessment. Johnson (1995) referred to it as the "analysis of information available," which consists of "the determination of salient parts and of the relationship of the various parts to each other and to the whole" (p. 71).

The next step in research is also analysis. If quantitative data were collected, statistical techniques will be used. With qualitative data, the information is sorted and categorized in order that the meanings will emerge. As in practice, the analysis step needs to be carried out systematically and conscientiously to avoid misinterpretations of results. Specific techniques are used to ensure that the results are free of bias. Johnson (1995) stated that, in practice, "the carrying out of the process (of analysis) generates new information" (p. 70). This effect also occurs in research: Results often generate new questions and issues.

Analysis of the data about children with AIDS may reveal that those in program X thought they had received more advocacy services than those from the comparison program Y, but that those in program X were less satisfied with the type of medical services available to them. Another phase of the research might include examining the source of this dissatisfaction and investigating whether this dissatisfaction extends to the adults with AIDS who receive services from program X. Organization of data and data analysis will be further discussed in Chapters 10, 11, 12, and 13.

Development of a Plan

In practice, the social worker takes the results of the assessment and develops a plan of action that often involves the formulation of goals. Johnson (1995) stated: "Goals take into consideration how the situation might be coped with in a manner that will minimize the negative aspects of the situation" (p. 71).

The comparable step in research is the writing of the report, which formally presents the analyzed results along with a description of the research method. The research report includes recommendations for further research, a logical extension of the process in which analysis of results generates new questions. An important part of the report in social work research is the section on the implications of the research for practice: How can the findings help social workers in the field? The researcher may recommend further research into reasons for the dissatisfaction with medical services, and more specifically the medical needs of children with AIDS. Report writing is further discussed in Chapter 14.

Implementation of a Plan

Implementation is the "action" part of social work practice; it takes place at the intervention stage. Unfortunately, in research this step tends to be downplayed, although research findings are of little use unless they are translated into some form of action.

Ideally, in our example, workers in program X would take the findings from the research and try to monitor more closely their medical referrals for the children, perhaps undertaking a more thorough follow-up with the families to ensure that the children's medical needs are being met. Chapter 15 discusses the various ways in which research can be utilized.

Evaluation of the Plan

The last step in practice is evaluation. Perhaps because it comes last, evaluation is often given little attention. We may find ourselves simply moving on to the next case instead. Johnson (1995) stated: "Evaluation of what happened can lead to an understanding that can be transferred to other situations and to more effective problem solving in those situations" (p. 72). The final step in the research

Table 2.1   **The relationship between research and practice**

Practice	Research
Preliminary statement of the problem	Deciding on the questions
Statement of preliminary assumptions	Developing questions
Selection and collection of information	Collecting the data, sampling, and design
Analysis of information available	Organizing the data, analyzing the data
Development of a plan	Research writing
Intervention/Implementation of a plan	Utilization of research findings
Evaluation of the plan	Evaluation of research

process is also often overlooked. This step involves evaluating the research by discussing its limitations and generally assessing its overall quality.

For example, one problem with the project concerning children and AIDS might have been that the caretakers were possibly influenced in their answers to the questionnaire about satisfaction with medical treatment. Wanting to please the researcher, the caretakers might have covered up some of the problems they experienced in caring for the children. Thus the answers might have been biased, making the program appear to be more effective than it was.

This step of evaluating the research will be further discussed in Chapter 15. See Table 2.1 for a comparison of these steps of research and practice.

VALUES IN RESEARCH AND PRACTICE

Besides the similarities in the processes of research and practice, there is a similarity in their values and ethics. Values relating to social workers' conduct and responsibilities to their clients, colleagues, employers, profession, and society are all reflected in social workers' ethical codes. In the United States, the NASW Code of Ethics (1997) includes ethical standards that apply to research. Many of these ethical standards are directly related to the values that underlie practice, values such as confidentiality, privacy, and self-determination. Some of these standards were listed earlier in this chapter. Here are the remaining standards.

- Social workers engaged in evaluation or research should carefully consider possible consequences and should follow guidelines developed for the protection of evaluation and research participants. Appropriate institutional review boards should be consulted.

- Social workers engaged in evaluation or research should obtain voluntary and written informed consent from participants, when appropriate, without any implied or actual deprivation or penalty for refusal to participate;

without undue inducement to participate; and with due regard for participants' well-being, privacy, and dignity. Informed consent should include information about the nature, extent, and duration of the participation requested and disclosure of the risks and benefits of participation in the research.

- When evaluation or research participants are incapable of giving informed consent, social workers should provide an appropriate explanation to the participants, obtain the participants' assent to the extent they are able, and obtain written consent from an appropriate proxy.

- Social workers should never design or conduct evaluation or research that does not use consent procedures, such as certain forms of naturalistic observation and archival research, unless rigorous and responsible review of the research has found it to be justified because of its prospective scientific, educational, or applied value and unless equally effective alternative procedures that do not involve waiver of consent are not feasible.

- Social workers should inform participants of their right to withdraw from evaluation and research at any time without penalty.

- Social workers should take appropriate steps to ensure that participants in evaluation and research have access to appropriate supportive services.

- Social workers engaged in evaluation or research should protect participants from unwarranted physical or mental distress, harm, danger, or deprivation.

- Social workers engaged in the evaluation of services should discuss collected information only for professional purposes and only with people professionally concerned with this information.

- Social workers engaged in evaluation or research should ensure the anonymity or confidentiality of participants and of the data obtained from them. Social workers should inform participants of any limits of confidentiality, the measures that will be taken to ensure confidentiality, and when any records containing research data will be destroyed.

- Social workers who report evaluation and research results should protect participants' confidentiality by omitting identifying information unless proper consent has been obtained authorizing disclosure.

- Social workers should report evaluation and research findings accurately. They should not fabricate or falsify results and should take steps to correct any errors later found in published data using standard publication methods.

- Social workers engaged in evaluation or research should be alert to and avoid conflicts of interest and dual relationships with participants, should inform participants when a real or potential conflict of interest arises, and should take steps to resolve the issue in a manner that makes participants' interests primary.

These values and ethics guiding research will be discussed throughout the book. Each chapter will include a section on ethics and how ethical standards relate to the topic being discussed in that chapter.

RESEARCH AND HUMAN DIVERSITY

By human diversity we mean to include the whole spectrum of differences among populations, including but not limited to gender, ethnicity, age, and sexual orientation. In practice we recognize the importance of understanding and appreciating group differences so we will not impose inappropriate expectations; we must also account for these differences in research. We discussed earlier that an important step in both research and practice is to clarify our assumptions. If we are not aware of our assumptions regarding certain groups, these assumptions can be disguised and undisclosed, causing biases in the research itself. Clarifying assumptions is only one way in which human diversity issues should be considered in the research process. As with ethics, each chapter in this book will discuss human diversity issues as they relate to research.

SUMMARY

In conclusion, research and practice follow parallel processes in approaching problems. When research methods are viewed in this way, they appear far less intimidating. We all know that practice can be frustrating; in truth, so can research. Just as practice has its great rewards, however, so does research. The road at times is a rocky one, but ultimately we all benefit.

STUDY/EXERCISE QUESTIONS

1. Discuss some of the ways you may find yourself engaged in research as a generalist social worker.

2. Select a research article from a social work journal. How could the findings from this research help you in your practice?

3. Select a research article from a social work journal. How would you change the research to make it more participatory?

4. Imagine you were asked to evaluate the program in which you were working (use your field placement as an example). How would you justify the importance of this research to a fellow student?

FURTHER READING

Causer, J., Cook, K. H., & Crouch, W. W. (1991). *Evaluating information.* New York: McGraw-Hill.

An excellent consumer's guide to social science research. Useful for each stage of the research process.

Felterman, D., Kaftasian, S., & Wandersman, A. (Eds.). (1996). *Empowerment evaluation.* Newbury Park, CA: Sage.

A collection of works on action, participatory, and empowerment forms of research, which includes some excellent case examples.

REFERENCES

Baer, B. L., & Federico, R. C. (1978). *Educating the baccalaureate social worker.* Cambridge, MA: Ballinger.

Causer, J., Cook, K. H., & Crouch, W. W. (1991). *Evaluating information.* New York: McGraw-Hill.

Chilman, C. (1995). Programs and policies for working poor families: Major trends and some research issues. *Social Service Review, 69* (3), 515–544.

Compton, B., & Galaway, B. (1994). *Social work processes.* Pacific Grove, CA: Brooks/Cole.

Egan, G. (1994). *The skilled helper: A problem management approach to helping.* Pacific Grove, CA: Brooks/Cole.

Hagen, J. L., & Lurie, I. (1995). Implementing JOBS: A view from the front line. *Families in Society, 4,* 230–238.

Johnson, L. (1995). *Social work practice: A generalist approach* (3rd ed.). Boston: Allyn & Bacon.

Landon, P. (1994). Generalist and advanced generalist practice. In National Association of Social Workers, *Encyclopedia of Social Work* (19th ed.). Washington, DC: Author.

Magura, S., & Moses, B. (1986). *Outcome measures for child welfare services.* Washington, DC: Child Welfare League of America.

Miley, K., O'Melia, M., & Dubois, B. (1995). *Generalist social work practice.* Boston: Allyn & Bacon.

National Association of Social Workers. (1997). *Code of ethics.* Washington, DC: Author.

O'Neil McMahon, M. (1996). *The general method of social work practice.* Boston: Allyn & Bacon.

Perlman, H. H. (1957). *Social casework: A problem solving process.* Chicago: University of Chicago Press.

Pincus A., & Minahan, A. (1973). *Social work practice: Model and method.* Itasca, IL: Peacock.

Schatz, M. S., & Jenkins, L. E. (1987). Differentiating generic foundation, generalist social work perspective, and advanced generalist practice in the generalist perspective (final report of a national Delphi study). Fort Collins, CO: Colorado State University, Department of Social Work.

Schatz, M.S., Jenkins, L. E., & Sheafor, B. (1990). Milford redefined: A model of initial and advanced generalist social work. *Journal of Social Work Education, 26* (3), 263–291.

Schulman, L. (1992). *The skills of helping individuals, families, and groups.* Itasca, NY: Peacock.

White, W. (1991). *Participatory action research.* Thousand Oaks, CA: Sage.

Deciding on the Question

■

H ow do I know whether this is a *real* research question? Is this what a research question should look like? I can't quite pin down what it is I need to find out." You will find yourself asking these kinds of questions when you are first confronted with the task of deciding on the research question. As a generalist social worker, you may not always participate in deciding on the question; this decision is often made within the agency prior to your involvement in the research. You need to be familiar with the procedure involved in deciding the question, however, so that you can understand (as in practice) how one step in the process leads to the next. You also need to learn this research stage so that you can evaluate your own practice, a process that is described later in this chapter.

As discussed in Chapter 2, the first step of the research process—deciding on the question—is equivalent to the first step in practice, developing a preliminary statement of the problem. This step, in research as in practice, is one of the most challenging. Often, this step is ongoing and involves continuously reworking and reevaluating the process.

This chapter will discuss the following topics:

- sources of questions
- research strategies
- types of questions
- the agency and deciding on the question
- ethical issues in deciding on the question
- human diversity issues in deciding on the question

SOURCES OF QUESTIONS

For generalist social workers, research problems or questions usually are determined by their agencies; these questions are directed at solving problems that arise in practice and are intended to produce practical outcomes. This type of research is known as **applied research.** When research is instead aimed at satisfying our intellectual curiosity, even if the results eventually will be applied to help solve practice problems, it is known as **pure research.**

An example will help clarify this definition. You are employed in an agency where a large proportion of the clients are victims of spousal abuse, and you see this as a growing problem. A pure research question would concern the causes of spousal abuse per se. As a generalist social worker employed in the agency, however, you would ask applied research questions, such as how well your agency serves the victims or what other services are needed by this client population.

If this distinction between pure and applied research still seems difficult to understand, some would argue that is because the distinction does not really exist in social work. Social work is in itself an applied field, so any question related to social work in any way will be some type of applied question. Some research, though, is more immediately applicable to social work practice than other research is. Rothman and Thomas (1994) actively promote forms of social work research called **developmental research** (also called **intervention research**). This type of research focuses on developing innovative interventions; research is used to design the interventions, test their effectiveness, and modify them based on recommendations that emerge from testing.

Personal experiences also come into play in the formulation of research questions. For example, you may find yourself working with a number of physically challenged young adults in the agency where you are employed. You become aware that some specialized type of housing needs to be established for these clients, and after consulting with your supervisor, you decide that it would make sense to carry out a needs assessment to determine the extent and type of need in the community. Your interest also may have stemmed in part from the fact that a member of your family is physically challenged.

The following is a checklist you can use to test whether the question you are thinking about can be successfully answered.

1. Does this topic really interest me? For example, am I choosing this topic to please someone else or do I have a genuine interest in it?

2. Is this a problem that is appropriate for scientific enquiry? For instance, if the question is along the lines of whether child abuse is morally wrong, the question may not be a suitable topic for scientific enquiry, as we discussed in Chapter 1.

3. Are adequate resources available to investigate this topic? For example, will your topic require large samples that will be costly to access or many time-consuming interviews? Do you or other people have the time and money to pursue the topic appropriately?

4. Will this topic lead to ethical problems? For instance, will the questions to be asked of subjects arouse potentially harmful emotions? Will the subjects feel coerced to participate?

5. Will you be able to secure permission—from the agency, community, clients, and so on—to carry out this research?

6. Are the results of the research going to be useful and have implications for the practice of social work?

RESEARCH STRATEGIES

Before you embark on the actual formulation of a research question, you need to identify the general research strategy that the question will adopt. The research strategy is determined by three factors: (1) the intent or goal of the research; (2) the amount of information we already have on the topic to be investigated; and (3) the intended audience. Two main strategies can be identified: descriptive and explanatory. Each of these will now be examined.

Descriptive Research

Descriptive research describes, records, and reports phenomena. Descriptive research can provide important fundamental information for establishing and developing social programs, but it is not primarily concerned with causes. Many surveys trying to determine the extent of a particular social problem—for example, the extent of child sexual abuse—are descriptive. In fact, an entire approach to research, called **survey research,** focuses on describing the characteristics of a group; this type of research will be discussed further in Chapter 5. Another example of descriptive research is students' recording their initial observations of an agency or case by keeping a log or journal. One method associated with descriptive research is **ethnography,** a method of describing a culture or society that is used in much anthropological research.

The interpretive approach lends itself very well to descriptive research. Because the interpretive approach generally uses words (qualitative data) rather than numbers or concepts that can be quantified (quantitative data), rich descriptions of phenomena can be produced. Often these descriptions emerge after carefully selecting the participants in the research—often, those who are best informed about the phenomenon being described. If the intention, however, is for the results to be generalized to wider populations and used as the justification for new or expanded services, the positivist approach would probably be more suitable. Here it would be more useful to collect relatively objective quantitative data describing the phenomena (rather than seeking people's subjective experiences) and to select the participants in the research according to how well they represent the population under study.

You will encounter descriptive research in social work journals. A considerable amount of policy evaluation and analysis is of this type. As a generalist practitioner, you may also be engaged in descriptive research. You could be asked to present some descriptive data relating to your agency (number of clients served, types of problems, and so forth) or to your community (the proportion of the population living below the poverty line, for example). Your supervisor may also require you to keep a journal describing your activities in the agency.

Interpretive Descriptive Research

Gregg (1994) explored the perceptions of women about their pregnancies. She conducted 31 interviews with pregnant women. Gregg wanted to explore the experience of pregnancy from the women's perspective. First she found that women she interviewed thought that it is after all possible to be a "little bit pregnant." They thought of pregnancy as starting prior to conception, when they were considering pregnancy. She also found that these women described pregnancy as resembling a "risk-laden obstacle course," rather than a relaxing, totally fulfilling experience. In this study new concepts emerged as a result of using an interpretive approach.

Positivist Descriptive Research

Levy (1992) examined lesbian parents' psychological resources, family functioning, and coping strategies used to deal with the stress of living in a heterosexual and homophobic environment. Data were collected using a number of different scales measuring family coping, self-esteem, self-mastery, and family environments. Coping patterns that emphasized social support, lesbian identity, and developing oneself were found to be most helpful. Women had high self-esteem and moderate levels of mastery. Family functioning was characterized by balanced levels of family cohesion and family organization. In this study, in contrast to Gregg's study of women and pregnancy, the concepts to be studied were defined prior to the research, and specific data collection instruments were used to measure these concepts.

Explanatory Research

Explanatory research aims at providing explanations of events in order to identify causes. This type of research requires the formulation of a **hypothesis:** a statement about the relationships between certain factors. Hypotheses usually have an "if *x*, then *y*" structure: for example, "if the ethnicity of the group leader is the same as the client, then success in the group will be more likely." We can accept or reject hypotheses depending upon the evidence produced through the research process.

A Hypothesis

Nash, Rounds, and Bowen (1992) studied the relationship between the level of parent involvement on early childhood intervention teams and social worker membership on the team. They stated: "This article hypothesizes that the presence of a social worker as a regular team member will be associated with a significantly higher level of parent involvement. It also hypothesized that this association will remain significant regardless of organizational or community setting" (p. 95). Both hypotheses were supported by the evidence resulting from the research.

As discussed in Chapter 1, the following conditions need to be met in order to establish **causality,** which is central to explanatory research. First, *two factors must be associated with one another.* Usually this association is established empirically. For example, you might determine that there is a relationship between the grade B.S.W. students received in the practice class and their grade in the field.

That relationship, however, does not necessarily mean that the practice grade caused the success in the field. The other conditions of causality also need to be met. The second condition is that *the cause precedes the effect in time.* In our example, you would need to demonstrate that students completed their practice courses prior to entering the field. The third element of causality is that *the relationship between the factors cannot be explained by other factors.* In our example, it is possible that other factors, such as past experience, had as much impact on field performance as the practice course grade.

In each step of the research process, explanatory research tries to address these conditions of causality. In reality, meeting all three conditions is often extremely difficult; the best we can expect is that only one or two of the conditions will be met. A positivist approach is often most appropriate to use when testing hypotheses and carrying out explanatory research. Qualitative data, however, can often be used to add depth and detail to the findings and so assist in the acceptance or rejection of the hypothesis.

Explanatory research is found in the social work literature, and as generalist practitioners, you may be directly involved in such research. Usually, you would not undertake such research alone but would participate as a member of a team—for example, in determining the effectiveness of a particular program or agency.

Explanatory Research

Smith, Smith, and Beckner (1994) evaluated the impact of an anger management workshop for medium-security women inmates. The results of the evaluation were that the workshop had a significant impact on the inmates. The most effective anger management skill learned was to walk away from a conflict and "cool down" in some other area of the prison.

Beyond the strategies of explanatory and descriptive research, another strategy, **exploratory research,** deserves mention. This strategy is undertaken when very little is known about the topic under study. Such studies can adopt either an explanatory or a descriptive strategy. Either an interpretist or a positivist approach is appropriate with exploratory research, although exploratory research is often associated with the former. Exploratory research often determines a study's feasibility and raises questions to be investigated by more extensive studies using either the descriptive or the explanatory strategy.

For example, you might suspect that the ethnicity of a group leader is important for success in the support group you have organized for children of alcoholics. The group leader is Puerto Rican. After interviewing some of the clients in the group to get their opinions, you find that the Puerto Rican clients were more likely than the others to state that the group was successful. Based on these results from the exploratory study, you plan to undertake more extensive research to evaluate the impact of the group leader's ethnicity on clients' perceptions of success.

Exploratory Research

Shongwe (1996) explored social workers' thoughts about their involvement in primary health care, a feature of the new health care policy in South Africa. When the study was carried out, there had been increasing pressure to involve social workers in urban areas in primary health care, which represented a shift from previous social work practice. This research was an important exploratory step in finding out social workers' feelings about the issue.

TYPES OF QUESTIONS

This section will explore the different types of applied research questions that are asked in generalist practice. The following questions from Chapter 1 provide examples of these different types of questions.

These questions evaluate the effectiveness of individual practice and are known as **practice evaluation studies.**

1. How effective is the grief counseling I am providing to Mrs. Garcia in helping her to cope with the death of her husband?
2. How is Mrs. Garcia experiencing the grief counseling I have been providing?

These questions evaluate the effectiveness of a program and are known as **program evaluations.**

1. How effective is program X in providing services that support and protect victims of domestic violence?
2. What are the experiences of the clients who receive services from program X?

These questions describe the extent of a social problem and are known as **needs assessments.**

1. What are the needs of adolescent fathers in city Y?
2. What is it like to be a teenage father in city Y?

Note that two examples are offered for each type of question. As we discussed in Chapter 1, the first example for each type of question is asked in a way that is more appropriate for a positivist approach—for example, "Program X received additional funding for next year. How can we show our program is effective and deserves more money?" The second example for each type of question is more appropriate for an interpretist approach—for example, "In what areas could our program be improved and what are our clients' experiences with the program?" The choice of which type of question to ask depends on the level of knowledge that already exists on the topic under study and the overall purpose of the research.

These types of questions, **practice evaluations, program evaluations,** and **needs assessments,** represent the different types of applied research encountered by generalist social workers in their practice. Although these questions appear diverse, they can be matched up with the three purposes of generalist social work as described by Baer and Federico (1978):

1. To enhance people's problem-solving, coping, and developmental capacities.
2. To promote effective and humane operation of systems that provide people with resources and services.
3. To link people with systems that provide them with resources, services, and opportunities.

The question evaluating individual practice is the one asking about visits to Mrs. Garcia. This question examines our ability to enhance a person's (in particular, Mrs. Garcia's) problem-solving, coping, and developmental capacities. The program evaluation question addresses the issues of the effective and humane operations of systems that provide people with resources and services. The third question, a needs assessment question about teenage fathers, is involved with linking people to resources. We will now discuss the different types of questions in more detail.

Practice Evaluation Studies

One type of research question that often occurs in social work practice is concerned with the effectiveness of an individual social worker's practice. As we have seen, this type of question directly relates to the enhancement of people's problem-solving, coping, and developmental capacities. Practice evaluations usually involve only one case, subject, or client system and require social workers to use specific criteria and methods in monitoring their own practice cases. For the generalist social worker, these cases include individuals, families, groups, or communities. Whatever the type of client system, only one is evaluated in a practice evaluation. This type of research can be either descriptive or explanatory, and either interpretive or positivist.

Increasingly, practice evaluations are being recognized as an integral element of social work practice. In part, this recognition has resulted from social workers' seeking a method of evaluation that could be integrated into their practice relatively easily. In addition to being easily integrated into practice, practice evaluations offer the generalist practitioner the advantages of low cost and availability of immediate feedback to both the social worker and client. Practice evaluations will be discussed more fully in Chapter 7.

A Practice Evaluation

Betchen (1992), in *Families in Society,* describes a case study concerning the use of short-term psychodynamic therapy with a divorced single mother. The intervention lasted 16 sessions. Two instruments were used to assess the client's progress: a client problem rating scale and a client adjective checklist to assess self-esteem and depression.

Program Evaluations

Program evaluation research questions are asked extensively in generalist social work practice and involve assessing a program's overall functioning rather than an individual practitioner's effectiveness. This type of question relates directly to the generalist social work function of promoting the effective and humane operation of the systems that provide resources.

Program evaluations play an increasing role in today's social work practice. During the federal government's War on Poverty of the 1960s and early 1970s, funding for social programs was high. Unfortunately, however, there was little accountability to funding sources regarding social programs' effectiveness in meeting client needs. Fischer (1976) conducted a review of the casework practice in social work. He concluded that approximately half of the clients receiving casework services either deteriorated to a greater degree or improved at a slower rate than did subjects who did not participate in the programs. Fischer's study jolted social workers and others into the awareness that adequate funding did not ensure a program's effectiveness. Fischer's work also disclosed that many of the studies he reviewed contained various methodological problems. As a result, the profession realized the necessity for more sophisticated research methods to assess service effectiveness and conduct program evaluations so that findings—positive or negative—would be reliable.

Program evaluation is primarily concerned with determining a program's effectiveness, which can be accomplished using any of three different strategies: formative, summative, or cost-benefit approaches. First, the **formative program evaluation** approach, or process analysis, examines a program's planning, development, and implementation. This type of evaluation is often performed as an initial evaluative step and is generally descriptive. Often the interpretive approach is used because it allows for a fuller understanding of the processes at work within the agencies and can address these processes from multiple perspectives—those of the client, the worker, and the administrator.

A Formative Program Evaluation

Rounds, Galinsky, and Stevens (1991) reported on an innovative method for linking people with AIDS in rural communities. Support groups were brought into the homes of rural residents through telephone conference technologies. The goals of the group were to increase information and social support, reduce feelings of isolation, and enhance the coping of individuals living with AIDS.

Although the authors briefly discussed an evaluation that was being carried out to assess the outcomes of the program, the article, published in *Social Work,* focused on describing the program's development and implementation.

The **summative program evaluation** approach, or outcome analysis, determines whether goals and objectives have been met and the extent to which program effects are generalizable to other settings and populations. This type of research is usually explanatory. Usually the positivist approach is more appropriate with summative evaluations, since the purpose is to establish causality (the program's effect). Often these types of evaluations are required by funding organizations, which are more interested in the kind of research evidence (generally quantitative) produced by positivist studies.

A Summative Program Evaluation

Hack, Osachuk, and De Luca (1994) evaluated the effectiveness of semistructured group work with adolescent boys who had experienced either extra- or intrafamilial sexual abuse. From pre- to post-group, the boys experienced decreased anxiety, decreased depression, increased self-esteem, and decreased internalizing and externalizing behaviors.

Cost-benefit or cost-effectiveness analysis can also be conducted. A **cost-benefit analysis** compares the program costs to the dollar value of the program results and computes a ratio of costs to benefits. A **cost-effectiveness study** compares program costs to some measure of program outcome and calculates a cost per unit.

The most comprehensive program evaluations combine a study of a program's implementation, outcomes, and cost-benefit aspects. As with summative evaluations, these types of studies usually require a more positivist approach, producing quantitative evidence. The design of program evaluations will be discussed in Chapter 6.

A Cost-Benefit Analysis Program Evaluation

Knobbe, Carey, Rhodes, and Horner (1995) conducted a cost-benefit analysis comparing services in community residences versus an institution for 11 individuals with severe mental retardation. Overall, the community-based program costs were lower and resulted in significant increases in the client's social networks, opportunities for integrated activities, and income.

Needs Assessments

Needs assessment questions are concerned with discovering the nature and extent of a particular social problem to determine the most appropriate response. This type of research is usually descriptive and, as previously mentioned, is also known as survey research. This kind of question is related to the practice function of linking people with systems.

An example of this type of needs assessment is the following: "I have talked to a couple of clients who need an alternative living situation for their adult developmentally delayed children. I wonder if there is a great enough need in the community to start a group home for the adult developmentally delayed?"

Reporting hearsay, citing individual cases, or simply acting on a hunch does not provide enough evidence for funding sources. Usually a funding source, whether a voluntary organization, a private foundation, or state government, requires documentation of the need for the program with evidence that the needs assessment has been performed scientifically.

Generally, a positivist approach is used for a needs assessment, since most needs assessments are concerned with generalizability of results rather than in-depth understanding of how people experience social problems. Sometimes, however, an interpretive approach can provide some important insights and new directions for assessing the needs of certain populations. Needs assessments can be designed in different ways; these design issues are discussed in Chapter 5.

A Needs Assessment

Nah (1993) examined the perceived problems of Korean families living in New York. Their responses were placed in the overall context of the problems of immigrants to the United States in order to differentiate needs common to all immigrants from the unique needs of Korean immigrants. The study included an examination of family relations, child-rearing, and practical aspects of language, employment, and health.

Although the types of research questions appear quite different, they all follow essentially similar research steps and strategies. Some differences in approach are sometimes required, particularly in the design stage. Thus a separate chapter is devoted to each of the three types of research questions.

The three types of research questions described here are not the only types of research questions social workers ask. If you look through any social work journal, you will find other types of research questions. You may find some pure research questions or historical studies. In addition, some articles may be theoretical and conceptual rather than empirical in nature.

In this book we focus upon practice evaluation studies, program evaluation, and needs assessment questions simply because these are the types of research questions you will be most likely to encounter as generalist social workers. Remember, though, that many other types of questions are possible in social work.

THE AGENCY AND DECIDING ON THE QUESTION

As we discussed earlier, except when conducting practice evaluations, you may have little or no choice in the research you will be doing as a generalist social worker. The question may have already been decided, and your task instead may be to conduct a needs assessment to help build a case for developing a new program in your community. Or perhaps your program's funding source demands that an evaluation be undertaken for funding to continue. You may find that you often have little opportunity to decide on research strategies or types of questions.

Despite this tendency for you to have little choice in the research, in many respects you are in an ideal position for conducting applied research. As an agency-based generalist social worker who is knowledgeable about research and familiar with the agency's workings and the community's concerns, you are well situated to conduct relevant research. You can also act as a resource person for outside researchers; when the opportunity arises, you may assist them in conducting research that is beyond the scope of your immediate responsibilities in the agency.

Collaboration Between a Researcher and a Practitioner

Galinsky, Turnbull, Meglin, and Wilner (1993) described an example of collaboration between researcher and practitioner to evaluate single-session groups for families of psychiatric inpatients. The article discussed some of the issues that can arise in this type of collaboration.

If you are asked to initiate a research study from the ground up, however, you must recognize that research is almost always a team effort, particularly at the stage of deciding on the question. Consult with agency staff, clients, and community to determine what they want from the evaluation or needs assessment. Don't forget to confer with those who are providing the funding for the project.

One strategy for ensuring that those who are affected by the research or its findings participate more fully in the research implementation is the use of **focus groups.** A focus group is a special group formed to help decide on the research question and the research method. A focus group is composed of people who are informed about the topic or will be affected by it in some way. A focus group can be used at any stage of the research process but is particularly useful in the beginning stages.

"A focus group can be defined as a carefully planned discussion designed to obtain perceptions of a defined area of interest in a permissive nonthreatening environment. It is conducted with approximately seven to ten people by a skilled interviewer. The discussion is relaxed, comfortable, and often enjoyable for participants as they share their ideas and perceptions. Group members influence each other by responding to ideas and comments in the discussion" (Krueger, 1988, p. 18).

The focus group is informal. The researcher asks participants focused questions with the emphasis on sharing information. The empowerment or action approach to research often uses focus groups, since a focus group enables clients to become directly involved in the research. For example, focus groups are an excellent way of involving community members in developing the research. The focus groups can themselves help identify other stakeholders and so expand the potential input.

The Use of Focus Groups

Ashery, Carlson, Falck, and Siegal (1995) used focus groups to examine how injection drug and crack cocaine users interact with the social services system. Participating in focus group sessions were 29 drug users. Findings revealed a very high rate of service use by the drug users.

ETHICAL ISSUES IN DECIDING ON THE QUESTION

Two ethical issues are central to the stage of the research process concerned with deciding on the question: the question's applicability to social work practice and the role of funding.

Applicability of the Question to Social Work Practice

One concern when you are deciding on a research question is whether and how the answer to the question is going to contribute to the field of social work. Usually applicability to practice is not too much of an issue, particularly for generalist social workers, because most questions derive directly from our practice in an agency. If your question has evolved from your personal experiences, however, you must ask whether answering the question is really going to assist the clients you serve. To determine the appropriateness of the question, discuss it with colleagues.

This issue presents another reason for adopting more participatory action research—research that is rooted directly in clients' concerns and in which they become active contributors.

Participatory Action Research

Mwansa, Mufune, and Osei Hwedie (1994) examined youth power and programs in Botswana, Swaziland, and Zambia. They used participatory research involving the youths in the programs, officials, and academics. The findings showed that most of the income-generating activities were inadequate, that teenage pregnancy was a serious problem, and that there were no viable programs for street children.

Another strategy to ensure that the research is applicable to social work practice is to use a developmental or intervention approach to research. This approach, which was discussed earlier in the chapter, uses research to help design and develop interventions. A number of different ways of conducting developmental research have emerged, but its basic principle is that effective interventions must be built systematically using the stages of design, continued testing, feedback, and modification. The focus is on using research to test and improve interventions—hence the alternative label *intervention research.*

Developmental Research

Bailey-Dempsey and Reid (1996) described a case study using developmental research to develop a case management intervention for problems of school failure. Six stages guided this project: (1) problem analysis and project planning; (2) information gathering and synthesis; (3) program design; (4) early development and pilot testing; (5) evaluation and advanced development; and (6) dissemination. As a result of using this approach, the research and the improvement of service were directly linked.

Availability of Funding

In agencies, research projects may be conducted because funding is available for these projects. Certain issues may be a priority at the local, state, or federal level, and funds consequently become available. You should be aware of the reason you are conducting research on these particular issues—namely, at least in part, the availability of funds. Presumably, it has already been established that this topic is a deserving one, but you need to realize that other issues are probably equally deserving and should not be ignored because of the convenience of funding. In other words, you should continue to act as advocates for those issues, regardless of the extent to which they are receiving fiscal support.

In addition, you may sometimes want to confirm for yourself whether a research program deserves an investment of time and money. Again, the best source for this type of information is the literature and colleagues.

HUMAN DIVERSITY ISSUES IN DECIDING ON THE QUESTION

During the stage of deciding on the question, you need to pay attention to human diversity issues. You should be aware that researchers' characteristics can influence their research and that agencies may also promote biases.

Characteristics of the Researchers

Traditionally there has been a predominance of studies conducted by white, middle-class men, resulting in an inherent bias in the types of research questions. In an article about methodological approaches to research on Hispanics, Becerra and Tambrana (1985) stated: "Clearly, the major advantage of having Hispanics conduct research on Hispanics is that, it assumes, Hispanic researchers will be sensitive to and understand the cultural norms and language" (p. 43). The authors also pointed out, however, that "being Hispanic" does not ensure cultural sensitivity or knowledge. The researcher also needs to be aware of subgroups (for example, some Hispanic subgroups are Cuban, Mexican-American, Spanish, and Puerto Rican), as well as the level of acculturation and socioeconomic class of those being studied.

Bowman (1983) addressed the issue of who conducts research, particularly with African Americans, by using two concepts: significant involvement and functional relevance. Significant involvement means that members of the group under study have a central role in the research, including decision making at each stage of the research process. Functional relevance means that the study promotes the expressed needs and perspectives of the study population. Significant involvement need not necessarily result in functional relevance or vice versa. Bowman argued that both these concepts must be considered in conducting research with minorities to ensure that minority concerns are addressed in research studies.

Similar arguments are presented in support of more women-centered research. Women tend not to conduct research in social work (Davis, 1986); those who do tend to be white, middle-class women. Consequently certain questions are not asked, and the content of research questions is not necessarily relevant to women. For example, when studies were conducted on work satisfaction, it was unusual to consider family issues, which are often of primary concern to women, but traditionally are not for men. Thus a biased picture was developed depicting women's lives in a male framework.

To broaden the idea of diverse group representatives conducting research, community members need to be involved as much as possible in the development of projects so that participants are empowered. In other words, more participatory action research needs to be undertaken. The Cornell Empowerment Project (1989) suggested that evaluation should be as inclusive as possible, involving (1) people who develop and use the program (for example, funders, agency boards, program staff); (2) direct and indirect beneficiaries of the program; (3) people who suffer a disadvantage related to the program.

A final point concerning who conducts the research relates to the potential problem of people's studying themselves—an issue when members of an organization or agency evaluate their own performance. Although the input and participation of organization members are essential, these evaluations do need to be counterbalanced by outsiders' evaluations.

Including Participants in the Research Design

Stevens (1996) used a participatory research approach to examine consultation in South African schools, with the intention of making consultations more relevant. Social workers were involved from the outset in planning the research, identifying what needed to be studied, and planning a workshop on consultation, as well as in the resulting evaluation. Focus groups were used in which the social workers were able to start thinking critically about what they were doing.

Bias in the Agencies

Most of our research questions derive from practice in agencies. We need to be aware that bias can also exist in agencies and that this bias can influence decisions about research questions.

For example, an agency's homophobic attitudes may result in ignoring the needs of lesbian clients, even though that group may require substantial social supports. Your supervisor may dismiss your request to carry out a needs assessment of this particular group. Watch for these biases; be aware that your agency's operation may be influenced by presuppositions and prejudices.

Including Diverse Populations and Their Issues in the Research Question

Arnold (1990) examined the early childhood, adolescent, and adult experiences of incarcerated African American women, in order to reveal the process of victimization, labeling, and subsequent criminalization of these women. She concluded: "If we are to witness a drop in the numbers of imprisoned women, legislators and policy makers need to reevaluate what happens to young girls who are victimized by gender, class, and race, and stop blaming the victim by processing and labeling her as deviant and/or criminal" (p. 163).

SUMMARY

This chapter described two research strategies: descriptive and explanatory. There is a distinction between applied research and pure research. Generalist social workers usually engage in three types of applied research: practice evaluations, program evaluations, and needs assessments.

Usually, in agencies, research questions have already been decided on, but it is important to ensure maximum input from those affected by the research and the resulting services. Focus groups are useful in ensuring this input, and participatory action research is recommended. Ethical issues in deciding on the research question include assessing the question's applicability to social work practice and availability of funding. Human diversity issues include the researcher's characteristics and the agency's biases.

STUDY/EXERCISE QUESTIONS

1. Look through a social work journal such as *Social Work Research and Abstracts* or *Affilia* and identify studies that adopt the research strategies described in this chapter (needs assessments, program evaluations, and practice evaluations). Discuss in class the reasons for your decisions.

2. If you are enrolled in a practicum or field placement, ask your supervisor about any program evaluations or needs assessments carried out by the agency. Find out why the evaluation or needs assessment was carried out. Who suggested it? Who was involved in that decision? Present the results of this discussion in class.

FURTHER READING

Alter, C., & Evens, W. (1990). *Evaluating your practice: A guide to self assessment.* New York: Springer.
A good discussion of the ways practice can be evaluated. Includes some excellent examples of evaluating client systems of different sizes and is consequently very appropriate for the generalist social worker.

Austin, M. J. (1982). *Evaluating your agency's programs.* Beverly Hills, CA: Sage.
A good introductory book on program evaluation.

Rothman, J., & Thomas, E. (1994). *Intervention research.* New York: Haworth Press.
A good collection of articles describing the application of intervention research. A good reference to ensure your research will be relevant and applicable to practice.

Soriano, F. (1995). *Conducting needs assessments.* Newbury Park, CA: Sage.
An introduction to needs assessments particularly suited to the generalist social worker.

REFERENCES

Arnold, R. A. (1990). Processes of victimization and criminalization of black women. *Social Justice, 17,* 153–166.

Ashery, R. S., Carlson, R. G., Falck, R., & Siegal, H. (1995). Injection drug users, crack cocaine users, and human service utilization: An exploratory study. *Social Work, 40* (1), 75–82.

Baer, B. L., & Federico, R. C. (1978). *Educating the baccalaureate social worker: Report of the undergrad-social work curriculum development project.* Cambridge, MA: Ballinger.

Bailey-Dempsey, C., & Reid, W. (1996). Intervention design and development: A case study. *Research on Social Work Practice, 6* (2).

Becerra, R. M., & Tambrana, R. E. (1985). Methodological approaches to research on Hispanics. *Social Work Research and Abstracts, 21* (2), 42–49.

Betchen, S. (1992). Short term psychodynamic therapy with a divorced single mother. *Families in Society, 73* (2), 116–121.

Bowman, P. J. (1983). Significant involvement and functional relevance. *Social Work Research and Abstracts, 19* (4), 21–26.

Cornell Empowerment Project. (1989). Evaluation consistent with the empowerment process. *Networking Bulletin.* Ithaca, NY: Cornell University, Cornell Empowerment Project.

Davis, L. (1986). A feminist approach to social work research. *Affilia, 1,* 32–47.

Fischer, J. (1976). *The effectiveness of social casework.* Springfield, IL: Charles C Thomas.

Galinsky, M. J., Turnbull, J. E., Meglin, D. E., & Wilner, M. E. (1993). Confronting the reality of collaborative practice research: Issues of practice, design, measurement, and team development. *Social Work, 38* (4), 440–449.

Gregg, R. (1994). Explorations of pregnancy and choice in a high tech age. In C. Riessman (Ed.), *Qualitative studies in social work research.* Newbury Park, CA: Sage.

Hack, T., Osachuk, T., & De Luca, R. (1994). Group treatment for sexually abused preadolescent boys. *Families in Society, 75* (4), 217–228.

Knobbe, C., Carey, S., Rhodes, L., & Horner, R. (1995). Benefit cost analysis of community versus institutional services for adults with severe mental retardation and challenging behaviors. *American Journal on Mental Retardation, 99* (5), 533–547.

Krueger, R. A. (1988). *Focus groups: A practical guide for applied research.* Newbury Park, CA: Sage.

Levy, E. (1992). Strengthening the coping resources of lesbian families. *Families in Society,* 23–31.

Mwansa, L., Mufune, P., & Osei Hwedie, K. (1994). Youth policy and programs in the SADC countries of Botswana, Swaziland, and Zambia: A comparative assessment. *International Social Work, 37* (3), 239–263.

Nah, K. (1993). Perceived problems and service delivery for Korean immigrants. *Social Work, 38* (3), 289–296.

Nash, J., Rounds, K., & Bowen, G. (1992). Level of parental involvement on early childhood intervention teams. *Families in Society,* 93–99.

Rothman, J., & Thomas, E. (1994). *Intervention research.* New York: Haworth Press.

Rounds, K. A., Galinsky, M. J., & Stevens, L. S. (1991). Linking people with AIDS in rural communities: The telephone group. *Social Work, 36* (1), 13–18.

Shongwe, C. H. L. (1996). *The relationship between social work and primary health care: An urban based study.* Coursework master's thesis, in progress, University of Natal, Department of Social Work, Durban, South Africa.

Smith, L., Smith, J., & Beckner, B. (1994). An anger management workshop for women inmates. *Families in Society,* 172–175.

Stevens, L. A. (1996). *Consultation as a social work method: Suggestions for practice.* Unpublished master's thesis, University of Natal, Department of Social Work, Durban, South Africa.

Developing the Question

■

S uppose your supervisor asked you to carry out a needs assessment to establish a health promotion program for a local business. You have some implicit assumptions about what the program will include—namely, seminars and information dispersal on wellness. After consulting with the staff of the business, however, you find that they are defining a health promotion program more broadly. Their idea of a health promotion program includes other services such as revising the business's health insurance coverage and providing discounts to local health clubs, counseling information and referral, and so forth.

This chapter will describe the research stage of developing the question, which is equivalent to the practice stage of stating preliminary assumptions. Developing the question involves clarifying the research question once it has been initially formulated. This clarification can help make explicit some initial assumptions inherent in research, in much the same way as is necessary in practice.

Here the question will be examined more closely. The following will be discussed:

- the literature review
- units of analysis
- naming the variables and values
- the relationship of variables
- defining and operationalizing the variable
- levels of measurement
- the agency and developing the question
- ethical issues in developing the question
- human diversity issues in developing the question

As discussed in the last chapter, often the research question has been decided on prior to your involvement. For example, the agency may have been asked by one of their funding sources to carry out an evaluation of the services, and you are to help with planning and implementing the study. Similarly, many of the stages discussed in this chapter may already have been completed by the time you are involved. It is still important for you as a participant in the project to understand the rationale behind these stages and, if you have the opportunity, to develop them yourself.

THE LITERATURE REVIEW

When conducting applied research—whether a program evaluation, a needs assessment, or single system study—we need to consult other sources of information. Sometimes information can come from colleagues who have had experience with the questions we are trying to answer. Our usual source of other information, however, is written material.

Undertaking a **literature review** means consulting with the written material relevant to a research problem. This written material can be found in a variety of places including libraries, public and private; city, state, and federal buildings; social agencies; private collections; and political, professional, social, and interest group organizations, such as the NASW.

In this section we will discuss the specific uses of the literature review; accessing the information; and writing the literature review.

Use of the Literature Review

The literature review assists with formulating the question in the following ways:

- generating the question
- connecting the question to theory
- identifying previous research
- giving direction to the project

Consulting the literature is useful not only in conducting research but in guiding practice, particularly if the literature is based on research. A thorough discussion of using the research literature to guide practice is the focus of Chapter 15.

Generating the Question

We described earlier how the generalist social worker is usually assigned a research project or question, and we noted that these questions derive directly from issues pertinent to the agency. Sometimes, however, you may be given considerable freedom in your choice of question, as when you are completing a research project for a class. Here it would make sense to consult the literature for ideas; often research articles include suggestions for future research.

Connecting the Research Question to Theory

As discussed in Chapter 1, science consists of both theories and research methods. Consequently, in any research, the connection to theory has to be made clear. In pure research, connecting a question to theory is a fairly obvious step. For example, if you are investigating the causes of spousal abuse, you need to be apprised of the human behavior theories that attempt to explain spousal abuse. This theoretical base can be found in the existing literature. In applied research, however, this step is not so obvious and can be easily overlooked. Illustrations of the use of the literature review for linking different types of social work research questions to theory will clarify this step.

Practice evaluations. When evaluating your own practice, you need to understand the theoretical base underlying your use of a particular intervention. For example, if you are using positive reinforcement to help a parent learn disciplining skills, you need to be familiar with the theory behind positive reinforcement—namely, behavior theory. The literature on behavior theory can then be consulted. In addition, you need to understand the theoretical link between the use of positive reinforcement in disciplining children and its appropriateness and effectiveness for this purpose, again turning to the literature for this information.

Program evaluations.   You recall that program evaluation can take several forms: summative, formative, or cost-benefit analyses. For each form, we need to consider how the research question links to theory. For example, you may be examining whether the agency in which you are employed is meeting one of its goals in providing support services to homebound elderly. You consult the literature to ascertain the theoretical basis for this type of care and examine studies of this type that have already been carried out. You may also find some of this material in the initial program proposal.

Connecting the Research Question to Theory: Program Evaluation

Schaffer and Lia-Hoagberg (1994) assessed the personal, family, and provider rewards and costs they experienced in obtaining prenatal care. Exchange theory provided the theoretical framework for this evaluation of prenatal services. The theory suggests that humans avoid relationships, interactions, and feeling states that are dissatisfying or costly and seek out experiences that are gratifying, pleasurable, or rewarding.

Needs assessment.   When assessing the need for a program, the literature can also be consulted to provide some theoretical substance. For example, in conducting a needs assessment to determine the number of homeless women and children in our community, a theoretical perspective and context can be gained by consulting the literature and determining the risk factors and problems experienced by homeless women and children.

Identifying Previous Research

When you choose or are assigned a research question, it is useful to find out whether a similar or identical question has already been answered. If it has, you may wish to reconceptualize the research question. For example, in conducting your needs assessment, you may find a report on a survey conducted in your community two years previously. This information will probably be useful, since the survey was done so recently. If the survey had been conducted ten years ago, however, you would need to **replicate** or repeat the study. Similarly, in a program evaluation, you may find that other evaluations of comparable programs have been conducted that would result in your evaluation's not necessarily contributing new and useful knowledge. Alternatively, you may find that the evaluations were conducted in communities very different from the one your agency serves, which would suggest that an evaluation would fulfill a useful purpose.

Note that when writing a thesis you will be required to include a section that includes a clear discussion of the relationship between your research topic and its theoretical framework.

Giving Direction to the Research Project

Although the concern here is primarily with the role of the literature review in developing the research question, you should also note that the literature review can give overall direction and guidance to the entire research project as well. You can, for example, review the literature to find out how researchers set up comparison groups in similar projects, or to get ideas about how samples can be selected. Using the literature review in this way, particularly in the early step of developing the question, can save considerable time later on and avoids "re-inventing the wheel."

Accessing Information

As we discussed previously, several literature sources are available to the social worker. Agencies and public and private organizations often maintain collections of materials. One good example is the National Association of Social Workers. The most extensive resource locations, however, are libraries. If you can find your way around a typical university library, you should have little trouble accessing information in other locations. Consequently, in this section the focus will be on locating information in a library. Most of the locating is carried out using computers; increasing numbers of computerized databases are being created, making access to information both easier and faster than in the past.

Library catalogs.   Most libraries have computerized catalogs that allow you access to the current holdings of that library. The computerized catalogs provide much the same information as the old card catalogs but are much easier to access.

Although different libraries have different systems, the general principles are similar. The author, title, or subject, or some combination of these, is entered. The computer then retrieves a list of potential sources of information. If you are starting out a literature review enter the key subject words, and then after finding a good source of information, look up the subject headings in this source. You can then use these subject headings to uncover more resources. Searching for published literature reviews on the topic you are investigating can also be useful. The catalogs will allow you to access journals, books, dictionaries, encyclopedias, and bibliographies, which are all excellent sources of information.

If your library contains a government document section, this will usually be accessed through a different system. Government documents are a great resource for social work researchers; these documents include census data, congressional proceedings, and other data not accessible in general libraries.

CD ROMs.   Most libraries now offer CD ROMs that contain citations for books and journals. They allow you to search a wide array of materials and are usually categorized according to the type of material they contain. Some examples of CD ROMs used by social workers include Psychlit, ERIC, and Social Work Abstracts. CD ROMs generally contain citations followed by a brief abstract. Some journals are beginning to publish entire articles on CD ROMs.

Interlibrary loan.   If there is a drawback to the increasing efficiency of computerized data retrieval methods, it is that libraries usually cannot hold all the materials that the computer databases contain. Although an increasing number of articles, rather than simply their abstracts, are accessible on CD ROMs, actually getting access to articles and books can be a problem. Hence the existence of the interlibrary loan system.

Libraries borrow from other libraries using the OCLC database, which contains most of the holdings of U.S. libraries as well as many foreign library holdings. Your library locates the desired article or book and then borrows it. Remember, though, that interlibrary loans can take some time. So start your search early using the computerized catalogs or CD ROMs, so that you will have time to obtain access to the book or article.

The Internet.   The Internet allows the researcher access to a seemingly endless supply of information. Many of the resources discussed earlier, such as government documents, can be accessed through the Internet. Many professional groups have bulletin boards and listservers that allow a researcher the ability to discuss issues with others. The World Wide Web also allows access to a vast amount of information and can allow you to research a topic internationally. Be careful when using the World Wide Web; there is a great deal of information to wade though and most of it is of little use to the researcher, makes its use a time-consuming undertaking.

Library staff.   When trying to access information do not forget to consult with the library staff. They are professionally trained in every aspect of library management and can be a tremendous resource. See Appendix A for list of library resources.

Summary of Accessing Information

1. State the topic, limit the range, and list all the relevant synonyms and keywords.
2. Using the computer catalog in your library, use the keywords to access some source of information.
3. When you access a relevant item, look at its subject headings and use these keywords to access further items.
4. Try to locate a literature review about the specific items.
5. If relevant, locate other material in government documents.

6. Access the computerized databases, such as Social Work Research and Abstracts.

7. Use the Internet and World Wide Web to track down other materials.

8. Access materials through the interlibrary loan system.

9. Ask a reference librarian for other ideas and help, if you need it, for each of these steps.

Writing the Literature Review

Although writing up your research, including the literature review, is discussed in Chapter 14, some guidelines for writing the literature review will be given here. Usually the first section of the research to be completed and written, the literature review should be completed before other stages of the research are undertaken. The literature review places the current research in its historical and theoretical context. It describes the background to the study and the relationship between the present study and previous studies conducted in the same area. The literature review should also identify trends and debates in the existing literature. It provides a link between past, present, and future, in addition to providing a context for the discussion of the results from the study. See Figure 4.1 for a checklist for writing the literature review (van Rooyen, 1996).

A literature review places the current research in its historical and theoretical context. It describes the background to the study and the relationship between the present study and previous studies conducted in the same area. It also identifies trends and debates in the existing literature.

The following are a few issues to consider when constructing a literature review (van Rooyen, 1996).

- Cite only research that you find specifically pertinent to the current study; be selective. Avoid reviewing or referring to sections of articles or texts that are not related to your study.

- Discuss and evaluate the literature you have selected.

- Show the logical continuity between existing literature and your study.

- Identify controversial issues or differences in the literature and your study.

- If there is a choice, cite the more recent literature, unless the older citations are needed for additional perspective.

- Write the literature review in the past tense.

- Refer to published studies for examples of literature reviews.

Figure 4.1   ***Literature review***

UNITS OF ANALYSIS

After examining the literature, it is important to start further developing the question. One of the first steps in this process is to determine the **unit of analysis.** The unit of analysis refers to what or whom is being studied. Three types of units of analysis are used in social work research: individuals, groups, and social artifacts.

Individuals.   These are the most common units of analysis. Descriptions of individuals are often aggregated to explain social group functioning. For example, in conducting a needs assessment for a community youth center, you may interview individual youths to assess their needs. This information would then be aggregated to document the needs of the group.

Groups.   Groups can also be the unit of analysis. Groups are of different types and include families, organizations, and communities. Families are often the unit of analysis in social work. For example, in an evaluation investigating the impact of a program on family cohesion, although individuals will be studied, the family group would make up the unit of analysis.

Social artifacts.   These are behaviors or products resulting from human activity. In social work, social artifacts may include books, divorces, birth practices, or ethical violations. For example, you are asked by your state NASW chapter to investigate unethical social work practice behavior. In the study, you look at the characteristics of those charged with such behavior: whether they are B.S.W.s or M.S.W.s, the field of practice in which they are employed, and so on. Here the unit of analysis is unethical social work practice.

NAMING THE VARIABLES AND VALUES

A **variable** is a characteristic of a phenomenon, and it is something that varies. Some common examples of variables often in social work research are income, ethnicity, and stress level. These characteristics vary or have different quantities, and these different quantities of variables are referred to as **values.** Note that our use of *value* in this context is not the usual meaning we assign to that term in social work practice, such as the social work value of self-determination.

Using the examples just given, possible values of income might include the following:

under $15,000/year
$15,000–$19,999/year
$20,000–$24,999/year
$25,000–$29,999/year
$30,000 and over/year

Ethnicity attributes might include the following:

> white (non-Hispanic)
> Hispanic
> African American
> Native American
> other

Stress level values might include the following:

> high
> medium
> low

Both the variables and the values that are used in research studies differ from study to study. In conducting a survey to assess the need for a day care center for developmentally delayed preschoolers, one variable might be income, so that you could assess the extent to which parents could pay for such a service. If you were carrying out the needs assessment in rural Kentucky, you might anticipate that incomes would be low. Consequently, the values included on the survey instrument would also be low; the levels presented in the above example might be too high. However, if the needs assessment were being performed in Santa Barbara, California, this categorization might be too low, and we would need to add much higher income levels.

In the same survey, ethnicity might also be considered a factor that would influence service need and consequently should be included in the study. As a variable, ethnicity is restricted in terms of the values that may be included, but there are still some choices. For example, if the study was carried out in New Mexico, the values for ethnicity listed earlier would need to be included. Alternatively, if the study was conducted in South Africa, completely different values would be used. Again, the values included depend on the purpose and context of the study.

One of the problems with naming values in this way is that information is lost in the process. For example, clustering all individuals in a category such as "Native American," leads to the loss of potentially critical information: the differences between different tribes, places of residence (on or off the reservation, rural or urban areas), and so on. This problem points to the importance of using the interpretist approach when appropriate, particularly when you are unsure about the nature of the values to be included in the study.

In interpretive studies the variables and values are not necessarily named prior to the research, but instead emerge from the study. For example in the pregnancy study cited in Chapter 3, the author concluded after carrying out extensive interviews with women that the key values relating to pregnancy were not simply "pregnant" and "not pregnant," but instead "not pregnant," "pregnant," and "a little bit pregnant," with the last condition's not having been suspected prior to the research's being undertaken. Even in interpretive studies, however, you need to have some idea of what variables are to be studied, even if other variables and their values are to be added later. In this example, the major variable studied was pregnancy.

One note of caution is in order about deciding variables to include in a study: Beware of what is called **reductionism,** or the extreme limitation of the kinds and numbers of variables to be considered as explaining or accounting for broad types of behavior. Reductionism is particularly problematic with the positivist approach, in which all the variables are named prior to the study and little allowance is made for the discovery of additional variables. For example, in a study on spousal abuse you may take many perspectives to explain this phenomenon. You might focus on economic factors, biological factors, family dynamics factors, or psychological factors, to name a few. According to the literature, all appear to play some role in spousal abuse. Incidentally, the literature review is key in the selection of these variables. Time and money constraints, however, often force us to consider only one group of factors. In this case, you may opt for the economic factors because the literature review disclosed these as being in need of further investigation. Choosing economic factors above the others is not, in itself, necessarily a problem; however, if you then suggest that these are the *only* factors in explaining spousal abuse, you would be guilty of reductionism. When you select the variables for a study, these variables may represent only one perspective on the explanation; in discussing your results, you need to acknowledge this. Social workers study human behavior, and human behavior is very complex. You cannot expect to come up with a complete explanation; you need to be aware of this limitation from the early stage of question development to the final stages.

THE RELATIONSHIP OF VARIABLES

Variables have different functions in a research study. The major distinction is between the roles of the independent and dependent variables. Independent and dependent variables are of primary concern in an explanatory study where specific variables are identified as contributing to specific outcomes—in other words, the study attempts to establish causality. In descriptive studies, such as a needs assessment, independent and dependent variables are often not identified as such. Also, interpretist studies often do not identify independent and dependent variables because they are usually not concerned directly with causality.

The **independent variable** is the presumed causal variable in a relationship. If you were studying the impact of social isolation on child sexual abuse, the independent variable would be social isolation. In a program evaluation, the independent variable is the program itself.

You can think of the **dependent variable** as the outcome variable that has presumably been affected by the independent variable. In a summative program evaluation where you are interested in whether program's goals are being met, the dependent variable would be those goals. In the example of the study attempting to identify the factors leading to child sexual abuse in a community, child sexual abuse would be the dependent variable. For each study, there may be a number of independent and dependent variables. In the study of child sexual abuse, income level (in addition to social isolation) may be another independent variable, and different types of child sexual abuse might be identified as different dependent variables.

As with the identification of variables and values, the literature review is extremely important in identifying the dependent and independent variables. In the study of child sexual abuse, any related theories need to be found in the literature and additional variables identified.

As in the case of different values, variables are not fixed as dependent or independent; the nomenclature depends on the study's purpose and context. Although child abuse is identified as a dependent variable in the example just given, in a study examining the factors that determine teenage pregnancy, child sexual abuse might well be identified as an independent variable.

Independent and Dependent Variables

Itzhaky and York (1995) studied the impact of apartment building committees in Israel. The house committees employed tenants as maintenance workers and administrators and also introduced professional workers. The researchers considered the dependent variable to be whether social activity of any kind for the residents of the building took place. One set of independent variables included the background variables of the number of families living in the apartment building and the community's typology. The second set included the functioning of the house committee, and such factors as how the committee was set up, how many meetings took place, and how dues were collected. A final independent variable considered whether a community social worker was in contact with the committee.

Defining and Operationalizing the Variables

Variables need to be defined in a clear and unambiguous manner, in much the same way we need to define concepts in practice.

A central tenet of the positivist approach is that variables must be clearly defined so they can be measured. Definition is less of a priority when using the interpretist approach, in which the definitions of concepts or variables emerge as the topic of inquiry is explored. Nevertheless, the focus of an interpretist study still must be clearly defined. In a study exploring people's beliefs about mental illness, the researcher would have to be clear about defining *mental illness,* even if the study itself ultimately explores and expands this definition.

Defining Variables in an Interpretive Study

Margareta Hyden (1994) in her interpretive study of woman battering in Sweden, clearly defined at the outset of her research the definition of assault or aggravated assault where the woman was the victim and the husband the perpetrator. Her study involved interviewing women about their experiences and how they made sense of violent action within their marriages. What emerged were different definitions and interpretations of the concept of marriage.

Many variables used in social work practice tend to be vague; they may seem open to a number of different interpretations depending on who is using them. In my first field practicum in a psychiatric hospital in Chicago, I was confused by such terms as *ego strength, depression,* and *independent living skills.* The definitions of these terms either were not provided or varied depending on who was doing the defining. In social work practice, we have to be careful that we clearly define our terms; otherwise confusion can result. A worker and client may think they both know what they mean by *independent living,* while their understandings are actually very different: The client may have in mind "living in my own apartment with no supervision," whereas the worker may mean "living in her own apartment with close supervision." In this example, no matter which definition is accepted, the term *supervision* will also need to be defined—perhaps as "the client's reporting to the social worker twice a week."

One danger of defining variables is that a definition appropriate in one culture may be inappropriate in another. So you have to be particularly careful about using definitions cross-culturally. Be especially careful with definitions when studying people in an unfamiliar culture (with *culture* not limited to describing nationality or ethnicity but also including groups of diverse types, such as single fathers or children of alcoholics). A more interpretive approach might even be advisable, so that definitions can emerge from the research.

As you did when naming the variables earlier, use the literature when defining variables. Consult both the previous research and theoretical writings on the topic for approaches to definitions.

A Concept That Is Difficult to Define

Seaberg (1990) wrote an article in *Social Work* devoted exclusively to the difficulties of defining a concept often used in social work: child well-being. He stated that according to the literature, the concept included aspects of family functioning, healthy/normal families, social indicators and quality of life, child protective service guidelines, moral philosophy, and scales for measuring child well-being.

He concluded: "Because it [child well-being] is highly abstract and value based, caution must be exercised in using the concept child well-being and in allowing it to become institutionalized in policy and decision making about families. . . . The likelihood of ever developing a specific conceptualization of child well-being that would achieve a high level of consensus throughout U.S. society seems remote" (p. 271).

Bear this example in mind when you consider some of the concepts often encountered in social work; global terms such as *child well-being* can de defined in many different ways.

Operationalizations

When using the positivist approach, the next step after defining the variables is to **operationalize** them—in other words, specifying how the variables are to be measured. This process is central to the positivist approach, where measuring and quantifying the study's variables is key. An interpretist approach is not concerned with this step, since the purpose of the study is to understand different dimensions of the variable.

Operationalizing becomes easier once variables have been formally defined. Even after definitions have been accepted, however, some ambiguities remain. For example, measuring the extent to which a client's independent living has been achieved would involve clarifying the issue of supervision. Would the client report by means of a telephone call or a face-to-face visit? How long would the client need to live independently in order to be considered successful? What kind of financial status would qualify as independent living? These are only a few of the questions that need to be answered before a satisfactory operational definition of the variable is achieved.

Measuring a variable could entail simply recording the presence or absence of a phenomenon. If reporting is defined as a telephone contact, either the contact was made or it was not. Or measurement might involve more elaboration, such as specifying the nature of the telephone contact. For example, if a prior arrangement was made regarding the time of the call and who was to initiate it, were these conditions fulfilled?

Operationalizing variables can be a challenge. Measuring a concept like depression may seem overwhelming to the social worker. A useful strategy in operationalizing a variable is to look in the literature and determine how others operationalized this concept. We refer to many variables in social work research over and over again. Depression is a good example; many measures of depression are available in the literature, including the Generalized Contentment Scale (Hudson, 1990), the Hamilton Rating Scale (Hamilton, 1967), and the CESED Scale (Radloff, 1977). Many of these measures can be adopted by social workers for evaluating their own practices.

Nevertheless, perhaps none of these measuring instruments is appropriate for the aspect of depression you are interested in examining. *Depression* is generally a label applied to specific behaviors being exhibited; to operationalize a variable like depression, often we must consider the behaviors that led to the label's original application. These behaviors might include excessive sleeping, loss of appetite, and so forth. A person's excessive sleeping is easier to measure than the person's level of depression. Excessive sleeping could be measured by the time spent sleeping.

The processes of defining and operationalizing the variables are closely related and can become circular. After defining a variable, the social worker may find that it is still difficult to operationalize the variable, and consequently the variable needs to be redefined. In fact, this circular process characterizes the entire research process, in the same way as it characterizes practice.

Operationalization

Cox (1995) compared the experiences of African American and white caregivers of dementia patients. Among the variables operationalized for the study were (1) attitudes toward caregiving, assessed by the extent to which elderly people should expect to receive care from their relatives and the extent to which relatives should be expected to provide such care; (2) patient status, assessed according to the level of cognitive functioning, disruptive behavior, social functioning, and physical functioning; and (3) caregiver stress, measured according to the caregiver's sense that his or her activities were restricted and relationships strained.

Defining and Operationalizing Goals and Activities

One type of defining and operationalizing that demands a separate discussion is when the generalist social worker conducts a summative program evaluation to determine whether a program has met its goals. As mentioned previously, the positivist approach might be the most appropriate here, and the program's goals and activities need to be defined and operationalized.

First, you need to specify what is meant by *goal* and *activity*. People use these terms in different ways, which confuses the matter. The term *goal* usually refers to the end product, "the end toward which effort is directed" (*Merriam-Webster's*, 1993). Occasionally, people use the terms *goal* and *objective* synonymously, or they use *goal* to refer to a long-term end product and *objective* to refer to a short-term end. *Activity*, in this context, refers to the means by which the goal is achieved.

The goals of a program called Adolescent Family Life might be to reduce the rate of high-risk babies born to adolescents and the rate of child abuse and neglect among teenage parents. The activities might include providing prenatal care and parenting classes to teenage parents.

The next step is to define and operationalize these goals and activities. The first goal, reducing the rate of high-risk babies born to adolescents, requires us to define *adolescents* and *high risk*. We might decide to define *adolescents* as those 18 years and under, and *high-risk babies* as low birth weight or premature infants. Of course, we would then need to operationalize these last two terms—*low birth weight* perhaps as under 5½ pounds at birth and *premature* as born after a pregnancy lasting 32 weeks or less. We would continue defining and operationalizing the other goals and the activities in a similar manner.

LEVELS OF MEASUREMENT

Another step in developing the research question is considering the level of measurement. The **level of measurement** is the extent to which a variable can be quantified and subsequently subjected to certain mathematical or statistical procedures. Obviously, determining the level of measurement for a variable is only of concern if quantitative data are being collected, so level of measurement usually is not considered in interpretive studies, where the data are generally qualitative. Quantification involves assigning a number to a variable; it depends, as you might guess, on how the variable is being operationalized. Using our example of measuring depression, we could count the number of hours the client sleeps each night, use an already developed measure such as the Generalized Contentment Scale, or have the client simply note each day whether or not she was depressed. Each measure involves assigning numbers in different ways, and consequently they result in different levels of measurement. Four different levels of measurement can be identified: nominal, ordinal, interval, and ratio (see Table 4.1).

Table 4.1   ***Levels of measurement***

Level of measurement	Definition	Example
Nominal	Data are assigned to categories based on similarity or difference.	Ethnicity, marital status, yes/no response
Ordinal	Data are sequenced in some order.	Many attitude and opinion questions
Interval	Data are sequenced in some order, and the distances between the different points are equal.	IQ, GRE scores
Ratio	Data are sequenced in some order, the distances between the different points are equal, and each value reflects an absolute magnitude. The zero point reflects an absence of the value.	Years of age, number of children, miles to place of employment

Nominal measures classify observations into mutually exclusive categories, with no ordering to the categories. Phenomena are assigned to categories based on some similarity or difference (for example, ethnicity, gender, marital status). Numbers are assigned to nominal categories, but the numbers themselves have no inherent meaning. For example, 1 is assigned to Hispanic and 2 to African American, but the numbers could be reversed and no meaning would be lost. The use of numbers with nominal data is arbitrary. In our example of depression, the client recording the absence (no) or presence (yes) of depression each day would result in a nominal level of measurement, as would other yes/no responses to questions.

Ordinal measures classify observations into mutually exclusive categories that have an inherent order to them. An ordinal level of measurement can often be used when we are examining attitudes. Respondents to a survey might be asked whether they agree with a particular statement, with the alternatives as follows:

strongly agree
agree
disagree
strongly disagree

These responses are ordered in sequence from strongly agree to strongly disagree (or vice versa) and numbered 1 to 4. Nevertheless, although these values are placed in sequence and are meaningful in that sense, the distance between each of the values is not necessarily equal and may be somewhat arbitrary.

Interval measures classify observations into mutually exclusive categories with an inherent order and equal spacing between the categories. This equal distance differentiates the interval level from the ordinal level of measurement. A good example of an interval scale is the IQ test: The difference between an IQ of 120 and 130 is the same between 110 and 120. Nevertheless, the interval level of measurement does not allow one to make any statements about the magnitude of one value in relation to another. It is not possible to claim that someone with an IQ of 160 has twice the IQ of someone with an IQ of 80.

Ratio measures possess all the characteristics of the interval level of measurement along with reflecting the absolute magnitude of the value. Put another way, at the zero point, the value is absent, or did not occur. Measurements of income, years of education, the number of times a behavior occurs—all are examples of ratio levels of measurement. In the depression example, counting the number of hours of sleep each night would result in a ratio level of measurement.

Note that most variables can be defined to allow different levels of measurement. Our example of depression is one case; anger is another. For example, a variable like anger can be measured at various levels. If the question "Do you think your child is angry?" is posed, and possible responses are yes and no, this constitutes a nominal level of measurement. But say the question is "To what extent do you think your child is angry?" and the respondent is offered the following scale:

very aggressive
aggressive
not aggressive

This would be an ordinal level of measurement. If anger is measured as one component in a personality test such as the Minnesota Multiphasic Personality Inventory (MMPI), the resulting level of measurement would be interval. Finally, if anger is defined in behavioral components, for example, the number of times the child hit another in an hour, it would be possible to use a ratio level of measurement.

These levels of measurement have important implications for the statistical analysis of research results. These implications will be examined in Chapters 12 and 13.

THE AGENCY AND DEVELOPING THE QUESTION

Much of the development of the research question occurs before you are involved. Variables may have already been identified, defined, and operationalized by those who initially conceived of the research question: our supervisors, the agency administrators, the funding organization, or individuals or groups in the community.

Don't be discouraged about not having had a role in that development. Work with what you have, and remember that this is only the beginning of the research. Often you can enhance the future development of the project through your research knowledge and your skills as an agency-based generalist practitioner. Don't forget that research is a team endeavor.

ETHICAL ISSUES IN DEVELOPING THE QUESTION

Giving Credit to Contributors

When drawing on information generated by others (for example, using a literature review or consulting with colleagues), you need to give credit to these sources of information when you write the research report. The technicalities of how to do this are discussed in Chapter 14. If you refer to someone else's ideas and do not give them credit, particularly if they are written ideas, you may be guilty of plagiarism.

Including Relevant Variables

The major ethical issue at the stage of the research process concerned with developing the question is determining what variables and values for them to include in the research question. You need to be certain you included all the important variables. In a needs assessment, it might be tempting to leave out some factors that you think may not support the need you are trying to document. In surveying a community to assess the need for an elder day care center, you want to leave out variables such as transportation need because, if such needs are great, the eventual funding of the project might be jeopardized. All variables perceived as important to the study should be included, however. Completeness is particularly critical when conducting positivist research, in which the variables are clearly defined before the research is undertaken. Including relevant variables is less of a problem with the interpretist approach, when the variables are often identified as a part of the study.

Avoiding Reductionism

An associated issue that we discussed previously is reductionism. You need to avoid looking at only one type of variable (for instance, economic factors) and claiming, if an association is found, that this variable alone is responsible for the particular outcome. Reductionism can be a danger when carrying out program evaluations because you are tempted to look only at the variables associated with the program, rather than considering others. For example, if you are evaluating a program that is intended to enhance self-esteem among high school dropouts, you would undoubtedly include the program-related variables such as length of time in the program and so on. You may not consider measuring outside factors that could also influence self-esteem, however, such as involvement in a local sports activity. These other factors may turn out to have far more impact than the program itself, but you may be reluctant to include them because they jeopardize the demonstrated efficacy of the program. Again, this problem of reductionism is more apparent in positivist research. In fact, a tendency to reductionism is one of the major drawbacks of this research approach and provides one of the rationales for social work to use more interpretive studies when attempting to answer many of the questions confronting social workers.

HUMAN DIVERSITY ISSUES IN DEVELOPING THE QUESTION

In developing the question, you must look carefully at human diversity issues to ensure that you are not building in biases against certain groups. The last chapter described the possible bias that exists when only certain groups undertake research in social work. Here will be discussed the potential bias in the literature.

Before you use materials to help guide a particular research project, you need to be aware of bias in the literature. Literature relating to human diversity issues has been scarce, although in recent years it has grown rapidly. For example, one social work journal is specifically devoted to human diversity issues: the *Journal of Multicultural Social Work*. Generally, though, we need to remember when consulting the literature that most social science research has been conducted by white, middle-class men; even when women have contributed, they have tended to be white, middle-class women. Overrepresentation of the views of these segments of the population, to the exclusion of others, constitutes a clear bias. Research questions developed by other groups may take a rather different course.

For example, until relatively recently, few studies had been conducted on the relationship between women's work and family lives, particularly those of minority women and their families. Studies of family functioning often did not examine women's experiences but instead focused on role relationships or parenting practices.

Bias in the Literature

Greif and Bailey (1990) pointed out in their article in *Families and Society* that the literature on fathers is scarce. They reviewed five major social work journals during a 27-year period. Fathers tended to be portrayed as perpetrators, missing, and embattled. The authors suggested that if the social work profession is committed to working with families, attention should be given to changing patterns of fatherhood.

SUMMARY

A critical step in the research process is the literature review, which assists in the generation of questions, connecting the question to theory, identifying previous research, and giving direction to the project. The unit of analysis needs to be determined at this stage in the research process. Variables and values must be distinguished. The definition and operationalization of variables includes defining goals and activities. Another step in developing the question involves determining the level of measurement: nominal, ordinal, interval, or ratio.

Often the generalist social worker does not have much influence over development of the research question. Ethical issues include ensuring the identification of relevant variables and avoiding reductionism. Human diversity issues in the development of the question include identifying potential bias in the literature.

STUDY/EXERCISE QUESTIONS

1. Look at research articles in *Social Work* and identify the unit of analysis used in the study. Also identify the independent and dependent variables when appropriate.

2. You are involved in an evaluation of a support group for parents of children with developmental disabilities.
    a. Identify some possible goals and activities of the group.
    b. Name at least five variables you would need to include in the evaluation.
    c. Define and operationalize these variables.

3. You have been asked to assist in designing and implementing a needs assessment for an elder day care facility in your community. Whom would you consult in the early stages of developing the assessment?

4. If you are in a field placement, talk to your supervisor; if not, talk to someone who is employed in a supervisory position in an agency in your community. Discuss with that person who they have involved in research projects at the agency and how they have involved those other people.

5. At your university library, meet with the social work reference librarian. Practice searching for a specific topic.

FURTHER READING

Burgess, R. G. (Ed.). (1986). *Key variables in social investigation.* London: Routledge & Kegan Paul.
Presents ten of the most commonly used social science variables and discusses their underlying concepts and the ways in which they have operationalized.

Kardas, E., & Milford, T. (1996). *Using the Internet for social science research and practice.* Belmont, CA: Wadsworth.
Up-to-date coverage of the use of the Internet for social work research.

Mann, T. (1987). *A guide to library search methods.* Oxford: Oxford University Press.
An excellent guide for completing literature reviews.

REFERENCES

Cox, C. (1995). Comparing the experiences of black and white caregivers of dementia patients. *Social Work, 40* (3), 343–349.

Greif, G. L., & Bailey, C. (1990). Where are the fathers in social work literature? *Families in Society: The Journal of Contemporary Human Services, 71* (2) 88–92.

Hamilton, M. (1967). A rating scale for primary depressive illness. *British Journal of School and Clinical Psychology, 6,* 178–296.

Hudson, W. W. (1990). *The clinical measurement package.* Homewood, IL: Dorsey Press.

Hyden, M. (1994). Woman battering as a marital act: Interviewing and analysis in context. In Riessman, C. (Ed.), *Qualitative studies in social work research.* Newbury Park, CA: Sage.

Itzhaky, H., & York, A. (1995). The autonomous apartment block: Israeli house committees. *International Social Work, 38,* 355–364.

Merriam-Webster's Collegiate Dictionary, 10th ed. (1993). Springfield, MA: Merriam-Webster.

Radloff, L. (1977). The CES-D Scale: A self report depression scale for research in the general population. *Journal of Applied Psychological Measurement, 1,* 385–401.

Schaffer, M., & Lia-Hoagberg, B. (1994). Prenatal care among low income women. *Families in Society,* 152–159.

Seaberg, J. R. (1990). Child well-being: A feasible concept? *Social Work, 35,* 267–272.

van Rooyen, C. (1996). *Taking the leap: A guide to higher degree research study in the Department of Social Work at the University of Natal.* Durban, South Africa: The University of Natal, Department of Social Work.

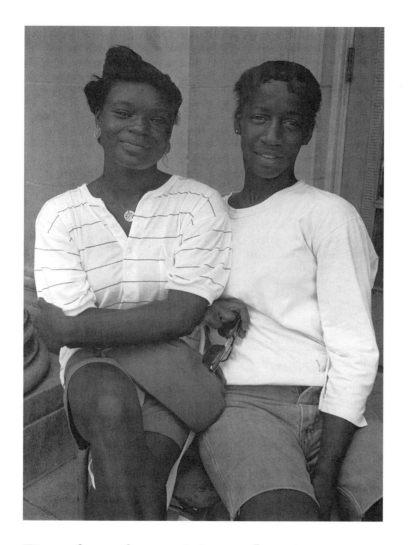

Designing Needs Assessments

■

The previous two chapters discussed designs for practice evaluations and program evaluations. This chapter will examine needs assessment designs. Needs assessments are concerned with describing the nature and extent of social problems and provide a clearer picture of the kinds of services and programs that can be most beneficial. Needs assessments are also known as **feasibility studies** or **front-end analyses.** Needs assessments were introduced in Chapter 3 as an important research strategy in social work. Social workers carry out needs assessments prior to designing a program, and for generalist social workers the need assessment is probably the most common type of research undertaken.

Needs assessments are often thought of as a type of **survey research.** Surveys measure people's attitudes, behaviors, or beliefs at one point in time; data are usually collected using questionnaires. In this chapter we will see that the survey is only one type of needs assessment design.

This chapter will include the following topics:

- reasons for conducting needs assessments
- types of designs for needs assessments
- the agency and needs assessments
- ethical issues and needs assessments
- human diversity issues and needs assessments.

REASONS FOR CONDUCTING NEEDS ASSESSMENTS

Sometimes it may seem unnecessary to conduct a needs assessment, because it seems obvious that a particular program is needed. For example, as a social worker working with families of children with mental retardation, for the last year the parents have been saying how increased respite care would help considerably to relieve some of the stress for themselves and their families. So why not just go ahead and develop a program? The answer is that since the early 1970s, there has been an unofficial (and sometimes official) requirement that any program proposal be accompanied by a needs assessment that systematically, and as objectively as possible, provides a rationale for a program's initial or further development. Thus, although you think you know what the needs are, this presumed knowledge is only subjective opinion and will not carry much weight with your proposed program's potential funders.

There are a number of different reasons for conducting needs assessments that go beyond just trying to figure out how many people can benefit from a proposed program. Being clear about the reason for conducting the study is important because that can help you more accurately plan, design, and implement the needs assessment. Five different reasons can be identified (Royse and Thyer, 1996):

To determine whether services exist;

determine whether there are enough clients to justify creating a new m;

ine who uses existing services;

4. To determine what barriers prevent clients from accessing existing services;
5. To document the existence of an ongoing social problem.

Needs assessments may be conducted for only one of these reasons, or for several. Each will be described in turn using the example of respite care for the parents of mentally retarded children as an illustration.

Determining Whether Services Exist in the Community

Just because you do not know of an intervention or program does not mean that it does not exist. Obviously this is more likely to be the case if you work in a large metropolitan area than if you are employed in a rural setting.

In order to make this determination, use your networking skills, the Internet, or other resources to search for programs. If your community does not already have a directory of social service agencies and programs, create one. Use your research skills to put together a directory of services that are available on computerized databases. This can be either a community-wide resource, or one specifically addressing the needs and concerns of the client population with which you work. In our example, this step would involve documenting services that are already available for families with mentally retarded children in your community.

Determining Whether There Are Enough Clients

One of the more common reasons for conducting a needs assessment is to find out whether enough clients have a particular problem to justify a new program. You may hear the need expressed for respite care from the majority of your clients, but your clients may not constitute enough of a need to start a new program. Perhaps your clients are not representative of clients of other agencies or other workers; in other words, your clients may be a nonrepresentative sample. The extent of the need should be systematically documented.

A Needs Assessment Determining the Number of Clients with a Particular Problem

Singer, Bussey, Song, and Lunghofer (1995) investigated the psychosocial issues of women serving time in jail. The study involved interviewing 201 randomly selected female inmates incarcerated at a municipal jail to establish the needs of this population. Of the women, 64% were in the clinical range for mental health problems, 83% were in the substance abuse range, and 81% had been sexually victimized at some time in their lives.

The authors made nine recommendations for services, including drug and alcohol treatment services, mental health services, education on sexually transmitted diseases, medical services, dental services, and parenting education.

Determining Who Uses Existing Services

Just because an agency or community runs a certain program does not mean that those who could benefit from it use the program. Respite services may be available, but parents may think they are ineligible or may simply not have heard of the program. Certain parents may use the program, but others may not; for example, older parents may use the services more than younger parents.

A Needs Assessment Determining Who Uses Existing Services

Barnes, Given, and Given (1995) examined use of services by daughters giving care to their elderly parents. The researchers compared employed daughters, daughters who were never employed while caregivers, and daughters who ended their employment to continue caregiving. The authors found that although all the caregivers could benefit from social work services, special attention is required for employed daughters, particularly those who are conflicted about their employment and caregiving roles.

Determining What Barriers Prevent Clients from Accessing Services

Sometimes clients know about services and may be referred to them by social workers but for various reasons do not use the services. Identifying these barriers can start the process of redesigning services or developing supplementary services. Often factors such as transportation and child care work as barriers. In the example of parents of children with mental retardation, one barrier might be parents' feeling of guilt concerning their children, in which case counseling and support to the families might be necessary before the families would actually use respite care.

A Needs Assessment Determining the Existence of Barriers to Use of Services

Rittner and Kirk (1995) carried out a survey of low-income, elderly people who attended daytime meal programs. The authors examined sociocultural and quality of life variables as they affected use of health care and transportation services. Most of the respondents self-reported their health as poor or very poor, and more than half had no medical care during the preceding six months. Social isolation from family and support systems exacerbated problems with transportation. Most relied on public transportation to gain access to health care services, but expressed fear in using this form of transportation.

Documenting the Existence of an Ongoing Social Problem

Sometimes it is not clear what problems people are confronting. This is a more fundamental question than documenting how many need a service (which assumes the nature of the problem is already known) and focuses on the characteristics of the social problem. In the respite care example, it was not until the parents started speaking out and expressing their need for support and assistance in the care of their children that the need for respite was recognized.

 A Needs Assessment Assessing the Nature of a Social Problem

Strober (1994) investigated the factors involved in the acculturation of Cambodian refugees in Los Angeles. Professionals involved in refugee services noted that Cambodian refugees were more severely psychologically distressed and slower to acculturate than other groups. The findings indicated that their adjustment difficulties were related to severe psychological distress. The Cambodian families and ethnic communities were ineffective at reducing this psychological distress, which the author suggested could be explained by the absence of a preexisting Cambodian community and the refugees' discomfort with existing culturally unfamiliar community agencies. (Note that this study also identified some barriers to existing service use.)

The author suggested that these refugees needed services that support family strengths, stronger worker-client bonds through more reciprocal interaction between the two, and greater worker community involvement.

TYPES OF DESIGNS FOR NEEDS ASSESSMENTS

A needs assessment is usually conceptualized as a descriptive survey, and as discussed in Chapter 3, does not require the types of explanatory designs needed for program evaluations. Some choices in design do need to be made, however. The first step is to understand why the study is being conducted. Use the options outlined in the previous section as a guide. Regardless of which of these questions is being addressed (with the exception of determining whether services already exist), almost all surveys, including needs assessments, rely on a probability sample from which results can be generalized. Since the primary purpose of a needs assessment is to document the need for services as accurately as possible, selecting the sample is critical. Refer to Chapter 8 for a full discussion of this aspect of the study.

The next step in deciding what type of design to use is to pose a number of questions.

1. Whose need is being assessed?
2. Who will have input into the design of the needs assessment?

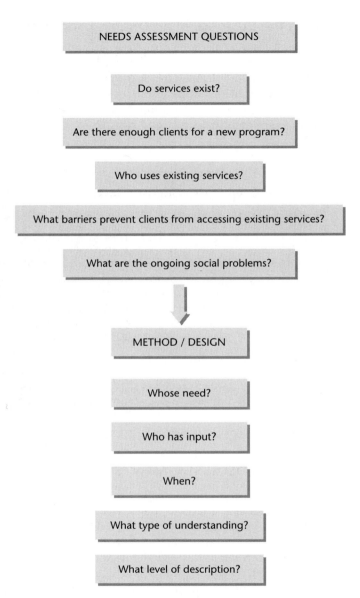

Figure 5.1 **Designing a needs assessment**

3. When will the needs assessment be carried out?
4. What type of understanding of the need is required?
5. What level of description is useful?

Each of these questions will be discussed next. (See Figure 5.1 for a chart depicting the different reasons for conducting a needs assessment and the different types of designs.)

Whose Need Is Being Assessed?

The first question, whose need the assessment is addressing, should be answered early on, since it determines who will be selected as participants in the research. Four different levels of needs can be studied: individual, organizational, community, and societal. Most needs assessments are concerned with individual needs of clients or potential clients, including basic needs such as food and shelter and needs for social services. A significant proportion of needs assessments carried out by social workers are concerned with organizational needs, the need for technical assistance or training of some type—for example, the need for an employee assistance program.

Assessing an Organization's Need

Rycraft (1994) investigated factors that may influence some caseworkers to continue employment in public child welfare when so many are leaving. From interviews with 23 caseworkers four factors of retention emerged: mission, goodness of fit, supervision, and investment.

Needs assessments are also carried out in communities, assessing the community's need for neighborhood development or services—for example, a community's need for a youth program. Societal needs are assessed at an even broader level—for instance, assessing the need for revisions in Social Security or in national policies related to services to the very old.

Who Will Have Input into the Design?

As with program evaluations, early on you need to determine who will be involved in designing and implementing the needs assessment. Clearly, this determination is partly related to the answer to the previous question, whose need is being assessed. The decision then becomes whether and to what extent participants will have input into planning the project. This book stresses the importance of participatory or action research. Involving the participants in the study design ensures their resulting "ownership" of the results. If participants are involved in designing and implementing a needs assessment, the results not only will have greater validity and relevance but also will be much more likely to be heard.

A Participatory Action Needs Assessment

Sarri and Sarri (1992) completed a participatory needs assessment in Bolivia. The study took place in a small, rural, poor agricultural community of Mallco Rancho. The core group designing the research consisted of five community members, the project consultant, and two staff members of a local nonprofit organization.

When Will the Needs Assessment Be Carried Out?

Two main choices exist about the timing of the data collection. The assessment may be cross-sectional or longitudinal.

With a **cross-sectional design,** a survey is carried out at one point in time. For example, parents are asked about their need for a respite care program. Although it may take a few months to collect the data, whether through a questionnaire or interview, data are collected from each parent just once. This is the most common type of design for a needs assessment.

A Cross-Sectional Study

Becerra and Chi (1992) examined the similarities and differences in the actual use of child care arrangements for infants and toddlers among low-income mothers of various ethnic groups (non-Hispanic whites, Mexican Americans, and Chinese Americans). The data indicated that in general, mothers of very young children of all groups prefer to have their infants cared for in their own homes by spouses, relatives, neighbors, or friends. (Note that this study also has an ex post facto design, which will be described later in this chapter.)

A **longitudinal design** might sometimes be necessary. Longitudinal studies are surveys conducted on multiple occasions over an extended period of time. There are three types of longitudinal studies: trend surveys, cohort surveys, and panel surveys.

Trend studies require multiple samplings from the same population over months or years to monitor changes or trends. For example, a trend study might examine how the characteristics of clients, or their problems that are served by a program, change over time, with the goal of changing the focus of the program to meet any changing needs.

A Trend Study

Caputo (1995) compared various measures of African American and white family income inequality and poverty for the periods 1969–1980 and 1981–1992.

Cohort studies examine specific subgroups as they change over time. These subgroups have specific characteristics in common; often this characteristic is age. For example, a cohort study may study the changing needs of families over time. In 1985 a group of families with parents in their early 20s were interviewed; in 1990 a group in their late 20s; and in 1995 families with parents in their early 30s. An analysis of changing needs could then be made.

Panel studies, unlike trend and cohort studies, study the same set of people over time. For example, graduates of a B.S.W. program might be asked about their further education needs two, four, and six years after graduation.

A Panel Study

Segal and Hwang (1994) completed interviews at 214 sheltered care facilities for the mentally ill in 1973 and then again in 1985. They wanted to compare the facilities' characteristics, residents, and communities before and after the licensing act in California. They found that licensure neither predicts quality nor apparently results in the development of higher quality facilities.

What Type of Understanding of the Need Is Required?

As with other types of research strategies, the decision about whether a positivist or interpretist approach is appropriate needs to be made.

Generally needs assessments adopt primarily a positivist approach. The goal after all is to provide documentation of need that will withstand the critical review of a funding organization or other monitoring body. As such, needs assessments usually involve either collecting new data through questionnaires (either mailed or face-to-face) or using secondary or already existing data, whether from government or nongovernment sources. (See Chapter 9 for a discussion of these data collection methods.)

Sometimes, however, a more in-depth understanding of a need is required. In such a case it may be necessary to use an interpretive approach or at least to collect more qualitative data than is usual in a needs assessment. For example, you may be interested in finding out more detail about what parents of mentally retarded children have in mind when they express the need for respite care.

What is their definition of respite care? What have been their experiences of respite care in the past?

Qualitative data collection methods often include interviewing key informants, using focus groups, a community forum, and observation, all of which are discussed in detail in Chapter 9. These types of needs assessments are less dependent on probability sampling because of the different type of understanding sought.

A Needs Assessment Using Qualitative Data

Chauncey (1994) collected data through individual interviews and group meetings on the emotional concerns and treatment needs of the male partners of female sexual abuse survivors. Concerns included conflicts about expressing needs, frustration with various aspects of their relationships, guilt and shame at having feelings, questions about how to deal with relatives, and sexual issues.

What Level of Description Is Useful?

You need to determine whether the relationship between certain variables in the study may be worth examining. For example, you might be interested in the relationship between the level of retardation in the child and the expressed need of the parents for respite care. It is not possible to carry out any of the group designs described in Chapter 6, but it is possible to carry out what is referred to as an **ex post facto design.** *Ex post facto* means "after the fact"; in this type of design, the subjects already possess the independent variable of interest before the study begins. Thus, for example, the children are characterized by a certain level of mental retardation before the needs assessment is carried out. Common variables in ex post facto designs include gender, ethnicity, ages, living situation, type of problem, and so on.

An Ex Post Facto Needs Assessment

De Anda and Smith (1993) examined data on 165 adolescents, 65 young adults, and 175 adults who called two suicide help lines in Los Angeles County. They compared the different types of problems reported by each age group. Adults and young adults reported depression as a primary reason for contemplating suicide; adolescents reported interpersonal problems.

A number of problems are associated with the ex post facto design, and it is important to note that this is not a form of experimental design. The independent variable is simply an attribute, not an experimental manipulation such as the random assignment to a program or to the group that is not in the program. In addition, any difference in the dependent variable could be due to many other factors that this design does not control for. Thus the relationship between the variables is simply as association. Statements about causality cannot be made with ex post facto designs. In other words, although there may be a relationship between parents' requesting respite care less frequently and parents' having less severely retarded children, it cannot be said that being a parent of a less severely retarded child *causes* the need for less frequent respite care.

THE AGENCY AND DESIGNING NEEDS ASSESSMENTS

A needs assessment is the type of research most often carried out by generalist social workers. The designs and variations offered in this chapter offer only a glimpse of what can be accomplished with needs assessments. When you need to carry out this type of research, be creative in your attempt to document need. Instead of just a mailed survey, think about some alternative strategies for collecting the data. Involve the participants as much as possible; remember, they are the ones who will be receiving the services.

ETHICAL ISSUES IN DESIGNING NEEDS ASSESSMENTS

A key ethical issue with needs assessments is ensuring that the needs documented in your report are those expressed by the participants in the research, rather than the needs the agency or administration would like to see met. Agencies do have their own agendas; sometimes there is a temptation to respond more to the source of funding than to the needs of the potential or actual clients. Again, as with ethical issues raised previously in this book, this problem can be avoided by ensuring that clients have input into the research. They must direct and design it as much as possible, with the result that they, rather than the agency, come to own it. This approach not only ensures an appropriate focus for the research but also can empower the participants in the study.

An Empowering (and Participatory) Needs Assessment

A group of students in Kwa Zulu Natal, South Africa, were placed for their field practicum in a community called Bhambayi. Bhambayi was originally a model community established by Gandhi. Now it is primarily a squatters' settlement,

(continued)

(continued)

with few formal services and extremely high unemployment. The students, in consultation with the community, wanted to assess the needs of the youth in Bhambayi. After interviewing 60 youths, all of whom were officially unemployed, more than half were found to have never attended high school. One of the questions asked about their skills. The responses included carpentry, needlework, shoemaking, and mechanics. It was also disclosed that many held informal jobs. The students and the community built on these skills by developing income-generating projects such as food production, concrete block making, and mechanical repairs. The research itself gave motivation and a sense of hope to the residents of Bhambayi as many commented that until asked about their skills, they had felt they did not possess skills that could result in income.

HUMAN DIVERSITY ISSUES IN DESIGNING NEEDS ASSESSMENTS

The primary purpose of a needs assessment is to identify "deficits" or problems in order that they can be addressed through new programs or modifications to existing programs. Identifying needs, while obviously a necessary step, can lead to certain groups' being stigmatized as consistently being associated with certain problems. For example, inner-city African American youths may be associated with crime, adolescent parents with inadequate parenting skills, refugee groups with acculturation problems, and so on. It is important to remember that needs assessments can also assess the strengths of the participants in the research and often should do this in addition to presenting the needs.

A "Strengths" Needs Assessment

Marin and Vacha (1994) examined self-help strategies and resources among people at risk for homelessness. They studied the practice of doubling up with friends and relatives and examined the relationships with those who housed them. Recommendations were made to enhance the living conditions among doubled-up households so they may continue to serve as a foundation in the prevention of homelessness.

SUMMARY

Designing needs assessments is a central research activity for generalist social workers. There are five reasons for carrying out needs assessments: to determine whether services exist; to determine whether there are enough clients to justify a program; to assess the barriers that prevent clients from accessing existing services; and to document the existence of an ongoing social problem. The type of design adopted depends on the reason for conducting the needs assessment; whose need is being assessed; who will have input into the design (that is, whether a participatory design will be used); when will the assessment be carried out (that is, whether it will be a longitudinal or cross-sectional study); what type of understanding is needed (interpretive or positivist); and what type of description is required. Ethical issues include ensuring that participants have maximum input into the design of the needs assessment. Human diversity issues include the importance of addressing strengths as well as deficits in the documentation of needs.

STUDY/EXERCISE QUESTIONS

1. Find an article in a social work journal and identify
   a. limitations in the methodology
   b. how you would have designed it differently
2. Talk with your fellow students about a service/program need that seems to exist at your university. Design a needs assessment for this issue.
   a. Design one using the positivist approach.
   b. Design one using the interpretist approach.

FURTHER READING

Royse, D., & Thyer, B. A. (1996). *Program evaluation* (2nd ed.). Chicago: Nelson Hall.
   This text has a good chapter on needs assessment.
Soriano, F. I. (1995). *Conducting needs assessments.* Newbury Park, CA: Sage.
   A good comprehensive guide to conducting needs assessments.

REFERENCES

Barnes, C. L., Given, B. A., & Given, C. W. (1995). Parent caregivers: A comparison of employed and not employed daughters. *Social Work, 40* (3), 375–381.

Becerra, R. M., & Chi, I. (1992). Child care preferences among low income minority families. *International Social Work, 35* (1), 35–47.

Caputo, R. K. (1995). Income inequality and family poverty. *Families in Society, 76* (10), 604–614.

Chauncey, S. (1994). Emotional concerns and treatment of male partners of female sexual abuse survivors. *Social Work, 39* (6), 669–676.

de Anda, D., & Smith, M. A. (1993). Differences among adolescent, young, adult, and adult callers of suicide help lines. *Social Work, 38* (4), 421–428.

Marin, M. V., & Vacha, E. F. (1994). Self help strategies and resources among people at risk of homelessness: Empirical findings and social service policy. *Social Work, 39* (6), 649–657.

Royse, D., & Thyer, B. A. (1996). *Program evaluation* (2nd ed.). Chicago: Nelson Hall.

Rittner, B., & Kirk, A. B. (1995). Health care and public transportation use by poor and frail elderly people. *Social Work, 40* (3), 365–373.

Rycraft, J. R. (1994). The party isn't over: The agency role in the retention of public child welfare caseworkers. *Social Work, 31* (9), 75–80.

Sarri, R., & Sarri, C. (1992). Participatory action research in two communities in Bolivia and the United States. *International Social Work, 35,* 267–280.

Segal, S. P., & Hwang, S. (1994). Licensure of sheltered-care facilities: Does it assure quality? *Social Work, 39* (1), 124–131.

Singer, M., Bussey, J., Song, L., & Lunghofer, L. (1995). *Social Work, 40* (1), 103–113.

Strober, S. B. (1994). Social work interventions to alleviate Cambodian refugee psychological distress. *International Social Work, 37* (1), 23–35.

Designing Program Evaluations

■

E arly in the research process you need to develop a research design. The design and sampling stages are comparable to the selection and collection of the information phase of practice. As with other steps of the research process, you may not be directly involved in designing the research for a program evaluation. At some point, however, your agency will undertake such an evaluation, and it is important that you understand the implications of selecting one type of design over another. In some cases, you may find yourself with the responsibility of initiating an evaluation.

There are two different types of program evaluations: formative and summative. These were discussed briefly in Chapter 3. A formative program evaluation focuses on description rather than on causality. For these types of evaluations, the interpretive approach is often more appropriate. A summative program evaluation is used in determining the extent to which the goals of the program were met—in other words, assessing the extent to which the program caused a specific outcome. Usually a positivist approach is adopted with this type of research. Causality demands that three basic conditions be met, as set out in Chapter 1. First, the cause precedes the effect in time. Second, the cause and the effect are related to one another. Third, this relationship cannot be accounted for by other factors. These three conditions are established by aspects of the summative research design, which includes the timing of the data collection and the formation of comparison groups. Different group designs can be used to establish causality. These are designs that help you assess the relationship of the program to a group of client systems, rather than one client system as in evaluating individual practice (a topic that will be discussed in Chapter 7).

Both formative and summative program evaluations are critical to assessing programs. A summative program evaluation, however, is usually required by a funding source, and the establishment of causality presents a major challenge. Consequently, the focus in this chapter will be upon these summative evaluations and their associated group designs.

Throughout this chapter a case example will be used to demonstrate the pros and cons of different designs. Assume you are employed by a program that offers high-risk adolescents a series of six birth control classes to increase knowledge of birth control practices. You are asked to evaluate the effectiveness of the program.

This chapter will discuss the following:

- formative program evaluations
- summative program evaluations
- types of summative program evaluation designs
- the agency and designing program evaluations
- ethical issues and designing program evaluations
- human diversity issues and designing program evaluations

FORMATIVE PROGRAM EVALUATIONS

Formative evaluations are generally very descriptive and provide detail about a program's strengths and weaknesses. Interpretive approaches using qualitative data are particularly useful with these types of evaluations.

In the adolescent birth control program, a formative evaluation would be undertaken if you were interested in finding out how the adolescents experienced the program: What did they perceive as its limitations and strengths? Alternatively a formative evaluation might examine how the parenting classes were being conducted, how the syllabus was developed, and whether the syllabus was being followed.

Formative evaluations make no attempt to establish any type of causality—in other words, no claim is made that the program resulted in specific outcomes. Also, no attempt is made to generalize the findings. Consequently, there are no dependent and independent variables and the sampling is generally purposive, rather than random. The focus is on in-depth description and analysis as a means of improving and strengthening the program. Thus much of the emphasis in a formative program evaluation is in assessing quality.

In understanding the adolescents' experiences with the birth control classes, in-depth interviews might be conducted to try to elicit the youths' reactions to the program. The classes could be observed and the facilitator interviewed in an attempt to understand how the classes were being implemented and to identify areas in need of development.

Often, formative evaluations can be strengthened by setting up some kind of comparison group. If clients' reactions to a program are found to be positive, it is difficult to avoid asking the question "compared to what?" One type of comparison could consist of comparisons with clients in different versions of the program. For example, if the birth control program had two classes with different leaders, those two could be compared. Another type of comparison could consist of comparing groups according to clients' characteristics—for example, comparing males and females, ethnic groups, socioeconomic groups, and so on. This type of design can be used for needs assessments and was discussed in Chapter 5.

Formative evaluations are extremely useful in the first year or so of a program's implementation, since findings from such a study can provide immediate feedback for improvement and growth. Thorough formative evaluations can lay the groundwork for later summative evaluations.

A Formative Program Evaluation

Siegel (1993) examined adoptive parents' reactions to open adoptions of their infants. Findings indicated overwhelmingly positive feelings about open adoption and some issues and concerns unique to the open adoption experience.

SUMMATIVE PROGRAM EVALUATIONS

Summative program evaluations and their associated group designs are primarily concerned with causality. As such, validity is a central issue. When considering the validity of a research design, two different validity issues are considered: internal validity and external validity.

Internal validity is the extent to which the changes in the dependent variable(s) are a result of the introduction of the independent variable(s) and not some other factor(s). For example, was the knowledge of birth control a result of the adolescents' participation in the birth control classes, or were other factors responsible for this increase in knowledge? This is an attempt to establish causality. In order to ensure internal validity in the birth control question, the three aspects of causality described in the previous section need to be addressed.

The first two conditions—that the cause precedes the effect and that there is a relationship between cause and effect—can be met by one aspect of the research design: the data collection time. With the adolescents, you can measure their level of knowledge about birth control before and after the classes. If you find that their knowledge level is low prior to the classes and high after the classes, this establishes that the classes preceded the increase in knowledge level.

The two measures also allow you to assess the extent of the relationship between a change in knowledge levels and participation in the classes. For example, 80% of those in the classes had a high level of knowledge after their participation. To decide whether this is a significant or important relationship, statistical tests are used (these will be discussed in Chapter 13). Even if you do determine that the relationship is significant, however, you still cannot say the classes caused a change in knowledge level, because the relationship could be explained by other factors. For example, the adolescents may have received some instruction at school on birth control at the same time as you were collecting data, which contributed to the change in knowledge level. This is where the second aspect of research design as it relates to causality becomes so important: comparison groups. **Comparison groups** either go through another type of program or else receive no type of bona fide intervention. These comparison groups can help strengthen causality claims. If the increase in knowledge level is greater among those who attended the classes than among those who were in the comparison group, you can begin to narrow down the factors responsible for that change as being the classes.

It is important that the comparison groups be otherwise equivalent to the group involved in the program being studied. The most reliable way of ensuring equivalence of the groups is to use random assignment of subjects into an **experimental group** (the group that receives the intervention being evaluated) and a **control group** (the group that does not receive the intervention being evaluated). **Random assignment** means that every subject has an equal chance of being assigned to either group. Equivalence of the groups is important because without it you cannot determine whether disparity in outcome between the two groups is due to the treatment or to the difference between the two groups. Later in this chapter some problems associated with random assign-

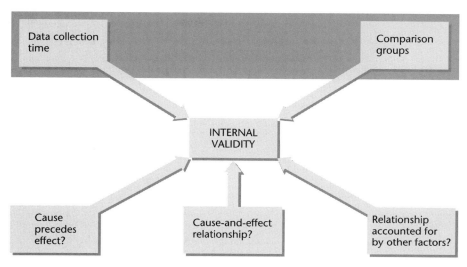

Figure 6.1   ***Internal validity in group design***

ment and some alternative strategies for setting up comparison groups will be discussed.

Do not confuse random assignment with random sampling. Random sampling involves creating a sample from a population, not assigning the experimental and control group, and will be discussed in Chapter 8. Random sampling and random assignment may or may not both be used in the same study. They are independent procedures and have different implications for the findings. Random sampling is concerned with the generalizability of the findings and the representativeness of the sample. Random assignment is concerned with the equivalence of the experimental and control groups and with establishing causality. You will see in our next discussion, however, that equivalence of the groups can *also* have an effect on the generalizability of the findings.

External validity is the other type of validity of concern in group design; it refers to the extent to which the research results are generalizable to the wider population. (See Chapter 1 for a discussion of generalizability.) External validity relates to the effectiveness of the treatment with other, similar client systems. As will be discussed in Chapter 8, generalizability is influenced by the sampling approach. In addition, however, generalizability depends on two other conditions: first, ensuring the equivalency of the groups, and second, ensuring that nothing happens during the course of the evaluation to jeopardize the equivalence of the groups or the representativeness of the sample.

The first condition for external validity is to ensure the *equivalency of the groups* being compared. You may decide that randomly assigning the comparison group is not feasible and that the comparison group should be made up of adolescents who are not eligible for the classes. This type of comparison group is problematic, however, because individuals in the comparison group might

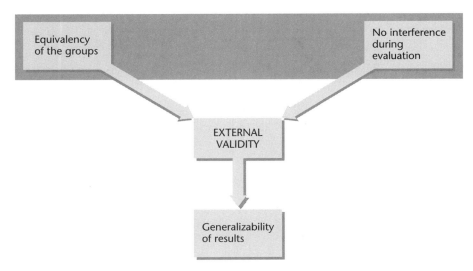

Figure 6.2   ***External validity in group design***

possess different characteristics from those who entered group therapy. Consequently, not only would any outcome showing differences between the two
groups have a lower internal validity than it might otherwise (that is, the causality would be questionable), but in addition the population to which the results
could be generalized would be limited. The results could only be generalized to
those eligible for the classes.

The second condition influenced by the research design and that affects external validity is ensuring that *no interference* occurs during the course of the evaluation that may decrease the distinction between the experimental and control
group. Interference of this kind is sometimes called **treatment diffusion.** It
can occur in three different ways. First, the adolescents may discuss the class
with their peers, some of whom may be in the comparison group. Then comparison between the two groups becomes problematic. Second, when the program is
not clearly defined, the distinction between the program group and the comparison group can be difficult. (This often points to the need for a formative evaluation in order to define the program components more clearly.) Finally, treatment
diffusion can result from reactivity effects. Changes occur when people are aware
they are participants in a study that blur the distinction between the program
group and the comparison group. Treatment diffusion leads to problems in gen-
eralizing the initial results to the wider population.

TYPES OF SUMMATIVE PROGRAM EVALUATION DESIGNS

In this section, different types of research design with their relative validity problems or threats will be examined.

Preexperimental Designs

A preexperimental design is a group design that often is the only feasible design to adopt, but from which no strong conclusion of causality can be drawn.

One-Group Posttest-Only Design

The **one-group posttest-only design** consists of one group (so that there is no comparison group) with one point of data collection (after the intervention). Figure 6.3 shows how this design might be visualized. Sometimes this design is referred to as a one-shot case study. Note that although the term *test* is used in the name of this design, this is simply a way of talking about the point at which data collection occurs. The data collection method may be any of the types discussed in Chapter 9, such as observing a behavior or administering a questionnaire.

The one-group posttest-only design can be useful in gathering information about how a program is functioning. This design can answer several questions: For example, how well are participants functioning at the end of the program? Are minimum standards for outcomes being achieved? This type of design is often used for **client satisfaction surveys,** in which clients are asked about how they experienced or perceived the program.

The one-group posttest-only design is very limited in its ability to explain or make statements about whether a program caused particular outcomes for clients and whether the results can be generalized to other client populations. Consequently, this design is viewed as having numerous threats to its validity—both internal and external.

A One-Group Posttest-Only Design

Frecknall and Luks (1992) used a mailed questionnaire to collect data on parents' impressions of the impact of a big brother/big sister program on their children.

Threats to Internal Validity

Remember that internal validity refers to whether it can be determined if the program caused a particular outcome. With the case example, we need to ask whether it was, in fact, the provision of birth control information that led to any increase in the knowledge.

Using the one-group posttest-only design results in the following threats to internal validity.

Selection. The kind of people selected for one group may differ from the kind selected for another. It may be that the clients who enrolled in the program were

Figure 6.3   ***One-group posttest-only design***

already highly motivated to learn about birth control. There was no pretest to measure this potential predisposition of the clients, so this possibility of **selection** threatens internal validity.

History.   **History** involves those events—other than the program—that could affect the outcome. Participants' high levels of knowledge about birth control may result from classes held in school or from some other factor. Without a comparison group, this possibility cannot be assessed.

Mortality.   Subjects may drop out of the groups so that the resulting groups are no longer equivalent; this possibility is called **mortality.** Some adolescents may have attended one class on birth control and then dropped out; however, they are still considered to be members of the experimental group. As a result, the group that ultimately receives the posttest is biased and perhaps shows a higher success rate than would be the case if the success rates of those who dropped out were also monitored. Consequently, the outcome of *all* participants must be assessed, which cannot be done without some type of pretest.

Note that mortality and selection are a little like mirror images. Selection is the bias involved when people initially choose to participate in the program. Mortality is the bias introduced by those who drop out of the program once they have begun.

As for our case example, because the data collection only occurs once (after the intervention) and because of the lack of a comparison group, the extent to which it can be stated that the program caused a change in birth control knowledge is limited with the one-group posttest-only design.

Threats to External Validity

The one-group posttest-only design poses some threats to external validity and generalizability of results. Possible problems include the following.

Selection-treatment interaction.   **Selection-treatment interaction** occurs when the ability to generalize is limited because the sample is not randomly selected or there is no pretest, so you cannot determine how typical the clients are. In our example, the adolescents may all be highly motivated to learn about birth control prior to enrolling in the program so that whether they complete the classes is irrelevant.

History-Treatment Interaction. **History-treatment interaction** occurs when other factors may be contributing to the outcome and so might affect the generalizability of the results (for example, if the positive outcomes resulted from a massive media campaign on pregnancy prevention rather than from the program). The program might have a negative outcome if the evaluation were carried out at a different point in time.

One-Group Pretest/Posttest Design

Another preexperimental design, the **one-group pretest/posttest design,** is similar to the preceding design except that a pretest is added. In the case example, the pretest might consist of a questionnaire given to all clients that asks about their knowledge of birth control prior to their attending the classes. This design helps answer several questions: not only how well participants are functioning at the end of the program, and whether minimum standards of outcome are being achieved, but also how much participants change during their participation in the program. This is a useful design, and certainly one that is often used in program evaluation characteristics. It is also a useful design to use when no comparison group is feasible (as, for example, in the Cushman, Kalmuss, and Namerow [1993] study of birth mothers placing their infants for adoption).

Some additional information can be gained from this type of design that can enhance statements of causality. The pretest allows selection to be ruled out as an alternative explanation, because any preexisting information on birth control would be identified. In the long run, however, this design often poses even more threats to validity than the one-group posttest-only design.

A One-Group Pretest/Posttest Design

Cushman, Kalmuss, and Namerow (1993) examined the experiences of 215 young birth mothers who placed their infants for adoption through different maternity residences and agencies. Both prebirth and postbirth interviews were conducted. The researchers suggested that several service-procedural variables were related to certain social-psychological outcomes for the birth mothers.

Figure 6.4   ***One-group pretest/posttest design***

Threats to Internal Validity

The one-group pretest/posttest design poses the following threats to internal validity.

History.   Because there is no comparison group, there is no way to tell whether other events may have affected the outcome.

Maturation.   Even though a change may be detected between the pretest and the posttest, this change may be due, not to the subjects' participation in the program, but rather to **maturation.** Subjects may change over the course of time due to lifelong learning rather than program effects. With adolescents, especially, the possibility of maturation is a potentially serious threat to internal validity.

In the case example, the adolescents' level of knowledge would have changed regardless of the program. Maturation is a particularly strong threat if the participants are young, or if there is a long time between the pretest and posttest. A comparison group helps control for maturation effects.

Testing.   The **testing** threat to validity may occur any time the subjects are exposed to a measuring instrument more than once. If the pretest gave the adolescents information that could increase their knowledge of birth control, this effect cannot be separated from the effect of the classes. A comparison group can help control for these testing effects because if they do exist, they exist for both groups; if the knowledge of the clients in the experimental group changed more than those in the comparison group, the researcher would be much more comfortable in concluding that the intervention was responsible for this change rather than the pretest.

Instrumentation.   The way in which the variables are measured, or **instrumentation,** may change during the course of the evaluation. For example, a questionnaire may change between its first and second administration. Sometimes, these changes are difficult to avoid. For example, the context in which the questionnaire is administered may change, as may the person administering it. This change, rather than the intervention, may account for any difference in the results.

Regression to the mean.   In the example, if eligibility for the birth control classes was determined as a result of taking a test on birth control knowledge (those with low knowledge levels would be eligible), then a posttest after the classes could exhibit a regression to the mean. This may occur because most people tend to perform close to their averages, but some days they score particularly high or low. When they take the test again, they will tend to regress to the mean, or be closer to their average score. Thus any change in score between the pretest and the posttest for the participants would not necessarily reflect the influence of the program but could simply be regression to the mean.

Interaction of selection and other threats.   Even if none of these previously discussed threats to internal validity are applicable to the general population, the threats may be relevant for those subjects selected to participate in the study. To take maturation as an example, it may not be the case that women in general become more knowledgeable about birth control as they mature. Adolescents who express a desire to receive more information through counseling, however, may also be more likely to become more knowledgeable just as a function of their age. This represents the interaction of selection and other threats—in this case, maturation.

Threats to External Validity

History-treatment interaction.   History-treatment interaction may be a problem with the one-group pretest/posttest design.

Reactive effects.   **Reactive effects** can occur when subjects change their behavior because they know they are participating in the study. The resulting outcomes may be distorted and cannot be generalized to a wider population. These reactive effects are difficult to overcome in any design because you cannot ethically engage in research without gaining the subject's consent. Consent will be discussed later in this chapter.

Static-Group Comparison Design

The **static-group comparison design** is a third type of preexperimental design. An extension of the posttest-only design, it includes a comparison group that also has a posttest (Figure 6.5). In this design, the groups are nonequivalent in that the comparison group was not randomly assigned, and there is no way of knowing how the groups are different or similar.

 A Static-Group Comparison Design

Itzhaky (1995) compared two types of community organizations in Israel. One community center was a project supervised by an interdisciplinary committee and a community social worker; the focus was on the participation of clients. In the other center, decisions were made by the staff and management with no social worker involvement. The experiences of the clients from each center were compared.

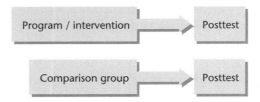

Figure 6.5   ***Static-group comparison design***

Several strategies can be adopted to achieve some equivalency of the comparison group even if random assignment does not occur. These strategies include baseline comparison, matching, cohort groups, and overflow comparison.

Baseline Comparison

Baseline comparison occurs when the comparison group is composed of cases handled prior to the introduction to the program. The problem with this approach is that it is difficult to determine whether cases identified as eligible in the absence of a program actually would have been referred to the program.

Matching

Matching involves selecting certain characteristics that are thought to have an important impact on outcomes—for example, gender or ethnicity—and ensuring these characteristics are equally represented in each group. In the example, based on previous research and our own experience, you may think that ethnicity—for instance, being Hispanic—is an important factor in determining the effectiveness of the program. Consequently, you make sure the program group has the same proportion of Hispanic adolescents as the comparison group. In a sense, matching is equivalent to quota sampling. Matching can also be combined with random assignment. When combined in this way, it is the equivalent of stratified random sampling. Needless to say, matching has the same problems as stratified or quota sampling. You need to ensure that the variables considered are, in fact, key variables. Often, it is difficult to determine the critical variables because of the lack of previous research or other sources of information to guide these decisions.

Matching

Teck-Hong (1992) examined the behavioral characteristics and health conditions of drug abusers in Singapore. The sample consisted of 100 drug abusers and 100 matched nonabuser controls. They were matched on the basis of sex, approximate age, ethnic group, education, and neighborhood.

Cohort Groups

Cohort groups provide another strategy for compiling comparison groups. A variation on matching, cohort groups are composed of individuals who move through an organization at the same time as those in the program being evaluated, but who do not receive the services of the program.

For example, you compare adolescents in the same class at school. Some are enrolled in the program—that is, the birth control class—and others are not; or one entire class is enrolled, and another class is not. Cohort groups can also be combined with matching.

Overflow Comparison

Sometimes people are referred to a program, but because the slots are filled, a waiting list is created. The **overflow comparison group** made up of people on the waiting list can then serve as a comparison group. However comparison groups are formed in the static-group comparison design, they are all nonequivalent—that is, not randomly assigned. This design offers one advantage over single-group designs: The threat from history is eliminated, because external events that may have an effect on the outcome will be occurring in both groups. The static-group comparison design still has other threats to internal and external validity, however.

Threats to Internal Validity

Selection. The major threat to the static-group comparison design's internal validity is selection, which results from not randomly assigning the groups and having no pretest. Consequently, it is not possible to determine how similar the two groups are to each other. Any difference that occurs in the outcome between the two groups may not be due to the presence or absence of the intervention, but to other differences between the groups.

For example, if the experimental group is made up of adolescents who elected to enroll in the birth control classes and the comparison group is made up of adolescents who did not want to attend the classes, the comparison group may be very different from the experimental group. The experimental group may later have greater birth control knowledge than the comparison group, but this may be less a function of the classes than a function of the experimental group's greater motivation to learn about birth control. The equivalency of the groups is not assured because of the absence of random assignment and the lack of a pretest.

Mortality. Because of the absence of a pretest and the absence of a randomly assigned comparison group, mortality is also still a problem with the static-group comparison design.

Threats to External Validity

Selection-treatment interaction. Selection-treatment interaction is a problem with this design.

Reactive effects. Reactive effects threaten the external validity of this design.

Quasi-Experimental Designs

These types of designs eliminate more of the threats to internal validity and can more strongly establish causality.

Time Series Design

A **time series design** overcomes some of the problems of the designs discussed previously, measuring several times before the intervention and then several times after the intervention (Figure 6.6). For example, the adolescents might be tested on their knowledge of birth control several times over the course of several months prior to the classes. Then the same test is given several times after the classes. The test might also be given during the time of the classes.

The advantage of the time series design is its ability to detect trends in the data before and after the intervention. In effect, this discounts the problems of maturation, testing, and instrumentation associated with the single pretest/posttest design because any trends in these effects could be detected. For example, if maturation is having an effect on the adolescents' knowledge of birth control, that effect will be reflected in a difference between the pretest scores.

Threats to Internal Validity

History.   Because of the absence of any type of comparison group, history is a major threat to internal validity in the time series design. Events external to the evaluation would have to be fairly powerful, however, in order to confound the effect of the classes.

Threats to External Validity

History-treatment interaction.   A potential threat to external validity is history-treatment interaction, as history interacts with the classes. An intervention that appears to work under some circumstances may not under others.

Reactive effects.   With repeated testing, reactive effects are also a problem.

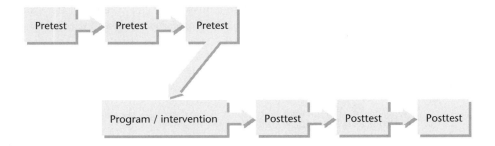

Figure 6.6   **Time series design**

Pretest/Posttest Comparison-Group Design

The **pretest/posttest comparison-group design** is a combination of the static-group comparison and the one-group pretest/posttest design (see Figure 6.7). The comparison group is still not randomly assigned, although this design can adopt any of the various methods used to set up comparison groups that are mentioned for the static-group comparison design. By combining features of both the static-group comparison and the one-group pretest/posttest design, this design becomes less problematic than either of them. History is controlled due to the comparison group, and the pretest identifies, to a certain extent, differences or similarities between the groups.

Threats to Internal Validity

Selection and maturation interaction. In the example, the pretest may indicate that the group that received classes had more knowledge about birth control than the comparison group prior to the intervention. If the posttest also indicates this difference between the groups, maturation may have been the cause of the treatment group's having even greater knowledge over time, whether or not they received the classes. This potential problem with internal validity depends a great deal on how the comparison group is selected and what the results indicate.

Threats to External Validity

Selection-treatment interaction. A potential problem is selection-treatment interaction, which can affect generalizability of the results.

Maturation-treatment interaction. Another potential problem is maturation-treatment interaction.

Reactive effects. Also a problem with the pretest/posttest comparison-group design are reactive effects.

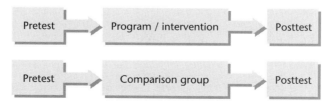

Figure 6.7 ***Pretest/posttest comparison-group design***

A Pretest/Posttest Comparison-Group Design

Riley and Greene (1993) studied the influence of education on self-perceived attitudes about HIV and AIDS among human service providers. Five different groups were studied.

Experimental Designs

These designs result in findings that can make the strongest claim for causality.

Pretest/Posttest Control-Group Design

The difference between the **pretest/posttest control-group design** and the previous design is that the comparison group and experimental groups are randomly assigned. When this occurs, the comparison group is referred to as a **control group** (see Figure 6.8). In the example, random assignment to either the control or experimental group might be made from high-risk students in a high school class. As a result of a randomly assigned control group, the threats to internal validity of history, maturation, mortality, selection, regression to the mean testing, and instrumentation are virtually eliminated.

A Pretest/Posttest Control-Group Design

Goodman (1990) evaluated the impact of a model telephone network program for caregivers of people with Alzheimer's disease. The study looked at caregivers' use of informal supports, perceived social supports, mental health, burden, and information about Alzheimer's disease. Participants were randomly assigned to the program or to an informational lecture series accessed over the telephone. In addition, the researchers combined a matching element along with the random assignment. The caregivers were matched initially for age (under 65 or 65 and older), gender, and relationship to the person with Alzheimer's (adult child, spouse, sibling). Then one of each pair was assigned randomly to the network or lecture component.

Only one potential external validity problem with the pretest/posttest control-group design remains. This involves the possible reactive effect of the pretest.

Despite the strength of this design, there are some difficulties in its implementation. Some of these problems are similar to those encountered in setting

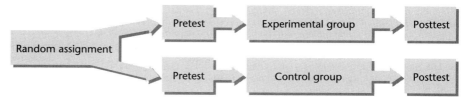

Figure 6.8 **Pretest/posttest control-group design**

up nonrandomly assigned comparison groups, including treatment diffusion and nonavailability of a list or pool of clients from which random assignment can occur. Some ethical issues with this design will be discussed later in this chapter.

Posttest-Only Control-Group Design

One way of eliminating the threat to external validity posed by the previous design is simply to eliminate the pretest. In the **posttest-only control-group design,** the two groups are again randomly assigned and consequently should be equivalent, and there should be no need for the pretests. Some researchers, however, are reluctant to eliminate what is essentially a safety measure to ensure the groups' equivalency.

A Posttest-Only Control-Group Design

Reid and Bailey-Dempsey (1995) examined the effect of monetary incentives on school performance. Teenage girls at risk of school failure were randomly assigned to a control group or to one of two experimental groups: one experimental group offering monetary incentives and the other a case management program. Posttest measures included GPAs and absences.

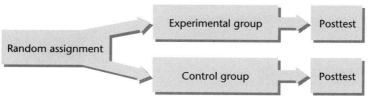

Figure 6.9 **Posttest-only control-group design**

The Solomon Four-Group Design

The **Solomon four-group design** is a combination of the previous two designs and as a result is extremely valid (see Figure 6.10). It is rarely used in social work research, however. It is usually difficult to find enough subjects to assign randomly between two groups, and the cost of the design exceeds the budgets of most social work program evaluations.

A Solomon Four-Group Design

Sawyer and Beck (1991) studied the effects of two types of educational videotapes on the perceived susceptibility of university freshmen to the AIDS virus, HIV. The research design consisted of two experimental conditions with pretests and posttests and two control groups, one with a pretest and a posttest, and one with a posttest only. The addition of the pretest to one of the control groups makes this design different from the four-group design illustrated in Figure 6.10.

The results indicated a significant increase in perceived susceptibility to HIV in the students who viewed the more affective videotape rather than the more cognitive one, particularly in those students who were not yet sexually active.

Table 6.1 summarizes each of the summative group designs and their threats to internal and external validity discussed in this chapter.

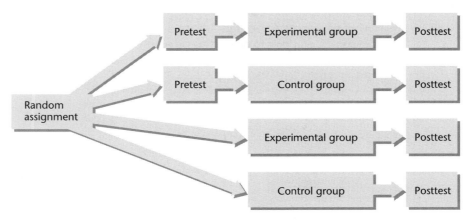

Figure 6.10 **Solomon four-group design**

Table 6.1   **Group research designs—threats to internal and external validity**

Type of design	Threats to internal validity	Threats to external validity
One-group posttest-only	Selection, history, mortality	Selection-treatment interaction, history-treatment interaction
One-group pretest/posttest	History, maturation, testing, instrumentation, regression to mean, interaction of selection, and other threats	History-treatment interaction, reactive effects
Static-group comparison	Selection and mortality	Selection-treatment interaction
Time series	History	History-treatment interaction, reactive effects
Pretest/posttest comparison	Selection and maturation	Selection-treatment interaction, maturation-treatment interaction, reactive effects
Pretest/posttest control-group	None	Reactive effects
Posttest-only control-group	None	None
Solomon four-group	None	None

THE AGENCY AND PROGRAM EVALUATION DESIGN

It should be clear from this chapter that experimental designs with randomly assigned control groups are preferable to use if you are interested in establishing whether a program or intervention, and not some other factor or factors, was responsible for a specific outcome. As generalist social workers, however, you may find that the textbook research examples are not practical, nor are they necessarily preferred. Don't be discouraged if you can't use a Solomon four-group design or, for that matter, random assignment; it may be that one of the other designs will give you the kind of information you need.

The challenge is to develop designs that are *feasible and appropriate for the research question,* and that is why this chapter includes some practical ideas on, for example, alternative ways of setting up comparison groups. Not only are these alternative strategies compatible with agency practice, but if the comparison groups received services or treatments (including simply part of the intervention being provided to the experimental group), many of these strategies become even more feasible and attractive to agencies. This approach is particularly useful with crisis-oriented or court-ordered services.

Another strategy that may result in the greater participation of agencies involves the use of unbalanced designs with fewer subjects assigned to the comparison or control group. Consequently, clients referred to the agency are more likely to receive services (Schilling, Schinke, Kirkham, Meltzer, & Norelius, 1988).

Finally, do not overlook the importance of formative program evaluations. They have an important role to play in the development of programs and should be the evaluation of choice for new programs.

Most important is to acknowledge your design's drawbacks and address them in the reporting of the evaluation. If research is conducted in this practical and responsible way, knowledge building in social work can progress with a solid agency-based foundation.

ETHICAL ISSUES IN PROGRAM EVALUATION DESIGN

Two major ethical issues are related to group design, both of them associated with control or comparison groups. First is the issue of whether establishing a comparison or control group involves denying services to clients. Second is the question whether the subjects' informed consent should be obtained so that a comparison group can be established.

Assignment to the Comparison or Control Group

The NASW Code of Ethics (1997) states that social workers should take appropriate steps to ensure that participants in evaluation and research have access to appropriate supportive services. Participants in the research should always be assured of some services. Whether they will be is an issue when participants are assigned to comparison or control groups.

This research strategy could be viewed as a denial of services, justified in the name of science; it poses an ethical dilemma that can have implications for administration of the evaluation. The personnel may see the creation of comparison or control groups as a way of manipulating clients and could consequently influence the evaluation. For example, in a situation where the comparison group is receiving a variation of the intervention to be evaluated, the staff—if they disagree with the creation of the comparison group—may not adhere to the guidelines governing this variation in an attempt to bring legitimate services to the subjects in the comparison group. In addition, clients simply may not be referred to the project.

Two arguments that use of comparison or control groups does not always pose a serious ethical problem can be made, however. First, the decision about who receives services in an agency is often arbitrary and political. Program services may run on demand, and the deprivation of services is not uncommon.

Second, by suggesting that clients are being denied valuable treatment, we are assuming that the intervention being evaluated is effective. Often, though, that assumption has no empirical basis. In fact, if it did, there would be little reason for carrying out the research in the first place. As in practice, however, the situation in research is often not this clear-cut. Usually some evidence—perhaps a combination of practice wisdom and research findings—indicates that the treatment is helpful to some extent. The purpose of the evaluation is then to determine how helpful it is. Consequently, our concern that we are violating subjects' rights by possibly denying them beneficial treatment involves other factors, such as individual judgments and values about how detrimental the denial could be. This is another example of the important role that values play in the scientific process.

Decisions relating to the establishment of control or comparison groups are probably governed by the seriousness of the problem. Under most circumstances, it would be hard to justify establishing a control group of emotionally disturbed children involved in self-destructive behaviors. In addition, the use of waiting lists and cohort groups, baseline comparison groups, and assignment to other types of interventions or programs can help ameliorate some of the potential ill effects of being assigned to the comparison or control group.

Informed Consent

Informed consent involves informing potential subjects fully of their role and the consequences of their participation in the research and seeking their permission. The NASW Code of Ethics (1997) states:

- Social workers engaged in evaluation or research should obtain voluntary and written informed consent from participants, when appropriate, without any implied or actual deprivation or penalty for refusal to participate; without undue inducement to participate; and with due regard for participants' well-being, privacy, and dignity. Informed consent should include information about the nature, extent, and duration of the participation requested and disclosure of the risks and benefits of participation in the research.

- When evaluation or research participants are incapable of giving informed consent, social workers should provide an appropriate explanation to the participants, obtain the participants' assent to the extent they are able, and obtain written consent from an appropriate proxy.

- Social workers should inform participants of their right to withdraw from evaluation and research at any time without penalty.

Informed consent is an issue, first of all, because of the difficulty of forming comparison groups. In seeking a comparison group, you may be reluctant to fully inform potential participants that they will not be receiving a service. In attempting to ensure their participation, you may justify your failure to inform them on the ground that their consent is not necessary if they are not receiving the service. Informed consent is less of a problem with control groups, in which participants will be randomly assigned to the control and experimental groups and therefore can be told they may or may not be receiving the service. *Consent must be gained at all times for any participation, however*—whether in the experimental group or the comparison or control group.

As discussed in the previous section, the effects of being in the control group can be improved somewhat by adopting alternative strategies—waiting lists, alternative programs, and so forth. These strategies can also help with the consent issue. In other words, the researcher will not be so tempted to avoid seeking informed consent in anticipation of the potential subject's refusing to participate, because ultimately the client will receive some type of intervention. The second issue relating to informed consent is the possibility that informing the subjects of the details of the evaluation will jeopardize the validity of the findings. For example, if the experimental group knows they are the experimental group and the control or comparison group knows that they are the control or comparison group, expectations can be set up that can affect outcomes. The experimental group may expect to change and, regardless of the actual impact of the intervention itself, may show improvement. This threat to validity was discussed earlier in the chapter as a reactive effect. Given the possibility of this threat, it is tempting to avoid giving subjects all the details of their participation. Informed consent should still be obtained, however. One way of dealing with the reactive problem is to inform the subjects that they will either be placed in a control or comparison or in an experimental group, but they will not be told which one in order to protect the validity of the findings. Of course, this is only an option if the control or comparison group is receiving at least some type of intervention, whether it is a variation of the one being evaluated or another intervention completely. If such intervention is not feasible, the researcher needs to acknowledge possible reactive effects rather than not inform the subjects.

HUMAN DIVERSITY ISSUES IN PROGRAM EVALUATION DESIGN

When developing a program evaluation and making decisions about the research design, the major issue relating to human diversity is ensuring that certain groups are not being exploited for the purpose of establishing comparison groups. Sometimes such exploitation can occur unintentionally. In social science research, the tendency is to assign members of disadvantaged groups, such as the poor, minorities, women, and others, to comparison groups. (This is not an issue for control groups when subjects are randomly assigned.)

Parlee (1981) argued that in psychology research (and this argument can be extended to social science research in general), the choice of particular comparison groups demonstrates the scientist's "implicit theoretical framework." She suggested that many of these frameworks are biased against women and that this bias becomes a real problem when we engage in matching. "Knowing" what variables to include entails biases that can favor certain groups over others. The choice of the comparison group defines the perspective that will dominate the research and in turn influence the findings.

Parlee (1981) cited a study in which a matched comparison group of women was sought for a 20-year-old men-only study of aging. One alternative was to match the women according to intelligence, education, and occupation. Another might argue for matching according to physiological similarities, for example, including the men's sisters. The former represented the social scientists' perspective while the latter reflected that of biomedical scientists. Clearly, these two alternatives involved two different perspectives on the causality underlying aging and would probably result in very different conclusions being drawn from the study.

It is critical to recognize this potential bias in comparison group selection. To counterbalance this problem, we should involve diverse people in conceptualizing the research, particularly if the program evaluation will have impacts on diverse populations. In this way, alternative viewpoints and perspectives can be fully incorporated into the group design.

SUMMARY

There are two main types of program evaluation: formative and summative. Formative evaluations are primarily descriptive, whereas summative evaluations focus on causality. When designing summative program evaluations, it is necessary to select a group design. Each design poses various threats to internal and external validity. Internal validity is the extent to which the changes in the dependent variable are a result of the independent variable. External validity refers to the generalizability of the research findings to a wider population. Research designs may have to be modified in agency settings. A design's drawbacks should be acknowledged in reporting the evaluation.

Ethical issues relating to group design include potentially denying services to clients when establishing comparison or control groups and obtaining informed consent from clients. Human diversity issues include not exploiting certain groups for use as comparison groups.

STUDY/EXERCISE QUESTIONS

1. The family service agency in which you are employed is planning to conduct an evaluation of its services. As the leader of a support group of parents of developmentally disabled children, you are asked to design an evaluation of this service.

   a. What design could you develop that would be feasible and would maximize the validity of your findings?

   b. Under what circumstances would a formative evaluation be appropriate and how would you carry this out?

2. Review an issue of *Social Work Research and Abstracts* and select an article that used one of the research designs described in this chapter.
   a. What are the threats to internal and external validity?
   b. Were these threats explicitly discussed?
   c. Propose an alternative design that would be feasible.

FURTHER READING

Cook, T. Q., & Stanley, J. (1963). *Experimental and quasi-experimental designs for research.* Chicago: Rand McNally.
A classic discussion of different research designs.

Fairweather, G. W., & Davidson, W. S. (1986). *An introduction to community experimentation: Theory, methods and practice.* New York: McGraw-Hill.
Specifically written for those involved with the evaluation of community programs.

Patton, M. Q. (1987). *How to use qualitative methods in evaluation.* Newbury Park, CA: Sage.
An excellent sourcebook for designing qualitative evaluations.

REFERENCES

Bailey-Dempsey, C., & Reid, W. J. (1996). Intervention design and development: A case study. *Research on Social Work Practice, 6* (2), 208–228.

Cushman, L. F., Kalmuss, D., & Namerow, P. B. (1993). Placing an infant for adoption: The experiences of young birth mothers. *Social Work, 38* (3), 264–272.

Frecknall, P., & Luks, A. (1992). Evaluation of parental assessment of the big brothers/big sisters program in New York City. *Adolescence, 27* (107), 715–718.

Goodman, C. (1990). Evaluation of a model self-help telephone program: Impact on natural networks. *Social Work, 35,* 556–562.

Itzhaky, H. (1995). Can social work intervention increase organizational effectiveness? *International Social Work, 38,* 277–286.

National Association of Social Workers. (1997). *Code of ethics.* Washington, DC: Author.

Parlee, M. B. (1981). Appropriate control groups in feminist research. *Psychology of Women Quarterly, 5,* 637–644.

Reid, W. J., & Bailey-Dempsey, C. (1995). The Effects of Monetary Incentives on School Performance. *Families in Society, 76* (6), 331–340.

Riley, J. L., & Greene, R. R. (1993). Influence of education on self-perceived attitudes about HIV/AIDS among human services providers. *Social Work, 38* (4), 396–401.

Sawyer, R. G., & Beck, K. H. (1991). Effects of videotapes on perceived susceptibility to HIV/AIDS among university freshmen. *Health Values, 15,* 31–40.

Schilling, R. F., Schinke, S. P., Kirkham, M. A., Meltzer, N. J., & Norelius, K. L. (1988). Social work research in social service agencies: Issues and guidelines. *Journal of Social Service Research, 11* (4), 75–87.

Siegel, D. H. (1993). Open Adoption of Infants: Adoptive Parents' Perceptions of Advantages and Disadvantages. *Social Work, 38* (1), 15–23.

Teck-Hong, O. (1992). Behavioral characteristics and health conditions of drug abusers: some implications for workers in drug addiction. *International Social Work, 35,* 7–17.

Designing the Evaluation of Practice

During the last 20 years, social workers have experienced increased pressure to evaluate their own practice. In part, this pressure stems from studies done in the 1960s and early 1970s, which suggested that social work practice was not as effective as many had expected (Fischer, 1973). On closer examination, the research studies themselves were found to have major methodological problems, raising questions about whether the findings from the studies should be viewed seriously and as an accurate reflection of the state of social work practice. First, the research studies often used no type of comparison group, which led to questions about the internal and external validity of the results. Second, because group designs used in program evaluations pooled the results from both successful and unsuccessful programs in order to determine average results, they were not able to determine what actually worked with whom and with what kinds of problems. Consequently, the results were often of little use to the practitioner. Third, the group designs generally relied on only two measures—one before the intervention and one after the intervention. There was no way of knowing what happened between these two measurement points. For example, a posttest may indicate that the target problem has not decreased in severity. It is possible, however, that at some point after the intervention but before the posttest, some decrease did occur. It could not be determined whether and why such an effect had occurred because of the way many of these studies were designed.

In addition to these methodological problems, other problems relating to ethical and social issues characterized these early studies. First, it was and is often difficult to get the support of agency personnel in assigning clients to control or comparison groups because of the ethical issues discussed in Chapter 6. Second, it was and is also often difficult to impossible for agencies to come up with the funds for a full-scale evaluation of even a moderate-sized program.

As a consequence of these problems and the continuing demand for accountability of the social services, social workers were increasingly required to evaluate their own practice. Different ways of implementing these evaluations emerged. At first, emphasis was on an approach adopted from psychology, a technology known as **single-system** or **single-subject studies.** These types of studies tried to assess the impact of interventions with client systems. Single-system designs relied heavily on the collection of empirical behavioral data and were grounded in the positivist tradition. They grew in popularity as they produced results identifying specific interventions and their effectiveness with specific clients with specific types of problems. An examination of the full range of single-system designs can be found in works such as Barlow and Hersen (1984) and Bloom, Fischer, and Orme (1995).

Later, after single-system designs were taught in departments and schools of social work, it was disclosed that many graduates tended not to use the single-system technology in their practice (Siegel, 1985). Reasons included the single-system design's perceived limited applicability to different interventions and target behaviors, and its lack of congruence with the realities of social work practice (Kagle, 1982). Alternative approaches to evaluating practice began to emerge. Instead of the single-system design approach of assessing the impact of interventions on client systems (that is, explanatory designs), descriptive methods were developed to monitor client progress and to monitor the intervention. Many of these methods used interpretive and qualitative approaches, differing significantly from the positivist approaches associated with single-system studies.

These new ways of evaluating practice give the social worker choices about which approach to use. As stressed in Chapter 1 and throughout this book, the choice in part depends upon the question being asked. Practice evaluation involves three major questions. First, how can the intervention be described? Second, how can the client's progress be monitored? Third, how effective is the intervention in bringing about client change? The first two questions are primarily descriptive, whereas the third is explanatory. Different types of descriptive and explanatory designs will be presented in this chapter.

This chapter will discuss the following:

- descriptive designs for evaluating practice
- explanatory designs for evaluating practice
- the agency and practice evaluation
- ethical issues in practice evaluation
- human diversity issues in practice evaluation

DESCRIPTIVE DESIGNS FOR PRACTICE EVALUATION

As just discussed, two types of questions in practice evaluation require descriptive designs: questions that focus on the nature of the intervention and questions that focus on monitoring any client change. Each of these will be presented in this section.

Monitoring Interventions

Often it is important to examine and reflect on the intervention being used; this is referred to as **monitoring interventions.** Evaluation then becomes a process of discovery rather than an experiment (as with a formative as opposed to a summative program evaluation). As a student social worker, you may be asked to evaluate how you are applying an intervention and to describe your activities to your supervisor. You can use various strategies to evaluate an intervention. Three methods can be used to monitor interventions: process recordings, practice logs, and case studies.

Process Recordings

Process recordings are written records based on notes or on a transcription of a recording (audio or video) of interactions between the worker and clients. These qualitative data then become an important source of information for improving practice.

Suppose you are just beginning your employment with Child Protective Services, and your supervisor has given you the go-ahead to visit a family alone. You are still unsure about whether you are conducting the interview appropriately, however. Consequently, immediately after the home visit you sit down and record the major interactions that occurred. You later share this process recording with your supervisor. This process can help identify the strengths and weaknesses in your interviewing skills; if you continue this type of monitoring for several cases, you may see patterns emerging.

Practice Logs

A variation on the process recording is an ongoing **practice log,** using self-reflection and analysis to understand how you and the client worked together in resolving issues raised. Papell and Skolnick (1992) discuss how practitioners' self-reflection can add to their understanding of practice. Practice logs go beyond a process recording in that the writer self-reflects and comments on his or her use of the intervention and the experience of practice. Practice logs are often required of students in their field practica. As a form of data collection, these will be discussed in Chapter 9.

Reflecting on Practice

Millstein (1993) cited Cook (1992):

> I have read through my logs. I like to read what I write, although I'm conscious of its being a point in time and I have moved beyond wherever I was. I am seeing my process unfold . . . a search for my own practice; a concern for fitting into my organization; a couple of forays into questions about what a family worker does and how to introduce myself to a patient; and finally a sense of method to reach a question. (p. 268)

For example, say you are involved in trying to organize a community center for youths but have never tackled anything like this before. Consequently, you carefully record all your activities, impressions, and thoughts connected with this endeavor, and you share this information with a more experienced community organizer whom you met at a NASW chapter conference the previous year. In this situation, rather than having to rely on anecdotes and your memory, your practice log gives you a systematic record of what occurred. This record can provide potential data for a more explanatory design you might want to attempt at a later date, in which you try to determine whether your strategy actually had the anticipated outcomes.

These types of evaluations are rarely published, since they are used primarily by individual workers and within agencies in order to enhance practice.

Case Studies

Case studies involve a more complete description of the application of the intervention, and tend to be more "objective" and less self-reflecting than the process recordings or practice log approaches. Detailed case studies of unusual cases, successful cases, or unsuccessful cases can yield some vital information. The type of information generated may either support existing practice principles or suggest new approaches and principles. Single case or multiple case studies can be used.

A Case Study: Support of Practice Principles

Burman and Allen-Meares (1994) presented a case study of two children who witnessed their mother being murdered by their father. The authors described how theories of psychosocial development and social learning guided the assessment and intervention phases. Behavioral and family intervention practices are also described. There is further discussion about the potential intergenerational cycle of violence and a sociocultural perspective on family violence within an ecological framework.

Multiple Case Studies: Suggestions for Innovations in Practice

Petr (1994) used nine case studies of families with children with serious emotional and behavioral disorders to examine placement-threatening crises. The findings suggested that placement prevention programs be reevaluated emphasizing the importance of informal support systems, long-standing family supports, and professionals' attitudes, as well as the role of medications.

One major advantage of monitoring interventions using any one of the three approaches described here is that it provides a means for practitioners to reflect on and study their own practice. The reflective method "would encourage practitioners to examine professional activity and the knowledge reflected in that activity against empirically-based theory as well as against their practice wisdom and tacit knowledge, using a range of methodologies." (Millstein, 1993, p. 257).

Monitoring Client Progress

Not only can you monitor an intervention, but also the client's progress. Information is gathered on the client while the intervention is taking place. As a result, decisions can be made as to whether the intervention should be continued, modified, or stopped. These data can be either qualitative, in the form of notes and narrative, or quantitative, in the form of behavioral observations or the different rapid assessment instruments described in Chapter 9, including target problem scales. Whichever data collection method is used, client goals must be clearly specified. Blythe and Tripodi (1989) make a useful distinction among three general types of goals in direct practice: change, maintenance, and prevention.

For example, in working with a group of adolescent mothers you may decide to monitor the clients' progress both during the months when the groups are held and after they stop. The change goal was to learn parenting skills, the maintenance goal was to practice those skills, and the prevention goal was to avoid future reporting for child abuse or neglect. The goals were monitored monthly for two years.

This type of practice evaluation is rarely published, although it is an extremely important strategy for evaluating practice as an ongoing activity. Often, the information gained from descriptive evaluations of individual practice can help to formulate hypotheses for future evaluations of our own practice. Consequently, descriptive studies can be viewed as an inductive mode of knowledge building (as discussed in Chapter 1).

EXPLANATORY DESIGNS FOR PRACTICE EVALUATION

Explanatory designs examine the impact of the intervention on the target behavior. These designs are now also called single-system studies or single-system designs. They involve three elements that help establish causality: a baseline, clear identification of the intervention, and target behaviors that can be operationalized and repeatedly measured.

Baseline

Rather than depending on control or comparison groups in their search for causality, single-system designs rely on the target behavior's being measured time and time again. In effect, the client system serves as its own control. A similar principle is in effect here as that used in the time series designs discussed in Chapter 6; with that group design, however, a group of client systems is monitored, whereas the single-system study monitors only one client system. The repeated measurement prior to the intervention is known as the **baseline.** The baseline allows you to compare target behavior rates before and after the intervention, thus allowing you to assess the impact of the intervention on the target behavior. Figure 7.1 demonstrates how results from explanatory single-system designs are usually displayed. The X axis records the incidents of the target behavior, and the Y axis shows the time interval over which the behavior is recorded. The vertical line represents the point at which the intervention was introduced.

For the assessment to have some validity, a stable baseline is needed prior to the implementation of the intervention. This consists of an observable pattern between the data points. Fluctuations may occur, but as long as they occur with some regularity this should constitute a stable baseline. An unstable baseline makes it difficult to interpret the study's results. A problem with interpreting the findings also occurs when the baseline is stable but is moving in the direction of the desired outcome prior to implementation of the intervention.

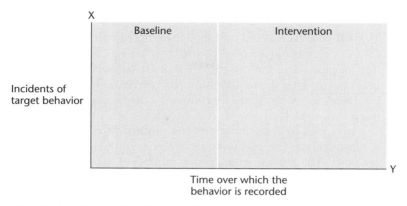

Figure 7.1   ***Displaying the results from explanatory single-system designs***

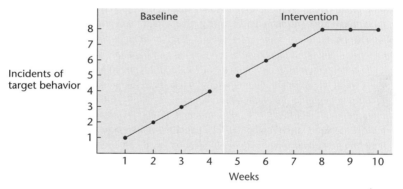

Figure 7.2   ***Example of a baseline moving the direction of the desired outcome***

Clearly Defined Intervention

Explanatory designs also require a clearly defined intervention, and the point at which it is introduced must be clearly presented.

Operationalization and Repeated Measure of Target Behavior

Explanatory designs also require that the target behaviors that are the focus of the intervention be clearly defined. For example, rather than a target behavior's being defined as a child's inattentiveness, a clearer definition would be the number of times a question is repeated to a child before he or she answers. In addition to being clearly defined, data about the target behavior need to be collected repeatedly.

Different types of explanatory designs will now be presented.

AB Design

The **AB design** is the simplest of the single-system designs. Data are collected on the target behavior prior to the intervention, and this constitutes the baseline, or phase A of the design. The B phase consists of measurements of the target behavior after the intervention has been introduced. The effectiveness of the intervention is determined by comparing the A measure of the target behavior to the B measure.

Let's look at a case in which the problem is a family's low attendance at a parenting class. The goal or target behavior of the intervention is to increase attendance. The A phase would be the number of times the family attends the class prior to the intervention. The class is held twice a week, and data are already available on the family's attendance over the previous three weeks. These data can be used as a baseline.

The point at which the intervention is introduced marks the beginning of the B phase. The intervention in this case might be to arrange for another family to help with transportation to the class. The frequency of the target behavior is then recorded for several weeks after intervention. An illustration of how these data might look if charted is given in Figure 7.3. The results can be analyzed by simply viewing the chart. An increase in attendance is clearly evident.

An AB Design

Slonim-Nevo and Vosler (1991) used an AB design to discuss the use of single-system designs with brief problem-solving systemic therapy. The case involved a woman who was experiencing constant jealousy over the relationship her husband had with his first wife. The authors developed a scale to measure the intensity of this obsession. After three weeks of baseline, an intervention was implemented using brief problem-solving therapy. An AB design was used in evaluating the impact of the intervention.

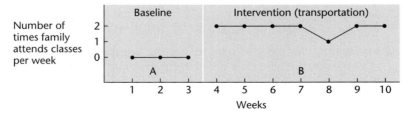

Figure 7.3   ***Example of an AB design***

One of the advantages of the AB design is its simplicity. In addition, the design can easily be integrated into the practice process, giving important information about those interventions that appear to work with particular client systems.

Some problems are associated with this design, however. The major problem is that you do not have any control over extraneous factors or the history threat to internal validity. In our example, it was possible that the classes suddenly became more interesting to the family or that the mother had convinced the father, who was exhibiting the most resistance to attending, of the benefits of the class. Or the results might have been due to a multitude of other factors. Thus the AB design is restricted in the information it can give about causality.

ABC Design

The **ABC design** is also known as the **successive intervention design** because the C phase represents the introduction of another intervention. Others can also be added on as D or E phases. The ABC design is simply the AB design with the addition of another intervention. With this design, the target behavior continues to be measured after the introduction of each intervention.

The ABC design can be convenient in that it often reflects the reality of practice. We introduce one intervention, and if it seems ineffective, we implement another intervention. The ABC design adds an empirical element to this common practice.

To continue with the example we have been using, transportation assistance did not increase attendance for another family. After further assessment it was found that the parents—although English-speaking—were native Spanish speakers and were having difficulty following the class. Consequently, a second intervention was the organization of a Spanish-speaking class for a number of Spanish-speaking families in the community. The families' attendance was monitored following this intervention and showed an increase.

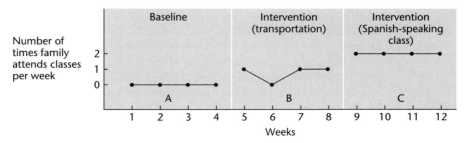

Figure 7.4   *ABC single-system design*

Although the ABC design nicely reflects the reality of practice, this design has the same types of problems associated with the AB design. You have no way of knowing whether the intervention or some other factor accounted for any change in the target behavior. This validity issue is complicated in the ABC design by not knowing whether it was the C intervention that resulted in the final outcome or a combination of the B and C interventions. Although you may not know specifically which intervention influenced the outcome, you do know about the effect of some combination of the interventions—a finding that in itself can enhance your practice and service to clients.

An ABC Design

Kazi and Wilson (1996) presented several examples of single-case evaluations from a project in Great Britain to train and encourage social workers to apply this type of evaluation to their practice.

One is a modification of the ABC design. The A B BC C design collected data on a 15-year-old's school attendance and the mother's feelings about her relationship with her daughter. Intervention B was weekly counseling sessions with the grandmother, the mother, the 15-year-old, and her boyfriend. These sessions did not improve school attendance although the mother's feelings about the relationship did improve. When intervention C was added to B (positive encouragement from teachers) both dependent variables improved and remained stable for the C phase.

ABAB Design

The **ABAB design** is also known as the **reversal design** or **withdrawal design;** it consists of implementing the AB design and then reversing—withdrawing the intervention and collecting baseline data again before implementing the intervention a second time. Suppose a school social worker works constantly with the problem of absenteeism. In the past, she has made regular home visits to the families involved, and she has a sense that this is working. She decides to test the intervention, starting with one case, that of a 12-year-old boy. The social worker monitors his attendance at school over a three-week period and then starts the home visits, which include counseling, information, and referral, twice a week. She collects data on attendance for another three weeks and then stops the visits, again monitoring attendance, for another three weeks. Finally, she once again introduces the intervention. The results, displayed in Figure 7.5, indicate that the intervention appears to have some impact on the student's school attendance.

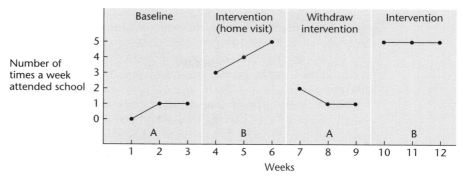

| | Baseline | Intervention (home visit) | Withdraw intervention | Intervention |

Number of times a week attended school

Weeks

Figure 7.5   **ABAB—reversal single-system design**

An ABAB Reversal Design

Dugan, Kamps, Leonard, Watkins, Rheinberger, and Stackhaus (1995) investigated the use of cooperative learning groups as a strategy for integrating two students with autism into a fourth grade class.

The baseline was 40 minutes of teacher-led sessions including lecture, questions and discussion, and the use of maps. The intervention was 10 minutes of the teacher's introducing the material followed by cooperative learning groups that included tutoring on key words and facts, a team activity, and wrap-up and review with the entire class.

The ABAB design showed increases for target students and peers in their scores on weekly pretests and posttests, academic engagement during sessions, and student interaction during the intervention.

The great advantage of the ABAB design is its ability to tell us about the impact of the intervention versus the impact of other possible factors; in other words, its ability to explain and imply causality is greater than the AB or the ABC designs.

The ABAB design does have a few problems, though. First, it cannot be applied to all target behaviors and all types of intervention. Some interventions cannot be reversed, particularly those that involve teaching a new behavior. For example, suppose you identify the target behavior as a second grader's tardiness, and you assess the problem as resulting from the mother's not being assertive with the child about getting ready for school. The intervention consists of the social worker's teaching the parent how to be assertive with the child. This would be a difficult intervention to reverse, since the mother's learned behavior could not be reversed.

Even if the intervention seemingly could be reversed, some residues of the intervention might remain. In the example of the 12-year-old boy's absenteeism, the home visits might have resulted in some carryover effects even after they were halted; in fact, this seems to have been the case. The interpretation of the results, as well as the precise impact of the intervention, then becomes more difficult.

With any explanatory single-system study, and particularly with the reversal design, you must spell out the details and possible consequences for the clients before the intervention is instituted. This procedure is similar to obtaining clients' informed consent prior to engaging in a group study.

Multiple Baseline Designs

A **multiple baseline design** involves replicating the AB design by applying the same intervention to two or more target behaviors, to two or more clients, or in two or more settings at different points in time. For example, a child is exhibiting problems at school; the target problem is identified as the teacher's concern that the child is not verbally participating in class. After assessment, it becomes apparent that this behavior is associated with the child's Navajo cultural background, which discourages speaking out. Intervention consists of discussion with the teacher about cross-cultural issues, including suggesting that she use some Navajo examples in teaching. This intervention could be tested *across client systems* by using the intervention with three different Navajo children. Alternatively, the intervention could be used *across target problems,* in which additional problems such as low grades and low socialization might be identified. These behaviors could be monitored before and after the implementation of the intervention. The intervention could also be tested *across settings* by, for example, looking at changes in one of the target problems in the day care center and at home in addition to the school setting. Figure 7.6 shows how data from a multiple baseline design might be displayed.

The multiple baseline design offers a great deal of potential for examining the effectiveness of particular interventions and can allow us to be more confident in our belief that the intervention was responsible for any measured change. In effect, the multiple baseline design involves the principle of comparison groups in group design, using either another client, another setting, or another target problem as a comparison. For example, if you find that the same intervention for the same target problem for the same setting was effective for two different clients, you would be more certain of the intervention's effectiveness than if you had simply looked at one client.

Nevertheless, there are some limitations on the extent to which you can hold the intervention responsible for any change in the target problem even with these designs. For example, when applying the multiple baseline design across clients, even if the change in the target problem resulted in a positive outcome for both clients, there is still no guarantee that it was the intervention and the intervention alone that resulted in the specific outcome. In fact, the validity

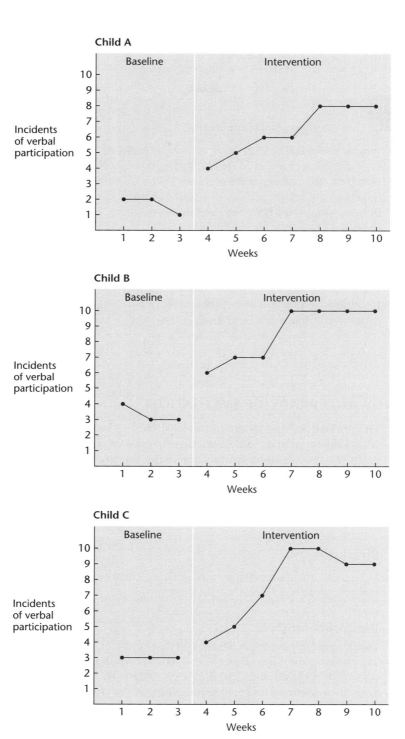

Figure 7.6   **Multiple baseline design**   123

limitations are similar to those associated with many of the nonexperimental designs discussed in Chapter 6.

 A Multiple Baseline Design

Warzak and Page (1990) used a multiple baseline design across behaviors to evaluate the acquisition of refusal skills by two developmentally disabled adolescent girls. The behaviors included eye contact, verbal refusal, specific statements regarding the unacceptability of sexual behavior, and leaving the situation. These behaviors were clearly defined and operationalized. The intervention consisted of using the behavioral techniques of rationale, modeling, rehearsal, feedback, and reinforcement. Baseline rates were low, and high frequencies of target behavior were observed as each behavior became the focus of training. The authors concluded that the girls' refusal skills were improved as a function of the training. See Figure 7.7 for the results of one of the girls. (This figure has been modified; unlike the authors' figure, it does not distinguish between behaviors demonstrated at the beginning of the session and those at the end.)

THE AGENCY AND PRACTICE EVALUATION

The evaluation of individual practice should of course, be extremely compatible with agency settings, although there seems to be some disagreement on this point. Much has been written about the relative strengths and limitations of practice evaluations and specific designs and about their applicability to practice and agency settings. A good overview is presented in an article by Corcoran (1993). These strengths and limitations follow.

Strengths

Strengths include feedback to the client, knowledge building for practice, and low cost and time factors.

Feedback to the Client

One benefit of practice evaluation is that feedback can be provided to the client. The intervention-monitoring and client-monitoring designs provide consistent feedback, and with single-system designs the client is provided with some tangible evidence that the intervention does or does not appear to have an impact on behavior. Feedback can result in longer-term effects and the clients' adopting self-help measures, avoiding further social work intervention.

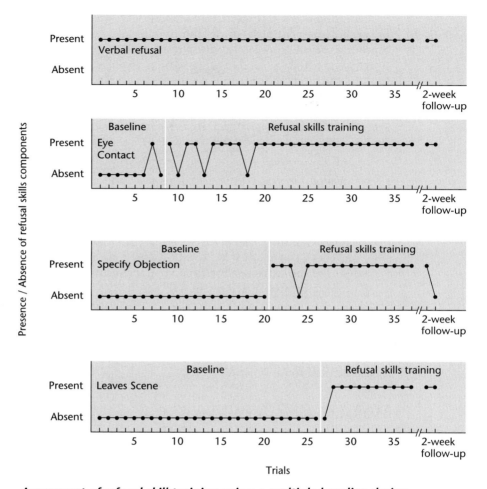

Figure 7.7   ***Assessment of refusal skill training using a multiple baseline design***

Source: Adapted from "Teaching Refusal Skills to Sexually Active Adolescents," by W. J. Warzak & T. J. Page, 1990, *Journal of Behavior Therapy and Experimental Psychology, 21,* p. 137. Copyright © 1990 with kind permission from Elsevier Science Ltd., The Boulevard, Langford Lane, Kidlington OX5 1GB, UK.

Knowledge Building for Practice

The activity of monitoring interventions or client progress can enhance workers' knowledge of their practice, by allowing workers to critically examine the values and assumptions underlying the use of theories and their associated interventions in practice. Questions that are critical in developing a knowledge of practice include these (Millstern, 1993): Am I doing what I think I'm doing? If not, what am I doing? What does my work tell me about how I make meaning of practice? What ways of knowing do I use?

The single-system explanatory studies offer information about the efficacy of specific interventions. Further information can be obtained by replicating or repeating the single-system studies—testing interventions with other clients, on other target behaviors, and in other settings. Replication increases internal validity (it is the intervention and not something else that is affecting the outcome) and external validity (the results are generalizable to a wider population).

Knowledge can be built through single-system studies by integrating single-system and group approaches in evaluating program effectiveness (Briar & Blythe, 1985). Berbenishty (1989) provided an example:

> The basic building blocks of the advocated methodology are single-case evaluation, intentionally designed, selected, and combined to form an assessment on the agency level. For each intervention, data on the characteristics of treatment, therapist, problem, and client are collected. These data from each single-case study are then aggregated to access the overall effectiveness of the group of cases. Further, in order to assess differential effectiveness, subgroups were identified and compared (as to their relative improvement), or certain background or treatment characteristics are correlated with outcome measures. (p. 33)

Time and Cost

Unlike group studies, which often require additional funds, evaluation of individual practice can be easily incorporated into practice with no extra expense or excessive time commitment.

Limitations

Evaluation of individual practice, then, offers some advantages in agency settings, but some arguments are also made against use of such evaluations in agencies. They do possess some limitations, including limited application, limited validity, and limited data analysis.

Limited Application

Historically, single-system explanatory designs were used almost exclusively for testing the effectiveness of behavioral intervention techniques. In part, their application was limited because of the emphasis in behavior theory on being able to define behaviors clearly so that any changes in the behaviors can be easily recorded. Many social workers, including generalist social workers, are deterred from using single-system studies because they have assumed the design is appropriate only for behavioral intervention and clearly observable and recordable behaviors. Designs that monitor intervention and client progress, however, can be used with a variety of different interventions and target behaviors.

In addition, some designs such as the withdrawal and multiple baseline designs, are often simply not practical. It is rarely possible to withdraw an intervention. Finally, often it is difficult to select a design when just beginning to work with a client; instead, designs are determined as practice evolves (Blythe and Rodgers, 1993). This is less of a problem with the monitoring designs described in this chapter, which are sensitive to the process of practice.

Limited Validity

Internal and external validity are a problem with the explanatory single-system designs, even when results are replicated. Single-system studies simply are not as valid as well-designed group designs used in program evaluations. As discussed in Chapter 6, however, well-designed group studies are rare. More often, less satisfactory designs (in terms of causality) are used, resulting again in internal and external validity problems. Consequently, in many instances single-system studies can be thought of as no worse in terms of validity than many group designs and certainly better than no design at all.

Another validity issue is the extent to which the use of self-report instruments, designed to measure subjective aspects of the client's problems, actually result in therapeutic reactive effects. Some claim that these effects are minimal (Applegate, 1992).

Analysis of Results

Another potential drawback of evaluating practice in agencies is that the analysis of findings is largely a matter of judgment, so that their applicability is limited. Some statistical analyses can be carried out for single-system designs, and these will be discussed in Chapters 12 and 13. As Schuerman (1983) pointed out, however, all these techniques have limitations: "Some require that we make assumptions about the data that are often not reasonable. Others are quite complicated mathematically and in addition require that we have many observations in each phase" (p. 57). Nevertheless, these statistical approaches do extend the evidence regarding the relative effectiveness of different interventions beyond judgment.

These criticisms focus on inferences about causality that can be made from evaluations. With the descriptive designs, analysis can be quite straightforward, particularly when monitoring client progress using quantitative measures.

ETHICAL ISSUES IN PRACTICE EVALUATION

Issues relevant to other types of social work practice are obviously applicable here, such as issues about confidentiality and informed consent, but two other ethical issues specifically relate to practice evaluation: the use of the reversal design and the issue of the interference with practice.

Reversal Design Issues

One could argue that withdrawing an apparently effective intervention, as we discussed in the reversal design section, is unethical. The counterargument is that withdrawal of the intervention will allow us to determine whether the intervention is responsible for any change in the target problem. This determination not only enhances the worker's knowledge of the intervention's effectiveness but also demonstrates its effectiveness to the client. As a result, the intervention may have a longer effect; parent training is a good example.

Interference with Practice

The second issue—the idea that practice evaluation procedures interfere with practice—has been raised consistently over the years. One response to this position is that practice evaluation studies can enhance practice and help direct and inform social workers in their day-to-day contact with client systems. For example, determining the data collection method may offer opportunities for other insights and further exploration with the clients regarding the target problem. In addition, the client's involvement in the research, particularly in the data collection, can result in the client's being engaged in the change process to a greater extent, simultaneously limiting the problem with confidentiality and informed consent. This effect constitutes not so much an interference with as an enhancement of practice.

Berlin (1983) provided an excellent example of a practice evaluation that demonstrated how "it is possible to keep the obligations of practice central, systematically assess the extent of change in the client's problem, and become a more sensitive, knowledgeable, credible practitioner in the process" (p. 251). In addition, the client- and intervention-monitoring designs offer no interference at all.

In conclusion, because of the joint participation of worker and client in several of the methods used in this chapter, ethical violations are far less likely than in group designs for program evaluations.

HUMAN DIVERSITY ISSUES IN PRACTICE EVALUATION

Throughout the process of evaluating individual practice, you need to pay attention to human diversity issues. This effort includes carrying out more studies on diverse clients, recognizing that what may be effective for one type of client is not necessarily effective for another. In fact, practice evaluations provide an excellent opportunity for exploring the richness of human diversity.

SUMMARY

There are two major approaches to evaluating practice: descriptive and explanatory. Descriptive methods include monitoring interventions and monitoring client progress. Explanatory approaches, or single-system designs, include the AB design, the ABC design, the ABAB design (reversal), and the multiple baseline design. The evaluation of individual practice in agency settings is advantageous because of the opportunity for direct client feedback, knowledge building for practice, and time and cost factors. Some problems are also associated with the evaluations, however, including limited analysis, limited validity, and limited application. Because of the partnership required between client and worker, ethical violations are less likely than with group design. Evaluations of individual practice offer many opportunities for exploring the great diversity among different groups.

STUDY/EXERCISE QUESTIONS

1. You are working with a family with an adolescent who is not attending school regularly. You want to evaluate your intervention with the adolescent and will collect data on her school attendance. What would be the advantages and disadvantages of the following designs for this evaluation?
   a. AB design
   b. ABC design
   c. ABAB design
   What would be the ethical issues in this case?

2. You would like to evaluate your practice as a generalist social worker in a hospital, but your supervisor objects, saying it would be too time consuming. Support your request and address her concerns.

3. Find an article in a social work journal that examines practice evaluation. Summarize the main points.

4. You have been facilitating a support group for teenage parents. The goal is for the group to continue without a facilitator. You will be monitoring attendance at the group as an indicator of its effectiveness. How would you do this?

5. Your supervisor asks you to monitor your practice focusing on the interventions you use. How would you do this?

FURTHER READING

Alter, C., & Evens, W. (1990). *Evaluating your practice: A guide to self-assessment.* New York: Springer.
   Useful to the generalist social worker because the authors apply single-system technology to different-sized systems, from communities to individuals.

Barlow, D. H., & Hersen, M. (1984). *Single case experimental designs: Strategies for studying behavioral change.* New York: Pergamon Press.
   A more technical book on single-system studies; a good reference.

Bloom, M., Fischer, J., & Orme, J. (1995). *Evaluating practice: Guidelines for the accountable professional* (2nd ed.). Englewood Cliffs, NJ: Prentice Hall.
   A thorough guide to single-system designs; emphasizes how the roles of researcher and practitioner can be combined.

Blythe, B., Tripodi, T., & Briar, S. (1994). *Direct practice research in human service agencies.* New York: Columbia University Press.
An excellent discussion and description of the different approaches to practice evaluation.

REFERENCES

Applegate, J. S. (1992). The Impact of Subjective Measures on Nonbehavioral Practice Research: Outcome vs. Process. *Families in Society: The Journal of Contemporary Human Services,* 100–108.

Berbenishty, R. (1989). Combining the single-system and group approaches to evaluate treatment effectiveness on the agency level. *Journal of Social Service Research, 12,* 31–48.

Berlin, S. (1983). Single-case evaluation: Another version. *Social Work Research and Abstracts, 19,* 3–11.

Bloom, M., Fischer, J., & Orme, J. (1995). *Evaluating practice: Guidelines for the accountable professional* (2nd ed.). Englewood Cliffs, NJ: Prentice Hall.

Briar, S., & Blythe, B. (1985). Agency support for evaluating the outcomes of social work services. *Administration in Social Work, 9,* 25–36.

Burman, S., & Allen-Meares, P. (1994). Neglected Victims of Murder: Children's Witness to Parental Homicide. *Social Work, 39* (1), 28–34.

Blythe, B., & Tripodi, T. (1989). *Measurements in Direct Practice.* Newbury Park, CA: Sage.

Blythe, B.J., & Rodgers, A. Y. (1993). Evaluating Our Own Practice: Past, Present, and Future Trends. *Single-System Designs in the Social Services.* 101–119.

Corcoran, K. J. (1993). Practice evaluation: Problems and promises of single-system designs in clinical practice. *Journal of Social Service Research, 18* (1/2), 147–159.

Cook, J. (1992). *Dilemma log.* Unpublished research assignment. Boston: Simmons College School of Social Work.

Dugan, E., Kamps, D., Leonard, B., Waskins, N., Rheinberger, A., and Stackhaus, J. (1995). Effects of cooperative learning groups during social studies for students with autism and fourth-grade peers. *Journal of Applied Behavior Analysis, 28,* 175–188.

Fischer, J. (1973). Is casework effective? A review. *Social Work, 18,* 5–20.

Kagle, J. D. (1982). Using single subject measures in practice decisions: Systematic documentation or distortion. *Aretê, 7* (2), 1–9.

Kazi, M. A., & Wilson, A. F. (1996). Applying single-case evaluation methodology in a British social work agency. *Research on Social Work Practice, 6* (1), 5–26.

Milstein, K. H. (1993). Building knowledge from the study of cases: a reflective model for practitioner self-evaluation. *Journal of Teaching, 8* (1/2), 255–277.

Papell, C. P., & Skolnick, L. (1992). The reflective practitioner: A comtemporary paradigm's relevance for social work education. *Journal of Social Work Education, 28* (1), 18–26.

Petr, C. G. (1994). Crises That Threaten Out-of-Home Placement of Children with Emotional and Behavioral Disorders. *Families in Society, 75* (4), 195–203.

Schuerman, J. R. (1983). *Research and evaluation in the human services.* New York: Free Press.

Siegel, D. (1985). Defining empirically based practice. *Social Work, 29,* 325–331.

Slonim-Nevo, V., & Vosler, N. (1991). The use of single-system design with systemic brief problem-solving therapy. *Families in Society: The Journal of Contemporary Human Services, 72,* 38–44.

Warzak, W. J., & Page, T. J. (1990). Teaching refusal skills to sexually active adolescents. *Journal of Behavior Therapy and Experimental Psychology, 12,* 133–139.

Selecting the Participants in the Research

N ow that you've decided on your research question and the type of design you will be using, who are going to be the participants in your research? In social work research, **sampling** involves determining who will be the participants in the study. Sampling is necessary because you usually cannot include everyone in the study, just as in practice you cannot interview or meet with all those involved. For example, you may be interested in determining the need for an afterschool program in your community, and you must identify and get opinions from all the families in the city who have school-age children 12 and under. Even in a small-sized city, this could be a large number of families, and you have a limited budget and only two months in which to complete the project. Consequently, you need to select a smaller group of participants, or **sample,** from this large group, or **population,** that is made up of all possible cases that you are ultimately interested in studying.

Sampling should be a familiar concept to you as generalist social workers. You often need to collect information relating to a target problem from a large number of people. When, due to time and other constraints, you cannot contact all of the relevant people, you select a sample. In research, there are specific ways to select a sample; the particular method we use depends on the nature and accessibility of the population and the type and purpose of the study we are undertaking.

Again, as with the steps of the research process already discussed, you may not be directly involved in sampling decisions. Knowledge of the process is essential, however, for two reasons: First, sometimes you will be involved in the sampling decision; second, you need to understand how sampling can affect use of the research findings in your practice.

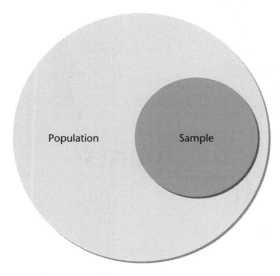

Figure 8.1   ***Population and sample***

This chapter will discuss the following:

- key concepts in sampling
- types of sampling methods
- sample size
- the agency and sampling
- ethical issues in sampling
- human diversity issues in sampling

KEY CONCEPTS IN SAMPLING

One of the key concepts of sampling is the extent to which the sample is representative of the population. A **representative sample** means that the sample has the same distribution of characteristics as the population from which it is selected. For example, in assessing the city's need for an afterschool program, you are interested in making statements applicable to the entire city, so your sample needs to be representative. Thus in this case it is important that the sample not be biased in any way. One way bias occurs is if only one neighborhood is selected. Neighborhoods tend to have specific socioeconomic and ethnic characteristics—for example, upper-middle-class suburbs, Hispanic barrios, retirement communities. As a result, they are not usually representative of the entire city population, at least not in terms of socioeconomic and ethnic structure. Neighborhood is only one example of possible bias. Other groupings, such as schools and churches, also may not be representative of the larger community.

If your sample is representative of the population, then you can generalize the findings from your sample to that population. When you **generalize,** you claim that the findings from studying the sample can be applied to the population. If you discover in your representative sample of families from your city that 70% express an urgent need for an afterschool program, you then generalize that 70% of the families in your city (that is, your population) will also express this need. In needs assessment studies such as this, it is critical that you are able to generalize your findings. Thus a positivist approach, which emphasizes generalizability of the findings, is taken when conducting many needs assessments.

In other studies, however, generalizability and representativeness are not such important issues. For example, rather than looking at the extent of need for an afterschool program, you instead might be concerned with exploring the experiences of families with children who spend part of the day unsupervised. Here you might use an interpretive approach, where the concern is less with the representativeness of the sample and the generalizability of the findings. In an interpretive study, the key concept is that the sample is **information rich;** that is, the sample consists of cases from which you can learn about issues central to the research question.

Before describing different sampling strategies, you need to become familiar with two other general sampling concepts. First, an **element** in sampling refers to the item under study in the population and sample. In generalist social work research, these items or elements may be the different client systems with which we work—individuals, families, groups, organizations, or communities. The element depends upon the unit of analysis. Elements may be more specific than these basic systems. In our example, families with school-age children 12 and under is a more specific element than simply families.

The second concept is **sampling frame:** a list of all the elements in the population from which the sample is selected. In the above example, the sampling frame would consist of a list of families in the city with school-age children 12 and under.

As you confront the realities of compiling a sampling frame, you may need to redefine the population. For example, you might have decided on families with children 12 and under as your element because the state in which you are conducting the study legally mandates that children of this age cannot be left without adult supervision. When you begin to compile a sampling frame, however, you run into problems because you find it very difficult to identify families with children of this age and younger. Instead, you discover that through the school system, you can more easily identify families with children in the first through the seventh grade. You may end up with a few 13-year-olds, but this isn't a problem if you redefine your population as families with children in the first through the seventh grades.

TYPES OF SAMPLING METHODS

The sample can be selected in two major ways: probability and nonprobability sampling. **Probability sampling** allows you to select a sample where each element in the population has a known chance of being selected for the sample. This type of sampling increases the representativeness of the sample and should be strived for when using the positivist approach.

Instead of a probability sampling method, you may choose a **nonprobability** or purposive sampling method. **Purposive sampling** allows the researcher to handpick the sample according to the nature of the research problem and the phenomenon under study. As a sampling method, purposive sampling is limited in terms of representativeness, in that the probability of each element of the population being included in the sample is unknown. It is, however, the sampling method of choice in interpretive studies, where generalizability of results is less important.

Probability and nonprobability sampling approaches will be presented in this chapter.

Probability Sampling

Probability sampling occurs when every element in the population has a known chance of being selected; thus, its representativeness is assured. In addition, no subject can be selected more than once in a single sample. There are four major types of probability sampling: (1) simple random sampling; (2) systematic random sampling; (3) stratified random sampling; and (4) cluster sampling. Table 8.1 includes each of the probability sampling methods along with their associated potential generalizability.

Table 8.1   ***Sampling methods and generalization of findings***

Sampling method	Generalizability
Probability	
Simple random	Can generalize; limitations minimal
Systematic random	Can generalize; limitations minimal—note how the elements are listed in the sampling frame
Stratified random	Can generalize; limitations minimal—make sure the strata involved are reflected in the analysis of the data
Cluster	Can generalize, but some limitations possible—note the characteristics of the elements because there is a possibility of sampling error with this type of probability sampling
Nonprobability	
Availability	Generalizations very limited
Quota	Generalizations limited
Purposive	Generalizations very limited
Snowball	Generalizations very limited

Simple Random Sampling

Simple random sampling is the easiest of the sampling methods, where the population is treated as a whole unit and each element has an equal probability of being selected in the sample. Because the sampling is random, each element has the same chance of being selected. When you toss a coin, there is an equal chance of its being heads or tails. In the afterschool program needs assessment example, a simple random sample would involve assigning identification numbers to all the elements (families with children in first through seventh grades) and then using a table of random numbers that can be generated by a computer. Most software packages for the social sciences have the ability to generate random number tables. If you did not have the random numbers table, you could literally put all the identification numbers of each element in a container and pick your sample from this.

Simple Random Sampling

Tam and Yeung (1994) studied community perceptions of social welfare in Hong Kong. They were interested in a representative sample and so used simple random sampling. Their sample consisted of 2326 households randomly selected from census information. Questionnaires were mailed to each of these households.

Simple random sampling is the most straightforward probability sampling method to use. It has some problems, though, which will become apparent as the other types of probability sampling are discussed.

Systematic Random Sampling

Systematic random sampling involves taking the list of elements and choosing every *n*th element on the list. The size of *n* depends upon the size of the sampling frame and the intended size of the sample. For example, if you had 400 elements in your sampling frame and you needed a sample of 100, every fourth element would be selected for the sample. If you needed a sample of 200, every second element would be selected.

Systematic Random Sampling

Rosenthal, Groze, and Curiel (1990)—in a study of race, social class, and special needs adoption—used different sampling procedures with different agencies. With a list of subsidized adoptions from the Illinois Department of Children and Family Services, the researchers used systematic random sampling by selecting every fifth child on the list for the study.

Generally, systematic random sampling is as random as simple random sampling. One potential problem with systematic random sampling arises, however, when the ordering of elements in the list being sampled from follows a particular pattern. A distortion of the sample may result. In the afterschool program example, students from the school district may be arranged into class lists of approximately 30 students, and all students who moved to the community within the last six months may be placed at the end of each of these lists. In some communities, these recent additions may be made up primarily of migrant workers. Consequently, if you were to select every 10th, 20th, and 30th element in each class list, your resulting sample would be made up of a disproportionate number of migrant workers, because even though each class has only three or four such students, they are more likely to be the 30th element in a class list.

Problems with the ordering of elements can usually be identified quite easily, and precautions can be taken. When lists are available, systematic random sampling may be easier than simple random sampling because it avoids the step of assigning identification numbers.

Stratified Random Sampling

Stratified random sampling is a modification of the previous two methods; in it the population is divided into strata, and subsamples are randomly selected from each of the strata. Sometimes you need to ensure that a certain proportion of the elements is represented, and stratified random sampling provides a greater chance of meeting this goal than either systematic or simple random sampling.

Selecting the Participants in the Research **139**

In the afterschool program study, you may be concerned about representation of the different ethnic groups of the families with children in first through the seventh grade. You identify 10% of the families as Native Americans. With a simple or systematic random sample, your sample should, if it is truly representative, include 10% Native American families. Unfortunately, due to the workings of probability theory, this is not always the result. At this point, we cannot delve into the depths of probability theory; but if we toss a coin 20 times, we might expect to end up with 10 heads and 10 tails. Often, however, results actually vary. We might end up with 12 heads and 8 tails.

To ensure that Native American families are representatively included in the sample, you can use stratified random sampling. Stratified random sampling requires two preconditions. First, you must be sure that membership in the group whose representation you are concerned about actually has an impact on the phenomenon you are studying. In our example, do you think that Native American families' viewpoints on afterschool programs will differ from those of other families? If not, their adequate representation in the sample may not be that important. Second, you need to know the proportion of this group relative to the rest of the population. In our example, 10% are Native American.

Stratified random sampling involves dividing the population into the groups or strata of interest; in this example, you would divide the population into Native Americans and non–Native Americans. (Note that you can create more than two strata if necessary. For example, you might also be concerned that Hispanic families be assured adequate representation in the sample. Knowing they make up 40% of the population, you would then create three strata: Native Americans, Hispanics, and others.) After creating the strata, simple or systematic random sampling is then carried out from each stratum in proportion to the stratum's representation in the population. In our example, to end up with a sample of 20, you would randomly select 2 from the Native American stratum, 8 from the Hispanic stratum, and 10 from the other stratum (see Figure 8.2).

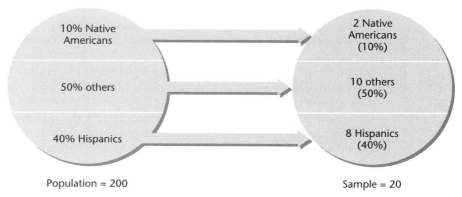

Figure 8.2 **Stratified random sampling**

Although under some circumstances stratified random sampling may be an improvement over simple random sampling, the disadvantages are the two preconditions described earlier—that is, the certainty that the characteristics with which you are concerned will impact the outcome and that you know the proportions of these characteristics in the population prior to the sampling.

Stratified Random Sampling

Larson, Richards, Raffaelli, Ham, and Jewell (1990) examined the nature of depression in late childhood and early adolescence by using a profile of daily states and activities. The sample consisted of fifth to ninth graders and included 406 randomly selected fifth to eighth graders (ages 10 to 15) stratified by gender, school grade, community, and time of year of participation. These students were selected from the populations of four Chicago-area schools—two in a working-class community on the edge of the city and two in an outlying white-collar suburb. The ninth graders were selected from the high schools serving the same residential neighborhoods.

Cluster Sampling

Cluster sampling involves randomly sampling a larger unit containing the elements of interest, and then sampling from these larger units the elements to be included in the final sample. Cluster sampling is often done in social work research because it can be used when it is difficult to get a sampling frame, and yet it is still a form of probability sampling. In the afterschool program example, suppose you are required to obtain the lists of students from each school rather than from the school district office. This could present a lengthy undertaking in a large school district with many schools. Or the lists may not be available either from the school or from the school district. In these cases, cluster sampling might provide a feasible solution.

In cluster sampling, a random sample of a larger unit is taken; in this case, the schools in which first through seventh graders are enrolled. This random sampling can be either simple, systematic, or stratified. In the afterschool program example, you use simple random sampling to select four schools. Then a random sample (again, either simple, systematic, or stratified) of the first through seventh grades in these four schools would be selected (Figure 8.3). Alternatively, if a student list is not available, all first through seventh graders in the four schools would be included in the final sample.

Cluster sampling can be useful in an agency setting, for example, when an agency serves a large number of clients over a yearly period (for example, 8,000 clients are referred). Instead of randomly selecting from this large sampling frame, three months (every fourth month) may be systematically ran-

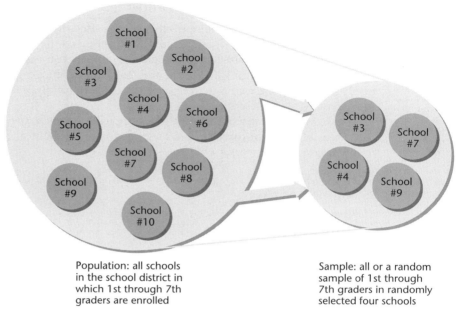

Population: all schools
in the school district in
which 1st through 7th
graders are enrolled

Sample: all or a random
sample of 1st through
7th graders in randomly
selected four schools

Figure 8.3   ***Cluster sampling***

domly sampled from the year, and the clients referred during those three
months included in the sample. Each month represents a cluster.

Cluster sampling has one potential problem. When a small number of units
is sampled (for example, four schools), there is greater probability of sampling
error. The four schools may consist of three white middle-class schools, whereas
the students' population (in ten schools) is a 50-50 mix socioeconomically. Consequently, the sample would be biased in favor of white middle-class students,
and other groups would be underrepresented.

Cluster Sampling

Tice (1994) studied a community's response to supported employment—employment for wages in the competitive marketplace with some supports, for individuals with severe disabilities or challenges. The sampling frame was the census tract
of a rural Ohio county. Using simple random sampling, one community was selected. The study's test population included all adult residents of households
in the selected community. A listing of adult individuals from the selected households was compiled, and one individual from each household was randomly
selected to serve as a study participant.

Nonprobability or Purposive Sampling

Purposive sampling allows the researcher to intentionally select those elements that are information rich, which makes the sampling method of choice in interpretive studies. In the afterschool program example, you may decide you are more interested in learning about the problems and experiences of families who need afterschool care rather than finding out the proportion of families who are in need of afterschool services.

There are a number of different types of purposive sampling methods. Patton discusses many of these (1990). Described here are eight of the most commonly used in social work:

1. typical case
2. criterion sampling
3. focus groups
4. key informants
5. community forum
6. quota
7. snowball
8. availability

See Table 8.2 for the different types of purposive sampling methods.

Typical Cases

Typical case sampling is the most often used method for purposive sampling. Typical cases are sought using the literature, previous research, or consultation with relevant groups. For the afterschool program example, families who appear

Table 8.2   ***Purposive or nonprobability sampling methods***

Method	Characteristics
typical cases	those with "typical" characteristics
criterion	participants selected according to some eligibility criteria
focus groups	those with an interest in the research topic
key informants	those with expertise on the research topic
community forum	open to a community; some can be purposively invited
quota	certain proportions of participants from different groups selected according to specific characteristics
snowball	some participants identified; these participants then identify others with certain characteristics
availability	those selected because they are available

typical in their need for services would be contacted through a local agency or schools.

A Typical Case

Wagner's (1994) study of the homeless in a New England city purposively selected a large group of homeless people. The resulting cohort "resembled the national demographic profile of the homeless population in terms of age, gender, education, marital status, rates of mental illness, substance abuse and place of birth; race was the sole exception" (p. 720).

Criterion Sampling

Criterion sampling involves picking all cases that meet some criterion—for example, including all families in an agency who meet eligibility criteria to receive services from that agency.

Criterion Sampling

Schwartz, AuClaire, and Harris (1991) used criterion sampling in their study of the effectiveness of an intensive home-based program. The client was eligible for participation in the study if he or she

1. was approved for out-of-home placement
2. was an adolescent (12–17 years)
3. was not a ward of the state
4. was not under court order into placement

Clients meeting each of the criterion constituted the pool of cases eligible for the study. During the sampling period, cases were assigned to treatment series or to a comparison group.

Focus Groups

Focus groups were discussed in Chapter 3 as a means of helping to formulate a question, and will be discussed further in Chapter 9 as a source of data collection. Focus groups are picked purposefully—those invited have some type of interest or expertise in the topic under study. Focus groups are also an excellent way of ensuring maximum participation and involvement by the community and by those on whom the research will have the most impact.

Focus Groups

Freedman, Litchfield, and Warfield (1995) studied the balancing of work and family responsibilities of parents of children with developmental disabilities. Four focus groups were convened to obtain the parents' perspectives.

Key Informants

Key informant sampling relies on people in the community identified as experts in the field of interest.

Key Informants

Rivera (1990) studied the extent to which knowledge about AIDS has been integrated into Mexican folk medicine (or *curanderismo*). Rivera interviewed three *curanderos* in Mexico and two owners of *botanicas* (healing artifact stores). He stated that the three *curanderos* had respected reputations and were well known where they lived (Guadalajara, Oaxaca, and close to Mexico City). The two owners of *botanicas* lived in barrios in Colorado and Texas.

Community Forum

The **community forum** involves publicizing a meeting or series of meetings at which individuals are briefed on the issues and then asked for input. Community members can be purposively invited.

A Community Forum

Buchanan and colleagues (1993–1994) described a new model of community-based planning developed by the Centro de Educacion, Prevencion y Accion (CEPA), an HIV prevention program for Puerto Ricans. A community forum was an important method used to collect needs assessment information, as were focus groups.

Quota Sampling

Quota sampling involves a certain proportion of elements with specific characteristics to be purposively included in the sample. In some respects, quota sampling is similar to stratified random sampling, except that no randomness is involved in selecting the elements. When examining the experiences of families with unattended school-age children in an interpretive study, you might be interested in ensuring that you interviewed families from all ethnic groups in the community. Like stratified random sampling, quota sampling requires that you know the proportion of these ethnic groups in the population. The problems associated with this form of sampling, as with stratified random sampling, are that the researcher needs to be sure that the categories or variables selected are important ones and that the proportions of these variables are known in the population. It may be that ethnicity is not a key variable that needs to be included.

Quota Sampling

Bentelspacher, Chiltran, and Rahman (1994) studied coping and adaptation patterns among Chinese, Indian, and Malay families caring for a mentally ill relative in Singapore. The sample was selected through case records in a psychiatric hospital of those diagnosed with schizophrenia, living with a family member, and admitted during one year. Out of the resulting 281 that met these criteria, the cases were stratified according to the three main ethnic groups in Singapore—Chinese, Indian, and Malay—with the objective of interviewing 10 caregivers from each group. On telephone contact, 7 (28%) of the 25 total Indian caregivers, 12 (29%) of the 41 total Malay caregivers, and 11 (27%) of the first 41 Chinese caregivers to be contacted agreed to participate.

Snowball Sampling

Snowball sampling involves identifying some members of the population and then having those individuals contact others in the population. This is a very useful strategy to adopt with less accessible populations—for example, the homeless—although it could also be used with the example of families with children who are unsupervised after school. You might identify and contact a few families and then ask those families to contact others they think are having problems.

Snowball Sampling

Danziger and Farber (1990) conducted a study investigating young black women's personal experiences and level of school success, and the kinds of supportive resources they receive. The researchers conducted in-depth interviews with 162 young women who live in the inner-city communities of Milwaukee and Detroit. In Milwaukee, a number of women were contacted who had participated in an earlier survey. From this core, snowball sampling was used to get referrals from other potential participants. In Detroit, referrals were received from agencies along with snowball sampling.

Availability Sampling

Availability or **convenience sampling** is used extensively in social work re-search and involves including available or convenient elements in the sample. Sometimes availability sampling is confused with random sampling, because su-perficially it appears random. A typical example of availability sampling is inter-viewing people in a shopping mall in an attempt to get a sample of the commu-nity. Alternatively, in an agency you are asked to conduct a program evaluation. The funds for the evaluation are available now, and you have two months to col-lect the data. Consequently, you decide to include in your sample clients referred to the program during the next 30 days. The population under study is all those referred to the program.

Research findings from availability samples cannot be generalized to the population under study. In the shopping mall example, you are going to be able to include in your sample only people who shop at the mall—maybe a small and not very representative sample of the community as a whole. In the program evaluation example, the clients referred to the agency in the month of the sam-pling may be different from clients referred at other times of the year; December may not be a very representative month of the entire year. Consequently, the sample is biased, making it difficult to generalize results to the entire commu-nity. Availability sampling is also problematic in that it does not possess the ad-vantages of a purposive sampling method. The elements are not picked for their information richness, but rather selected on the basis of convenience. Availabil-ity samples, however, often present the only feasible way of sampling.

 Availability Sampling

A study by Schilit, Lie, Bush, Montagne, and Reyes (1991) examined inter-generational transmission of violence in lesbian relationships. The researchers used an availability sample. Probability sampling would have been difficult with this population—lesbians living in the region—because complete lists do not exist. The availability sample consisted of a mailing list for a lesbian organization in Tuc-son, which contained approximately 350 names and addresses in the Tucson area.

Availability sampling is often the sampling method to use when evaluating your own practice. One case or more is selected and the effectiveness of the in-tervention assessed. This type of research will be discussed in more detail in Chapter 7.

Studying Complete Populations

Sometimes, particularly when conducting program evaluations, it is possible to study the entire population rather than a sample. For example, you could define the population in such a way that you can include all the elements in that population in your study. If the program is relatively small, all the clients served during a certain period (say, six months) could be defined as the population, and all could be studied. (Remember, the definition of the population is in part up to you.) Or if the program is new, it might be quite feasible to study the entire population—namely, all who have been served since the program's inception. It is also possible to study the entire population if the population is quite specific— for example, children with Down's syndrome in a medium-sized city.

Studying an Entire Population

Levin and Herbert (1995) studied the different work assignments of B.S.W. and M.S.W. social workers in hospitals in four Canadian provinces. They sent a questionnaire to the directors of social work departments in all 89 hospitals in the four provinces.

SAMPLE SIZE

Statisticians devote a considerable amount of energy to determining how large or small samples should be. Some of the kinds of research that generalist social workers usually conduct, such as program or practice evaluations, do not require you to make a decision about sample size because the sample is fixed—namely, a small program or your own practice.

The size of the sample in part depends on its homogeneity, or the similarity among different elements. If you can be assured that the characteristics of the sample elements are similar on the dimensions you are interested in studying, then the sample can be smaller. In the example of unsupervised children, if all the children are similar in the characteristics in which you are interested—ethnicity, socioeconomic status, and family configuration—then the sample size can be small. If, however, you are interested in comparing the afterschool program needs of different types of families—for example, across family configuration, income, and so on—then you would probably need a larger sample to ensure that you have enough subjects in each category. As we saw in Chapter 3, a minimal number of cases is required in each category to allow certain statistical analyses to occur.

The size of the sample also depends on the research approach used. In positivist studies using probability samples, sample sizes usually need to be quite large, whereas in interpretive studies the sample size is small. As Patton (1990) stated: "The validity, meaningfulness, and insights generated from qualitative inquiry have more to do with the information-richness of the cases selected and the observational/analytical capabilities of the researcher than with sample size" (p. 185).

In interpretive studies (or qualitative inquiry, using Patton's terminology), the sample size depends on the amount of information generated; the size of the sample is no larger than that needed to gather the information of interest (Patton, 1990). Redundancy is to be avoided (Lincoln & Guba, 1985).

Also important to consider when deciding on sample size is the issue of sampling error. **Sampling error** is the extent to which the values of the sample differ from those of the population. The margin of error refers to the precision needed by the researcher. A margin of error of 5% means the actual findings could vary in either direction by as much as 5%. For example, a client satisfaction survey that finds 55% of clients were "very satisfied" could have actual results anywhere from 50% to 60%. If the sample is large enough, the sampling error and margin of error can be reduced. With 100 tosses of a coin, you are more

Table 8.3   **Size of sample required at 5% confidence interval**

Population Size	Sample Size
50	44
75	63
100	80
150	108
200	132
250	152
300	169
400	196
500	217
750	254
1,000	278
2,000	322
4,000	351
5,000	357
10,000	370
15,000	375
20,000	377
25,000	378
50,000	381
100,000	384
1,000,000	384

Source: From *Educational and Psychological Measurement,* by R. V. Krejcie and D. W. Morgan, pp. 607–610. Copyright © 1970 Sage Publications, Inc. Reprinted by permission of Sage Publications, Inc.

likely to end up with 50% heads and 50% tails than you are with 20 tosses. In reporting the results of large-scale surveys, it is important to report the extent of sampling error.

A number of quite complicated formulas can assist in determining sample size. If you have concerns about the size of your sample, consult with a statistician or refer to a good statistics text (see Chapters 12 and 13 for some references). Refer back to Table 8.1 for some guides as to sample size and sampling error.

Table 8.3 gives different sample sizes and their associated **margin of error.** The margin of error reported in this table is 5%. This means the actual findings could vary as much as 5% either positively or negatively. Another way to view this is to state that the findings, using the sample sizes in the table, have a 95% **confidence level,** which expresses how often you would expect similar results if the research were repeated. For example, in a sample with a 95% confidence level and a 5% margin of error, the findings could be expected to miss the actual values in the population by more than 5% only five times in 100 surveys.

THE AGENCY AND SAMPLING

As generalist social workers engaging in research, you may need to use sampling methods that are not textbook examples. Two cases of these modifications are discussed in this section: limited probability sampling and combining sampling methods.

Often, an integral part of a needs assessment is the ability to generalize the findings to an entire community, county, or larger area. Unfortunately, it is often not possible to obtain representative samples due to most agencies' time and money constraints. Sometimes, however, it is possible to obtain a **limited probability sample**—for example, from a neighborhood or agency—and then compare the characteristics of this sample with the characteristics of a sample drawn from a larger population. In this way, some tentative generalizations of the findings can be made. Sometimes similarities are not found between the smaller and larger samples. For example, in Schilit and colleagues' (1991) study on lesbian violence, discussed earlier, the authors found that when they compared the ethnicity, income, and education of their subjects to these characteristics in the population of Tucson, there were large differences, thus limiting any generalizations.

A Limited Probability Sample

Smith and Kronauge (1990), in their study of who is involved in decision making about abortion, drew a random sample from women who received abortions through one agency in St. Louis, Missouri. The researchers then compared two characteristics of this sample—marital status and age—with a national sample. The similarity they found allowed them to tentatively generalize the findings from their sample to the wider population.

This method of expanding generalizations suffers from some problems similar to those of stratified random sampling: the assumption that we know what the important characteristics are when comparing a smaller sample with a larger sample. Consequently, this method should be used with caution.

Another often-needed modification of sampling is to combine sampling methods. Sometimes practical constraints do not allow you to proceed with the type of sampling planned; it may be possible to sample one group using a planned method but not another group.

Combined Sampling Methods

Kruk (1994) studied disengaged noncustodial fathers in the United States, Canada, and Great Britain. He managed to secure court records in Canada in order to select a probability sample. In Great Britain, however, he did not have access to these records and had to use an availability sampling method, placing advertisements in newspapers and seeking referrals from legal and social work practitioners.

ETHICAL ISSUES IN SAMPLING

Two ethical issues relate to sampling: first, responsible reporting of the sampling method and, second, obtaining the subject's consent to the research.

Reporting the Sampling Method

It is the researcher's responsibility when reporting research findings—whether in a journal article, a report, or a presentation—to ensure that the research methods used in the study are described as accurately as possible. Details of reporting will be described in Chapter 14. Some discussion is necessary here, however, because inaccuracies and ambiguities in research reports often concern the sampling method.

Sometimes authors write about supposedly random methods of sampling that are really availability or some other form of nonprobability sampling. When reading reports and articles, look for an explicit description of the sampling method along with a frank description of the generalization limitations, particularly if a nonprobability sampling method is used. It is unethical to claim even implicitly that the results of a nonprobability sample are generalizable to a wider population. Such a claim is misleading and can have some serious negative implications. Nonprobability and probability sampling methods have very different purposes as discussed in this chapter.

Informed Consent

Whenever any type of social work research is undertaken, it is critical that no coercion is exerted and that the subject voluntarily agrees to participate. The subjects or participants must always be told about the purpose and goals of the research. As discussed in Chapter 6, voluntary, informed consent should always be obtained from the participants. Figure 8.4 is an example of a consent form.

Many ethical guidelines present dilemmas. You may feel that by disclosing information about the research project to the participant, you will jeopardize the research results. For example, if you are using observation to collect data about a specific behavior and if participants know they are being observed, their behavior might change considerably. Another problem arises when you inform participants that their involvement in the research is voluntary: A certain number may choose not to participate. The researcher then does not know whether the results from the participants who agreed to participate are different from those who refused.

Sometimes—and these times are *not* frequent—the voluntary participation ethical standard may need to be modified. If this is necessary, you must clearly

---

CONSENT TO PARTICIPATE IN RESEARCH

The purpose of this research is to learn more about the needs of families who are in the process of reuniting with their children. I would also like to learn about the services that were provided to you and your family and the meaning each has for you. I would like to hear about how you have coped with your experiences and what you believe would help other families who may one day experience a similar situation.

I am a graduate student social worker and am working independently on this research project, however, with the permission and knowledge of my field placement agency (Department of Children, Youth and Families) and the Department of Social Work at New Mexico State University. I will protect your identity by using fictitious names and disguising incidents. I plan to share the results of this study with other helping professionals through presentations and possible publication.

*   *   *   *   *   *   *   *   *   *   *

I hereby acknowledge that I am 18 years or older and agree to participate in this research project. I acknowledge that the information obtained in the interview will be used to prepare a research project and that every precaution will be taken to protect my identity and assure confidentiality. I acknowledge my participation as voluntary and know that I may withdraw my participation at any time.

RESPONDENT _____   RESEARCHER _____

DATE _____   DATE _____

Figure 8.4   ***A form for obtaining participants' informed consent***

understand and explain the reasons. In particular, you must be careful that researchers do not use their power or authority to exploit the subjects. Suppose a professor who is carrying out research on students' experiences of sexual harassment requests that all the students in her class complete a questionnaire that she estimates will take about 15 minutes. She states that participation is voluntary, but those who choose not to participate will be required to write a five-page research paper. This is clearly a form of coercion, with the professor using her authority to force participation. A similar situation can be envisioned with a social work researcher requiring the participation of individuals who are dependent upon the social worker for services. The decision to forgo the participant's consent must be very carefully considered to ensure that no blatant coercion is occurring.

Another way of viewing the issue of the subject's consent is to modify our perspective on the distinction between researcher and participant. The relationship between researcher and participant can be seen as egalitarian, rather than viewed, as traditionally, as a relationship in which researchers wield power and authority over subjects. When an even footing is adopted, the question of the participant's consent becomes a nonissue. Instead, researchers make their research skills accessible to participants, participants become active contributors in the research, and each gains from being involved. Emphasizing the egalitarian relationship between researcher and participant is one way of incorporating this connectedness into research methodology. This type of relationship can be created by using sampling methods such as the key informant, the focus group, and the community forum, in all of which community members have an opportunity to serve both as participants and as contributors. An egalitarian relationship between researcher and participant is a characteristic of participatory research, as discussed in previous chapters.

When evaluating individual practice, the way the research is presented to the client is important and can affect the researcher-participant relationship. If you present the research as something special, different or separate from practice, then the client will see it that way and often resist being involved (or used) in a research project. But if you stress the integration between research and practice and point out how the client will benefit from feedback on the relative effectiveness of the intervention, then you will be more accurately depicting the whole idea of evaluating practice. In addition, you will be engaging in a true partnership with the client, benefiting all involved.

Breaking down the distinction between researcher and participant has other advantages apart from the issue of the participant's consent. First, it addresses the concern that research is not always responsive to the needs of oppressed groups. When a partnership between researcher and participant is created, responsiveness is more assured. Second, the validity of the research may be enhanced. The more traditional relationship between researcher and participant, which emphasizes separateness, may result in a greater likelihood of the participant's giving invalid responses out of a lack of understanding of the researcher's intent. This problem is avoided by building the partnership. Third, this approach seems to be particularly compatible to social work practice, where emphasis is placed on establishing a relationship with the client.

Creating an egalitarian relationship between subject and researcher thus seems a reasonable approach to adopt and one that offers several advantages. As a final note, however, we should add that in practice an egalitarian relationship can sometimes be difficult to achieve. Srinivasan and Davis (1991) commented on this in an article reporting on the organization of a women's shelter. This study, incidentally, is a good example of the application of feminist research principles. They stated:

> Although my intent was to establish egalitarian relationships with all participants in the study, I was not always successful in this regard. The staff readily accepted and treated me as another volunteer, but the residents had more difficulty accepting me as an equal. The residents were skeptical about why I was there. (p. 41)

HUMAN DIVERSITY ISSUES IN SAMPLING

Unfortunately, the social science literature, at least prior to the early 1970s, does not provide many examples of studies with heterogeneous samples. For example, Holmes and Jorgensen (1971) found that subjects were males twice as often as females, a ratio even higher than the ratio of college student subjects to non–college student subjects. Not only were the samples homogenous, but also the findings from these samples were generalized to the population as a whole— populations that included non–college graduates, women, and minorities. These generalizations should never be made because the samples were simply not representative of the populations.

A classic example of this problem is presented by Kohlberg's study of the development of morality. In his initial study, he selected a sample of Harvard male graduates (1969). Based on this study, Kohlberg developed a model and theory of moral development that he used as a template to assess the moral development of *all* individuals. Moreover, as a result of applying this model to women, he concluded that women often did not reach the higher level of moral development and were, therefore, deficient morally. Later, Gilligan (1977) challenged these conclusions and studied moral development in a sample of women. She proposed alternative moral developmental stages for women, concluding that women were not deviant or deficient in their moral development but simply followed a different course.

Similar assumptions and erroneous generalizations have been made relating to minority populations. White middle-class samples have been studied, and the findings have been generalized and presented as the norm by which to evaluate minorities. Such improper generalizations are not always made explicitly by the researchers themselves, but often by others who draw assumptions from the findings and apply them to other groups.

Historically, such generalizations have been made about the effectiveness of social programs. If a program is demonstrated to be ineffective with a minority urban sample, it may be concluded that consequently the program would be ineffective with all minorities. It is critical that we recognize diversity within minority groups. Program ineffectiveness with some urban minorities does not mean program ineffectiveness with other minorities or with rural minorities.

The danger of improper generalizations can in part be avoided if research consumers enhance their knowledge. This includes you! Researchers, as discussed in the previous section, can also help by being explicit about the limitations of their sampling method. It is often easier, however, to be critical of existing studies than to avoid such pitfalls in our own research. The erroneous assumptions that Kohlberg made seem almost obvious now, but that is because we have an increased sensitivity to gender issues. Additionally, there is an increasing awareness of ethnic and racial diversity when applying research methods. Be cautioned that other dimensions of diversity are less evident. For example, ageism and homophobia are still pervasive in our culture, even among social workers. Sometimes we are not even aware of all the dimensions of diversity. The issue goes beyond consciously excluding a particular group.

SUMMARY

Key concepts in sampling are representativeness, generalizability, and information richness. The two different types of sampling strategies are probability and purposive methods. Probability sampling includes simple random sampling, systematic random sampling, stratified random sampling, and cluster sampling. Purposive sampling includes typical case, community forum, focus groups, key informants, quota, snowball, and availability sampling.

When conducting sampling in an agency, sampling methods may need to be modified. Ethical issues include accurate reporting of the sampling method and the subject's consent. Human diversity issues relate to whether the sampling represents diverse populations adequately.

STUDY/EXERCISE QUESTIONS

1. A local agency has asked you to help them conduct a survey to determine whether the city needs an elder day care facility. The population of the city is 65,000. About 20% of the city's population lives below the poverty level. All persons over the age of 60 would be eligible for the center.
   a. Define the population.
   b. Will probability sampling be possible? If not, why not? If so, what method would you use?
   c. Discuss the pros and cons of each of the following suggestions made by various members of the board of the agency:
      (i) Interview elders who frequent the local shopping mall early in the morning for exercise.
      (ii) Mail questionnaires to members of the local branch of the American Association of Retired Persons (AARP).
      (iii) Conduct a telephone interview using the telephone directory as a sampling frame.

2. Review an issue of *Social Work,* and answer these questions about the re-
    search articles.
    a. What was the sampling method used?
    b. What are the limitations with each of the sampling methods?
    c. Were these limitations made explicit in the articles?

FURTHER READING

Johnson, J. C. (1990). *Selecting ethnographic informants.* Newbury Park, CA: Sage.
A systematic guide to selecting nonprobability samples. Excellent for the
generalist social worker who often cannot use probability samples.

REFERENCES

Buchanan, D., Apostal, E., Balfour, D., Claudio, C., Marinoff, J., O'Hare, N.,
Rodriguez, M., & Santiago, C. (1993–1994). The CEPA project: A new model
for community-based program planning. *International Quarterly of Community Health Education, 14* (4), 361–377.

Bentelspacher, C. E., Chiltran, S., & Rahman M. (1994). Coping and adaptation
patterns among Chinese, Indian, and Malay families caring for a mentally
ill relative. *Families in Society: The Journal of Contemporary Human Service,*
287–294.

Danziger, S. K., & Farber, N. B. (1990). Keeping inner-city youths in school:
Critical experiences of young black women. *Social Work Research and
Abstracts, 26* (4), 32–39.

Freedman, R. I., Litchfield, L. C., & Warfield, M. E. (1995). Balancing work and
family: Perspectives of parents of children with developmental disabilities.
Families: The Journal of Contemporary Human Services, 507–514.

Gilligan, C. (1977). In a different voice: Women's conceptions of self and of
morality. *Harvard Educational Review, 47,* 481–512.

Holmes, D. S., & Jorgensen, B. W. (1971). The personality and social psychologists study men more than women. *Representative Research in Social Psychology, 2,* 71–76.

Kohlberg, L. (1969). *Stages in the development of moral thought and action.* New
York: Holt, Rinehart & Winston.

Krejcie, R. V., & Morgan, D. W. (1970). Determining sample size for research
activities. *Educational & Psychological Measurement, 30,* 607–610.

Kruk, E. (1994). The disengaged noncustodial father: Implications for social
work practice with the divorced family. *Social Work, 39,* 15–24.

Larson, R. W., Richards, M. H., Raffaelli, M., Ham, M., & Jewell, L. (1990). Ecology of depression in late childhood and early adolescence: A profile of daily
states and activities. *Journal of Abnormal Psychology, 99* (1), 92–102.

Levin, R., & Herbert, M. (1995). Differential Work Assignments of Social Work Practitioners in Hospitals. *Health & Social Work, 20,* 21–30.

Lincoln, Y. S. & Guba, E. G. (1985). *Naturalistic Inquiry.* Newbury Park, CA: Sage.

National Association of Social Workers. (1997). NASW Code of Ethics. *NASW News, 25,* 24–25.

Patton, M. Q. (1990). *Qualitative Evaluations & Research Methods.* Newbury Park, CA: Sage.

Rivera, G., Jr. (1990). AIDS and Mexican folk medicine. *Sociology and Social Research, 75* (1), 3–7.

Rosenthal, J. A., Groze, V., & Curiel, H. (1990). Race, social class, and special needs adoption. *Social Work, 35,* 532–538.

Schilit, R., Lie, G., Bush, J., Montagne, M., & Reyes, L. (1991). Intergenerational transmission of violence in lesbian relationships. *Affilia, 6* (1), 72–87.

Smith, H. W., & Kronauge, C. (1990). The politics of abortion: Husband notification legislation, self-disclosure, and marital bargaining. *The Sociological Quarterly, 31* (4), 585–598.

Srinivasan, M., & Davis, L. V. (1991). A shelter: An organization like any other. *Affilia, 6* (1), 38–57.

Tam, T. S. K., & Yeung, S. (1994). Community perception of social welfare and its relations to familism, political alienation, and individual rights: The Case of Hong Kong. *International Social Work, 37* (1), 47–60.

Tice, C. (1994). A community's response to supported employment: Implications for social work practice. *Social Work, 39* (6), 728–735.

Wagner, D. (1994). Beyond the pathologizing of network: Alternative activities in a street community. *Social Work, 39* (6), 718–726.

Collecting the Data

■

N ow that you have decided on the research design and the way participants will be selected, you need to decide how you will gather the information or data. Do you go out and interview people directly? Do you use forms and questionnaires to collect information, or do you need to observe?

After defining and conceptualizing the problem in generalist practice, you must decide how information will be collected. This information is referred to in both practice and research as **data** (singular **datum**), and they are collected using a **measuring instrument,** or data collection method. These methods include questionnaires, observation, logs and journals, interviews, scales, and secondary data. All these will be described in this chapter.

As a generalist social worker, you may or may not actually collect the data. The plan and perhaps even the data collection may have already been implemented. Even if you don't direct the collection of the data, and certainly if you are responsible for collecting data, you will need to know what instruments are used under what circumstances.

This chapter will include a discussion of the following topics:

- qualitative and quantitative data
- ways of collecting data
- who collects the data
- combining data collection methods
- determining reliability and validity
- the agency and data collection
- ethical issues in collecting the data
- human diversity issues in collecting the data

QUANTITATIVE AND QUALITATIVE DATA

As discussed in Chapter 1, the positivist and interpretist approaches tend to involve the collection of different types of data. The former emphasizes the collection of quantitative data, and with the latter the emphasis is on qualitative data. Sometimes the terms *qualitative research* and *quantitative research* are used synonymously with *interpretist research* and *positivist research,* respectively. Strictly speaking, though, *quantitative* and *qualitative* refer to the type of data rather than an entire research approach. Sometimes studies using the positivist approach will collect partly or completely qualitative data, and sometimes interpretive studies will involve the collection of some quantitative data. So using the data collection type to describe the entire research approach can be misleading.

WAYS OF COLLECTING DATA

Six major methods of collecting data, or measuring instruments, will be described in this section (see Figure 9.1): interviews, questionnaires, observation techniques, logs and journals, scales, and secondary data.

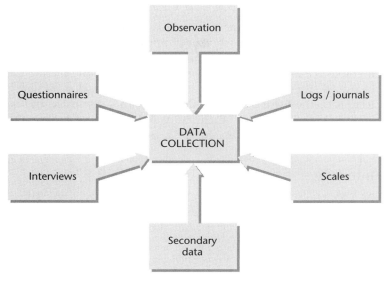

Figure 9.1 **Methods of data collection**

At this point, note that you can either construct your own data collection instrument using one or more of the methods listed here, or else use an already existing measure. Whenever possible, use an existing measure, particularly if it is standardized. A standardized instrument is uniform throughout. It includes items uniformly administered and scored according to an agreed-upon procedure. This type of instrument not only is convenient to use but also has established reliability and validity, two measurement concepts discussed at the end of this chapter.

As they are described, each of the six methods will be assessed for both **neutrality** and **applicability.** Patton (1990) proposed the term *neutrality* as an alternative to either *objectivity* or *subjectivity.* Objectivity is one of the central premises of the positivist approach. As discussed in Chapter 1, however, objectivity is virtually impossible to achieve, and even the positivist admits it is a problematic term. Interpretism is more concerned with the subjective experiences of the subjects in the study. *Subjective,* however, is also a problematic term, with negative connotations implying bias and relevance only to specific subjects. *Neutrality* appears to be a more useful term and is defined by Patton as characterizing research in which "the researcher does not seek out to prove a particular perspective or manipulate the data to arrive at predisposed truths" (p. 55).

Patton suggests adopting the term *empathetic neutrality* for the interpretive approach (which he calls the qualitative approach). Here, though, we maintain that *neutrality* is a useful term for both the positivist and interpretist perspectives.

Apart from neutrality, the other criterion by which the data collection methods will be discussed in the next section is applicability. The **applicability** of a measuring instrument is whether or not it is appropriate and suitable for a particular type of problem. For example, observation would typically not be a useful method to employ if we were collecting information on child abuse, but would be suitable for collecting information on child behavior problems. Each data collection method will be described, along with a discussion of both its strengths and weaknesses in terms of neutrality and its relative applicability for the kinds of research questions we encounter as generalist social workers.

Interviews

As a generalist social work student, you are already quite skilled at conducting interviews. Interviews are structured, semistructured, or unstructured. Often, the questions may be very similar, but the interviews are distinguished based on how they are conducted.

Structured Interviews

In a **structured interview,** the interviewer knows in advance the questions to ask and in many cases is simply administering a verbal questionnaire. Often this questionnaire is already developed by the agency workers.

A Structured Interview

First, Rife, and Toomey (1994) studied the rural homeless. During the six-month data collection period, 919 homeless adults were interviewed in 21 counties. To ensure standardized use of the instruments, training sessions were held for all the interviewers.

Semistructured Interviews

In a **semistructured interview,** the interviewer has more freedom to pursue hunches and can improvise with the questions. Semistructured interviews often use interview schedules consisting of the general types of questions to ask, but they are not in a questionnaire format. Sometimes semistructured interviews are referred to as open-ended interviews.

A Semistructured Interview

Johnson (1995) examined the nature of the relationship between elders and their caregivers by comparing their attitudes toward the definition, criminalization, and treatment of elder abuse. She collected the data using face-to-face semi-structured interviews designed to gather both qualitative and quantitative data. Results suggested the perceptions of the two groups were similar.

Unstructured Interviews

Completely **unstructured interviews** can also be used. This type of interview is similar to a conversation except that the interviewer and interviewee know that an interview is being conducted and that the interviewee is privy to information of interest to the interviewer.

Neutrality

Although structured and semistructured interviews are more neutral than unstructured interviews—because asking specific questions minimizes some bias—in general, the neutrality of interviewing is limited. We know that we respond differently to different people depending on how we are approached. The answer to an interviewer's question will be influenced by several factors: the interviewer's age, gender, ethnicity, and dress; the context in which the interviewer approaches the interviewee; the manner in which the interviewer speaks; and so forth. In addition, these characteristics will not have a constant effect on all the interviewees. Instead, each interviewee will respond differently to these characteristics depending on previous experiences, and there is no way of knowing exactly how these responses differ. This is referred to as the **reactive effect:** the interviewer influences the interviewee, and the interviewee responds in a particular way, which will then have a feedback effect on the interviewer. With the positivist approach, the reactive effect can be a serious limitation and can jeopardize the data collection method's objectivity, which as you will remember is important in the positivist approach.

If you are using the interpretive approach, reactivity is not necessarily a problem, since the approach involves a recognition that the relationship between the researcher and subject exists and not only enhances the quality of the data but also can itself create the data. Using the interpretive approach, the researcher and subject explore the topic together, each contributing to the process and each working in different ways. "The researcher and subject are interconnected in an ongoing relationship that influences the data that are produced. No 'objective' data can be collected because all data depend on the specific individuals and their relationship to one another" (Davis, 1986, p. 37).

Thus, when using the interpretive approach, you must acknowledge that objectivity will be lost. Neutrality is still important, however. In fact, interpretist researchers often state "up front" the type of relationship they strive for with their subjects. Gregg (1994) in her study of pregnancy stated:

> I continued (quite consciously) to refrain from developing friendships with the women during the course of the study, even though this sometimes seemed artificial and contrived. I did not want them to feel they had to continue with the study or to feel that they were obliged to reveal things to me

out of loyalty or friendship. . . . When I ran into someone I had interviewed, we would say hello, I would ask her how she was, and we would go on. These encounters were awkward for me. (Gregg, 1994, p. 55)

Some of the problems undermining the neutrality of interviews can be overcome by training the interviewers. They can be given an explicit protocol or format that they are required to follow. As a generalist social worker, you may be required to conduct interviews of this type. Also, audio recordings allow the interviews to be reviewed. Recordings can sometimes inhibit the interviewees, however, resulting in a distortion of their responses.

The advantage of interviews is that they allow ambiguous questions to be clarified. This opportunity does not exist when questionnaires are administered, particularly by mail. Then respondents interpret the question in their own way, which may be very different from the intention of the researchers when they developed the questions.

Interviewing also has a positive effect on the response rate, the proportion of people who respond to the questions in either a questionnaire or interview. We have all been asked to participate in research—on the telephone, on the street, or through the mail. Sometimes we agree, and sometimes we refuse to participate. For researchers, a problem arises when many people refuse to participate, because these people might turn out to be very different from those who do. For example, if you send out 100 questionnaires asking about people's experiences of childhood sexual abuse, but only 25 people respond—all of whom state they were not abused as children—you have no way of knowing whether the nonrespondents were all abused and were reluctant to disclose this on their questionnaire, or were not abused and decided not to respond, or were distributed between abused and not abused. Because you do not know, you have to be cautious and assume that the results may well be biased. Interviews, however, generally obtain a high response rate. This is particularly true for face-to-face interviews, less so for telephone interviews.

Nevertheless, the high response rate of even face-to-face interviews is not always assured. The response rate does not just depend on the method of data collection; other factors include the characteristics of the subjects, the purpose and nature of the research question or project, and the characteristics and training of those applying the data collection instruments.

One form of interviewing involves **focus groups.** These were described in Chapter 3 as a means of helping to develop the research question and in Chapter 8 as a sampling method; they can also be used as a way of collecting data.

Applicability

Interviewing may be preferred to other techniques in the following circumstances:

- You are interested in a high response rate.

- You want to gather in-depth information. Interviewing is one of the main methods for collecting qualitative data and is a key data collection method in many interpretive studies, where the focus is on collecting information that discloses the richness of the subject's experience.

■ Anonymity is not of primary importance. If your research involves a sensitive issue—such as the incidence of spousal abuse in a community—and the community is relatively small, anonymity may be important, and interviewing would not be an appropriate data collection method. People are less reluctant to share such sensitive information with strangers.

■ Time and money are of no great object. Interviews are time consuming, particularly if you are interested in getting responses from a large geographic area. In addition, interviewers often need to be trained. Consequently, this data collection method is expensive. If the budget is low and the sample large, interviewing would not be the data collection method of choice.

■ The respondent is not comfortable with writing or is illiterate.

Questionnaires

In general, questionnaires have many advantages that interviews do not have; at the same time, they lack the strengths of interviews. There are several types of questionnaires.

Mailed Questionnaires

Mailing questionnaires is a popular method of distributing questionnaires. Agencies often use this method to survey their clients as part of a program evaluation or needs assessment.

 A Mailed Questionnaire

Peterson (1990) carried out a survey of 476 members of the NASW to determine their characteristics, educational background, and perceptions of the field of aging. A mailed questionnaire was used to collect the data. Respondents perceived that the field of aging would be much larger and more important in the future, and they recommended increased gerontological preparation for all social work students.

Face-to-Face Questionnaires

Face-to-face questionnaires may be administered much as structured interviews are. Structured interviews can be thought of as verbally administered questionnaires.

A Face-to-Face Questionnaire

Oliveira, Baizerman, and Pellet (1992) studied street children and their helpers in Brazil. They were particularly interested in the street children's aspirations for their futures. They administered face-to-face questionnaires with closed-ended and open-ended questions.

Group Questionnaires

These questionnaires are administered to groups. For example, if you are interested in getting feedback on a foster parent training session, you might administer questionnaires to the entire group at one time.

A Group Questionnaire

In a study by Anderson, Kann, Holtzman, Arday, Truman, and Kilbe (1990), students completed self-administered questionnaires in their classroom under the direction of trained data collectors in an effort to gather information on high school students' knowledge about HIV and AIDS and their sexual behavior.

Bilingual Questionnaires

In many communities and with certain populations, bilingual questionnaires are essential.

A Bilingual Questionnaire

Salgado de Snyder, Cervantes, and Padilla (1990) examined gender and ethnic differences in psychosocial stress and generalized distress in a group of 593 people consisting of Hispanic immigrants, Mexican Americans, and Anglo Americans. The researchers administered the data collection instrument (a demographic checklist, an inventory, and a scale) either in Spanish or English, depending upon the respondents' language proficiency.

Neutrality

Questionnaires are relatively neutral. Interviewer bias is absent, and the responses are clear and usually unambiguous. The neutrality of the responses, however, depends a great deal on the care with which the questionnaire has been constructed. Ambiguities can be minimized by stating questions as clearly and simply as possible. For example, avoid questions containing double negatives, such as "Do you disapprove with the refusal to build a day care center in your neighborhood?" Also avoid double-barreled questions, such as "How many children under the age of 12 do you have, and do you have problems with child care?"

In addition, avoid leading and biased questions, such as "There is a great deal of community support for the new youth center; are you in favor of it?" Also, ask only questions respondents are capable of answering, in that they have some knowledge of the issue being researched. Try not to ask questions about future intentions, instead focus on the present. Finally, in an effort to maintain maximum neutrality, avoid response sets—in other words, don't phrase a series of questions in such a way that the answers will probably all be the same (for example, all yeses or all nos), since people tend to become set in a certain way of responding.

Just as interviews generally have high response rates, questionnaires—particularly those that are mailed—have low response rates. You can take some precautions to help improve the response rate, though. Such precautions include taking care with the questionnaire's length, the structure of the questions, the content of the questions, the format of the questionnaire, the cover letter, and follow-up.

Length.   Make the questionnaire as short as possible and eliminate unnecessary questions. When constructing a questionnaire, for each question ask yourself, "How is this question relevant to my research question?" If you cannot come up with a good answer, drop the question.

Structure of the questions.   Questions can be structured in two ways: closed-ended and open-ended. A **closed-ended question** gives the respondent a limited number of categories to use as answers. For example:

Name those who help you with child care:

_____ parents

_____ older children

_____ other relatives

_____ day care center

_____ family day care

_____ unrelated babysitter

_____ other

These are easy for the researcher to understand once the questionnaire is returned, but it is important to ensure that all possible categories are included for the respondent. Closed-ended questions result in quantitative data.

An **open-ended question** leaves it up to the respondent to create a response. No alternatives are given. For example:

What kinds of improvements would you suggest the day care center make in this next year? _____

Open-ended questions can be intimidating to respondents and they may be put off by them, but this type of question ensures that respondents can answer in ways that accurately reflect their views—that is, they are not forced to respond using the researcher's categories. Open-ended questions are particularly useful when you do not know a great deal about the subject that you are investigating. They also provide a way of collecting qualitative data.

The content of the questions. One strategy for increasing the response rate is to limit sensitive questions, or if they have to be included, to embed them within the questionnaire. The same holds true for many demographic questions such as gender and educational level. Instead of starting the questionnaire with these questions, place them at the end. Most respondents are not interested in these questions and can be discouraged if they are the first questions.

New Mexico State University
Department of Social Work
3SW, PO Box 30001
Las Cruces, NM 88003-8001

I would like to ask you to take about 10 minutes to complete this questionnaire. This is part of a study on women and employment. Your answers will help in the planning of services and programs in order to assist working women like yourself.

Please do not write your name on the questionnaire.

This questionnaire will be picked up tomorrow, or you can mail it to the above address.

If you have any questions about the study, please ask the person who is distributing the questionnaire, or call me at 555-2143.

Also, if you are interested in the results of this study or would be willing to be interviewed, complete and mail the attached postcard to me.

Christine Marlow, Ph.D.
Professor of Social Work

Figure 9.2 **Example of a cover letter**

Format of the questionnaire. The response rate can also be enhanced by the overall packaging of the questionnaire. Make sure it is free of typographical and spelling errors. Ensure that the layout is clear and uncluttered.

Cover letter. If you are mailing the questionnaire, include a cover letter that very briefly describes the purpose of the study and encourages the person to respond. You may want to include a small incentive, such as a quarter, coupons, or a pen. Of course, the person should never be coerced to respond. Also, emphasize in the cover letter that responses will be kept confidential. An example of a cover letter is shown in Figure 9.2.

Follow-ups. Second mailings can enhance the response ratio of mailed questionnaires by about 10%, but of course they add to the cost of the project.

A checklist for constructing a questionnaire or an interview schedule is given in Table 9.1.

Even with a carefully designed and administered questionnaire, response rates can still suffer. As we discussed in relation to interviews, other facts can influence the response rate besides the structure of the instrument or the way it is administered. These factors include the topics and variables included in the research itself.

Table 9.1   **Checklist for constructing questionnaire and interview questions**

_____ The questions are short.	_____ Consent has been given to answer the questions.
_____ There are no double-barreled questions.	_____ Anonymity and confidentiality have been assured.
_____ The questions are clear and focused.	If mailed:
_____ There are no sensitive questions.	_____ A cover letter is attached.
_____ There are no leading questions.	_____ The questionnaire is clearly formatted.
_____ The respondents are capable of answering the questions.	_____ The questionnaire is short.
_____ The questions are focused on the present.	_____ There are mostly closed-ended questions.
_____ There are no questions containing double negatives.	_____ There is a return date.
_____ The response categories are balanced.	_____ A stamped, addressed envelope is included.
_____ The questions are in a language that can be understood by the respondent.	

Applicability

Questionnaires can be used in preference to other data collection techniques when

- a high response rate is not a top priority
- anonymity is important
- budgets are limited, although extensive mailings of questionnaires can also be expensive
- the respondents are literate

Observation

Not all phenomena can be measured by interviews or questionnaires. Examples of these types of phenomena include illegal behaviors or children's behavior. If we are interested in a child's behavior in the classroom, interviewing or administering a questionnaire to the child would probably not elicit objective responses. As a social work student, you probably realize that observation is an integral part of social work practice, and you have already learned to be a good observer. Observation can be structured or unstructured.

Structured Observation

When behaviors are known and categorized prior to the observation, and the intention is to collect quantitative data, **structured observation** is the method of choice. In this method, behaviors are categorized prior to the observation according to their characteristics, including their frequency, direction, and magnitude. These categories can then be quantified.

Take the example of trying to measure a child's inattention in the classroom. First, inattention needs to be clearly defined, perhaps as talking with other children without the teacher's permission. Frequency would be the number of occasions, during a specified period of time (for example, one hour), that the child talked with other children without permission. Duration would be the length of time the child talked. Magnitude would be how loudly the child talked within a specified period of time. Clearly, selection of the method of observation depends on what behavior is being measured, how the behavior is defined, and how often it occurs.

Observation

Soloman (1994) used observation as one of several data collection methods in her study of welfare workers' responses to homeless welfare applicants. She observed 25 interviews between welfare recipients and their caseworkers. She spent 100 hours at the welfare office watching the exchanges. She also noted her impressions of the workplace physical facilities, two staff meetings, and two in-service training sessions.

Unstructured Observation

When little is known about the behaviors being observed, or when an interpretive approach is adopted and the goal is to focus primarily on collecting qualitative data, **unstructured observation** is used. This method is used extensively in anthropology for studying unfamiliar cultures.

The observer interacts to varying degrees with those being observed. When the observer fully submerges him- or herself to become one of the observed group, this is known as **participant observation.** A classic example of participant observation in social work is the observer's becoming a member of a gang in order to observe gang behavior.

 Participant Observation

Sands (1995) studied the parenting experiences of low-income single women with serious mental disorders. Several methods of data collection were used; one of these was participant observation by the researcher and her assistant at the "social rehab" program. Each observer spent four to five hours a day on separate occasions for eleven days over a period of four months observing the children, teachers, and mothers. At times the observers assisted the teachers with the children.

Neutrality

Observation varies in its neutrality. The degree of neutrality depends a great deal on the type of observation, level of training, and control for reactivity.

Type of observation.   Generally, structured observation is more neutral than unstructured observation is, because in structured observation, the behaviors are defined beforehand. With unstructured observation, behaviors are not so clearly defined. In addition, in unstructured observation, the observer's involvement in the behavior can further bias the observation.

The level of training.   The more training the observers receive regarding the procedures to be followed for the observation, the greater the neutrality. Often, particularly in structured observation, the categories are not immediately apparent, no matter how much care was taken in their development. Observers may need to be instructed in what is meant by, for example, asking for the participant's opinion.

Control for reactivity.   Reactivity, or the reactive effect, is the problem of subjects changing their behavior in some way as a result of the observer's observing them. (This effect was discussed earlier in regard to interviewing.) Reactivity can be partly controlled by using one or more of the following four strategies: videotapes, one-way mirrors, time with observer, and participant observation. A videotape recorder can be used to record behavior, but this may further inhibit the subject.

Second, sometimes one-way mirrors can be used, although we must be sure to obtain consent from those being observed. A third method for controlling reactivity is for the observer to spend some time with the subject so that the subject can become more comfortable with the observation. For example, if you want to observe classroom behavior, sit in the classroom for some time before you actually make the observation. Finally, we can overcome some reactivity effects with participant observation.

One further comment regarding neutrality is that observation need not always be visual. Sometimes enough information can be gained by listening to audio recordings. Maybe you have already used this method of observation as a means of improving your practice. Remember that since you are then without the nonverbal part of the interaction, neutrality can decrease from possible misinterpretation of the communication.

Applicability

Observation can be used in preference to other data collection techniques when behaviors are difficult to measure using other techniques, and observers and funds are available for training.

Logs and Journals

Sometimes logs, journals, or diaries can be used to collect data. These could be considered forms of self-observation but really warrant a separate discussion from observation. Logs, journals, or diaries—like observation—can be structured or unstructured.

The client may record his or her own behavior, or the social worker may record the client's behavior. Social workers also use logs and journals to record their own behavior. In Figure 9.3, the social worker is assessing her feelings and reactions in a home visit by recording in a journal. This log is unstructured and can allow for a stream of consciousness type of data collection; often these types of data are very valuable in an interpretive study. Logs can also be used to collect quantitative data. Service logs are of this type, where the entries involve checking or noting numbers next to categories.

Neutrality

Neutrality of logs and journals can be fairly limited, particularly if they are not structured or guided in some way. Neutrality can be enhanced by the use of more structured journals and logs so that the client or worker responds to specific questions. It is also helpful to encourage the client to record behaviors as soon as they occur rather than relying too much on retrospective information.

Applicability

Logs and journals can be used in preference to other data collection techniques when detailed personal experiences are required from subjects, and subjects are literate.

SOCIAL WORKER'S JOURNAL RECORD OF A HOME VISIT TO A CLIENT
Thursday, February 15

Tonight I visited Art A. again. The house looked dark when I pulled up, and I felt kind of uneasy. I went through all the safety precautions I had learned previously and then went to the door and knocked. My stomach felt jittery. Finally, after several minutes, I heard footsteps inside and Art opened the door. He looked kind of disheveled and I sensed that he was upset about something, but he asked me very politely to come in and sit down. The house was so dark! I asked him to turn on some lights, and I sat near the door, just in case. Something just didn't feel right. Then it hit me—his dog Spike hadn't barked when I knocked and that dog was his constant companion. I didn't want to ask him about Spike because I was sure it was bad. I felt a lump forming in my throat. What a great social worker I am! I'm supposed to be calm, cool, and collected! I guess if I didn't empathize though, I wouldn't have been there in the first place. Sure enough, Spike was dead—he'd been run over by a car.

CLIENT'S LOG OF DRINKING BEHAVIOR
Monday

10:00   I took my break at work and had a couple of sips of George's beer (he brings it in his lunch pail).

12:00   Drank 2 beers with lunch.

5:00   Stopped after work at Charlie's Grill and had 3 beers and 2 or 3 shots of whiskey, which my friends bought for me.

7:00   Jack Daniels before dinner (on the rocks).

8:00   3–4 beers watching the Broncos whip the Cowboys.

11:00   Went to buy cigs and stopped at Fred's bar, had a couple of beers.

1:00   Had a shot of whiskey before bed to help me get to sleep.

Figure 9.3   **Examples of journal and log recordings**

A Log

Burack-Weiss (1995) examined the memoirs and journals of people who have cared for severely ill and disabled parents, mates, and children. She concluded that the experiences have multiple meanings, many of them positive and life enhancing.

Scales

Most variables are not clear-cut and cannot be contained in one question or item; instead, they are composed of a number of different dimensions or factors. Level of functioning, marital satisfaction, and community attitudes are all of this complex type. Composite measures consisting of a number of items are called **scales.** Scales can be used in interviews and questionnaires—sometimes even in structured observation—and they are important when you need to collect quantitative data.

Standardized scales are a type of scale that is uniform and tested extensively. (Some sources of standardized scales are found in the Further Reading section at the end of this chapter.) Usually, published scales are accompanied by information about what they are intended to measure and with what type of population.

Scales are composed of several questions or observations "that have a logical or empirical structure to them" (Ruben & Babbie, 1989, p. G7). The most common form for social science research is the **Likert Scale.** The respondent is shown a series of statements and is then asked to respond using one of five response alternatives, usually "strongly agree," "agree," "no opinion," "disagree," "strongly disagree," or some variant of these. An example of a standardized scale including Likert measures is given in Figure 9.4. This is the F-COPES scale (McCubbin & Thomson, 1991) used to measure family coping.

Sometimes you may need a scale to measure a specific variable—for example, child well-being or aggression. Whenever possible, as with other types of data collection methods, try to use existing scales; they can eliminate considerable work. There are some drawbacks to using existing scales, though: They may not be designed to measure the variables in your study. For example, a family coping scale would not be appropriate for measuring family cohesion. The other problem is the temptation to design research around a standardized instrument—for example, changing your study to look at family coping rather than family cohesion.

Three specific types of scaling are commonly used in social work research, particularly in practice evaluations: target problem scales, goal attainment scales, and rapid assessment instruments.

Target Problem Scales

Target problem scales are a means to track changes in a client's target behavior. This type of scale is particularly useful when actual outcomes are difficult to identify. The scale involves identifying a problem, applying an intervention, and then repeatedly rating the extent to which the target problem has changed (Mutschler, 1979). One such target problem scale is shown in Figure 9.5 on p. 176. This example includes a global improvement scale that summarizes the amount of change that actually took place in the target problem.

Goal Attainment Scale

Goal attainment scales (GAS) reflect the achievement of outcomes and are used both to set client goals and to assess whether goals have been met. Kiresuk and Lund (1977) were among those who first suggested using these for social work research. Goal attainment scaling involves four steps:

Purpose:

The Family Crisis Oriented Personal Evaluation Scales is designed to record effective problem-solving attitudes and behavior which families develop to respond to problems or difficulties.

Directions:

First, read the list of response choices one at a time.

Second, decide how well each statement describes your attitudes and behavior in response to problems or difficulties. If the statement describes your response very well, then circle the number 5 indicating that you STRONGLY AGREE; if the statement does not describe your response at all, then circle the number 1 indicating that you STRONGLY DISAGREE; if the statement describes your response to some degree, then select a number 2, 3, or 4 to indicate how much you agree or disagree with the statement about your response.

WHEN WE FACE PROBLEMS OR DIFFICULTIES IN OUR FAMILY, WE RESPOND BY:	Strongly disagree	Moderately disagree	Neither agree nor disagree	Moderately agree	Strongly agree
1. Sharing our difficulties with relatives	1	2	3	4	5
2. Seeking encouragement and support from friends	1	2	3	4	5
3. Knowing we have the power to solve major problems	1	2	3	4	5
4. Seeking information and advice from persons in other families who have faced the same or similar problems	1	2	3	4	5
5. Seeking advice from relatives (grandparents, etc.)	1	2	3	4	5
6. Seeking assistance from community agencies and programs designed to help families in our situation	1	2	3	4	5
7. Knowing that we have the strength within our own family to solve our problems	1	2	3	4	5

(continued on next page)

Figure 9.4   **Family Crisis Oriented Personal Evaluation Scales (F-COPES)**

Source: From "F-COPES: Family-Crisis Oriented Personal Evaluation Scales," by H. McCubbin, D. Olson, & A. Larsen. In H. I. McCubbin, A. I. Thompson, & M. A. McCubbin (Eds.), *Family Assessment: Resiliency, Coping, and Adaptation: Inventories for Research and Practice.* Copyright © 1996 University of Wisconsin System. Reprinted with permission.

WHEN WE FACE PROBLEMS OR DIFFICULTIES IN OUR FAMILY, WE RESPOND BY:	Strongly disagree	Moderately disagree	Neither agree nor disagree	Moderately agree	Strongly agree
8. Receiving gifts and favors from neighbors (e.g., food, taking in mail, etc.)	1	2	3	4	5
9. Seeking information and advice from the family doctor	1	2	3	4	5
10. Asking neighbors for favors and assistance	1	2	3	4	5
11. Facing the problems "head-on" and trying to get solutions right away	1	2	3	4	5
12. Watching television	1	2	3	4	5
13. Showing that we are strong	1	2	3	4	5
14. Attending church services	1	2	3	4	5
15. Accepting stressful events as a fact of life	1	2	3	4	5
16. Sharing concerns with close friends	1	2	3	4	5
17. Knowing luck plays a big part in how well we are able to solve family problems	1	2	3	4	5
18. Exercising with friends to stay fit and reduce tension	1	2	3	4	5
19. Accepting that difficulties occur unexpectedly	1	2	3	4	5
20. Doing things with relatives (get-togethers, dinners, etc.)	1	2	3	4	5
21. Seeking professional counseling and help for family difficulties	1	2	3	4	5
22. Believing we can handle our own problems	1	2	3	4	5
23. Participating in church activities	1	2	3	4	5

(continued on next page)

Figure 9.4 Continued

WHEN WE FACE PROBLEMS OR DIFFICULTIES IN OUR FAMILY, WE RESPOND BY:	Strongly disagree	Moderately disagree	Neither agree nor disagree	Moderately agree	Strongly agree
24. Defining the family problem in a more positive way so that we do not become too discouraged	1	2	3	4	5
25. Asking relatives how they feel about problems we face	1	2	3	4	5
26. Feeling that no matter what we do to prepare, we will have difficulty handling problems	1	2	3	4	5
27. Seeking advice from a minister	1	2	3	4	5
28. Believing if we wait long enough, the problem will go away	1	2	3	4	5
29. Sharing problems with neighbors	1	2	3	4	5
30. Having faith in God	1	2	3	4	5

Figure 9.4   *Continued*

1. identifying the problem
2. specifying the areas where change is desired
3. making specific predictions for a series of outcome levels for each area
4. by a set date, scoring the outcomes as they are achieved (five possible outcomes are designated, from least to most favorable.)

Goal attainment scales can be used for a wide variety of problem situations. Figure 9.6 on p. 177 shows a modification of a goal attainment scale used by the New Mexico Human Services Department. In identifying the problem, positive terms should be used, as in this example. Instead of stating that the client lacks parenting skills, it is stated that she would like to learn new methods or techniques for parenting. The 0 level is the expected outcome for this goal, with two less successful (-2, -1) and two more successful ($+1$, $+2$) possible outcomes, with their respective criteria for attainment. At the initial time of scoring, this client was scored at a -2, or the most unfavorable outcome, but at a later date, the score was $+2$, indicating the client had achieved the best anticipated successful outcome for this goal. The GAS is an excellent way for both social worker and client to monitor progress and to determine the desirability of specific outcomes.

TARGET PROBLEM (rated by client)	TARGET PROBLEM RATING					GLOBAL IMPROVEMENT
	Degree of Severity				Degree of Change	
	Session #					
	1	2	3	4	Month	
Difficulty in talking about feelings	ES	ES	S	S	S	3
Getting to work on time	ES	S	S	NVS	NP	5
Fear of leaving house in daytime	ES	S	S	NVS	NP	5
	TOTAL					13 / 3 = 4.3
						Somewhat to a lot better

Severity Scale			Improvement Scale		
NP	=	No problem	1	=	Worse
NVS	=	Not very severe	2	=	No change
S	=	Severe	3	=	A little better
VS	=	Very severe	4	=	Somewhat better
ES	=	Extremely severe	5	=	A lot better

The global improvement rating is obtained by totaling the change scores and dividing by the number of target problems. This yields a number that reflects the client's overall improvement on all problems.

Figure 9.5   **Example of a target problem and global improvement scale for one client**

Rapid Assessment Instruments

A **rapid assessment instrument (RAI)** is a standardized series of structured questions or statements administered to the client to collect data in practice evaluations. Rapid assessment instruments are short, easy to administer, and easy to complete (see Levitt & Reid, 1981). Some examples include the Beck Depression Inventory, the Rathus Assertiveness Schedule, and the Multi-Problem Screening Inventory (Hudson, 1990). The MPSI can be used in conjunction with practice to collect data on several variables, including generalized contentment and marital satisfaction. These scales are computerized. Other types of scales can be found in the list of scales at the end of this chapter.

Neutrality

Scales are designed to be as neutral as possible, particularly those that are standardized.

Family Name: ___Vin___ Social Worker Name: ___Remington/Drake___

Goal Number: ___1___ Goal: To increase knowledge of parenting
skills to reduce the family's need for the services of the Human
Services Department.

Statement of problem: The client is requesting new methods or
techniques to help parent her children.

Date Goal Scaled: During first week Date when scored: Weekly

Rating of Client when goal was first scaled: ___-2___

Rating of Client when goal was last scored: ___+2___

Whose goal?: Client and Family Preservation Services team

Outcome Categories	Client's Attainment Criteria
Most unfavorable outcome thought likely* (−2)	The client totally disregards her parenting skills or tools when interacting with her children.
Less than expected success (−1)	The client listens to and understands new parenting skills and techniques presented but does not follow through with applying them.
Expected level of success (0)	The client learns a new parenting skill or technique suggested by Family Preservation Services.
More than expected success (+1)	The client applies one new skill or technique suggested by Family Preservation Services.
Best anticipated success* (+2)	The client applies two new skills or techniques suggested by Family Preservation Services.

*Unlikely, but still plausible.

Figure 9.6 **Example of a goal attainment scale**

Source: From "Goals and Attainment Scaling in the Context of Rural Child Welfare," by W. C. Horner and J. L. Pippard. Copyright © 1982 Child Welfare League of America. Used with permission. This article was originally published in *Child Welfare, 61* (7), 1982, p. 419.

Applicability

Scales are useful in studies where the emphasis is on collecting quantitative data. They are also useful for measuring multifaceted concepts. Scales are helpful when there is not a great deal of time available for data collection.

Secondary Data

Secondary data are data collected for purposes other than the present research. They may be data collected for another research project or data that were not collected with research in mind at all. With computers, secondary data have become more accessible even to the most humble of researchers. We use secondary data all the time in generalist practice—by consulting case records written by others and by referring to agency statistics when writing up reports. In fact, case records provide an important secondary data source for agency-based social worker research. Other sources of secondary data include U.S. census data and the numerous reports generated by state and federal government.

Secondary Data Use

Caputo (1995) studied the relationship between gender and race with regard to economic conditions and employment opportunities between 1969 and 1991. The study used data contained in the *Economic Report of the President* and the U.S. Department of Commerce's *Money Income of Household, Families and Persons in the United States* to examine annual mean differences in black and white, male and female employment opportunity and median income in the 1970s and 1980s.

Using Case Records as Data

Grigsby (1994) studied whether protective service workers recognize and emphasize the importance of maintaining parent-child or other attachment relationships. She examined the closed case records of children who had experienced foster care placements.

Agencies—both private and public—are creating data banks in increasing numbers and storing information about their operations, including the number of clients served, types of target problems, outcomes, staffing patterns, and budgets. Additionally, information can be obtained on crime rates, child abuse and neglect rates, and so forth.

These types of data are particularly useful when conducting a needs assessment. Two strategies can be adopted using secondary data in a needs assessment: rates under treatment and social indicators. The **rates under treatment** approach uses existing data from agencies to determine the needs of a community. The problem with this approach is that use of existing services may not, in fact, reflect unmet needs.

Rates Under Treatment

Benbenishty and Oyserman (1995) examined the present state of children in foster care in Israel in order to design future programs and develop policy. Data for the study consisted of existing information generated from the clinical information system set up for Israel's foster care service in 1988–1989. Under the system, each worker is expected to gather information about each of the children in his or her care on a series of standardized forms. The study was based on workers' annual reports on each child's situation and on plans for that child's immediate and long-term future.

The **social indicators** approach selects demographic data from existing public records to predict a community's needs. Existing statistics relating to people's spatial arrangement and facilities in a community, housing patterns, crime patterns, and so on, can help us determine where, for example, to place a community center.

Social Indicators

Ozawa (1995) investigated the economic status of vulnerable older women. She used a number of existing data sources that provided various economic indicators for older women. Data included surveys carried out by the Social Security Administration.

Indirect Sources

Indirect sources refer to information that can be used for research but that was initially collected for some other purpose. Indirect sources include case records, newspapers, and other media reports. For example, we may be interested in studying an agency's attitudes toward the developmentally disabled, so we consult case records on this topic. The most common way of dealing with indirect sources is to subject it to content analysis. **Content analysis** is a method of coding communication to a systematic quantifiable form. It will be discussed further in Chapters 10 and 11.

Neutrality

When using secondary data, we need to be aware that sometimes these data have limited neutrality. Indirect sources can often be particularly biased because they were not initially collected for research purposes. For example, there may be gaps in a record that we are using. In addition, because records were made for a purpose other than ours, information relating to our research question may be missing. For example, if we were gathering information on agency attitudes toward the developmentally disabled, that information may be missing from case records.

Direct sources are more neutral, but the researcher needs to verify the exact form of the questions that were initially asked. The form of questions asked later by the secondary researcher may be different; we need to know what this difference is. For example, you may be interested in the number of juveniles seen by the local juvenile probation office who had a previous record of substance abuse. You may be interested primarily in alcohol use, whereas the data collected did not distinguish between alcohol and other types of substance abuse. When using secondary data, you cannot assume that the first researcher's questions are similar to your own.

Colby (1982) discussed some of these problems in her article on secondary analysis. She also pointed out that secondary analysis is especially valuable for the study of women because theories about women, and women themselves, have undergone substantial change. Consequently, it is important to reanalyze data to determine the extent to which different results are due to a different interpretation or in fact due to changes that have occurred over time.

Applicability

Secondary data can be used when the data are available (this is not always the case). Secondary data also can be applied when the definition of the secondary data variables and the form of the questions are the same (or similar) to yours; if not, you must at least be aware of the differences. Secondary data can be helpful when a needs assessment is required, and the budget is limited. Secondary data can yield much information when you are interested in conducting a historical study—for example, the history of an agency or of the way a particular problem has been addressed in the past.

WHO COLLECTS THE DATA

As with the other decisions to be made concerning data collection, the decision about who should collect the data depends greatly on the type of research question asked. We tend to think of the researcher as the only person who should collect the data, as when interviewing or administering a questionnaire.

Apart from the researcher, the client or subject can also collect the data. Journals or diaries can be used in this way. Questionnaires can be self-administered; mailed questionnaires are the obvious example. Clients can also observe and record their own behavior using scales or checklists. Engaging the client in the data collection process is particularly valuable in conducting single-system studies, and as we saw in Chapter 7, can provide opportunities for feedback on changes in the client's behavior.

Earlier reactivity effects were discussed. This reactivity effect can also be a problem when the client collects data on his or her own behavior or uses **self-monitoring.** This reactivity can be quite strong, resulting in self-monitoring being used as an intervention device. Kopp (1988) presented an interesting review of the literature on how self-monitoring has been used both as a research and as a practice tool in social work.

COMBINING DATA COLLECTION METHODS

Methods and instruments can and should be used in conjunction with one another. As mentioned earlier in the chapter, both qualitative and quantitative data can be collected. In addition, a number of different methods can be used in the same study.

Using Multiple Measures

A study of the maltreatment of school-age children was carried out by Wodarski, Kurtz, Gaudin, and Howing (1990). Measures included

- a caseworker report, including child well-being scales
- a child behavior checklist
- a child interview schedule
- the child's permanent school record
- the Teoness Inventory (a self-report measure for delinquency)
- a parent interview schedule
- the Piers-Harris Children's Self-Concept Scale
- scales of independent behavior
- composite adjustment indices

Through the use of these instruments, the researchers were able to collect data concerning the children's school performance, socioemotional development, and adaptive behavior, as well as for control and demographic variables.

Table 9.2   **Characteristics of data collection methods**

	unstructured interviews	mailed question-naire	participant observation	standardized observation	logs	face-to-face administered standardized scales
high response rate	yes	no	n/a	yes	maybe	yes
anonymity assured	no	yes	no	no	no	no
low reactivity effects	no	yes	maybe	maybe	yes	yes
illiterate subjects	yes	no	yes	yes	no	no
semilegal or illegal behavior	no	maybe	maybe	no	no	no
large sample or limited funds	no	yes	no	no	no	yes
in-depth, "thick description"	yes	no	yes	no	yes	no

Combining measures can enrich your study and help ensure that you are tapping a maximum number of dimensions of the phenomenon under study. Using a number of data collection methods is sometimes called **triangulation.** Other forms of triangulation include using a number of different theories, researchers, or research methods—for example, a mix of interpretive and positivist approaches. Triangulation, particularly in interpretive studies, can help enhance the validity of findings.

DETERMINING RELIABILITY AND VALIDITY

Before a measuring instrument is used in the research process, it is important to assess its reliability and validity. This is important regardless of whether an interpretive or positivistic approach is used, although the way in which they are assessed does vary according to the approach and according to whether the data are qualitative or quantitative. Quantitative data—particularly scales and highly standard interview, questionnaire, and observation schedules—lend themselves most easily to the tests for reliability and validity presented here. Standardized scales are always accompanied by the results of validity and reliability tests. Open-ended, qualitative instruments, however, are more difficult to assess for reliability and validity. The principles presented here, if not the specific tests themselves, can still be used as guidelines with open-ended instruments to improve their validity and reliability.

Reliability

Reliability indicates the extent to which a measure reveals actual differences in the phenomenon measured, rather than differences inherent in the measuring instrument itself. Reliability refers to the consistency of a measure. To illustrate, a wooden ruler is a reliable measure for a table. If the ruler were made of elastic, however, it would not provide a reliable measure, because repeated measures of the same table would differ due to the ruler's expanding and contracting. If a client is chronically depressed and you measure the degree of depression at two points in time, the instrument is reliable if you get close to the same score each time, provided the level of depression has not in fact changed. Clearly you need to establish the instrument's reliability before you can determine true changes in the phenomena under study.

As generalist social workers, you need to assess the extent to which the data collection instrument is reliable. There are two major ways to assess the instrument's reliability: assessing sources of error and assessing the degree to which the instrument's reliability has actually been tested. Each of these will be discussed in turn.

Sources of Error

When assessing the reliability of an instrument, you need to determine whether there is evidence of certain sources of error. The following are four major types of error: unclear definition of variables, use of retrospective information, variations in the conditions for collecting the data, and structure of the instrument.

Unclear Definitions of Variables

As we saw in Chapter 4, variables can be difficult to define because many social work terms tend to be vague. If a variable is not clearly operationalized and defined, its measurement lacks reliability: The possible outcome can be interpreted differently by different social workers. The wording of questions in questionnaires often creates problems with unclear definitions of variables. A question might be phrased in such a way that two individuals interpret it differently and provide two different answers, even though the actual behavior they are reporting is the same. For example, people might be asked, "Do you often use public transportation in the city?" In responding, people may interpret *often* in different ways. Interpretive studies where the variables are not necessarily clearly defined and operationalized clearly pose a particular challenge. Extensive use of interviews in these types of studies overcomes some of the problems, because the unstructured data collection method allows exploration of the concepts to take place. If the variable described by the respondent is unclear, the respondent can be asked to elaborate and define. The definition comes from the subjects, rather than from the researcher.

Use of Retrospective Information

Retrospective information is gathered through subject recall, either by a questionnaire or an interview. These data are almost inevitably distorted. Moreover, sometimes subject recall is hampered because of the nature of the topic under study—as you might expect if you were investigating an adult's experience of childhood sexual abuse, for example. Case records are one form of retrospective data collection, and they are consequently subject to considerable error. Case records usually reflect the idiosyncratic recording practices of the individual social worker. The worker will select out certain aspects of the case for recording, resulting in impaired reliability.

Variations in Conditions for Collecting the Data

When interviews are used to collect data, interview conditions can also affect reliability. The subject may respond differently depending on whether the interviewer is male or female. (This is the reactive effect we discussed earlier.) Similar problems may arise due to the ethnicity and age of the interviewer. Where the interview is conducted may also cause disparities in responses. Even with questionnaires (for example, mailed questionnaires), lack of control over the conditions under which they are administered can result in low reliability.

Structure of the Instrument

Certain aspects of the data collection method itself may enhance or decrease reliability. An open-ended questionnaire that requires that responses be categorized and coded can present reliability problems.

Testing Reliability

In addition to identifying the sources of error in an instrument, we can also assess the extent to which the instrument's reliability has been tested. As generalist social workers, you will need to be able to understand what reliability tests, if any, others have conducted. In addition, you may be able to use these tests on some of the instruments you develop.

Reliability is determined by obtaining two or more measures of the same thing and seeing how closely they agree. Four methods are used to establish the reliability of an instrument: test-retest, alternate form, split half, and observer reliability.

Test-Retest

Test-retest involves repeatedly administering the instrument to the same set of people on separate occasions. These people should not be subjects in the actual study. The results of the repeated administrations are then compared. If the results are similar, reliability of the instrument is high. A problem associated with this method of testing reliability is that the first testing has influenced the second. For example, during the second testing the individuals may be less anxious, less motivated, or less interested, or they may simply remember their answers from the first test and repeat them. In addition, they may have learned from the first testing, particularly with attitude questions. To avoid these problems, some have suggested (Bostwick & Kyte, 1989) that measuring instruments that are strongly affected by memory or repetition should not be tested for reliability using this method.

Alternate Form

With **alternate form** tests, different but equivalent forms of the same test are administered to the same group of individuals—usually close in time—and then compared. The major problem with this approach is in the development of the equivalent tests, which can be time consuming. In addition, this approach can still involve some of the problems associated with the test-retest method.

Split Half

With the **split half** method, items on the instrument are divided into comparable halves. For example, a scale could be divided so the first half should have the same score as the second half. This testing method looks at the internal consistency of the measure. The test is administered and the two halves compared. If the score is the same, the instrument is probably reliable. A major problem with this approach is ensuring that the two halves are equivalent. Equivalency is problematic with instruments other than scales.

Observer Reliability

Observer reliability involves comparing administrations of an instrument done by different observers or interviewers. To use this method effectively, the observers need to be thoroughly trained; at least two people will code the content of the responses according to certain criteria.

Each of these methods of testing for reliability involves comparing two or more results. Usually, this comparison uses some kind of **correlation coefficient.** This is a statistic that measures the extent to which the comparisons are similar or not similar—that is, the extent to which they are related or correlated. The concept of correlation will be discussed in more detail in Chapters 12 and 13. For our purposes now in assessing reliability, the correlation coefficient can range from 0.0 to 1.0, the latter number reflecting a perfect correlation, or the highest level of reliability possible. Generally, a coefficient of .80 suggests the instrument is reasonably reliable. Table 9.3 summarizes the criteria that can be used to assess an instrument's reliability.

Table 9.3   ***Criteria for assessing the reliability of measuring instruments***

1	Is the variable clearly defined?
2	Is retrospective information avoided?
3	Are there controlled conditions under which the data are collected?
4	Is the question format closed?
5	Are reliability tests used? Is so, is the correlation coefficient greater than 0.5?

If the answer is yes to most of these questions, then the instrument is probably reliable.

Instruments with High Reliability

The scales included in the Multi-Problem Screening Inventory developed by Hudson (1990) all have a test-retest and split half reliability correlation coefficients of at least .90. The scales were developed for a variety of behaviors, including child problems, guilt, work problems, and alcohol abuse.

Validity

The **validity of a measuring instrument** reflects the extent to which you are measuring what you think you are measuring. This is a different idea than reliability. To take the example used previously, if a wooden ruler is used to measure the dimensions of a table, it is a reliable and valid instrument. If you use the ruler to measure ethnicity, however, the instrument maintains its reliability, but it is no longer valid. You would not be measuring ethnicity but some other variable (for example, height), which has no relationship to ethnicity as far as we know.

Validity is not as straightforward as reliability because there are different types of validity, and each one is tested in a different way. The three main types of validity are criterion validity, content validity, and construct validity. Each type of validity relates to different aspects of the overall validity of the instrument, and each addresses different dimensions of the problem of ensuring that what is being measured is what was intended to be measured. These types of validity will be discussed along with the ways in which each can be tested.

Validity testing can be quite complex, and sometimes entire articles in the social work literature are devoted to testing the validity of specific instruments. For example, Guttmann and Brenna (1990) assessed the validity of the Personal Experience Inventory (PEI), an instrument for assessing the level and nature of substance abuse in adolescents. Seaburg (1988) examined the validity of Child Well-Being Scales and concluded that due to the complexity of the concept of child well-being, the validity of the scale is somewhat questionable and should be used cautiously. As generalist social workers, you will need to understand what type of validity testing has been carried out and in some cases test instruments you have developed.

Criterion Validity

Criterion validity describes the extent to which a correlation exists between the measuring instrument and another standard. To validate an instrument developed to assess a program that helps pregnant teenagers succeed in high school, a criterion such as SAT scores might be used as a comparison. Similarities in scores would indicate that criterion validity had been established.

Content validity

Content validity is concerned with the representativeness of the content of the instrument. The content included in the instrument needs to be relevant to the concept we are trying to measure. For example, the content validity of an instrument developed to measure knowledge of parenting skills could be obtained by consulting with various experts on parenting skills—perhaps social workers who run parenting groups and a professor at the department of social work. They could then point out areas in which the instrument may be deficient. Clearly, content validity is partly a matter of judgment, depending upon the knowledge of the experts who are available to you.

Construct validity

Construct validity describes the extent to which an instrument measures a theoretical construct. A measure may have criterion and content validity but still not measure what it is intended to measure. Construct validity is the most difficult to establish, because as we mentioned earlier, many research variables are difficult to define and theoretically vague. Constructs used in social work include aggression, sociability, and self-esteem, to name just a few. With construct validity, we are looking not only at the instrument but also at the theory underlying it. The instrument must reflect this theory.

For example, in testing the construct validity of an instrument to measure aggression in preschoolers, the associated theoretical expectations need to be examined by referring to the literature and research on the topic. One explanation that may be found is that the highly aggressive children will not be achieving well in the classroom. If the instrument does not reflect this dimension of the topic, the instrument probably does not have construct validity. IQ tests provide an example of a measure with low construct validity. IQ tests were created to measure intelligence. Since their development, however, it has become apparent that they measure only one dimension of intelligence—the potential to achieve in a white middle-class academic system. Other dimensions of intelligence remain untapped by IQ tests, resulting in their limited validity for measuring intelligence.

One way of more fully ensuring construct validity is to define the construct using small, concrete, observable behaviors (Duncan & Fiske, 1977). Such definition helps avoid some of the wishy-washiness associated with many constructs used in social work practice. For example, if both the verbal and non-verbal behaviors of preschoolers are recorded, and certain patterns of these behaviors become apparent in those children previously labeled aggressive, you can be more fully assured that your label does in fact have construct validity.

Once you are familiar with this information on validity and the ways it can be tested, you are then in a position as a generalist social worker to assess the validity of the measuring instruments you read about or that you propose to use. Table 9.4 presents a checklist that can be used to assess the validity of instruments.

Feedback

Feedback is an important way of testing the validity of quantitative data collected from interpretive studies. In this type of research, the concepts under study may not be clearly defined at the outset. Moreover, the intent of the research may well be to define and elaborate on these concepts. However, data must be understandable and relevant to the participants in the research. The participants should be allowed to verify the data. This feedback can be carried out both formally (for example, through focus groups or community meetings) or informally (for example, through meetings and informal gatherings with the participants).

Note that often in the collection of qualitative data, responsibility for validating the data lies directly with the researcher rather than being assured

Reporting of Reliability and Validity of a Standardized Measuring Instrument

McCubbin and Thomson (1991) reported on the reliability and validity of the Family Crisis Oriented Personal Evaluation Scales (F-COPES). They reported that the F-COPES has good stability with a four-week test-retest correlation of .81. The individual subscales have test-retest correlations ranging from .61 to .95. The authors also reported that the scale has good concurrent validity, correlating with several other family measures.

Table 9.4   **Criteria for assessing the validity of quantitative measuring instruments**

1	Was the instrument tested for criterion validity?
2	Was the instrument tested for content validity?
3	Was the instrument tested for construct validity?
4	Is the variable defined as clearly and concretely as possible?

If the answer is yes to most of these questions, then the instrument is probably valid (that is, if the findings from the tests support the validity of the instrument).

through the use of prescribed methods, such as a criterion validity check. Therefore it is even more important for the researcher to act responsibly and ethically.

THE AGENCY AND DATA COLLECTION

As generalist social workers, you often do not have much of a choice when it comes to selecting a data collection method. You may be asked to help develop a questionnaire for a needs assessment, in which case the decision about the data collection has already been made.

Because of time and money constraints, some of the more complicated and time-consuming data collection techniques—such as lengthy questionnaire and scale construction, participant observation, and extensive interviews—cannot be considered by the generalist social worker engaged in research. Instead, consider using rapid assessment instruments, case records, and self-observation (by the client) as much as possible.

It should not be forgotten, however, that generalist social workers can be key players in the data collection process. After all, it is they who have access to critical data, both directly from the clients and indirectly from the agency records. Thus the challenge for generalist social workers becomes to explore the opportunities offered in the agencies for data collection and research by either undertaking research themselves or encouraging their agencies to explore research possibilities.

ETHICAL ISSUES IN COLLECTING DATA

When collecting data for a research study, we need to be concerned about three ethical issues: potential harm to the subjects, anonymity and confidentiality, and justification for research.

Harm to the Subjects

Clearly, we need to avoid harming the subjects in any way. The NASW Code of Ethics (1997) states:

- Social workers engaged in evaluation or research should carefully consider possible consequences and should follow guidelines developed for the protection of evaluation and research participants. Appropriate institutional review boards should be consulted.
- Social workers engaged in evaluation or research should protect participants from unwarranted physical or mental distress, harm, danger, or deprivation.

As simplistic as these mandates may seem, on closer examination these things are easier said than done. When asking questions in whatever form—whether interviewing or using a questionnaire—you are often requiring subjects to examine and assess their own behavior. Questions relating to childhood abuse may be painful for the respondent. Other questions that are difficult to answer concern income and the ability to pay for a proposed service.

Consequently, assessing the extent of discomfort for the subject can be difficult. Some projects—for example, federally funded research and research conducted at universities—require the proposed research to be reviewed by **human subjects committees** or **institutional review boards.** During the review process, the researcher must answer specific questions regarding potential harm to subjects. Even when an outside review is not required, we need to be sensitive to the impact of our data collection method on subjects.

Anonymity and Confidentiality

Both anonymity and confidentiality help participants avoid harm. Again, the NASW Code of Ethics (1997) states:

- Social workers engaged in evaluation or research should ensure the anonymity or confidentiality of participants and of the data obtained from them. Social workers should inform participants of any limits of confidentiality, and when any records containing research data will be destroyed.

Anonymity means that the researcher cannot identify a given response with a given respondent. It was mentioned previously that an interview can never be anonymous, and when identification numbers are put on questionnaires to facilitate follow-up and increase the response rate, anonymity is also jeopardized. Ensuring anonymity not only reassures the subjects but can also enhance the objectivity of the responses. For example, if you are asking questions about deviant behavior, the respondent is more likely to give a response that accurately reflects the behavior if anonymity can be assured.

Confidentiality means that the researcher knows the identity of the respondents and their associated responses but ensures not to disclose this information. Obviously, confidentiality becomes particularly critical when conducting interviews, for which anonymity is impossible to ensure. The principle of confidentiality should be explained to respondents either verbally or in a cover letter accompanying the questionnaires. Do not confuse confidentiality and anonymity; they are different and are both extremely important.

Justification of the Research

The NASW Code of Ethics (1997) states:

- Social workers should never design or conduct evaluation or research that does not use consent procedures, such as certain forms of naturalistic observation and archival research, unless rigorous and responsible review of the research has found it to be justified because of its prospective scientific, educational, or applied value and unless equally effective alternative procedures that do not involve waiver of consent are not feasible.

Informed consent was discussed in Chapter 6. Using data that is not collected directly from the participants (such as client records and other secondary data) does not exempt the researchers from another ethical responsibility: ensuring the research is needed and justified.

HUMAN DIVERSITY ISSUES IN COLLECTING THE DATA

Awareness and knowledge of human diversity issues during the data collection stage of the research process. Some of the central issues to which we need to pay attention are the selection of the data collection method for diverse populations; the relevance to diverse populations of the content of the data collection method; and the application of the data collection method to diverse populations.

Selection of Data Collection Methods for Diverse Populations

The extent to which data collection methods may or may not be applicable to certain groups within a population needs to be considered. Some groups may be uncomfortable with the notion of being administered a questionnaire or being interviewed; you need to be sensitive to the ways in which different cultural groups might regard different methods.

For example, Myers (1977) recommended the use of in-depth interviews instead of questionnaires with certain groups, including respondents who are poor, of an ethnic or racial minority, or socially distant from the researcher. Using in-depth interviews rather than other data collection methods can enhance the validity of the responses. Myers suggested that sometimes, because of the time-consuming nature of this approach, in-depth interviews can be combined with more structured questionnaire methods.

Gilligan's (1982) analysis of the development of men's and women's resolutions of moral conflicts concluded that women develop a mode of thinking that is "contextual and narrative" and their understanding is based on the individual in the context of their relationship with others. This way of thinking is contrasted with men's, which is seen as focusing on autonomy and separation from others. Some authors (such as Davis, 1986) have suggested that women's different ways of thinking require different approaches to research—particularly different data collection techniques. Male research methodology—the traditional approach—emphasizes the abstract and formal and lends itself to quantification and the use of the positivist approach, whereas the female approach, with its emphasis on connection, lends itself more easily to an interpretive approach and its associated qualitative data.

Relevance to Diverse Populations of the Content of the Data Collection Method

In addition to the appropriateness of a particular data collection instrument, taking account of human diversity requires considering the content of that instrument and its appropriateness to the group under study.

Certain words or phrases—whether in interview or questionnaire form, whether conducted under the auspices of a feminist or traditional research approach—may be interpreted by the respondent in a different way from that intended by the researcher. In many cases, this divergence of interpretations may be due simply to the researcher's lack of understanding or insensitivity to the cultural group that is being studied. For example, some groups may interpret questions about mothers as including mothers-in-law. Serious validity problems can result, since the researcher is thinking of *mother* in one sense, and the subject is defining *mother* very differently. Reliability problems also arise.

Another perhaps less obvious problem might occur when conducting, for example, a research project concerned with methods and problems of disciplining children. You would need to acknowledge the methods and problems experienced by gay and lesbian parents (unless we purposefully *intend* to exclude them) in addition to those of heterosexual parents, because some of the problems gay and lesbian parents encounter might be different. Consequently, you would need to include questions relevant to this group so as not to exclude problems such parents might be experiencing and thus jeopardize the validity of your findings.

Earlier, we discussed the usefulness of rapid assessment instruments and other instruments that have already been developed. Check to see whether the instruments you use have been used with diverse populations and whether their reliability and validity have been tested with these groups.

Many of these issues are an extension of the discussion in Chapter 3 about the need to include relevant variables in the study. You must not only account for all the relevant variables but also be aware of human diversity issues in phrasing or constructing the data collection instrument.

Validating an Instrument with Diverse Populations

Briggs, Tovar, and Corcoran (1996) assessed the validity and reliability of the Children's Action Tendency Scale with Latino youth. They concluded that it may be usefully employed with Latino sixth and seventh graders.

Application of the Data Collection Method to Diverse Populations

Even if the data collection method and the structure and content of this method are sensitive to the needs of diverse populations, the way in which the instrument is administered still may not be.

For example, you may be carrying out a needs assessment for socially isolated, recently immigrated Asian women. To obtain valid and reliable information, you would need not only to include questions relevant to this population, but also to ensure that the interviews are conducted so that they elicit the required information. This necessitates the use of people who are sensitive to the population under study as interviewers, administrators of questionnaires, and observers. For example, with the Asian women, an interviewer would need to be familiar with this group's language, gender role, and intergenerational role expectations in order to engage the subject in the interview and obtain valid and reliable data.

SUMMARY

Quantitative approaches create categories of the phenomenon under study and assign numbers to these categories. Qualitative approaches examine the phenomenon in more detail. Data collection methods include interviews, questionnaires, observation, logs and journals, and secondary data. Scales can measure complex variables. There are several techniques for checking the reliability and validity of data collection methods.

When collecting data in an agency, data collection methods that are compatible to the practice need to be used. Ethical issues include considering potential harm to the subjects and the issues of confidentiality and anonymity. When considering human diversity issues, the selection, relevance, and application of the data collection method need to be considered.

STUDY/EXERCISE QUESTIONS

1. Develop a questionnaire to assess the campus needs (such as parking, day care, and so on) of students in your class. Include both open-ended and closed-ended questions.
   a. How do you decide what questions to include?
   b. How would you administer the questionnaire?

2. Have another student in the class critique your questionnaire and comment on its reliability and validity.

3. Using the source books listed in this chapter and others located at the library, find a suitable instrument to measure adolescents' self-esteem.
   a. Report on its validity and reliability.
   b. Are there any groups for which the instrument may not be reliable or valid?

4. Your agency has asked you to participate in planning a program for adults with a history of childhood sexual abuse.
   a. How would you collect data that would demonstrate a need exists for such a program?
   b. How would you ensure confidentiality?

5. Design a structured interview to assess the satisfaction of clients who have just finished receiving services from a family service agency.
   a. Conduct this interview with a classmate.
   b. Would other methods of data collection be more reliable or valid in this case?

6. Design a way of observing a Head Start student who is reported to be disrup-
    tive in the classroom.
    How would you check the validity and reliability of this method?

FURTHER READING

Beere, C. A. (1990). *Women and women's issues: A handbook of tests and measures.*
San Francisco: Jossey-Bass.
A collection of instruments that have been used for studies concerned with
women and women's issues.

Fischer, J., & Corcoran, K. (1994). *Measures for clinical practice: A sourcebook*
(Vols. 1–2) (2nd ed.). New York: The Free Press.
A collection of scales for research and practice.

Gordon, R. L. (1987). *Interviewing, strategy, techniques, and tactics* (4th ed.).
Homewood, IL: The Dorsey Press.
A useful reference book on research interviewing.

Irwin, D. M., & Bushness, M. M. *Observational strategies for child study.* New York:
Holt, Rinehart & Winston.
Includes some exercises to give experience in observation.

Levitt, J., & Reid, W. J. (1981). Rapid assessment instruments for practice. *Social
Work Research and Abstracts, 17,* 13–19.
A collection of instruments that can be used in the evaluation of individual
practice.

Lockhart, D. C. (Ed.). (1984). *Making effective use of mailed questionnaires.*
San Francisco: Jossey-Bass.
Discussion of the design and administration of mailed questionnaires.

Magura, S., & Moses, B. S. (1986). *Outcome measures for child welfare services:
Theory and applications.* Washington, DC: Child Welfare League of Amer-
ica, Inc.
A collection of scales for research and practice.

Miller, D. C. (1991). *Handbook of research design and social measurement.*
Newbury Park, CA: Sage.
A comprehensive collection of issues in research design and measurement.

Mueller, D. (1986). *Measuring social attitudes: A handbook for researchers and
practitioners.* New York: Teachers College Press.
Information on how to construct scales and examples of existing scales.

Warren, C. A. B. (1988). *Gender issues in field research.* Newbury Park, CA: Sage.
An excellent little book on conducting field research and gender. Includes
chapters on the sexual politics of field work and women's place in fieldwork
methodology.

REFERENCES

Anderson, J. E., Kann, L., Holtzman, D., Arday, S., Truman, B., & Kilbe, L.
(1990). *Family Planning Perspectives, 22* (6), 252–255.

Benbenishty, R., & Oyserman, D. (1995). Children in foster care: Their present situation and plans for their future. *International Social Work, 38* (2), 117–131.

Bostwick, G., & Kyte, N. (1989). Validity and reliability. In R. M. Grinnel (Ed.), *Social Work Research and Evaluation* (3rd ed., pp. 111–136). Itasca, IL: Peacock.

Briggs, H., Tovar, D., & Corcoran, K. (1996). The CATS: Is it reliable and valid with Latino youngsters? *Research in Social Work Practice, 6* (2), 229–235.

Burack-Weiss, A. (1995). The caregiver's memoir: A new look at family support. *Social Work, 40* (3), 391–396.

Caputo, R. (1995). Gender and race: Employment opportunity and the American economy, 1969–1991. *Families in Society, 76* (4), 239–247.

Colby, A. (1982). The use of secondary analysis in the study of women and social change. *Journal of Social Issues, 38* (1), 119–123.

Duncan, S., & Fiske, D. (1977). *Face-to-Face Interaction.* Hillsdale, NJ: Erlbaum.

Davis, L. V. (1986). A feminist approach to social work research. *Affilia, 1,* 32–47.

First, R. J., Rife, J. C., & Toomey, B. G. (1994). Homelessness in rural areas: Causes, patterns, and trends. *Social Work, 39* (1), 97–107.

Gilligan, C. (1982). *In a different voice.* Cambridge, MA: Harvard University Press.

Gregg, R. (1994). Explorations of pregnancy and choice in a high-tech age. In C. Riessman (Ed.), *Qualitative studies in social work research.* Newbury Park, CA: Sage.

Grigsby, K. (1994). Maintaining attachment relationships among children in foster care. *Families in Society, 75* (5), 269–276.

Guttmann, D. R., & Brenna, D. C. (1990). The personal experience inventory: An assessment of the instruments' validity among a delinquent population in Washington State. *Journal of Adolescent Chemical Dependency, 1* (2), 6–10.

Hudson, W. (1990). *The multi-problem screening inventory.* Tempe, AZ: Walmyr Publishing.

Johnson, I. (1995). Family members' perceptions of and attitudes toward elder abuse. *Families in Society, 76* (4), 220–229.

Kiresuk, T. J., & Lund, S. H. (1977). Goal attainment scaling. In C. C. Attkisson, W. A. Hargreave, M. J. Horowitz, & S. E. Sorenson (Eds.), *Evaluation of human service programs.* New York: Academic Press.

Kopp, J. (1988). Self-monitoring: A literature review of research and practice. *Social Work,* 8–21.

Levitt, J., & Reid, W. J. (1981). Rapid assessment instruments for practice. *Social Work Research and Abstracts, 17,* 13–19.

McCubbin, H. I., & Thomson, A. I. (Eds.). (1991). *Family assessment inventories for research and practice.* Madison: University of Wisconsin.

Mutschler, E. (1979). Using single-case evaluation procedures in a family and children's service agency: Integration of practice and research. *Journal of Social Service Research, 3,* 115–134.

Myers, V. (1977). Survey methods for minority population. *Journal of Social Issues, 33,* 11–19.

National Association of Social Workers. (1997). NASW code of ethics. *NASW News, 25,* 25.

Oliveira, W., Baizerman, M., & Pellet, L. (1992). Street children in Brazil and their helpers: Comparative views on aspirations and the future. *International Social Work, 35* (2), 163–176.

Ozawa, M. (1995). The economic status of vulnerable older women. *Social Work, 40* (3), 323–331.

Patton, M. (1990). *Qualitative evaluation and research methods.* Newbury Park, CA: Sage.

Peterson, D. A. (1990). Personnel to serve the aging in the field of social work: Implications for educating professionals. *Social Work, 35* (5), 412–415.

Ruben, A., & Babbie, E. (1989). *Research methods for social work.* Belmont, CA: Wadsworth.

Salgado de Snyder, V. N., Cervantes, R. C., & Padilla, A. M. (1990). Gender and ethnic differences in psychosocial stress and generalized distress among Hispanics. *Sex Roles, 22* (7/8), 441–453.

Sands, R. (1995). The parenting experience of low income single women with serious mental disorders. *Families in Society, 76* (2), 86–96.

Seaburg, J. R. (1988). Child well-being scales: A critique. *Social Work Research and Abstracts, 24* (3), 9–15.

Solomon, C. (1994). Welfare workers' response to homeless welfare applicants. In C. Riessman (Ed.), *Qualitative studies in social work research.* Newbury Park, CA: Sage.

Wodarski, J. S., Kurtz, P. Q., Gaudin, J. M., Jr., & Howing, P. T. (1990). Maltreatment and the school age child: Major academic, socio-emotional, and adaptive outcomes. *Social Work, 35* (7), 506–513.

Organizing the Data

ometimes you get so caught up in designing the project and in planning the data collection that once the data is in hand, you may wonder what to do with it all. The three types of research discussed in this book—practice evaluation, program evaluation, and needs assessment—all have the potential to overwhelm you with data.

This chapter is concerned with organizing the data once they are collected. This stage bridges the gap between data collection and data analysis. In generalist practice, we can make the analogy to collating and organizing the data prior to attempting an assessment.

How the data are analyzed depends to a great extent on whether the data are qualitative or quantitative. As discussed in Chapter 1, quantitative data are the result of fitting diverse phenomena into predetermined categories. These categories are then analyzed using statistical techniques. Qualitative data, on the other hand, produce a mass of detailed information in the form of words rather than numbers. Such data must be subjected to forms of analysis that will help make sense out of these words.

These different data also require different strategies for their organization before they can be analyzed.

This chapter includes the following topics:

- organizing quantitative data—coding and basic programming
- organizing qualitative data
- the agency and organizing the data
- ethical issues in organizing the data
- human diversity issues in organizing the data

ORGANIZING QUANTITATIVE DATA

You work for a public agency that provides assistance to foster care families. Your supervisor has just asked you to develop a questionnaire to mail to all foster families in the area served by the agency to identify their unmet needs. There are 300 foster families in your area. You send out a two-page questionnaire to all 300 families and receive 150 back. These questionnaires contain a considerable amount of valuable data for your agency. These data are in raw form, however, and as such are not very useful to you. Imagine trying to tally answers to 30 questions for 150 questionnaires by hand—a very time-consuming and tedious process. This mass of quantitative data can be analyzed using statistical procedures, which can be further facilitated through the use of the computer.

You need to be thinking about how the data will be organized as early in the research process as possible. This is especially important when you use a questionnaire to collect data because the way questions are structured can influence the way data can ultimately be organized. Organizing quantitative data involves coding the data and basic programming in preparation for analysis.

Coding the Data

Referring to the foster family questionnaire, the first step to transferring the information from the questionnaire to the computer is to code it. **Coding** involves organizing the collected information so that it can be entered into the computer. Coding is accomplished in three steps: (1) converting the responses to numerical codes; (2) assigning names to the variables; and (3) creating a code book.

Converting the Responses to Numerical Codes

In the foster care example, one question on the questionnaire is: "How many times in the last month were you contacted by a worker in the agency?" The response to this type of question is very straightforward; it simply entails entering the number reported into the computer. Note that this response is at the ratio level of measurement and reflects the absolute magnitude of the value (see Chapter 3). The level of measurement determines the type of statistical analysis that we can perform. With ratio data, you have a great deal of latitude in that responses can be manipulated in a variety of ways: They can be added, subtracted, multiplied, and divided. They represent real numbers and are not strictly codes.

When you look at the other types of questions and their responses, however, often the number that is assigned to the response is a code, and there is a certain amount of arbitrariness in its assignment. This is the case with data at the nominal and ordinal level of measurement. For example, the questionnaire might read: "How would you gauge your overall level of satisfaction with the services our agency provides? (Circle the most applicable response.)

very satisfied   satisfied   somewhat satisfied   not satisfied"

This information can be entered more easily if you assign numeral codes to each of the possible responses—for example:

very satisfied   1
satisfied   2
somewhat satisfied   3
not satisfied   4

Note that the level of measurement of this variable is ordinal. The numbers are ranked, but the distance between the numbers is not necessarily equal. Thus our use of these numbers in statistical analysis will be more limited than it was for those in the previous question. Note that this satisfaction question constitutes one variable with four different possible responses or values, coded 1 to 4.

Another question on the questionnaire is this: "Specifically, which services could be expanded to meet any of your needs more to your satisfaction? Please check all that apply.

_____   Individual counseling
_____   Family counseling
_____   Training—preparation for foster child
_____   Other, please specify: _____ "

For this question, more than one response could be checked. The easiest way to deal with this type of question is to divide it into three subquestions or three variables, rather than one. The three would consist of individual counseling, family counseling, and training. A number would be assigned (1 or 2) according to whether the respondent checked or did not check each item. Note that here we are dealing with variables that are at the nominal level of measurement. The numbers have been assigned arbitrarily to the responses, and they are not ranked in any way.

		numerical code
individual counseling	checked (yes)	1
	not checked (no)	2
family counseling	checked (yes)	1
	not checked (no)	2
training	checked (yes)	1
	not checked (no)	2

Another characteristic of this question that demands special attention is the "other" item, which directs respondents to write in an answer. One solution is to categorize the response to this subquestion or variable into finite (countable) groups (for example, individual services, group services, information and referral, and so on) and then assign numbers to each of these groups. Alternatively, the data can be fitted into existing categories. We need to be careful not to lose the meaning intended by the respondent. An alternative strategy is to treat this item as qualitative data. After all, this is essentially a qualitative mode of collecting data, in that it is attempting to seek information from the subject's perspective rather than imposing previously constructed categories on the subject's behaviors. Organization of qualitative data will be discussed later in this chapter.

Whatever type of question you are coding, two guidelines need to be followed: The coding categories should be mutually exclusive and exhaustive. When categories are mutually exclusive, a given response can be coded in one way only for each variable. That is why in the last example the question needed to be treated as several variables to accommodate the fact that more than one yes response was possible.

The codes should also be exhaustive; in other words, all the data need to be coded in some way. Coding is a tedious task in research. Do not omit coding some responses because you think you will not need them in the analysis. (If this is the case, the questions should not have been asked.) Moreover, it is very difficult to perform coding later and to add to the data set once data analysis has begun. So, although it can be tiresome, coding must be done with care. Any mistakes would lead to a misrepresentation of the results.

Assigning Names to the Variables

It is too cumbersome to enter the entire question into the computer. Also, the computer cannot read questions in this way. Consequently, the variables themselves need to be coded or named so that they can be understood by the computer. This means translating the questions into words that are of a certain length—for example, usually no more than seven characters. Generally, the first character has to be a letter; it cannot be a numeral. It is useful to pick a variable name that relates to the question. Say the question was this: "How would you gauge your overall level of satisfaction with the services our agency provides?" A possible variable name could be SATISFY. For the question that asked about individual counseling, family counseling, and training services, these three variables could be denoted SERVICE1, SERVICE2, and SERVICE3.

Developing a Code Book

The code book is used to record how responses are coded and how each variable is named. The code book provides a reference for you and other researchers who would need to know or remember to what the codes originally referred. Sometimes, particularly on smaller projects, a code book may not be needed because the codes can be included on the questionnaire. When designing the questionnaire, bear this in mind; it can save work later. In the last example, you would need to note in the code book that the code for a yes response to the question about expanding individual counseling, family counseling, and/or training services is 1; for a no response, the code is 2.

The next step is to enter the information into the computer. In order to do this, you need to select a statistical software package.

Basic Programming Using a Statistical Software Package

Statistical software packages can be used to make data analysis a simple and efficient task. Data are collected and then organized to be entered into the computer and analyzed by the statistical software, producing statistical results.

Many statistical programming packages are available today, such as SPSS for Windows, SYSTAT, MINITAB, and MICROCASE. (See Appendix B for sources for this software.)

Many of the programming principles are similar, whatever particular package you use. Some packages are more user-friendly than others. For all of them, the following general steps are followed:

1. Data are usually entered in rows (although some statistical packages do not require this). Columns are assigned to variables. The first few columns are usually assigned to the ID number of the questionnaire or interview schedule. In the previous example, if 150 questionnaires were returned, three columns will be needed for the ID number in order to cover the ID numbers 001 to 150. The next variable, SATISFY, needs only one column since the codes range only from 1 to 4.

2. Names can be given to each of the variables. There are usually restrictions on the form and length of these variable names.

3. The program is run choosing from the menu of commands. Each command refers to a specific statistical test. You can also use the commands to recode the data—for example, to convert ratio level data into categories at the nominal level, or to give instructions concerning what to do about missing data.

4. You will receive **output** from running the program. The output will appear on the screen, or you can produce hard copy (a printed version) that contains the results of the statistical analysis.

To gain familiarity and confidence with computers and software packages, check out university computer centers. They usually provide workshops and instruction in the use of specific software packages. If you plan to do statistical analysis using a computer, these workshops, which are usually free to students, can be very helpful.

ORGANIZING QUALITATIVE DATA

Organizing qualitative data can be even more overwhelming than organizing quantitative data simply because of the nature of this type of information. Quantitative data by definition are pieces of information that fit into certain categories, which in most cases have been previously defined. Consequently, organizing the data is a matter of ensuring that the data are correctly assigned to the categories and are in a form that the computer can read. On the other hand, qualitative data, once collected, are usually completely uncategorized in order to capture as much in-depth information as possible. Analysis becomes a much more complex process.

Use of the computer is not confined to quantitative data, but is equally useful for organizing and analyzing qualitative data. A word processor is very helpful for recording field notes. Word processing programs such as WordStar, WordPerfect, and MacWrite allow you to move text around easily. Different types of files can also be maintained and cross-referenced with minimal effort.

In addition, software packages are designed specifically for analyzing qualitative data, such as ETHNOGRAPH and NUDIST. (See Weitzman and Miles, 1995, in the Further Reading section at the end of this chapter for more examples. Also see Appendix B for sources of software to use with both qualitative and quantitative data.)

Before you start collecting data, it is a good idea to decide what role the computer is going to play in your project and what software you will be using. Then you will be able to organize your field notes and codes accordingly.

Four different elements involved in the organization of qualitative data will be described: note keeping, organizing files, coding notes, and identifying gaps in the data.

Note Keeping

As discussed in Chapter 9, the primary mode of collecting qualitative data is through observation or interviewing. Much note keeping is involved. Sometimes, particularly in the case of participant observation or informal interviewing, these notes are haphazard. Consequently, one of the first steps is to organize and rewrite these field notes as soon as possible after you have taken them. Rewriting the notes will help jog your memory, and the result will be more detailed, comprehensive notes than you could have produced in the field. Bernard (1988), an anthropologist, suggested five basic rules in the mechanics of note taking and managing field notes:

1. Don't put your notes in one long commentary; use plenty of paper and keep many shorter notes.

2. Separate your note taking into physically separate sets of writing.

    ■ Field jottings—notes actually taken in the field. These provide the basis of field notes.

    ■ Field notes—write-up from your jottings.

    ■ Field diary—a personal record of your experience in the field, chronicling how you feel and how you perceive your relations with others in the field.

    ■ Field log—a running account of how you plan to spend your time, how you actually spend it, and how much money you spend.

3. Take field jottings all the time; don't rely on your memory.

4. Don't be afraid of offending people when you are taking field jottings. (Bernard made an interesting point about this: Being a participant observer does not mean that you *become* a fully accepted member of the group, but rather you *experience* the life of your informants to the extent possible.) Ask permission to take notes; usually it will be given. You can also offer to share your notes with those being interviewed.

5. Set aside some time each day to write up your field notes.

Field Notes

Skucas (1996) examined the reactions of informal support networks of five women who had been assaulted. She used field notes while audio recording semi-structured interviews. When the recordings were transcribed, the subject's emphases were not captured in the transcriptions; the field notes were used to assist in identifying emerging themes.

When collecting qualitative data, you can **transcribe** interviews, or write down verbatim a recording of the interview. Transcriptions are extremely time consuming. It takes six to eight hours to transcribe a one-hour interview. Sometimes, in the case of process recordings (discussed in Chapter 7), you can complete a shorthand transcription, writing down the main interactions in sequence. This results in something more than field notes but less detailed than a full transcription.

Of course, there may be occasions when the transcription is necessary and central to the study. For example, Marlow (1983) transcribed from a videotape a behavior therapy interview to look at the relationship between nonverbal and verbal behaviors. The transcription included very small behaviors—for example, intonation and slight movements of the hands and facial features. Descriptions can give some important, detailed information that can enrich our understanding of client and worker experiences.

Using a Transcription

Depoorter (1996) transcribed five interviews she conducted with social workers when investigating how they understood the concept of success in therapy. Although time consuming, transcription allowed her to identify more clearly the elements of this concept.

Organizing Files

Your rewritten field notes will form your basic or master file. Always keep backup copies of these notes as a precautionary measure. As you proceed with the data collection, you will need different types of files or sets of notes. Generally, at a minimum you will need five types of files: descriptive files, methodological files, biographical files, bibliographical files, and analytical files.

The descriptive file includes information on the topic being studied. In the case of a program evaluation, this file would include information on the program itself, its history, its development, and so forth. Initially, this file will contain most of your notes.

The methodological file or set of notes deals with the techniques of collecting data. It gives you the opportunity to record what you think has improved or damaged your interviewing and observation techniques.

The biographical file includes information on individuals interviewed or included in the study. For example, it might include information about clients, the director, and so on.

The bibliographical file contains references for material you have read related to the study. This file is very similar to the type of file you might keep when completing a research term paper.

Finally, the analytical file provides the beginnings of the analysis proper. It contains notes on the kinds of patterns you see emerging from the data. For example, when interviewing the clients from a family service agency, you may have detected the relationship between their perceptions about the benefits of the program and the specific type of problem they brought to the agency. Consequently, you may start a file labeled "Benefit-Problem." Your analytical set of notes will initially be the smallest file.

Do not forget to cross-reference your files. Some materials in the "Benefit-Problem" file pertaining to a particular client may need to be cross-referenced with a specific biographical client file. A note in each will suffice. This preparation and organization will help the analysis later on.

Coding the Notes

In addition to cross-referencing the five main types of notes, additional coding will help when you come to the analysis stage. As you write up the field notes, use codes for categorizing the notes. These codes can be recorded at the top of each page of notes or in the margin and can be either numbers or letters. Don't forget, though, to keep a code book just as you would for quantitative data.

Obviously, these codes will vary in their precision and form depending on the purpose of the study. In a program evaluation, the codes may refer to the different channels of authority within the organization, the different types of clients served, or any other aspect of the program that is of concern in the evaluation. In a practice evaluation where you may be monitoring the application of an intervention, codes can be used to categorize the content of the interview or meeting.

Identifying Gaps in the Data

Throughout the organization of the data, you need to keep notes on gaps in the data or missing information. Keeping track of gaps is not so necessary in a quantitative study when decisions pertaining to data collection are made early in the study. With a qualitative study, however, you often do not know what data need to be collected until well into the project, when new insights and ideas relating to the study become apparent.

THE AGENCY AND ORGANIZING THE DATA

The central message of this section is to make optimal use of computers if you have them available in your agency. They can save an enormous amount of time, and for larger projects, they are indispensable.

If your agency does not have computer access, lobby for it. Fairly inexpensive computers and software are available. Not only are computers essential to organize and analyze data, but they can be used for many aspects of practice and research, including literature reviews, writing reports, clinical assessment, and Internet and World Wide Web access.

ETHICAL ISSUES IN ORGANIZING THE DATA

Two ethical issues are involved in data organization—one for each type of data, quantitative and qualitative. For quantitative data, ethical issues are minimized because most decisions about how to handle the data have been made prior to this stage. The major problem is how to deal with the "other" responses. As mentioned before, you can create categories for these responses, or they can be fitted into existing categories. In adopting the latter approach, you need to be careful that we preserve the integrity of the data and that you do not try to put the data into categories that are inappropriate or that simply reflect your preferences.

Ethical issues relating to the organization of qualitative data are more pervasive. At each stage you must be careful that your biases do not overtly interfere. For example, when compiling field notes from your field jottings, ensure that the field notes reflect as closely as possible your observations in the field and are not molded to fit your existing or developing hypothesis. This is a difficult process because one of the underlying principles governing the interpretive approach (which usually involves qualitative data) is that objectivity is not the overriding principle driving the research. Instead, the researcher recognizes the role of subjectivity and that the nature of the data is in part a product of the relationship between the researcher and participant.

When coding the notes, be aware of the same issue. If you doubt your objectivity, you may want to consult with someone who can examine part of your notes or your coding scheme and give you some feedback. What you are doing here is conducting a reliability check, which in itself can serve the purpose of ensuring that the research is being conducted in an ethical manner.

HUMAN DIVERSITY ISSUES IN ORGANIZING THE DATA

The primary human diversity issue parallels the ethical issues concerning quantitative data that were just discussed. When ambiguous data are categorized, such as responses to "other" questions, attention needs to be paid to ensuring that the categorization adequately accounts for the various human diversity issues that may be involved in the responses.

Human diversity issues arise in different stages in the organization of qualitative data. Field notes need to reflect any human diversity elements, although this depends on from whom you are getting your information. The coding also needs to tap this dimension. And you may wish to pay particular attention to whether or not human diversity issues were addressed when trying to determine whether gaps exist in your data. For example, in collecting data on clients' perceptions of the services they are receiving from a family service agency, it may be important to ask clients about how significant their social worker's ethnicity is to them or about whether clients feel that their social worker and the agency are sensitive to cultural differences.

SUMMARY

Organizing quantitative data includes coding the data and identifying statistical software packages. Organizing qualitative data also involves identifying appropriate software, in addition to note keeping, organizing the files, coding the notes, and identifying gaps in the data. Ethical and human diversity issues include ensuring that the integrity of the data is preserved.

STUDY/EXERCISE QUESTIONS

1. The agency in which you are employed has no computers available to the social workers. As a means of lobbying for computers, draw up a list of the ways in which the computer could be used for research and practice in the agency.

2. Construct a questionnaire of about five items to find out students' attitudes on combining research with practice. Administer the questionnaire to five students in the class.
   a. Create a code book.
   b. Enter the data in a computer using statistical software.

3. Interview five students in the research class about their attitudes on combining research with practice. How would you organize these data?

FURTHER READING

Hedderson, J. (1991). *SPSS/PC+ made simple.* Belmont, CA: Wadsworth. An excellent introduction to SPSS/PC+.

Weitzman, E. A., & Miles, M. B. (1995). *Computer programs for qualitative data analysis.* Newbury Park, CA: Sage.

REFERENCES

Bernard, H. R. (1988). *Research methods in cultural anthropology.* Newbury Park, CA: Sage.

Depoorter, A. (1996). *How practitioners define success.* Unpublished master's research project, New Mexico State University, Las Cruces.

Marlow, C. R. (1983). *The organization of interaction in a behavior therapy interview.* Unpublished doctoral dissertation, University of Chicago, Chicago.

Skucas, L. (1996). *Female sexual assault victims and their informal support networks: Family preservation's potential.* Unpublished master's thesis, New Mexico State University, Las Cruces.

Analysis of Qualitative Data

■

N o matter how you collect qualitative data—through interviews, open-ended questionnaires, or personal logs—the amount and apparent lack of order of the data can be overwhelming. This chapter describes ways that qualitative data can be analyzed. The primary focus of this chapter will be on analyzing data in interpretive studies, where the data are usually qualitative. Although interpretive studies will be the focus, some techniques and approaches discussed in this chapter can also be used to analyze qualitative data collected as part of positivist studies.

This chapter discusses the following topics:

- approaches to analyzing qualitative data
- the agency and qualitative analysis
- ethical issues in qualitative analysis
- human diversity issues in qualitative analysis

APPROACHES TO ANALYZING QUALITATIVE DATA

Analysis of qualitative data and analysis of quantitative data differ in a number of important ways. First, the distinctions among data collection, data organization, and data analysis are much more difficult to define when the data are qualitative. For example, data analysis can often begin before data collection is completed. Second, the methods of analysis are much less structured than with quantitative data. As a result, qualitative data analysis is much more challenging and at times very difficult to complete successfully. Many decisions are left to the researcher's discretion. Third, the primary mission in the analysis of qualitative data is to look for patterns in the data, noting similarities and differences. Various techniques can be used to identify these patterns, and they will be discussed in the next section of this chapter. Fourth, it is important to keep the data in context to avoid the temptation to present emerging data patterns as independent conclusions that will stand on their own. This contextual analysis is central to interpretist research. Data must always be presented in context by referring to the specific situations, time periods, and persons in which the identified pattern occurred. Fifth, qualitative data analysis tends to be inductive rather than deductive. Careful observation leads to the description of connections and patterns in the data that can in turn enable us to form hypotheses and ultimately develop them into theoretical constructs and theories. The findings are grounded in real-life patterns—hence the term *grounded theory* is also used to refer to qualitative data analysis (Glaser & Strauss, 1967).

Five dimensions will be presented as guidelines for the analysis of qualitative data. The researcher may choose to use all these dimensions, or just one or two, depending on the purpose of the study. These dimensions include presenting the data as a descriptive account; constructing categories or themes; carrying out logical analysis; proposing hypotheses; and validating the data. (See Figure 11.1.)

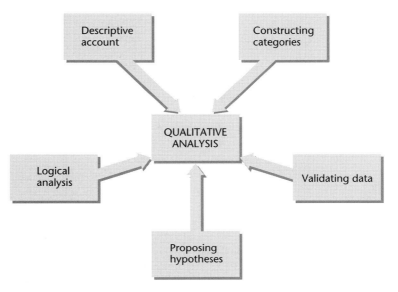

Figure 11.1   ***Dimensions of qualitative analysis***

Descriptive Accounts

The basis of qualitative analysis often consists of a description. This narrative includes all the materials you have collected: observations, interviews, data from case records, or impressions of others. These descriptive accounts are also called **case studies.**

Patton (1987) suggested three steps for constructing a case study. First, the raw case data are assembled. These data consist of all the information collected for the case study. The second step is constructing a case record; the case data are organized, classified, and edited into an accessible package. The third step is writing the case study narrative. The narrative can be chronological or thematic (or both). The narrative should be a holistic portrayal of a person or program.

The case study can take the form of any of the types of research we have considered in this book: a practice evaluation, a description of the problem for a needs assessment, or a description of a program for a formative program evaluation.

A Case Study for Evaluation of Practice

Sefansky (1990) described a case study that involved work with the family of a young survivor of a plane crash. She discussed the use of crisis intervention and family-centered social work practice with this case. She also described the effects of the media on the staff and the institution and her personal reactions and involvement with the family.

A Case Study for Needs Assessment

Sklar and Hartley (1990) studied the bereavement of people who have experienced the death of a close friend. Their findings indicated that these "survivor friends" experienced bereavement patterns similar to those of people who have suffered the loss of family members. The authors argued that the experience and needs of this bereavement group need to be addressed.

A Case Study for Program Evaluation

Mwansa, Mufune, and Osei-Hwedie (1994) examined, using a case study approach, youth policies and programs in the countries of Botswana, Swaziland, and Zambia. These youth programs are designed to deal with three challenges faced by the youths: work and employment, education and skills training, and social life. The authors concluded, first, that a formally constituted governmental base is integral to the success of youth development and, second, that more research in these countries is called for to determine needs from the youths themselves.

One type of case study is ethnography. As described in Chapter 9, ethnography is a description of a culture. Ethnography is also regarded as a specific approach to interpretive research (see Patton, 1990, for a presentation of the different approaches to qualitative or interpretive research). Historically, ethnography was the domain of anthropology. Anthropologists relied on participant observation to produce ethnographic studies or monographs of exotic cultures. Social workers have recognized the value of this approach in describing the different cultures with which they are involved—for example, the culture of the homeless or of gangs. In anthropology, ethnographies are often long and detailed, but social work researchers have produced "mini-ethnographies." Note that ethnographies (both full-length and short ones) can also be a useful resource for social workers and can help acquaint them with the cultures with which they work.

Ethnography in Social Work

Rojiani (1994) used an ethnographic approach to describe the experiences of a patient who had received community-based long-term care, services, and planning. Rojiani described the formal care provided by professionals as a distinct culture from the care provided by friends and families.

Constructing Categories

As mentioned earlier, interpretive studies and analysis of qualitative data generally use an inductive rather than a deductive approach. Patterns, themes, and categories emerge from the data rather than being developed prior to collection. There are two main strategies for identifying categories once the data have been collected: indigenous and researcher-constructed categories.

Indigenous Categories

Indigenous categories, which use the **emic** approach, involve identifying the categories used by those being observed, or adopting the natives' point of view. In many ways, this approach is very compatible to the practice skills of building rapport and developing empathy so that the worker can see the world from the client's point of view. These indigenous categories are often referred to as themes or recurring patterns in the data.

Indigenous categories are constructed from data collected using the frame elicitation technique. **Frame elicitation** involves framing questions in such a way that you find out from your subjects what *they* include in a particular topic or category. An approach that works well for needs assessments is to ask subjects "what kinds of" services are needed. For example, if you are interested in finding out the needs of the physically challenged in your community, you can ask: "What kinds of services for the hearing impaired are needed?" Categories of responses are then elicited from the respondents rather than being imposed by the researcher. To identify overlapping areas of different responses, the researcher can ask whether one category of response is "the same as" or "part of" another category. Using our example, the question would be framed thus: "Is afterschool care the same as respite care?" Such questions elicit data with which you can construct a taxonomy of the respondent's perception of services needed by the physically challenged.

You need to be aware of a number of issues when constructing taxonomies or categories in this way. First, interinformant variation is common; that is, different informants may use different words to refer to the same category of things. Second, category labels may be fairly complex, consisting of a phrase or two rather than simply a word or two. Third, for some categories, informants may have no label at all. Fourth, the categories overlap.

Once these issues have been considered, however, indigenous categories can be useful to the generalist social worker. You can be assured that the case is being presented from the client's perspective and not being interpreted inappropriately by the researcher.

The use of indigenous categories is essential to the specific interpretive approach called phenomenology. The details of this approach (see Patton, 1990) will not be discussed here except to note that it is concerned with answering the question: "What is the experience of this phenomena for these people?" To capture this experience, the researcher should use indigenous categories or identify themes.

Using Indigenous Categories or Themes

Abramson and Mizrahi (1994) examined collaboration between social workers and physicians. They described analysis of their data as follows:

> As we immersed ourselves further, patterns of collaborative behavior and attitudes emerged. Collaborators and collaborative relationships could be classified along a continuum that we have ultimately identified as traditional, transitional and transformational. The dramatic differences among types of physicians became apparent first (we were initially unclear whether the continuum applied to social workers). As we returned to the data, we saw collaborative characteristics of social workers could be classified similarly. (p. 38)

Researcher-Constructed Categories

Researcher-constructed categories are categories that researchers apply to the data. These categories may be relatively meaningless to the people under study, but the categories do provide a good overall picture of the phenomenon being investigated. Studies using researcher-constructed categories can be considered interpretive or qualitative as long as the study follows the major principle of interpretive research—namely, that data are considered in context rather than through rigidly imposed categories.

Using Researcher-Constructed Categories

Biller and Rice (1990) studied people who had survived multiple losses of persons with AIDS. They used a three-stage model of grief that had already been developed. This model included the phases of avoidance, confrontation, and reestablishment. The researchers used information gathered by interviewing seven respondents—five gay males and two lesbian females—and noted how these data fitted into the predeveloped phases.

One approach to researcher-constructed categories is **content analysis.** Content analysis involves coding written and oral communications and then making inferences based on the incidence of these codes. This approach was first mentioned in Chapter 9 when discussing the use of secondary data. Content analysis can be performed on transcribed recorded interviews, process recordings on a case, published articles in newspapers or journals, and so forth.

Alter and Evens (1990) suggested six steps for content analysis:

1. Select the constructs of interest and define them clearly.
2. Select a unit of analysis (word, sentence, phrase, theme, and so on) to be coded.
3. Define the categories. They should be mutually exclusive and should be fairly narrow.
4. Test this classification scheme on a document.
5. Revise if reliability is low and test again until an acceptance level of reliability is achieved.
6. Code the text of interest and do a category count.

Allen-Meares (1984) discussed the important role content analysis can have in social work research. An early example of content analysis is provided by Hollis (1972), who used a coding typology. Hollis was interested in describing and understanding the communications that take place in social casework interviews. Interviews were transcribed and coded line by line using the following codes:

U = unclassified
A = sustainment
B = direct influence
C = exploration, description, ventilation
D = person-situation reflection
E = pattern-dynamic reflection
F = developmental reflection

Interviews could then be understood depending upon the frequency of the different types of communication. These codes were developed specifically for casework practice; thus, different categories would need to be developed to do content analysis on generalist practice interviews.

 Content Analysis

Petr and Barney (1993) reported the results of a content analysis of focus group interviews of parents of children with developmental disabilities, emotional disorders, and technology-supported needs. Categories included special needs (2241 statements); reasonable efforts in crisis situations (92); parent-professional relationships (278); and definition of reasonable efforts (82). Each of these categories also had four or five subcategories.

Although content analysis is often used in social work research, it has a number of problems. First, the validity of the codes, like any other researcher-constructed category, may be an issue. Second, the coding of the text can be unreliable if it is done by only one coder. Intercoder reliability should be established, which often means training the coder. Third, the coding almost inevitably involves lifting concepts out of context, which essentially negates much of the value of qualitative research.

Logical Analysis

Logical analysis involves looking at the relationships between variables and concepts. This is similar to the quantitative processes of correlation and cross-tabulation, described in Chapter 9, which extend the one-dimensional picture of the data. In qualitative analysis, a similar process, called **cross-classification,** is used to look at these relationships. Patton (1987) described cross-classification as

> creating potential categories by crossing one dimension or typology with another, and then working back and forth between the data and one's logical constructions, filling in the resulting matrix. This logical system will create a new typology, all parts of which may or may not actually be represented by the data. (p. 155)

An important aspect of examining the data this way is to display the data in a table or matrix.

Cross-Classification

Patton (1987) used a hypothetical example of cross-classification in evaluating a juvenile justice program.

> Suppose we have been evaluating a juvenile justice program which places delinquent youths in foster homes. We have visited several foster homes; observed what the home environments are like; and interviewed the juveniles, the foster home parents, and the probation officers. A regularly recurring theme in the interviews is the importance of the process of "letting kids learn to make their own decisions." A regularly recurring outcomes theme is "keeping the kids straight" (reduce recidivism). The blank cell in a matrix created by crossing the program process ("kids making their own decisions") with the program outcome ("keeping kids straight") creates a data analysis question: What actual decisions do juveniles make that are supposed to lead to reduced recidivism? We then carefully review our field notes and interview quotations looking for data that help us understand how people in the program have answered this question based on their actual behaviors and practices. By describing what decisions juveniles actually make in the program the decision makers to whom our findings are reported can make their own judgments about the strength or weakness of this linkage between this program process and the desired outcome. (p. 156)

Proposing Hypotheses

Interpretive research is primarily concerned with developing hypotheses, rather than testing them. Part of qualitative and interpretive analysis, however, does involve speculation about causality and linkages. One way of representing and presenting this causality is to construct **causal flowcharts.** These are visual representations of ideas that emerge from studying the data, seeing patterns, and seeing possible causes for phenomena. We have been using causal flowcharts in this text to illustrate some of the research methods. Often, causal flowcharts consist of a set of boxes connected by arrows. The boxes contain descriptions of states (attitudes, perceptions, ages, and so on), and the arrows tell how one state leads to another.

A Causal Flowchart Analysis

Tomlinson (1991) carried out a qualitative research study about concerned parents of teenagers who were acting out. Tomlinson provided a profile of parents' characteristics, including a multidimensional view of parent competence, an analysis of the main components of the conflict between parent and adolescent, and a theory that perceived vulnerability provides a context in which the conflict flourishes. Tomlinson depicts these elements in a causal flowchart (see Figure 11.2).

The development of hypotheses and causal statements should be firmly rooted in the data, and not imposed on the data or overly influenced by the researcher's theoretical biases. If a researcher uses a category previously defined

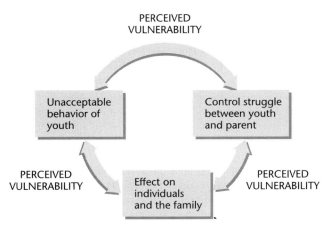

Figure 11.2   ***Main elements of the parent-adolescent conflict process***

Source: From "Unacceptable Adolescent Behavior and Parent-Adolescent Conflict," by R. K. Tomlinson, 1991, *Child and Adolescent Social Work, 8,* p. 44. Copyright © 1991 Human Sciences Press, Inc. Reprinted with permission.

theoretically, the qualitative nature of the research can be ensured by the nature of the data collection methods and the manner in which those data are used either to support or to refute the categories. The context of the data must be taken into full consideration. The researcher should try to avoid the linear thinking associated with quantitative analysis. One strength of qualitative analysis is its potential for revealing contextual interrelationships among factors and their circular and interdependent natures.

Validation

Validation of qualitative data requires rather different processes than validation of quantitative data. Processes for validation of qualitative data include consideration of rival or alternative hypotheses, consideration of negative cases, the process of triangulation, and preservation of the context of the data.

Rival Hypotheses

After a hypothesis has been developed and proposed, **rival hypotheses** need to be explored and compared to the proposed hypothesis. Rival hypotheses can emerge from the literature or from the data. The rival hypotheses and the proposed hypothesis are both tested by looking at the data and considering which hypothesis appears to most closely reflect the data. In some cases, both hypotheses appear to be supported.

Rival Hypotheses

Gregg (1994) stated: "When initiating the study, I planned to explore how women make choices about genetic information and prenatal diagnosis: Do they use a rational, cost benefits model . . .? My research was able to answer the original question: For the most part women did use a rational, cost benefits approach. But the research also provides additional, unanticipated answers" (p.63). Gregg found that women experienced pregnancy as a risk-laden path and also experienced a state defined as "a little bit pregnant"—two outcomes or rival hypotheses that Gregg did not anticipate.

Negative Cases

Patterns in data emerge when researchers look at what occurs most often. Almost always, however, there are exceptions, or **negative cases,** that do not fit the patterns. These need to be examined and explained. When you encounter a case that does not fit your theory, ask yourself whether it is the result of (1) normal social variation, (2) your lack of knowledge about the range of appropriate behavior, or (3) a genuinely unusual case. Force yourself to think creatively on this issue. As Bernard (1994) stated, "If the cases won't fit, don't be too quick to throw them out. It is always easier to throw out cases than it is to reexamine one's ideas, and the easy way out is hardly ever the right way in research" (p. 321).

A Negative Case

Depoorter (1996) studied practitioner's views of success and found one negative case. This worker, rather than suggesting that lack of success was due to some difficulty in establishing reachable goals with the client, tended to blame the client for not cooperating. This case led Depoorter to speculate that some characteristic of the worker could explain this perspective. The negative case gave Depoorter some directions for future research—for example, comparing male and female views of success.

Triangulation

Triangulation involves the use of different research approaches to study the same research question. One way to use triangulation is to collect different kinds of data, such as interviews and observations, which may include both qualitative and quantitative data. Another approach is to have different people collect and analyze the data or to use different theories to interpret the data. Finally, data from different sources can be compared, such as examining consistent and inconsistent information from different informants.

Using triangulation may result in what appears to be conflicting information. Such conflicts do not automatically invalidate the proposed hypotheses. Instead, such conflicts may simply indicate that new and different information has been acquired, adding another dimension to our understanding of the phenomenon being studied.

Triangulation Using Multiple Data Interpreters

Gutiérrez , DeLois, and GlenMaye (1995) examined the concept of empowerment through the perspectives of human service workers. They stated:

> The data were independently analyzed by three readers. . . . The three readers then met to discuss their findings and to work toward a common understanding. Areas of agreement and disagreement were noted during each meeting and became the focus for discussion. When the readers were satisfied that all themes from an interview had been identified they moved on to the next transcript. After all transcripts were completed, notes from the analytic meetings were used to identify common themes across interviews. These themes then became the central findings of the study. (p. 516)

Triangulation Using Different Data Sources

Soloman (1994) used six different data collection methods in her study of welfare workers and homeless welfare applicants. By comparing the results of these six methods she was able to partly validate her findings. The six methods included (1) discussions with eight key informants; (2) observations in a welfare office; (3) observations of 47 application interviews; (4) observation of 25 interviews between welfare recipients and their caseworkers; (5) individual interviews with four welfare application intake workers; and (6) interviews with 15 homeless applicants.

Preserving the Context of the Data

One central purpose of interpretive research and qualitative data analysis is that the data are kept in context. This contextualization provides a greater level of assurance that the findings are not distorted. The context of each response needs to be considered. Additionally, it is important to recognize the limitations of the sampling method used, for these limitations can affect the external validity of the findings. Generally, sampling methods are purposive in interpretive studies. The context of the findings is limited; to put it another way, the findings have limited generalizability.

The Limited Context of the Findings

Ejaz (1991) studied social work education in India and its relevance for the culture of that country. The findings were somewhat unexpected. Graduates did not overwhelmingly state that their education was too Westernized or culturally unsuitable. But the author adds that these findings may reflect that members of the sample were residents of a large, cosmopolitan, highly urbanized city. This factor, along with others such as being Indian and part of a diverse cultural heritage, could have resulted in the respondents' recognizing the importance of universally applicable social work principles, rather than specific, indigenous principles. The author noted that "it is important to replicate this study in other parts of the country to get a more realistic picture of what the Indian social work scene is like and what needs to be done to improve it further" (p. 309).

THE AGENCY AND QUALITATIVE ANALYSIS

Qualitative data and its subsequent analysis can be invaluable to the generalist social worker. By its nature, it is very compatible with practice. We interview as part of our practice, and we keep logs as part of our practice. Both are important sources of qualitative data.

One preconception about qualitative analysis is that it is not as complex as quantitative analysis and that it does not require as sophisticated skills as quantitative analysis does. One goal of conducting qualitative research in an agency setting is to dispel this notion, both to enhance the credibility of qualitative studies and to earn the time and support necessary to conduct qualitative data analysis, thereby producing reports that can make a meaningful contribution to the agency.

ETHICAL ISSUES IN QUALITATIVE ANALYSIS

There are ethical issues in the analysis of qualitative data that you don't encounter in the analysis of quantitative data. Quantitative analysis is protected by the nature of statistical analysis and the rules that govern whether or not findings are statistically significant. Without this kind of objective guide, the interpretation and analysis of qualitative data depend a great deal more on judgment; consequently, the possibility that ethical standards might be violated increases.

Personal, intellectual, and professional biases are more likely to interfere with qualitative data analysis, despite the existence of validation controls. For example, we discussed earlier the use of negative cases as a method of validation. Sometimes it can be tempting to ignore negative cases, implying that there is more agreement than actually exists among the findings so as to make the proposed hypothesis or argument appear stronger.

There may be a fine line between violating an ethical standard intentionally and simply missing a particular avenue of inquiry. For example, a negative case may not have been examined because the researcher did not see it as an exception but in fact interpreted it as supporting the proposed hypothesis.

On the other hand, qualitative analysis can sometimes expose distortions in previous research. Consequently, qualitative studies can make an important ethical contribution to our knowledge. Srinivasan and Davis (1991) conducted research on the organization of shelters for battered women. They stated that these shelters have tended to be idealized as collectivist organizations that empower both residents and staff. Their qualitative research at one shelter indicated that despite an implicit philosophy of empowerment, a shelter is an organization like any other: An egalitarian, collectivist structure existed for relationships among staff members, and a hierarchical structure existed for relationships among staff and residents. The authors concluded by recommending that feminist social workers continuously assess how ideology affects the organizational environment in which services are delivered.

HUMAN DIVERSITY ISSUES IN QUALITATIVE ANALYSIS

As with ethical issues, analysis of qualitative data provides more opportunities to ignore human diversity issues than the analysis of quantitative data does. Data can be analyzed and hypotheses generated that directly reflect the researcher's biases, which may reflect negatively on certain groups. Although such biases can also appear in quantitative research, they are more likely in qualitative research, and additional precautions need to be taken. Researchers conducting qualitative analysis should constantly use self-examination to determine whether they are perpetuating stereotypical or negative images of the subjects in their studies. The purpose of validation procedure is partly to ensure that stereotyping and other forms of bias do not occur.

Qualitative analysis can actually be an asset in ensuring that human diversity issues are recognized. The qualitative approach can provide a richer and more diverse picture of phenomena.

Overcoming biases can be a difficult task, even through the use of careful qualitative strategies. Sometimes it is very hard for us to identify these biases in our thinking; even the definition of a bias can be problematic. As social workers, we know that the environment and society in which we live profoundly affect the way we think, including the way we think about different groups. Our upbringing and social environment may result in our unconscious exclusion of certain groups. This effect provides the foundation for discourse analysis.

Discourse analysis focuses on ways in which all analyses are embedded in the researcher's biographical and historical location (Warren, 1988). A great deal of emphasis in discourse analysis has been placed on how women have been marginalized (Keller, 1985):

> "Our laws of nature" are more than simple expressions of the results of objective inquiry or of political and social pressures; they must also be read for their personal—and by tradition, masculine—content. (p. 10)

This perspective relates to the discussion in Chapter 1 concerning the difficulty of achieving true objectivity and the impact of values on how we carry out and interpret science.

SUMMARY

The primary mission in qualitative data analysis is to look for patterns in the data while maintaining the context of the study. Approaches to qualitative analysis include descriptive accounts (case studies), constructing categories (indigenous categories and researcher-constructed categories—including the use of content analysis), logical analysis (cross-classification), proposing hypotheses (using causal flowcharts), and techniques of validation (using rival hypotheses, negative cases, triangulation, and contextualization).

Although qualitative data analysis is naturally compatible with practice, the myth persists that it is unduly time-consuming, unsophisticated, and nonproductive. Researchers in agency settings have the responsibility of dispelling this myth. Due to the unstructured nature of qualitative analysis, we must ensure that personal, intellectual, and professional biases do not interfere with the process. We must also take care that diverse groups are recognized at the analysis stage.

STUDY/EXERCISE QUESTIONS

1. Conduct an interview with a fellow student, gathering information on what he or she considers to be his or her family's culture.
    a. Use the indigenous category approach discussed in this chapter.
    b. Compare your findings with others in the class.
    c. Is it possible to propose a hypothesis based on these findings?
    d. How would you validate your findings?
2. Carry out a content analysis on ethics and research using issues of a social work journal. Note that you will need to define *ethics* and *research,* and specify the number and type of journal. What conclusions can you draw from your findings?

FURTHER READING

Bernard, H. R. (1994). *Research methods in cultural anthropology.* Newbury Park, CA: Sage.
Although written for anthropologists, social workers also will find this book a useful and clear introduction to qualitative data collection and analysis.

Denzin, N. K., & Lincoln, Y. S. (1994) *Handbook of qualitative research.* Newbury Park, CA: Sage.
The reference book for qualitative research methods. Very comprehensive—a book that can tell you "anything you ever wanted to know."

Glaser, B. G., & Strauss, A. L. (1967) *Discovery of grounded theory: Strategies for qualitative research.* Chicago: Aldine.

Patton, M. Q. (1987). *How to use qualitative methods in evaluation.* Newbury Park, CA: Sage.
A useful guide for program evaluations applying qualitative methods—which is a perspective usually not taken by program evaluation guides.

Sherman, E., & Reid, W. J. (Eds.). (1994). *Qualitative research in social work.* NY: Columbia University Press.
An interesting collection of readings on qualitative research, including a few chapters on ethnographies in social work.

Silverman, D. (1993). *Interpreting qualitative data.* Newbury Park, CA: Sage.
A good guide to analyzing different types of qualitative data.

Tutty, L., Rothery, M., & Grinnell, R. (1996). *Qualitative research for social workers.* Allyn & Bacon.

REFERENCES

Abramson, J. S., & Mizrahi, T. (1994). Examining social work/physician collaboration: An application of grounded theory methods. In C. Riessman (Ed.), *Qualitative studies in social work research.* Newbury Park, CA: Sage.

Allen-Meares, P. (1984). Content analysis: It does have a place in social work research. *Journal of Social Science Research, 7,* 51–68.

Alter, C., & Evens, W. (1990). *Evaluating your practice.* New York: Springer.

Bernard, H. R. (1994). *Research methods in cultural anthropology.* Newbury Park, CA: Sage.

Biller, R., & Rice, S. (1990). Experiencing multiple loss of persons with AIDS: Grief and bereavement issues. *Health and Social Work, 15,* 283–290.

Depoorter, A. (1996). What factors contribute to a therapist's decision to rate a client as successful? Unpublished research project. Department of Social Work, New Mexico State University.

Ejaz, F. K. (1991). Social work education in India: Perceptions of social workers in Bombay. *International Social Work, 34* (3), 299–311.

Gregg, R. (1994). Explorations of pregnancy and choices in a high-tech age. In C. K. Riessman (Ed.), *Qualitative studies in social work research.* Newbury Park, CA: Sage.

Gutiérrez, L. M., DeLois, K. A., & GlenMaye, L. (1995). Understanding empowerment practice: Building on practitioner based knowledge. *Families in Society, 76* (9), 534–542.

Hollis, F. (1972). *Casework: A psychosocial therapy.* New York: Random House.

Keller, G. F. (1985). *Reflections on gender and science.* New Haven, CT: Yale University Press.

Mwansa, L. K., Mufune, P., Osei-Hwedie, K. (1994). Youth policy and programmes in the SADC countries of Botswana, Swaziland and Zambia: A comparative assessment. *International Social Work, 37,* 239–263.

Patton, M. Q. (1987). *How to use qualitative methods in evaluation.* Newbury Park, CA: Sage.

Patton, M. Q. (1990). *Qualitative evaluation and research methods.* Newbury Park, CA: Sage.

Petr, C. G., & Barney, D. D. (1993). Reasonable efforts for children with disabilities: The parents' perspective. *Social Work, 38* (3), 247–254.

Rojiani, R. H. (1994). Disparities in the social construction of long-term care. In C. K. Reissman (Ed.), *Qualitative studies in social work research.* Newbury Park, CA: Sage.

Sefansky, S. (1990). Pediatric critical care social work: Interventions with a special plane crash survivor. *Health and Social Work, 15,* 215–220.

Sklar, F., & Hartley, S. F. (1990). Close friends as survivors: Bereavement patterns in a "hidden" population. *Omega, 21,* 103–112.

Soloman, C. (1994). Welfare workers' response to homeless welfare applicants. In C. K. Reissman (Ed.), *Qualitative studies in social work research.* Newbury Park, CA: Sage.

Srinivasan, M., & Davis, L. V. (1991). A shelter: An organization like any other? *Affilia, 6,* 38–57.

Tomlinson, R. K. (1991). Unacceptable adolescent behavior and parent-adolescent conflict. *Child and Adolescent Social Work, 8,* 33–55.

Warren, C. (1988). *Gender issues in field research.* Newbury Park, CA: Sage.

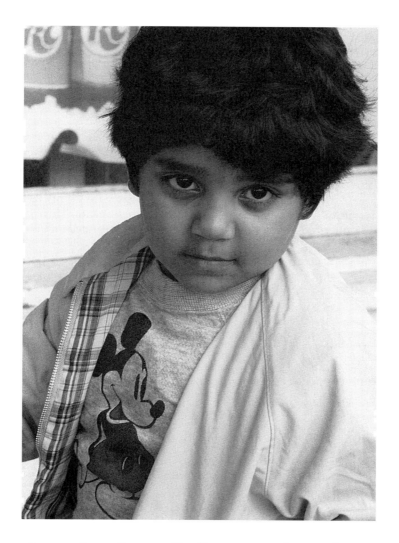

Analysis of Quantitative Data: Descriptive Statistics

T his chapter and Chapter 13 discuss how quantitative data can be analyzed. As discussed in Chapter 1, these are data that can be counted or quantified. The analysis stage of the research process makes some sense out of the information collected. This research stage compares to the assessment stage in practice.

Meaning can be derived from quantitative data in two ways. One is through the use of **descriptive statistics,** which summarize the characteristics of the sample or the relationship among the variables. During this process, you want to get as full a picture as possible of the data. A number of different statistical techniques allow you to do this. You can also use **inferential statistics,** which are techniques for determining whether generalizations or inferences about the population can be made using the data from your sample. This chapter discusses descriptive statistics, whereas the next chapter discusses inferential statistics.

The focus of these two chapters is twofold. First, they focus on understanding which statistics are useful for which purpose. Some statistics are simply not appropriate and are meaningless when used with certain types of data. This approach to statistical understanding prepares you to become an informed and observant consumer of research—a critical role for the generalist social worker. Part of using findings for practice involves understanding and interpreting statistical analysis of the data in various studies. A second focus of these chapters is on how to run different statistical tests using statistical software. Many different statistical software packages are available, which all use similar procedures and commands.

This chapter discusses the following topics:

- frequency distributions
- measures of central tendency
- measures of variability or dispersion
- measures of association
- descriptive statistics and practice evaluation
- the agency and descriptive statistics
- ethical issues and descriptive statistics
- human diversity issues in descriptive statistics

FREQUENCY DISTRIBUTIONS

As discussed in Chapter 4, each variable possesses values. The variables' names, along with their values, are entered into the computer as described in Chapter 10. One of the first things you need to do in statistical analysis is to get an idea about how these values are distributed for each variable. In order to do so, you use frequency distributions. These are descriptions of the number of times values of a variable occur in a sample.

For example, say you have collected data on the need for a day care center on a local university campus. Let's assume that 25 students with preschool children were interviewed. Each of these students represents one **observation,** or case; this is equivalent to a unit of analysis. The variables included number of preschool children, ethnicity, expressed need for day care on campus, and miles from campus. The ethnic groups are represented by codes: 1 for white non-Hispanic; 2 for Hispanic; and 3 for African American. Expressed need for day care on campus is coded on a 4-point scale, with the number 4 representing greatest need, and 1 the least need. The number of preschool children in a family and miles from campus are represented by the actual numbers of children and miles. We could present the data as in Table 12.1.

Table 12.1   **Data on four variables by each observation**

Observation number	Number of children	Ethnicity	Need for day care	Miles from campus
1	2	1	3	2
2	1	1	4	1
3	1	3	4	10
4	1	1	4	23
5	1	2	3	4
6	1	1	3	2
7	2	2	4	1
8	2	1	3	1
9	1	2	2	6
10	3	1	4	40
11	2	1	3	2
12	1	2	1	1
13	1	1	2	3
14	2	1	4	7
15	2	1	4	8
16	1	3	4	9
17	1	1	3	15
18	2	1	4	12
19	1	2	1	23
20	2	1	1	1
21	2	1	4	2
22	1	2	4	1
23	2	1	4	3
24	1	1	4	1
25	2	1	3	6

Simply reviewing this table does not make it easy to understand what the data really look like. Several frequency distributions can be constructed for the previous example: one for the variable ethnicity (see Table 12.2), one for expressed need for day care (see Table 12.3), and one for number of preschool children (see Table 12.4). One can also be constructed for miles from campus (see Table 12.5); rather than list each distance separately, however, you can categorize values to make data more readable. Try to use categories that make some intuitive or theoretical sense. You also need to ensure that categories are of same size. For example, you might use categories such as "less than 5 miles," "5–9 miles," "10–14 miles," and "15 miles and over." By grouping data points into categories in this way, of course, some information is inevitably lost.

An example of a frequency distribution table that resulted from the use of a statistical software package is presented in Figure 12.1. This table shows

Table 12.2   **Frequency distribution of ethnicity**

Label	Value	Frequency	%
non-Hispanic white	1	17	68
Hispanic	2	6	24
African American	3	2	8
	Total	25	100

Table 12.3   **Frequency distribution of need for day care**

Label	Value	Frequency	%
no need	1	3	12
a little need	2	2	8
some need	3	7	28
great need	4	13	52
	Total	25	100

Table 12.4   **Frequency distribution of number of preschool children in the household**

	Value	Frequency	%
	1	13	52
	2	11	44
	3	1	4
	Total	25	100

Table 12.5 **Frequency distribution of miles from campus**

Value	Frequency	%
less than 5 miles	14	56
5–9 miles	5	20
10–14 miles	2	8
15 miles and over	4	16
Total	25	100

```
AGEGR      AGE AT GRADUATION

VALUE LABEL            VALUE           FREQUENCY        PERCENT

                        20               1               1.0
                        21              16              16.2
                        22              23              23.2
                        23              15              15.3
                        24              10              10.1
                        25               5               5.1
                        26               1               1.0
                        27               1               1.0
                        28               1               1.0
                        29               1               1.0
                        30               1               1.0
                        31               2               2.0
                        32               6               6.1
                        33               1               1.0
                        35               1               1.0
                        37               2               2.0
                        40               1               1.0
                        41               1               1.0
                        44               1               1.0
                        45               1               1.0
                        46               1               1.0
                        48               2               2.0
                        49               1               1.0
                        50               1               1.0
                        51               1               1.0
                        62               1               1.0
                         .               1               1.0
                                        ──              ─────
                       Total            99             100.0
```

Figure 12.1 **An example of a frequency distribution**

distribution of ages of B.S.W. graduates over a period of two years. In this example, again, the data could have been grouped to make frequency distribution easier to read, this time according to the age of graduates.

Note that one respondent did not respond to the question about age. The missing response is represented by a dot at the bottom of the value column. These incomplete data are referred to as **missing values.**

Sometimes frequency distributions can be displayed as graphs or charts. Chapter 14 discusses how to do so. An example of a frequency distribution from a published article is displayed in Table 12.6. This table presents some of the results of a study carried out by Anastas, Gibeau, and Larson (1990), concerning problems experienced by working families in their provision of elder care. Note that both raw number (n) and percentage (%) are presented.

Table 12.6 **Work and caregiving conflict ($n = 419$)**

Conflict and Work Adjustments Among Working Caregivers		
Measure	%	n
Conflict score		
no conflict (0)	53	223
conflict (1)	39	164
considered quitting (2)	8	32
Work adjustments because of caregiving		
used vacation time	64	269
changed work schedule	33	138
used personal leave	32	132
missed work meetings	18	77
missed outside conferences	14	57
missed overtime	13	54
called in sick	8	35
refused a more responsible position	7	30
unable to seek a new job	6	27
left a job	5	21
declined a job offer	4	15
taken a leave of absence	3	14

Source: From "Working Families and Eldercare," by J. W. Anastas et al., 1990, *Social Work, 35* (5), 405–411. Copyright © 1990 National Association of Social Workers, Inc. Reprinted with permission.

MEASURES OF CENTRAL TENDENCY

Another important perspective on data is the location of the middle of the distribution, or the average value. There are three different types of averages, each determined in a slightly different way. These three types are mode, median, and mean.

Mode

The **mode** is the value possessed by the greatest number of observations. In Table 12.2, non-Hispanic white is the mode for ethnicity because this category or value occurred most often. In Table 12.3, "great need" is the mode for expressed need for day care, and in Table 12.5, "less than 5 miles" for distance from campus. The mode can be used regardless of the level of measurement. It can be used for ethnicity (a nominal level of measurement), expressed need for day care (an ordinal level of measurement), and for miles from campus (a ratio level of measurement). In contrast, other measures of central tendency and other statistics discussed in this chapter (measures of variability and measures of association) are restricted in terms of levels of measurement that they can use.

Median

The median, another type of average, can be used only with ordinal, interval, and ratio level data. **Median** is that value at which 50% of observations lie above it and 50% of observations lie below it. The median is thus the value that divides the distribution in half.

The median cannot be used for nominal levels of measurement because it has meaning only with ranked data. Nominal data cannot be ranked, and consequently it cannot be determined whether cases lie above or below a particular nominal value. Numbers are often assigned to nominal data, but these numbers do not have any inherent meaning. We cannot rank, say, the values of ethnicity in any order from highest to lowest, and thus we cannot determine the middle or median value. The median is a popular measure of central tendency primarily because it is not influenced by extreme values that can be a problem with the mean (see the following section). In addition, the median is more stable than the mode, although less stable than the mean. Salaries are often described using the median. (See Appendix C for the formula for the median.)

Mean

The mean, the third type of measure of central tendency, is even more restrictive in the level of measurement that can be used. It can be computed only from interval and ratio levels of measurement (although some will argue that it can also be used with ordinal level data). The **mean** is a result of summing the values of observations and then dividing by the total number of observations. The mean miles from campus for our participants in the needs assessment (Table 12.1) is 7.36 miles. (See Appendix C for the formula for the mean.)

The major strength of the mean is that it takes into consideration each value for each observation. Extreme values, however, either high or low, can distort the mean, particularly if sample size is relatively small. Let's look at the example of miles from campus again but substitute one high value (60 miles) for a middle-range value (6 miles). The mean now becomes 9.52 (238/25 = 9.52), a two-mile difference in the mean as a result of one observation. The mean is the most stable measure of central tendency, however, and in addition is the prerequisite for computation of other statistics.

A Study Using The Mean

Wasik, Ramey, Bryant, and Sparling (1990) assessed the relative impact of two interventions. One was family education and a center-based family educational day care program, and the other was a less intensive intervention group consisting of home-based family education on child-rearing attitudes only. Table 12.7 shows the means and standard deviations (which we will discuss in the next section) of three groups—those receiving intensive intervention, less intensive intervention, and no intervention—on their child-rearing attitudes.

Table 12.7   ***Means and standard deviations on parent child-rearing attitudes***

	Center day care and family education		Family education		Control	
	M	*SD*	*M*	*SD*	*M*	*SD*
	(*n* = 14)		(*n* = 21)		(*n* = 22)	
progressive scale score on combined form (36 months)	30.3	6.1	29.2	5.7	28.5	4.9
authoritarian scale score on combined form (36 months)	22.6	5.7	23.9	4.6	23.3	5.3
modernity score on combined form (36 months)	59.7	8.4	57.3	5.6	57.2	6.7

Source: From "A Longitudinal Study of Two Early Intervention Strategies: Project CARE," by B. H. Wasik et al., 1990, *Child Development, 61.* Copyright © 1990 The Society for Research in Child Development, Inc. Reprinted with permission.

In summary, to determine which measure of central tendency to apply, you need to consider how you are going to use the information. For example, means are appropriate when you are interested in totals. If you know the national average is 2.3 children per family, then you can guess that a town of 100 families should have about 230 children. If you know that the mode is 1 child per family, then any family you choose at random will probably have 1 child. The reason the average household income is often reported as the median rather than the mean is that often we are interested in an individual comparison of our own financial situation to other normal-range incomes. The mean is inflated by the few unusual persons who make millions. Mean income, however, is more useful in comparing different countries' gross national product (GNP).

Visual Distribution of Data

Data can sometimes be presented as a **normal distribution,** or a bell-shaped curve. Properties of a normal distribution are as follows:

1. The mean, median, and mode have the same score value.
2. It is symmetrical: The right half of the distribution is the mirror image of the left half.
3. Most scores are concentrated near the center.

If distributions have most scores concentrated at one end of distribution rather than at the middle, this is referred to as a **skewed distribution** (see Figure 12.2). The assumption that a distribution is normally distributed underlies many inferential statistical tests, which will be discussed in the next chapter.

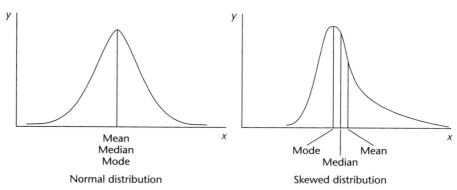

Figure 12.2 ***Normal and skewed distributions***

MEASURES OF VARIABILITY OR DISPERSION

Another dimension for describing data is the extent to which scores vary or are dispersed in distribution. Figure 12.3 depicts three distributions. They have the same measure of central tendency, but they differ in the extent to which they are spread out, or in their variability.

Like measures of central tendency, measures of variability differ, with each one more appropriate in some situations than in others. Two types of measures of variability are discussed here: the range and the standard deviation.

Range

The **range** is the easiest measure of variability to compute and to understand: It is simply the distance between the largest or maximum value and the smallest or minimum value. The range is computed by subtracting the lowest value from the highest value. The range can be used only with interval and ratio levels of data because it assumes equal intervals.

The problem with the range is its extreme instability. Different samples drawn from the same population may have very different ranges. Consequently, the range does not give you a very reliable view of what variability is in population. The range for the age variable in Figure 12.1 is 42 (62 minus 20). If you changed either the highest or lowest score to an extreme value, the range would be dramatically affected.

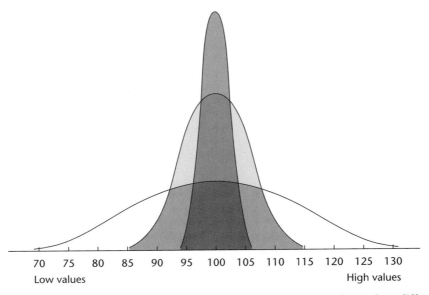

Figure 12.3   ***Three distributions with the same measure of central tendency but different variabilities or dispersions***

Table 12.8   **Demographic characteristics of the farm households**

Characteristic	Pennsylvania (n = 22)		Iowa (n = 20)		Combined (n = 42)	
	Median	Range	Median	Range	Median	Range
age of heads of household[1]	41	20 to 69	48	20 to 79	45	20 to 79
age of parents	49	20 to 69	50	30 to 79	49	20 to 79
families' income[2]	20,100	<9,999 >40,000	22,667	<9,999 >40,000	21,062	<9,999 >40,000
household size	2.5	2 to 7	2.5	1 to 7	2.5	1 to 7
acreage[3]	165	30 to 500	300	120 to 1200	180	30 to 1200
length of residence on farm	22.5 years	1 year– 60 years	19.5 years	2 months– 70 years	21.5 years	2 months– 70 years

[1] Includes children older than age 21 working the farm, living in the same house, and acting as heads of households. In Pennsylvania, there were 22 households containing 24 families.

[2] Income median was computed from group data. Modal income for Pennsylvania and Iowa was $10,000 to $17,999.

[3] Includes rented, owned, or custom.

Source: From "Farm Families' Preferences Toward the Personal Social Services," by E. Martinez-Brawley and J. Blundall, 1989, *Social Work, 34* (6), p. 514. Copyright © 1989 National Association of Social Workers, Inc. Reprinted with permission.

Table 12.8 presents data from a study by Martinez-Brawley and Blundall (1989), who studied farm families' preferences for personal social services. The table presents demographic characteristics of farm households and includes the median and range for a number of variables.

Standard Deviation

The standard deviation is a measure that averages together each value's distance from the mean. Calculating the **standard deviation** involves the following steps:

1. Calculate the mean.
2. Measure the distance of each score from the mean.
3. Square these distances (to eliminate negative values).
4. Add the squared differences from the mean.
5. Divide by the *n*, thus calculating a mean of the differences from the mean.
6. Take the square root of the result.

(See Appendix C for the formula for the standard deviation.)

Because the standard deviation uses the mean and is similar to the mean in many respects, it can be used only with interval and ratio level data. The standard deviation is the most stable of the measures of variability, although it too, because it uses the mean, can be affected by extreme scores. Refer back to Table 12.7 for an example that includes the standard deviations of outcome measures.

MEASURES OF ASSOCIATION

Up to this point we have been looking only at **univariate measures,** which measure one variable at a time, and we have been trying to develop a picture of how that one variable is distributed in a sample. Often, though, we want to measure the relationship between two or more variables; such measures are, respectively, **bivariate** and **multivariate measures.**

Often, when carrying out a program evaluation, you are interested in the relationship between two or more variables. For example, you may want to study the effect of a special program for high school students on their self-esteem. You would need to look at the relationship between the independent variable (the special program) on the dependent variable (self-esteem). Or you may wish to compare the dependent variables of an experimental and control group—that is, outcomes from two different programs. To do so, you need to use bivariate statistics.

Similarly, in needs assessments, sometimes you are interested in examining the relationship among variables. For example, in investigating a community's need for a YMCA/YWCA, you want to know not only how many people express this need but also the characteristics of these individuals—ages of their children and so forth. Here the two variables are expressed need and ages of children.

Multivariate analysis involves examining the relationships among more than two variables. This text does not discuss this type of analysis, but sources cited in the Further Reading section at the end of this chapter offer some guidance. Try to enroll in a statistics course if at all possible.

Two bivariate measures of association are discussed in this section: cross-tabulation and correlation.

Cross-Tabulation

Cross-tabulation is probably the most widely used bivariate statistic, because it is simple to use and extremely versatile. Cross-tabulations are also known as **contingency tables.** Cross-tabulations may be used with any level of measurement. If interval and ratio (and sometimes ordinal) levels of measurement are used, however, they must be collapsed into a smaller number of categories (the meaning of *smaller* here is discussed a little later).

An example of a cross-tabulation, shown in Figure 12.4, is from a study that examined the workplace service needs of women employees. This particular contingency table looks at the relationship between how the women perceived their husband's participation in household chores (CHORE) and their need for flexible work hours (FLEX).

Generally, the dependent variable (in this case, the need for flexible work hours) is displayed in columns, and the independent variable (husband's participation in chores) is displayed in the rows. The row totals plus percentages and column totals plus percentages are written at the end of each row and column respectively. CHORE has three values (low, medium, and high participation), and FLEX has two values (yes, a need; no, no need). Consequently, we have what is called a 3 by 2 (3 values by 2 values) contingency table, with 6 cells or boxes. If the variables had more values, the table would be larger. You need to be careful that the table is not too large; we also cannot let the number of cases in any of the cells get too low (five or less) because then there are problems in the use of inferential statistics. (Inferential statistics will be discussed in Chapter 13.) Sometimes several values need to be combined to reduce the number of values and so reduce the size of the table. As a result, the number of cases in each cell increases.

Let's continue reading the table. The top number in each cell refers to the number of cases. In the top left-hand cell in Figure 12.4, the number of cases is 75. The second number is the row percentages—that is, for the percentage of women who stated their husbands were low participants in household chores, 83.3% requested flexible work hours. The third number in the cell is the column

CHORE		FLEX		
	Count Row Pct Col Pct Total Pct	YES	NO	Row Total
Low Participation	1	75 83.3 65.8 53.6	15 16.7 57.7 10.7	90 64.3
Medium Participation	2	15 83.3 13.2 10.7	3 16.7 11.5 2.1	18 12.9
High Participation	3	24 75.0 21.1 17.1	8 25.0 30.8 5.7	32 22.8
Column Total		114 81.4	26 18.6	140 100.0

Figure 12.4 **Cross-tabulation of two variables: FLEX and CHORE**

percentage: In our example, this represents the percentage of women who requested flexible work hours—65.8% reported low participation of their husbands in household chores. The bottom number in the cell is the total percentage. In other words, the number of cases in the cell, 75, is 53.6% of the total number of cases. The total number of cases can be found in the lower right-hand corner. In Figure 12.4, this number is 140 and, as is recorded immediately below 140 in the cell, represents 100% of cases. You can go through and read each of the cells in this manner. To the extreme right are the row totals and percentages, and at the bottom of the table, the column totals and percentages. Note that the labels on the table help guide your interpretation.

The availability of percentages allows you to compare groups of unequal size. A sense of association can be gained by comparing these percentages. For example, a slightly lower proportion of those reporting high participation of their husbands in household chores requested flexible work hours (75%) than those who reported medium and low participation (83.3% for both). Is this difference big enough to signify a relationship between the variables, or is it simply due to change? This question is answered in the next chapter when the topic of inferential statistics is discussed.

Correlation

Correlation is another common way of looking at the relationship between variables, which can be used only with interval and ratio level data. In our example of a study investigating the impact of a program directed at increasing the adolescent participants' self-esteem, it was hypothesized that the number of sessions adolescents attended would have an impact on their level of self-esteem measured on an equal interval scale. Ten adolescents were tested on their level of self-esteem before and after the program (see Table 12.9).

These data can then be plotted on a chart called a **scattergram** (Figure 12.5). The horizontal axis (X) represents the client's length of time in the program, and the vertical axis (Y) represents the difference in the client's level of self-esteem before and after participation in the program.

In Figure 12.5, the line connecting the dots is perfectly straight. In this case, there is a **perfect correlation** between the two variables: When one variable increases or decreases, the other does so at the same rate. A perfect correlation very rarely occurs; usually you find that the dots do not perfectly follow the line but are scattered around it. The direction of the relationship can vary. Figure 12.5 demonstrates a **positive correlation** between the number of sessions attended and the level of self-esteem. As the number of sessions attended increased, so did the level of self-esteem. A **negative correlation** can also occur; this is depicted in Figure 12.6. Here the high values of one of the variables, self-esteem, are associated with the low values of the other variable, the number of sessions attended.

The extent to which data points are scattered gives us an indication about the strength of the relationship between the two variables. There is a formula to

Table 12.9   **Self-esteem scores and number of weeks in the program (n = 10)**

Client ID	Self-esteem score	Number of weeks in program
1	8	1
2	10	2
3	12	3
4	14	4
5	16	5
6	18	6
7	20	7
8	22	8
9	24	9
10	26	10

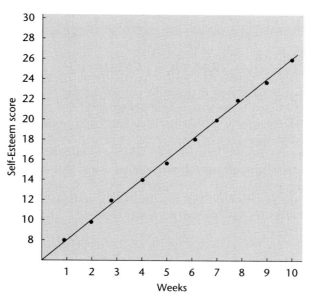

Figure 12.5   **Scattergram of relationship between self-esteem score and time in program (a perfect positive correlation)**

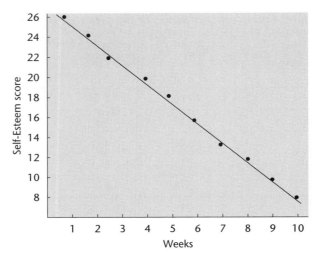

Figure 12.6 **Scattergram of relationship between self-esteem score and time in program (a perfect negative correlation)**

precisely measure the strength of this relationship; again, it involves inferential statistics and will be discussed in the next chapter.

The line passing through the dots is used to predict certain values. This prediction involves **regression analysis,** which will be discussed briefly in the next chapter.

DESCRIPTIVE STATISTICS AND PRACTICE EVALUATION

Descriptive statistics are not necessarily limited in their application to group studies. They can also be used in single-system studies when quantitative data are collected. Many measures of central tendency and of variability can be used in single-system designs. For example, mean measures during baseline and intervention can be calculated. Calculating mean measures, however, does involve losing much data through aggregation—something that single-system studies are in fact designed to avoid. Consequently, the most effective way to describe the results of single-system studies is to display the results visually. You can think of data charts as possessing certain properties (Bloom, Fischer, & Orme, 1995), as follows.

Level. The magnitude of data is the level. Differences in levels can occur between the baseline and the intervention. A change in level is called a **discontinuity** (see Figure 12.7).

Stability. Where there is clear predictability from a prior period to a later one, the data are stable. Stability occurs if the data can be easily represented by a

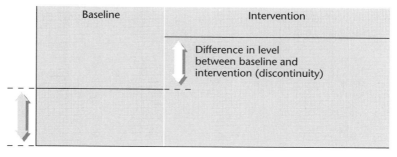

Figure 12.7   **Levels of data**

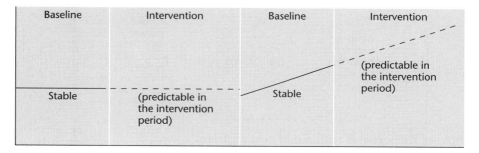

Figure 12.8   **Stability of data between baseline and intervention**

mean line. Data lines can still be stable even if they change in magnitude. See Figure 12.8 for two examples of stability of data between baseline and intervention periods.

Trends.   Where the data tend in one direction—whether the pattern is increasing or decreasing—a trend is present. Trends are called **slopes** when they occur within a given phase and **drifts** when they occur across phases. See Figure 12.9 for variations of trends.

Improvement or deterioration.   Specific comparisons between the baseline and intervention periods can show improvement or deterioration in the target behavior. Of course, a determination of what is improvement and what is deterioration depends on whether greater or lesser magnitudes of the behavior are desired. Figure 12.10 illustrates this idea.

Other factors that need to be considered when describing findings from the charts include the following:

The timing of the effects.   Sometimes effects occur immediately after the baseline and sometimes they are delayed (Figure 12.11).

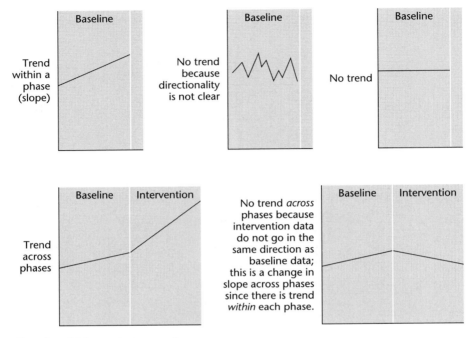

Figure 12.9   Trends within and across phases

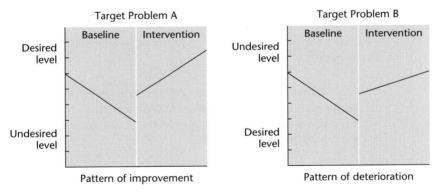

Figure 12.10   Patterns of improvement and deterioration

The stability of the effects.   The effect of the intervention may wear off. If so, implementation of a different intervention is indicated (Figure 12.12).

Variability in the data.   This often happens but needs to be treated cautiously, particularly when the variability occurs during the baseline period. In both examples in Figure 12.13, it is difficult to interpret the effects due to variability in the baseline data.

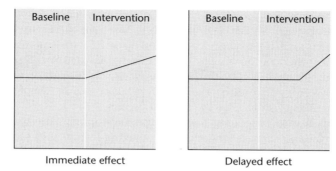

Figure 12.11 **Immediate and delayed effects**

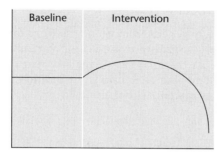

Figure 12.12 **Unstable effects**

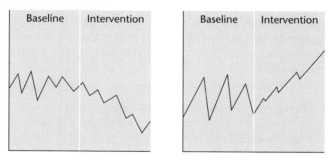

Figure 12.13 **Variability in data**

The next chapter will discuss how data from single-system studies can be analyzed using specifically designed statistical techniques. These techniques then give you an indication of the data's statistical significance. This is particularly useful when the data are variable, as in Figure 12.13.

When displaying results, you need to ensure that you accurately graph the data. Computer packages specifically designed to handle data from single-system designs are very helpful. One is the Computer Assisted Practice Evaluation (CAPE) (Bronson & Blythe, 1987), which is based on the Lotus 1-2-3 program. This program plots the data on a graph and does the statistical tests that the user specifies. Another computer option is Computer Assisted Social Services (CASS), which combines the ability to do single-system data analysis with the Multi-Problem Screening Inventory (Hudson, 1990) discussed in Chapter 9. This package produces graphs that plot the results of scales.

Great advances are being made in the development of computer aids for practice evaluation. These strides are encouraging in that they facilitate analysis of data from single-system studies and prompt social workers to evaluate their own practice.

THE AGENCY AND DESCRIPTIVE STATISTICS

Descriptive statistics can be easily generated in agency settings for needs assessments and program evaluations. Obviously, using a computer enhances the generation of such statistics. Discuss the analysis of single-system data with your colleagues. They can help validate your conclusions. In addition, you can show them how single-system designs can enhance their practice.

ETHICAL ISSUES IN DESCRIPTIVE STATISTICS

One major ethical issue in the use of descriptive statistics is ensuring that the correct—that is, the appropriate—statistic is being used to portray the data. In addition, you must avoid distorting the data to fit any preconceived ideas. Beware of leaving out data that do not support your hypothesis—this is completely unethical. Accurate reporting of the methods you use and the results you obtain is the backbone of good science. Only in this way can we replicate studies and add to the knowledge base of social work. The NASW Code of Ethics (1997) states:

■ Social workers should report evaluation and research findings accurately. They should not fabricate or falsify results and should take steps to correct any errors later found in published data using standard publication methods.

HUMAN DIVERSITY ISSUES IN DESCRIPTIVE STATISTICS

In categorizing values—for the purpose of constructing frequency distribution tables or for cross-tabulations—care must be taken that differences between groups of individuals are respected. Often, the number of subjects in some minority groups is small, and there is a temptation to collapse these groups into one. In doing so, however, we may lose critical information about human diversity. Consequently, it is important to devise a means to retain this information. One strategy would be to add a qualitative or interpretive dimension to your study.

SUMMARY

Descriptive statistics summarize the characteristics of a sample. Frequency distributions are descriptions of the number of times the values of a variable occur in a sample. The measures of central tendency are the mode, median, and mean. Data can be distributed in a normal or bell-shaped curve or in a skewed pattern. Measures of variability are the range and standard deviation. The measures of association are cross-tabulation and correlation. One of the most effective ways to use descriptive statistics with single-system studies is to present the results visually, although statistical analyses can also be conducted.

STUDY/EXERCISE QUESTIONS

1. Look for articles in social work journals that use
   a. the mean/median or mode
   b. the standard deviation
   c. correlation
   d. cross-tabulations

2. One of the Study/Exercise Questions in Chapter 10 asked you to develop a questionnaire for measuring student attitudes on combining research and practice, to administer the questionnaire, and to construct a code book. Construct a frequency distribution table for two of the variables included in this questionnaire.

3. Find an article in a social work journal that uses a single-system design. Are the data presented visually? Are the results clear as a result of this visual presentation?

FURTHER READING

Blalock, H. M. (1979). *Social statistics*. New York: McGraw-Hill.
   A good source book for delving into the intricacies of statistical analysis.

Blythe, B., Tripodi, T., & Briar, S. (1994). *Direct practice research in human service agencies*. New York: Columbia University.
   Includes much content on the analysis of data in practice evaluations.

Dileonardi, J., & Curtis, R. (1992). *What to do when the numbers are in*. Chicago: Nelson Hall.

Graft, J. L. (1990). *Statistics and data analysis for social workers* (2nd ed.). Itasca, IL: Peacock.

An easy-to-read introduction for social workers; includes most of what you will need.

Pilcher, D. (1990). *Data analysis for helping professions.* Newbury Park, CA: Sage. An excellent basic statistics text.

Weinbach, R. W., & Grinnell, R., Jr. (1989). *Statistics for social workers.* New York: Longman.
Basic statistics for social workers, very readable.

REFERENCES

Anastas, J. W., Gibeau, J. L., & Larson, P. J. (1990). Working families and elder-care: A rational perspective in an aging America. *Social Work, 35,* 405–411.

Bloom, M., Fischer, J., & Orme, J. (1995). *Evaluating practice: Guidelines for the accountable professional* (2nd ed.). Boston: Allyn & Bacon.

Bronson, D. E., & Blythe, B. J. (1987). Computer support for single case evaluation of practice. *Social Work Research and Abstracts, 23,* 10–13.

Hudson, W. (1990). *Computer assisted social services.* Tempe, AZ: Walmyr.

Martinez-Brawley, E., & Blundall, J. (1989). Farm families preferences toward personal social services. *Social Work, 34* (6), 513–522.

Wasik, B. H., Ramey, C. T., Bryant, D. M., & Sparling, J. J. (1990). A longitudinal study of two early intervention strategies: Project CARE. *Child Development, 61* (6), 1682–1696.

Analysis of Quantitative Data: Inferential Statistics

Now that you have an understanding of how to describe quantitative data, when you are evaluating a program or your own practice you might ask: How important is a difference in outcome between those who received the intervention and those who did not? Can we generalize these findings to a wider population? These questions can be answered with inferential statistics. **Inferential statistics** allow us to determine whether an observed relationship is due to chance or whether it reflects a relationship between factors, and they allow us to generalize the findings to the wider population.

Chapter 12 was concerned with describing the profile of the sample or population. In this chapter, quantitative analysis is taken one step further, and hypotheses are tested using statistical procedures or tests. This type of analysis is critical in assessing the effectiveness of programs and practice. Hypotheses, as discussed in Chapter 3, are specific ways of structuring and stating research questions. In the case of a program evaluation, the hypothesis might be something like this: "If pregnant adolescents complete the prenatal classes provided by program A, then they will be less likely to give birth to low birth-weight babies than those adolescents who do not complete the program."

It is important to know whether this type of hypothesis can be supported by data. Descriptive statistics can be used to present the characteristics of the sample—for example, their ages, marital status, other children, and other demographic information. In order to test hypotheses, however, inferential statistics are needed.

As generalist social workers, you are not necessarily involved in direct analysis of data. Thus the emphasis of this chapter, as in the last, is not on computing statistics but rather on understanding which statistics are useful for which purpose.

This chapter will discuss the following:

- sources of error and the role of inferential statistics
- types of hypotheses
- significance levels
- statistical power
- steps in the computation of the statistical tests
- types of statistical tests
- inferential statistics and practice evaluations
- the agency and inferential statistics
- ethical issues in inferential statistics
- human diversity issues in inferential statistics

SOURCES OF ERROR AND THE ROLE OF INFERENTIAL STATISTICS

Throughout the research process, there are possibilities for error in our conclusions. Errors can come from three different sources, and each source of error can be addressed by specific strategies.

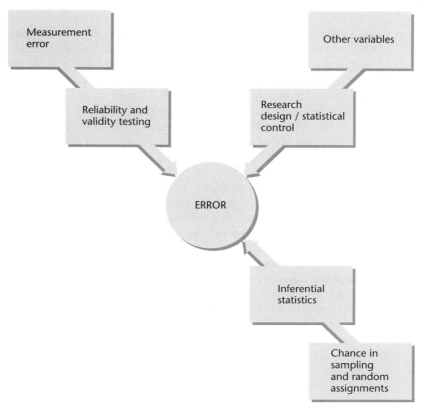

Figure 13.1 **Sources and corrections for error**

First, a measurement error may affect data collection; this possibility can be assessed by checking the reliability and validity of the data collection instrument (see Chapter 9 for a discussion). Second, other variables might be responsible for the relationship, and they need to be controlled. Variables can be controlled by the research design or, as we discussed in the last chapter, statistically. The third source of error is chance. Chance has to do with sampling variability, as was discussed in Chapter 8. A randomly drawn sample and a population may differ due to chance. The role of chance factors can be assessed through the use of inferential statistics, which relies on probability theory. (The specific statistical tests involved are described later in this chapter.) These three sources of error and the strategies for their assessment are illustrated in Figure 13.1.

TYPES OF HYPOTHESES

A hypothesis suggests that two or more variables are associated in some way. There are two types of hypotheses. First, the **two-tailed** or **nondirectional hypothesis** simply states that there is an association between two or more variables but predicts nothing about the nature of the direction of the association. One such example would be the hypothesis that gender has an impact on the likelihood of hospitalization for depression. A **one-tailed** or **directional hypothesis** specifies not only that the variables are associated but also the nature or direction of the relationship or association—whether it is positive or negative. For example, we might hypothesize that women are more likely than men to be hospitalized for depression. The state of prior knowledge drawn from the literature and theory will in part determine whether one-tailed or two-tailed hypotheses are developed. Remember that when developing hypotheses you do need to draw on existing knowledge; hypotheses should not be based on impulse or initial impressions.

A type of hypothesis that is central in inferential statistics is the null hypothesis, which is derived from either the one-tailed or two-tailed hypothesis. The **null hypothesis** states there is no association between the variables. The null hypothesis is formulated only for testing purposes. Using our previous example of a one-tailed hypothesis, the null hypothesis would be that women are not more likely than men to be hospitalized for depression. Statistical analysis then allows the null hypothesis to fail to be rejected. If the null hypothesis is not rejected, then it is concluded that no relationship exists between the variables. On the other hand, if the null hypothesis is rejected, there does appear to be a relationship between the variables that is not a result of chance.

This process may seem unnecessarily complicated. The concept of the null hypothesis is important, however, because it reminds us that statistical tests are intended to determine to what extent a relationship is due to chance, rather than whether or not the hypothesis is true.

SIGNIFICANCE LEVELS

When data are first examined it is not possible to draw clear conclusions based on the findings. For example, in the question relating to gender and hospitalization for depression, the results may disclose that of the people hospitalized for depression, 55% were women versus 45% men. Just looking at these results does not disclose whether this 10% difference between the men and women is simply due to chance or is due to the effect of the program or some other variable. A statistical test must be used for this purpose.

A finding is **statistically significant** when the null hypothesis is rejected and the probability that the result is due to chance in the sample or population falls at or below a certain cutoff point. This cutoff point has been established by statistical convention to be .05. In other words, if a relationship occurs due to chance no more than 5 times out of 100, the null hypothesis is rejected. In this case, it is very unlikely that the relationship is based on chance, and the hypothesis acknowledges that the variables named in it are having an impact on the outcome. Sometimes the significance level is set at lower levels (for example, .01) or, under special circumstances, higher levels (.10). The important thing to remember is that the significance level is set prior to the statistical testing.

The observed level of significance is signified by $p < .05$ (or $p < .01$), and any level below .05 (or .01) is regarded as statistically significant. Establishing statistical significance at the .05 level or less does not mean there is a proven relationship between the variables but rather that there is only a 5% probability that the relationship is a result of chance occurrence. Avoid stating that a hypothesis has been proved. A more accurate statement is that the hypothesis is statistically significant at the .05 level.

STATISTICAL POWER

Sometimes decision errors can be made in either failing to reject or rejecting the null hypothesis. These two errors are referred to as Type I and Type II errors. **Type I error** is the rejection of the null hypothesis and the false conclusion that a relationship exists between the variables when in fact no "real" relationship does exist. **Type II error** is the failure to reject the null hypothesis and so the failure to identify any "real" relationship between the variables (see Figure 13.2). Obviously these errors can present some serious problems.

A statistical test's ability to correctly reject a null hypothesis is referred to as the test's **power.** Generally, the power of the test increases as sample size increases. The test's power is also greater the higher the level of measurement—that is, tests using ratio level data will be more powerful than those using nominal level data.

STEPS IN THE COMPUTATION OF STATISTICAL TESTS

The computation of statistical tests all involve similar steps:

1. Identify the appropriate test and identify its formula.
2. Enter the raw data into the formula and compute the statistical score. (The formulas for the statistical tests can be found in Appendix C.)

		What the "real" relationship is between the variables.	
		True	False
Researcher decision about the relationship between the variables	Fail to reject null hypothesis	Correct decision	Type II error
	Reject null hypothesis	Type I error	Correct decision

Figure 13.2 **Type I and Type II errors**

3. Compute the degree of freedom, which is related to the size of the sample and the power of the test.

4. Use the probability tables (see Appendix D) to assess the probability level and statistical significance of the statistics score.

These steps are completed rapidly and accurately by whichever statistical software you may be using. Generally, the statistics score and its statistical significance are reported.

TYPES OF STATISTICAL TESTS

In this section will be described the most common statistical tests encountered in the social work literature and those needed for the analysis of most of your data. Four tests will be discussed: t-tests, analysis of variance (ANOVA), correlational analysis (including regression analysis), and chi-square.

Each test is appropriate only under certain conditions. When selecting a test, you need to consider four factors: first, the structure of the null hypothesis; second, the need to use certain tests only with certain levels of measurement; third, the size of the sample; fourth, the distribution of the responses—whether or not the distribution is normal. A summary table of the tests and their conditions for use is presented in Table 13.1.

Table 13.1   ***Types of statistical tests and some conditions for use***

	T-test	ANOVA	Correlation coefficient	Chi-square
Comparing means of two populations	Yes	No	No	No
Comparing means of more than two populations	No	Yes	No	No
All variables at interval /ratio level of measurement	No	No	Yes	No
One variable only at interval /ratio level of measurement	Yes	Yes	No	No
All variables at ordinal /nominal level of measurement	No	No	No	Yes

The T-Test

Conditions of Use

The t-test is used under the following conditions:

1. You are interested in testing a null hypothesis to find whether two samples have the same mean.

2. The dependent variable is at the interval level of measurement at least (although some argue that the ordinal level of measurement is acceptable), and the other variable (usually the independent variable) is at the nominal level of measurement.

3. The sample size can be small.

These conditions often occur in social work. Many program evaluation designs include comparison groups. Each group that is compared represents a value at the nominal level of measurement. Program evaluations often measure the outcome or dependent variable (for example, the number of months an individual has held a job, or the score on a standardized test) at the interval or ratio level. The null hypothesis in such a program evaluation could be that the intervention had no effect; in other words, the two groups had similar outcomes or mean scores. Just on the basis of probability, though, outcomes are likely to be different. The t-test discloses whether this difference could be due to chance. Similarly, you would want to use this test when comparing two groups such as males and females, urban and rural residents, or married and unmarried people, and looking at their differing outcome variables. This type of t-test is known as an independent samples t-test or a groupwise comparison t-test.

Another type of t-test is the paired samples or pairwise comparison t-test. Also commonly used in social work research, the paired samples t-test compares two means at different points in time for the same sample. For example, such a test might compare academic and cognitive scores for children at the beginning of a Head Start program with their scores at the end of a year.

The degrees of freedom for the t-test is accomplished by subtracting 2 from the *n* (the total number of participants in both groups).

The Use of T-Tests in the Literature

Jamison and Virts (1990) used a t-test in their study of the influence of family support on chronic pain. Two groups of chronic pain patients were compared—those who described their family as being supportive (233 patients) and those who stated they had family conflicts (275 patients). The outcome, or dependent variables, included demographic, medical, behavioral, and psychological factors (all at the ratio or interval level of measurement). A t-test analysis comparing the supportive and nonsupportive groups disclosed that several of the independent variables—sleep disturbances ($t = 3.73$), depression ($t = 6.54$), and irritability ($t = 8.21$)—were found to be significant at the $p < .05$ level.

Analysis of Variance (ANOVA)

Conditions of Use

The analysis of variance statistical test (ANOVA) is used under these conditions:

1. You are interested in testing a null hypothesis to find whether or not the means in more than two samples are the same.
2. The dependent variable is at least the interval level of measurement, and the other variable, usually the independent variable, is measured at the nominal level.
3. The sample size can be small.

Sound familiar? The t-test is in fact a special case of ANOVA, and the conditions of the use of ANOVA are consequently very similar to those of the t-test, except that ANOVA is used to compare more than two groups. The ANOVA results in an *F*-test statistic.

ANOVA is useful if, for example, you are comparing the outcomes of three or more programs in different parts of the state and the outcome is being measured at the interval level or above.

The Use of ANOVA

Hopper and McCarlnielson (1991) carried out an interesting study that investigated factors contributing to people's recycling behavior. The study also evaluated the impact of different recycling program strategies, including block leaders, prompts, and information. The randomly selected sample of 240 households were randomly assigned to the five different recycling programs. Outcomes variables included a recycling score, a social norm score, and an awareness of consequences score. Whether or not the households actually participated in recycling was also recorded.

The data showed that recruited block leaders had the greatest impact on the recycling score, prompts had a somewhat smaller effect, and information had the least impact. The data indicated that only the recruited block leader group resulted in statistically significant increases in both the social norm and personal norm scores. None of the groups showed significant increases in awareness of consequences.

Correlational Analysis

Conditions of Use

The correlation coefficient gives an indication of the strength of the correlation between two variables. It is used under the following conditions:

1. You are interested in testing the null hypothesis to find out whether two variables are not correlated.

2. Both variables are at the interval level of measurement or a higher level.
3. A normal distribution of responses is not required.

Chapter 12 discussed the use of the scattergram to look at the relationship between two variables. This relationship was described as a correlation. The correlation coefficient examines the strength and direction of the relationship between two variables and discloses whether the relationship is statistically significant. The correlation coefficient statistic is represented by *r*, also referred to as the Pearson *r*. The coefficient is in the range of −1.0 to +1.0. The −1.0 represents a perfect negative correlation, and +1.0 represents a perfect positive correlation.

The degrees of freedom for the Pearson *r* is simply the *n*. You need to remember that the *r* statistic is simply looking at the strength and relationship between two variables; under no circumstances is it to be used to imply causation. Level of self-esteem and performance on an aptitude test for social work might be highly correlated but this does not mean that one causes the other; the other conditions of causality also need to be met (see Chapter 3).

Correlational Analysis

Abelsohn and Saayman (1991) examined the relationship of four family-based clinical dimensions to the adjustment of 45 adolescents during the first 18 months of parental separation. There was a significant correlation between perceived post-separation family structure and adolescent adjustment. One surprising finding was that the adolescents do better when exposed to the mother's distress. The authors suggest that such exposure is an indication of a mutually supportive process where the mother is attuned to the adolescent's vulnerability.

Regression Analysis

One of the main strengths of the *r* statistic is with prediction. Regression analysis is used for this purpose, and involves finding the straight line that best fits the data. Such lines show how much change in the dependent variable is produced by a given change in an independent variable or several independent variables. Regression produces coefficients that indicate the direction and amount of change in the dependent variable to be expected from a unit change in the independent variable.

Regression Analysis

Poulin and Walter (1993) carried out a longitudinal study of social worker burnout. Using regression analysis, the authors found that low and high burnout is associated with a number of organizational, client, and personal factors. The authors suggested that burnout not only can be prevented but also can be reversed.

Chi-Square Analysis

Conditions of Use

Chi-square analysis is one of the most widely used statistical tests in social work research, in part because it is a test that can be used with the ordinal or nominal levels of measurement.

The chi-square is used under these conditions:

1. You are interested in testing the null hypothesis to find whether there is no relationship between two variables.
2. The variables are both measured at the nominal or ordinal level. Although chi-square can be used with data at any level of measurement, often at the interval or ratio level of measurement the data will need to be collapsed into categories.

In the last chapter, cross-tabulation was discussed, which is a way of describing the relationship between two variables measured at the nominal or ordinal level. With cross-tabulation, we are eyeballing or estimating the relationship. The chi-square statistic can be applied to cross-tabulation to give us a more accurate reflection of the significance of the relationship between two variables.

Chi-square analysis assesses the extent to which the frequencies in our cross-tabulation, called the **observed frequencies,** differ from what we might expect to observe if the data were distributed in the cross-tabulation according to chance. These chance frequencies are called the **expected frequencies.** The chi-square statistic is represented by χ^2. The degrees of freedom for the chi-square are related to the number of cells rather than to the *n*. They are computed using the following formula:

df = (r−1) (c−1)
r = number of rows
c = number of columns

Exercise caution when using chi-square analysis. If the sample is too small or if one or more of the cells has an expected value of less than 5, chi-square should not be used.

Chi-Square Analysis

Bryan and Ajo (1992) used both chi-square analyses and correlational analyses to examine the social and contextual factors influencing the role perceptions of African American fathers. Results indicated no significant relationship between age or education and role perceptions, whereas number of hours fathers worked per week and income were found to be significantly related to the saliency of role perceptions. Some of these results are displayed in Table 13.2.

Table 13.2   **Relation between role perceptions of respondent African American fathers and education and type of employment**

Variable	χ^2	Significant level
Education	16.56041	0.071
Type of employment	15.26178	0.073

Source: From "The Role Perception of African American Fathers," by D. L. Bryan and A. A. Ajo, *Social Work Research & Abstracts, 28* (3), p. 19. Copyright © 1992 National Association of Social Workers, Inc.

Inferential Statistics and Practice Evaluations

Chapter 12 discussed how results from practice evaluations, particularly single-system studies, can lend themselves to the use of descriptive statistics and how various software packages can facilitate this process. It is also possible to use certain statistical techniques with the results from single-system studies that give us some indication about the effectiveness of our interventions.

Before describing some of these techniques, a distinction needs to be made between three types of significance, which can be encountered in the analysis of group data but often are more relevant in single-system studies: These types of significance are practical or clinical, visual, and statistical. **Practical** or **clinical significance** is attained when the specified goal of the intervention has been reached. For example, the goal of an intervention may be to increase a child's school attendance from 50% to 90%. Anything below this goal may not be of practical significance, even though that figure may be higher than what is needed for statistical significance.

Hersen and Barlow (1984), who wrote a comprehensive text of single-system studies, stated that "applied interventions strive for change that ordinarily surpasses statistical significance" (p. 267). By the way, this distinction between practical and statistical significance is also relevant to the analysis of group data, not just single-system data.

Chapter 12 discussed the importance of visual presentation of the data from single-system studies. If the results look significant, this is known as **visual significance.** As with practical significance, there can be some discrepancy between visual significance and statistical significance. Occasionally, visual significance may not represent statistical significance; we may be looking for even a very slight visual trend.

Some have argued that statistical analysis cannot be conducted on data from single-system studies (Campbell & Stanley, 1966) because of the completely different nature of single-system and group data. Another potential problem with using inferential analysis with single-system data is that often we find that outcome scores are related to one another. This relationship, called **autocorrelation,** occurs when scores are related so that if we know what happened in the past, we can predict what will happen in the future. Autocorrelation can result in misleading findings and can complicate any statistical analysis.

In recent years, however, attempts have been made to accommodate these potential problems involved in analyzing single-system data. For example, Bloom, Fischer, and Orme (1995) described methods to manage and interpret autocorrelation in some detail.

The three following analytical procedures will be discussed: celeration line approach, standard deviation approach, and relative frequency approach.

Celeration Line Approach

This approach for analysis of single-system data was developed by Gingerich and Feyerherm (1979). It involves connecting the midpoints of the two values of baseline data with a line and projecting this line into the intervention period. The line may either accelerate or decelerate depending upon its direction— hence the term **celeration line.** If a certain proportion of the data are on the desired side of the celeration line, then an estimate can be made of the statistical significance using tables developed by Bloom (1975). Details of this method can be found in Gingerich and Feyerherm (1979), Behling and Merves (1984), or Bloom, Fischer, and Orme (1995).

The celeration line approach has the advantage of not being influenced by autocorrelation, but it is subject to a number of limiting conditions. These include the fact that the number of observations in the baseline and intervention phases should be approximately the same number. Second, celeration lines cannot be used when the baseline is bounded—that is, when the line reaches either the maximum or the minimum. In these cases, the line obviously cannot be extended into the intervention phase. See Figure 13.3 for a visual representation of the celeration line.

Standard Deviation Approach

This approach is based on the standard deviation, which measures the dispersion of scores around the mean (see Chapter 12). With this approach for analyzing data of single-system studies, if the possible intervention mean is more than two standard deviations from the baseline mean then there is a statistically signifi-

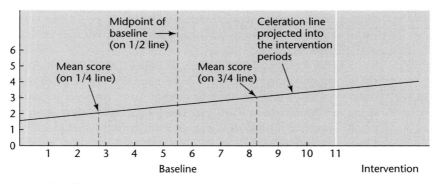

Figure 13.3 **Celeration line approach**

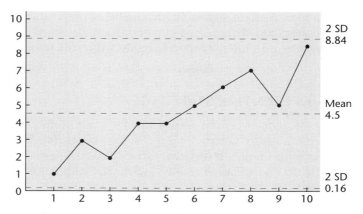

Figure 13.4   **Standard deviation approach**

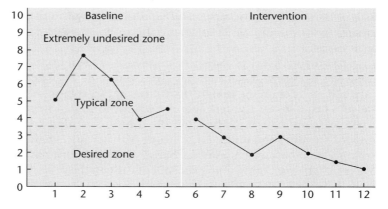

Figure 13.5   **Relative frequency approach**

cant change. Figure 13.4 illustrates this procedure. See Bloom, Fischer, and Orme (1995) for details of how to compute this approach.

This simple procedure can be used for almost any number of data points. This approach cannot be used with data that is autocorrelated, however, unless the adjustments mentioned earlier are made (see Bloom, Fischer, & Orme, 1995).

Relative Frequency Approach

This approach assumes that typical behavior is represented by the middle two-thirds of the baseline behavior. The proportion of scores that fall outside this range during the intervention period is calculated, and the proportion is located on a probability table. The value from the probability table is the estimate of statistical significance of the change. See Bloom, Fischer, and Orme (1995) for details on the computations involved in this approach. The relative frequency procedure is illustrated in Figure 13.5.

As with the celeration approach, the number of observations in the baseline and intervention period should be approximately the same. Also, autocorrelation can interfere with interpretation of results using this approach.

THE AGENCY AND INFERENTIAL STATISTICS

Commonly, the outcomes from agency-based research studies are not subject to much in-depth analysis. Often, the report simply contains descriptive statistics. This results from a number of different factors: first, the need to focus on practical over statistical significance; second, lack of statistical knowledge; and third, lack of access to computers.

The focus on practical significance is understandable in an agency setting. Often, this practical significance can be thought of as political significance. If an agency is carrying out a program evaluation, the agency may not be concerned with whether the results are statistically significant but rather with whether the goals of the program have been met. Demonstrating statistical significance could enhance practical findings considerably, however, and therefore strengthen the agency's case.

Unfortunately, lack of statistical knowledge in agency settings is all too common. This overview of statistics has given you some basic knowledge that you can build on by enrolling in statistics courses or by exploring the many available statistics texts. If you still feel at a loss when confronted with analysis of your data, seek consultation. Universities often have statistical consultants, or you can look in your community for someone with statistical know-how. If you are writing a grant or research proposal, budget in the cost of a statistical consultant. Whenever possible, bring in the consultant early in the project's planning stage. As we have seen, the type of analysis you carry out is contingent upon other aspects of the research process—the levels of measurement, design, and sample size. Thus, utilizing the consultant from the start will ultimately help the data analysis itself. Statistical consultation groups also exist on the Internet.

Lack of access to computers and software is another potential stumbling block to data analysis in an agency setting. As generalist social workers you need to lobby for their inclusion in the budget.

ETHICAL ISSUES IN INFERENTIAL STATISTICS

Two ethical issues need to be considered in the use of inferential statistics: first, the selection of the most appropriate test; and second, the presentation of statistical significance.

Selection of the Test

Selection of the most powerful test is critical. For example, if a less powerful test is used in place of a more powerful one—assuming conditions allow use of the latter—then there is a smaller likelihood that the null hypothesis will not be rejected when, in fact, it should have been. In other words, a Type II error may be committed. Essentially, a Type II error is a distortion of the results and can be regarded as unethical.

You also must be careful to avoid selecting only tests that support your hypotheses. Watch for this not only in your own research but when you are reading articles.

Statistical Significance

Several authors have commented on how important it is to recognize that statistical significance is not a concrete entity or property of a particular set of data (MacRae, 1988). The presence of statistical significance may or may not indicate strong relationships and depends on a number of factors, many of which we have already discussed, including sample size, type of question being asked, and the influence of other factors. Consequently, we need to be careful in how we present results and in how we draw conclusions when referring to statistical significance.

Weinbach (1989) stated: "If practitioners are to make intelligent and informed discussions regarding whether a finding is meaningful for them, they must know more than just whether a relationship between variables is statistically significant" (p. 35). He stressed the importance of responsible reporting of results, including a statement of the sample size and whether this size falls within the usual-size range for which the test is best suited. Such reporting would help the reader assess the appropriateness of the particular test for the research. The strength of the relationship should be presented as clearly as possible—as a percentage difference or an actual correlation. Weinbach concluded: "The ethical researcher who invites replication and feels comfortable in the use of statistical testing should not object to any of these requirements" (p. 35).

HUMAN DIVERSITY ISSUES IN INFERENTIAL STATISTICS

Human diversity issues in inferential statistics relate to your interpretation and understanding of statistical findings, however clearly and responsibly they are reported. Occasionally, findings can seduce us into believing that something is related to something else when actually the findings are partial or otherwise open to question. You must be careful that these results are used responsibly and that they have acknowledged their potential bias against certain groups. As we have discussed throughout this book, the sources of these biases can exist at each stage of the research process.

SUMMARY

One possible source of error in research is chance. The role of chance factors can be assessed with inferential statistics and the use of probability theory. Hypotheses can be two-tailed, one-tailed, or null. A finding is statistically significant when the null hypothesis is rejected and the probability that the finding will occur due to chance falls at or below a certain cutoff point. The ability of a statistical test to correctly reject a null hypothesis is the power of the test.

Four statistical tests are t-tests, ANOVA, correlational analysis, and chi-square analysis. Techniques for analyzing the results from single-system studies include the celeration line approach, the standard deviation approach, and the relative frequency approach. Ethical issues involved in inferential statistics are the selection of the most appropriate test and the notion of statistical significance. We must also ensure that the findings are used responsibly and that they acknowledge potential bias against certain groups.

STUDY/EXERCISE QUESTIONS

1. Look in social work journals and find two articles reporting on program evaluations that used inferential statistics.
    a.   What hypotheses were being tested?
    b.   What inferential statistics were used?
    c.   Did they seem to be appropriate tests?
    d.   What was the statistical significance of the findings?
2. Under what circumstances would you need to undertake the statistical analysis of findings from a single-system study?

FURTHER READING

See Chapter 12 for further reading on statistical analysis.

Bloom, M., Fischer, J., & Orme, J. (1995). *Evaluating practice: Guidelines for the accountable professional* (2nd ed.) Boston: Allyn & Bacon.
One of the more detailed accounts of how to analyze data from single-system studies.

REFERENCES

Abelsohn, D., & Saayman, G. S. (1991). Adolescent adjustment to parental divorce: An investigation from the perspective of basic dimensions of structural family therapy theory. *Family Process, Inc., 30* (2), 177–191.

Behling, J. H., & Merves, E. S. (1984). *The practice of clinical research: The single case method.* New York: University Press of America.

Bloom, M. (1975). *The paradox of helping: Introduction to the philosophy of scientific practice.* New York: Wiley.

Bloom, M., Fischer, J., & Orme, J. (1995). *Evaluating practice: Guidelines for the accountable professional* (2nd ed.). Boston: Allyn & Bacon.

Bryan, D. L., & Ajo, A. A. (1992). The role perception of African American fathers. *Social Work Research & Abstracts, 28* (3), 17–21.

Campbell, D. T., & Stanley, J. C. (1966). *Experimental and quasi-experimental designs for research*. Chicago: Rand McNally.

Gingerich, W., & Feyerherm, W. (1979). The celeration line technique for assisting client change. *Journal of Social Service Research, 3,* 99–113.

Hersen, M., & Barlow, D. H. (1984). *Single-case experimental designs*. New York: Pergamon Press.

Hopper, J. R., & McCarlnielson, J. (1991). Recycling as altruistic behavior: Normative and behavioral strategies to expand participation in a community recycling program. *Environment and Behavior, 23,* 195–220.

Jamison, R. N., & Virts, K. L. (1990). The influence of family support on chronic pain. *Behavior Research and Therapy, 28,* 283–287.

MacRae, A. W. (1988). Measurement scales and statistics: What can significance tests tell us about the world? *British Journal of Psychology, Family Practice, 79,* 161–171.

Poulin, J., & Walter, C. (1993). Social worker burnout: a longitudinal study. *National Association of Social Work, 29,* 5–11.

Weinbach, R. W. (1989). When is statistical significance meaningful? A practice perspective. *Journal of Sociology and Social Welfare, 16* (1), 31–37.

Research Writing

Y ou've analyzed the research results, and in front of you are several computer printouts or, in the case of qualitative data, masses of notes and coded material. Inevitably, there comes a time when you need to write up your research results. Writing the research report is necessary both for yourself—particularly when you are evaluating your own practice—and for others. In fact, for needs assessments and program evaluations, the writing of the report is a critical research stage; as a generalist social worker, you may be more involved in this stage than any other. In addition, you may be asked to assist with developing research proposals, often as part of larger grant proposals. Alternatively, as a student, you will need to write up research reports and, in a graduate program, a thesis or dissertation. Finally, you may decide to submit an article, based on a completed research project, for publication in one of the many professional journals in social work or a related field.

Writing about research is the focus of this chapter. The two basic types of research writing—proposal writing and reporting research results—are analogous to similar steps in practice: first, the writing of an assessment and intervention plan; and second, the reporting of the results of the intervention.

This chapter discusses the following:

- general principles of research writing
- the research proposal
- the research report
- disseminating the report
- the agency and research writing
- ethical issues in research writing
- human diversity issues in research writing

GENERAL PRINCIPLES OF RESEARCH WRITING

Four general principles of research writing are addressed here: knowing your audience; using appropriate citations and references; the structure of the report or proposal; and, finally, the process of writing.

Knowing Your Audience

One of the basic principles of writing, research or otherwise, is to identify your audience. The content and style of the written product should differ according to your intended readers. For example, in writing a research proposal for a needs assessment to establish a date rape prevention program on a university campus, clarify from the outset to whom the proposal is directed—the university administration, a local chapter of NASW, or some other audience. Obviously, audiences are very different. The university administration might need considerable information about the phenomenon of date rape and a discussion of its potential impact on student recruitment, whereas the NASW chapter might require more emphasis on the social and psychological costs of the problem, such as date rape's impact on women's self-esteem.

Your audience influences not only the content of your proposal or report but also the style you adopt. If writing for the university administration, your writing style would be more formal than if you were writing a report for a group of parents in the community.

Referencing Sources of Information

When you are writing any type of report that refers to work by other authors, whether quoting them directly or through indirect reference, it is critical that you appropriately cite your sources of information. Although you can use a number of different referencing styles, the one most widely used in social work literature is the American Psychological Association (APA) referencing method. This is the style used in this book.

The *Publication Manual of the American Psychological Association,* 4th ed. (1994) is the guidebook for the APA style. This book contains a great deal of information; therefore some of the more important and common rules will be summarized here, using examples.

Quotations from a Source

He stated, "A test of discrimination on the grounds of disability is whether a person treats an individual with mental retardation less favorably in identical or similar circumstances than he or she treats or would treat other people" (Tse, 1994, p. 359).

Referencing Citations in the Text

Textor (1995) discussed the changes occurring in the German child welfare system as a result of the passage of the Child and Youth Welfare Law enacted in 1991.

These citations in the text, whether direct quotes or ideas, are then listed in a bibliography. The sources are listed alphabetically by author, using the following format:

Journal articles

1. One author

MacPherson, S. (1996). Social work and economic development in Papua, New Guinea. *International Social Work, 39,* 55–67.

2. Two authors, journal paginated by issue

Ribner, D. S., & Schindler, R. (1996). Ethiopian immigration to Israel: The apparatus of absorption. *Journal of Multicultural Social Work, 4* (1), 75–88.

Books

Payne, M. (1991). *Modern social work theory: A critical introduction.* Chicago, IL: Lyceum Books.

Articles or chapters in edited books

Solomon, C. (1994). Welfare workers' response to homeless welfare applicants. In C. K. Riessman (Ed.), *Qualitative studies in social work research* (pp. 153–168). Thousand Oaks, CA: Sage.

Reports

National Institute on Drug Abuse. (1992). *Socioeconomic and demographic correlates of drug and alcohol use* (DHHS Publication No. ADM 92-1906). Washington, D.C.: U.S. Government Printing Office.

The Structure of the Proposal or Report

This section outlines some general principles relating to the structure of the report. (The specifics of the content of both the proposal and the report are discussed in the following section.) Again, the APA manual is useful since it not only contains details about referencing sources but also describes each component of the report or proposal.

In general, these conventions should be followed:

- *Title* Use a clear and concise title.

- *Authorship and sponsorship* Credits should be inclusive. Don't forget anyone!

- *Abstract* An overview of the contents of the report or proposal is provided in the form of an abstract to prepare the reader for what follows. Two abstracts are included in Appendix E. One is for a qualitative study, and one is for a quantitative study.

- *Appendices* Sometimes the report may include material that is relevant but too bulky to include in the text of the proposal or report. These materials are then included as appendices. Common materials to place in the appendices are the data collection instruments and statistical tables that do not relate directly to the findings.

- *Bibliography and referencing* As was discussed in the previous section, be sure to cite all your sources appropriately.

Remember that your report or proposal should maintain a consistent style. For instance, if you use the APA style for references, you should also use this manual for instructions in how to structure titles and abstracts.

The Process of Writing

Research reports and proposals should be written as clearly and as concisely as possible. This is not the place for flamboyant writing. Remember that you want others, possibly from very diverse backgrounds, to read and understand the results of your research. A long and convoluted report may not only cloud comprehension of the findings but also discourage some from even trying to read the report. Be as straightforward in your writing as possible. The following sugges-tions can help you achieve this clarity:

- Keep a research log to facilitate the process of the report or proposal writing as well as the process and development of the research itself. A **research log** is an informal but systematic record of ideas and progress relating to the research. Once the research is completed, it may be difficult to remember ex-actly why one research strategy was adopted over another or what doubts there were about a particular approach. The research log can help jog the memory.

- Prepare an outline (details will be discussed in the next section). You may not end up following your outline exactly, but that's OK. The idea is to at least have a rough idea in your mind and on paper of how the report or pro-posal is structured. The outline helps avoid a written product that wanders from one topic to another.

- Write a first draft, then revise and revise and revise, if necessary. Do not ex-pect your first draft to be anything like the final one.

- Ask colleagues, faculty, or students to read early drafts and give their com-ments. Do not be afraid of criticism at this point. Generally, the more input you receive, the higher the quality of the written product. Have your readers comment on structure, content, style, grammar, and spelling.

- Have someone proof the final copy—primarily for grammar and spelling.

THE RESEARCH PROPOSAL

A **research proposal** is a paper proposing the undertaking of a specific type of research. This is often necessary to obtain permission and funds to conduct the study.

Writing the proposal can also directly assist the researcher in conceptualiz-ing the research. By systematically thinking through each step of the research process, as is required in the research proposal, the researcher can gain new in-sights and clarifications regarding the research itself.

The format required for a research proposal varies depending upon the specific conditions under which the proposal is being written. These include the following:

- The funding agency may provide application forms that specify the infor-mation being requested.

- The funding agency may request a letter of intent, which requires the re-searcher to describe the proposal briefly. The funding source, based on this letter, may or may not ask the researcher to submit a full-fledged proposal.

- Sometimes, funding agencies send out requests for proposals (RFPs) that specify what they are interested in funding and how proposals should be submitted.

Taking these conditions into consideration, generally a standard outline is used for writing research proposals. The different components include these:

- statement of the research topic
- literature review
- research questions and hypotheses
- research design
- sampling strategy
- data collection
- data analysis
- presentation of the results
- administration and budget
- credentials of the researcher and other relevant personnel

These outlines tend to have a quantitative or positivist bias. Although it could be argued that the outline could also accommodate an interpretive or qualitative study, many funding agencies are, in reality, still primarily interested in more traditional approaches. As discussed in Chapter 1, however, researchers are increasingly adopting a number of different methods of inquiry, which will eventually influence the format and expectations of RFPs.

Each step of the outline has been explained sequentially in this book. A few items should be clarified, though. First, the literature review varies according to what type of research is being proposed (as was also discussed in Chapter 4). In the case of a program evaluation, this section would report why the program is being evaluated and would include findings from the evaluations of similar programs. For a needs assessment, this section would include a description of prior research that has reported on the extent of the social problem to be investigated. Some of this information could be found in the social work literature, but it may also be found in various government document depositions or in agencies' archives. The literature review for a less applied study—for instance, looking at the impact on a child's self-image of one parent being physically challenged (a possible thesis topic)—would be different. Here the literature review would include a discussion of the various theories that have suggested a relationship may occur, in addition to reporting similar research and their findings. This information could be found in the social work and social science literature in university libraries.

In the data collection section, you are generally required only to state the method you will use to collect data. For example, if the data collection requires the development of an instrument—such as an interview schedule or a questionnaire—typically this does not need to be completed for the proposal, but you will need to state what types of variables you will be including. If you plan to use scales or other instruments that have already been developed, then you would include these in an appendix to the proposal.

The data analysis section clearly cannot be discussed in any detail in the proposal except to indicate which statistical tests or other forms of analysis will be used. The presentation of results section should include a discussion of how and to whom the results will be presented. The budget section should itemize all expenses, including supplies, personnel costs, mailing costs, computer costs, and so forth. Finally, you usually need both to summarize your credentials as they relate to the project and to include a curriculum vitae.

THE RESEARCH REPORT

As with the research proposal, the organization of the research report depends in part upon the demands of the agency or the funding source. In general, however, this outline is followed:

- statement of the research topic
- literature review
- research questions and hypotheses
- research design
- sampling strategy
- data collection method(s)
- results
- discussion
- limitations
- recommendations for future research
- implications for practice

These sections apply whether you are reporting on a practice evaluation, needs assessment, or program evaluation study and regardless of whether the study employs a primarily quantitative or qualitative approach.

Obviously, this outline is very similar to the proposal. In fact, if you have a well-structured and well-informed proposal, the research report will be much easier to complete. Some differences do exist between the proposal and the report. The report includes four additional sections: the results of the study, a discussion of the findings, the limitations of the study, and suggestions for future research.

Results Section

Regardless of your audience and the type of research, the focus of your report will be on the results. How results or findings are reported depends on whether the study has adopted a positivist or interpretist approach, and reference will be made to this distinction throughout the following sections. Reporting findings often involves the use of tables, graphs, and charts. These visual representations are particularly useful for presenting quantitative data. In the following section, we will describe some forms visual representations can take.

Tables

Statistical tables are the most common form of reporting quantitative findings and are essentially types of frequency distributions. Several principles need to guide the presentation of the data. First, clearly display the data and do not clutter the table with unnecessary details. Second, make the table as complete as possible, usually including both raw numbers and percentages (percentages facilitate comparison). Third, provide a summary of the statistical tests at the bottom of the table when appropriate. Finally, clearly label the table, including footnotes where appropriate. Ziesemer, Marcoux, and Marwell (1994) examined the differences in academic performance, adaptive functioning, and problem be-

Table 14.1   **Range of mean scores of self-perception profile for children**

Subscale	Low-SES national norm	Homeless (n = 42)	Matched sample* (n = 41)	Comparison sample (n = 40)
global self-worth				
M	2.66–3.24	3.17	2.99	3.05
SD	.44–.85	.63	.64	.63
scholastic				
M	2.61–2.95	2.84	2.81	2.92
SD	.56–.86	.65	.68	.72
social				
M	2.56–3.00	2.79	2.91	2.79
SD	.47–.92	.67	.69	.65
athletic				
M	2.47–3.21	2.94	2.81	2.82
SD	.54–.88	.71	.77	.68
physical appearance				
M	2.62–3.16	3.16	2.84	2.76
SD	.58–.94	.63	.74	.66
behavior				
M	2.75–3.32	3.00	2.87	3.04
SD	.34–.72	.55	.73	.59

Note: SES = socioeconomic status.

* Students with low SES who were geographically mobile.

Source: From "Homeless Children: Are They Different from Other Low-Income Children?" by C. Ziesemer, L. Marcoux, and B. E. Marwell, 1994, *Social Work, 39* (6). Copyright © 1994 National Association of Social Workers, Inc. Reprinted with permission.

haviors of 145 elementary school children who had experienced homelessness and a matched group of 142 mobile children with low economic status. The authors used tables along with other visual aids to present the results. Table 14.1 indicates the range of mean scores on a self-perception profile for the children in the study.

Graphs

Graphs are an alternative or a supplement to tables that present the data more visually. Similar guidelines apply to graphs as apply to tables. One drawback of graphs is that they lack the detail of tables; but their advantage is that they present a visual image of the data that makes the results apparent at a glance. Graphs are particularly useful in presenting data from practice evaluation studies. Some of the principles of graphing were discussed in Chapter 7.

Various types of graphs can be used. The **line graph** connects various data points with lines. Figure 14.1 represents some of the results from a study comparing families receiving family preservation services with families in a control group.

Another type of graph is the **bar graph.** Bar graphs are useful visual means of displaying data at the nominal level of measurement. In the Ziesemer,

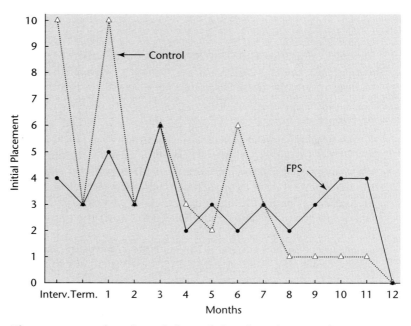

Figure 14.1 **Placement as a function of elapsed time from intervention**

Source: From "Evaluating the Impact of Intensive Family Preservation in New Jersey," by L. H. Feldman. In K. Wells and D. E. Biegel (Eds.), *Family Preservation Services,* Figure 3.3. Copyright © 1991 Sage Publications, Inc. Reprinted by permission of Sage Publications, Inc.

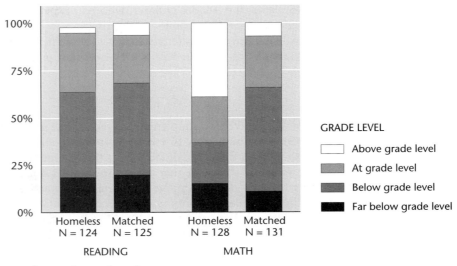

Figure 14.2 **Teacher ratings of performance**

Source: From "Homeless Children: Are They Different from Other Low-Income Children?" by C. Ziesemer, L. Marcoux, and B. E. Marwell, 1994, *Social Work, 39* (6). Copyright © 1994 National Association of Social Workers, Inc. Reprinted with permission.

Marcoux, and Marwell (1994) study described earlier, bar graphs were used to display the teacher's ratings of performance between the two groups in both reading and math. These bar graphs are displayed in Figure 14.2.

Pie Charts

A final type of pictorial or visual presentation of data is the pie chart. **Pie charts** can be used when we want to show the relative contributions of each value to the whole variable. Pie charts are particularly useful for displaying a budget. If too many values need to be included, however, pie charts can look cluttered and be confusing. Figure 14.3 is an example of a pie chart used in the Ziesemer, Marcoux, and Marwell (1994) study. The chart shows the proportion of the samples in student functioning risk categories.

Many computer programs can generate graphs and charts, often in different colors. Remember when constructing these visual aids that the goal is to make the data more accessible and clearer to the reader.

Apart from reporting the results using visual aids, the other part of presenting findings is to describe them in writing. This description need not be extensive and can simply consist of translating the findings as straightforwardly as possible. When describing the findings, it is important to avoid interpreting the data; simply report the information and, when necessary, the statistical tests and their results.

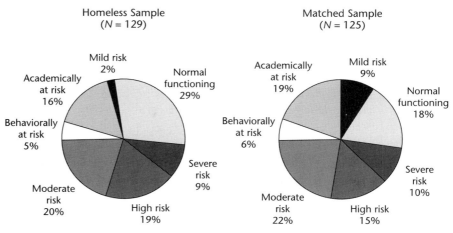

Figure 14.3   **Proportion of samples in student functioning risk categories**

Source: From "Homeless Children: Are They Different from Other Low-Income Children?" by C. Ziesemer, L. Marcoux, and B. E. Marwell, 1994, *Social Work, 39* (6). Copyright © 1994 National Association of Social Workers, Inc. Reprinted with permission.

Reporting Results from a Positivist or Quantitative Study

North and Smith (1994) compared homeless white and nonwhite men and women. The Diagnostic Interview Schedule and Homeless Supplement was used in interviewing 900 homeless people. The authors' presentation of the results followed the usual format for reporting the results of a positivist or quantitative study.

First, the authors described the sample demographics using a table:

Table 1 shows selected sociodemographic information. The majority of the subjects (70 percent of men, $n=418$, and 84 percent of women, $n=252$) were African American; 3 percent ($n=18$) of men and 4 percent ($n=12$) of women were of other ethnicities. . . ." (p. 641)

Then the authors presented the results from each set of questions from the interview schedule, including questions about employment and financial resources, history of homelessness, family and childhood, psychiatric disorders, and psychiatric treatment history. Each set of results was accompanied by a table. For example, part of the reporting of the results for the section on history of homelessness reads as follows:

Table 3 shows subjects' histories of homelessness. White men and women reported more episodes of homelessness than nonwhites, and white women had experienced more years of homelessness than nonwhite women. . . . (p. 643)

Reporting Results in an Interpretive or Qualitative Study

Farber (1990) reported on the significance of race and class in marital decisions among unmarried adolescent women. The data were collected through semi-structured interviews. The first section of her presentation of the findings related to the young women's view of marriage as an ideal:

> Nearly all of the teens, regardless of their class or race, view marriage and marital childbearing as an ideal type of family. Their attitudes are typified by this 16-year-old white middle-class mother: "When I got pregnant and I decided to bring Joshua home with me, it didn't seem nice . . . for a little boy or little girl to have one of what he should have—you know, half of what he should have. . . . I wouldn't wish that on anybody. A child was meant to have a mother and a father. . . . I can't imagine myself having only my mother. My life wouldn't be the same without my mother and my father."
>
> This young woman expresses traditional values about families being composed of two parents. Most teens expressed similar attitudes suggesting that, for them, being a single mother does not reflect changed values about how families should be formed. This ideal is also evident in their childhood memories of how they imagined their adult lives would be. The same white middle-class mother said: "I always wanted to be married and have kids when I was older. When I was done with school and things like that. I always imagined that after I was a big person, all grown up, never young, you know." A similar childhood goal was expressed by a 16-year-old black middle-class teen: "I wanted to be married and have a career before I even had a baby. That's how I wanted it to be. I wish it wasn't like this."
>
> Like the middle-class and working-class teens, the black lower-class mothers had childhood dreams of living in the ideal American family, as defined here by a 16-year-old black lower-class mother: "I thought I would be married, and I had at least two kids—a boy and a girl. I would be married to this one person I was in love with, you know, and we had our own house and stuff." The white lower-class 16-year-old mother stated: "I seen myself before I had a kid, you know, I would be married. And I would have babies, but not until I was married. I was pretty sure about that."
>
> The young mothers from all backgrounds described ideal visions that are congruent with traditional values about family formation. These childhood reflections suggest that their present judgments about the undesirability of out of wedlock childbearing are not simply responses to the stress of single motherhood. Most of these teen mothers grew up valuing a way of life from which they have deviated. They were unable to, or chose not to, act in accordance with these ideals. (p. 54)

Sometimes studies include both qualitative and quantitative results. The quantitative results might be presented followed by a description of the qualitative findings. A discussion section would then integrate the two.

Reporting Quantitative and Qualitative Results

Vera (1990) studied the effects of divorce groups on individual adjustment. She reported the qualitative and quantitative findings in the following manner:

Analysis of Group Data

A paired-comparison t-test ($p < .05$) was computed from the scores obtained in the Index of Well-Being at the first and last group meetings. These scores indicated that, taken as a group, the subjects on the average show significant improvement on the Index of Well-Being. Differences between group A and group B on the Index of Well-Being were not significant. Further, no significant differences were found between subjects who completed and who did not complete the follow-up instrument.

Analysis of Qualitative Data

Qualitative data were obtained from the screening interview and from information elicited during the group meetings. Analysis of these data revealed that some factors reoccurred in the subjects' histories. These factors have been identified in the literature as interfering with the adjustment to divorce and psychosocial well-being (B. F. Fisher, 1976). Analysis of the researcher's notes suggested that factors such as the passage of time, divorce-related losses, other life events, characteristics of the divorce event, and the presence of support may have interfered with divorce recovery. The 11 cases were rank ordered according to the number of factors present (Table 1). Subjects with the largest number of factors appeared to show less improvement in divorce adjustment and psychosocial well-being than did those with fewer factors. (p. 16)

Discussion Section

Unlike a research proposal, a research report always contains some kind of discussion section. The discussion section follows and is closely linked to the results section, and it provides an explanation of the results. This section is important whether you are discussing the results of an evaluation of your own practice, a needs assessment, or a program evaluation. The findings are related to the hypotheses (if there are any) and to the theoretical premise of the study itself. Part of this process involves comparing your research findings to findings from comparable research in the literature and pointing out similarities and differences in the results and conclusions. In this way, you can make connections among various empirical findings, thereby providing collective support and evidence for theories (see Figure 14.4).

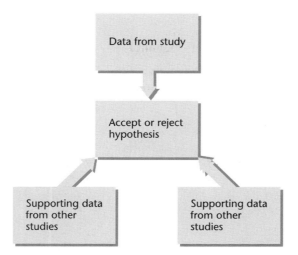

Figure 14.4 **Structure of the discussion section of a research report**

A Discussion Section from a Positivist or Quantitative Study

Slonim-Nevo, Cwikel, Luski, Lankry, and Shraga (1995) examined caregiver burden among three-generation immigrant families in Israel. Data were collected using a face-to-face questionnaire including a Caregiver Strain Index. After presenting the results, the authors proposed that they were best explained by a model including four variables: the health condition of the elderly person, the amount of care provided by the caregivers, the psychological condition of the children in the family, and the length of stay in the new country. This model includes universal components shared by both immigrant and nonimmigrant caregivers as well as elements specific to the immigrant group.

The authors refer to the literature in describing the universal components:

> As shown in other studies, caregiver strain increases when the health condition of the elderly deteriorates and the caregiver has to provide more care (Baruch and Barnett, 1983; Mindel and Wright, 1982). . . . Observing the severe condition of close relatives (usually parents or spouses) often creates feelings of despair, guilt, hopelessness and fear about one's own future (Feinauer et. al. 1987). Such feelings are likely to increase caregiver strain. (p. 198)

In qualitative studies, the distinction between describing the results and discussing the findings can be fuzzy. In part, this fuzziness may result from our attempt to provide an insightful description of the phenomenon under study. We still need to make a careful distinction between the description and the interpretation.

A Discussion Section from a Qualitative Study

Walzer (1995) presented pregnant daughters' reports about how their mothers influenced their own identities as mothers. In the discussion section Walzer states:

> For the women in this sample, the first pregnancy appears to be a transition during which daughters reflect on their relationships with their mothers while coming to terms with their own notions of motherhood. Most of the women in this sample did not articulate a sense of feeling closer to and more identified to their mothers. The mixed feelings that daughters reported regarding the caretaking they received from their mothers and the role of this ambivalence in their own conceptions of motherhood may partly reflect the unattainable expectations that our culture places on mothers (O'Connor, 1990). (p. 601)

Limitations Section

By now, it should be very evident that no research is perfect. Flaws and limitations may result from the nature of the question that is being asked, but often—and particularly in social work research—these imperfections simply reflect the social and political context of the studies. For example, random assignment into the experimental and control groups is not always feasible, as discussed in Chapter 6. Sometimes there simply is not time to carry out in-depth interviews with as many people as you would like. In reporting the limitations, go through the research process and point out the drawbacks of the method at each stage. Some common limitations have been discussed in previous chapters, but here is a summary of these problems:

- *Problems associated with the research strategy or approach*   The study's approach—descriptive, explanatory, positivist, interpretist—needs to be made explicit, and the approach's drawbacks need to be acknowledged.

- *Limitations of the sampling method*   Nonprobability sampling will result in limited generalizability of the findings; but probability sampling may not yield information-rich cases.

- *Limited response rate*   A response rate of less than 50% limits generalizations even if probability sampling is used.

- *The reliability and validity of the data collection methods*   These need to be specified.

- *The problems associated with internal and external validity*   Validity problems can occur when the research is explanatory (rather than descriptive) and often result from the lack of a comparison group, particularly one that has been randomly assigned. These problems need to be acknowledged.

- *The problems associated with the interpretation of the results*   It is important to point out that interpretations are just that, interpretations; other people may interpret the results rather differently. Interpretive problems may arise whether statistical tests have been used or the data are qualitative.

Obviously, there are other limitations, which will be explored further in the next chapter. The ones presented here provide a general guideline to follow when writing the limitations section of your report, paper, or article.

The extent to which you discuss limitations depends on your audience. You must devote at least a paragraph to addressing these issues. If you are writing up the results of a needs assessment or a program evaluation, the limitations section can be minimal. But if your audience is more knowledgeable about research, you must provide a more extensive limitations section.

A Limitations Section

Greenberg (1995) examined the role of adult children with severe mental illness as a source of support for their aging parents. The data were collected through face-to-face interviews with 105 mothers aged 55 and older who were living with and caring for an adult child with a serious mental illness. The author discussed in some detail the limitations of the study. Excerpts from this discussion follow:

> There are several limitations to this study. First, this study is based on a nonprobability sample of mothers who volunteered to participate in the study. Thus, caution should be exercised in generalizing the findings. Second, as with all survey studies, the findings are based on self report data and have all the limitations of such data. . . . Third, there is a potential confound between the mother's report of the adult child's assistance and her level of subjective burden. Finally, and most important, the study is cross sectional and therefore cannot establish causal relationships. (p. 421)

Recommendations Section

The next section of the report consists of recommendations for further study and explicitly states the questions that have arisen from the research itself. In a needs assessment report (and sometimes in program evaluation reports), this section is critical because all the research is, in fact, building up to this conclusion.

Recommendations for Further Research Section

Tracy, Whittaker, Pugh, Kapp, and Overstreet (1994) described network characteristics and support resources from a sample of 40 families receiving family preservation services. In the final section of the article they recommended future research:

Future research in this area might include experimental studies of social network interventions in combination with family treatment services. Such studies would need to incorporate valid and reliable measures of social support and social networks, longitudinal designs, and adequate control over the implementation of the intervention by different workers and different program models. (p. 489)

Implications for Practice

An implications for practice section can also be included in social work research reports, papers, or articles. Here you need to explain the connection between the specific findings of your research and practice. Usually this section is included only in reports that are published in the social work literature. In the reports written by generalist social workers that are typically disseminated to community, agency, or funding representatives, this section is often not included.

An Implications for Practice Section

In my needs assessment of employed clerical workers (Marlow, 1990), I concluded:

The major result of this study is the information that it provides on the characteristics that affect employed women's service needs. This information can contribute to policy development to support employed women, an area in which social workers increasingly are becoming involved. Such policies have received increasing support in recent years and include public policies such as the development of federal day care funding programs, and developments in the private sector, such as the growth of employee assistance programs. The findings from this study indicate that the service needs of this group of clerical workers are relatively uniform, regardless of ethnicity, countering some assumptions about the needs of Mexican-American women. This study consequently can remind social workers who are advocates for people in the workplace that information is needed from employees themselves to guide the development of programs and policies that will be truly responsive to their needs. (p. 264)

The order and structure of these last few sections can vary. Often the discussion section includes the implications for practice section, the limitations section, and the suggestions for further research section.

DISSEMINATING THE REPORT

Disseminating or distributing the research report is an essential prerequisite to incorporation of research into practice (see Chapter 15). The dissemination of a report can take several forms: Reports can be orally presented; distributed internally in written form; and published in journals.

Oral Presentation

You may be required to present your research results orally at a community meeting, at a meeting of the agency's board of directors, or to legislators. In the case of practice evaluations, usually the results are discussed more informally with the client and others who might be involved. When presenting orally at a formal meeting, keep the following items in mind:

- Know how much time you have to give the report and stick to this time. Rehearsing your presentation will help.

- Allow time for questions and discussion. Know in advance how much time will be allocated for discussion.

- Use visual aids (overheads, slides, and so on) and handouts (containing a summary of the results and perhaps some charts and scales) when appropriate.

- Try not to become defensive about the research if someone criticizes it during discussion or question time. Simply answer the questions as clearly and as straightforwardly as possible. You should already be aware of the limitations and have thought them through, but you may have missed some.

Distributing Written Reports Internally

The appearance of the report is important even if it is only to be distributed in-house. The term *in-house* can encompass anything from a small agency to a large government department. Be sure that the original report is clear and will reproduce good copies; it can be frustrating to read a report that has been poorly copied. Make sure that everyone who is meant to receive the report actually does.

Publishing the Report

You should strive to publish whenever possible. Publication undoubtedly allows the profession the best access to research findings. Social work journals are making a conscious effort to solicit and publish articles written by practitioners. As a practitioner, you have important contributions to make that can be very different from academicians'.

There are some ways to assess whether or not your report has potential for publication. Consider the following:

- Is it investigating a problem that has received little attention in the past in the research literature? Many journals devote entire issues to research on a newly explored topic.

- Does it have a new slant or perspective on a problem? For example, there may have been many program evaluations on the effectiveness of parent training on reducing incidence of child abuse and neglect. But if your agency has a program that serves a large number of Puerto Rican clients and you have been involved in evaluating the program, you might have excellent material for publication if none has previously been published on this type of intervention with this particular client group.

■ Is it an innovative research method or combination of methods?

Use participatory principles in disseminating the report. Petersen, Magwaza, and Pillay (1996) used the following methods:

> The participants decided that the results of the epidemiological study needed to be made accessible to the community via pamphlets which could be distributed in the community as well as an audiotape which could be played at the district hospital. On a more regional and national level it was decided that the results needed to be made accessible to other communities experiencing violence via the media such as the national/public radio as well as an article published in a black national Sunday newspaper. The participants agreed to distribute the pamphlets to the parents of the pre-school children. Due to the lack of community resources, the researchers were requested to ensure that the other above-mentioned tasks were carried out. (p. 71)

If you are considering publishing, you should know that different journals are interested in different types of articles. To get a sense of who is interested in what, refer to the *NASW Guide to Social Work Authors*. This gives information on many journals and lists their specific requirements in terms of length of article, reference style, number of copies, and so on.

THE AGENCY AND RESEARCH WRITING

Very often the agency for which you are completing the research will give you specific requirements on how to write the report. Usually, an in-house report on a program evaluation or needs assessment will focus on the results section. A needs assessment may also concentrate on the implications of the findings for practice. If you are writing the report for publication and wider distribution, you may want to emphasize the methods section over the results and devote some attention to a discussion of how the results support or reject previous research. This will enable other researchers to replicate or augment your study.

As a generalist social worker employed in an agency, you will most often write reports on individual cases. These are also research reports if you used some type of evaluation as part of your practice. So start now—combine research and practice and contribute to social work knowledge.

Also, don't forget that another important way in which you can contribute is to give presentations at conferences. For example, your state NASW chapter probably holds conferences every year and strongly encourages practitioners to contribute.

ETHICAL ISSUES IN RESEARCH WRITING

Two major ethical issues arise in research writing. The first issue is appropriately referencing material that is included in a report. The second is confidentiality of results. We will discuss each of these issues in turn.

Referencing Appropriately

Existence of Previous Work

Whenever research is being planned and conducted, it is imperative that you consult other work that has been completed in the target area. For example, you may have been asked by your supervisor to conduct a needs assessment for an afterschool program in your community. You are excited about the opportunity to show off some of your newly acquired research skills. But the next day an ex-classmate calls you from a neighboring city; after you tell her about your assignment, she tells you she has just finished conducting such a study in her community. You are tempted to ignore this piece of information and continue with your own plans because that way you could do your survey alone and collect the credit. Ethically, however, you need to acknowledge your friend's information as useful assistance in the development of your needs assessment; perhaps you may even be forced to recognize that there is no need for this type of study in your community at this time.

Citing References Appropriately

Given that you do decide to use information from your friend's study, it is imperative that you give her credit for her work. This applies to a study published locally as a report, as well as to more widely distributed publications. Recognizing others' contributions can present dilemmas. It would be impossible to credit everyone who has contributed to our intellectual and professional development. In the case of specific research endeavors, however, you must recognize the contributions of others; otherwise, you may be guilty of plagiarism.

Confidentiality of Results

Just as confidentiality needs to be ensured during the data collection phase, you also need to preserve confidentiality when writing and disseminating the report. Subjects' identities should not be disclosed without their permission. Confidentiality may be problematic in qualitative reports with extensive quotes that inadvertently reveal the subject's identity. It is also an issue with practice evaluations. The NASW Code of Ethics (1997) states:

- Social workers engaged in the evaluation of services should discuss collected information only for professional purposes and only with people professionally concerned with this information.

- Social workers who report evaluation and research results should protect participants' confidentiality by omitting identifying information unless proper consent has been obtained authorizing disclosure.

Another related issue is **copyright.** Copyright law applies not only to published materials but also to in-house reports. Be sure to check on the restrictions that might pertain to distribution and publishing before you disseminate a report more widely.

HUMAN DIVERSITY ISSUES IN RESEARCH WRITING

Three human diversity issues are involved in research writing. First, you must ensure that bias against certain groups is not contained in the report. Second, you should avoid using exclusive language. Third, you must consider to whom the results are being disseminated.

Bias Against Certain Groups

Be careful to exclude biases in the writing that tend to stereotype groups in our society. You are less at risk for this if you paid careful attention to human diversity issues throughout the research process. Then you simply ensure the data are accurately presented and equitably and nonjudgmentally discussed.

Exclusive Language

The issue of exclusive language involves acknowledging our differences and avoiding sexism. Although the predominant use of the male pronoun as a generic pronoun is becoming increasingly less acceptable, we do need to ensure that nonsexist terms are employed consistently. This involves not only the appropriate use of male, female, and plural pronouns, but also the use of terms that are gender neutral, such as *chair* instead of *chairman*.

We also need to ensure that terms do not reflect ethnic or cultural biases or a lack of sensitivity to human diversity. Use a descriptor of a cultural group that is recognized by the group itself. For example, using the term *Mexican American* in New Mexico to refer to Hispanics could be offensive to some individuals who view themselves as Spanish Americans with minimal connections to Mexico. Accuracy often requires that we not lump groups of people together under one label.

Disseminating the Results

The final human diversity issue relating to research writing is the question of who should receive the results. There is a growing argument in favor of giving the findings to the participants included in the research rather than just to the practitioners and other researchers. This is of course critical when conducting participatory or action research.

This does not necessarily entail making the entire research report available to the participants, particularly if it is extensive or excessively technical. Instead, a smaller report can be written specifically for those participating in a needs assessment or program evaluation, in which the results could potentially influence an entire community. One advantage of practice evaluations is that the results are routinely shared with the client (usually verbally).

Advocates of the feminist perspective point out that sharing the results with the participants is another dimension of how "the researcher and subject can work in different ways to explore a 'truth' that they mutually locate and define" (Davis, 1986). This results in a participatory and consensual style attributed to feminist approaches, not only in research but also in administrative style and social work practice (Norman & Mancuso, 1980).

Giving participants access to findings is also being increasingly viewed as a minority issue. It is being recognized that research results can be empowering to subjects. Historically, minority subjects have often been used by the researcher and have reaped no benefits. Apart from making the results accessible to the participants, researchers need to pay more attention to repaying the participants. Of course, in social work research, the results of needs assessments, program evaluations, and practice evaluations all directly contribute to the development or improvement of interventions designed to assist those who are studied. Sometimes, though, benefits can be extended further—for example, by returning a proportion of the royalties from book sales to the community or by paying participants for the time they spend being interviewed.

SUMMARY

Four general principles of research writing are to know your audience, to use appropriate citations and references, to structure your research report or proposal correctly, and write the report as clearly and as concisely as possible. The research proposal is a paper proposing undertaking a specific type of research. The funding agency may have requests for proposals (RFPs) that list the projects they are interested in funding and how the proposals should be submitted. Like the research proposal, the research report should follow an outline structure: statement of the research topic, theoretical framework, research questions and hypotheses, data collection methods, sampling strategy, research design, results, discussion, limitations, recommendations for future research, and implications for practice. Reports may be presented orally, distributed internally (in-house), or published.

In an agency, generalist social workers are involved in writing not only formal reports and proposals but also case reports. The ethical issues involved in research writing include appropriately referencing material and ensuring confidentiality of the results. Human diversity issues of concern in research writing are eliminating stereotyping of certain groups, avoiding exclusive language, and disseminating results to subjects.

STUDY/EXERCISE QUESTIONS

1. Request sample grant applications from organizations in your city or state that fund research efforts related to social work. Share these in class and discuss their similarities and differences.

2. Select a social work journal article and critique it, using the structure of a research report presented in this chapter as a guide.

3. Select research articles from social work journals that contain tables or charts.
    a. Do they clearly illustrate the results of the research?
    b. What changes would you make to improve them?

FURTHER READING

Booth, W. C., Colomb, G. G., & Williams, J. M. (1995). *The craft of research.* Chicago: The University of Chicago Press.
An excellent and practical guide to writing research reports.

Strunk, W., & White, E. B. (1994). *The elements of style* (2nd ed.). New York: Macmillan.
A classic reference on writing; an invaluable guide.

Westerfeld, A., & Dietz, T. (1996). *Planning and conducting agency-based research.* New York: Longman.
A very practical guide to agency research.

Wolcott, H. (1990). *Writing up qualitative research.* Newbury Park, CA: Sage.
A good little book specifically dealing with the task of writing up qualitative results.

REFERENCES

Davis, L. V. (1986). A feminist approach to social work research. *Affilia, 1,* 32–47.

Farber, N. (1990). The significance of race and class in marital decisions among unmarried adolescent mothers. *Social Problems, 37,* 51–63.

Greenberg, J. S. (1995). The other side of caring: Adult children with mental illness as supports to their mothers in later life. *Social Work, 40* (3), 414–423.

Marlow, C. R. (1990). Management of family and employment responsibilities by Mexican-American and Anglo-American women. *Social Work, 35,* 259–265.

National Association of Social Workers. (1997). NASW code of ethics. *NASW News, 25,* 24–25.

Norman, E., & Mancuso, A. (1980). *Women's issues and social work practice.* Itasca, IL: Peacock.

North, C. S., & Smith, E. M. (1994). Comparison of white and nonwhite homeless men and women. *Social Work, 39* (6), 639–647.

Petersen, I., Magwaza, A. S., & Pillay, Y. G. (1996). The use of participatory research to facilitate a psychological rehabilitation programme for child survivors of violence in a South African community. *Social Work/ Maatskaplike Werk, 32* (1), 67–74.

American Psychological Association. (1994). *Publication Manual of the American Psychological Association* (4th ed.). Washington, DC: Author.

Slonim-Nevo, V., Cwikel, J., Luski, H., Lankry, M., & Shraga, Y. (1995). Caregiver burden among three-generation immigrant families in Israel. *International Social Work, 38* (2), 191–204.

Tracy, E. M., Whittaker, J. K., Pugh, A., Kapp, S. N., & Overstreet, E. J. (1994). Support networks of primary caregivers receiving family preservation services: An exploratory study. *Families in Society, 75* (8), 481–489.

Vera, M. I. (1990). Effects of divorce groups on individual adjustment: A multiple methodology approach. *Social Work Research and Abstracts, 26,* 11–20.

Walzer, S. (1995) Transition into motherhood: Pregnant daughters' responses to their mothers. *Families in Society, 76* (10), 596–603.

Ziesemer, C., Marcoux, L., & Marwell, B. E. (1994). Homeless children: Are they different from other low-income children? *Social Work, 39* (6), 658–668.

Using Research Findings in Practice and Evaluating Research

With Patricia Sandau-Beckler, M.S.W.

One more stage of research needs to be discussed—the use and evaluation of the research findings. This step's equivalent in practice is implementation and evaluation of the plan. As discussed in Chapter 2, practice is enhanced when social workers are producers and consumers of research.

Using the results of research in our practice necessitates evaluating the research itself. Conducting research is not a flawless endeavor, as we have seen throughout this text. An important step in the research process is critically assessing research results to identify their strengths and weaknesses. Remember, too, that although this chapter focuses on research findings that result from using science, remember from Chapter 1 that other sources of understanding can be used in practice: values, intuition, experience, and authority.

The two final tasks of evaluating the research and using the results in practice are linked. By first evaluating the research, you can assess the findings' applicability to your particular practice situation.

Both steps will be discussed in this chapter, along with the other topics listed here:

- using research findings in practice
- evaluating research
- the agency in the use and evaluation of research findings
- ethical issues in the use and evaluation of research findings
- human diversity issues in the use and evaluation of research findings

USING RESEARCH FINDINGS IN PRACTICE

Case Examples

We will consider five cases, each dealing with different client systems: individual, family, group, organization, and community.

- *Individual client system* Sue—an adolescent female who is a substance abuser
- *Family client system* The Kickingbird family—a Native American family in which an incident of a child's physical abuse has been reported
- *Group client system* Parent support group—a number of parents who have expressed concerns about their children who have attention deficit disorder
- *Organization client system* The Children's Center—an agency to plan and develop foster care services for children with AIDS
- *Community client system* STOP—a community-wide task force formed to reduce teen suicide

For cases such as these, research findings can be used during each stage of the problem-solving process. A summary of the stages and the relevance of research findings for each stage follow.

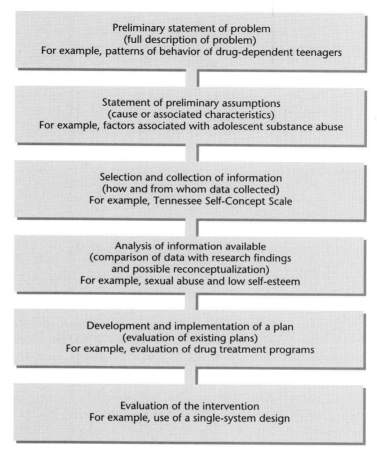

Figure 15.1   **Use of research findings in practice**

Preliminary statement of the problem.   The initial step in deciding on a course of action is to clarify the problem. This step can be facilitated by consulting existing research.

Statement of preliminary assumptions.   Consult the research to determine the cause of the problem or at least some of the factors associated with it.

Selection and collection of information.   Ideas about how to collect information and from whom can be obtained from research.

Analysis of information available.   Organize the material so that a plan can be developed. Alternatively, the analysis may lead to a reconceptualization of the problem or reveal a need for further information. Again, research findings can be used, perhaps to compare them with the data from the case.

Development and implementation of a plan.   Before the plan can be developed and implemented, research findings are used to determine whether similar plans and interventions have been successful in the past.

Evaluation of the intervention.   Once the intervention has been implemented, we need to consider its effectiveness with each case. Again, existing research can help in evaluating practice.

Individual System

Client: Sue

Presenting problem: Dependence on drugs

Referral: Sue, a 15-year-old Hispanic adolescent, was referred to a drug treatment program for substance abuse at her local high school. She was suspended from school and cannot return until she completes treatment. At the treatment intake the worker assessed Sue's drug use pattern and family relationships. A review of her drug use patterns indicated that she has started using drugs only in the past six months. Her use of drugs has increased recently, and she admits that she cannot place limits on her behavior and is preoccupied with drug use. She stated that she has many reasons to stop using but worries that she will lose her friends.

Preliminary Statement of the Problem

In attempting to clarify the problem with Sue, the worker used research to determine whether the patterns of behavior were consistent with a drug-dependent individual. The behaviors were found to be similar to those outlined by Jellinek (1960), who developed a model of alcoholism as a disease that progresses according to certain symptoms and behaviors (Acoca & Barr, 1989). The worker also wondered about the relatively short duration of the substance-abusing behavior. She found that the average time from initiation to addiction is significantly shorter for women than men (Ellinwood, Smith, & Vaillant, 1966). She also found that clients make the decision to change based on assessing the pros and cons. Prochaska, DiClemente, and Norcross (1992) developed a stages of change model that included precontemplation, contemplation, preparation, action, and maintenance. Their research indicates that motivation to change can be increased by assisting clients to see more risks than benefits if they continue their current substance abuse behavior. Consequently, this research began to provide some basis for understanding the problem.

Statement of Preliminary Assumptions

The worker wondered what problems might be associated with adolescent substance abuse; she found that sexual victimization affects about 75% of women in treatment for substance abuse (Yandow, 1989). In addition, a study of female adolescents who entered drug treatment showed that sexual abuse victims used drugs more frequently than nonvictims did. Sexual abuse victims also appeared to begin drug use at an earlier age than their peers (Harrison, Hoffman, & Edwall, 1989). Research also suggests that addicted women under 30 are more likely than those 30 and over to have histories that include dropping out of school, unemployment, welfare dependence, and psychophysiological problems (Harrison & Belille, 1987). Substance abuse in women is also often associated with low self-esteem (Beckman, 1978; Beckman, Day, Bardsley, & Seeman, 1980; Cuskey, Berger, & Densen-Gerber, 1977; McLachlan, Walderman, Birchmore, & Marsden, 1979). This research then helped the worker understand some of the underlying problems associated with teen female drug abuse.

Selection and Collection of Information

The research literature can be consulted to identify assessment tools that can assist in the collection of information on Sue's problem. For example, the tool used by the Chemical Dependency Adolescent Assessment Project in St. Paul, Minnesota (Nakken, 1989), or the Tennessee Self-Concept Scale that has been used for female substance abusers (Wheeler, Biase, & Sullivan, 1986) may be appropriate in this case. Using standardized tools can help us compare clients to other groups of clients experiencing the same or similar issues; this provides a basis for the total assessment of Sue's substance abuse. The worker also found a tool developed by Velicer, DiClemente, Prochaska, & Brandenburg (1985) that assists in identifying both the stage of change for the individual and the person's readiness for change.

Analysis of Information Available

From the worker's assessment, which included standardized assessment tools, it was found that Sue had been sexually abused and had low self-esteem. This supported the research findings cited earlier that found an association between substance abuse and sexual victimization and low self-esteem. She also found that Sue was in a contemplation stage and was considering the pros and cons of taking action to stop her substance use. The analysis of this information thus laid the foundation for the intervention plan.

Development and Implementation of a Plan

The worker developed a plan to include information about the risks of continuing the behavior and research-based strategies of motivational interviewing (Miller & Rollnick, 1991) to assist Sue in moving toward taking action. When Sue made the decision to take action, she moved into a preservation stage of change, and the worker assisted her in developing a plan to attend an inpatient drug treatment program specifically for women. The plan also addressed the problem of sexual abuse. Research findings indicate that unless women receive treatment for the sexual abuse their risk of relapse is increased (Young, 1990). Research indicates that the success rate for the recovery of female substance abusers is only 20% to 30% (Bowman & Jellinek, 1974; Pattison, 1974), suggesting that traditional programs may need to be redesigned to meet the special needs of women

(Doshan & Bursh, 1982; Reed, 1987). Root (1989) discussed how programs are not designed for women who experience posttraumatic stress. The cultural background of the client also needs to be considered. In a discussion of drug abuse treatment for Hispanics, Marin (1991) suggests that many drug treatment programs do not include culturally relevant material. Thus these evaluations need to be considered when selecting a program for Sue.

Evaluation of the Intervention

This case would be appropriate for a single-system study. Behaviors such as the reduction or abstinence of substance use or improved self-esteem could be monitored. Bloom, Fischer, and Orme (1995) presented a large array of single-system research designs along with a selection of data collection methods that would be appropriate for this case. The research limitations and the problems with obtaining accurate data collection for the substance abuse depend on Sue's ability and that of her parents and peers to be accurate reporters. Also, intervening variables, such as discovering a parental chemical abuse problem, may influence the outcomes of a single-subject design.

Family System

Client: The Kickingbird family

Presenting problem: Report of physical abuse of a child

Referral: The Kickingbird family was referred to a Native-American health and social services agency due to an incident of physical abuse. The family had physically abused their 12-year-old child for leaving the home and not caring for her three younger siblings while the parents were away. One sibling had played with matches and had started a fire in the kitchen. The father spanked the 12-year-old until she was black and blue. The incident was reported to the agency by school officials. The family is described as having few friends and no contact with their extended family.

Preliminary Statement of the Problem

To identify the problems in the Kickingbird family, the worker must first acknowledge that defining physical abuse of a child is sometimes difficult and can be affected by many factors. One such factor might be cultural variations in its definition. Existing research can be consulted to help understand these various definitions. Long (1986) suggested that physical abuse of children within their own families is "a culture-bound issue" (p. 131). Community standards are different for different cultural groups, and the definition of what constitutes abuse is defined within the context of the group. She also suggested that abuse must be assessed and treated within the cultural context.

Statement of Preliminary Assumptions

To determine the factors associated with the abuse in this family, it was useful for the worker to examine the research that has been conducted on child abuse and neglect, particularly among Native Americans. A multitude of contributing factors have been identified. Mannes (1990b) reported:

> According to the Milwaukee Indian Health Board, Inc. . . . , some of the more general problems that Indian families confront are: (1) perpetuating cycles of violence, (2) social isolation, (3) economic deprivation, (4) poor child-rearing skills, (5) personal frustration, (6) guilt, (7) emotional trauma, (8) marital problems, (9) too many children, (10) rigid sex roles, (11) drug and alcohol abuse and consumption, (12) psychoses, and (13) poor health. (p. 11)

These factors are, in fact, similar to the patterns of behavior associated with abuse outlined by the National Institute of Mental Health (Gelles, 1987). Research on the relationship between social supports and child abuse suggests a relationship between parental isolation and physical abuse (Chan, 1994; Corse, Schmid, & Trickett, 1990; Gaudin & Pollaine, 1983). This relationship is more strongly linked in the area of neglect (Seagull, 1988). These studies have not been conducted with Native American families, however.

Selection and Collection of Information

The worker needed to select a risk assessment tool to help determine the areas of family strength and collect information on the family's service needs; in this way the worker would be able to consistently document the necessary information for the analysis. Risk assessment tools have been developed to assess the risk for a child's entry into foster care: The Washington Risk Assessment (English, 1989) and the Family Risk Scales (Magura & Moses, 1986) are two examples. The Family Risk Scales consist of 26 items designed to measure a child's risk for entry into foster care, including child-related, parent-related, and economic risk factors. Other items covered are living conditions, family residence, social support, parental health, use of physical punishment, use of verbal discipline, sexual abuse of child, child's health, mental health, and school adjustment. The Family Risk Scales may need to be used in conjunction with other assessment tools (Fraser, 1990). Many instruments lack documentation of their reliability and validity; thus care is recommended when selecting instruments (Rzepnicki, Schuerman, & Littell, 1991). In order to balance the information on the family, the worker supplemented the risk assessment tool, with a newly developed strengths assessment tool, which is part of a Family Centered Assessment Tool (1996). This tool, however, also needs to be used with care because it is currently in the process of validation. This research process will include Native American families of the Southwest. The diversity and variation within Native American cultures must also be taken into account for this tool to be effective. A social network tool was also selected to assess the family's resources and support systems (Tracy and Whittaker, 1990).

Analysis of Information Available

Existing research on high-risk Native American families reviewed by the worker identified a great need for Native American families to obtain counseling and transportation (English, 1989). Using this information, the worker paid attention to those elements of the risk assessment tool and that identified these particular needs. Both of these needs were found to be clearly apparent for the Kickingbird family. The strengths assessment tools identified as strengths the family members' commitment to one another and the beliefs and traditions that connected them. The social network map assisted the family and the worker in identifying some extended family support that previously had not been seen as a resource.

Development and Implementation of a Plan

The worker developed a plan for the delivery of in-home family preservation services that would build on the family's strengths. This type of program was designed for families whose children are at imminent or high risk for placement. Research carried out on home-based programs indicates an average of 79% effectiveness (Nelson, Landsman, & Deutelbaum, 1990). Barth and Berry (1987) and Magura (1981) stated that evaluations of family preservation services programs conclude that these have only limited success. These tentative findings, however, are partly due to the lack of a precise operationalization of *imminent risk* for out-of-home placement (Wells & Biegel, 1992; Tracy, 1992; Stein & Rzepnicki, 1983). Workers who determine what imminent risk is may be motivated by a variety of influences, such as cost cuts, program waiting lists, worker relationships with the family preservation services program, or worker caseload size. Another problem with evaluating the findings from family preservation programs is the lack of adequate control groups in many of the studies, making it difficult to conclude whether the program or some other factor is responsible for outcomes (Rossi, 1992; Wells & Biegel, 1992). Random assignment of cases to different groups and services is the best way of achieving equivalence of the groups and increases the internal and external validity of the findings (Rzepnicki, Schuerman, & Littel, 1991). More recently, a meta-analysis of the effect size in the research results of eight quasi-experimental and experimental designs found a statistically significant outcome representing more positive results in the family preservation program evaluations (Blyth, Salley, & Jayaratne, 1994). None of these programs evaluated were, however, focused on evaluating family preservation services with the Native American population. While seen as a potentially culturally sensitive response, programs designated specifically for Native-American families may also vary in their effectiveness (Mannes, 1990a; Tafoya, 1990; Mannes, 1993). By recognizing these limitations of the family preservation research findings in developing and implementing a plan, the worker may remain flexible to other service options if this one is unsuccessful.

Understanding the tentative nature of the findings from the evaluation of family preservation services, the worker considered a short-term intensive in-home program to be the least restrictive for this family. The program was developed by Homebuilders in Tacoma, Washington, and provided intervention within 24 hours of referral, around-the-clock availability of therapists, low caseloads (maximum of three), and brief services (30 to 45 days) in the home environment (Haapala & Kinney, 1979). The plan also included culturally specific parenting skills based on the family's beliefs and traditions, as well as extensive work with the Kickingbirds' extended family to increase contact and support for the Kickingbirds.

Evaluation of the Intervention

As in the previous case, the use of a single-system design would be appropriate here. Goal attainment scaling to address the father's increased use of appropriate discipline might be used. Some scales from the Multi-Problem Screening Inventory (Hudson, 1990) could be used to demonstrate any changes in parental attitudes. A pretest and posttest using the Child Well-Being Scales (Magura & Moses, 1986) could also be used for evaluating any discipline change in the family. The Relative and Friend Support Index could assess the changes in social support of the family (McCubbin & Thompson, 1987). The worker could choose from a variety of single-system designs; Alter and Evens (1990) provided a number of alternatives. Some of the descriptive, least rigorous designs enable the worker and family to monitor progress, while the more rigorous designs—including withdrawal and multiple baselines designs—allow the worker to assess which aspects of services or techniques are most beneficial. Ethical issues may be encountered with withdrawal of services in high-risk child abuse situations (Rzepnicki, Schuerman, & Littel, 1991), however. Also, generalizability is low from single-system studies.

Group System

Client: Parents in a community

Presenting problem: Concern with children who have attention deficit disorder (ADHD)

Referral: A group of parents from a school district are concerned about services and support for families of children with attention deficit disorder (ADHD). They have asked the school social worker to help them develop a plan to meet their children's needs.

Preliminary Statement of the Problem

The first step for the worker is to clarify the problem and assess its magnitude. Research findings can be an important resource for problem definition. The fourth edition of the *Diagnostic and Statistical Manual of Mental Disorders* (DSM-IV) is a reference manual that lists definitions and research findings for psychological disorders (American Psychiatric Association, 1994). Although the DSM can be a useful resource, workers must acknowledge the potentially negative effects on clients by placing diagnostic labels on them. According to the DSM criteria, ADHD refers to a condition in which developmentally inappropriate degrees of inattention, impulsiveness, and hyperactivity are evident. These symptoms must last over a six-month time period and occur in two or more settings (American Psychiatric Association, 1994). The DSM-IV estimates that 3% to 5% of children have ADHD; other estimates have ranged up to 14.3% (Schachar, Rutter, & Smith, 1981). Shapiro and Garfinkel (1986) screened an elementary school population (315 children) and found that 8.9% of the children qualified for a diagnosis of attention deficit disorder or conduct disorder. The DSM-IV suggests ADHD occurs more frequently if a first-degree family member has ADHD or other psychiatric challenges such as mood and anxiety disorders, learning disorder, substance abuse–related disorders, and emotional and personality disorders (American Psychiatric Association, 1994; Frick, Lahey, Christ, Lobber, & Green, 1991; Seidman, Biederman, & Faraone, 1995).

Statement of Preliminary Assumptions

The worker needs to look at the current research to identify the causes of this problem and its associated characteristics. Chess and Thomas (1984) view behavior disorders as a result of difficulty of fit between the capacities of the child and environmental pressures. Others argue for the biological underpinnings of ADHD (Brickman et al., 1985; Dubey, 1976; Rapport & Ferguson, 1981; Tramontana & Sherrets, 1985). In one study, Green (1990) noted that the style of interaction and communication in ADHD families is characterized by the following: lack of clear and consistent rules for rewards and punishment; disciplinary responses based on parental moods; attempts to resolve arguments through increased threats and counterthreats; communication characterized by intensity of physical action and sound, such as gestures and yelling instead of words and logic; compliance demanded through the use of force; and finally, disruption of the orderly flow of ideas in communication due to frequent and sudden topic changes. The worker should be cautious about adopting this view of ADHD as a family problem, however, because it can reinforce feelings of guilt and inadequacy by the parents and may harm children by stressing a treatment approach that is ineffective unless balanced with other treatments (Johnson, 1988). The worker should be prepared to assist parents who may have unrecognized ADHD and other psychiatric disorders (Kaplan & Shachter, 1991).

Selection and Collection of Information

Several instruments may be appropriate for obtaining information about children with ADHD. Tools for assessing children who show disruptive behavior include interviews with parents; reports from schools and community agencies; medical history and physical examination; neurological examination; psychological testing; allergy evaluation; laboratory studies; interviews with and observation of the child; behavior rating scales completed by parents, teachers, and significant others in the child's life; and self-report scales (Shekim, 1986). The Connors Scales are often used for assessing hyperactivity and attention deficit disorders (Benton & Sines, 1985). The Self-Report Delinquency Scale (Elliott & Ageton, 1980), the Child Behavior Checklist (Achenbach & McConaughy, 1987), the Adolescent Antisocial Behavior Checklist (Curtiss et al., 1983), and the Parent Daily Report (Patterson, Chamberlain, & Reid, 1982) also may be useful in this case.

Analysis of Information Available

The information that the worker gathered for this case can be compared with existing research findings. Between 1960 and 1975, 2,000 articles were published regarding children with hyperactivity or minimal brain dysfunction. When the nomenclature was reviewed and ADHD became identified, 7,000 more articles were published (Weiss, 1985). The validity of the psychological testing used in many of these research articles is complicated by the possibility of racial and ethnic bias, however (Cronbach, 1975). These issues need to be considered when comparing findings from individual cases to the findings in the literature.

Development and Implementation of a Plan

Parent support groups offering child management skills could be considered for this case. In a study in one state, parents requested concrete management skills training from professionals (New Mexico Children's Services Subcommittee, 1991). Parent support groups and advocacy groups have been developed to monitor schools, boards of education, and state agencies to ensure that handicapped children receive services (Johnson, 1988). As a group, parents "can organize and exert political pressure, and they can provide parents with the often desperately needed support that comes through finding out that many have similar problems and that such problems do not always have to be defined in terms of the failure of individual parents and individual children" (Johnson, 1988, p. 354). Parents can provide support, assistance in problem solving, access to useful information, and solutions to social isolation problems (Johnson, 1988). Although the effectiveness of these particular groups for parents has recently been established through limited research, extensive literature is available on the use of support groups in general (Pisterman et al., 1989; Pollard, Ward, & Barkley, 1983; Bennett, DeLuca, & Allen, 1996; Toseland & Rivas, 1984).

Evaluation of the Intervention

The support group for parents could be evaluated with parent satisfaction inventories. Existing inventories could be modified to meet the needs of this particular group (Toseland & Rivas, 1984). Group designs could be adopted using sources such as Campbell and Stanley (1963).

Organization System

Client: The Children's Center

Presenting the problem: Need for foster parents for HIV-infected children

Referral: The Children's Center, in a large urban area, has had increased demand for foster care services for HIV-infected babies. Large numbers of children have been abandoned in local hospitals, and the rate of HIV-infected mothers is increasing. The agency is asking a group of workers to develop strategies for foster care recruitment of these children.

Preliminary Statement of the Problem

According to statistics from the Centers for Disease Control (CDC) in Atlanta, the number of children with HIV infection is rapidly increasing (1992). Health officials estimate that 25% to 35% of these children will require substitute care (National Adoption Information Clearinghouse, 1989). It is estimated that 80,000 children will be orphaned as a result of AIDS by the year 2000 (Michaels & Levine, 1992)

Statement of Preliminary Assumptions

Planning foster programs for HIV-infected babies requires an understanding of why so many of these children are in need of foster care. In New York City, 80% of the infants with AIDS are born of drug-using parents, and 42% are African American and Hispanic. Many of these families live in poverty, and family systems are chaotic; support is often unavailable since other family members are not knowledgeable about AIDS (Rowe & Ryan, 1987). The mode of the disease's transmission also contributes to an increasing number of children in need of care: "Ninety percent of children with AIDS acquire the infection in the womb from infected mothers who are intravenous drug users or the sexual partners of intravenous drug users" (Child Welfare League of America, 1988, p. 1). The CDC (1992) confirmed similar rates of 85%. Women infected with HIV have a 15% to 40% chance of giving birth to an infected baby or transmitting HIV through breast feeding (Johnson et al., 1989; Husson, Comeau, & Hoff, 1990; Brown, 1990; Oxtoby, 1994; Mofenson, 1994). New uses of drugs such as zidovudine have decreased this probability to 8.3% (Connor et al., 1994).

The worker reviewed a study by Groze, McMillen, & Haines-Simeon (1993), which suggested that compared to foster parents who were not providing foster care for HIV-infected children, those that did choose to do so were highly motivated because they had work-related experiences with HIV-infected children and scored higher (38%) in beliefs that they "had something to offer children" compared to the control groups (20%). They also had higher rates of willingness to provide care again for the foster care system (95%) compared to the control groups (87%).

Selection and Collection of Information

A useful initial strategy in this case would be to assess the knowledge of AIDS by foster parents or potential foster parents; this would assist in the recruitment program. The Child Welfare League of America has a tool that assesses knowledge and attitudes toward HIV and AIDS (Annin, 1990). Beckler (1990) adapted this tool for use by foster parents.

Analysis of Information Available

The agency's survey of foster and potential foster parents indicated that the number of families willing to provide care for HIV-infected children was low. In addition, families' knowledge of the transmission and symptoms of HIV and AIDS was limited. These data corresponded to the research findings cited earlier. The families also indicated the need for increased financial assistance for medical costs, transportation, education on hygiene and safety, respite care, and counseling for the stress resulting from caring for such children. These data also corresponded to the recommendations from the New Jersey Department of Human Services (1989).

Development and Implementation of a Plan

Model programs exist that use intensive care management for biological parents, recruitment of foster-adoptive parents, and training of foster parents (Ford & Kroll, 1990). Consulting these programs and assessing their ability to recruit and train foster parents in the care of HIV-infected babies would be a productive use of the existing research.

In addition, other model programs—such as the New Jersey Special Home Services Provider Program, which supplies financial support, intensive training, counseling, and in-home support—can give ideas for foster parent recruitment (New Jersey Department of Human Services, 1989). Finally, it has been suggested that the recruitment program should include an educational component (Anderson, 1990) in addition to attitude and skills training in caring for HIV-infected babies. This education seems particularly appropriate with the families in this community whose knowledge of HIV and AIDS is limited. Much of the information for the educational component can be drawn from existing research—for example, information on the symptoms of AIDS, such as chronic diarrhea, fatigue, and weight loss (Lockhard & Wodarski, 1989; Oleske, 1987; Rogers, 1985, 1987a, 1987b; Scott, 1987; Shannon & Animann, 1985). The recruitment plan for this agency largely involved efforts to recruit families in the helping professions that would have experiences with HIV-infected children, including nurses, hospital personnel, clergy, and professional and paraprofessional caregivers. The second strategy was a public media campaign that focused on advertising for parents who felt they had resources to offer children.

Evaluation of the Intervention

Program evaluation techniques can be used to assist the effectiveness of the training and recruitment program. Models such as those used by Groze, McMillen, and Haines-Simeon (1993) offer some examples of evaluation methods.

Measures could include knowledge and attitude inventories for the foster parents, a count of the number of HIV-infected children actually placed, continued commitment to provide foster care for HIV-infected children, and qualitative methods using such research strategies as phenomenology to capture families' experiences.

Community System

Client: STOP, a community task force

Presenting problem: Teen suicide in community

Referral: A task force has been developed in a rural community after three suicides were committed in three months. Community leaders, school officials, and interested community members have joined together to develop a comprehensive community plan for assisting their youth.

Preliminary Statement of the Problem

An overview of the problem of teen suicide is available in the research findings. According to U.S. Vital Statistics (1992), the third leading cause of death for 15- to 24-year-olds is suicide. In an interview, Garfinkel stated that in the past 30 years the number of childhood suicides has increased by 300%, and the number of suicide attempts has increased by 350% to 700% (Frymier, 1988). The scope of the problem suggested by Hepworth, Farley, and Griffiths (1986) is that half a million young people attempt suicide each year, and of that number approximately 5,000 succeed.

Statement of Preliminary Assumptions

Much research has investigated the causes of suicide and may provide useful information for this case. An interaction of factors—such as chronic adjustment problems, dislocation, and stress associated with adolescence—and a recent traumatic event seem to contribute to adolescent suicide. Alcohol is a further factor to be considered. Grueling and DeBlassie (1980) found that more than 50% of teenagers who had committed suicide had a history of moderate to severe drinking. Garfinkel stated that rural youth kill themselves at a higher rate than do urban youth (Frymier, 1988). More recent studies have not found statistically significant differences between rural and urban populations but have suggested further longitudinal studies (Albers & Evans, 1994).

Selection and Collection of Information

The community task force to prevent teen suicide would need to gather local statistics on the incidence of suicide in their community. In addition, assessment instruments for individuals, such as the Beck's Depression Inventory, the Suicide

Intent Scale (SIS), and the Children's Depression Inventory (CDI) can measure depression and suicidal ideas (Beck et al., 1961; Teri, 1982; Pierce, 1977; Pierce, 1981; and Kovacs, 1980–1981). The ability of this instrument to accurately measure depression must be assessed for members of diverse cultural groups. Allen-Meares (1987) noted that the items were derived from white and African American psychiatric patients between the ages of 15 and 44. More research is needed with diverse cultural groups.

Analysis of Information Available

The survey of community teens indicated high rates of depression. These rates were then compared to the literature. Garfinkel stated that between 6% and 8% of junior and senior high schoolers have been severely or profoundly depressed (Frymier, 1988). The males were found to consider suicide more indirectly and were more likely to use drugs as a coping mechanism. These findings were comparable to those of Harlow, Newcomb, and Bentler (1986). The survey results also indicated that most students wanted to learn more about suicide. This was also consistent with the research findings completed with 25,000 high school students (Smith, 1976; Carlson, 1981; Elkind, 1984a, 1986b).

Development and Implementation of a Plan

The high rates of suicidal thinking and drug abuse indicated in the survey may lead the community task force to choose educational strategies. One successful program educated teens to monitor their own depression and helped them to identify coping styles and mechanisms (Frymier, 1988). Peer helpers are resources that can be used in this process; 75% of teenagers who are severely depressed or suicidal turn to peers for help, compared to 18% who turn to parents and only 7% who choose to see a mental health professional (Frymier, 1988). Another successful program (Cliffone, 1993) demonstrated shifts in attitudes toward more positive attitudes about suicide prevention, such as seeing suicidal thinking as treatable. Students learned to prepare themselves to assist others by encouraging them to obtain help from professionals.

Evaluation of the Intervention

The reduction of teen suicide in this community can be evaluated through a number of methods, including the use of mental health statistics concerning children at risk for suicide; evaluation of students' level of understanding of stress symptoms and safety issues, including supporting other students in obtaining professional assistance; and parental and/or recognition by parents and school personnel of the signs of suicide risk. Evaluation of students seeking assistance and being referred by peers may also assist the community in understanding the results of intervention methods.

LIMITING CONDITIONS

We may find that the extent and manner in which we use research findings depends on a number of factors, many of which are beyond our control. Mullen (1988) referred to four of these limiting conditions: tradition, philosophy, technological skills, and quality of information.

Traditionally, social workers have not relied on information drawn from research, but rather from theory and experience. Incorporating research into practice still seems alien to many social workers. Philosophically, research may seem to be dramatically opposed to the practice of social work. Research can be viewed as mechanistic and devoid of a humanitarian perspective. As research methods in social work become more sophisticated in their ability to tap the intricacies of human interactions, however, this perceived gap between social work practice and social work research will narrow.

Technological skills are another limiting condition. Many social workers simply do not understand the complexities of research methods. This problem will gradually lessen as graduates of social work programs are required by the Council on Social Work Education (CSWE) to have completed at least one course in social work research methods. The knowledge and skills discussed in this text provide more than enough information for the social worker to use research in practice.

The limitation on quality of information refers to the social work research findings themselves. There are both problems with existing research and great gaps in the research literature. Again though, we can optimistically assume that as social workers become more knowledgeable about research through the incorporation of research content into the social work curriculum, so the body of research literature will gradually expand. In the interim, research findings need to be incorporated as much as possible into practice. The limitation of poor quality research is addressed in the next section, in which we discuss how to evaluate research information.

EVALUATING RESEARCH

Although the evaluation of research is discussed here as a separate step in the research process, as is true of steps in the practice process, this step can merge or overlap with other research stages—particularly the step of evaluating the intervention). It is not only the findings per se that are of interest, but also the quality of the research. No research study is completely flawless. One of the researcher's responsibilities in writing up the results of the study is to include a limitations section, to guide readers in their assessment of the research. Often, however, the limitations section is incomplete. Identifying all the limitations in a research study is critical if you are to effectively use research findings in social work practice.

Use the guide in Figure 15.2 to help you evaluate research studies. Also refer to the sources listed in the Further Reading section at the end of this chapter.

A. Statement of the Problem
1. What is the problem under study?
2. Is the problem clearly stated, identified, and understandable?
3. Is the importance of the problem clearly presented?
4. Is the research question or hypothesis clearly stated?

B. Research Approach
1. Is the research strategy/approach clearly presented?

C. Literature review
1. Does the literature review include a thorough coverage of the problem?
2. Are the findings and their sources clearly referenced?
3. Does the literature review use current references? If older references are used, are they important links to the history of the problem?
4. Does the literature review provide information on how concepts should be defined and measured?

D. Variables
1. When applicable, are the dependent and independent variables clearly identified?
2. When applicable, are the dependent and independent variables defined and operationalized?

E. Sampling
1. What is the population in the study?
2. What sampling method was used?
3. Is the sampling method appropriate for the research approach?

F. Study Design
1. Is the design of the study clearly presented?
2. Is the design appropriate for the research approach?

G. Data Collection
1. Are the data collection methods clearly specified?
2. Are the data qualitative, quantitative, or both?
3. What procedures were used to ensure reliability and validity of the data?
4. Are there additional sources of data that could have been used?

H. Data Analysis
1. When present, are tables and graphs understandable?
2. Is there an orderly and clear interpretation of research findings?
3. For quantitative data, were appropriate statistical tests used?
4. For qualitative data, is the method of analysis clearly described?
5. Do the conclusions follow logically from the data analysis?
6. Are the data sufficient to warrant the conclusions?

(continued on next page)

Figure 15.2 **Guidelines for evaluating journal articles**

Source: From an unpublished outline by Rose Rael.

I. Ethical Issues
   1. Are the consequences for human beings considered?
   2. Was informed consent obtained from the subjects?
   3. Are the participants protected from harm?
   4. Is there assurance that the data will be kept confidential?
   5. Who is given credit for the research?

J. Human Diversity Issues
   1. Is the research question of interest or does it apply to diverse groups?
   2. Is the data collection method relevant for the group(s) under study?
   3. Is the sample diverse?
   4. If there are comparison groups, what is their membership?
   5. Is the subject involved in the research project beyond simply being a subject?
   6. Does the categorization of data maintain diversity?
   7. Is the research report written in an exclusive or stereotypical manner?
   8. To whom were the results disseminated?
   9. Was there maximum participation from many groups in the research?

K. Limitations of the Study
   1. Are the limitations of the study clearly stated?
   2. If the limitations are not clearly stated, what limitations can you, the reader, assign to the study?

L. Conclusions and Recommendations
   1. Are the conclusions substantiated by the research findings? Are the conclusions significant and relevant to the problem and population under study?
   2. What are the recommendations for future studies? Does the study identify implications for social work?

THE AGENCY IN THE USE AND EVALUATION OF RESEARCH FINDINGS

To be responsible generalist practitioners we need to take research seriously; this includes using and evaluating research findings. Although there is no denying that time is a factor in agencies, the challenge is to carry out research within your time constraints. Here are some guidelines:

1. Use computer searches as much as possible to locate research on specific topics. You can also use the Internet to identify listservs relevant to your topic, and of course the World Wide Web can yield some good sources. As noted earlier, the Web also contains some not so good sources, so be selective in your search.

2. Be specific in identifying relevant research. There is an enormous amount out there. For example, if you are researching the second case in this chapter

(the Kickingbird family), don't look for everything on child abuse, but specifically for physical abuse in Native American families. Being specific will considerably limit the amount of literature you need to review. If you come up with nothing in the specific area, broaden your search.

3.　List only those findings that are relevant to the practice issues. Be concise. Next, comment on the quality of the evidence. At this point you can refer to the frameworks described earlier. Don't be too compulsive in their use, though; simply note some of the major problems with the research.

4.　Keep this record of the findings, limiting conditions, and quality of the research as brief as possible. Enter the information into a computer and create files for different topics.

ETHICAL ISSUES IN THE USE AND EVALUATION OF RESEARCH FINDINGS

Although social workers can benefit from applying research findings to their practice, research cannot always provide the answers. Sometimes the questions that interest you have not yet been investigated, for any number of reasons. Funding may not have been available, for example. Even if your topic has been researched, this research may have been constrained by a particular theoretical framework or a particular type of research method, limiting the usefulness of the findings.

Due to these gaps in the knowledge, you cannot always use research. You need to explicitly acknowledge this patchiness, recognizing that every stage of the practice process cannot be supported with information derived from research. An intellectual and personal honesty is required in acknowledging where the gaps in your practice knowledge exist. This honesty also provides a means for developing a personal research agenda—program evaluation, needs assessment, evaluating your own practice, or pure research.

HUMAN DIVERSITY ISSUES IN THE USE AND EVALUATION OF RESEARCH FINDINGS

When referring to research studies to enhance your practice, you need to be sure that these studies are themselves sensitive to human diversity issues. You may be able to ascertain this when assessing the quality of the research. For example, in the research studies on physical abuse, you note that none of the samples include Hispanic families; consequently, any results from these studies would be limited in their ability to be generalized to a wider population. When evaluating research studies, bear in mind the comments relating to human diversity issues made in each chapter regarding each step of the research process.

SUMMARY

Using the results of research in practice necessitates evaluating the research it-self. The process of using research in practice is explored with five different client systems: individual, family, group, organization, and community. At each stage of practice, research findings can assist. Four limiting conditions deter the use of research in practice, however: These are tradition, philosophy, technological skills, and quality of information. Several frameworks have been suggested to as-sist in the evaluation of research.

Agency issues include advocating the importance of using research in prac-tice. As generalist practitioners, we are faced with the challenge of conducting re-search within the agency's time constraints. Ethical issues involve recognizing the gaps in our research knowledge; we cannot support every stage of the prac-tice process with research. Human diversity issues relate to the existing research. We must be sensitive to human diversity when assessing the quality of research.

STUDY/EXERCISE QUESTIONS

1. Select an article in a social work journal and apply the framework for the evaluation of research displayed in Figure 15.2.

2. Take a case in which you have been involved either as a volunteer or a practicum student and describe how you would use research findings at each step of the practice process.

FURTHER READING

Katzet, J., Cook, K., & Crouch, W. (1991). *Evaluating information.* New York: McGraw-Hill.
A great consumer's guide to the research literature.

Stern, P., & Kalof, L. (1996). *Evaluating social science research.* (2nd ed.). New York: Oxford University Press.
A good guide to evaluating social science studies; includes many examples from the literature.

York, R. (1997). *Building basic competencies in social work research.* Boston: Allyn & Bacon.

Szafran, R. (1994). *Social science research.* Los Angeles: Pyrczak.
A collection of articles with some critical evaluative guides and questions.

REFERENCES

Achenback, T. M., & McConaughy, S. H. (1987). *Empirically based assessment of child and adolescent psychopathology: Practical applications.* Newbury Park, CA: Sage Publications.

Acoca, L., & Barr, J. (1989). *Substance abuse: A training manual for working with families.* New York: Edna McConnell Clark Foundation.

Albers, E. & Evans, W. (1994). Suicide ideation among a stratified sample of rural and urban adolescents. *Child and Adolescent Social Work Journal, 11* (5), 379–389.

Allen-Meares, P. (1987). Depression in childhood and adolescence. *Social Work, 32* (6), 512–516.

Alter, C., & Evens, W. (1990). *Evaluating your own practice: A guide to self-assessment.* New York: Springer.

American Psychiatric Association. (1994). *Diagnostic and statistical manual of mental disorders* (4th ed.). Washington, DC: Author.

Anderson, G. R. (1990). Foster parent education: Preparing for informed and compassionate caregiving. In G. R. Anderson (Ed.), *Courage to care: Responding to the crisis of children with AIDS.* Washington, DC: Child Welfare League of America.

Annin, J. B. (1990). Training for HIV infection prevention in child welfare services. In G. R. Anderson (Ed.), *Courage to care: Responding to the crisis of children with AIDS.* Washington, DC: Child Welfare League of America.

Barth, R., & Berry, M. (1987). Outcome of child welfare services under permanency planning. *Social Service Review, 61,* 71–90.

Beck, A., Ward, C., Mendelson, M., Mock, J., & Erbaugh, J. (1961). An inventory for measuring depression. *Archives of General Psychology, 4,* 561–571.

Beckler, P. (1990). Resources for HIV/AIDS education: Cases. In G. R. Anderson (Ed.), *Courage to care: Responding to the crisis of children with AIDS.* Washington, DC: Child Welfare League of America.

Beckman, L. J. (1978). The psycho-social characteristics of alcoholic women. *Drug Abuse and Alcoholism Review, 1* (5–6), 1312.

Beckman, L. J., Day, T., Bardsley, P., & Seeman, A. (1980). The personality characteristics and family background of women alcoholics. *The International Journal of the Addictions, 15* (1), 147–154.

Bennett, T., DeLuca, D., & Allen, R. (1996). Families of children with disabilities: Positive adaptation across the life cycle. *Social Work in Education, 18* (1), 31–44.

Benton, A. L., & Sines, J. O. (1985). Psychological testing of children. In H. Kaplan & B. Sadock (Eds.), *Comprehensive textbook of psychiatry* (4th ed., pp.1625–1634). Baltimore: Williams & Wilkins.

Bloom, M., Fischer, J., & Orme, D. (1995). *Evaluating practice: Guidelines for the accountable professional.* Englewood Cliffs, NJ: Prentice Hall.

Blyth, B., Sally, M., & Jayaratne, S. (1994). A review of intensive family preservation services research. *Social Work, 18* (4), 213–224.

Bowman, K. M., & Jellinek, E. M. (1974). Alcohol addiction and treatment. *Journal of Studies on Alcoholism, 35* (2), 98–176.

Brickman, A. S., et al. (1985). Neuropsychological assessment of seriously delinquent adolescents. *Journal of the American Academy of Child Psychiatry, 23,* 453–457.

Brown, P. (1990, October 13). HIV may claim fewer babies. *New Scientist,* 10.

Campbell, D., & Stanley, J. (1963). *Experimental and quasi-experimental designs for research.* Chicago: Rand McNally.

Carson, G. A. (1981). The phenomenology of adolescent depression. *Adolescent Psychiatry, 9,* 411–412.

Centers for Disease Control. (1992). HIV/AIDS Surveillance Report, January 1–22.

Chan, Y. C. (1994). Parenting stress and social support of mothers who physically abuse their children in Hong Kong. *Child Abuse and Neglect, 18,* 261–269.

Chess, S., & Thomas, A. (1984). *Origins and evolution of behavior disorders.* New York: Brunner/Mazel.

Child Welfare League of America. (1988). Report of the CWLA task force on children and HIV infection: Initial guidelines. Washington, DC: Author.

Cliffone, J. (1993). Suicide prevention: A classroom presentation to adolescents. *Social Work, 38* (2), 197–203.

Connor, E., Sperling, R., Gelber, R., Kiselev, P., Scott, G., O'Sullivan, M. J., VanDyke, R., Bey, M., Shearer, W., Jacobson, R., Jimenez, E., O'Neil, E., Bazin, B., Delfraissy, J., Culnane, M., Coombs, R., Elkins, M., Moye, J., Stratton, P., & Balsley, J. (1994). Reduction of maternal-infant transmission of human immunodeficiency virus type 1 with zidovudine treatment. *New England Journal of Medicine, 331,* 1173–1180.

Corse, S., Schmid, K., & Trickett, P. (1990). Social network characteristics of mothers in abusing and nonabusing families and their relationships to parenting beliefs. *Journal of Community Psychology, 18,* 44–59.

Cronbach, L. J. (1975). Five decades of public controversy over mental testing. *American Psychologist, 30,* 1–14.

Curtiss, G., et al. (1983). Measuring delinquent behavior in inpatient treatment settings: Revision and validation of the adolescent antisocial behavior checklist. *Journal of the American Academy of Child Psychiatry, 22,* 459–466.

Cuskey, W., Berger, L., & Densen-Gerber, J. (1977). Issues in the treatment of female addiction: A review and critique of the literature. *Contemporary Drug Problems, 6* (3), 307–371.

Doshan, T., & Bursh, C. (1982). Women and substance abuse: Critical issues in treatment design. *Journal of Drug Education, 12* (3), 229–239.

Dubey, R. (1976). Organic factors in hyperkinesis: A cortical evaluation. *American Journal of Orthopsychiatry, 48,* 353–366.

Ellinwood, E. H., Smith, W. G., & Vaillant, G. E. (1966). Narcotic addiction in males and females: A comparison. *The International Journal of the Addictions, 1,* 33–45.

Elliott, D. S., & Ageton, S. S. (1980). Reconciling race and class differences in self-reported and official estimates of delinquency. *American Sociological Review, 45,* 95–110.

Elkind, D. (1984a). *All grown up and no place to go.* Reading, MA: Addison-Wesley.

Elkind, D. (1984b). *The hurried child.* Reading, MA: Addison-Wesley.

English, D. J. (1989, August). *An analysis of characteristics, problems and services for CPS cases by ethnicity.* Paper presented at the American Public Welfare Association 3rd Roundtable on Risk Assessment, San Francisco.

Family Centered Assessment Tool. (1996). Santa Fe, NM: Children, Youth and Families Department.

Ford, M., & Kroll, J. (1990). *Challenges to child welfare: Countering the call for a return to orphanages.* St. Paul, MN: North American Council on Adoptable Children.

Fraser, M. (1990). Program outcome measures. In Y. Y. Yuan & M. Rivest (Eds.), *Preserving families: Evaluation resources for practitioners and policymakers.* Newbury Park, CA: Sage.

Frick, P., Lahey, B., Christ, M., Loeber, R., Green, S. (1991). History of childhood behavior problems in the biological relatives of boys with attention-deficit hyperactivity disorder and conduct disorder. *Journal of Clinical Child Psychology, 42* (4), 445–451.

Frymier, J. (1988). Understanding and preventing teen suicide: An interview with Barry Garfinkel, M.D. *Phi Delta Kappan, 70* (4).

Gaudin, Jr., J. M. & Pollane, L. (1983). Social networks, stress and child abuse. *Children and Youth Services Review, 5,* 91–102.

Gelles, R. J. (1987). *Family violence* (2nd ed.). Newbury Park: CA: Sage.

Green, R. J. (1990). Family communication and children's learning disabilities: Evidence for Cole's theory of interactivity. *Journal of Learning Disabilities, 23* (3), 146.

Groze, V., McMillen, J. C., Haines-Simeon, M. (1993). Families who foster children with HIV: A pilot study. *Child and Adolescent Social Work Journal, 10* (1), 67–87.

Grueling, J., & DeBlassie, R. R. (1980). Adolescent suicide. *Adolescence, 15,* 589–601.

Haapala, D., & Kinney, J. (1979). Homebuilders approach to the training of in-home therapists. In S. Maybanks & M. Boyce (Eds.), *Homebased services for children and families.* Springfield, IL: Charles C Thomas.

Harlow, L. L., Newcomb, M. D., & Bentler, P. M. (1987). Depression, self-derogation, substance use, and suicide ideation: Lack of purpose in life as a mediational faction. *Journal of Clinical Psychology, 42* (1), 5–21.

Harrison, P. A., & Belille, C. A. (1987). Women in treatment: Beyond the stereotype. *Journal of Studies on Alcohol, 48* (6), 574–578.

Harrison, P. A., Hoffman, N. G., & Edwall, G. D. (1989). Differential drug use patterns among sexually abused adolescent girls in treatment for chemical dependency. *The International Journal of the Addictions, 24* (6), 499–514.

Hepworth, D. H., Farley, O. W., & Griffiths, J. K. (1986). Research capsule. *Social Research Institute Newsletter.* Salt Lake City: Graduate School of Social Work, University of Utah.

Hudson, W. (1990). *The multi-problem screening inventory.* Tempe, AZ: Walmyr.

Husson, R. N., Comeau, A., Hoff, R. (1990). Diagnosis of human immuno-deficiency virus infection in infants and children. *Pediatrics, 86* (1), 1–10.

Jellinek, E. M. (1960). *The disease concept of alcoholism.* New Brunswick, NJ: Hillhouse Press.

Johnson, H. C. (1988). Drugs, dialogue, or diet: Diagnosing and treating the hyperactive child. *Social Work Journal, 33,* 349–355.

Johnson, J. P., Nair, P., Hines, S. E., Seidan, S., Alger, L., Review, D., O'Neil, K., & Hebel, R. (1989). Natural history and serologic diagnosis of infants born to human immunodeficiency virus-infected women. *American Journal Of Diseases of Children, 143,* 1147–1153.

Kaplan, C. & Shachter, E. (1991). Adults with undiagnosed learning disabilities: Practice considerations. *Families in Society, 72* (4), 195–201.

Kovacs, M. (1980–1981). Rating scales to assess depression in school-aged children. *Acta Paedopsychiatrica, 46,* 305–315.

Lockhart, L. L., & Wodarski, J. S. (1989). Facing the unknown: Children and adolescents with AIDS. *Social Work, 34* (3), 215–221.

Long, K. A. (1986). Cultural considerations in the assessment and treatment of intrafamilial abuse. *American Journal of Orthopsychiatry, 56* (1), 131–136.

Magura, S. (1981). Are services to prevent foster care effective? *Children and Youth Services Review, 3,* 193–212.

Magura, S., & Moses, B. S. (1986). *Outcome measures for child welfare services: Theory and applications.* Washington, DC: Child Welfare League of America.

Mannes, M. (1990a). Implementing family preservation services with American Indians and Alaskan natives. In M. Mannes (Ed.), *Family preservation and Indian child welfare.* Albuquerque, NM: American Indian Law Center, Inc.

Mannes, M. (1990b). Linking family preservation and Indian child welfare: A historical perspective and the contemporary context. In M. Mannes (Ed.), *Family preservation and Indian child welfare.* Albuquerque, NM: American Indian Law Center, Inc.

Mannes, M. (1993). Seeking the balance between child protection and family preservation in Indian child welfare. *Child Welfare League of America, 72* (2), 141–151.

Marin, B. (1991). Drug abuse treatment for Hispanics: A culturally-appropriate, community-oriented approach. In R. R. Watson (Ed.), *Drug and alcohol abuse prevention.* Totowa, NJ: Humana Press.

McCubbin, H. & Thompson, A. (Ed). (1987). *Family assessment for research and practice.* Madison: University of Wisconsin.

McLachlan, F. C., Walderman, R., Birchmore, B., & Marsden, L. (1979). Self-evaluation, role satisfaction and anxiety in the woman alcoholic. *The International Journal of the Addictions, 14* (6), 809–832.

Michaels, D., & Levine, C. (1992). Estimates of the number of motherless youth orphaned by AIDS in the United States. *Journal of the American Medical Association, 268,* 3456–3461.

Miller, W. & Rollnick, S. (1991). *Motivational interviewing: Preparing people to change addictive behavior.* New York: Guilford Press.

Mofenson, L. (1994). Epidemiology and determinants of vertical HIV transmission. *Seminar in Pediatric Infection Disease, 5,* 252–265.

Mullen, E. J. (1988). Constructing personal practice models. *Social Work Research and Evaluation.* Itasca, IL: Peacock Publishers.

Nakken, J. M. (1989). Issues in adolescent chemical dependency assessment. In P. B. Henry (Ed.), *Practical approaches in treating adolescent chemical dependency: A guide to clinical assessment and intervention.* New York: Haworth Press.

National Adoption Information Clearinghouse. (1989). *Adoption and foster care of children with AIDS: An analysis of existing state policies.* Washington, DC: Administration for Children, Youth, and Families, U.S. Department of Health and Human Services.

Nelson, D. E., Landsman, M. J., & Deutelbaum, W. (1990). Three models of family-centered placement prevention services. *Child Welfare, 69* (1), 3–21.

New Jersey Department of Human Services Division of Youth and Family Services. (1989). *A practice guide to caring for children with AIDS.* Trenton, New Jersey: Office of Policy, Planning and Support.

New Mexico Children's Services Subcommittee. (1991). *Parents survey results.* Santa Fe: New Mexico Health and Environment Department.

Oleske, J. (1987). Natural history of HIV infection II. In K.B. Silverman & A. Waddell (Eds.), *Report of the surgeon general's workshop on children with HIV infection and their families* (pp. 24–25). Washington DC: U.S. Department of Health and Human Services, Public Health Service.

Oxtoby, M. J. (1994). Vertically acquired HIV infection in the United States. In Pisso, P.A. and Wilfert, C.M. (Eds.), *Pediatric AIDS: The challenge of HIV infection in infants, children, and adolescents.* Baltimore, MD: Willima & Wilkens.

Patterson, G. R., Chamberlain, P., & Reid, J. B. (1982). A comparative evaluation of a parent training program. *Behavior Therapy, 13,* 638–650.

Pattison, E. M. (1974). The rehabilitation of the chronic alcoholic. In B. Kissen & H. Begletter (Eds.), *Biology of alcoholism: Vol. III. Clinical Pathology.* New York: Plenum Press.

Pierce, D. (1977). Suicidal intent in self-injury. *British Journal Of Psychiatry, 130,* 377–385.

Pierce, D. (1981). The predictive validation of the suicide intent scale: A five year follow-up. *British Journal of Psychiatry, 139,* 391–396.

Pisterman, S., McGrath, P., Firestone, P., Goodman, J., Webster, I., & Mallory, R. (1989). Outcome of parent-mediated treatment of preschoolers with attention deficit disorder with hyperactive. *Journal of Consulting and Clinical Psychology, 57,* 628–635.

Pollard, S., Ward, E., & Barkley, R. (1983). The effects of parent training and Ritalin on the parent-child interactions of hyperactive boys. *Child and Family Therapy, 5,* 51–69.

Prochaska, J., DiClemente, C., & Norcross, J. (1992). In search of how people change: Applications to addictive behaviors. *American Psychologist, 47* (9), 1102–1114.

Rapport, J. L., & Ferguson, H. B. (1981). Biological validation of the hyperkinetic syndrome. *Developmental Medicine and Child Neurology, 23,* 667–682.

Reed, B. (1987). Developing women-sensitive drug dependence treatment services: Why so difficult? *Journal of Psychoactive Drugs, 19,* 151–164.

Rogers, M. F. (1985). AIDS in children: A review of the clinical epidemiologic and public health aspects. *Pediatric Infectious Disease, 4,* 230–236.

Rogers, M. F. (1987a). AIDS in children. *The New York Medical Quarterly, 21,* 68–73.

Rogers, M. F. (1987b). Transmission of human immunodeficiency virus infection in the United States. In K. B. Silverman & A. Waddell (Eds.), *Report of the surgeon general's workshop on children with HIV infection and their families* (pp. 17–19). Washington, DC: U.S. Department of Health and Human Services, Public Health Service.

Root, M. (1989). Treatment failure: The role of sexual victimization in women's addictive behavior. *American Journal of Orthopsychiatry, 59* (4), 542–549.

Rossi, P. H. (1992). Assessing family preservation programs. *Children and Youth Services Review, 14,* 77–98.

Rowe, M., & Ryan, C. (1987). *A public health challenge: State issues, policies and programs, I.* Intergovernmental Health Policy Project. Washington, DC: George Washington University.

Rzepnicki, T. L., Schuerman, J. R., & Littell, J. H. (1991). Issues in evaluating intensive family preservation services. In E. M. Tracy, D. A. Haapala, J. Kinney, & P. J. Pecora (Eds.), *Intensive family preservation services: An instructional sourcebook.* Cleveland: Mandel School of Applied Social Sciences, Case Western Reserve University.

Schachar, R., Rutter, M., & Smith, A. (1981). The characteristics of situationally and pervasively hyperactive children: Implications for syndrome definition. *Journal of Child Psychology and Psychiatry, 22* (14), 737–753.

Scott, G. B. (1987). Natural history of HIV infection I. In K. B. Silverman & A. Waddell (Eds.), *Report of the surgeon general's workshop on children with HIV infection and their families* (pp. 22–23). Washington, DC: U.S. Department of Health and Human Services, Public Health Service.

Seagull, E. (1987). Social support and child maltreatment: A review of the evidence. *Child Abuse and Neglect, 11,* 41–52.

Seidman, L., Biedermans, J., & Faraone, S. (1995). Effects of family history and comorbidity on the neuropsychological performance of children with ADHD: Preliminary findings. *Journal of the American Academy of Child and Adolescent Psychiatry, 34* (8), 1015–1024.

Shannon, K. M., & Animann, A. G. (1985). Acquired immune deficiency syndrome in childhood. *Journal of Pediatrics, 106,* 332–342.

Shapiro, S. K., & Garfinkel, B. D. (1986). The occurrence of behavior disorder in children: The interdependence of attention deficit disorder and conduct disorder. *Journal of the American Academy of Child Psychiatry, 25,* 809–819.

Shekim, W. O. (1986). Dimensional and categorical approaches to the diagnosis of attention deficit disorder in children. *Journal of the American Academy of Child Psychiatry, 25,* 653–658.

Smith, D. (1976). Adolescent suicide: A problem for teachers? *Phi Delta Kappa, 57,* 539–542.

Stein, T. T., & Rzepnicki, T. (1983). *Decision making at child welfare imbalance: A handbook on practitioners.* New York: Child Welfare League of America.

Tafoya, N. (1990). Home-based family therapy: A model for Native American communities. In M. Mannes (Ed.), *Family preservation and Indian child welfare.* Albuquerque, NM: American Indian Law Center, Inc.

Teri, L. (1982). The use of the Beck inventory with adolescents. *Journal of Abnormal Child Psychology, 10,* 227–284.

Toseland, R. W., & Rivas, R. F. (1984). *An introduction to group work practice.* New York: Macmillan.

Tracy, E. (1992). Defining the target system for family preservation services. In K. Wells and D. E. Beigel (Eds.), *Family preservation services: Research and evaluation.* Newbury Park, CA: Sage Press.

Tracy, E. M. & Whittaker, J. K. (1990). The social network map: Assessing social support in clinical practice. *Families in Society: The Journal of Contemporary Human Services, 71,* 461–470.

Tramontana, M. G., & Sherrets, S. D. (1985). Brain impairment in child psychiatric disorders: Correspondences between neuropsychological and C.T. scan results. *Journal of the American Academy of Child Psychiatry, 24,* 590–596.

U.S. Vital Statistics. (1992). Washington, D.C.: National Center for Health Statistics.

Velicer, W. F., DiClemente, C. C., Prochaska, J. O., & Brandenburg, N. (1985). A decision balance measure for assessing and predicting smoking status. *Journal of Personality and Social Psychology, 48,* 1279–1289.

Weiss, G. (1985). Hyperactivity: Overview and new directions. *Psychiatric Clinics of North America, 8,* 737–753.

Wells, K., & Biegel, D. (1992). Intensive family preservation research: Current status and future agenda. *Social Work Research & Abstracts, 28* (1), 21–27.

Wheeler, B. L., Biase, D. V., & Sullivan, A. P. (1986). Changes in self-concept during therapeutic community treatment: A comparison of male and female drug abusers. *Journal of Drug Education, 16* (2), 191–196.

Yandow, U. (1989). Alcoholism in women. *Psychiatric Annals, 19,* 243–247.

Young, E. B. (1990). The role of incest in relapse. *Journal of Psychoactive Drugs, 22,* 249–258.

Library Resources

Compiled by Donnelyn Curtis
Interim Head of Collection Management,
New Mexico State University Library

Included in this appendix are listings of the following resources:

- dictionaries, encyclopedias, and handbooks
- statistical sources
- selected bibliographies and guides
- indexes, abstracts, and databases
- journals

BACKGROUND SOURCES: DICTIONARIES, ENCYCLOPEDIAS, AND HANDBOOKS

Barker, R. L. (1995). *The social work dictionary* (3rd ed.). Silver Spring, MD: National Association of Social Workers.

This volume provides social work definitions and identifies and describes organizations, trends, philosophies, and legislation relevant to social work. It gives concise definitions of terms as they are used by social work practitioners and offers a chronology of important events in the history of social work and the NASW Code of Ethics.

Briere, J., Berliner, L., Bulkley, J. A., Jenny, C., & Reid, T. (Eds.) (1996). *APSAC handbook on child maltreatment*. Thousand Oaks, CA : Sage Publications.

This handbook is published in cooperation with the American Professional Society on the Abuse of Children. It includes a bibliography and indexes.

Contemporary world issues series. Santa Barbara: ABC-CLIO.

These specialized handbooks provide preliminary background information, including overviews, chronology, biographical information about important people in the field, lists of organizations, and annotated resource lists.

Selected titles:

Costa, M. *Abortion: A reference handbook* (2nd ed.).

Hall, R. (1995). *Rape in America: A reference handbook.*

Hombs, M. E. (1994). *American homelessness: A reference handbook* (2nd ed.).

Kinnear, K. L. (1995). *Childhood sexual abuse: A reference handbook.*

Kinnear, K. L. (1995). *Violent children: A reference handbook.*

McCue, M. L. (1995). *Domestic violence: A reference handbook.*

Newton, D. E. (1994). *Gay and lesbian rights: A reference handbook.*

Reeves, D. L. (1992). *Child care crisis: A reference handbook.*

Woods, G. (1993). *Drug abuse in society: A reference handbook.*

Corsini, R. J. (Ed.). (1994). *Encyclopedia of psychology* (2nd ed., 4 vols.). New
    York: Wiley.
    This set contains 2500 entries on subjects and people. Cross-references and
    further readings are given for many entries, referring the user to an exten-
    sive bibliography in an appendix.

Encyclopedia of social work (19th ed., 3 vols.). (1995). Silver Spring, MD: National
    Association of Social Workers.
    This is the only encyclopedia devoted entirely to social work. It contains
    290 articles, some lengthy, and 142 bibliographies. In addition, it provides
    a good overview of issues and activities in social work and social welfare,
    serving as an excellent starting point for background information or a liter-
    ature search. It has a separate biographical section and an index.

Facts on File encyclopedias. New York: Facts on File.
    Each of these specialized one-volume encyclopedias is edited by an author-
    ity in the field and provides an overview of its subject, encompassing con-
    cepts as well as particulars. Each provides definitions, information about or-
    ganizations related to the topic, various appendices, and sources for more
    information.

Selected titles:

Adamec, C. A. & Pearce, W. L. (1991). *The encyclopedia of adoption.*

Clark, R. E., & Clark, J. F. (1989). *The encyclopedia of child abuse.*

DiCanio, M. (1989). *The encyclopedia of marriage, divorce and the family.*

DiCanio, M. (1993). *Encyclopedia of violence: Origins, attitudes, consequences.*

Evans, G., & Farberow, N. L. (1988). *The encyclopedia of suicide.*

Fantasia, R., & Isserman, M. (1994). *Homelessness: A sourcebook.*

Kahn, A. P., & Fawcett, J. (1993). *Encyclopedia of mental health.*

O'Brien, R., & Chavez, M. (1991). *The encyclopedia of alcoholism.*

O'Brien, R., & Cohen, S. (1992). *The encyclopedia of drug abuse.*

Roy, F. H., & Russell, C. (1992). *The encyclopedia of aging and the elderly.*

Garland reference library of social science series. New York: Garland Press.
> The formats of these titles vary. Some are straightforward bibliographies, while others are encyclopedias or handbooks, providing background information and facts as well as sources for further information.

Selected titles:

Bullough, V. L., & Bullough, B. (Eds.) (1994). *Human sexuality: An encyclopedia.*

Gilmartin, P. (1994). *Rape, incest, and child abuse: Consequences and recovery.*

Henslin, J. M. (1993). *Homelessness: An annotated bibliography.*

Jacobson, C. K. (1995). *American families: Issues in race and ethnicity.*

Nuba, H., Searson, M., & Sheiman, D. L. (Eds.) (1994). *Resources for early childhood: A handbook.*

Rebach, H., Bolek, C. S., Williams, K. L., & Russell, R. (1992). *Substance abuse among ethnic minorities in America : A critical annotated bibliography.*

Ginzberg, L. (1995). *Social work almanac* (2nd ed.). Washington, DC: National Association of Social Workers.
> This volume combines national and some international information on population, children, crime and corrections, education, health and mortality, mental health, older adults, and the social work profession. Most of the data comes from government publications, with additional information extrapolated from publications by organizations such as the American Public Welfare Association. It includes detailed NASW membership data and many charts and graphs.

Kuper, A., & Kuper, J. (Eds.) (1996). *Social science encyclopedia* (2nd ed.). London: Routledge & Kegan Paul.
> This one-volume encyclopedia is international in scope, and includes short and long articles by authorities in their fields. A "discipline and subject" index provides additional access to the alphabetically organized articles. Each article is followed by a short list of references.

Levinson, D. (Ed.) (1995). *Encyclopedia of marriage and the family* (2 vols.). New York: Macmillan.
> This interdisciplinary encyclopedia covers all aspects of marriage. The articles are written by authorities and include bibliographies. There is a detailed subject index.

Ramachandran, V. S. (Ed.) (1994). *Encyclopedia of human behavior* (4 vols.). San Diego, CA: Academic Press.
> The articles and the accompanying articles are long, with subdivisions. Both psychiatric and psychological perspectives are included, along with articles about neurological research. The subject index is detailed.

STATISTICAL SOURCES

American statistics index. Washington, DC: Congressional Information Service (published annually since 1973).

This is a comprehensive, descriptive guide and index to the statistics published by all government agencies, congressional subcommittees, and statistics-producing programs. Each issue consists of an abstracts section and an index section which provides access to the abstracts by detailed subjects, names, categories, titles, and report numbers.

Statistical handbook series. Phoenix, AZ: Oryx Press.

Selected titles:

Chadwick, B. A., & Heaton, T. B. (1996). *Statistical handbook on adolescents in America.*

Chadwick, B. A., & Heaton, T. B. (1992). *Statistical handbook on the American family.*

Dobrin, A. (Ed.) (1995). *Statistical handbook on violence in America.*

Schick, F. L., & Schick, R. (1994). *Statistical handbook on aging Americans.*

Taeuber, C. M. (Ed.) (1996). *Statistical handbook on women in America* (2nd ed.).

Statistical record series. Detroit: Gale.

Selected titles:

Darnay, A. J. (Ed.) (1994). *Statistical record of older Americans.*

Reddy, M. A. (Ed.) (1993). *Statistical record of native North Americans.*

Schmittroth, L. (Ed.) (1994). *Statistical record of children* (2nd ed.).

——— (Ed.) (1995). *Statistical record of women worldwide* (2nd ed.).

Statistical record of black America. Biennial.

Statistical record of Hispanic America. Biennial.

U.S. Bureau of the Census. *Statistical abstract of the United States.* Washington, DC: U.S. Government Printing Office (published annually since 1987).

This is a standard work for locating statistical information. It includes data from both private and government sources. Emphasis is on national data; however, many tables reflect state or regional data (look up "state data" in the index to find the charts that differentiate among states). References in the index are to chart number, not to page number. Often the original work from which the statistics were taken is cited.

FURTHER RESOURCES: SELECTED BIBLIOGRAPHIES AND GUIDES

The following are examples of the numerous specialized bibliographies of interest to social work researchers. To find a bibliography in an online library catalog, use the subject term with the subheading "bibliography."

AIDS bibliography. Bethesda, MD: National Medical Library (published monthly since 1989).

Alcohol, tobacco, and other drugs: Resource guide series. (1994). Rockville, MD: Center for Substance Abuse Prevention, U.S. Department of Health and Human Services.

Hayslip, B., Servaty, H. L., & Ward, A. S. (Eds.) (1995). *Psychology of aging: An annotated bibliography.* Westport, CT: Greenwood Press.

Herron, N. L., & Zabel, D. (1995). *Bridging the gap: Examining polarity in America.* Englewood, CO: Libraries Unlimited.

Frazier, B. H., & Hayes, K. C. (1994). *Selected resources on sibling abuse: An annotated bibliography for researchers, educators, and consumers.* Beltsville, MD: National Agricultural Library.

Nordquist, J. (Ed.). *Contemporary social issues* series. Santa Cruz, CA: Reference and Research Service.

Selected titles:

———— (1996). *Asian Americans: Social, economic, and political aspects—a bibliography.*

———— (1993). *The African American woman: Social and economic conditions—a bibliography.*

———— (1994). *Latinos in the United States: Social, economic, and political aspects—a bibliography.*

———— (1995). *Recent immigration from Latin America: Social, economic, and political aspects—a bibliography.*

———— (1994). *Violence in American society: A bibliography.*

———— (1994). *Women and aging: A bibliography.*

———— (1993). *Women and AIDS: A bibliography.*

Social welfare. Washington, DC: U.S. Government Printing Office (published annually since 1994).

Stanton, G. W. (Ed.) (1994). *Children of separation: An annotated bibliography for professionals.* Metuchen, NJ: Scarecrow Press.

Weitzman, E. (1995). *Computer programs for qualitative data analysis.* Thousand Oaks, CA: Sage.

IDENTIFYING THE LITERATURE: INDEXES, ABSTRACTS, DATABASES

Many of these indexes are available in both print and electronic format. The electronic version is often updated daily or weekly; print indexes are usually updated quarterly. Computerized databases are issued to libraries on CD-ROM, and many are also or alternatively made available through the World Wide Web.

Abstracts in social gerontology. Newbury Park, CA: Sage Periodicals (published quarterly since 1990).

> The quarterly publication is organized in broad subject categories, with a keyword index. It gives abstracts for journal articles, books, pamphlets, government publications, legislative research studies, and other types of publications. It includes an author index.

Agricola

Bibliography of agriculture. Phoenix, AZ: Oryx Press (published since 1941).

> Primarily a source for agricultural references, *Agricola* also indexes articles, reports, books, and government documents in the areas of home economics, nutrition, and rural sociology. There are citations to articles, for instance, on the prevention of teenage pregnancy, the WIC program, and prenatal nutrition. Both the print and online versions are maintained by the National Agricultural Library and updated quarterly.

Guide to resources and services. Ann Arbor, MI: Inter-university Consortium for Political and Social Research (published annually since 1977).

> This annual index refers to numerical computer files such as "Violence research data from the National Institute of Justice." The files are available from member universities of the ICPSR.

ERIC. Various vendors, 1966–.

CIJE (Current index to journals in education). Phoenix: Oryx Press (published since 1969).

RIE (Research in education) 1966–1974; (*Resources in education*) (published since 1975).

> *ERIC,* widely available through the internet and as a CD-ROM database, combines the *CIJE* and *RIE* indexes, which are still available in print versions that are updated monthly. The subject terms that organize the print indexes are known as "descriptors" in *ERIC,* and they can be found in an online (or print) thesaurus, to help with precision in online retrieval. The user can also search by keyword, author, or title and can limit the search by date of publication. The database contains references (with abstracts) to journal articles (indexed in *CIJE*) and ERIC Documents (indexed in *RIE*), and the full text of ERIC Digests, which summarize current issues. ERIC Documents include research reports and studies, conference proceedings, some dissertations and theses, and other nonjournal literature of interest to those in the field of education. They are available in many libraries on microfiche.

Current contents: Social and behavioral sciences. Philadelphia: Institute for Scientific Information (published since 1974).

This product, available on disk as well as in print, reproduces the content pages in approximately 1300 international journals grouped within broad categories as well as articles from multi-authored books. It is indexed by keyword and author, and it can be searched using words that would appear in titles or abstracts.

PsycLIT, PsycInfo, Psychological abstracts. Washington: American Psychological Association (published since 1927).

The print version is a comprehensive monthly compilation of nonevaluative summaries of the world's literature in psychology and related disciplines, containing abstracts listed under 16 major classification categories. An author and brief subject index appear in each issue. These are then cumulated at the end of the year. The final subject index is much expanded from the monthly issues. The computerized versions are available on CD-ROM and the Internet, with various search interfaces. *PsycInfo* is the expanded version of *PsycLIT,* containing abstracts of dissertations and other resources as well as the journal articles and book chapters that are abstracted in the latter product. In order to derive the greatest benefit from *Psychological Abstracts, PsycInfo,* or *PsycLIT,* the *Thesaurus of Psychological Index Terms* should be used.

Public affairs information service bulletin (PAIS). New York: Public Affairs Information Service (published since 1915).

The semi-monthly print version of this index includes journal articles, books, pamphlets, and U.S. government documents. The annual cumulation includes an author index. The subjects that are covered include: crime, poverty, umemployment, divorce, work, women, culture, and race relations. It is also available on CD-ROM and through the Internet.

Social sciences index. New York: H. W. Wilson (published since 1929).

This is an author and subject index to over 350 journals in the fields of anthropology, sociology, and related fields. A separate section at the end of each quarterly print issue indexes book reviews. It is also available on CD-ROM and through the Internet.

Social work abstracts. Silver Spring: National Association of Social Workers (published since 1977).

Lengthy abstracts are organized in broad categories in the quarterly (and annually cumulated) print version, with author and subject indexes. Each quarterly issue begins with a research section, comprised of articles and "research notes." The CD-ROM and internet versions can be searched by keyword and limited by dates.

Society for Research in Child Development. *Child development abstracts and bibliography.* Chicago: University of Chicago Press (published since 1928).

Issued three times a year with annually cumulated author and subject indexes, this source contains abstracts of articles about child development from U.S. and international periodicals, also a section of book notices.

Sociofile.

Sociological abstracts. San Diego, CA: Sociological Abstracts (published since 1952).

This source includes abstracts to articles, papers presented at sociological meetings, books, book reviews, and bibliographies. The print version is organized in broad subject categories with a subject index.

Women studies abstracts. Rush, NY: Rush Publishing (published since 1972).

This index, with abstracts, has recently been made available electronically. It describes articles from a wide range of periodicals, and includes additional listings of articles not abstracted. The print version is organized by subject and is updated quarterly.

SELECTED LIST OF CURRENT JOURNALS

Administration in Social Work

Affilia: The Journal of Women and Social Work

Advances in Alcohol and Substance Abuse

AIDS Education and Prevention: An Interdisciplinary Journal

Alcohol Health and Research World

Alcoholism Treatment Quarterly

The American Journal of Drug and Alcohol Abuse

American Journal of Family Therapy

American Journal of Orthopsychiatry

Aretê

The British Journal of Social Work

Canadian Social Work Review: Revue Canadienne de Service Social

Child Abuse & Neglect: The International Journal

Child and Adolescent Social Work Journal

Child and Youth Care Forum

Child and Youth Services

Child Welfare

Children and Society

Children Today

Clinical Social Work Journal

Computers in Human Services

Crime and Delinquency

Day Care and Early Education

Death Studies

Ethnic and Racial Studies

Evaluation and Program Planning: An International Journal

Exceptional Children

Families in Society: The Journal of Contemporary Human Services

Family Perspective

Family Planning Perspectives

Family Process

Family Relations: Journal of Applied Family and Child Studies

The Gerontologist

Hastings Center Report

Health and Social Work

Hispanic Journal of Behavioral Sciences

Hospice Journal

Human Services in the Rural Environment

Information and Referral: The Journal of the Alliance of Information and Referral Systems

International Journal of Aging and Human Development

International Journal of the Addictions

International Social Work

Journal of Aging and Social Policy

The Journal of Analytic Social Work

Journal of Applied Gerontology

Journal of Applied Psychology

Journal of Applied Social Psychology

Journal of Child and Adolescent Substance Abuse

Journal of Continuing Social Work Education

Journal of Divorce and Remarriage

Journal of Family Issues

Journal of Gerontological Social Work

Journal of Homosexuality

Journal of Independent Social Work
Journal of Marital and Family Therapy
Journal of Marriage and the Family
Journal of Multicultural Social Work
Journal of Progressive Human Services
Journal of Social Policy
Journal of Social Service Research
Journal of Social Work and Human Sexuality
Journal of Social Work Education
Journal of Sociology and Social Welfare
Journal of Studies on Alcohol
Journal of Teaching in Social Work
Journal of Women and Aging
Journal of Youth and Adolescence
Journals of Gerontology: Series B, Psychological Sciences and Social Sciences
Marriage and Family Review
Omega: Journal of Death and Dying
Public Administration Review

Public Welfare
Research on Social Work Practice
Residential Treatment for Children and Youth
School Social Work Journal
Smith College Studies in Social Work
Social Forces
Social Policy
Social Problems
Social Psychology Quarterly
Social Service Review
Social Work
Social Work Education: Development and Training for Social Care and Social Services
Social Work in Education
Social Work in Health Care
Social Work Research
Social Work with Groups
Suicide and Life Threatening Behavior
Youth and Society

Software Resources

QUANTITATIVE

Simstat
Porvalis Research
5000 Adam Street
Montreal, QC
CANADA H1V 1W5

Voice/Fax: (514) 899-1672

Stata
Stata Corporation
702 University Drive East
College Station, TX 77840

Telephone: (800) 782-8272
          (that's 800-STATAPC, U.S.)
          (800) 248-8272 (Canada)
          (409) 696-4600 (Worldwide)
Fax: (409) 696-4601 (Worldwide)
e-mail: Stat@stata.com

NCSS
NCSS Statistical Software
329 North 1000 East
Kaysville, UT 84037

Telephone: (800) 898-6109
          (801) 546-0445

Fax: (801) 546-3907
e-mail: ncss@ix.netcom.com

Statistica
StatSoft
2300 East 14th Street
Tulsa, OK 74104

Telephone: (918) 749-1119
Fax: (918) 749-2217
e-mail: info@statsoft.com

BMDP
Parallel Performance Group Inc.
450 Jordan Rd., Apt. 3a
Sedona, AZ 86336

Telephone: (520) 282-6300
e-mail: mail@ppgsoft.com

SPSS
444 North Michigan Avenue
Chicago, IL 60611

Telephone: (800) 543-2185
Fax: (800) 841-0064

SAS
SAS Institute Inc.
SAS Campus Drive
Cary, NC 27513-2414

Telephone: (919) 677-8000
Fax: (919) 677-8123

QUALITATIVE

QSR NUD.IST
In the Americas:
Sage Publications, Inc
2455 Teller Road
Thousand Oaks, CA 91320-2218

Telephone: (805) 499-0721
Fax: (805) 499-0871
e-mail: nudist@sagepub.com

In Europe and the U.K:
Sage Publications, Ltd.
6 Bonhill Street
London EC2A4PU
UK

Telephone: 44(0)171 330 122
Fax: 44(0)171 374 8741
e-mail: nudist@sageltd.co.uk

Hyper RESEARCH
ResearchWare, Inc.
P.O. Box 1258
Randolph, MA 02368-1258

Voice/Fax: (617) 961-3909
e-mail: researchwr@aol.com

Ethnograph
Qualis Research Associates
P.O. Box 2070
Amherst, MA 01004

Telephone: (413) 256-8835
Fax: (413) 256-8472
e-mail: qualis@MCImail.com
          qualis@qualisresearch.com

QED
MiMiC/TriMM
P.O. Box 1208
7500 BE ENSCHEDE
The Netherlands

Fax: 31 53 4353027

Statistical Formulas

Pearson *r*

$$r = \frac{e - \frac{(a)(b)}{N}}{\sqrt{\left[c - \left(\frac{a^2}{N}\right)\right]\left[d - \left(\frac{b^2}{N}\right)\right]}}$$

where r = Correlation coefficient
a = Sum of values of x
b = Sum of values of y
c = Sum of values of x^2
d = Sum of values of y^2
e = Sum of values of x and y
N = Number of cases

t-test

$$t = \frac{Ma - Mb}{\sqrt{\left(\frac{(Sa)^2 + (Sb)^2}{Na + Nb - 2}\right)\left(\frac{Na + Nb}{(Na)(Nb)}\right)}}$$

where t = t value
Na = Number of cases in Group A
Nb = Number of cases in Group B
Sa = Sum of squares of raw scores in Group A
Sb = Sum of squares of raw scores in Group B

Mean

$$\bar{x} = \frac{\sum X_1}{N}$$

where $\sum$ = scores added together
X_1 = score for subjects
N = number of subjects

Median

Given an ordered list of n values, the median equals the value at position $\frac{(n+1)}{2}$.
If n is odd, a single value occupies this position. If n is even, the median equals
the mean of the two middle values.

Standard Deviation

$$S = \sqrt{\frac{\sum (x-\bar{x})}{n-1}}$$

where s = sample standard deviation
n = sample population
$\bar{x}$ = sample mean
x = total scores

Chi-square

$$\chi^2 = \sum \frac{(O-E)^2}{E}$$

where χ^2 = Chi-square value
O = Observed frequency
E = Expected frequency
$\sum$ = Sum of (for all cells)

$$E = \frac{(R)(C)}{(N)}$$

where E = Expected frequency in a particular cell
R = Total number in that cell's row
C = Total number in that cell's row
N = Total number of cases

Probability Tables

Critical values of chi-square

	Level of significance for a one-tailed test					
	.10	.05	.025	.01	.005	.0005
	Level of significance for a two-tailed test					
df	.20	.10	.05	.02	.01	.001
1	1.64	2.71	3.84	5.41	6.64	10.83
2	3.22	4.60	5.99	7.82	9.21	13.82
3	4.64	6.25	7.82	9.84	11.34	16.27
4	5.99	7.78	9.49	11.67	13.28	18.46
5	7.29	9.24	11.07	13.39	15.09	20.52
6	8.56	10.64	12.59	15.03	16.81	22.46
7	9.80	12.02	14.07	16.62	18.48	24.32
8	11.03	13.36	15.51	18.17	20.09	26.12
9	12.24	14.68	16.92	19.68	21.67	27.88
10	13.44	15.99	18.31	21.16	23.21	29.59
11	14.63	17.28	19.68	22.62	24.72	31.26
12	15.81	18.55	21.03	24.05	26.22	32.91
13	16.98	19.81	22.36	25.47	27.69	34.53
14	18.15	21.06	23.68	26.87	29.14	36.12
15	19.31	22.31	25.00	28.26	30.58	37.70
16	20.46	23.54	26.30	29.63	32.00	39.29

(continued)

Critical values of chi-square *(continued)*

df	.10	.05	Level of significance for a one-tailed test .025	.01	.005	.0005
	.20	.10	Level of significance for a two-tailed test .05	.02	.01	.001
17	21.62	24.77	27.59	31.00	33.41	40.75
18	22.76	25.99	28.87	32.35	34.80	42.31
19	23.90	27.20	30.14	33.69	36.19	43.82
20	25.04	28.41	31.41	35.02	37.57	45.32
21	26.17	29.62	32.67	36.34	38.93	46.80
22	27.30	30.81	33.92	37.66	40.29	48.27
23	28.43	32.01	35.17	38.97	41.64	49.73
24	29.55	33.20	36.42	40.27	42.98	51.18
25	30.68	34.38	37.65	41.57	44.31	52.62
26	31.80	35.56	38.88	42.86	45.64	54.05
27	32.91	36.74	40.11	44.14	46.94	55.48
28	34.03	37.92	41.34	45.42	48.28	56.89
29	35.14	39.09	42.69	46.69	49.59	58.30
30	36.25	40.26	43.77	47.96	50.89	59.70
32	38.47	42.59	46.19	50.49	53.49	62.49
34	40.68	44.90	48.60	53.00	56.06	65.25
36	42.88	47.21	51.00	55.49	58.62	67.99
38	45.08	49.51	53.38	57.97	61.16	70.70
40	47.27	51.81	55.76	60.44	63.69	73.40
44	51.64	56.37	60.48	65.34	68.71	78.75
48	55.99	60.91	65.17	70.20	73.68	84.04
52	60.33	65.42	69.83	75.02	78.62	89.27
56	64.66	69.92	74.47	79.82	83.51	94.46
60	68.97	74.40	79.08	84.58	88.38	99.61

Source: From Table IV of R. A. Fisher and F. Yates, *Statistical Tables for Biological, Agricultural, and Medical Research,* published by Addison Wesley Longman Ltd. Reprinted by permission of Addison Wesley Longman Ltd.

Code of Ethics, approved by the National Association of Social Workers (NASW), January 1, 1997, Section 5.02 Evaluation and Research

(a) Social workers should monitor and evaluate policies, the implementation of programs, and practice interventions.

(b) Social workers should promote and facilitate evaluation and research to contribute to the development of knowledge.

(c) Social workers should critically examine and keep current with emerging knowledge relevant to social work and fully use evaluation and research evidence in their professional practice.

(d) Social workers engaged in evaluation or research should carefully consider possible consequences and should follow guidelines developed for the protection of evaluation and research participants. Appropriate institutional review boards should be consulted.

(e) Social workers engaged in evaluation or research should obtain voluntary and written informed consent from participants, when appropriate, without any implied or actual deprivation or penalty for refusal to participate; without undue inducement to participate; and with due regard for participants' well-being, privacy, and dignity. Informed consent should include information about the nature, extent, and duration of the participation requested and disclosure of the risks and benefits of participation in the research.

(f) When evaluation or research participants are incapable of giving informed consent, social workers should provide an appropriate explanation to the participants, obtain the participants' assent to the extent they are able, and obtain written consent from an appropriate proxy.

(g) Social workers should never design or conduct evaluation or research that does not use consent procedures, such as certain forms of naturalistic observation and archival research, unless rigorous and responsible review of the research has found it to be justified because of its prospective scientific, educational, or applied value and unless equally effective alternative procedures that do not involve waiver of consent are not feasible.

(h) Social workers should inform participants of their right to withdraw from evaluation and research at any time without penalty.

(i) Social workers should take appropriate steps to ensure that participants in evaluation and research have access to appropriate supportive services.

(j) Social workers engaged in evaluation or research should protect participants from unwarranted physical or mental distress, harm, danger, or deprivation.

(k) Social workers engaged in the evaluation of services should discuss collected information only for professional purposes and only with people professionally concerned with this information.

(l) Social workers engaged in evaluation or research should ensure the anonymity or confidentiality of participants and of the data obtained from them. Social workers should inform participants of any limits of confidentiality, the measures that will be taken to ensure confidentiality, and when any records containing research data will be destroyed.

(m) Social workers who report evaluation and research results should protect participants' confidentiality by omitting identifying information unless proper consent has been obtained authorizing disclosure.

(n) Social workers should report evaluation and research findings accurately. They should not fabricate or falsify results and should take steps to correct any errors later found in published data using standard publication methods.

(o) Social workers engaged in evaluation or research should be alert to and avoid conflicts of interest and dual relationships with participants, should inform participants when a real or potential conflict of interest arises, and should take steps to resolve the issue in a manner that makes participants' interests primary.

(p) Social workers should educate themselves, their students, and their colleagues about responsible research practices.

AB design   A single-system design in which there is a comparison between the baseline (A) and an intervention period (B).

ABAB design   A single-system design that is also known as a withdrawal or reversal design where the AB design is duplicated in order to increase the validity of the results.

ABC design   A single-system design in which the baseline (A) is followed by one intervention period (B) and a second intervention period (C).

Alternate form   A method of testing an instrument's reliability where different but equivalent forms of the same test are administered to the same group of individuals, usually close in time, and then compared.

Anonymity   A condition in which the researcher cannot identify a given response with a given respondent.

Applicability   Whether or not a measuring instrument is appropriate and suitable for a particular type of problem.

Applied research   Research that produces practical outcomes and is directed at solving problems encountered in social work practice.

Authority   Referring to outside sources of knowledge.

Autocorrelation   The relationship between the outcome or dependent variable scores in single-system studies.

Availability sampling (convenience sampling)   A nonprobability sampling method where available or convenient elements are included in the sample.

Bar graph   A visual means of displaying data at the nominal level of measurement.

Baseline   Repeated measurement before the introduction of the intervention that allows the comparison of target behavior rates before and after the intervention.

Baseline comparison   A strategy for comparing the equivalency between experimental and comparison groups where the comparison group is composed of cases handled prior to the introduction to the program.

Bivariate measure   A method of measuring the relationship between two variables.

Case studies   A description of the application of an intervention.

Causal flowcharts   A visual means of representing causal connections of qualitative data.

Causality   A principle that involves meeting three conditions: first, two factors are empirically related to one another; second, the cause precedes the effect in time; and third, the relationship between the factors cannot be explained by other factors.

Celeration line   A means of predicting the dependent variable in single-system studies.

Changing criterion design   A single-system design that involves setting goals for the client that change over time.

Client satisfaction survey   A design used to ask clients how they experienced or perceived a program.

Clinical significance (practical significance)   Significance level that is achieved when the specified goal of the intervention has been reached.

Closed-ended questions   Questions that provide respondents with a fixed set of alternatives from which they choose.

Cluster sampling   A form of probability sampling that involves randomly sampling a larger unit containing the elements of interest and then sampling from these larger units the elements to be included in the final sample.

Coding   A means of organizing and collecting information so that it can be entered into a computer.

Cohort groups   A strategy for increasing the equivalency between experimental and comparison groups where the comparison groups move through an organization at the same time as those in the program being evaluated but do not receive program services.

Cohort studies   Cohort studies examine specific subgroups as they change over time.

Community forum   A public meeting or series of meetings where individuals are briefed on the issues and then asked for input—a form of purposive sampling.

Comparison groups   Subjects who receive another type of intervention or who receive no type of bona fide intervention and who have not been randomly assigned. Comparison groups can be used to increase the internal and external validity of group designs.

Confidence level   How often you would expect to find similar results if the research were repeated.

Confidentiality   A state in which the researcher knows the identity of the respondents and their associated responses but guarantees not to disclose this information.

Construct validity   A means of testing an instrument's validity; involves examining the extent to which an instrument measures a theoretical construct.

Contamination   The difficulty of distinguishing between the experimental and comparison groups, either due to contact between the subjects of each group or due to no clear distinction between the program experiences of the clients in each group.

Content analysis   A method of coding written communication to a systematic quantifiable form.

Content validity   A method of testing an instrument's validity that involves ensuring the content of the instrument to the concepts being measured.

Contingency table   A measure of association, also known as cross-tabulation.

Control group   Subjects who do not receive the intervention being evaluated and who have been randomly assigned.

Construct validity   The extent to which an instrument measures a theoretical construct.

Convenience sampling   A nonprobability sampling method where available or convenient elements are included in the sample.

Copyright   Laws that apply not only to published material but also to in-house reports.

Correlation   A measure of association used with interval or ratio level data.

Correlation coefficient   A statistic that measures the extent to which the comparisons are similar or not similar, related or not related.

Cost-benefit analysis   Program costs compared with the dollar value of the program results; a ratio of costs to benefits is computed.

Cost-effectiveness study   Program costs compared to some measure of program output; a cost per unit is calculated.

Cover letter   Sent with a questionnaire to briefly describe the purpose of the study and the principle of confidentiality.

Criterion sampling   Selecting all cases that meet some criterion.

Criterion validity   The extent to which a correlation exists between the measuring instrument and another standard.

Cross-classification   A method of qualitative data analysis that creates categories by crossing one dimension or typology with another.

Cross-sectional design   A method of measuring behavior as it occurs at one point in time or over a relatively short period of time.

Cross-tabulation   A measure of association, also known as contingency tables.

Data   Information that is collected for research.

Deduction   A process of drawing conclusions from the general to the particular; opposite to the process of induction.

Dependent variable   The outcome variable that has been presumably affected by the independent variable.

Descriptive research   A process of recording and reporting phenomena; not primarily concerned with causes.

Descriptive statistics   A means of summarizing the characteristics of a sample or the relationship among the variables.

Developmental research (intervention research)   Research specifically focused on developing innovative interventions by actually using research to design the interventions, test their effectiveness, and modify them based on recommendations that emerge from testing.

Directional hypothesis (one-tailed hypothesis)   A hypothesis that specifies not only that there is an association between variables but also predicts whether the relationship is negative or positive.

Discontinuity   A difference in data levels between the baseline and intervention periods.

Discourse analysis   A way of understanding how the researcher's social context can influence how data are understood and analyzed.

Drifts   Trends that occur across the intervention and baseline periods.

Ecological fallacy   The danger of reaching conclusions in your study using a unit of analysis other than that used by the study.

Element   The item under study in the population and sample; in social work, a client system.

Emic   A system of organizing and developing categories of qualitative data that are derived from those being studied rather than constructed by the researcher.

Empiricism   Observation through the use of the senses.

Ethnography   A method of describing a culture or society.

Etic   A system of organizing and developing categories of qualitative data that are developed by the researcher rather than derived from those being studied.

Ex post facto design   Ex post facto ("after the fact") refers to designs where subjects already possess the independent variable of interest before the study begins.

Expected frequencies   Cross-tabulations that are what one might expect to observe according to probability.

Experience   A form of knowledge that includes firsthand, personal participation in events.

Experimental designs   Group research designs that randomly assign to the control group and experimental group.

Experimental group   In a program evaluation, the group that receives the intervention being evaluated.

Explanatory research   Studies directed at providing explanations of events to identify causes.

Exploratory research   A form of research that generates initial insights into the nature of an issue and develops questions to be investigated by more extensive studies.

Exploratory single-system design   A design focused on assessing an intervention's impact on a target behavior.

External validity   The extent to which research results are generalizable to the wider population.

Feasibility studies   Another name for a needs assessment. (See *needs assessment.*)

Feedback   An important way of testing the validity of data from interpetive studies and making certain that the data is understandable to and relevant to the participants in the research.

Fixed format   In computer programming, a format in which each code has its specific column assignment in each row of data.

Follow-up   A second mailing can enhance the response ratio of mailed questionnaires.

Focus group   A group formed to help develop the research question.

Formative program evaluation   An examination of the planning, development, and implementation of a program.

Frame elicitation   A means of framing questions to elicit from subjects what they include in a particular topic or category.

Frequency distribution   A description of the number of times the values of a variable occur in a sample.

Front-end analyses   Another name for a needs assessment. (See *needs assessment.*)

Generalist social work practice   A form of social work practice taught in B.S.W. programs that involves practice with different-size client systems and uses a number of different interventions and practice roles.

Generalization   The application of research findings to other situations.

Generalize   The ability to apply the findings from studying the sample to the population.

Goal attainment scales (GAS)   Scales used in single-system studies that reflect the achievement of outcomes; they both set client goals and assess whether the goals have been met.

Group design   The effect of a variable or variables on another variable or variables for a number of different client systems or elements.

History   A threat to the internal validity; those events that occur, other than the intervention, to affect the outcome.

History-treatment interaction   A threat to the external validity.

Human diversity   The whole spectrum of differences among people, including but not limited to gender, ethnicity, age, and sexual orientation.

Human subjects committees   Committees that review the ethical implications of research.

Hypothesis   A probability statement about the relationships among certain factors.

Independent variable   The presumed causal variable in a relationship.

Induction   The use of observation to examine the particular and then develop a generalization to explain the relationship among many of the particulars; the opposite of deduction.

Inferential statistics   A means to determine whether an observed relationship is due to chance or in fact reflects a relationship among factors; allows us to generalize the findings to the wider population.

Information-rich sampling (purposive sampling)   Picking cases from which you can learn about the issues central to the research question—the sampling method of choice in interpretive studies.

Informed consent   Subjects' permission, obtained after fully informing potential participants of their research role and the consequences of their participation.

Institutional review boards   Boards that review the ethical implications of research being conducted at that institution.

Instrumentation   A threat to internal validity; the way in which the variables are measured may change when measures are taken more than once.

Internal validity   The extent to which the changes in the dependent variable(s) are a result of the introduction of the independent variable(s) rather than other factor(s).

Interpretism   An approach to science that emphasizes the subjective, descriptive, inductive, and qualitative aspects of inquiry.

Interval measures   Measures that classify observations into mutually exclusive categories in an inherent order and with equal space between the categories.

Intervention research (developmental research) Research specifically focused on developing innovative interventions by actually using research to design the interventions, test their effectiveness, and modify them based on recommendations that emerge from testing.

Intuition   A form of insight not based on specialized training or reasoning.

Key informant sampling   Picking someone in the community identified as an expert in the field of interest; a form of purposive sampling.

Level of measurement   The extent to which a variable can be quantified and subsequently subjected to mathematical or statistical procedures.

Likert scale   A common measurement scale consisting of a series of statements with five response alternatives.

Limited probability sample   A sample whose characteristics are compared with the characteristics of a sample drawn from a larger population, allowing some tentative generalizations of the findings to be made.

Line graph   A graph that uses a line to connect the data points.

Literature review   A resource for consulting with the written material relevant to the research problem.

Logical analysis   In qualitative data analysis, the process of looking at the relationships between the variables and concepts.

Longitudinal design   A study that tracks behavior over a significant period of time.

Margin of error   Measure of the precision the researcher needs.

Matching   A strategy for increasing the equivalency of experimental and comparison groups; certain characteristics thought to be important in impacting outcomes are selected, and these characteristics are equally represented in each group.

Maturation   A threat to internal validity; a change that is not a result of the intervention but of the subject's becoming more mature with the passage of time.

Mean   A measure of central tendency; the result of summing all values of the observations and then dividing by the total number of observations.

Measuring instrument   The method or means by which data are collected.

Median   A measure of central tendency; a value where 50% of the cases lie above the value and 50% of the cases lie below the value.

Missing values   Incomplete data.

Mode   A measure of central tendency; the value possessed by the greatest number of observations.

Monitoring client progress   Examine and reflect on client progress; used in practice evaluation.

Monitoring interventions   Examine and reflect on interventions used in practice evaluation.

Mortality   A threat to internal validity; subjects dropping out of groups, resulting in a lack of equivalency between the groups.

Multiple baseline design   A replication of the AB design where the same intervention is applied to two or more target problems, to two or more clients, or in two or more settings at different points in time.

Multivariate analysis   Involves examining relationships between more than two variables.

Multivariate measure   A method of measuring the relationship of two or more variables.

Needs assessment   Questions concerned with discovering the nature and extent of a particular social problem to determine the most appropriate type of response.

Negative cases   A means of validating findings from qualitative research.

Negative correlation   A relationship between two variables; as the values of one variable increase, the values of the other variable decrease.

Neutrality   When the researcher does not seek a particular perspective in order to draw conclusions.

Nominal measures   Measures that clarify observations into mutually exclusive categories with no ordering to the categories.

Nondirectional hypothesis (two-tailed hypothesis)   A hypothesis that states there is an association between two or more variables but predicts nothing about the direction of that association.

Nonprobability sampling   The process of selecting a sample where each element in the population has an unknown chance of being included in the sample.

Normal distribution   A bell-shaped curve that is symmetrical; the mean, median, and mode are the same, and most of the scores cluster around the mean, median, and mode.

Null hypothesis   A hypothesis that there is no association between the variables.

Objectivity   The condition in which to the greatest extent possible, the researcher's values and biases do not interfere with the study of the problem.

Obscure variable   A third variable that has hidden the real degree of association between the independent and dependent variables.

Observation   A way of collecting information separate from philosophizing or speculating.

Observed frequencies   Frequencies in a cross-tabulation derived from the sample.

Observer reliability   The comparison of different administrations of the same instrument by different observers or interviewers.

One-group posttest-only design   A type of quasi-experimental group design.

One-group pretest/posttest design   A type of quasi-experimental group design.

One-tailed hypothesis (directional hypothesis)   A hypothesis that specifies not only that there is an association between variables but also predicts whether the relationship is negative or positive.

Open-ended questions   Questions that do not provide respondents with responses, leaving them free to formulate their own responses.

Operationalize   A means of specifying the manner by which the variable is to be measured.

Ordinal measures   Measures that classify observations into mutually exclusive categories with an inherent order.

Output   The final product obtained from submitting a computer program to the computer; this can be displayed on the screen or as hard copy (printout).

Overflow comparison groups   A strategy for increasing the equivalency of comparison and experimental groups where the comparison groups are those who are referred to a program but who cannot be served at that time.

Panel studies   Studies that look at the same set of people over time.

Participant observation   An observation method involving the observer's fully submerging himself or herself to become one of the observed group.

Participatory action research   An opportunity for the subjects' involvement in the research process—an approach to research that has several aims, all intended to empower participants.

Perfect correlation   A relationship between two variables where the values of each variable increase or decrease at the same rate as each other.

Pie charts   A visual representation of data used to show the relative contributions of each of the values to the whole variable.

Population   All possible cases that are of interest to the researcher.

Positive correlation   A relationship between two variables where, as the values of one variable increase, the values of the other variable also increase.

Positivism   An approach to science that adheres to the principles of objectivity, causality, deduction, collecting quantitative data, and producing generalizable results.

Posttest-only comparison group   A type of preexperimental group design.

Posttest-only control-group design   A type of experimental design.

Power   The probability of correctly rejecting a null hypothesis.

Practical significance (clinical significance)   Significance level that is achieved when the specified goal of the intervention has been reached.

Practice evaluation   The type of research that assesses an individual social worker's practice.

Practice logs   A type of process recording where the practitioner keeps an ongoing record of their practice.

Preexperimental designs (quasi-experimental designs)   Designs that use comparison groups rather than control groups, or that use no type of comparison group or control group, and thus have limited internal and external validity.

Pretest/posttest comparison-group design   A type of preexperimental group design.

Pretest-posttest control-group design   A type of experimental design.

Probability sampling   The process of selecting a sample where each element in the population has a known chance of being included in the sample.

Problem-solving process   Specific steps in generalist social work practice.

Process recording   A written record of what transpired with a client system.

Program evaluation   A type of research concerned with the assessment of a program's overall functioning.

Provisionality   A scientific principle involving realization that all scientific findings are tentative and that no ultimate truths can be established.

Pure research   Research centered on answering questions about human behavior to satisfy intellectual curiosity with little concern for the practical benefits that might result.

Purposive sampling (information rich)   A nonprobability sampling method that includes purposively including in the sample elements of interest.

Qualitative data   The nonnumerical examination of phenomena focusing on the underlying meanings and patterns of relationships.

Quantitative data   The creation of categories of phenomena under study prior to investigation and the assignment of numbers to these categories.

Quasi-experimental designs (preexperimental designs)   Designs that use comparison groups rather than control groups, or that use no type of comparison group or control group, and thus have limited external validity.

Quota sampling   A nonprobability sampling method that includes a certain proportion of elements with specific characteristics in the sample.

Random assignment   The process by which every subject has an equal chance of being assigned to a control group or the experimental group.

Range   A measure of variability; the distance between the largest and the smallest value.

Rapid assessment instrument (RAI)   A standardized series of questions or statements to connect data in single-system studies.

Rates under treatment   A type of secondary data that uses existing data from agencies to determine the needs of the community.

Ratio measures   Measures that classify observations into mutually exclusive categories with an inherent order and equal spacing between the categories; the ratio measure reflects the absolute magnitude of the value (and has an absolute zero point).

Reactive effect   The degree to which the researcher's presence affects the behavior being observed.

Reactivity   The problem of the observer's behavior inhibiting or affecting the subject's behavior.

Reductionism   The extreme limitation of the kinds and numbers of variables to be considered when explaining or accounting for broad types of behavior.

Regression analysis   A statistical analysis that allows an estimate of how much change in the dependent variable is produced by a given change in the independent variable or variables.

Regression to the mean   A threat to external validity; the tendency of test scores to regress to the mean.

Reliability   The extent to which a measure reveals actual differences in what is being measured, rather than differences that are inherent in the measuring instrument itself.

Replicate   To repeat a study in order to determine if the same results are found.

Representative sample   A sample that accurately represents the distribution of relevant variables in the population.

Research log   Informal but systematic records of ideas and progress relating to a research study.

Research methods   Means of systematically organizing observations and replicating studies.

Research proposal   A paper proposing undertaking a specific type of research.

Response rate   The proportion of the sample that responds to a questionnaire or interview.

Reversal design   A design that is the same as ABAB single-system design.

Rival hypothesis   A means of validating findings from qualitative research.

Sample   A group of subjects chosen from the population.

Sampling   A means of determining the subjects of the study.

Sampling error   The extent to which the values of a sample differ from those of the population.

Sampling frame   A list of all the elements in the population from which the sample is selected.

Scales   A measurement technique that combines a number of items into a composite score.

Scattergram   A means of plotting the relationships between two interval or ratio level data.

Science   A system for producing knowledge and the knowledge produced from that system.

Secondary data   Existing forms of information that have been previously collected.

Selection   A threat to internal validity; the possibility that the group of people selected for one group will differ from those selected for the other group.

Selection-treatment interaction   A threat to external validity.

Self-monitoring   A process in which a client collects data on his or her own behavior.

Semistructured interview   An interviewing situation in which the interviewer is freer to pursue hunches and improvise in asking questions.

Simple random sampling   A form of probability sampling in which the population is related as a whole unit and each element has an equal chance of being included in the sample.

Single-system design or study   The type of design used in practice evaluation.

Skewed distribution   A distribution in which most of the scores are concentrated at one end of the distribution rather than in the middle.

Split half method   Items on the instrument are divided into comparable halves.

Slopes   Trends that occur in the data within the baseline or within the intervention period.

Snowball sampling   A form of nonprobability sampling that identifies some members of the population and then has those individuals contact others in the population.

Social indicators   A form of secondary data collection that involves selecting demographic data from existing records to predict a community's needs.

Social work ethics   Values and ethical standards recognized by the profession of social work and codified by the National Association of Social Workers (NASW).

Solomon four-group design   A type of experimental group design.

Standard deviation   A measure of variability that averages the distance of each value from the mean.

Standardized observation   An observation technique in which behaviors are categorized prior to the observation according to their characteristics, including their frequency, duration, or magnitude. These categories can then be quantified.

Standardized scales   Uniform scales that are tested extensively.

Static-group comparison design   A type of quasi-experimental group design.

Statistically significant   Characteristic of a finding when the null hypothesis is rejected and the probability that the result was due to chance falls at or below a certain cutoff point—usually 5%, or the .05 significance level.

Stratified random sampling   A form of probability sampling in which the population is divided into strata and subsamples are randomly selected from each stratum.

Structured interview   An interviewing situation in which the interviewer knows ahead of time the questions to be asked and in many cases is simply verbally administering a questionnaire.

Structured observation   Behaviors are categorized prior to the observation according to their characteristics, including their frequency, direction, and magnitude. These categories can then be quantified.

Subjective   Reality as perceived by the subject; the researcher's biases and values are explicitly stated.

Successive intervention design   A design that is the same as the ABC single-system design.

Summative program evaluation   An assessment that determines whether goals and objectives have been met and the extent to which program efforts are generalizable to other settings and populations.

Survey research   Studies focusing on describing the characteristics of a group.

Systematic random sampling   A form of probability sampling in which every *n*th element of the sampling frame is selected for the sample.

Systematic steps   The ordered steps in research methods.

Target problem scales   Scales used in single-system studies to track the changes in a client system's target behavior.

Testing   A threat to internal validity; the effect the testing itself may have on the subject.

Test-retest   The repeated administration of the instrument to the same set of people on separate occasions.

Theories   Scientific descriptions and explanations of logical relationships among phenomena.

Time series design   A type of quasi-experimental design in which a number of measurements are made both before and after the intervention.

Transcribe   The act of writing down verbatim a recording of the interview.

Treatment diffusion   The act of ensuring that there are no interferences during the course of the evaluation that may affect either the equivalence of the groups or the representativeness of the sample.

Trend studies   Multiple samplings from the same population over months or years to monitor changes or trends.

Triangulation   A means of validating findings from qualitative research.

Two-tailed hypothesis   A hypothesis that states that two or more variables are associated, but does not predict whether the association is negative or positive.

Type I error   An erroneous rejection of the null hypothesis—the conclusion that a relationship exists between the variables when no relationship in fact exists.

Type II error   An erroneous failure to reject the null hypothesis—a failure to identify a relationship between variables.

Typical case sampling   The most often-used type of purposive samples. Typical cases are sought using the literature, previous research, or consultation with relevant groups. Cases that appear typical in need for services would be contacted through a local agency or schools.

Unit of analysis   The situation or person who is the object of the study.

Univariate measures   Measures that examine variables one at a time.

Unstructured interviews   Interviews that are similar to conversations except that the interviewer and interviewee know that an interview is being conducted and the interviewee is privy to information of interest to the interviewer.

Unstructured observation   Observation that is used when little is known about the behaviors being observed and no categorization of the behaviors has been done before the interview.

Validity of a measuring instrument   The extent to which we are measuring what we think we are measuring.

Value   The quantitative measure attached to a variable.

Values   Beliefs about what is right and wrong.

Variable   Characteristic of a phenomenon; something that varies and subsequently has different values.

Visual significance   A state that occurs when the visual presentation of results from a single-system study looks significant.

Withdrawal design   A design that is the same as an ABAB single-system design.

TO THE OWNER OF THIS BOOK:

I hope that you have found *Research Methods for Generalist Social Work*, Second Edition, useful. So that this book can be improved in a future edition, would you take the time to complete this sheet and return it? Thank you.

School and address: _____

Department: _____

Instructor's name: _____

1. What I like most about this book is: _____

_____

_____

2. What I like least about this book is: _____

_____

_____

3. My general reaction to this book is: _____

_____

4. The name of the course in which I used this book is: _____

_____

5. Were all of the chapters of the book assigned for you to read? _____

   If not, which ones weren't? _____

6. In the space below, or on a separate sheet of paper, please write specific suggestions for improving this book and anything else you'd care to share about your experience in using the book.

_____

_____

_____

_____

_____

Optional:

Your name: _____ Date: _____

May Brooks/Cole quote you, either in promotion for *Research Methods for Generalist Social Work,* Second Edition, or in future publishing ventures?

Yes: _____ No: _____

Sincerely,

Christine Marlow

IN-BOOK SURVEY

At Brooks/Cole, we are excited about creating new types of learning materials that are interactive, three-dimensional, and fun to use. To guide us in our publishing/development process, we hope that you'll take just a few moments to fill out the survey below. Your answers can help us make decisions that will allow us to produce a wide variety of videos, CD-ROMs, and Internet-based learning systems to complement standard textbooks. If you're interested in working with us as a student Beta-tester, be sure to fill in your name, telephone number, and address. We look forward to hearing from you!

In addition to books, which of the following learning tools do you currently use in your counseling/human services/social work courses?

_____ **Video** _____ in class _____ school library _____ own VCR

_____ **CD-ROM** _____ in class _____ in lab _____ own computer

_____ **Macintosh disks** _____ in class _____ in lab _____ own computer

_____ **Windows disks** _____ in class _____ in lab _____ own computer

_____ **Internet** _____ in class _____ in lab _____ own computer

How often do you access the Internet? _____

My own home computer is:

_____ Macintosh _____ DOS _____ Windows _____ Windows 95

The computer I use in class for counseling/human services/social work courses is:

_____ Macintosh _____ DOS _____ Windows _____ Windows 95

If you are NOT currently using multimedia materials in your counseling/human services/social work courses, but can see ways that video, CD-ROM, Internet, or other technologies could enhance your learning, please comment below:

_____

_____

_____

Other comments (optional): _____

_____

Name _____Telephone _____

Address _____

School _____

Professor/Course_____

You can fax this form to us at (408) 375-6414; e:mail to: info@brookscole.com; or detach, fold, secure, and mail.

FOLD HERE

BUSINESS REPLY MAIL

FIRST CLASS   PERMIT NO. 358   PACIFIC GROVE, CA

POSTAGE WILL BE PAID BY ADDRESSEE

ATT: ___MARKETING___

**Brooks/Cole Publishing Company
511 Forest Lodge Road
Pacific Grove, California 93950-9968**

FOLD HERE